Philosophies of Religion

EXPANDING PHILOSOPHY OF RELIGION

Series Editors

J. Aaron Simmons, Furman University, USA
Kevin Schilbrack, Appalachian State University, USA

A series dedicated to a global, diverse, cross-cultural, and comparative philosophy of religion, Expanding Philosophy of Religion encourages underrepresented voices and perspectives and looks beyond its traditional concerns rooted in classical theism, propositional belief, and privileged identities.

Titles in the series include

Philosophical Hermeneutics and the Priority of Questions in Religions, by Nathan Eric Dickman

Philosophies of Religion, by Timothy Knepper

Diversifying Philosophy of Religion, edited by Nathan R. B. Loewen and Agnieszka Rostalska

Philosophies of Religion

A Global and Critical Introduction

Timothy Knepper

BLOOMSBURY ACADEMIC
LONDON • NEW YORK • OXFORD • NEW DELHI • SYDNEY

BLOOMSBURY ACADEMIC
Bloomsbury Publishing Plc
50 Bedford Square, London, WC1B 3DP, UK
1385 Broadway, New York, NY 10018, USA
29 Earlsfort Terrace, Dublin 2, Ireland

BLOOMSBURY, BLOOMSBURY ACADEMIC and the Diana logo are trademarks of Bloomsbury Publishing Plc

First published in Great Britain 2023

Cover design by Louise Dugdale
Cover image © northlightimages/Getty Images.

A catalogue record for this book is available from the British Library.

A catalog record for this book is available from the Library of Congress.

ISBN: HB: 978-1-3502-6295-9
PB: 978-1-3502-6296-6
ePDF: 978-1-3502-6297-3
eBook: 978-1-3502-6298-0

Series: Expanding Philosophy of Religion

Typeset by RefineCatch Limited, Bungay, Suffolk
Printed and bound in Great Britain

To find out more about our authors and books visit www.bloomsbury.com and sign up for our newsletters.

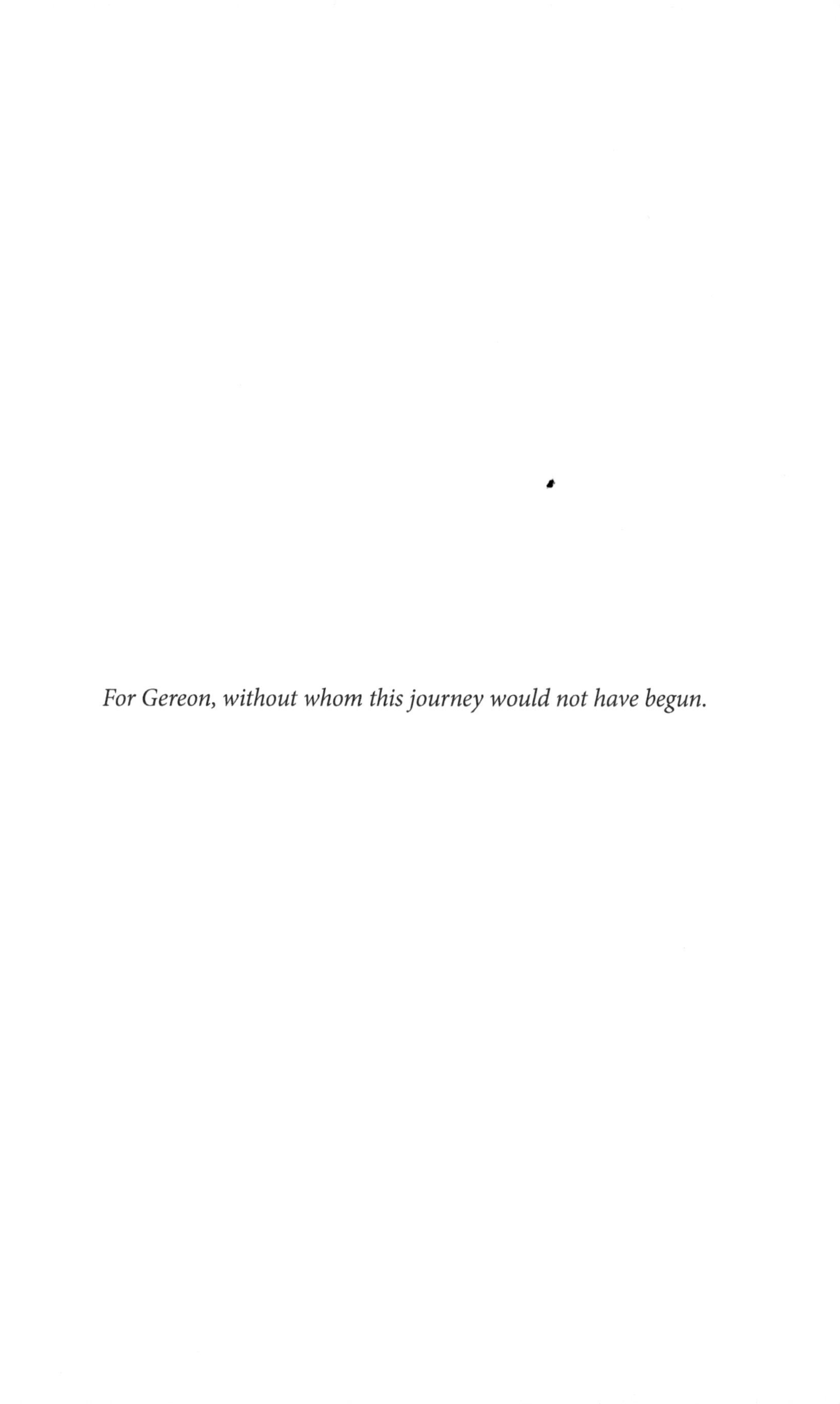

For Gereon, without whom this journey would not have begun.

Contents

List of Figures and Tables ix
Preface xii
Abbreviations, Diacritics, Pronunciations xiii

Introduction 1

Part I What Is Philosophy of Religion?

1 **The Traditions of Philosophy of Religion** 13

2 **What Is Religion?** 39

3 **What Is Philosophy?** 65

Part II Journeys of the Self

4 **Who Am I?** 97

5 **Where Do I Come From?** 123

6 **Where Am I Going To?** 151

7 **How Do I Get There?** 179

8 **What Obstacles are in My Way?** 207

Part III Journeys of the Cosmos

9 What Is the Cosmos? 237

10 Where Does the Cosmos Come From? 267

11 Where Is the Cosmos Going To? 295

12 How Does the Cosmos Get There? 321

13 What Obstacles are in the Way of the Cosmos? 347

Glossary 375
Notes 415
Select Bibliography 449
Index 463

Figures and Tables

Figures

1	Babaláwo Performing Ifá Divination. Rodolfo Contreras. "Fa Divination System," January 17, 2017, Alamy Stock Photo.	31
2	*Yīn/Yáng* and Eight Trigrams. Machine Elf 1735, "Fuxi 'Earlier Heaven' *bagua* Arrangement," July 9, 2010, CC BY-SA 3.0, Public Domain, Wikimedia Commons.	50
3	The Circle of Comparison. Timothy Knepper, March 11, 2022.	81
4	Muḥammad's Miʿrāj. Khamseh of Nizami, "Ascent of Muhammad to Heaven," *c.* 1539–43, Public Domain, Wikimedia Commons.	112
5	Face of Mars. Viking 1, NASA, Public domain, Wikimedia Commons.	145
6	Resurrection of the Dead. Luca Signorelli, "Resurrection of the Flesh," *c.* 1500, Chapel of San Brizio (Duomo di Orvieto), Public domain, Wikimedia Commons.	164
7	White Buffalo Calf Woman. Dennis Jarvis, "DSC01043, White Buffalo Calf Woman," August 7, 2018. CC BY-SA 2.0, flickr.com. https://www.flickr.com/photos/22490717@N02/43612608584.	182
8	Sĕpîrôt of Jewish Kabbalah. AnonMoos, "Kabbalistic 'Tree of Life,'" July 26, 2014, Public Domain, Wikimedia Commons.	226
9	Jain Cosmic Person (*Loka Puruṣa*). Wellcome Collection, "Sanskrit Delta 82," sixteenth century, CC BY 4.0. https://wellcomecollection.org/works/bt4wcdrf.	245
10	Zhōu Dūnyí's "Diagram of the Supreme Polarity/Ultimate (*Tàijítú*)." Edescas2, "El taijitu," July 2, 2006, Public domain, Wikimedia Commons.	271
11	Amitābha. Tịnh Tông Học Viện, "Amitabha 013," May 4, 2017, CC BY-NC-SA 2.0, flickr.com. https://www.flickr.com/photos/154345899@N03/33629271933.	307
12	Kṛṣṇa in Universal Form (*viśvarūpa*). The Picture Art Collection, "Vishvarupa1910: M A Joshi and company," *c.* 1910, Alamy Stock Photo.	331

13 Lisbon Earthquake and Tsunami, 1755. Science History Images, May 4, 2016, Alamy Stock Photo. 364

Tables

0.1 Ten Sets of Categories and Questions for Global-Critical Philosophy of Religion 7
1.1 Traditions of Philosophy of Religion 15
1.2 Component Parts of a Tradition of Philosophizing about Religion 16
1.3 Schools of South Asian Philosophy of Religion 26
1.4 The "Three Teachings" of China 29
1.5 Metaphorical and Philosophical Questions about the Journey of the Self 35
1.6 Metaphorical and Philosophical Questions about the Journey of the Cosmos 36
2.1 Contemporary Forms of Indigenous South Asian Religion 48
2.2 The Four Corners of Thick Description 59
3.1 Areas of Inquiry for Western Philosophy 67
3.2 Potential Sources of Valid Knowledge in South Asian Philosophy of Religion 72
3.3 Ten Sets of Categories and Questions for Global-Critical Philosophy of Religion 79
3.4 The Four Corners of Thick Description 79
3.5 Epistemic Virtues of True Theories 86
4.1 Scriptural Terms for "Soul" and "Spirit" in Abrahamic Religions 109
4.2 Four Types of "Selves" 120
4.3 Epistemic Virtues of True Theories 120
5.1 Mencius's Four Sprouts 135
6.1 Types of Liberation in South Asian Philosophy of Religion 156
6.2 Lakȟóta Terms for What Happens to the "Soul/s" after Death 161
7.1 Seven Sacred Rites of the Lakȟóta 183
8.1 Four Virtues and Seven Feelings 218
8.2 Types and Examples of Obstacles 231
9.1 Six Pan-Yorùbá *Òrìṣà* 242
9.2 South Asian Cosmologies 248
9.3 Abrahamic Cosmologies 257
10.1 Daoist Cosmogony/Cosmology 270

10.2 Udayana's Nine Arguments for the Existence of *Īśvara* 277
10.3 Rāmānuja's Refutations of Proofs for the Existence of *Brahman* 279
10.4 Aristotle's Proof from Motion (as adapted by Aquinas) 280
10.5 Aristotle's Proof from Causation (as adapted by Aquinas) 280
10.6 Ibn Sīnā's "Proof of the Truthful" 281
10.7 Al-Ghazālī's *Kalām* Cosmological Argument 281
10.8 Aquinas' Five Ways 283
10.9 Descartes' First Proof 285
10.10 Descartes' Second Proof 285
10.11 Locke's Proof 285
10.12 William Lane Craig's Kalām-Cosmological Proof 287
10.13 Alvin Plantinga's Modal Version of the Ontological Proof 288
11.1 Japanese Buddhist Teachings during the *Mappō Dharma* 308
11.2 Scientific Eschatologies 316
12.1 Abrahamic Exemplars and Experiences for Mystical Re-enactment 326
12.2 Eight-Limbs of Yoga 328
12.3 Three Bodies Theory 332
13.1 Logical Problem of Evil 364
13.2 Evidential Problem of Evil 1: Absolute Version (Rowe) 366
13.3 Evidential Problem of Evil 2: Relative Version (Draper) 367

Preface

Little did I realize what I was getting into when I began the journey of this textbook. Little has winded me more than struggling to ascend peak after peak of religio-philosophical tradition, text, and thinker. Little have I so frequently abandoned old paths and maps for new ones.

Fortunately, my journey was not alone.

For orienting me to my diverse subject matter, more than anyone I thank our seminar in global-critical philosophy of religion, especially co-founder Gereon Kopf and co-organizer Nathan Loewen, though also many core members over the last eight years: Purushottama Bilimoria, Fritz Detwiler, Eric Dickman, Marie-Hélène Gorisse, Leah Kalmanson, Louis Komjathy, Nathan Loewen, Herbert Moyo, Ayodeji Ogunnaike, Oludamini Ogunnaike, Jin Park, Parimal Patil, Agnieszka Rostalska, Kevin Schilbrack, Aaron Simmons, Nikky Singh, Laura Weed, and Wesley Wildman.

For daring to test-drive earlier models of this textbook with their students, reporting back its flaws and imprecisions, more than anyone I am grateful to Storm Bailey, Cody Dolinsek, Gereon Kopf, and Nathan Loewen, as well as the four anonymous reviewers.

At Bloomsbury, I thank Colleen Coalter and Suzie Nash, my editor Roza I. M. El-Eini, Merv Honeywood for his patience and diligence throughout the proofreading stage, and series editors J. Aaron Simmons and Kevin Schilbrack.

I also thank Agnieszka Rostalska for creating the index and Drake University's Center for the Humanities for funding this work.

And for supporting me through this five-year journey, I am indebted to Daria, James, Frances, and those with whom I now travel.

Abbreviations, Diacritics, Pronunciations

I have tried to keep abbreviations to a minimum, using them mostly to denote the languages of key terms (when they are not otherwise clear by context):

Ar. Arabic
Ch. Chinese
Gk. Greek (ancient)
Hb. Hebrew (ancient)
Lk. Lakȟóta
Lt. Latin
Jp. Japanese
Sk. Sanskrit
Yr. Yorùbá

For reasons mentioned in my introduction, I use diacritical marks for non-English terms. Here, I provide a brief language-by-language explanation and pronunciation guide (for those non-English languages for which I utilize diacritical marks, i.e., all above except Latin).

Arabic

For Arabic, I employ the standard system used by the *International Journal of Middle Eastern Studies* (IJMES): https://www.cambridge.org/core/services/aop-file-manager/file/57d83390f6ea5a022234b400/TransChart.pdf. I thank Mohammed Rustom for his kind help with this. Also, I consulted the pronunciation guide here: https://wordadayarabic.com/2012/12/17/notes-on-arabic-pronunciation-and-transliteration/. Of the Arabic terms that you will encounter below, these are the relevant diacritic marks:

ʾ the letter *hamsa*; a glottal stop (like the break in the middle of "uh-oh")
ʿ the letter *ʿayn*; pronounced like the "a" sound in "tab," though as if "choked"

ā, ī, ū long vowel sounds
ḥ, ṣ, ṭ raspy, "pharyngealized" sounds (made by constricting the pharynx or epiglottis during articulation)

Chinese

I use the standard "Pinyin" (*hànyǔ pīnyīn*, 漢語拼音) transliteration system of Mandarin Chinese, also including the traditional Chinese characters in parentheses on my first use of a transliterated term, except in cases where a single English term transliterates different Chinese characters (e.g., *lǐ* for 禮 [rites, rituals, customs] and 理 [principle-pattern], and *shì* for 事 [thing, phenomenon], 是 [right/correct, be/exist], and ± [knightly class]). Pinyin utilizes diacritical marks (macron, acute, caron, grave) over vowels to denote tones as follows:

ā first tone: flat or high-level
á second tone: rising or high-rising
ǎ third tone: falling-rising or low
à fourth tone: falling or high-falling
a fifth tone: neutral

Greek (Ancient)

For ancient Greek terms, macrons are employed for long vowels (e.g., *psychē*).

Hebrew (Ancient)

With five exceptions, I use the "Transliteration Standards of *The SBL Handbook of Style*" for ancient Hebrew terms: http://www.viceregency.com/Translit.htm. Thanks to my colleague Brad Crowell for his assistance with this. The five exceptions are terms either with no biblical use (*shevirah*, *Shekhinah*) or with common usage in English (*Kabbalah*, *mitzvah*, *mitzvot*). Here are the diacritic marks that you will encounter in this book:

ʾ the letter ʿ*ayin*; a glottal stop
ʿ the letter ʾ*ālep*; a weak stop indicating a "breathing"
ĕ, ē, ê most vowels can be marked with a caron, macron, or circumflex; in general, these correspond to increasing degrees of strength and length (with the circumflex indicating a diphthong)

ṣ "ts" or "tz" sound (as in "cats" or "hertz")
š "sh" sound (as in "shop")
ḥ, ṭ raspy, "pharyngealized" sounds (made by constricting the pharynx or epiglottis during articulation)

Lakȟóta

I consulted the online version of the *New Lakota Dictionary* for the spelling and diacritical marks of most of the Lakȟóta terms in this book: https://nldo.lakotadictionary.org/. These diacritical marks are of three main types. First, acute accents over vowels (e.g., á, é, í, ó, ú) indicate a stressed syllable. Second, the consonant *n* with a "hook" (*ŋ*) gives the preceding vowel a nasal sound. Third, caron accents over the consonants *č*, *ǧ*, *ȟ*, and *š* are a bit more complicated; here is a brief guide to the ones that you will encounter below, which has been kindly provided to me by Fritz Detwiler:

č like "ch" in "rich"
čh like "ch . . . h" in "much haste"
ǧ a soft "g" followed by a "zee" sound
ȟ like the Spanish "x" sound in "Mexico"
pȟ "sp" sound in "spin" followed by Spanish "x" sound in "Mexico"
š like "sh" in "shop"
tȟ "t" in "still" followed by Spanish "x" sound in "Mexico"
ž like "s" in "pleasure"

Japanese

As with Greek above, macron accents over vowels indicate they are long (e.g., *shūkyō*).

Sanskrit

I use the standard International Alphabet of Sanskrit Transliteration (IAST) and also consulted the following pronunciation guide: https://fpmt.org/wp-content/uploads/education/translation/guide_to_sanskrit_transliteration_and_pronunciation.pdf. I thank Marie-Hélène Gorisse for her gracious help with this. The diacritic marks that you will encounter below fall into two broad cases, macrons over long vowels (ā, ī, ō, ū) and an assortment of diacritics for consonants as follows:

ṅ velar "n," as in "king"

ñ palatal "n," as the first "n" in "onion"

ś palatal sibilant "sh," as in the German "ich"

ṭ, ḍ, ṇ retroflex stops, as English "t," "d," "n" (the tip of the tongue strikes the front of the palate)

t, d, n dental stops, as French "t," "d," "n" (the tip of the tongue strikes the edge of the teeth)

ṣ retroflex sibilant "sh," as in "shop"

ṛ vocalic r, as in "ri" in "cringe"

ṃ nasalization of the vowel sound that precedes, as in "yum"

ḥ voiceless aspiration, as English "h," but after the vowel sound, like a fainted echo

Yorùbá

As with Chinese (above), Yorùbá is a tonal language that utilizes diacritics largely to indicate the tone of vowels, with acute, grave, and macron accents denoting high, low, and mid tones, respectively, as well as a circumflex for a rising tone and a caron for a falling tone. A dot or vertical line below vowels indicates open variants of vowels, and a dot or vertical line below the consonant *s* makes the "sh" sound in English. To give just one example, here is the range of pronunciations of the English vowel *o*:

ó high tone
ò low tone
ō mid tone
ô rising tone
ǒ falling tone
ọ/o̩ open variantṅ

Introduction

What Is this Textbook?

This is an undergraduate textbook in global-critical philosophy of religion. It is an *undergraduate textbook*, designed for undergraduate students and courses. It is a textbook in *philosophy of religion*, intended for courses in which philosophical questions of meaning, truth, and value are raised about religious ideas, reasons, and worldviews. It is a textbook in *global* philosophy of religion, inclusive of religious reasons and ideas from many different religious traditions, texts, and thinkers. And it is a textbook in *critical* philosophy of religion, attentive to the socio-historical contexts and rhetorical-political ends of religious reason-giving, as well as some of the conceptual perspectives and methodological tools used to theorize and study it.

Why Was this Textbook Written?

Very few textbooks in philosophy of religion are both global and critical.[1] Why is there a need for such a book?

Textbooks in philosophy of religion should be global since religion is global. It exists around the world and throughout time in many different forms and expressions, most of which neither reduce to our contemporary "Western" understanding of religion nor occur in sociolinguistic contexts where there is even a word for religion. If we are going to philosophize about religion, we should include as many of its different forms and expressions as possible, avoiding the temptation to limit religion to the forms and expressions that we know best or think best.

Since there is such a strong temptation to limit religion to what we know best or think best, philosophy of religion should also be critical. Consider the following: When many twenty-first-century English-speaking people think about religion, they often think about what the term "religion" has come to mean in twenty-first-century English—an individually chosen, privately held, system of beliefs pertaining to "God." But the forms and expressions of religion around the globe and through time go well beyond this understanding of religion. Most religious practices and ideas were not—and arguably still are not—individually chosen and privately held; rather, they were given through culture or family and enmeshed in societies and polities. Many religious traditions were—and still are—more concerned with what is done with the body than what is thought with the mind. And a fair number of religious traditions either deny "God" outright or find "God" irrelevant to religious practice. So, if we want to philosophize about religion globally, we need to think about religion critically.

To philosophize about religion "critically" does not mean to "criticize" religion—at least not as we typically understand what "criticize" means: "to indicate the faults of (someone or something) in a disapproving way." Indeed, this is the first definition of "criticize" found in present-day English dictionaries. The second definition of "criticize," however, is closer to what is meant when we talk about philosophizing about religion "critically": "to form and express a sophisticated judgment of (a literary or artistic work)." Of course, global-critical philosophy of religion does not form and express sophisticated judgments *of literary or artistic works*. But it does form and express *sophisticated judgments*, which require sophisticated—not naïve—understandings of what religion is and how it works. This includes the example above: if you think that religion is everywhere and always a matter of individually chosen, privately held, organized systems of belief about "God," then you are not thinking sophisticatedly about religion.

To express sophisticated judgments about religion is also to think critically about the term that I have so far been putting in quotes: "God." Here, a global-critical philosophy of religion faces three critical issues from the get-go. First, the English term "God"—from the Proto-Germanic **guđán*, which scholars believe ultimately derives from the Proto-Indo-European root **ǵ^{h}eu̯*, meaning to pour (a libation for a deity), or **ǵ^{h}au̯*, meaning to invoke (a deity)—is increasingly used to refer to a dizzying diversity of deities: Which one, exactly, is meant by "God"? Second, the English term "God" is often used with an upper-case "G" to refer to "the supreme being" and with a lower-case "g" to denote "a superhuman being" or "lesser deity" (or in the plural—"gods"—as a collective noun): Which "Gods" are candidates for "the supreme being" and therefore should be referred to as "God" (rather than "god")? Third, among the "God-like things" of different cultures and communities, some are viewed as person-like beings who intend, perceive, think, emote, act, etc., others, as impersonal powers, causes, principles, or realities that are more nature-like than person-like (depending on how these terms are understood). In some cases, this matter is contested, for example, the Chinese term translated as "Heaven" (*Tiān*, 天), which some Chinese philosophers have understood as a quasi-anthropomorphic God, others, as the impersonal, mysterious workings of nature. Given the English convention of capitalizing the proper names of beings but not natural processes, should *Tiān* only be capitalized when referring to a person-like God ($Tiān_1$)? If we capitalize *Tiān* when it refers to the impersonal workings of nature ($Tiān_2$), are we likely to misunderstand it? Or is $Tiān_2$ sufficiently "ultimate" (as power, cause, principle, or reality) to warrant capitalization?

Hopefully, this short discussion gives you some inkling of the critical issues we will encounter in doing philosophy of religion globally and critically. Likely, it also shows you how power dynamics are always implicated in these critical issues: Who gets to decide how "God" is used and when it is capitalized? Who is included? Who is excluded? Whose religion is normalized? Whose is abnormalized? (Note for starters that Gods are seldomly female or feminized—more on this matter throughout this book, especially Chapter 10.) We can hardly plumb the depths of all these critical issues in the introduction of this textbook, though we will get to them in time. For now, however, we do need some practical solutions regarding capitalizing ultimate beings, powers, causes, principles, and realities, as well as for disambiguating occurrences of "God." Here, I opt for simplicity and specificity. With respect to simplicity, I will capitalize all occurrences of "God," "Gods," and other terms for what I take to be ultimate beings, powers, causes, principles, and realities. With respect to specificity, I will try my best always to specify which "God" is being referred to by "God."

How Was this Textbook Written?

To philosophize about religion globally and critically is no easy task. Nor is writing an undergraduate textbook in global-critical philosophy of religion. The forms and expressions of religious ideas, reasons, and traditions are so numerous, detailed, and diverse that no one scholar possesses the expertise needed to write such a book. What to do? In 2015, a group of scholars decided to begin working together on projects and publications in "global-critical philosophy of religion," especially as related to undergraduate teaching and learning. This group included specialists in the philosophies of religion of different religious and philosophical traditions, philosophers of comparative religion and comparative philosophy of religion, and scholars who work on critical issues and perspectives in the study of religion and philosophy. I am fortunate for the guidance and advice they have offered me in writing this textbook.

One of the biggest hurdles that our group faced involved rethinking the basic questions and categories of philosophy of religion. As you will soon learn in Chapter 1, the label *philosophy of religion* was first used by European philosophers during the European Enlightenment. This was a time when the growing success of science and fledgling separation of church and state led philosophers to begin asking which religious beliefs if any were true. The religions that these philosophers knew best were those practiced in Europe—Christianity mostly; Abrahamic religions more broadly. These philosophers therefore asked philosophical questions about what they believed to be the core beliefs of these religious traditions and expressions—the nature and existence of different kinds of Western-philosophical and Christian-creator Gods, as well as the problem of evil and the immortality of the soul.

Topics like God, evil, and the soul have remained central to Euro-American philosophy of religion up to the present. But they are not usually central to philosophies of religion in other places and at other times. Take Buddhist and Confucian traditions, for example, which arguably have no creator God(s), no immortal soul, and no problem of evil as such. If Buddhism and Confucianism were to be included in a philosophy of religion that asks about the nature and existence of a Western-philosophical or Christian-creator God, the problem of evil, and the immortality of the soul, they would appear wanting, weird, or wrong. (The same would happen if Christianity and Islam were to be included in a Buddhist philosophy of religion that asks about the ultimate nature of the *dharma*, the specific mechanics of *karma*, and underlying psycho-phenomenal constituents of reality-as-experienced.

Our group decided, therefore, that new sets of topics and questions for global-critical philosophy of religion were in order. As will be explained in Chapter 1, my own set of topics and questions come from the basic metaphor *life is a journey*, which can be used to generate philosophical topics and questions that are inclusive of many different religious traditions and communities, not just those most prominent in twenty-first-century English-speaking countries. These topics and questions allow these many different religious traditions and communities to stand on relatively equal footing in a global-critical philosophy of religion. Or so this textbook argues. More importantly, this textbook proffers a set of topics and questions for global-critical philosophy of religion that other global-critical philosophies of religion can *argue against*. As a colleague quipped when I first set out on the task of writing this book, if I were indeed able to accomplish it, then others would surely begin doing the same in hopes of doing better. I certainly hope so, for there are countless ways to reimagine global-critical philosophy of religion, many of which are no doubt much more global or critical than my own.

Who Is this Textbook Written For?

This textbook is designed for undergraduate students who optimally have a little bit of exposure to the academic study of philosophy and religion. It is not necessary for you to have taken a philosophy or religious-studies class before reading this book, but you will find it easier to understand the content of this book if you have had such a class (especially one that has introduced you to "non-Western" religions or philosophies). In other words, this book is ideally suited for, though not necessarily restricted to, mid-level or upper-level undergraduate courses with one prerequisite in philosophy or religious studies.

What about the practice of religion? Is it necessary or preferable that the reader of this book practices or has practiced some religious tradition? No. Nor is it necessary or preferable that the reader of this book is agnostic or atheistic. Why? On the one hand, anyone can come to an understanding of the contexts, forms, meanings, and uses of any religious reason or idea, at least in principle. Just as we are able to understand histories and cultures that are not our own (e.g., the American Civil War or the Warring States period in China), so we are able to understand religious reasons and ideas that are not our own. On the other hand, everyone comes to understandings of every religious reason or idea with certain preconceptions, biases, and interests. This is as true for your understanding of your own religious reasons and ideas as for your understanding of someone else's.

The key here is to see that understanding occurs *by means of*—rather than in lieu of—our preconceptions, biases, and interests. The goal therefore is to become aware of and "own" our preconceptions, biases, and interests, at least insofar as this is possible (while also recognizing that we may never come to see some of our most fundamental preconceptions, biases, and interests). But how does that happen? In my experience, one way is when we genuinely attempt to understand and value what is "other" than ourselves. Another way is to scrutinize and question the ideas and values that we take as "common sense." To do both—understand what is other, question what is familiar—is to philosophize, or at least to begin to philosophize. Anyone can do it. You do not need to be religious or non-religious to philosophize about religion. You just need to be willing to understand what is other and question what is familiar.

How Should You Read this Textbook?

It is important to learn how to do philosophy of religion before actually doing philosophy of religion. I therefore strongly encourage you to read the first three chapters of this book before the last ten chapters. Know, though, that these preliminary chapters contain abundant material about the religious philosophies of the world, and that in learning this content you will already be engaging philosophical questions and issues about it. In other words, you will be philosophizing about religion from the very beginning of Chapter 1 (if you are not already).

Chapter 1, "The Traditions of Philosophy of Religion," introduces you to the six (meta)traditions of philosophizing about religion that we will study throughout this book: *East Asian Philosophy of Religion*, *South Asian Philosophy of Religion*, *Mediterranean/Abrahamic Philosophy of Religion*, *African Philosophy of Religion*, *Indigenous American Philosophy of Religion*, and *European/Academic Philosophy of Religion*. As you become familiar with these (meta)traditions, you will see how their cultural-historical contexts shape their philosophical goals or ends, which in turn inform their philosophical methods and contents. What this means is that the questions and topics of some philosophy of religion are never simply natural or essential; rather, they are the products of cultural-historical contexts and political-rhetorical ends. The same is true for my own questions and topics for global-critical philosophy of religion, which I develop from the structure of the metaphor *life is a journey*, specify as philosophical questions, and apply to both the self and the cosmos. In expectation that some of you will want to know now what these metaphorical categories and philosophical questions are, I provide here Table 0.1.

Chapter 2, "What is Religion?" examines the religious content that we philosophize about when we philosophize about religion. We begin with a

Table 0.1 Ten Sets of Categories and Questions for Global-Critical Philosophy of Religion

Chapter No.	Journey Category	Philosophical Questions
Chapter 4	Who am I?	What is the nature of humans? Are they individuals? Are they substances?
Chapter 5	Where do I come from?	What is the original condition of humans? Are they free, good, or enlightened?
Chapter 6	Where am I going to?	Do humans survive death? If so, how?
Chapter 7	How do I get there?	By what paths do humans reach their destinations? Can only one path, at most, be true or effective?
Chapter 8	What obstacles are in my way?	What obstacles prevent humans from reaching their destinations? Is religion itself an obstacle?
Chapter 9	What is the cosmos?	What is the fundamental nature of the cosmos? Is it designed for the religious paths of humans?
Chapter 10	Where does the cosmos come from?	Is the cosmos eternal, created by one or more Gods, or otherwise generated? Can the creation or causation of the cosmos be proved?
Chapter 11	Where is the cosmos going to?	Does the cosmos have an end? If so, what happens afterwards?
Chapter 12	How does the cosmos get there?	How does the cosmos function? Are anomalous events and extraordinary experiences part of that functioning?
Chapter 13	What obstacles are in the way of the cosmos?	Is there disorder, suffering, or "evil" in the cosmos? How is it reconciled with the existence of one or more Gods?

series of introductions to religious histories, practices, and ideas in our six traditions of philosophizing about religion. Then, we examine a question that has vexed recent scholars of religion: Should the term *religion* be abolished given that it arguably distorts and colonizes many of the religious traditions of the world? Finally, we "learn lessons" from the critical study of religion and religions for the practice of global-critical philosophy of religion, especially how the global-critical philosopher of religion should "robustly describe" religious reason-giving with respect to what I call the "four corners" of description: logical form, conceptual meaning, cultural-historical context, and rhetorical-political ends.

Chapter 3, "What is Philosophy?" turns to the philosophical methods that we utilize when we philosophize about religion. This chapter first looks at philosophy in the "West," again demonstrating how contexts inform ends, which influence forms and contents. We then explore some issues and insights from non-Western philosophy. The chapter finally culminates in the assembly of a robust set of tools from both Western and non-Western philosophies for the practice of global-critical philosophy of religion. In particular, we examine what it means to formally compare religious ideas and reasons cross-culturally, as well as how we might critically evaluate philosophical ideas and reasons in comparative, cross-cultural perspective. Chapters 1–3 therefore collectively provide you with the methods, contents, and topics of global-critical philosophy of religion: a three-step method of philosophizing about religion (robust description, formal comparison, critical evaluation); six traditions of philosophizing about religion (see above), and ten sets of categories and questions (also see above).

Chapters 4–13 then get to the business of philosophizing about religion, each taking up one of ten sets of questions and topics for global-critical philosophy of religion, with Chapters 4–8 focusing on the self, Chapters 9–13, on the cosmos. Chapter 4 asks, "Who am I?" examining whether we are a "self" that is individual and substantial. Chapter 5 asks, "Where Do I Come From?" inquiring whether humans are naturally or originally good, free, or enlightened. Chapter 6 asks, "Where am I Going to?" focusing on whether humans survive death and if so how. Chapter 7 asks, "How do I Get There?" looking at whether only one religio-philosophical path, at best, can be true or effective. Finally, Chapter 8 asks, "What Obstacles are in My Way?" considering, among other things, whether and when religion itself becomes an obstacle for humans.

With Chapter 9, we turn to the cosmos, asking, "What is the Cosmos?" looking at whether and how religious and scientific cosmoses are designed for religious paths and practices. Chapter 10 asks, "Where Does the Cosmos Come From?" raising a central question of Western philosophy of religion: Is the cosmos created or caused by one or more Gods or some other kind of "ultimate reality"? Chapter 11 asks, "Where is the Cosmos Going to"? focusing on the relationship between theories about the end of the cosmos and social contexts of suffering. Chapter 12 asks, "How Does the Cosmos Get There?" examining the nature and role of anomalous events ("miracles") and extraordinary experiences ("mysticism") within the ordinary operation of the cosmos. Finally, Chapter 13 asks, "What Obstacles are in the Way of the Cosmos?" wrestling with the classical problem of evil, while also noting its absence from most religious traditions.

In reading this material, you will encounter terms and names that might be new or foreign to you. I have therefore provided a glossary at the end of this book. To aid in your learning, each chapter begins with learning objectives, ends with discussion questions and suggested primary and scholarly sources, and includes tables throughout.

Over the final year of writing this book, I went back and forth about whether to include diacritical marks for non-English terms. On the one hand, there was the issue of respect for these non-English languages and fidelity to the pronunciation of their key religio-philosophical terms; on the other hand, the issue of accessibility and ease for English-language readers. In the end, I decided for the former, in large part because this is an introduction to global-*critical* philosophy of religion. Thus, I also provide (above, in the front matter) a pronunciation guide for diacritically inflected letters in Arabic, Chinese, Greek, Hebrew, Japanese, Lakȟóta, Sanskrit, and Yorùbá.

Why Should You Read this Textbook?

Why should you read this textbook? One reason is simply my motivation in writing this textbook: there are few, if any, textbooks that approach the philosophy of religion both globally and critically, taking seriously the philosophical dimensions of the religious traditions and communities of the world. This is not just a reason why you should read this textbook; it is also a reason why you should practice global-critical philosophy of religion. Religious traditions and communities perennially ask and answer philosophical questions. We take these religions seriously when we take seriously their answers. You might then ask, why should the religions of the world be taken seriously? To that question, colleges and universities typically invoke learning ideals such as "global citizenship" or "intercultural development." The more you know about the religions of the world, the better a global citizen you will be and the more you will contribute to the flourishing of a global world. I agree.

Still, there are two more answers to the question "Why should you be a global-critical philosopher of religion (by reading this textbook)?" The first answer involves your neighbor—perhaps not your literal neighbor, but probably someone in your neighborhood or at least your town or city. Like no time before in human history, humans live in relative proximity to those who belong to different religious traditions or communities. Taking seriously the religions of the world (especially in their philosophical dimensions) is therefore taking seriously your neighbor. And taking seriously your neighbor (by understanding something about the philosophical dimensions of her religion) helps the two of you live in greater peace and harmony and collaborate together for the public good.

Global-critical philosophy of religion is also an indispensable means of taking ourselves seriously. Let me tell you a story to illustrate this point. When I had my very first job interview to teach philosophy, I was asked what I would say if student asked me why they should study philosophy. As I floundered with an answer, the interviewer abruptly cut me off and bluntly asserted: because it is something they bring with them. (Needless to say, I did not get that job.) This now is my answer to you: philosophy—in the sense of wonder about what is real, true, and good—is something you "bring with you" as a human being (especially as a young adult). For most of our adolescent lives we learn answers to these questions from those who raise us and teach us. Eventually, though, we seek answers for ourselves—either to understand why the reasons we grew up with should also be our reasons, or to look for new reasons that make better sense to us. I believe that philosophy of religion is of unparalleled use in this quest, for it is philosophy of religion that asks and answers questions about what is real, true, and good with respect to the ultimate concerns of humans. And by doing philosophy of religion *globally and critically*, you will learn about many such visions of the real, true, and good, not just those of the dominant culture and religion around you.

So, this is why you should do global-critical philosophy of religion by reading this book: the fate of the world, your neighborhood, and yourself depend on it.

Part I

What Is Philosophy of Religion?

1 The Traditions of Philosophy of Religion
2 What Is Religion?
3 What Is Philosophy?

1

The Traditions of Philosophy of Religion

Learning Objectives

- Explain the relationship between the four component parts of a tradition of philosophizing about religion: context, end, method, content.
- Describe some of the basic features of our six traditions of philosophizing about religion.
- Show how the contexts and ends of our six traditions of philosophizing about religion shape their methods and contents.
- Explain how the journey metaphor offers categories for global-critical philosophy of religion.
- Explore how the context and ends of your own philosophy of religion shape its method and content.

I. Traditions of Philosophy of Religion and their Component Parts

This chapter introduces you to some of the ways in which humans have philosophized about religion at different times and in different places. In doing so, we focus on six of the many "traditions" of philosophy of religion.

As a quick visit to Merriam-Webster will show, there are several definitions of *tradition*, the most relevant of which for us are "cultural continuity of social attitudes, customs, and institutions," and "characteristic manner, method, or style." Putting these together, we can deduce that each tradition of philosophy of religion has *characteristic manners, methods, or styles* that are *passed down and continued through social attitudes, customs, and institutions*. To elaborate, a tradition of philosophy of religion involves: (1) groups of people who inherit similar families of religious practices, ideas, and institutions; (2) who enact philosophy of religion to similar ends, in similar ways, and about similar contents; (3) and who pass down and preserve their philosophizing about religion through similar social institutions of some sort.

How many traditions of philosophy of religion are there in the history of the world? It is impossible to say. Many—perhaps most—are lost forever to our gaze. Moreover, how one itemizes traditions of philosophy of religion depends on how widely one "casts the net." Whereas we could call all South Asian philosophy of religion just one tradition, we could just as easily specify dozens, perhaps hundreds, of traditions of philosophizing about religion in South Asia among the varieties of Hinduism, Buddhism, and Jainism, not to mention Islam, Sikhism, Zoroastrianism, Christianity, Marxism, Western scholarship, postcolonialism, and so forth. Because this is an introductory textbook, I have decided to cast the net wide, focusing on the six traditions of philosophizing about religion in Table 1.1, while at the same time treating the philosophers and philosophies within them with contextual specificity.

Obviously, these are only thumbnail sketches for now. Moreover, giving names to each of these traditions suggests that they are singular and separate, when in fact each is internally diverse and increasingly intertwined with others. Some of these traditions are more like meta-traditions that are themselves constituted by different traditions; some cross geographic boundaries, influencing and being influenced by other traditions. In the cases of African and indigenous American philosophy of religion, there were no continent-wide traditions prior to European colonialism, and there now are such continent-wide traditions only to the extent that they are products of sociopolitical movements or academic scholarship. (For this reason, as I explain below, I focus on Yorùbá and Lakȟóta philosophy of religion, respectively.) Nevertheless, outlining these broad traditions makes it possible to examine how different philosophers and philosophies within them take up similar questions and issues, allowing us to appreciate the singularity of these philosophers and philosophies within their general cultural-historical contexts. It also helps us see the ways in which philosophies of religion often differ considerably between traditions.[1]

Table 1.1 Traditions of Philosophy of Religion

East Asian philosophy of religion	Traditions that begin in China before the Common Era and include the religious philosophies of Confucianism, Daoism, and Buddhism
South Asian philosophy of religion	Traditions that begin on the Indian subcontinent before the Common Era and include the religious philosophies of Hinduism, Buddhism, Jainism, and Sikhism
Mediterranean/Abrahamic philosophy of religion	Traditions that begin in the Mediterranean region before the Common Era, are influenced by ancient Greek and Roman philosophy, and include the Abrahamic religions of Judaism, Christianity, and Islam
African philosophy of religion	Traditions that begin in Africa before European colonization and intensify afterwards in response to European philosophy and religion
Indigenous American philosophy of religion	Traditions that begin in the Americas before European colonization and intensify afterwards in response to Euro-American philosophy and religion
European/Academic philosophy of religion	Traditions that begin in Enlightenment Europe, philosophize about the religions of Enlightenment Europe (Christianity mostly), and are eventually passed down and disseminated to other parts of the world through Western scholarship

It is through these traditions that we will practice global-critical philosophy of religion in this textbook. Every chapter will include sections about religious philosophers and philosophies from each of these traditions. Chapter by chapter, your knowledge about these traditions will deepen, as you develop and refine your own global-critical philosophy of religion in relationship to them. For now, though, let us begin gently—with a simple introduction to these traditions of philosophizing about religion. The goal of this chapter is just this. But it is also to show you how these traditions of philosophizing about religion are products of their historical and cultural contexts. This is a crucial point. There is no "natural" or "essential" content for philosophy of religion. Rather, the religious ideas and issues that people reason about and contest vary from place to place and time to time. In some cases, it is some kind of creator God (as typically found in the Abrahamic religions)—what the nature of this God is, whether this God exists, whether the existence of this God is compatible with evil, and so forth. But in other cases, it is how to escape the cycle of rebirth, how to cultivate virtue, how to preserve tradition against change, how to live in harmony with nature, how to discern one's destiny, how to cure sickness, and more.

Let us give this insight some analytical precision. The traditions of philosophy of religion are composed by four features: context, end, method, and content. If it helps, you can pair each feature with one or more of the questions that detectives ask:

1 Context = *where* and *when*;
2 End = *why*;
3 Method = *how*;
4 Content = *what*.

Context is the historical and cultural setting of some tradition of philosophy of religion at some place (*where*) and time (*when*). *End* is the reason *why* people philosophize about religion in this context—what they hope to achieve or do. *Method* is the means by which (*how*) people attempt to achieve this end in this context (for example, philosophical logic, textual interpretation, intuitive insight, argumentative debate). *Content*, finally, is *what* people philosophize about in some context, to some end, with some method. See Table 1.2 for a summary of all four.

Here, then, is our analytical claim about the traditions of philosophy of religion: *context shapes end, which in turn informs method and content.* With this claim, we can restate our insight above with a bit more precision: what humans choose to philosophize about and the methods they use to philosophize about this content are products of both their cultural and historical context and the social and personal goals they hope to attain in that context.

Table 1.2 Component Parts of a Tradition of Philosophizing about Religion

Context (*where*/*when*)	Historical and cultural setting of some tradition of philosophy of religion
End (*why*)	Reason why people are philosophizing about religion in this context
Method (*how*)	Means by which people attempt to achieve this end in this context
Content (*what*)	What is philosophized about, in some context, to some end, with some method

II. European/Academic Philosophy of Religion During and After the European Enlightenment

Now we turn to our six traditions of philosophizing about religion, beginning in the European Enlightenment, a time during which the title "philosophy of religion" was first deployed.[2] For our purposes, I map this period from the early seventeenth century through the middle nineteenth century. It was characterized, above all, by the championing of "reason" as the primary source of authority and legitimation of knowledge. It was a time of "scientific revolution," with respect to not only the remarkable growth of scientific knowledge but also a growing confidence in the scientific method as the only reliable means of producing knowledge. It was also a period in which the rule of absolute monarchs and the authority of the Roman Catholic Church was challenged, with constitutional democracies sprouting and spreading in place of divinely sanctioned monarchies.

In this context religion was "belief-ified" and "privatized." The former term, *belief-ification*, designates the growing tendency to reduce religion to its supposedly core beliefs, which were then evaluated to discern if any could be rationally proved. Increasingly, this became the goal of philosophy of religion during and after the Enlightenment—to show which beliefs were true and therefore compatible with what science was revealing about the natural world. No longer were the church and its theology the source and standard of knowledge. Rather, the tradition-specific beliefs of religious traditions became a matter of mere "opinion" or "faith"; only what agreed with reason was true. In the case of the religion of the Enlightenment—Christianity—this meant that tradition-specific beliefs about, say, the divinity of Jesus or the Trinitarian nature of the Christian God were matters of opinion (at least for some philosophers). Only supposedly core, tradition-neutral beliefs like the existence of a philosophically rarefied, creator God and the immortality of the soul were thought to be provable (or disprovable).

In the case of "privatization," Enlightenment religion increasingly became a matter of what people did in their private lives. Religion was gradually removed from the public realm of the state, as constitutional democracies began to legislate the "separation of church and state." Citizens were "free" to practice whichever religion they chose, just so long as it did not interfere with the workings of the state. For the first time in the history of humankind, there was a sharp distinction between the secular (public) and the religious (private).

What does this context of "belief-ification" and "privatization" mean for the method and content of Enlightenment philosophy of religion? In the case of method, religious beliefs were interrogated from the standpoint of Western philosophy to determine which could be proved true or false. Western philosophical methods were paramount in this endeavor, as was agreement with what science revealed about the natural world. "Appeals to authority" were therefore ruled out, especially where those authorities involved the dogmatic teachings of some church.

It should come as no surprise, then, to learn that the content of Enlightenment philosophy of religion was "lowest common denominator religion"—the religious beliefs that Enlightenment thinkers took to be common to all (European) religious traditions at the time. These beliefs included, first and foremost, the nature and existence of the God of European Christianity: Who or what exactly is this God, and can "His" existence be proved? Related to the nature and existence of this God was the problem of evil: If this God does exist and is all-powerful and all-loving, then why is evil as prevalent and random as it seems to be? Another set of issues concerned the nature of the self: Can we prove the immortality of the soul? Can we give a rational account of how humans should behave and why (ethics)?

These questions have remained the core issues for much of "Western" philosophy of religion right up to today. This is not to say that other issues have not been added to this list. Given the privatization of religion, the topic of religious experience has been of increasing importance to Western philosophy of religion, especially insofar as mystical experience is claimed to be a common core of all religious traditions. The topic of religious pluralism has also been of growing significance, particularly with respect to whether and how it is possible for all religious traditions to be "true" in some way. In both cases, it should again be clear how context and end influence content.

Not only have new issues been added to the docket of Western philosophy of religion over the last fifty years, but new forms or sub-traditions of philosophizing about religion have appeared, too. The dominant form of Western philosophy of religion remains "analytic" or "Anglo-American" philosophy of religion, which inherits, or just is, the form of philosophy of religion that we have already explored in this section. Since the 1970s, however, there has been a rival form of philosophy of religion known as "Continental" philosophy of religion since it draws upon the religious insights of twentieth-century philosophers from the continent of Europe. Whereas analytic philosophy of religion privileges analysis and logic, aspiring for rigor and clarity, Continental philosophy of religion employs tools from the twentieth-century philosophical movements of phenomenology and hermeneutics, seeking experiential intuition and interpretive insight. We will look further at all these methods in Chapter 3 as we develop tools for philosophizing about religion.

Although there are several other recent forms of philosophizing about religion in Western scholarship—e.g., fideist, process, comparative, non-Western—we will limit ourselves here to only two more, both of which are crucial for practicing philosophy of religion in a manner that is critical and therefore will feature in most of our chapters below. The first, *feminist philosophy of religion*, has confronted patriarchal conceptions and symbols of Gods mostly in Abrahamic religions and Western philosophies; however, it has been and can be applied more broadly to critique religious ideas, texts, and institutions that normalize male perspectives and powers over against those of women. Such feminist critiques are of utmost importance in global-critical philosophy of religion since nearly all of the traditional religious ideas, texts, and institutions from nearly all of the "world religions" were (and still largely are) patriarchal—created and legitimated by men, sometimes as a means of marginalizing and controlling women. A second critical perspective looks more broadly at those voices that are absent and excluded from, if not reviled and vilified in, religious texts and institutions whether due to race, ethnicity, gender, sexual orientation, class, or something else. Over the last fifty or so years, this critical perspective has become known as *postcolonialism* insofar as it is frequently deployed with respect to those marginalized and oppressed by colonial and imperial powers and institutions. Note, however, that such powers and institutions are not exhausted by the colonialism and imperialism of modern Europe; they run back through time to include all empires, states, and religio-political orders.

Why did the latter half of the twentieth century witness the birth of philosophies of religion such as feminism and postcolonialism? This is a complex issue, of course. In the very least, however, explanations include the waning of European colonialism, global and local redistributions of power and control, burgeoning critical cultural-historical scholarship, and increased concern with equality and liberty. Once again, therefore, it should be clear how changing sociopolitical contexts shape the aims, methods, and contents of philosophies of religion.

III. Antecedents to the European Enlightenment Tradition: Greco-Roman and Abrahamic Philosophy of Religion

The Enlightenment tradition of philosophy of religion (and its legacy in contemporary analytic philosophy of religion) did not of course come from nowhere. Its origins stretch back through the Middle Ages to ancient Rome and Greece. We now examine this tradition of philosophy of religion, showing how the philosophical issues of Mediterranean/Abrahamic philosophy of religion have roots in ancient Greek and Roman philosophy and are subsequently developed and debated in the Middle Ages by Jews, Christians, and Muslims. Once again context shaped end, which informed method and content. Thus, even though some content seems to be shared between Mediterranean/Abrahamic and European/Academic philosophy of religion, this content is constituted and engaged very differently by these two traditions of philosophy of religion.

In the case of ancient Greek philosophy, nothing had more impact on Abrahamic philosophy of religion than the concepts and proofs of God-like beings in the writings of Plato (427–347 BCE) and Aristotle (384–322 BCE). Plato's dialogue *Republic* speaks about "the Good" as that which is beyond all existing things, whereas his dialogue *Timaeus* features a "Demiurge" that fashions the cosmos out of preexisting materials. Much like Plato's "Good," Aristotle's "Unmoved Mover" is the end or goal (Gk. *telos*) of the cosmos, "thought that thinks itself" and thereby maintains the eternal intelligible truths of the cosmos. Unlike Plato's "Good," however, Aristotle's "Unmoved Mover" was buttressed with systematic proofs for Its/His existence, one of which argues from the motion of physical objects to the necessity of an Unmoved Mover that keeps them in motion, the other, from chains of cause-and-effect to an Uncaused Cause that is the ultimate source of all causation.

Note, however, that Aristotle's Unmoved Mover is not a creator of the cosmos, which for Aristotle is eternal; rather, the Unmoved Mover merely guarantees the perpetual motion of celestial bodies and the eternal existence of the biological species, logical truths, and metaphysical principles of the cosmos. Abrahamic philosophers of religion therefore devoted considerable attention to Aristotle's "God" and the proofs for Its/His existence, especially since Aristotle's philosophy was esteemed as science by many medieval philosophers of religion. This attention was most sustained in Islamic philosophy (Ar. *falsafa*) and theology (*kalām*). Whereas the former tended to employ versions of Aristotle's proofs that were claimed to be valid regardless of whether the cosmos was created or eternal, the latter preferred a simple argument from the existence of the cosmos to the necessity of a creator. Ultimately, Aristotle's proofs also influenced both the Jewish philosopher Moses ben Maimon (Latinized as Maimonides, 1135–1204) and the Christian philosopher and Dominican monk Thomas Aquinas (1225–74), the latter of whom offered five Aristotelian-influenced "ways" of proving the existence of a God. But just as Muslims argued about which proofs were effective, so did Christians, with Dominicans following the "Five Ways" of Aquinas and Franciscans instead preferring the "ontological" proofs of the Benedictine monk Anselm (1033–1109). What is fascinating about all this is that a topic that now divides theists from atheists—proofs for the existence of a God—once divided Abrahamic philosophers and theologians within themselves, primarily over the status given to Aristotle's "reason" vis-à-vis scriptural revelation. Here lies one important context and end of medieval Abrahamic philosophy of religion.

Roman philosophy also exerted influence on Abrahamic philosophy of religion, especially with respect to the question of free will, which became a topic of keen interest due in part to the influence of the Hellenistic philosophical school of Stoicism. For Stoics, especially the early founders of the school, God (Gk. *theos*) was held to be immanent throughout the cosmos (*kosmos*), directing its recurring expansion from and contraction back to pure creative fire, always in accordance with reason (*logos*), apparently in the same exact way every single time.[3] Does this mean that all events in the cosmos are causally determined and that we therefore have no free will? Stoic positions on this matter are by no means clear, especially given the emphasis in Stoic ethics on rationally choosing to live in accordance with nature. It would seem, though, that a gap had begun to open between what humans will (internally) and what actually occurs (externally).

This gap arguably provides the vocabulary for Christians such as the Apostle Paul (5–67) and the theologian/philosopher Augustine (354–430) to speak about the difference between the freedom to choose what to do and the ability to carry out that choice. For these Christians, "original sin" did not affect the human ability to freely choose what to do; it did however make it impossible for humans to effect that choice in action until the will was redeemed by a Christian God. Again, though, it was in Islamic theology and philosophy that these Greco-Roman issues played out most dramatically.

Here, the free will debate did not involve the Christian concept of original sin; instead, it centered on the justice and omnipotence of Allah. Whereas the Muʿtazilite school of theology declared that Allah can only justly reward and punish humans if they are free and therefore morally culpable for their behavior, the Ashʿarite school of theology deployed the notion of *kasb* (acquisition) to walk a fine line between divine justice and omnipotence: Although Allah is the actual cause of all events (and therefore omnipotent), humans "acquire" these events and therefore moral culpability for them insofar as they do choose to do (what Allah actually does).

What is once again interesting is that an issue that is still "live" for contemporary philosophy began in a very different context and with very different ends. Moreover, the *method* and *content* of the problem of free will are also very different in medieval and contemporary philosophy of religion. In the former case, scriptural testimony and theological terminology were used to figure out how human free will could be reconciled with divine omnipotence; in the latter case, the cognitive sciences are increasingly employed to determine if the appearance of free will can be reconciled with brain science. We will look at this issue in depth in Chapter 5.

IV. Philosophy of Religion Outside "Western" Traditions

Thus far, we have only considered some of the Western traditions of philosophy of religion—origins as such in the European Enlightenment and antecedents in Greco-Roman and Mediterranean-Abrahamic philosophy of religion. How do we look for philosophy of religion outside these traditions? How do we look for philosophy of religion where nothing is identified as "philosophy" or "religion," let alone "philosophy of religion"?

Although full-blooded explorations of philosophy and religion will wait until Chapters 2 and 3, respectively, we can for now employ starter definitions of these terms that will enable us to look for examples of philosophizing about religion that were not originally named as such. For now, let us simply define "philosophy" as the providing, defending, and examining of reasons, and "religion" as concern for ultimate problems and solutions, paths and destinations, realities and truths. (Again, please note that this is just a start; we will specify and complexify these definitions of religion and philosophy in Chapters 2 and 3, respectively.) With these definitions, we can now look for cases of philosophizing about religion in which reasons are provided, defended, and examined about ultimate problems and solutions, paths and destinations, realities and truths. In each case, you should be mindful of the analytic claim from the first section above: the historical-cultural contexts of a philosophy of religion shape its political-rhetorical ends, which in turn inform its method and content. This means that the contents of the philosophies of religion below might look quite different from those of "the West."

A. Philosophy of Religion in South Asia

Arguably, there were no terms for "religion" and "philosophy" in South Asia prior to the introduction of the Western concepts of "religion" and "philosophy" during British colonization and rule (1757–1947). During that time, the Sanskrit terms *dharma* and *darśana* were increasingly used to translate "religion" and "philosophy," respectively. Neither term, however, is a tight fit.

On the one hand, *dharma* is a wide-ranging, multi-valent term that encompasses ethical meanings relating to sacred duty and law, epistemological meanings concerned with truth and its teaching, and metaphysical meanings pertaining to the fundamental nature of reality. From a Western standpoint, we might therefore say that it is a term with as many philosophical senses as religious ones. On the other hand, *darśana* first applied to the auspicious seeing of a God in the form of a statue (*mūrti*) and was later extended to schools of "philosophy" that took different "views" or "perspectives" about what was good, true, and real. These "philosophical" schools, however, address as many topics that are religious as are philosophical (at least as "religion" and "philosophy" are understood from a modern Western viewpoint).

In short, therefore, there is no clear-cut distinction between "religion" and "philosophy" in South Asian "philosophy of religion." Nevertheless, there are schools in which philosophizing about religion (as well as a great number of other matters) occurs—the previously mentioned *darśana*-s. Moreover, these schools were renowned for their vigorous debates with one another. This, therefore, will be our focus for the tradition—or traditions, more exactly—of philosophy of religion in South Asia.

Although debates between rival religio-philosophical schools and positions in South Asia are evident well before the Common Era, it is apparently not until early in the Common Era that the procedures and rules of debate were codified in writing, perhaps first in in a medical treatise called the *Charaka Saṃhitā*, but more systematically in the founding text for one of these religio-philosophical schools, the *Nyāya Sūtras*. By this point in time, there was a flourishing diversity of these schools—ones that eventually come to be thought of as "Hindu," as well as ones that are Buddhist and Jain, probably also a materialist-skeptic school called Cārvāka or Lokāyata, possibly others, too. The context is one in which these schools engaged in public debate (*kathā*), often before rulers or assemblies, usually for reward or prestige. For two of these kinds of debates, disputation (*jalpa*) and refutation (*vitaṇḍā*), the objective was victory. For a third kind of debate called "discussion" (*vāda*), however, the goal was truth. We will have more to say about this third kind of debate—*vāda*—in Chapter 3 when we look at tools for philosophizing about religion.

Over time, six of these schools become known as *āstika*, which literally means "affirmer," though often gets translated as "orthodox." Among other reasons, this is because these schools accept the authority of the *Vedas*, a collection of books that were taken as revealed scripture in Vedic religion, a precursor of Hinduism.[4] Interestingly, though, four of these schools are not very concerned with the *Vedas*. The first, Nyāya, is a school of logic and epistemology that examines the many different means of attaining knowledge (*pramāṇa*), e.g., perception, inference, and testimony. Vaiśeṣika, which later merges with Nyāya, looks instead to the basic stuff of reality, positing an atomistic theory of reality that includes nine types of substances and six kinds of objects of experience. By contrast, the third school, Sāṁkhya, forwards a dualistic metaphysics, showing how the entire cosmos evolves from two fundamental existents, a pure experiencer and that which is experienced. Yoga, which later merges with Sāṁkhya, is instead occupied with how to use yogic techniques to liberate the innermost self. That leaves only the fifth and sixth schools, both of which concern themselves with proper interpretation of the *Vedas*. Although the fifth school, Mīmāṃsā, focuses on the earlier sections of the *Vedas*, maintaining the efficacy of sacrificial fire rituals for liberation, the sixth school, Vedānta, limits itself to the last section of the *Vedas*, the *Upaniṣads*, often claiming that understanding the relationship between the innermost self (*Ātman*) and ultimate reality (*Brahman*) can bring release (*mokṣa*) from the cycle of rebirth (*saṃsāra*).[5] As you will learn in Chapter 5, Vedānta comes in three main forms: the "non-dual" (*advaita*) Vedānta of Śaṅkara (*c.* 788–*c.* 820), for which everything just is *Ātman-Brahman*; the "qualified non-dual" (*viśiṣṭādvaita*) Vedānta of Rāmānuja (1017–1137), which holds that finite souls and material things exist as temporary qualifications of *Brahman*; and the "dual" (*dvaita*) Vedānta of Madhva (1238–1317), which maintains that *Brahman*, souls, and material things are entirely and eternally different substances.

The other three main "schools" eventually became known as *nāstika*—literally "denier," though often translated as "heterodox"—since they rejected the authority of the *Vedas*. For the first, Cārvāka (or Lokāyata), only one text survives to the present, so most of what we know about it comes from rival *darśana*-s that attempted to refute it. Nevertheless, it seems reasonable to assume that Cārvāka philosophers—whether or not they were ever organized as a "school"—rejected not only the authority of the *Vedas* but also the existence of a non-material soul and therefore the soul's ultimate release from the cycle of rebirth. Moreover, as we will see in Chapter 3, Cārvāka also provided a devastating critique of the reliability of inferential reasoning.

In the case of the other two *nāstika* "schools," Jainism and Buddhism, we know quite a bit more, not only because of an abundance of textual materials but also because they survive to the present day in robust and differentiated forms. Much like Sāṁkhya, Jainism—which is constituted by two main branches, Śvētāmbara ("white-clad," the monks of which wear only a loin cloth) and Digambara ("sky-clad," the monks of which go naked)—teaches a dualistic theory of reality: everything is composed of souls (*jīva*-s) that are entrapped in and deluded by matter (*pudgala*). When souls liberate themselves from matter, they ascend to the apex of the cosmos where they enjoy omniscience. In other words, liberated souls do not return to some ultimate reality or enter into the presence of some God. In fact, Jains deny and even offer arguments against the existence of an ultimate reality or first cause. This is not to say that all the "orthodox" schools of Hindu philosophy do believe in a first cause or ultimate reality; some tend to, while others do not. Regardless, the existence of a first cause or ultimate reality is one topic about which these schools debate. (More on this in Chapter 10.)

The final "school," Buddhism, is more like a meta-school that encompasses within it many different monastic and philosophical divisions. This need not concern us yet, for there are some central religio-philosophical issues about which most Buddhist traditions agree, many of which are points of contention with other South Asian schools. For one, Buddhists generally reject, or at least do not posit, the existence of some ultimate reality or first cause, especially if it is understood to be permanent in nature, since everything in Buddhism is generally regarded as fundamentally impermanent. This means that Buddhists also reject, or at least do not posit,

Table 1.3 Schools of South Asian Philosophy of Religion

Name of School	Teachings of School
Nyāya	Focuses on valid sources of knowledge
Vaiśeṣika	Atomistic theory of reality that posits nine types of substances and six kinds of objects of experience
Sāṁkhya	Shows how the entire cosmos evolves from two fundamental existents
Yoga	Explains how to use yogic techniques to liberate the innermost self
Mīmāṃsā	Maintains the efficacy of the sacrificial fire ritual for liberation
Vedānta	Focuses on the relationship between the innermost self and ultimate reality
Cārvāka	Argues against an immaterial soul and release of the soul from rebirth
Jainism	Teaches that souls must extricate themselves from matter to be liberated; rejects the existence of a first cause or ultimate reality
Buddhism	Holds that all things are impermanent, even the self-soul; rejects (or does not posit) the existence of a first cause or ultimate reality

the existence of a permanent or immortal soul; the "self," rather, is a label for a composite of changing processes.

Although the existence of a first cause and an eternal soul are two issues about which Buddhists disagree with many of the other schools of religio-philosophy in South Asia, we should not assume that these are the sole issues of debate in South Asian philosophy of religion, for to do so would be to make South Asian philosophy of religion too much like European Enlightenment philosophy of religion. In fact, the issues of the "soul" and "God" are not generally as important as other issues in South Asian philosophy of religion. One such issue concerns the method that is effective for obtaining release from the cycle of rebirth. Another is the nature of phenomenal and ultimate reality—what really exists and how. A third encompasses logic, language, and epistemology; a fourth, causality. We will turn to some of these issues in Chapters 2 and 3 when we look more closely at religion and philosophy. For now, Table 1.3. provides a nutshell summary of all these South Asian schools of philosophy of religion.

B. Philosophy of Religion in East Asia

Not only were terms for religion not introduced into Japanese and Chinese until the late nineteenth century; those terms—*shūkyō* and *zōngjiào* (宗教),

respectively—were coined by translators of European texts who needed a term for religions like Christianity that are rooted in doctrine and exclusive of other doctrine-based religions. It should not be surprising, then, to learn that in the case of China four of the five state-recognized instances of the category *zōngjiào* are not native to China: Buddhism, Catholicism, Islam, and Protestantism. Along with Daoism—the only *zōngjiào* that is native to China—these are the five "sectarian teachings" of contemporary China (with *zōng* meaning "sect"; *jiào*, "teaching").

In China, however, there is a much earlier and entirely native classification of teachings that goes back at least as far as the Ming Dynasty (1368–1644): the "three teachings" (*sānjiào*, 三教) of the Confucian or "scholar" (*rú*) tradition (*rújiā*, 儒家), the Daoist tradition (*dàojiā*, 道家), and the Buddhist tradition (*fójiā*, 佛家). As a classification of religions in China, *sānjiào* is not without its own issues since it not only excludes so-called "Folk Religion," a category that encompasses more Chinese religious behavior than all three teachings combined, but also includes Confucianism, which continues to be debated by scholars (both Chinese and not) with respect to whether it constitutes religion. Nevertheless, each of the *sānjiào*, even Confucianism, offers robust philosophical theories and arguments about ideas and issues of religious significance, whereas "Folk Religion" remains a heterogeneous category containing many different practices and beliefs, none of which has received sustained philosophical attention. Our engagement with the "traditions" of East Asian philosophy of religion, therefore, will be limited to the *sānjiào*: Confucianism, Daoism, and Buddhism. Although we will occasionally look at these traditions in Japan and Korea, we will usually stick to China, the area of East Asia in which Confucianism and Daoism first began and Buddhism first spread.

The first two "teachings," Confucianism and Daoism, date back to a period of ancient Chinese history that was so rich in philosophical disputation that it was later known as the period when "100 Schools Contended." In reality, there were far fewer than 100 distinct philosophical positions, most of which were not organized into cohesive schools. Still, the philosophical contention was real, driven by the increasing social chaos and outright civil warfare brought by the slow demise of the Zhou Dynasty (1122–256 BCE) during its later periods known as Spring and Autumn (722–476 BCE) and Warring States (475–221 BCE). During these periods, the central ruler and kingdom could no longer maintain control over its feudal lords and states, which battled one another for power and survival, inflicting widespread suffering and upheaval in the process. This was the formative context of early Chinese philosophy (of religion), the ends of which centered on solutions this problem. It was not uncommon for sages and teachers to present their solutions to local rulers in hopes that their programs might be adopted and they themselves might be employed.

The first philosophical response to this social and political deterioration was that of Kǒng Qiū, who was later known in China simply as Kǒngzǐ (孔子), meaning "Master Kong," which was later Latinized by Europeans as "Confucius" (551–479 BCE). In essence, Confucius' answer was simple—to return to the tried and true ways of old, the way of the scholars (*rú*), who studied and taught the rituals and ceremonies (*lǐ*, 禮) of the early Zhou Dynasty. In fact, though, Confucius innovated a new path by which a "profound person"—literally "gentleman" (*jūnzǐ*, 君子)—could cultivate virtue, foster order in society, and thereby bring harmony between himself, Heaven (*Tiān*, 天), and earth (*dì*, 地), all by expressing human-heartedness (*rén*, 仁) through the rituals, conventions, and customs of society (*lǐ*). Three generations later, a Confucian known in China as Mèngzǐ ("Master Meng," 孟子, 372–289 BCE), which was later Latinized as "Mencius," maintained that *Tiān* bestows innate propensities toward virtue on humans, who are therefore naturally good. In both cases, however, *Tiān* is less of an anthropomorphic deity than a cosmic principle (such as "nature").

During the Warring States period, the main rivals of Confucians included both the Mohist tradition (*mòjiā*, 墨家), which maintained the practical utility of human behavior and the equality of all people before *Tiān*, and the Legalist tradition (*fǎjiā*, 法家), which held that people were naturally and fundamentally selfish and that the state must therefore impose strict laws and harsh punishment. Soon thereafter, however, both schools faded into oblivion, eventually leaving first Daoists and later also Buddhists as the primary sparring partners for Confucians.

Although Daoism was probably not an organized school of thought or practice before the Common Era, the term for Daoist tradition or school (*dàojiā*) was later applied to a group of texts from the period when "100 Schools Contended," the most famous of which are the *Dàodéjīng* (道德經) and the *Zhuāngzǐ* (莊子). The former, which is traditionally ascribed to the mythical sage known as Lǎozǐ ("Old Master," 老子, *c.* sixth century BCE), is an elliptic and enigmatic, poetic-mystical text that speaks about the *Dào* (Way, 道) as the source of all reality and the force by which natural changes occur in a harmonious manner. Humans in general and rulers in particular can live and rule in accord with *Dào* by acting in ways that are as spontaneous, natural, and effortless as possible, not by assiduously cultivating virtue and ordering society, as the Confucians taught. By contrast, the *Zhuāng*, part of which was written by the historical figure Zhuāngzǐ (Master Zhuāng, 莊子, *c.* 368–*c.* 286 BCE), is unconcerned with, if not antagonistic toward, rulers, focusing instead on individual human beings who "walk" in *Dào*-like ways by navigating reality according to context and circumstance, avoiding fixed positions and absolute perspectives, understanding the relativity and complementarity of all judgments about goodness and reality.

This leaves only the third of the three teachings—Buddhism, about which you have already learned a little in the preceding section. Suffice it to say here, that most forms of Buddhism in East Asia took distinctly East Asian forms that were markedly different from Buddhism in South Asia. Among other things, the South Asian Buddhist emphasis on "suffering" (Sk. *duḥkha*) was displaced by an inherently good and all-pervasive "Buddha-nature" (Ch. *fóxìng*, 佛性), with enlightenment therefore becoming easily, even "suddenly," attained rather than requiring arduous effort and innumerable lifetimes.

Nevertheless, Buddhism remained focused on the mind; thus, Buddhism was considered the teaching that brought internal harmony, whereas Confucianism restored harmony to the family and society, Daoism, to the body and nature. These are the "three teachings" of Chinese religio-philosophy (as summarized in Table 1.4), which are eventually viewed as complementary teachings rather than oppositional philosophies. With this change, we have new contexts and ends for philosophy of religion—contexts in which social stability and order are not so fragile, ends for which different religio-philosophies work in tandem to bring harmony to society, nature, and mind.

Table 1.4 The "Three Teachings" of China

Name	Teaching
Confucianism	Taught that the virtue of the self and the harmony of society could be restored by expressing human-heartedness in social rituals and behaviors
Daoism	Taught that individuals and societies should act in spontaneous and effortless ways that are aligned with *Dào*, the cosmic source and force of reality
Buddhism	Taught that an original "Buddha-nature" can be recovered and that release from rebirth can be attained through meditative practices, devotional acts and utterances, or other ritual means

C. Philosophy of Religion in Africa

In the case of African traditions of philosophizing about religion, we focus on just one people—the Yorùbá, an ethnic group located in the West African countries of Nigeria, Benin, Togo, and Ghana. Why? For one, we want to respect the individualities and particularities of different African philosophies of religion rather than creating some overgeneralized, monolithic, ahistorical "African philosophy of religion." Also, unlike the meta-traditions above, we do not possess robust extant sources from which to reconstruct a meta-tradition of philosophizing about religion in sub-Saharan Africa prior to the twentieth century (which is of course not to say that it did not happen).[6] But why the Yorùbá, you might still wonder. These reasons are a bit more practical and personal: first, there now is an abundance of Yorùbá philosophizing of religion; second, Yorùbá cultures and religio-philosophies are significantly present in and interact with "Western" (and indigenous) cultures and philosophies in the Americas; third, two core members of our "global-critical philosophy of religion" seminar are Yorùbá and study Yorùbá philosophy of religion.

"Yorùbá" is in fact a term of Arabic origin, first used by the Hausa people of Northern Nigeria to refer to residents of the city of Ọ̀yọ́.[7] In the nineteenth century, however, the Anglican Church Missionary Society used "Yorùbá" as the name for all the people in the region who spoke similar languages, shared common cultures, and believed in a common descent from another city, Ifẹ̀. This was of course in order to colonize and missionize. Thus, we find in "Yorùbáland" what occurred in so many places around the world in the nineteenth century—ethnic groups and religions created and named by European Christians to missionize, colonize, and control.

In the case of the Yorùbá, it was also to enslave. The Yorùbá were the largest ethnic group to be exported to the Americas as slaves. For this reason, there are significant Yorùbá populations in Central and South American countries such as Cuba, Dominican Republic, Saint Lucia, Jamaica, Trinidad and Tobago, Venezuela, Brazil, and Grenada. In fact, given the success of Christianity and Islam in sub-Saharan Africa during the twentieth century, the traditional religio-philosophical beliefs and practices of the Yorùbá are now more common in "New World" religions of the Americas such as Santería in Cuba (aka, Lucumí or Regla de Ocha) and Candomblé in Brazil. Due to the Cuban diaspora of the latter half of the twentieth century, Yorùbá religion is now also common in the United States, especially Miami and the New York metro.

The Yorùbá trace a common origin to the sacred city of Ifẹ̀, where deities called *Òrìṣà* first descended to earth after having created it. By the early second millennium, a kingdom had been established at Ifẹ̀ (fl. 1100–1450), marking one estimation of the origins of "Yorùbáland." Ifẹ̀'s political and military power was eventually surpassed in the latter half of the second millennium by the Ọ̀yọ́ Empire. Due to a series of civil wars, however, the Ọ̀yọ́ Empire weakened and collapsed in the late eighteenth and early nineteenth centuries, rendering the Yorùbá easy targets for slave raiders.

If there is a "philosopher of religion" in traditional Yorùbá society, the chief candidate is a diviner known as a "father of secrets" (*babaláwo*), who, according to one anthropologist, was the "intellectual" of traditional Yorùbá society, possessing remarkable memory, intelligence, and insight.[8] The services of a *babaláwo* were sought especially when a person wanted to redress some sickness or misfortune by learning about the destiny (*àyànmọ̀*) that was fixed to her inner self or head (*orí*) before birth. To ascertain this destiny, the *babaláwo* cast palm nuts or a divining chain to determine from which of 256 collections of sacred scripture (*Odù Ifá*) to recite, explain, and interpret verses relevant to the issue at hand. According to some contemporary philosophers of Yorùbá religion, this makes Ifá divination an essentially interpretive endeavor, one involving no small amount of creative and critical thinking (Figure 1).

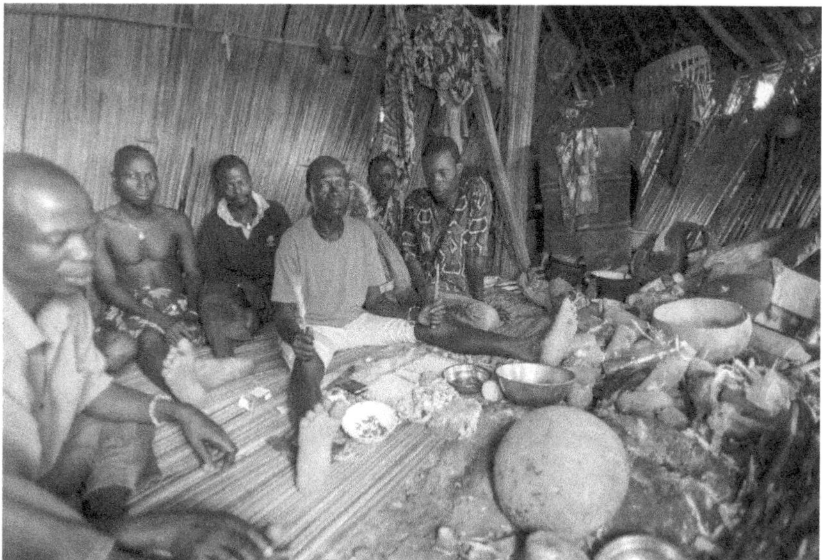

Figure 1 Babaláwo Performing Ifá Divination. Rodolfo Contreras. "Fa Divination System," January 17, 2017, Alamy Stock Photo.

Here we see one end of traditional Yorùbá philosophy of religion—to learn about one's destiny, usually to address some malady. The context that drives this end concerns uncertainty and instability—the fragility of human life due to sickness and disease, natural vicissitudes and disasters, and social conflict and war. Later, during twentieth-century colonial occupation and subsequent postcolonial freedom, another relevant end of African philosophy was to emerge, one that involves the relationship between philosophy and religion, specifically whether the worldviews or "ethnophilosophies" of traditional African culture are sufficiently critical and interrogative to constitute philosophy. As we will see in Chapter 3, this debate has much to teach us about the forms and ends of philosophy of religion more generally.

D. Philosophy of Religion in the Americas

With respect to traditions of philosophizing about religion in the Americas, we avoid ahistorical over-generalization by focusing on just one tribe of one nation: the Lakȟóta-speaking "Sioux" of the North American plains (for reasons very similar to those mentioned above about Yorùbá philosophy of religion). At the time of European contact (mid-1600s), this tribe was one of the "Seven Fireplaces" (Očhéthi Šakówiŋ)—as this nation originally referred to itself—who lived at the headwaters of the Mississippi River. Sometime after contact, the Seven Fireplaces migrated to the central plains, where they were increasingly referred to as "Sioux," a pejorative term meaning "snakes in the grass" that was given to them by their Algonquian-speaking neighbors to the east. The Lakȟóta (or Teton) are one of three linguistic groups of Sioux, which also includes Dakȟóta (or Yankton) and Nakȟóta (or Santee). The Lakȟóta themselves consist of seven bands: Oglála, Sičháŋǧu, Húŋkpapȟa, Mnikȟówožu, Sihásapa, Oóhenuŋpa, and Itázipčho.

Although the Lakȟóta were originally granted the entire western portion of South Dakota—including the Black Hills (Pahá Sápa), which are sacred to them—by the US government in the 1868 Treaty of Fort Laramie, this Treaty was reneged after gold was discovered in the Black Hills. Now, the Lakȟóta mostly live on five reservations in western South Dakota (none of which are in the Black Hills): Pine Ridge, Rosebud, Lower Brule, Cheyenne River, and Standing Rock.

As in the case of Yorùbá philosophy of religion, precolonial, Lakȟóta traditions of philosophizing about religion are largely inaccessible to scholarship. However, as in the case of Yorùbá philosophy of religion, they involved a special class of people—in this case, the "holy man" (*wičháša wakȟáŋ*), which is more commonly, though inaccurately, known as the "medicine man."[9] Holy men received revelations, performed miracles, and otherwise communicated with the spiritual world through dreams and visions. Among their powers included the ability to control the weather, to heal, to communicate with spirits and other species, to predict the future, and to find lost objects.

As interesting as these phenomena are, you might say that none constitutes philosophizing about religion, at least not with respect to the providing, defending, and examining of reasons. Perhaps. Maybe it is simply the case that Western scholarship does not have access to the reasons that were provided, defended, and examined by traditional holy men. Or maybe Lakȟóta philosophy of religion, like Yorùbá philosophy of religion, necessitates a reconceptualization of our understanding of what philosophy of religion is and does.

We will examine this issue in detail when we look at the methods and contents of philosophy in Chapter 3. For now, we stick to matters of context and end. What can we say about the context and end of precolonial Lakȟóta philosophy of religion? The context involved the semi-nomadic life of a community of people on the high plains of North America; the ends therefore concerned the surviving and thriving of this community in this context. Holy men (and women) helped the community understand and navigate their relationship to the natural world around them, especially with respect to its mysterious, sacred dimensions.

Later, as Euro-Americans began segregating the Lakȟóta onto reservations, this context changed, generating new ends for Lakȟóta philosophy of religion. One such aim is similar to that of postcolonial Yorùbá philosophy of religion: understanding and defending traditional philosophy of religion over against Western thought and culture. In the case of the Lakȟóta, this sometimes took the form of religio-philosophical resistance to and critique of Euro-American religion and philosophy, particularly as inspired by the "American Indian Movement" (AIM) of the latter half of the twentieth century. Some of the material on Lakȟóta philosophy of religion in Chapters 4–13 will come from those who were part of, or were impacted by, this movement—most of all, the prolific Lakȟóta historian and philosopher Vine Deloria, Jr. (1933–2005). Other material will instead come from traditional "holy men" who still seek to preserve and defend traditional Lakȟóta ways.

V. Categories for Global-Critical Philosophy of Religion

You should now have some cursory familiarity with the six traditions of philosophy of religion that we will explore throughout the remainder of this book. Rest assured that we have only begun our journey, so there is no need to have mastered this information just yet. Chapter by chapter, you will increase this familiarity, so that by the end of this book you will have a robust understanding of the range of questions, issues, and answers of each tradition.

For now, we can re-emphasize that the content of European/Academic philosophy of religion—the attributes of, proofs for the existence of, and problem of evil for an omnipotent, omniscient, and omnibenevolent creator-God—is not the content of other philosophies of religion. Nor is this content somehow "natural" or "essential"; rather, it is the product of social-historical contexts and epistemic-political ends. Hence, this content should not be the norm by which other philosophies of religion are judged. Nor should it provide the categories through which "global" philosophy of religion is conducted.

What then to do? Where might we find categories by which to philosophize about religion globally and critically?

As you know from the Introduction of this book, I propose utilizing the *journey metaphor*, drawing on its component parts for the basic categories and questions of global-critical philosophy of religion. Why? One reason is the journey metaphor is used in many different religious traditions to structure paths of religious growth and maturation.[10] Another reason is the journey metaphor is arguably fundamental to cognition and therefore culturally widespread.[11] Perhaps the best reason, however, is simply that the journey metaphor works to restructure the philosophy of religion in a globally inclusive manner. Or so, I will show throughout this book.

By *journey metaphor*, I mean, more exactly, the metaphor *life is a journey*, which utilizes the conceptual structure of a journey to understand and express the temporal dimension of people's lives. Although there is much to say about this metaphor,[12] here I stick to its core, constituent parts: journeys have a point of origin and destination, a route that is planned, obstacles and sights that are encountered along the way, and a traveler who is accompanied by and encounters other travelers. Each of these constituent parts can be used to generate philosophical questions, first vaguely in terms of the metaphor itself, second more precisely for philosophizing about religion, both as represented in Table 1.5.

Table 1.5 Metaphorical and Philosophical Questions about the Journey of the Self

1. Who am I?	What is the nature of humans? Are they individuals? Are they substances?
2. Where do I come from?	What is the original condition of humans? Are they free, good, or enlightened?
3. Where am I going to?	Do humans survive death, and if so, how?
4. How do I get there?	By what paths do humans reach their destinations? Can only one path, at most, be true or effective?
5. What obstacles are in my way?	What obstacles prevent humans from reaching their destinations? Is religion itself such an obstacle?

You might notice, however, that although these questions encompass some of the topics and issues addressed by our six traditions above, they largely neglect the central topics and issues of "Western" philosophy of religion, especially the attributes of its God, proofs for the existence of its God, and the problem of evil for its God. We can therefore reduplicate the vague questions in the left-hand column above with respect to the cosmos, recognizing that in some philosophies of religion the cosmos can be thought of as being on a journey of sorts, at least in the sense of having an origin, destination, path, and obstacles, and that in other philosophies of religion there is a crucial, central relationship between humans as microcosm and cosmos as macrocosm. Most importantly, in reduplicating these questions in terms of the cosmos, we can generate five more specified questions that are productive for philosophizing about religion, as represented in Table 1.6.

You might protest that although Abrahamic philosophies of religion tend to posit an origin and end to the cosmos, many others do not. True enough. Does this second set of questions then unfairly privilege Abrahamic philosophies of religion? Not so, at least not if we recognize the power of what I call the "null result." Consider that the correct answers to Questions 7 and 8 might simply be "nowhere"—the cosmos does not have an origin or an end. In other words, to ask where the cosmos comes from or goes to is not to presume that it has an origin or end. It might, and it might not. (The same holds true in the case of philosophies of religion that reject that notion that the self is some essential and unique substance-soul that has some ultimate destiny beyond death.)

Table 1.6 Metaphorical and Philosophical Questions about the Journey of the Cosmos

6. What is the cosmos?	What is the fundamental nature of the cosmos? Is it designed for the religious paths of humans?
7. Where does the cosmos come from?	Is the cosmos eternal, created by one or more Gods, or otherwise generated? Can the creation or causation of the cosmos be proved?
8. Where is the cosmos going to?	Does the cosmos have an end? If so, what happens afterwards?
9. How does the cosmos get there?	How does the cosmos function? Are anomalous events and extraordinary experiences part of that functioning?
10. What obstacles are in the way of the cosmos?	Is there disorder, suffering, or "evil" in the cosmos? How is it reconciled with the existence of one or more Gods?

If it helps, therefore, you can tack a parenthetical subjunctive clause to the end of every question above as follows:

1. Who am I (if anyone/anything)?
2. Where did I come from (if anywhere)?
3. Where am I going to (if anywhere)?
4. By what path (if any)?
5. Around which obstacles (if any)?
6. What is the cosmos (if anything)?
7. Where did it come from (if anywhere)?
8. Where is it going to (if anywhere)?
9. By what path (if any)?
10. Around which obstacles (if any)?

VI. And What About You?

Before drawing this chapter to a close, allow me to propose one final set of questions, which in this case concerns *you*: What are the contexts and ends of *your* philosophy of religion? How do these contexts and ends shape the methods and contexts of *your* philosophy of religion?

I imagine that many readers inhabit socio-historical contexts that involve religious diversity, conflict, and innovation. You might live in proximity to practitioners of religious traditions that are not your own. You might be bombarded with media accounts of religious conflict from around the globe. You might have available to you forms of spirituality that "think outside the box" of institutionalized religion.

How does this affect the ends of your philosophy of religion? Perhaps these ends remain the traditional-academic ones of figuring which religious ideas, arguments, and theories are real, true, and good. Maybe, though, they instead involve the ends of peaceful co-existence, of understanding difference, or of meaningful personal existence. Whatever the case, I invite you to end this chapter by reflecting on how the context of your philosophizing about religion affects its ends, which in turn impacts its method and content.

Questions for Discussion

1 Choose one of the six traditions of philosophizing about religion. Explain how the context of this tradition shapes its ends, which influence its method and content. Do additional research if necessary.
2 Sketch the content of two or more of the six traditions of philosophy of religion. Where do you find significant similarity and difference? How do you explain this significant similarity and difference?
3 Use one of the ten categories/questions of global-critical philosophy of religion to investigate some of the religious philosophies with which you are already familiar. Which questions are easy to answer and why? Which questions are difficult to answer and why?
4 Which aspects of your own cultural-historical context are relevant to your own philosophy of religion? How does this context shape the ends or aims of your own philosophy of religion? How do your context and ends inform the methods and content of your philosophy of religion?

Primary and Scholarly Sources

East Asia

Graham, A. C. *Disputers of the Tao: Philosophical Argument in Ancient China*. La Salle, IL: Open Court, 1989.

Schwartz, Benjamin I. *The World of Thought in Ancient China*. Cambridge, MA: Belknap Press of Harvard University, 1985.

European/Academic

Collins, James. *The Emergence of Philosophy of Religion*. New Haven, CT: Yale University Press, 1969.

Oppy, Graham and Nick Trakakis, *The History of Western Philosophy of Religion*, 5 vols. New York: Oxford University Press, 1999.

Westphal, Merold. "The Emergence of Modern Philosophy of Religion." In the *Blackwell Companion to Philosophy of Religion*, eds. Philip L. Quinn and Charles Taliaferro, 111–17. Malden, MA: Blackwell Publishers, 1997.

Lakȟóta

Powers, William K. *Oglala Religion*. Lincoln, NE: University of Nebraska Press, 1977.

Powers, William K., James Garrett, and Kathleen J. Martin. "Lakota Religious Traditions." In *Encyclopedia of Religion*, vol. 8, 2nd ed., ed. Lindsay Jones, 5295–8. New York: Macmillan, 2005.

Mediterranean/Abrahamic

Foltz, Bruce, ed. *Medieval Philosophy: A Multicultural Reader*. New York: Bloomsbury, 2019.

Marenbon, John. *Medieval Philosophy: An Historical and Philosophical Introduction*. London: Routledge, 2007.

South Asia

Gupta, Bina. *An Introduction to Indian Philosophy: Perspectives on Reality, Knowledge, and Freedom*. New York: Routledge, 2012.

Matilal, Bimal Krishna. *The Character of Logic in India*, eds. Jonardon Ganeri and Heeraman Tiwari, chapter 2. Albany, NY: State University of New York Press, 1998.

Yorùbá

Abímbọ́lá, Kọ́lá. *Yorùbá Culture: A Philosophical Account*. Birmingham: Iroko Academic Publishers, 2005.

Hallen, Barry. *A Short History of African Philosophy*, 2nd ed. Bloomington, IN: Indiana University Press, 2009.

2

What Is Religion?

Learning Objectives

- Describe some of the basic religious practices and ideas in the religious traditions of the Mediterranean region (Abrahamic religions), South Asia, East Asia, Native America (Lakȟóta), and West Africa (Yorùbá).
- Explain why the question "Should 'religion' be abolished?" matters for the academic study of religion in general and global-critical philosophy of religion in particular.
- Evaluate whether "religion" should be abolished for the academic study of religion in general and global-critical philosophy of religion in particular.
- Explain the four component parts of the "robust description" of religious reason-giving.

I. Introduction

The goal of this chapter is to introduce you to religion. Although this might sound easy enough, the academic study of religion is contentious in a number of ways, many of which involve the fact that *religion* is a European-language word and concept. The English term *religion*—just like the terms for religion in many other European languages—derives from the Latin word *religio*, which originally applied to correct worship of, not belief in, the Gods (of the Roman Empire). For next two thousand or so years, *religio* took on many other meanings, most of which continued to pertain to practice, not belief. Not until the European Enlightenment did *religion* come to mean what it generally means today—an individually chosen and privately held system of beliefs about a creator God.

Why is this a problem? For starters, religion around the world and through time is not usually a matter of holding correct beliefs (orthodoxy); correct practice (orthopraxy) is generally much more important. Another problem is that religion around the world and through time is usually neither personally chosen nor a compartmentalized component of culture; it is just part and parcel of the way that people are raised and live their lives. Perhaps the biggest problem is that there were no terms and concepts for religion in non-European languages—especially not if what is meant by religion is "an individually chosen and privately held system of beliefs about a creator God." The question, then, is this: Can we study religion, or even say that there is religion, in places and times where there are no terms and concepts for religion? To put the question in the terms in which scholars of religion often debate it: If *religion* is a modern Western concept that does not fit premodern and non-Western "religion" and, moreover, serves to colonize and inferiorize such "religion," should *religion* be abolished?

We take up this contentious question later in this chapter. First, though, we begin with a survey of "religion" in our areas of philosophical focus—the Mediterranean region, India, China, West Africa, the North American plains, and the contemporary "West"—for it is only possible to critically assess the concept of religion after learning about the diversity of religion around the world and through time. Does this mean that we are assuming there is religion without "religion"? Not necessarily. It is simply that you need to encounter some relevant "data" before you can competently answer the question "Should *religion* (the term) be abolished?" If it helps, therefore, you can think for now of these "religions" as constituted by practices, ideas, and institutions that have religious dimensions insofar as they involve ultimate problems and solutions, paths and destinies, and realities and truths, thus deferring the question about whether these things really are religions.

II. Religion in Our Six Traditions of Philosophizing About Religion

A. Religion in the Mediterranean Region: Abrahamic

By "religion in the Mediterranean region," we include those religious traditions that originated in the eastern Mediterranean region and the

Arabian Peninsula, especially Judaism, Christianity, and Islam. These traditions are referred to as "Abrahamic" since they all look to a man named Abraham—who, if he lived, did so in the early second millennium BCE—as a common forefather or "patriarch." Abraham was called by the God YHWH to leave his home in Mesopotamia and resettle in what is now in present-day Israel. As a reward for his faithfulness, Abraham was promised progeny, property, and prosperity through a covenantal bond with YHWH.

For Judaism, this covenantal bond is central, especially in the form through which it was given to a later patriarch named Moses on Mount Sinai in the middle of the second millennium BCE. By this point in time, YHWH had rescued the descendants of Abraham—who were then arranged into twelve tribes—from captivity in Egypt and had begun leading them on a forty-year journey through the wilderness of the Arabian Peninsula back to present-day Israel. While in route, YHWH commanded the leader of these tribes, Moses, to ascend a sacred mountain variously named Sinai or Horeb, on which YHWH gave Moses the 613 commandments (Hb. *mitzvot*) that would henceforth constitute the covenantal relationship between the Jewish people and YHWH. Ten of these laws are the well-known "Ten Commandments"; the others cover matters as diverse as religious ritual and festivals, priestly attire and behavior, sacrificial law, dietary laws, family law, criminal law, employment law, business law, property law, tax law, judicial procedures, agriculture and animal husbandry, laws of war, and ethical behavior

A few generations after the twelve tribes settled in present-day Israel, a monarchy was established and a temple was erected in the city of Jerusalem. In the first half of the first millennium BCE, religious practice centered around worship of YHWH in this temple. Three times a year, the people traveled to Jerusalem to make offerings and sacrifices, which were administered by a class of priests. When this temple was later destroyed by the Babylonians in 587 BCE, those Jews who were exiled to Babylon began learning how to practice their religion without a temple. It was at this time that study and observance of the commandments started to become important. Thus, even after the Jews were freed from captivity and allowed to return to present-day Israel (in 538 BCE) and rebuild a temple in Jerusalem (which was completed in 515 BCE), the study and observance of the commandments (which were soon thereafter codified in the Torah, the first five books of the Hebrew Bible) remained as important as temple worship and offering. Moreover, after this second temple was destroyed by the Romans in 70 CE, Torah study and observance became the main form of practice. This "Rabbinic Judaism" involves the leadership of rabbis (teachers) who study and interpret the commandments and lead worship in local synagogues.

There is much more to say about Rabbinic Judaism, especially since almost all of the Jewish philosophers of religion whom we will examine in future chapters belong to this "Rabbinic" period of Judaism (which reaches all the way to the present). But this will need to wait until we encounter these philosophers. So, let us turn now to Christianity.

Although Christianity shares the same early history with Judaism, it places much less emphasis on the laws that were given to Moses and became the basis of the covenantal relationship between the Jewish people and God. Instead, Christians in general see the first-century man Jesus (*c.* 5 BCE–*c.* 33 CE) as the means by which to establish relationship with their God. Scholars debate what exactly can be known about the historical figure Jesus. Most, though, seem to agree that such a person existed, spent his adulthood teaching and performing extraordinary deeds in present-day Israel, attracted crowds and followers, and was eventually executed on a cross by the ruling Romans. Christians believe that Jesus then rose from the dead, appeared to his closest followers (disciples), and taught for forty more days before ascending into heaven. It is through Jesus' death and resurrection that Christians establish their relationship with their Trinitarian God. Although there is much disagreement about exactly how this happens, one common explanation is that Jesus' death and resurrection redeem humans from their sins and absolve them of (most of) the laws of the Mosaic covenant.

Christians take the life of Jesus as an example to be followed. Thus, two ritual actions, above all, are crucial to the practice of most branches of Christianity: baptism and communion. Through the former, Christians not only model Jesus' baptism before he began his career by a man called John the Baptist; they also symbolically cleanse themselves of sin either through immersion of their entire body in water or the sprinkling of water on their head. Unlike baptism, which is usually performed when one begins the Christian faith, communion can be performed daily, weekly, monthly, or in some other regular fashion. No matter how frequently it is performed, the act of communion models the "Last Supper" of Jesus with his disciples before his crucifixion. Christians partake of bread and wine (or juice or water), the former of which either becomes or represents Jesus' body, the latter of which either becomes or represents Jesus' blood. Where this relationship is one of representation—as is the case in many newer Protestant, Evangelical, and Restorationist churches—communion is largely symbolic in nature. But in the oldest forms of Christianity—Eastern Orthodoxy and Roman Catholicism, in particular—the bread and wine are believed to transform into Jesus body and blood during the ritual of communion. Thus, Christians become united with Jesus by eating his body and drinking his blood.

The major point of disagreement in the history of Christianity, however, did not concern whether the bread and wine were transformed into the body and blood of Jesus during the ritual of communion but rather who exactly Jesus was. Whether due to the influence of Greek philosophy or the fact that the Roman Empire eventually made Christianity its state religion, the reconciliation of doctrinal disagreements was central to the history of first-millennium Christianity, with emperors calling seven "Ecumenical Councils" from the fourth to eighth century to forge unity. The first two councils took up the relationship between Jesus and God: against those Christian theologians who held that Jesus was merely "like" God or the first of God's creations, these councils held that the three persons of the Trinity—God the Father, Jesus Christ, and the Holy Spirit—were one essence (Gk. *homoousious*) in three substances or persons (*hypostases*). The third through sixth councils then tackled the relationship between Jesus' divine and human natures; against those Christian theologians who held that Jesus' human and divine natures were somehow united or that Jesus' divine nature somehow supplanted his human nature, these councils maintained that Jesus' was one person with two distinct natures—fully God and fully human. Not everyone agreed of course. Along the way, plenty of Christian branches fell outside of the bounds of orthodoxy as defined by these councils. Most notably, the Oriental Orthodox Christian Church—which includes churches from northeastern Africa, the Middle East, and India—refused to agree that Jesus had two separate natures, holding that the divine and human coexist in Jesus in one nature.

As with Judaism, there is much more that can be said about Christian history, practice, and belief; however, as with Judaism, these things must wait until later in the context of our exploration of particular Christian philosophers of religion in subsequent chapters.

Instead, we turn now to Islam. Although Islam does not share as much pre-common-era history with Judaism as Christianity, it does look back to Abraham as a forefather or patriarch. Moreover, it attempts to restore the pure monotheism of Abraham in a society that was largely polytheistic at the time. That society was located in the city of Mecca on the Arabian Peninsula during the sixth–seventh century, the time when the final prophet of Islam, Muḥammad ibn ʿAbd Allāh (570–632), lived. Mecca was the hub of trading routes; perhaps for that reason, the ruling Quraysh tribe retained the statues of many different local, regional, and distant deities in a building called the *Kaʿbah*, which was said to have been built by Abraham himself.

Although Muḥammad was a member of the Quraysh tribe, he spent his time in the hills outside Mecca meditating on the one God, Allah (which is the Arabic word for "God," probably derived from Hebrew words for God[s] such as *ʾĒl*, *ʾĔlôah* [sing.], and *ʾĔlohîm* [pl.]). During one of these occasions (in 610), the angel Gabriel (Ar. Jibrīl) began revealing to Muḥammad the Qurʾān. These revelations would continue throughout the remainder of Muḥammad's life. They would also anger Muḥammad's fellow Quraysh, who took Muḥammad's revelations as a threat to their power and way of life. Eventually Muḥammad and his followers were forced to flee Mecca for the neighboring city of Medina in 622. A war with Medina ensued, with the smaller forces of Muḥammad ultimately prevailing. When Muḥammad re-entered Mecca in 630, his first order of business was to smash all the idols in the Kaaba since there was "no God but God (Allah)," who could not be represented in any physical form whatsoever.

Although Muḥammad lived only two more years, he was to leave a blueprint for the practice of Islam after his death. Like Judaism, Islam is a religion of law and a complete way of life, with the Qurʾān and the sayings and doings of Muḥammad (*ḥadīth*) forming its basis. This law (*sharīʿa*) applies to all aspects of life—not just religion but also personal and family life, business and trade, political and legal matters. The core of this way of life, though, is the "Five Pillars of Islam": first, to recite the Muslim creed (*shahādah*); second, to pray five times a day toward Mecca (*ṣalāh*); third, to give 2.5 percent of one's wealth annually to those less fortunate (*zakāt*); fourth, to fast during the month of Ramadan from before sunrise to sunset (*ṣawm*); fifth, to make a pilgrimage to Mecca at least once in life if physically and financially able (*ḥajj*).

Islam was to endure only one major division, which occurred relatively early in its history—the splintering of Sunni and Shīʿa Islam. Whereas the Sunni recognized all four of the leaders (caliphs) who were chosen to rule after Muḥammad, the Shīʿa maintained that the leader must be of the same bloodline as Muḥammad. Consequently, the Shīʿa reject the first three caliphs after Muḥammad, recognizing only the fourth, ʿAlī ibn Abī Ṭālib, who was Muḥammad's cousin and son-in-law. We will look at this division further in Chapter 11.

More significant for our purposes is what is variably referred to as Sufism, Sufi Islam, or mystical Islam. Like the other Abrahamic religious traditions,

Islam possesses "mystical" sub-traditions, composed largely of adherents who sought a more direct and experiential encounter or union with Allah. Just as with Jewish and Christian mystics, Sufis sometimes ran afoul of more orthodox forms of religion in this quest for direct experiential encounter of Allah. More will be said about this in later chapters.

B. Religion in South Asia

The earliest discernable traces of religion in South Asia reach at least as far back in time as a civilization that flourished in the Indus Valley around 2000 BCE. But it is not until the later Vedic civilization (roughly 1500 to 500 BCE) that we begin to see significant traces of what will, over time, become "Hinduism." In fact, one way to understand Hinduism is the process by which regional and village deities from all over the Indian subcontinent were "grafted" onto Vedic religion for several thousand years.

What is Vedic religion? Like most things Indian, it is many different things. It begins as a set of polytheistic and ritualistic practices, with a panoply of deities that were petitioned by professional priests through fire rituals called *yajña*-s (by burning grains and other vegetables and plants or by pouring clarified butter [*ghee*] into the fire). Myths about these Gods and instructions for performing these rituals were contained in sacred books called the *Vedas*.

By the time that the fourth and final section of the *Vedas* were written (from about the eighth–sixth century BCE to about the third–first century BCE), there had been increased scrutiny and criticism of these practices. Many of these texts, called *Upaniṣads*, voice this critical attitude; some also advance the counterview that many different Gods, indeed the entire cosmos, are manifestations of an underlying ultimate reality, *Brahman*, and that this ultimate reality is one with the innermost or universal self, *Ātman*. For some of these *Upaniṣads*, the way of liberation (*mokṣa*) comes through meditative knowledge of the words of the *Upaniṣads*, especially the fundamental truth that *Ātman* is *Brahman*. Only so—and not through the fire ritual—can humans be released from *saṃsāra*, the wheel of rebirth, to which they are bound by *karma*, the law of cause and effect.

The *Upaniṣads* are not the only movement to criticize the Vedic system; Jainism and Buddhism do so, too, as does a materialist-skeptic movement called Cārvāka, not to mention some other ascetic movements that do not survive. But unlike the *Upaniṣads*, which were later drawn into and reconciled with Vedic religion, Jainism, Buddhism, and Cārvāka rejected the claim that the *Vedas* were revealed and therefore authoritative. As you learned last chapter, these traditions were therefore eventually called *nāstika* (literally "denier"; more commonly "unorthodox").

The origins of Jainism predate the appearance of historical Buddha by at least a quarter-century, perhaps much longer. Although the twenty-fourth and final "conqueror" (*jina*) or "ford-maker" (*tīrthaṅkara*) of Jainism—a man referred to as Mahāvīra, meaning "great hero"—is traditionally believed to have lived from 599 to 527 BCE, Jains believe that twenty-three *tīrthaṅkara*-s preceded Mahāvīra, the first of whom lived over 8 million years ago. As for Mahāvīra, he lived during the time when Vedic religion had fallen under critique. Unlike the philosophy of the *Upaniṣads*, however, Mahāvīra taught that there was no first cause or ultimate reality. Rather, there were only souls (*jīva*-s) entrapped in and deluded by matter (*pudgala*) through the force of *karma*, which is a material stuff that sticks to the soul in Jainism. Souls—and note that everything has a soul in Jainism—must therefore work to liberate themselves from *karma*. For humans, this requires a fourteen-stage process involving the "Three Jewels" of Jain practice—deep faith, pure conduct, and right knowledge—after which the soul is isolated (*kevala*) from the body and ascends to the apex of the cosmos where it enjoys complete omniscience. It is the stages of "pure conduct," however, for which Jainism is best known, especially as reflected in the "Five Great Vows" of non-hurting (*ahiṃsā*), truthfulness (*satya*), non-stealing (*asteya*), sexual purity (*brahmacarya*), and non-grasping (*aparigraha*).

Much like Mahāvīra, the historical Buddha—whose given name was Gautama of the Śākya clan (*c.* 563–*c.* 483 BCE)—renounced a life of comfort for one of asceticism. Unlike Mahāvīra, however, the Buddha did not find enlightenment in such a life, instead choosing a "Middle Way" between over-indulgence and asceticism. Ultimately, the Buddha attained enlightenment (*nirvāṇa*), "waking up" to the world as it is—a world of impermanence and the suffering that comes from clinging to impermanent things as if they were permanent. After waking up, the Buddha taught this "Middle Way" for some forty years, making many disciples. His teachings are best codified in two central Buddhist doctrines: The Four Noble Truths and the Eightfold Path. The Four Noble Truths are that suffering exists, is caused by our clinging to and ignorance about impermanent things, but has a solution, which is achieved by the Eightfold Path, which itself is constituted by components of wisdom, virtue, and concentration: Right View, Right Intention, Right Speech, Right Action, Right Livelihood, Right Effort, Right Mindfulness, and Right Meditation.

As you know from Chapter 1, Jainism, Buddhism, and Cārvāka constitute three of the nine major schools of Indian philosophy that debated with one another for hundreds of years, usually for royal patronage. The other six are the *āstika* or "orthodox" systems of Nyāya, Vaiśeṣika, Sāṃkhya, Yoga, Mīmāṃsā, and Vedānta. It is with these nine "schools" and their intensive debates with one another that Indian philosophy reaches an apex. (In fact, there were several different philosophical schools of South Asian Buddhism, some of which we will examine in later chapters.)

Although we will focus most of our attention on these South Asian philosophical schools throughout the remainder of this book, here we should point out that the (modern) Hinduism that is practiced today is mostly devotional in nature. The rise of devotional movements was a slow and steady process that cannot be precisely pinpointed. As Vedic religion spread throughout the subcontinent, regional and village deities were incorporated into the Vedic pantheon. Over time, three deities, none of whom were very prominent in the *Vedas*, became central for devotional Hinduism. Vaiṣṇavite Hindus worship Viṣṇu or one of his many "descents" (*avatāra*-s) into bodily form, especially Kṛṣṇa and Rāma. Śaivite Hindus worship Śiva and other members of his family. And Śaktite Hindus worship the Mother Goddess (Mahādevī) in one of her many forms, particularly Kālī and Durgā. In many types of devotional Hinduism, devotees believe that deities can cut *karma* for them, thereby delivering them from rebirth, usually into a heavenly realm. This is the way of *bhakti* (devotion), which is contrasted from the way of *jñāna* (knowledge), which is pursued by the *darśana*-s mentioned above.

Finally, a few words should be said about the South Asian religion of Sikhism, whose origins lie after the philosophical debates on which we focus in this book, though should not be ignored entirely, since it constitutes the world's fifth largest religion, larger even than Judaism. Sikhism begins with a series of ten gurus who lived in the fifteenth through seventeenth centuries in the northwestern Punjab region (which is now divided between India and Pakistan). These gurus taught a path of monotheism, rejecting the "idol worship" of some Hindu traditions, while embracing the more general South Asian worldview in which the "soul" is trapped in a cycle of rebirth by *karma*. For Sikhs, this way of release involves "Three Pillars": *nām japō*, to meditate on and recite the names of their God, *Waheguru*; *kirat karō*, to honestly earn; and *vaṇḍ chhakō*, to share and consume together. Table 2.1 offers a summation of Sikhism and the other forms of South Asian religion discussed above.

Table 2.1 Contemporary Forms of Indigenous South Asian Religion

Name	Practice
Vaiṣṇavite Hinduism	Devotional form of Hinduism that worships Viṣṇu or one of his many "descents" (*avatāra*-s) into bodily form, especially Kṛṣṇa and Rāma
Śaivite Hinduism	Devotional form of Hinduism that worships Śiva and other members of his family
Śaktite Hinduism	Devotional form of Hinduism that worships the Mother Goddess in one of her many forms, particularly Kālī and Durgā
Jainism	Fourteen-stage path by which the soul liberates itself from matter; focuses on deep faith, pure conduct, and right knowledge
Buddhism	Eightfold path by which the "self" understands all things to be impermanent, its own "self" included
Sikhism	Monotheistic religion that teaches three central "pillars": meditating on the God *Waheguru*, honestly earning, and sharing and consuming together

C. Religion in East Asia: China

As you learned last chapter, terms for religion were not introduced into Japanese and Chinese until the late nineteenth century, and when they were, they were primarily used to categorize "foreign" religions that were perceived to be doctrinally rooted and mutually exclusive. As you also learned last chapter, the major Chinese "teachings" were much earlier categorized by the Chinese under the heading *sānjiào*—the "three teachings" of Confucianism, Daoism, and Buddhism. In Chapter 4–13, we will see how these three teachings each make important contributions to global-critical philosophy of religion with respect to the understanding the self and the cosmos. Here, though, we focus on the practices of these teachings, especially as they concern ultimate problems and solutions, paths and destinies, and realities and truths. First, though, we look at religious behavior that does not fall squarely under the headings of any of the *sānjiào*—so-called "Folk Religion," which traditionally encompassed more religious behavior in China than all three teachings combined.

Some of this behavior goes back to our earliest evidence of religion in China—oracle bones from the Shang Dynasty (*c.* 1550–1045 BCE). Large bones, often of oxen that had been ritually sacrificed, were heated until they cracked. The patterns in the bones were then read by ritual diviners as the answers to questions asked prior to the ritual and later carved into the bones. These divinations were conducted for the Shang royal court, usually to discern or influence the outcome of some future event, whether natural or social. Although all such events were ultimately under the control of a supreme deity called *Shàngdì* (Lord on High, 上帝), prayers and sacrifices were also directed toward "lower" nature deities or royal ancestors, through whom the Shang royal court sought to appease and control the unpredictable and capricious *Shàngdì*.

With the passing of power from the Shang to the Zhou Dynasty (1046–256 BCE) came changes to these beliefs and practices. The supreme deity of the Zhou was known as *Tiān*, a term commonly translated as "Heaven." Whereas *Shàngdì* acted capriciously, *Tiān* was thought to reward moral behavior, as evinced by *Tiān*'s withdrawal of support from the immoral Shang and bestowal of the right to rule on the Zhou through the "Mandate of Heaven" (*Tiānmìng*, 天命). Although *Tiān* was earlier spoken of as quasi-anthropomorphic God, He/It appears to have been increasingly understood as an impersonal natural force, especially by Chinese philosophers (of religion). Relatedly, divination was gradually mechanized and popularized—the former, through the use of a divination manual called the *Yìjīng* (易經) that paired divination outcomes with combinations of broken (*yīn*, 陰) and unbroken (*yáng*, 陽) lines that were generated numerically; the latter, with divination being practiced beyond the royal court. Likewise, the veneration of and communication with ancestors was not only extended beyond the royal family to the common people but also interpreted morally as a form of filial piety.

Many of these beliefs and practices continue through time to the present, albeit in altered forms. Veneration of and communication with the ancestors is still central, with Qīngmíng (清明), the springtime festival of sweeping the ancestors' graves, serving as a major public holiday. Divination and possession also still occur, with divination often employing simple divining blocks, usually in combination with fortune sticks. Although the ultimate cosmic force is thought of impersonally as *Dào* or *Tàijí* (Supreme Polarity/Ultimate, 太極), popular belief also includes a celestial bureaucracy of deities that parallels that of former Chinese empires. At the top is the Jade Emperor (Yù Huáng, 玉皇), followed by a retinue of lesser deities that include judges of the underworld (e.g., Yánluó Wáng, 閻羅), each city's "God of Walls and Moats" (Chénghuángshén, 城隍神), each village's "God of the Soil and the Ground" (Tǔdìgōng, 土地公), and each household's "Stove God" (Zàoshén, 灶神), who reports the deeds of the household to the Jade Emperor every New Year. Traditional cosmology and medicine understand everything to be permeated by two opposite but complementary forces of *qì* (vital energy, 氣): *yīn*, the "negative" or passive, the force of earth, which brings all things to completion; and *yáng*, the "positive" or active, the force of heaven, which is the great beginning. These polar forces are commonly conjoined with five material phases (*wǔxíng*, 五行), together which produce all physical and moral change—wood, the process of bending and straightening; fire the process of flaming and rising; earth, the process of growth and fructification; metal, the process of yielding and molding; and water, the process of wetting and sinking—as well as the "eight trigrams," combinations of broken (*yīn*) and unbroken (*yáng*) lines that represent the fundamental principles of reality (Figure 2).

Some of these "folk" beliefs and practices infused Confucianism and Daoism over time. The springtime cleaning of the graves in particular and the veneration of the ancestors in general are both associated with Confucianism and its virtue of filial piety, whereas divine pantheons, Chinese

Figure 2 *Yīn/Yáng* and Eight Trigrams. Machine Elf 1735, "Fuxi 'Earlier Heaven' *bagua* Arrangement," July 9, 2010, CC BY-SA 3.0, Public Domain, Wikimedia Commons.

cosmology and medicine, and divination and possession have all become elements of Daoist teaching and practice. Although Confucianism often seems to Westerners only like moral-political philosophy, it is important to recognize not only that Confucian worship was instituted in Confucian temples as early as the Han Dynasty (206 BCE –220 CE) but also that the Confucian philosophers of the Song Dynasty (960–1280), who are now commonly referred to as "Neo-Confucians," systematized a Confucian metaphysics and innovated Confucian meditative practices.

The history of Daoism, by contrast, is witness to the organization of several Daoist movements and the production of countless Daoist scriptures. What distinguishes these movements and scriptures in general and Daoism in particular is an emphasis on achieving longevity, if not immortality, by bringing the self into greater degrees of alignment with the *Dào*. Several practices were used to this end: meditation to return the self to and unite it with the *Dào*, breathing techniques to slow down the breath and redirect it throughout the body, dietary regimens to balance *qì* in the body, yogic bodily postures, and therapeutic techniques.

Finally, there is Buddhism, which although foreign to China, not only impacted Chinese culture and religion in profound ways but also became its largest ism-ized religion. Of the four main distinctly Chinese schools of Buddhism, two are crucial for the philosophical underpinnings of East Asian Buddhism in general. The school of Huáyán (華嚴) understands reality as a grand harmony of phenomena (Sk. *dharma*-s; Ch. *shì*, 事) that are interdependent and interpenetrative expressions of an absolute principle-pattern (*lǐ*, 理) that is identified with both emptiness (Sk. *śūnyatā*; Ch. *kōng*, 空) and Buddha-nature (Sk. *tathāgatagarbha* or *buddhadhātu*; Ch. *fóxìng*). Tiāntāi (天台) recognizes that all things are both empty of self-existence (Sk. *svabhāva*; Ch. *zìxìng*, 自性) and provisionally existent, that all things possess Buddha-nature and are therefore originally enlightened, and that all things are present in every moment of thought. By contrast, the other two main schools of Chinese Buddhism focus more on practice. Chán (禪), which is known in Japan as Zen, places importance on a simple style of "just sitting" meditation, the goal of which is to penetrate one's innermost core and recover one's original Buddha-nature, whereas Pure Land (Jìngtǔ, 淨土) is a popular lay movement that ritually chants the name of a Buddha named Amitābha (Ēmítuófó, 阿彌陀佛), who generated a "Pure Land" into which his devotees can be reborn and from which it is easier to attain *nirvāṇa*. We will spend more time with each of these schools of Chinese Buddhism throughout this book.

D. Religion in the Americas: Lakȟóta

The first thing to say about religion for the Lakȟóta people—at least before significant exposure to European culture and religion—is that it was not religion, at least not if we think of religion as a compartmentalized component of culture, especially one that pertains to the beliefs that people individually choose and privately hold. Rather, religion for the Lakȟóta just is part and parcel of Lakȟóta culture, involving ritualized action that mostly occurs in the public sphere. The Lakȟóta term that was later used to mean "religion," *wóčhekiye*, once simply meant "to cry for"—a common feature of Lakȟóta rituals.

Another way in which Lakȟóta religion is different from what is typically thought of as religion (in the modern West) is that there probably once was not a/one "God" in Lakȟóta religion. Although the Lakȟóta term that is now translated as "God," *Wakȟáŋ Tȟáŋka*, has been increasingly conceptualized as Christian-like since Euro-American contact, evidence suggests that *Wakȟáŋ Tȟáŋka* did not originally resemble such a God. Rather, *Wakȟáŋ Tȟáŋka*, which means something like "great mysterious sacred," was probably the sum total of the sacred mysterious powers of the cosmos, most of all the *tobtób kiŋ* or "four times four," a group of sixteen sacred, mysterious beings and forces. Collectively, these sacred, mysterious beings and forces were responsible for creating the world as we know it, humans included.[1]

Much more important than myths of creation, however, is the myth of the sacred pipe (*čhaŋnúŋpa wakȟáŋ*), which was given to the Lakȟóta by White Buffalo Calf Woman, who is herself one of the *Wakȟáŋ Tȟáŋka* (as Wóȟpe). With the pipe and its rituals, the Lakȟóta not only first established a relationship between human beings and spirits but also re-establish that relationship every time they perform the rituals. Through the pipe and its rituals, the Lakȟóta also orient their world in time and space and structure their society relationally with one another and the rest of creation.

Although there are seven sacred rituals that are given by White Buffalo Calf Woman, three are especially prominent: "making spirit," "crying for a vision," and the Sun Dance. "Making spirit" (*inípi*), now sometimes known as "sweat lodge," is a rite of purification that effects a transition from the mundane to the sacred, often in preparation for other rituals. "Crying for a vision" (*haŋbléčeyapi*), now commonly known as "vision quest," is a four-day period of solitary fasting and prayer during which one receives a vision from the spirits. And the Sun Dance (*wiwáŋyaŋg wačhipi*) is a four-day ritual in which men dance around a pole until they break free from the rope that attaches their chest to the pole, thereby offering their pierced flesh to *Wakȟáŋ Tȟáŋka*.

E. Religion in Africa: Yorùbá

Much like the Lakȟóta, the Yorùbá did not "have religion" as a distinct part of their culture(s), especially one that pertained to individually chosen sets of beliefs about higher powers. Nor did the Yorùbá have "one religion." Rather, much like Hindu religious traditions, Yorùbá religion varied considerably from region to region, with different deities (*Òrìṣà*) worshipped in different towns and cities. Islam was also influential on Yorùbá religion, especially Ifá divination, at least by the early nineteenth century, as was Christianity in the later nineteenth century.[2] Not until the twentieth century would more exclusive forms of Islam and Christianity take root. It was at this time that a term for "religion" was introduced—*ẹsin*, a variant of the term *isin* (service).

All this is to say that the study of traditional "Yorùbá religion" is complicated in two fundamental ways: traditionally, there was neither "religion" nor "Yorùbá" (the latter of which, as you know from Chapter 1, first designated just the residents of the city of Ọ̀yọ́ and only much later applied to all the people of the area). Nevertheless, there are a number of religiously significant practices and beliefs that were fairly widespread throughout "Yorùbáland": the practice of Ifá divination, a select number of *Òrìṣà* with "pan-Yorùbá" representation, sacrifices to and possession by these and other *Òrìṣà*, and rituals for ancestors. These aspects of "Yorùbá religion" will be our focus in this book.

In the case of Ifá divination, issues of sickness, misfortune, and uncertainty are brought to a diviner called a *babaláwo*, who then casts nuts or throws a chain in order to produce a number that reveals which collection (*odù*) of a sacred scripture called *Odù Ifá* contains a solution to that problem. This scripture, which traditionally did not exist in written form but rather was memorized by diviners, is divided into 256 collections, each of which contains a number of poems (*ẹsẹ*) about mythical precedents, several of which the priest recites and interprets. The client then chooses for themself which poem best suits their issue, after which the *babaláwo* and client discuss the next steps to be taken, most importantly which sacrifice (*ẹbọ*) must be made to which *Òrìṣà* to ensure that the divination will come to pass.

Some *Òrìṣà* personify natural phenomena (rivers, thunder) or human activities (ironworking, childbearing), whereas others are legendary ancestors. Each, however, is associated with a particular part of the body, particular personalities and characteristics, and particular abilities and virtues. In the case of Ifá divination, therefore, the choice of which *Òrìṣà* to which to sacrifice is determined by which affliction one suffers. *Òrìṣà* worship, however, extends well beyond Ifá sacrifice, including daily, annual, and other routine rituals, sacrifices, and festivals.

Above all the *Òrìṣà*, so to speak, is a "high God" usually called Olódùmarè (in the *Ifá* corpus) or Ọlọrun (elsewhere). Together with three primordial *Òrìṣà*—Ọrunmila, the *Òrìṣà* of Ifá divination; Èṣù, the *Òrìṣà* who delivers sacrifices to the other *Òrìṣà*; and Ọbàtálá, the *Òrìṣà* who creates humans—Olódùmarè created the heavens. After the heavens were populated with all 400 primordial *Òrìṣà*, some of them descended from the heaven to make dry land over the primordial waters (at the city of Ifẹ̀), to create humans, and to settle cities and towns. Most of the *Òrìṣà* now inhabit a "lower heaven" under the crust of the earth, from which they can rise to respond to invocation and sacrifice, sometimes "mounting" (*gùn*) their devotees and possessing them in ecstatic states of trance. Olódùmarè, however, remains in "upper heaven," where he serves as the judge of every human life upon death (at least according to the tradition of Ifá).

Olódùmarè not only plays the role of judge; he also enlivens every human being by blowing into them his life-breath (*èmí*) and fixing to them an "inner head" (*orí*), which contains a destiny (*àyànmọ́*) that determines their personality and life-trajectory. It is critically important, therefore, to learn this destiny through Ifá divination, especially when confronted with illness and adversity.

F. Contemporary Religion in the "West"

We would be remiss if we did not briefly examine some of the more notable recent developments of religion, especially in the "West." First and foremost, as you already know, religion in the modern West was progressively reinvented as a system of belief that is individually chosen and personally held. This reduction of religion to the mental and the individual has in turn given rise to non-institutionalized expressions of religion, which are often categorized by the phrase "spiritual but not religious" or the term "NONE." Those who are "spiritual but not religious" are said to possess certain beliefs about "Higher Powers," even though they do not identify with any organized, institutionalized, ism-ized form of religion. When answering surveys that ask them whether they identify with any of the ism-ized forms of religion, such people often tick the box labeled "NONE."

Another notable recent religious phenomenon is that of "multiple belonging"—people who identify as belonging to two or more religious traditions. Of course, this phenomenon is not new in the sense that many of the religious traditions of the world were not mutually exclusive of one another. As you now know, for example, the Chinese were commonly said to be Confucians, Daoists, and Buddhists all at once, as well as to observe certain "folk traditions." Nevertheless, the last few decades have witnessed a rise in the number of people who avowedly identify as belonging to multiple religious traditions—Jews who are also Buddhists, Christians or Muslims who are also Hindu, Yorùbá who are Muslims or Christians, and so forth.

The flipside of multiple belonging is a phenomenon known as hybridity (or syncretism). Hybridity, to some degree, is simply a fact of religion (and more generally, culture). As a religion/culture travels to different places and encounters different religions/cultures, it is affected, to some degree, by those religions/cultures. To the extent that this process produces something distinctly new, in which there are recognizable pieces of different religious practices or beliefs from different religions or cultures, we have hybridity. Afro-Caribbean religion is the hybrid product of West African religion, Catholic Christianity, and indigenous Caribbean religion. Cao Đài is a recent Vietnamese religion that combines elements of Buddhism, Christianity, Daoism, Confucianism, and Islam. Some have even called American Christianity the hybrid product of European Christianity, Gnostic spirituality, and American individualism.

III. Should "Religion" be Abolished?

We are now ready to return to where we began: Should *religion* be abolished? First, note what should be obvious: this question does not ask whether religious traditions or expressions should be abolished; rather, it asks whether the category of *religion* should be abolished. Also appreciate that this is primarily a question for scholarship, not for everyday discourse, one that asks whether scholars should avoid using the category of *religion*, not whether the "language police" should stop "ordinary people" from uttering the word *religion*. Finally, consider that this is not a question about what is practically feasible; rather, it is a question of what *ought* to be done. With these distinctions in place, let us look three of the reasons why some scholars of religion believe that *religion* should be abolished.[3]

First, there is the fact that religion is not a natural entity but rather a social construction. Religion is not like plum trees and pit bulls; rather, it is like baseball and politics. *Religion* is used to refer to certain things that people do, certain institutions that people create, and certain ideas that people have. Moreover, *religion* has been used to refer to lots of different kinds of behaviors, institutions, and ideas throughout time and space. Originally, the

Latin term *religio* referred to correct practice of the rituals and observances pertaining to the Roman Gods. During the Middle Ages, *religio* was sometimes applied exclusively to monastic institutions and practices—monks and nuns were religious; others were not. Not until the Enlightenment did European terms for religion begin to refer to systems of belief (as well as a distinct aspect of culture). And not until the nineteenth and twentieth centuries did terms for religion begin to be introduced into non-European languages, either by coining new words or by adding new meanings to existing words. (It was also during the nineteenth century that the "ism-ized" terms for many of the religions of the world were first coined—e.g., Hinduism, Buddhism, Jainism, Sikhism, Daoism, Confucianism, etc.) Can there be religion where there is no term for religion? Is there *really* any such thing as religion in the first place?

The second type of reason why scholars argue that *religion* should be abolished is that the modern Western concept of religion does not fit and therefore distorts so-called religious practices, institutions, and ideas elsewhere in time and space. As you already know, this modern Western concept of *religion* has several core components: (1) religion is primarily a matter of beliefs; (2) religious beliefs are about a creator God; (3) these beliefs form a structured whole that does not vary (much) through space and time; (4) each religion is constituted by a different, mutually exclusive set of beliefs; (5) religion is one of many distinct and universal elements of culture; (6) believing or not believing in some particular religion is a matter of private, individual choice. Hopefully, our survey of religion above has showed that, indeed, the modern Western concept of *religion* does not fit many of the so-called religious traditions of the world: religions are often about practice (at least as much as belief); religions are internally diverse and temporally changing; religions intertwine and overlap; religion is often just a matter of cultural and familial tradition. Thus, we should ask whether the term *religion* can be used to identify and analyze "religions" that are so different from the modern Western construction of religion.

The third reason why some scholars think that *religion* should be abolished is that this modern Western construction is an ideologically motivated means of maintaining the dominance of Western culture. According to this argument, so-called religions must conform to the standard of modern Western religion if they are to count as instances of the category *religion*. They must be belief-centered and scripturally based. Their beliefs must be thought of as forming a structured whole that is homogenous and unchanging. Their systems of belief must be mutually exclusive of one another. Most importantly, they must be rooted in personal, private experience, which is cordoned off from the secular, public sphere of the state and the market, in which Western institutions continue to dominate. The modern Western category of *religion* therefore serves as a tool of Western imperialism, a means of relegating the religions and cultures of "others" to realms in which they are politically and economically insignificant. Thus, some scholars argue that if religion is to be studied at all, it should be studied as an ideological tool of oppression.

Of course, there are also scholars who argue that *religion* is a term and concept that is useful to human inquiry and therefore ought to be retained and reformed, not abolished and abandoned. In response to the first argument above, these scholars maintain that even though *religion* is a human construction, it can be used to refer to certain kinds of human actions in the world, and that even though *religion* is a modern Western construction, the practices, institutions, and ideas of non-modern and non-Western traditions can (in certain cases) be interpreted as religious. In response to the second and third arguments above, these scholars hold that even though *religion* has been and often still is understood in a narrow modern Western manner and deployed to support an oppressive modern Western agenda, the term can be reformed to be more broadly and justly applicable.

Although I count myself in the latter camp (retain and reform), I nevertheless have strong sympathies with the former camp (abolish and abandon), which has important lessons for the study of religion in general and the practice of global-critical philosophy of religion in particular. I believe it is crucial for us to learn to see religion beyond its modern Western construction, as well as to notice when modern Western constructions of religion are being used for ethnocentric or imperialistic ends. Religion is not (just) a set of beliefs about God(s). Religion does not (always) come in mutually exclusive, ism-ized forms. Religion is not (usually) something that is personally chosen and privately held vis-à-vis the public, secular state. Religion is never free from cultural, societal, economic, and political biases, interests, uses, and abuses.

These lessons are as important for religions as they are for "religion." No religious tradition is constituted by a singular and unchanging set of beliefs; philosophers of religion must be mindful of matters of internal diversity, historical change, and bodily practice so as not to homogenize, ossify, and intellectualize religious traditions. (Beware when somebody tells you that, e.g., Hinduism is everywhere and always just such-and-such a set of beliefs.) No religious tradition can be extricated from its wider context; philosophers of religion must be mindful of the cultural-historical embeddedness of religious traditions so as not to spiritualize, compartmentalize, and de-historicize them. (Beware when somebody tells you that, e.g., the core of Islam can be distinguished from its "corrupt" cultural aggregations.) Most importantly, no religious tradition is free of the dynamics of power; philosophers of religion must be mindful of who does and does not get to speak for, represent, and define some religious tradition. (Beware when somebody tells you that, e.g., his version of Christianity is the only real or true one.)

IV. Upshot for Global-Critical Philosophy of Religion: Robust Description

In light of these "lessons" (concerning context, diversity, change, practice, and power), our philosophizing about religion in Chapters 4–13 will try to focus on *individual acts of religious reason-giving*, describing them as robustly as possible in terms of what I call the *four corners of thick description*: logical form, conceptual content, contextual setting, and political use. As we will see in Chapter 3, such "robust description" is the first in a three-step method for practicing global-critical philosophy of religion. Here, we examine robust description in an effort to "bring home" this chapter's lessons about religion and religious traditions for the practice of global-critical philosophy of religion.

In theory, acts of religious reason-giving could involve practically anything—any reason why someone does or does not practice or believe something somehow related to religion. That said, reason-giving about religion comes into clearest focus when it involves the *reasonableness* of some religious practice or belief, which usually happens when there is *disagreement* about whether that practice or belief is reasonable. Think about it. If we grow up practicing and believing *religion x*, never encountering anyone who does not practice and believe *religion x* (which in this case is really just a way of life), then we have little need to give reasons why we practice and believe *religion x*. But if we encounter people (whether in person or through stories or texts) who do not practice and believe *religion x*, then we might begin to feel the need to give reasons why we practice and believe what we do. These reasons could be for the sake of trying to "convert" others. Most likely, though, they are simply for the sake of showing to ourselves that our religious practices and beliefs are reasonable. Either way, we now have reason-giving about the reasonableness of religion.

In taking acts of religious reason-giving as our primary object of inquiry, the global-critical philosopher of religion seeks first to describe some particular instance of religious reason-giving by some particular person or text in some particular cultural-historical context. Thus, the global-critical philosopher of religion avoids a naïve (un-critical) philosophy of religion that generalizes about religious traditions and abstracts religious ideas out of context. At the same time, however, the global-critical philosopher of religion must be mindful that acts of religious reason-giving contain ideas and are embedded in traditions, both of which extend beyond the context of some particular act of religious reason-giving.

How does the global-critical philosopher of religion strike this balance between particularities and generalities? I recommend a "robust description" of religious reason-giving that attends to the "four corners" of acts of religious reason-giving listed in Table 2.2: *logical form*, *conceptual meaning*, *contextual setting*, and *political use*.

Logical form: Break the argument down into its steps. What are its premises and conclusion(s)? What is its logical form? Is it a deductive argument in which the conclusion necessarily follows from the premises? Or do the premises only make the conclusion more likely or probable? By breaking the argument down into steps, you will better be able to evaluate the truth of its premises, the validity of its form, and the truth or likeliness of its conclusions. We will examine logical form further in Chapter 3 when we look at the evaluation of religious reason-giving.

Conceptual meaning: What are the key terms in the premises of the argument? What do they mean? Traditionally, Western philosophy arrived at the meaning of a concept by determining its necessary and sufficient conditions. In the example of a triangle, *having three sides* and *having internal angles that add up to 180 degrees* are each necessary conditions and

Table 2.2 The Four Corners of Thick Description

Logical form	Representation of the logical form of the argument
Conceptual meaning	Meaning of the key concepts in the argument
Contextual setting	Knowledge of the cultural-historical setting of the argument
Political use	Awareness of how the argument serves or contests structures of power

collectively sufficient conditions of *being a triangle*. This is easy enough when it comes to definitions of triangles and other mathematical objects, but what about the religious ideas and practices of humans? We will explore this issue further in Chapter 3.

Contextual setting: This is a bit of a "kitchen sink" category. It centrally includes knowing about the historical and cultural context of an act of religious reason-giving: What are the key historical events? What is the pertinent social order? What are the relevant cultural values and norms? Importantly, though, this category also includes matters of religious context: What are the prominent forms of religious practice? How are the related religious traditions structured and ordered? Where is there religious disagreement and conflict? Ideally, such an analysis is both synchronic and diachronic. To analyze synchronically is to look at something at a particular time—when the reason was given. By contrast, to analyze diachronically is to look at something through time—whether and how the reason gets contested, changed, or abandoned over time.

Political use: This category could easily get collapsed into the previous category. After all, how an argument gets used is part of its context. But the political uses of an argument are so important to global-*critical* philosophy of religion that they deserve their own category. By *political*, try not to think only about politics in the twenty-first-century sense: political parties, campaigns, elections, and so forth. Rather, something much more expansive is meant—political in the sense of involving power. How does an act of religious reason-giving involve power? Does it come from a place of power, or does it challenge power? Does it serve to marginalize, inferiorize, demonize, or just the opposite? Note that answering these questions requires knowing a bit about how power is distributed in the contextual setting of an act of religious reason-giving, as well as what the status of the reason-giver is with respect to this distribution of power. This requires paying attention to issues of race, class, and gender (among other things).

V. Summing Up: So What Is Religion?

As you recall, I forwarded a provisional definition of religion last chapter: "concern for ultimate problems and solutions, paths and destinations, realities and truths." Here I complexify this definition in three ways. First, "concern" should not be understood individually or mentally; rather, it includes many different "dimensions" of human behavior, including bodily practices and rituals, experiences and emotions, narratives and myths, doctrines and philosophies, ethics and laws, institutions and societies, art and other material culture.[4] We might say that the more something encompasses these dimensions, the more robustly religious it will be. Second, the adjective "ultimate" registers a cluster of related meanings—most foundational, most final, most extreme, most important—and therefore captures a wide diversity of "problems and solutions, paths and destinations, realities and truths." Most notably, it includes what is most foundational, final, extreme, or important for some person or community with respect to how they live their lives, as well as what that person or community believes to be most foundational, final, extreme, or important "in reality."[5] Third, the phrase "problems and solutions, paths and destinations, realities and truths" allows us to include religious traditions for which person-like creator Gods are not present or important, while also recognizing that "Gods, Spirits, and Ancestors"—to use a standard phrase from the academic study of religion—are common features of many religious traditions. In particular, the term "ultimate realities" should be understood to include person-like superhuman beings (Gods, Spirits, Ancestors) as well as non-person-like ultimate realities, forces, and principles such as *Brahman*, *Dào*, and *Buddha-nature*.

No definition, however, is perfect. No doubt you can find flaws in the one above. It is not easy to "reform" *religion*, which is yet another reason why some scholars advocate its "abolition." What do you think? Should "religion" be abolished and abandoned or retained and reformed? Regardless of where you stand, you will hopefully see that there are strong arguments on each side and important lessons to be learned in general.

And what if you choose to abolish? Does that mean that you can no longer engage in global-critical philosophy or religion? Well, maybe not as such. But I argue that the ten questions that we will examine in Chapter 4–13 have relevance to your life and your world regardless of whether you understand them as "religious" or not. I also argue that the ways in which these questions have been answered in traditions in South Asia, East Asia, the Mediterranean region (Abrahamic), West Africa (Yorùbá), the North American plains (Lakȟóta), and contemporary Euro-centric scholarship are worth examining regardless of whether you understand these traditions as "religious" or not. Ultimately, it does not matter much whether some philosopher or philosophy is labelled as "religion" or not, at least not for this global-critical philosophy of religion. It only matters whether this philosopher or philosophy offers interesting and important ways of answering questions about some of our central questions: who we are, where we come from, where we are going, how we get there, what obstacles stand in our way, what the cosmos is, where the cosmos comes from, where the cosmos is going, how the cosmos gets there, and what obstacles stand in its way.

We will get to these questions soon. First, however, we have one final preliminary investigation to conduct: What is philosophy?

Questions for Discussion

1 Should the category or term for religion be abolished in the academic study of religion? Defend your answer against the opposing side in this debate.
2 Why does a critical understanding of religions and the concept of *religion* matter for global-critical philosophy of religion?
3 Provide three instances of religion that do not fit the modern Western understanding of religion. What makes them instances of religion if they do not fit the modern Western understanding of religion?
4 Find some instance of religious reason-giving. Describe its logical form, conceptual meanings, historical context, and political ends as completely as possible. What do you learn in doing so?

Primary and Scholarly Sources

East Asia

Adler, Joseph A. "Chinese Religions." In *Encyclopedia of Religion*, 2nd ed., ed. Lindsay Jones 1580–1613. Detroit, MI: Macmillan Reference USA, 2005.

Poceski, Mario. *Introducing Chinese Religions*. New York: Routledge, 2009.

European/Academic

Fitzgerald, Timothy. *The Ideology of Religious Studies*. New York: Oxford University Press, 2003.

Schilbrack, Kevin, "Religions: Are there Any?" *Journal of the American Academy of Religion* 78/4 (2010): 1112–38.

Lakȟóta

DeMallie, Raymond J. "Lakota Beliefs and Rituals in the Nineteenth Century." In *Sioux Indian Religion*, eds. Raymond J. DeMallie and Douglas R. Parks, 25–43. Norman, OK: University of Oklahoma Press, 1987.

Feraca, Stephen E. *Wakinyan: Lakota Religion in the Twentieth Century*. Lincoln, NE: University of Nebraska Press, 1998.

Mediterranean/Abrahamic

Corrigan, John, Frederick M. Denny, Carlos M. N. Eire, and Martin S. Jaffee, *Jews, Christians, Muslims: A Comparative Introduction to Monotheistic Religions*, 2nd ed. New York: Routledge, 2011.

Corrigan, John, Carlos M. N. Eire, Frederick M. Denny, and Martin S. Jaffee, *Readings in Judaism, Christianity, and Islam*. Upper Saddle River, NJ: Pearson, 1998.

South Asia

Clothey, Fred. *Religions of India: A Historical Introduction*. New York: Routledge, 2007.

Koller, John. *The Indian Way: An Introduction to the Philosophies and Religions of India*, 2nd ed. New York: Prentice Hall, 2006.

Yorùbá

Abímbọ́lá, Kọ́lá. *Yorùbá Culture: A Philosophical Account*. Birmingham: Iroko Academic Publishers, 2005.

Peel, J. D. Y. *Christianity, Islam, and* Oriṣa *Religion: Three Traditions in Comparison and Interaction*, chapter 11. Oakland, CA: University of California Press, 2015.

3

What Is Philosophy?

Learning Objectives

- Describe the basic contexts, ends, forms, and contents of Western philosophy, evaluating whether philosophy is entangled in "religion" and "rhetoric."
- Explain some of the chief contributions from non-Western philosophy for global-critical philosophy of religion.
- Understand the three-step method of global-critical philosophy of religion, especially formal comparison and critical evaluation.
- Explain the different ways in which religious reason-giving can be evaluated "however possible," evaluating the nature and role of critical evaluation in global-critical philosophy of religion.

I. Introduction

Now that we have looked at what philosophy of religion philosophizes about, we turn to what philosophy of religion philosophizes with. We begin with the tradition of philosophy that was first named *philosophy*: ancient Greek philosophy. From there, we follow the trajectory of philosophy in the "West" through medieval, modern, and postmodern stages. After that, we examine some philosophical issues and insights from the other traditions of our book: South Asia, East Asia, North America (Lakȟóta), and Africa (Yorùbá). We then turn to a three-step method for doing global-critical philosophy of religion, especially the final step of evaluation, exploring what it means to evaluate religious reason-giving "however possible." Finally, we evaluate evaluation itself: should a global-critical philosophy of religion aspire only to understand global philosophies of religion in their cultural-historical contexts or also to raise philosophical questions of meaning, truth, and value about them?

II. Western Philosophy: A Quick Tour

A. Ancient Greek Philosophy

The first systematic and extensive use of the term *philosophy* was by the ancient Greek philosopher Plato (427–347 BCE), who differentiated philosophy—literally the "love of wisdom"—from mythology and rhetoric. In opposition to mythology—stories about the Greek Gods—philosophy allegedly gives reasoned arguments for its claims rather than appealing to divine revelation. And in contrast to rhetoric—the art of persuasion—philosophy allegedly strives to ascertain what is real, true, and good, rather than what is merely apparent, rhetorically persuasive, and conventionally expedient.

The context for all three is of course ancient Greece, more narrowly Athens, where, for a brief period, democracy was the rule of law. Since all male and free citizens, regardless of occupation or education, were expected to serve in a legislative body called the Assembly, it was crucial for members of the aristocracy to be able to persuade commoners of their proposals. Hence, there was a need not only for rhetorical and argumentative training but also for statesmanship and general education. Plato's Academy was one such school; Plato apparently wrote his dialogues for his students to hone their reasoning and orating skills. Plato's most famous student, Aristotle (384–322 BCE), later opened his own school, the Lyceum, after first serving as the personal tutor of Alexander the Great.

Although argumentative persuasion and general education were undoubtedly two goals of early Greek philosophy, Plato and Aristotle spoke of philosophy as going beyond this to provide "enlightenment" for the soul. Moreover, philosophy was, in the words of one recent scholar, "a way of life."[1] For Plato, knowledge of what is ultimately true and real (Forms) effected release of the (immortal) soul from embodied reincarnation and, therewith, other-worldly happiness. For Aristotle, knowledge of logical principles and scientific essences brought the (mortal) soul into closest proximity with the Unmoved Mover and, therewith, this-worldly happiness. In this respect, ancient Greek philosophy was not unlike religion (especially as religion is often thought of today).

Table 3.1 Areas of Inquiry for Western Philosophy

Metaphysics	The study of what is real, especially that which goes beyond physical reality, including the most general features of reality itself (time, space, substance, generality, causality, numbers), the nature of the self or soul (including free will and determinism), and the existence of God
Epistemology	The study of what is true, encompassing the nature, sources, limits, justification, and structure of knowledge; traditionally included logic as well
Axiology	The study of what is good or, more generally, valuable; a collective term for ethics (the study of what is right and good), aesthetics (the study of what is beautiful), and political philosophy

Given the importance of persuasion and debate, ancient Greek philosophy developed and delineated forms of argumentation, most basically the distinction between deductive arguments, where the conclusion necessarily follows from the premises, and inductive arguments, where the conclusion is only ever probable given the premises. (We explore these below in section V.) But given the importance of education and knowledge more generally, the content of ancient Greek philosophy was expansive, covering the real (physics and metaphysics), the true (logic and epistemology), and the good (ethics, political philosophy, and aesthetics, all of which were later subsumed under the category of "axiology"). As summarized in Table 3.1, these were to become the chief areas of inquiry for Western philosophy.

What can be learned from this selective picture of ancient Greek philosophy? First, its contexts and ends did matter for its methods and content. Second, philosophy and religion were not as neatly separable then as they supposedly are now. Third, philosophy was not a-political or a-rhetorical; rather, it played a significant role in the education of the aristocracy and the politics of the state.

B. The Rest of the West

For the sake of space, we now pick up the pace, treating the other three major time periods of Western philosophy in this one section. (In subsequent chapters we will "dig in" to medieval/Abrahamic philosophy and modern/Academic philosophy of religion.) Again, we analyze these periods of Western philosophy in terms of their contexts, ends, methods, and contents.

One important context of medieval Western philosophy involved the way in which ancient Greek philosophy lived on past its original cultural milieu, impacting medieval Western philosophy as a body of knowledge that was contended with in relation to the Abrahamic religious traditions. This meant that one important end of medieval Western philosophy was that of "faith seeking understanding," rejecting or reconciling ancient Greek philosophy with religious revelation and doctrine. The methods of medieval Western philosophy therefore continued to concern the forms of argumentation passed down by ancient Greek philosophy, while also investigating which premises could be proved by reason and which could only be known by revelation. Finally, the content of medieval Western philosophy pertained in part to those issues of potential harmony and conflict between reason and religion—e.g., the eternality of the cosmos, the immortality of the soul, and proofs for the existence of an Abrahamic God.

The context for modern philosophy, which runs roughly from the seventeenth century up through the mid-twentieth century, involves the unparalleled success of the sciences, the rise of modern secular democracies, and European colonialism of much of the globe. This context drove several ends, most justificatory in nature: the justification of science (given its success), the justification of religion (given its lack of success), and the justification of Western philosophy itself (given the discovery of other philosophies through expansionist endeavors). As for the methods of modern Western philosophy, one interesting addition concerns increasing efforts to purge or restrict religion from it. The contents of modern Western philosophy were focused above all on matters of epistemology (given all the emphasis on justification), with ethics/politics running a close second (given the rise of modern democracies and the colonization of much of the rest of the world).

This brings us to the present, a period sometimes called "postmodern" since the epistemic foundations and ideals of modern philosophy have come under increasing criticism. In the words of one postmodern philosopher, postmodernity is broadly characterized by an "incredulity toward meta-narratives."[2] No longer do "we" believe any philosophical, religious, political, or scientific "narratives" that offer totalizing accounts of the capital-T Truth about capital-R Reality. Postmodern, postcolonial, and feminist philosophers therefore often engage in critical interventions of philosophical "meta-narratives," especially those deployed to legitimate Euro-centric and male-centric perspectives.[3] To some extent, "difference" now serves as an end, whether simply as greater recognition of non-Western forms of philosophy or as active efforts to undermine modern colonial forms of philosophy. The methods of postmodern philosophies therefore involve a blurring of the distinction between philosophy and other forms of inquiry, especially those that were traditionally denigrated by philosophers like rhetoric and literature. Thus, the contents of philosophy have come to include critical investigation of Western philosophy itself, Western ideals of truth, and the power dynamics that inhabit all philosophies, especially Western philosophy.

With postmodern, postcolonial, and feminist philosophies, Western philosophy therefore "comes full circle," at least in certain respects, as these philosophies reveal how reason is not only interested and powered but also entangled in allegedly non-philosophical discourses such as religion and rhetoric. Moreover, the very attempt to protest that reason is not these things—interested, powered, entangled—is itself seen as motivated by interests, powers, and entanglements. Of course, this is not the only way of viewing and doing Western philosophy today; in many respects, the ends, methods, and contents of modern philosophy remain alive and well, even in our so-called postmodern context. Nevertheless, the philosophical criticism of philosophy is a unique feature of philosophy today. Once again, therefore, it should be clear how context shapes end, which influences method and content.

III. Philosophy "Outside the West"

We turn now to philosophy "outside the West," focusing on examples from our South Asian (Indian), East Asian (Chinese), Native American (Lakȟóta), and West African (Yorùbá) traditions, particularly as they inform the practice of global-critical philosophy of religion. As we do, we are immediately faced with a difficulty not unlike that of the last chapter—viz., just like "religion," "philosophy" is a Western term that is not present as such elsewhere. In this sense, there is technically no "philosophy" outside the West, at least not until the term was introduced. Can there be philosophy where there is no "philosophy"?

As we look for philosophy outside the West, we are faced with another difficulty. The Western traditions of philosophy are unique in that ancient Greek philosophy lost its original cultural-religious mooring yet remained a viable tradition of thinking that was applied to other traditions, especially the Abrahamic religious traditions during the Middle Ages. This did not generally happen elsewhere in the world. Hence, the distinction between philosophy and religion, which often looms large in the modern West, is rather new and porous elsewhere.

Nevertheless, if philosophy just is inquiry about what is real, true, and good, then it stands to reason that there is no culture without philosophy. Just as we might say that every culture exemplifies concerns and ritualizes actions with respect to ultimate problems and solutions, paths and destinies, realities and truths (and therefore has religion), so every culture possesses views about what is real, true, and good (and therefore has philosophy). You will recall, however, that Chapter 1 offered a different definition of philosophy, one that involves the explicit giving, defending, and examining of reasons. Do all cultures have this, too? As we will soon see, this can be a contentious issue, particularly in twentieth-century African philosophy.

A. South Asian Philosophy

Of the many fascinating features of South Asian philosophy, two are especially important for the practice of global-critical philosophy of religion. The first pertains to Jain philosophy, which worked out three interrelated "doctrines of relativity" over the course of the first millennium CE—the first concerning the nature of things that exist (ontology); the second, our knowledge of these things (epistemology); the third, our assertions about these things (language).

According to the *doctrine of non-one-sidedness* (*anekāntavāda*), reality consists of innumerable things or substances (*dravyas*-s), each of which possesses innumerable essential qualities (*guṇa*-s) and non-essential modes (*paryāya*-s).[4] Since reality is non-one-sided, the *doctrine of standpoints* (*nayavāda*) holds that the things of reality can only be known from a variety of perspectives (*naya*-s).[5] And given the non-one-sidedness of reality and the different standpoints from which it can be viewed, the third and final *doctrine of conditional assertion* (*syādvāda*) maintains that assertions about reality are only correct from a certain perspective or in a certain sense.[6]

Collectively, these three "doctrines of relativity" offered effective argumentative tools for Jains, especially in debates with proponents of certain Hindu and Buddhist philosophical schools. The former (Hindus) were accused of emphasizing permanence vis-à-vis impermanence; the latter (Buddhists), just the opposite; both therefore were guilty of the philosophical error of one-sidedness (*ekāntatā*). For some Jains—such as eighth-century philosopher Haribhadra—these "doctrines of relativity" also served an irenic end insofar as they entailed the recognition that all the religio-philosophies of medieval South Asia were partially valid and useful means toward enlightenment or release. For us, therefore, these doctrines not only provide useful tools of analysis for epistemological claims and linguistic assertions, means by which we can consider these claims and assertions from different perspectives, but also encourage is us an air of humility, reminding us that we each only have a partial and perspectival view of what is real, true, and good.

Although these "doctrines of relativity" are unique to Jainism, a second contribution for global-critical philosophy of religion from South Asian philosophy of religion was shared by all schools, even though it was formulated by Nyāya, which posited four reliable sources of knowledge (*pramāṇa*): perception, inference, comparison, and testimony. Not all schools accepted all four of these sources of knowledge, and some schools added other sources of knowledge. Nevertheless, all contended with these four sources, accepting or rejecting them.

The first, perceptual knowledge (*pratyakṣa*), is established by contact between the senses and objects of perception. These objects of perception include physical objects (e.g., table), the properties of objects (e.g., solidity), internal states (e.g., pain), and three "extraordinary" objects of perception: the natures of objects (e.g., table-ness), cross-sensory objects (e.g., the visual perception of ice as cold), and perception of the past and present through yogic powers. The second source of knowledge, inference (*anumāna*), was codified as a five-step proof as follows:

1. state the position (*pratijñā*) to be demonstrated (e.g., this hill has fire);
2. provide the cause or reason (*hetu*) for this statement (e.g., because it has smoke);
3. give the invariable concomitance between (no. 1) and (no. 2) (*udāharaṇa*) (e.g., whatever has smoke has fire);
4. offer a similar example of (no. 3) (*upanaya*) (e.g., as in the case of a campfire);
5. restate the initial position as demonstrated (*nigamana*) (e.g., therefore, this hill has fire).[7]

The third source of knowledge is comparison or analogy (*upamāna*), knowledge based on similarity (between, e.g., two species of mammals). Finally, the fourth source of knowledge is verbal testimony or simply "words" (*śabda*), which to count as knowledge not only must come from an honest, reliable, competent, and authoritative source (whether human or divine) but also must be articulated in such a manner that the words can be understood by the hearer or reader. Table 3.2. sums up all four.

Table 3.2 Potential Sources of Valid Knowledge in South Asian Philosophy of Religion

Name	Description
Perceptual knowledge	Contact between the senses and objects of perception
Inference	Five-step inference: (1) state position; (2) provide reason; (3) give invariable concomitance; (4) offer example; and (5) restate position
Comparison	Similarity between two examples of a general category
Testimony	Report by an honest, reliable, competent, and authoritative source

Three things here are important for us. First, for many schools of South Asian philosophy, testimony (*śabda*) is recognized as a valid source of knowledge, provided that the speaker is reliable and knowledgeable and that the hearer can understand. This is in stark contrast to a common stance in Western philosophy according to which "appeal to authority" is an informal fallacy. In truth, however, we rely on authorities for most of our knowledge. Consider, for example, what you read in books about historical events, hear on the news about current events, and learn from teachers about scientific facts. The question, then, concerns not whether we rely on authorities at all but whether these authorities are reliable.

Second, as we mentioned in Chapter 1, the Cārvāka *darśana* criticized inference (*anumāna*) as a valid source of knowledge (*pramāṇa*) given that the necessary concomitance in step 3 can never be proved.[8] How do we know that whatever has smoke also has fire *in all cases* since we can never perceive all cases? How can we know that smoke and fire are necessarily connected since we only perceive particular associations of smoke and fire, never the necessary connection between them?[9] We return to this issue below (section V.A.) when we look at inductive argumentation.

Third and more generally, the itemization of sources of knowledge (*pramāṇa*) by Nyāya in particular and by South Asian philosophy in general motivates the global-critical philosopher of religion to pay attention to what is recognized as legitimate sources of knowledge in different philosophies of religion. This is especially true when entering into discussion or debate with another global-critical philosopher of religion: Which sources of knowledge will the two of you recognize as legitimate? We return also to this issue below (section V.E.).

B. East Asian Philosophy

As you know from preceding chapters, the latter half of the first millennium before the Common Era in China was known as the period when "100 Schools Contended." These contentions were most fierce between Confucians and Mohists. Whereas Confucians emphasized the recovery of traditional rituals and conventions (*lǐ*, 禮), Mohists stressed the practical consequences of human behavior, arguing that the proper measure of human action is not whether it accords with tradition but "benefits all under *Tiān*" (Heaven). And while Confucians called for a "rectification of names" through which people would know their hierarchical roles in the "Five Great Relationships"—father/son, elder brother/younger brother, husband/wife, elder/younger, and ruler/ruled—Mohists maintained that "everyone is equal before *Tiān*" and that humans should therefore seek to imitate *Tiān* by practicing "inclusive care" (*jiān ài*, 兼愛) for all without respect to kinship or status.

One byproduct of this debate involved the development of Mohist epistemology.[10] Given their rejection of traditional rituals and mores (*lǐ*, 禮), which they took to be nothing more than the consensus of the scholarly (*rú*) class, Mohists needed to produce their own objective ethical standards. Ultimately, Mohists used the concept "the benefit of all under Heaven" as the criterion for identifying what is morally right (*yì*, 義). This criterion is just one example of a larger class of models, paradigms, and standards that Mohists called *fà* (法), which encompasses any tool or aid for guiding an action or making a judgment. This includes rules or definitions, prototypes or pictures, actual tools or measuring devices, concepts such as "the benefit of the world," and role models such as *Tiān*, who, for the Mohists, was a perfect moral agent and therefore the highest ethical standard.

The process by which *fà* were employed in cognition and judgment was referred to by Mohists as "distinguishing what is 'this' [*shì*] from what is 'not' [*fēi*]." Some particular *fà* was used as a pattern by which similar things could be distinguished from dissimilar things. The *fà* of pine tree, for example, could be used to determine what is "this" (*shì*, 是) or "not" (*fēi*, 非) a pine tree. More relevantly, the *fà* of moral rightness (*yì*) could be used to judge whether some set of actions was "this" (*shì*) or "not" (*fēi*) morally right. But how was the *fà* for moral rightness established in the first place, you might ask. For Mohists, this involved looking to the "root," "source," and "use" of a *fà*: in the first case, historical precedents were consulted, especially among the ancient sages; in the second, what was actually experienced was witnessed, mostly among the common people; in the third, practical consequences were calculated, particularly whether benefit was produced.

It was in these terms—*shì*/this and *fēi*/not—that Confucians and Mohists debated. Confucians might assert, for example, that music was "this" (*shì*) with respect to moral rightness (*yì*), whereas Mohists would deny "not" (*fēi*). For the (proto) Daoist sage Zhuāngzǐ (*c.* 368–*c.* 286 BCE), however, both judgments were examples of a "that's it which deems" (*wéi shì*, 為是), which he contrasted to a "that's it that goes by circumstance" (*yīn shì*, 因是). These are tricky phrases to translate, especially *yīn shì*, which is translated as variably as a "that's it that goes by circumstance," a "that's it that is mutually dependent," a "this that is dependent," a "this according to what you go by," and a "relying on 'so.'"[11] The underlying gist, though, is that *yīn shì* is "dependent" on context—"based on prior or enacted commitments, gestalts orientations, and inner processes," as one scholar explains, rather than the "arbitrarily posited" *wéi shì*.[12] Whereas *wéi shì* is fixed, rigid, absolute, and dogmatic, *yīn shì* is fluid, supple, relative, and fallible.

As scholars of Zhuāngzǐ are quick to point out, this does not mean that judgments are entirely arbitrary and thoroughly relative.[13] Rather, every judgment is delivered by some particular person with some particular personal interests and experiences, who is embedded in some particular sociolinguistic context and circumstances. We should not, therefore, refrain from judgments about what is "this" (*shì*) or "not" (*fēi*); rather, we should "adopt an attitude of epistemic modesty in making perspective-based choices."[14] Nor should we refrain from judging the judgments of others; rather, we should do so from our own perspective, again with modesty, in recognition that the judgments of others are delivered from their own perspectives, which are different from ours.

Here, we have more insights that are useful for the practice of global-critical philosophy of religion: humans form beliefs and make judgments about the way the world is and how to live in it; to refrain from doing so is simply not possible. But since all such beliefs and judgments are contextual, and since the contexts of others can be quite different from our own, we should forward our own judgments with an attitude of epistemic humility and contextual awareness.

C. American Indian (Lakȟóta) Philosophy

If there were traditions of philosophical discussion and debate in precolonial Lakȟóta traditional ways, they are inaccessible to the historian and anthropologist. It is reasonable to assume some measure of discussion and debate of sacred beliefs and practices among Lakȟóta "holy men" (*wičháša wakȟáŋ*), but we have no record of this prior to the late nineteenth century. We therefore focus on recent Lakȟóta philosophy, especially that of Vine Deloria, Jr. (1933–2005), arguably the highest regarded Lakȟóta historian and philosopher.

According to Deloria, one of the key principles of American Indian epistemology comes from the Lakȟóta phrase "all my relations" (*mitákuye oyásiŋ*), which is pronounced at the end of every Lakȟóta ceremony.[15] For Deloria, this phrase constitutes nothing less than the American Indian principle of observation and interpretation, a method of inquiry and inference about the natural world. How does it work? In essence, it establishes relationships between things in the natural world, reasoning therefrom. Deloria provides the example of the Pawnee, who knew when to return from hunting in the high plains to their corn crops in the Missouri River valley by inspecting milkweed, which matured two weeks before corn—precisely the length of time that it would take for the Pawnee to return to their corn. This is just one example of how the American Indians recognized that the universe was alive and interrelated, which Deloria argues does and should inform an American Indian epistemology whereby the relational patterns between natural phenomena are observed, generalized, and employed as a guide for life.

Deloria's second epistemological method also comes from an American Indian phrase, in this case one spoken by the Lakȟóta holy man Black Elk after he recited the story about how White Buffalo Calf Woman revealed the sacred pipe and its rituals. At the end of the story, Black Elk first fell silent then said: "This they tell, and whether it happened so or not, I do not know; but if you think about it, you can see that it is true."[16] For Deloria, the phrase "if you think about it, you will see that it is true" is not just a statement of faith but also an epistemological principle. How? For Deloria, it shows that everything has instructive value and therefore must be considered. The task of American Indian epistemology is therefore to find proper patterns of interpretation for our experiences, including not just ordinary ones but also extraordinary ones that concern the behavior of higher powers as revealed in dreams, visions, and prophecies.

In sum, American Indian epistemology, at least according to Vine Deloria, Jr., looks for patterns of relatedness in natural and extraordinary phenomena, omitting nothing, remaining open to instruction and correction, and affirming the centrality of each person's "seeing what is true." We return to these insights below.

D. African (Yorùbá) Philosophy

We save African (Yorùbá) philosophy for last, because no tradition of philosophy has taken up the relationship between philosophy and culture as extensively and rigorously as African philosophy.[17] This encounter begins in earnest in the mid-twentieth century with what was later characterized as "ethnophilosophy"—the philosophy of some ethic group, usually from sub-Saharan Africa, which is said to be their "timeless tradition," especially as contrasted to Western culture and philosophy. Placide Tempels's *Bantu Philosophy* (1945) is widely regarded as the first attempt to articulate an African ethnophilosophy, in this case that of the Bantu people of central and southern Africa. According to Tempels, the Bantu perceived and conceived the world in terms of "vital forces" rather than scientific mechanisms, though were unable to express these beliefs by means of discursive statements that could be subjected to philosophical analysis and evaluation. For Tempels, Bantu culture therefore constituted "ethnophilosophy" (rather than full-blooded Western philosophy).[18]

By the 1970s, many African philosophers had begun criticizing the deployment of "ethnophilosophy," objecting to the cooption of philosophy by anthropology, not to mention the subjugation of African ethnophilosophy to Western philosophy. In 1976, Kwasi Wiredu's essay "How Not to Compare African Traditional Thought with Western Thought" undermined comparisons between "African rationality" and "Western rationality" that represented the former as precolonial "folk philosophy," contrasting it to modern, Western science. Later, Peter Bodunrin's 1981 essay "The Question of African Philosophy" questioned whether African philosophy could be based on traditional African culture given that philosophy is critical, argumentative, and reflective in nature. Two years after that, Paulin Hountondji's *African Philosophy: Myth and Reality* (1983) coined the term "ethnophilosophy," accusing "ethnophilosophers" such as Tempels of taking to be true what is simply held traditionally, thereby portraying African philosophy as devoid of rational argumentation and critical analysis.

Several of these critics of ethnophilosophy went on to develop philosophies that defended rationality as culturally universal. Kwasi Wiredu, for example, argued that although every culture has its own distinctive folk philosophy of traditional beliefs, philosophy demonstrates the rational principles that are universal to all cultures (e.g., the law of non-contradiction, the principle of induction, and the harmonization of the interests of the individual with those of society). Philosophy should not therefore be mistaken as the culturally imperialistic folk philosophy of the West. On the contrary, philosophy is the means of liberating Africa from Western cultural stereotypes.

Other philosophers, however, questioned the universality of rationality, maintaining that African conceptual and cognitive systems were not only sufficiently unique but also genuinely alternative pathways to the truth. In the case of the Yorùbá philosophy of religion, Moses Makinde maintained that Ifá divination and scientific methodology are completely different yet equally true ways of knowing and engaging reality, whereas J. Olubi Sodipo and Barry Hallen's study of everyday Yorùbá discourse concluded that the criteria for knowing (versus merely believing) are much different than in Western philosophy, with Yorùbá knowledge consisting only of firsthand or personal experience, not of what can be demonstrated by logic or generalized as scientific law. More broadly, H. Odera Oruka challenged Hountondji's dismissal of ethnophilosophy, asserting that there has always been reflection on issues of importance to human existence by *some* people in *all* societies. Oruka called this traditional reflection "philosophical sagacity," which involves those "sages" who reflect critically on the traditional beliefs and values of a society's folk philosophy.

These different positions also pattern Yorùbá philosophy of religion, especially the two Yorùbá philosophers of religion whom we will consult most frequently in this book, Kọ́lá Abímbọ́lá and Segun Gbadegesin. The former—much like Makinde, Sodipo, and Hallen—regards his "philosophical account" of traditional Yorùbá culture as an exercise in "cultural philosophy." Differentiating "cultural philosophy" from "ethnophilosophy," Abímbọ́lá claims that Yorùbá diviners engage their sacred text, *Odù Ifá*, in a hermeneutical manner—interpreting, analyzing, and evaluating it critically and reflectively.[19] By contrast, Segun Gbadegesin maintains that "African philosophy is first and foremost a philosophical activity," one that is African insofar as it is directed at "issues relating to African realities—traditional or contemporary."[20] For Gbadegesin, the chief criterion of philosophical activity is critical reflection. In cases, where critical reflection is not present and traditional worldviews are simply accepted without evaluation, philosophy is absent.

What can we take from these debates? Three things. First, given a content-based understanding of philosophy, it is clear that "indigenous cultures" have perspectives about what is real, true, and good. Indeed, this is what matters most for our own global-critical philosophy of religion—how traditions of philosophy of religion (like Yorùbá) answer our core questions about the self and the cosmos. Second, if we take an activity-based approach to philosophy, we should recognize a diversity and degree of philosophical behavior including questioning, scrutinizing, analyzing, interpreting, reflecting, examining, evaluating, theorizing, and debating, all about what is real, true, and good. It is also difficult to imagine human cultures absent of at least some of this philosophical activity. Third, as we ourselves philosophize about religion, we will be doing more than just coming to understand global religious philosophies in their cultural contexts; we will also be philosophizing about them. This involves the behavior listed above, especially evaluation, which is the primary topic of the rest of this chapter.

IV. A Method for Global-Critical Philosophy of Religion

We turn now to the method by which we will practice global-critical philosophy of religion in the subsequent chapters of this book. As you already know from last chapter, this method has three steps: robust description, formal comparison, and critical evaluation. Robust description involves the contextual understanding of some act of religious reason-giving. Formal comparison is the process of identifying important differences and similarities between it and others. And critical evaluation raises philosophical questions of truth and value about it in comparative perspective.

Before explicating these three steps, let us recall our ten sets of categories and questions, which we learned about in Chapter 1. In each case, there are both a vague metaphorical question and more precise philosophical questions (see Table 3.3).

With respect to each of these sets of questions, our first step is to describe the relevant forms of religious reason-giving in each of our six traditions of philosophizing about religion. As you know from last chapter, this "robust description" addresses the "four corners" of religious reason-giving, at least insofar as time and space allow (see Table 3.4).

Our next (second) step is to compare these "robust descriptions" against one another in order to learn about their similarities and differences. How? Comparison is a circular process, one that moves back and forth between a category of comparison and the objects of comparison. For the sake of simplicity, however, let us begin with the comparative category, using *self* as an example (thus anticipating the topic of our next chapter). First, we want

Table 3.3 Ten Sets of Categories and Questions for Global-Critical Philosophy of Religion

Chapter No.	Journey Category	Philosophical Questions
Chapter 4	Who am I?	What is the nature of humans? Are they individuals? Are they substances?
Chapter 5	Where do I come from?	What is the original condition of humans? Are they free, good, or enlightened?
Chapter 6	Where am I going to?	Do humans survive death? If so, how?
Chapter 7	How do I get there?	By what paths do humans reach their destinations? Is only one path, at most, true or effective?
Chapter 8	What obstacles are in my way?	What obstacles prevent humans from reaching their destinations? Is religion itself ever an obstacle?
Chapter 9	What is the cosmos?	What is the fundamental nature of the cosmos? Is it designed for the religious paths of humans?
Chapter 10	Where does the cosmos come from?	Is the cosmos eternal, created by one or more Gods, or otherwise generated? Can the creation or causation of the cosmos be proved?
Chapter 11	Where is the cosmos going to?	Does the cosmos have an end? If so, what happens afterwards?
Chapter 12	How does the cosmos get there?	How does the cosmos function? Are anomalous events and extraordinary experiences part of that functioning?
Chapter 13	What obstacles are in the way of the cosmos?	Is there disorder, suffering, or "evil" in the cosmos? How is it reconciled with the existence of one or more Gods?

Table 3.4 The Four Corners of Thick Description

Logical form	Representation of the logical form of the argument
Conceptual meaning	Meaning of the key concepts in the argument
Contextual setting	Knowledge of the cultural-historical setting of the argument
Political use	Awareness of how the argument serves or contests structures of power

to get clear about the meaning of comparative category of *self*, which for the sake of this example we will initially define as a substantial, individual, and autonomous locus of identity—absolutely permanent and unchanging over time (substance), radically distinct and separate from everything else (individual), and in complete control and power over itself (autonomous).

Second, we want to ask how the objects of comparison are similar and different from one another with respect to being instances of the comparative category *self*. In doing so, we might notice that many of the "selves" of religious philosophies are not individual, substantial, autonomous loci of identity. In some cases, they are not isolated individuals but rather webs of external relationships with other beings; in other cases, they are not permanent substances but rather clusters of ever-changing, internal processes. Thus, we will need to modify or replace our comparative category to include these different kinds of "selves." Regardless of which we do (modify/replace), our new comparative category will ideally be broad enough to encompass a variety of "selves" without unduly biasing or favoring any of them over against the others. Note that this might take several iterations. Also note that every comparative category will always bias or favor its comparative results in some way (since every category comes from somewhere—some language, culture, history, system of valuation, etc.). Nevertheless, comparative processes must end somewhere. For us, that "somewhere" is a place from which we can understand the important and interesting similarities and differences between the objects of comparison with respect to the category of comparison—e.g., that (1) individual-substantial souls, (2) webs of external relationships, and (3) clusters of internal processes are three different ways in which philosophies of religion have conceptualized what it means to be a "self." This process, in sum, is what is meant by "formal comparison"—comparison that formally scrutinizes categories of comparison to facilitate critical understanding of the similarities and differences between objects of comparison, ideally without unduly biasing or favoring any of them vis-à-vis the others. It is a circular, oscillating process that looks like what is depicted in Figure 3.

Once we have attained this comparative understanding, we are ready for our third and final step, critical evaluation. At its most basic, you can think of evaluation as answering the "so what?" question. Why do any of these descriptions and comparisons matter to me and the world? More precisely, critical evaluation is the process by which philosophers raise and pursue questions of truth and value about acts of religious reason-giving in comparative perspective.

Here, you might have two initial objections. First, *how dare we* make judgments of truth and value about the religious ideas and practices of others? Second, *how can we* make judgments of truth and value religious ideas and practices since they are matters of personal opinion without relevant empirical evidence.

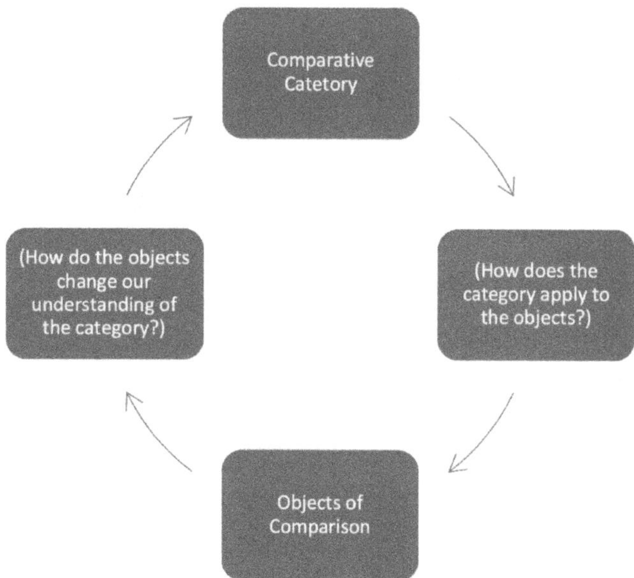

Figure 3 The Circle of Comparison. Timothy Knepper, March 11, 2022.

My response to this first question addresses two common misunderstandings about critical evaluation. First, critical evaluation is not for the sake of proving others wrong or inferior; rather, it is a way of taking seriously both ourselves and others by critically examining what we hold to be real, true, and good, and by making those beliefs vulnerable to what other people hold to be real, true, and good. We do this out of respect for others, recognizing that other religious traditions and people do make claims about what is real, true, and good, and that they want these claims to be taken seriously, not carelessly dismissed or summarily set aside. We also undertake critical evaluation out of respect for ourselves, recognizing that if we care about what is real, true, and good, then we will want not only to learn about the beliefs of others but also to ask whether there is any truth or value in those beliefs for us. For me, this is the ultimate goal of global-critical philosophy of religion—to critically evaluate whether and how the realities, truths, and goods of religious traditions, texts, and thinkers *matter for me*. I will come back to this in the very last section of the chapter.

This brings us to the second common misunderstanding about critical evaluation—that it is for the sake of arriving at some absolute or objective truth. In turn, this brings us to the second objection above—that there can be no critical evaluation of the truth and value of religions ideas and practices since religion is a matter of opinion or absent of evidence. My response to this second misunderstanding and second objection will be much longer, involving the next section of this chapter.

V. Critical Evaluation: However Possible

Let us begin by tacking "however possible" onto the end of our definition of critical evaluation above: critical evaluation is the process by which philosophers raise and pursue questions of truth and value about acts of religious reason-giving in comparative perspective *however possible*. How ever is it possible to evaluate acts of religions reason-giving?

A. Argument Analysis

One tried and true way that philosophers practice critical evaluation involves breaking down an argument into its premises and conclusion, then asking whether the premises are true, whether the argument is valid, and whether the conclusion is true. In section III.A. above we looked at the five-step argument that was employed in South Asian philosophy; here we will examine some of the argumentative forms employed in Western philosophy.

First, there are deductive arguments, in which the truth of the premises and validity of the argument necessitate the truth of the conclusion. Here is the most famous example of a deductive argument from Western philosophy (for which the variables *a*, *c*, and *S* will stand for the *antecedent*, *consequent*, and Socrates, respectively):

- P1: All humans (*a*) are mortal (*c*);
- P2: Socrates (*S*) is a human (*a*);
- C: Socrates (*S*) is mortal (*c*).

Since the form of this argument is valid and its premises are true, its conclusion is true, i.e., the truth of the conclusion necessarily follows from the truth of the premises. Not all deductive arguments, however, have valid forms. One small change in argument above makes it invalid:

- P1: All humans (*a*) are mortal (*c*);
- P2: Socrates (*S*) is mortal (*c*);
- C: Socrates (*S*) is a human (*a*).

Where did this argument go wrong? Intuitively, we know it went wrong since Socrates could be mortal and not be human (e.g., if Socrates were the name of your cat). In technical terms, this fallacy is known as *affirming the consequent* since the second premise affirms of Socrates (*S*) the consequent (*c*) instead of the antecedent (*a*). Likewise, there is a fallacy of *denying the antecedent* in arguing "if Socrates is not human, then Socrates is not mortal":

- P1: All humans (*a*) are mortal (*c*);
- P2: Socrates (*S*) is not human (~*a*);
- C: Socrates (*S*) is not mortal (~*c*).

In both cases we can put the fallacy simply: although all humans are mortal, not all mortals are human.

In contrast to deductive arguments, the truth of the premises of an *inductive argument* does not necessitate the truth of its conclusion. Inductive arguments are therefore not valid or invalid; rather, they are strong or weak, depending on the relative strength of the conclusion given the truth of the premises. The category of inductive argument is therefore something of a "kitchen sink" into which all non-deductive arguments are placed. One of the more common kinds of inductive argument is an *inductive generalization*:

- P1: Object *x* accelerates at 9.8 meters/sec^2 in free fall (in a vacuum);
- P2: Object *y* accelerates at 9.8 meters/sec^2 in free fall (in a vacuum);
- P3: Object *z* accelerates at 9.8 meters/sec^2 in free fall (in a vacuum);
- C: All objects accelerate at 9.8 meters/sec^2 in free fall (in a vacuum).

No matter how many objects are observed accelerating at such a rate in free fall, the conclusion is never proved, for one can never observe all cases. The conclusion of an inductive generalization is only ever probable.[21]

In addition to *inductive generalizations*, there are other types of non-deductive arguments, the most important of which for philosophy of religion are *arguments from analogy* and *inferences to the best explanation*. *Arguments from analogy* argue from the shared properties of two things to their shared possession of some additional property.

- P1: Max and Fido, both dogs, are similar with respect to having two ears, two eyes, and a nose;
- P2: Max also has four legs;
- C: Therefore, Fido probably has four legs.

Inferences to the best explanation, by contrast, involve hypothesizing the best explanation for some relevant facts. Supposing you wake up one morning to find an empty beer bottle on the table (P1). Knowing that you have only one roommate (P2), you will infer to the best explanation that your roommate drank the beer (C). Although inferences to the best explanation are often classified into their own argumentative group of *abduction*, what matters most of us is that just like inductive generalizations and arguments from analogy, they are only ever probable, never conclusive. (Perhaps you drank the beer in your sleep, perhaps a robber broke in and drank it, perhaps it was aliens, etc.)

We will encounter all four of these argumentative forms in this book (deduction, inductive generalization, arguments from analogy, inference to the best explanation). Your ability to identify their form is the first step in ascertaining the truth or likeliness of their conclusion. But you will also need to determine whether the premises are true. How do you do that in the case of arguments about religious ideas and practices?

Here is one example relevant to our comparison above of theories of "self." The sixteenth-century French philosopher Descartes (1596–1650) maintained that a person is not their body, which is divisible, material, and mortal, but is rather their mind/soul, which is indivisible, immaterial, and immortal. One of his arguments involved a thought experiment in which he tried to doubt first the existence of his body, then the existence of his mind/soul, concluding that since he could doubt the existence of the body but not the existence of his mind/soul, then he must be a mind/soul, not a body. Here is one way to put one aspect of this argument into deductive form:

- P1: Those things whose existence cannot be plausibly doubted truly exist;
- P2: The existence of the soul/mind cannot be plausibly doubted;
- C: The soul/mind truly exists.

Since this is a formally valid deductive argument, we know that if the premises are true, then the conclusion is true. Are the premises true? You might object that before we can ask if these premises are true, we need to clarify the meanings of the key terms. What do we mean by "soul/mind," "plausibly doubted," and "truly existing"? Western philosophers have typically approached the analysis of concepts by asking about their necessary and sufficient conditions (see Chapter 2). Can we provide the criteria of *soul/mind*, *plausibly doubted*, or *truly existing*? As we know from our survey of world philosophies above, philosophers as diverse as the fourth-century BCE Daoist Zhuāngzǐ, the eighth-century Jain Haribhadra, and the twentieth-century Lakȟóta Vine Deloria, Jr., have underscored the perspectivalism and contextualism involved in the definition of all concepts (as have plenty of Western philosophers). So, as we try our best to make ideas clear throughout this book (many of which appear in the Glossary), we must remain aware that most definitions are up for debate, subject to perspective, and relative to context.

What then about the truth of the premises in the Cartesian argument above, for example, that the existence of the soul/mind cannot be plausibly doubted (P2)? Here, we are fortunate to be practicing global-critical philosophy of religion, as the history of religion is not without examples of "souls" that have been doubted. Most notably, Buddhist philosophers through time have argued that there is no permanent soul or self since there is no part of ourselves that does not change over time. In particular, the second-century BCE Buddhist monk Nāgasena argued in his famous "Chariot Sermon" that although we give names and identities to ourselves, we are in fact nothing but an ever-changing set of five "bundles"—those of our bodies, senses, perceptions, desires, and awareness. Which theory, Descartes' or Nāgasena's, is correct (if either)? Are we permanent, unchanging, immortal souls, or impermanent, ever-changing, mortal non-souls? This question takes us to our next way of practicing critical evaluation "however possible."

B. Theory Assessment

If we want to assess the truth of some premise, especially as it involves a general theory, we can ask about its "epistemic virtues" or "truth-conducive properties." These are the characteristics that humans often take true theories to possess. You might think that what is true is simply what fits the world, so to speak. But even scientific theories cannot be proved true in this direct, empirical manner since scientific theories make predictions about what happens in *all cases*, and all cases can never be empirically experienced. (This is just the problem of inductive generalization that we looked at above.) Moreover, scientific theories assume auxiliary hypotheses, depend on the truth of other theories, and in some cases have no direct, empirical verification or falsification. For this reason, "epistemic virtues" (or "truth-conducive properties") beyond simple empirical accuracy are often employed, especially when assessing one theory against another. These epistemic virtues include external coherence, practical usefulness, internal consistency, theoretical simplicity, and explanatory scope. (See Table 3.5.)

All these virtues are potentially relevant for our own critical evaluation of religious theories, especially as they are implicated in the premises of

Table 3.5 Epistemic Virtues of True Theories

Name	Central Question
Empirical accuracy	Is the theory accurate with how we experience empirical reality?
External coherence	Does the theory cohere with other forms of knowledge?
Practical usefulness	Is the theory useful to the way we live our lives, whether socially or individually?
Internal consistency	In the theory internally consistent?
Theoretical simplicity	Is the theory conceptually simple?
Explanatory scope	Does the theory help explain other aspects of natural or social reality?

arguments. Take, for example, our two theories of "self" above: the permanent, unchanging, immortal soul of Descartes; and the impermanent, ever-changing, mortal non-soul of Nāgasena. We can evaluate these theories with respect to their epistemic virtues independently of or over against each other. Is there any empirical evidence that bears on the truth of these theories, say from neuroscience or evolutionary biology? How do these theories cohere or fit with other widely accepted practices, values, and ideas, for example, those of criminal law and developmental psychology? How useful are these theories to the ways in which we live our lives, whether individually or socially? Are these theories internally consistent, absent of any logical or conceptual contradictions? Are they theoretically simple, avoiding excess explanatory entities unless necessary? Do they help us explain other aspects of natural and social reality?

Of course, these epistemic virtues are not a calculus that "spits out" a correct answer if one or more theories are input into them. Nevertheless, they offer a second means of critically evaluating religious reason-giving, in this case by assessing the truth-conducive properties of religious theories, especially as they are or are involved in the premises of arguments.

C. Probability Calculation

Our third means of critical evaluation in fact is a calculator, one called Bayes' Theorem, which is used to calculate the probability of a hypothesis, especially in light of new evidence that bears on the hypothesis' probability. It can also be used to measure how some new piece evidence affects two rival hypotheses.

Bayes' Theorem get pretty complicated pretty quickly. But here is how it goes in a nutshell. The probability of some hypothesis given the evidence (P [H/E]) is a function of the probability of the evidence given the hypothesis (P [E/H]), multiplied by the prior probability of the hypothesis before or without the evidence (P [H]), divided by the probability of the evidence apart from the hypothesis (P [E]).

$$P(H/E) = \frac{P\,(E/H) * P\,(H)}{P(E)}$$

As we will see in future chapters, Bayes' Theorem has been used by contemporary philosophers of religion to calculate the probability of the existence of some God given relevant information about the cosmos (Chapters 9 and 10) and to measure the degree to which the existence of evil affects the probability of the rival hypotheses of theism and naturalism (Chapter 13). Here, however, let us stick with the example from this chapter: theories about the self. Suppose the new piece of evidence in this case is neuroscience's ability to map correlations between neurophysiological states and phenomenological experiences (e.g., when the brain is in such-and-such a state, you feel sad). How does this new piece of evidence affect our rival hypotheses: the permanent, unchanging, immortal soul of Descartes; and the impermanent, ever-changing, mortal non-soul of Nāgasena? In each case, the probability of the hypothesis given the evidence (P [H/E]) can be calculated by estimating the probability of the evidence given the hypothesis (P [E/H]), multiplied by the probability of the hypothesis apart from the evidence (P [H]), divided by the probability of the evidence apart from the hypothesis (P [E]). The values that you derive will no doubt be influenced by personal factors, most of all how probable you find these hypotheses to be in the first place. Nevertheless, it would seem that this new piece of evidence from neuroscience decreases the probability of the soul of Descartes and increases the probability of the non-soul of Nāgasena.

D. Experiential Intuition and Interpretive Insight

Our fourth set of tools for critical evaluation swings to the very opposite side, attending to our own personal experiences of religious ideas and reasons. Here we focus on two tools that come from the twentieth-century Western philosophical movement called Continental philosophy: *experiential intuition*, and *interpretive insight*. (Note, however, that we have already seen above an emphasis on experiential intuition and interpretive insight in Lakȟóta and Yorùbá philosophy.)

By *experiential intuition*, I refer to the Western philosophical approach known as Phenomenology, which studies the "lived experience" or "life world" of people, especially as "phenomena" show up to consciousness prior to reflection and categorization. Although Phenomenology can be quite technical and often contentious, it offers a simple tool for the practice of global-critical philosophy of religion: attend to the lived experiences of those you study, including yourself. As psychologists of religion have demonstrated, we humans usually do not reason ourselves into or out of religious beliefs; rather, we find them convincing or not because of our life experiences. Most of the time, however, we are oblivious about how our life experiences shape our beliefs. For this reason, phenomenology offers a powerful tool for the practice of global-critical philosophy of religion: search your own life experiences to see how they inform your beliefs, values, and attitudes. Take, for example, our example above: Supposing you believe that you are a permanent, unchanging, immortal soul, what life experiences inform this belief? How and why do you experience yourself this way prior to reflection or categorization?

Thus far, we have been considering experiential intuition solely as a means of investigating one's own life world. In fact, Phenomenology is also used to attend to the life worlds of others. But a second tool from Continental philosophy is even more useful to the study of the life world of the other, particularly as that life world comes into dialectical relationship with one's own life world. This tool, which we will call *interpretive insight*, comes from the field of Hermeneutics, which is technically "the art and science of textual interpretation," though is often applied to all experience in general. The most famous hermeneutical philosopher, Hans Georg Gadamer (1900–2002), understood the act of textual interpretation as a "fusion of horizons." On the one hand, there is the horizon of the text, which includes its context of production and history of interpretation. On the other hand, there is the horizon of the reader of the text, who brings her own "prejudices" to the act of interpretation. For Gadamer, these prejudices are not to be understood negatively but rather as the "pre-judgments" that we bring to the interpretation of texts in particular and experience in general. It is impossible to escape these pre-judgments since they constitute who we are. There is no interpretation, indeed no experience, without prejudgment. Nevertheless, we should try to become aware of the prejudgments that we bring to texts in particular and experience in general, especially when they appear to distort our interpretations and experiences of what is "other" (the text, a person, the world). This requires making our prejudgments vulnerable to correction by this "other." How do we do this in the case of our example above? Supposing you think of yourself as a permanent, unchanging, immortal soul, and you encounter an "other"—whether in text or in person—that articulates the perspective of an impermanent, changing, mortal, non-soul. How does a "fusion of horizons" occur in this case? First, you must take this other seriously, regarding it as possibly holding some truth for you. Second, you must make yourself vulnerable to this other, allowing it to reveal your pre-judices about it. Finally, you must be willing to change, at least in some small way, adjusting your pre-judices that do fit the other. Which pre-judices might change in this case? Perhaps at least this: you no longer think of your own view of the self as the exclusive or normative view, recognizing that others think differently about it.

E. Authority Clarification

The case study immediately above brings us to our fifth and final tool, which we will call "authority clarification." When you are philosophizing with some "other"—again, whether in text or in person—you might reach a point at which you discover that you disagree not only about the truth of a premise, idea, or theory but also about the sources of knowledge upon which it rests. To reverse the case study above, suppose your main source of knowledge for your belief that you are a non-soul is Buddhist scripture (in this case, the Pāli Canon) and that the main source of knowledge for your dialectical partner's belief that they are a soul is the Bible. How do you reconcile this disagreement?

The typical solution from Western philosophy is simply to toss out all so-called "appeals to authority" like religious scriptures and sages. That is certainly an option. But we should proceed with caution in global-critical philosophy of religion, where one person's legitimate source of knowledge is another person's illegitimate appeal to authority, and where sources of knowledge include not just the scriptures and testimonies of diverse religious traditions but also dreams and omens, mystical experiences and shamanistic trances, prophecy and prognostication.

A very different solution comes from medieval debating tradition of South Asia, especially the *vāda* ("discussion") debate in which truth rather than victory was the goal (see Chapter 1). According to one contemporary philosopher, *vāda* debates required the investigation of the opponent's argument "in and on its own terms" by stepping into her shoes, thereby providing a forum for an exchange of opinions and clarification of perspectives.[22] How does that provide a solution for our example? Recall the first four sources of knowledge (*pramāṇa*-s) in South Asian philosophy: perceptual knowledge, inference, comparison, and testimony. In stepping into the shoes of one's opponent, one had to recognize their sources of knowledge as valid, at least for the sake of the debate—for example, that the testimony of the *Vedas* (especially the *Upaniṣads*) is a valid source of knowledge for a "Hindu" from the school of Vedānta who believes in an immortal, unchanging, permanent "soul" (*Ātman*). Rather than *tossing out* sources of knowledge that were not held in common, debating partners *took on* sources of knowledge that were not their own. Can this be done in the case of our disagreement above? Can you "take on" the Christian New Testament or the Buddhist Pāli Canon as a source of knowledge, even if you do not find it a credible authority? Why not, at least for the sake of understanding, if only for the duration of the debate, especially if your goal is truth rather than victory? Even if not, the debating tradition of South Asia shows us the importance of clarifying our sources of knowledge, especially when philosophizing with others.

VI. Why do we Philosophize about Religion?

This concludes my answer to second objection above. By means of the five tools above, we can critically evaluate religious reason-giving, though not in a manner that arrives at some absolute or objective truth and not for the sake of proving others wrong of inferior. Rather, philosophy of religion—or at least the global-critical philosophy of religion practiced here—is contextual, humble, fallible, and personal. *Contextual* refers to an awareness of one's own and others' personal and social backgrounds and biases. *Humility* is a function of contextual awareness: if we are aware of the backgrounds and biases that influence what we are inclined to accept as true or valuable, then we can better understand and respect how others with different contexts and biases are inclined to accept different things as true and valuable. Such awareness not only fosters a sense of humility but also displays the *fallibilisitic* nature of philosophizing about religion—no claim has exclusive purchase on absolute truth; all claims are open to correction, revision, dialogue, and debate. Taken together, the contextual, humble, and fallible nature of philosophy of religion reveal the essentially and irreducibly *personal* quality of philosophy of religion, which is a key means of taking seriously your own quest for meaning, truth, and value. This is not to say that there might not one day be widespread certainty and agreement about what is religiously true and valuable. Regardless of whether that day ever comes, however, philosophy of religion here and now offers an indispensable set of tools for figuring out how to live our lives in light of what we find ultimately true and valuable.

Questions for Discussion

1. Why does Western philosophy seem to end up from where it starts—i.e., entangled in rhetoric/literature and mythology/religion? Is this somehow necessary or merely accidental?
2. Explain some of the non-Western philosophical contributions explicated in section II. Which do you find most useful to global-critical philosophy of religion? Which do you find least useful?
3. Explain the overall method of global-critical philosophy of religion, focusing on formal comparison. Develop a comparative category and use it to compare two or more (religious) objects of comparison. What do you learn in doing so?
4. Can philosophers of religion critically evaluate religious ideas and arguments? Should they? Which tools do you find most and least useful in doing so?

Primary and Scholarly Sources

East Asia

Fraser, Chris. "Mohism." In *The Stanford Encyclopedia of Philosophy,* ed. Edward N. Zalta, Winter 2015 ed. Available online: https://plato.stanford.edu/archives/win2015/entries/mohism/ (accessed March 11, 2022).

Hansen, Chad. "Zhuangzi." In *The Stanford Encyclopedia of Philosophy*, ed. Edward N. Zalta, Spring 2017 ed. Available online: https://plato.stanford.edu/archives/spr2017/entries/Zhuangzi/ (March 11, 2022).

Mòzǐ, chapter 4. In *Mo Zi: The Book of Master Mo,* trans. Ian Johnston, 14–16. New York: Penguin Books, 2010.

Zhuāngzǐ, chapter 2.5–6. In *Wandering on the Way: Early Taoist Tales and Parables of Chuang Tzu*, trans. Victor H. Mair, 14–17. New York: Bantam Books, 1994.

European/Academic

Kelly, David. *The Art of Reasoning: An Introduction to Logic and Critical Thinking*, 4th ed. New York: W. W. Norton & Co., 2013.
Palmer, Richard. *Hermeneutics: Studies in Phenomenology and Existential Philosophy*. Evanston, IL: Northwestern University Press, 1969.

Lakȟóta

Deloria, Vine, Jr. "Relativity, Relatedness, and Reality." In *Spirit and Reason*, 32–9. Golden, CO: Fulcrum Publishing, 1999.
Deloria, Vine, Jr. "If You Think About It, You Will See That It is True," In *Spirit and Reason*, 40–60. Golden, CO: Fulcrum Publishing, 1999.

Mediterranean/Abrahamic

Oppy, Robert Graham and Nick Trakakis, eds. *The History of Western Philosophy of Religion*, 5 vols. New York: Oxford University Press, 2009.

South Asia

Gautama, Akṣapāda. *Nyāya Sūtras*, I.1. In *A Sourcebook in Indian Philosophy*, eds. Sarvepalli Radhakrishnan and Charles A. Moore, 358–63. Princeton, NJ: Princeton University Press, 1957.
Long, Jeffrey D. *Jainism: An Introduction*, 117–71. New York: I.B. Tauris, 2009.
Malliṣeṇa. *Syādvādamañjarī*, XXIII. In *A Sourcebook in Indian Philosophy*, eds. Sarvepalli Radhakrishnan and Charles A. Moore, 262–5. Princeton, NJ: Princeton University Press, 1957.
Matilal, Bimal Krishna. *The Character of Logic in India*, eds. Jonardon Ganeri and Heeraman Tiwari, chapter 2. Albany, NY: State University of New York Press, 1998.
Umāsvāti. *That Which Is: Tattvārtha Sūtra*, I.35, ed. Kerry Brown and Sima Sharma, 24–7. San Francisco, CA: HarperCollins Publishers, 1994.

Yorùbá

Abímbọ́lá, Kọ́lá. *Yorùbá Culture: A Philosophical Account*, preface. Birmingham: Iroko Academic Publishers, 2005.

Gbadegesin, Segun. *African Philosophy: Traditional Yoruba Philosophy and Contemporary African Realities*, chapter 1. New York: Peter Lang, 1991.

Hallen, Barry. "Contemporary Anglophone African Philosophy: A Survey." In *A Companion to African Philosophy*, ed. Kwasi Wiredu, 99–148. New York: Wiley-Blackwell, 2006.

Part II

Journeys of the Self

4 Who Am I?
5 Where Do I Come From?
6 Where Am I Going To?
7 How Do I Get There?
8 What Obstacles are in My Way?

4

Who Am I?

Learning Objectives

- Understand, compare, and evaluate some of the important and interesting ways in which religious thinkers, texts, and traditions answer the question "Who am I?"
- Explain some of the ways in which these answers challenge the notion that the self is individual and substantial.
- Explain how understandings of "self" are related to other questions about it: where it comes from, where it is going to, how it gets there, and what obstacles are in its way.

I. Introduction

For the remaining ten chapters of the book, we will be philosophizing about ten topics of global-critical philosophy of religion, the first five of which concern the self. Now is as good a time as any, therefore, to talk about what we mean by "self."

In keeping with the journey metaphor, it would be more accurate to use the term "journeyer." In this section of the book, we want to know how different philosophies of religion understand who the journeyer is (if anyone), where the journeyer comes from (if anywhere), where the journeyer is going to (if anywhere), how the journeyer gets there (if by any means), and what obstacles are in the journeyer's way (if any). But "journeyer" does not quite grab us the way "self" does. Moreover, using the term "self" allows us to reflect critically on the notion of self. What is this notion?

For better or worse, many of us inherit the idea that we are a "self"—individual, substantial, and autonomous. As we will soon see, however, many religious and philosophical traditions, texts, and thinkers do not affirm this understanding of the self. In some cases, the "self" is not understood as a discrete individual but rather a set of external relationships with other beings, whether human or other. In other cases, the "self" is not thought to be a substantial being but rather a set of internal parts or processes. In still other cases, the "self" is not posited as an autonomous being but rather significantly determined or affected by forces, principles, or beings outside its control.

Here, we consider the first two of these issues: external relationships and internal components, saving the third, autonomy, for the next chapter. In this chapter, we learn that what seems like the easiest question to answer—Am I?—is not at all so.

II. South Asian Philosophy of Religion

One of the core issues of early South Asian philosophy of religion concerns what the "self" is and how it is liberated from the cycle of rebirth. As you know from Chapter 2, some of the *Upaniṣadic* sages of the first millennium BCE, whose ideas came to constitute one root of Hinduism, posited a universal or innermost self or soul called *Ātman*.

Although different *Upaniṣads* describe *Ātman* differently, they share enough in common to sketch a set of overlapping features, at least for our purposes. *Ātman* is not the body or senses; nor is it self-awareness or the mind that perceives and conceives. Rather, *Ātman* is the power and unity behind all bodily and mental functions. *Ātman* is therefore a pure subject that can never be objectified. It is a knower that knows, though cannot itself be known, at least not through ordinary mental knowing, which is always of some object. *Ātman* is also, at least for some *Upaniṣadic* sages, one with ultimate reality, *Brahman*. In the words of the *Bṛhadāraṇyaka Upaniṣad*, one can only say "not this, not this" (*neti neti*) about *Ātman*, for *Ātman* is ungraspable, undecaying, unencumbered, and unbound. The person who comes to see *Ātman* in herself and all things in *Ātman* becomes "calm, composed, cool, patient, and collected," "is not burnt by evil" but rather "burns up all evil," and becomes "the world of *Brahman*."[1]

How does one come to know *Ātman* and that it is *Brahman*? For some proponents of the later Hindu school of Vedānta philosophy, which systematized the teaching of the *Upaniṣads*, *Ātman/Brahman* is known by coming to understand the words of the *Upaniṣads*. Maybe this is also what happened with the original oral communication of the *Upaniṣads*: As students listened to their guru's teachings about *Ātman-Brahman*, they came to know *Ātman-Brahman*. Perhaps as some *Upaniṣads* suggest, this involved years of yogic concentration on their words, especially by means of the sacred syllable *Oṃ*, the three phonemes of which (A-U-M) are symbolic of the creation, maintenance, and destruction of the cosmos, together which constitute the essence of innermost consciousness and ultimate reality (*Ātman-Brahman*). Regardless, what is important for us are the reasons that *Upaniṣadic* sages provided for the existence and nature of *Ātman*.

These reasons are best categorized in three ways. First, there is the need to make sense of ourselves as a substance-self—*Ātman* as that which provides a sense of unity to our mental and bodily actions, despite the fact that our bodies, perceptions, thoughts, desires, and even self-awareness change over time. Second, there is the need to make sense of reincarnation—*Ātman* as that which inherits the karmic consequences of former actions and therefore reincarnates from body to body. Finally, there is the need to make sense of final death—*Ātman* as that which achieves liberation or release (*mokṣa*) from rebirth upon the least death of the mind-body.

The historical Buddha (*c.* 563–*c.* 483 BCE), however, saw things differently. As you also remember from Chapter 2, the Buddha taught Four Noble Truths, the first of which is that "suffering" exists. The Sanskrit word for suffering (*duḥkha*)—which literally means "painful," encompassing physical, emotional, and mental pain—is arguably best understood as "unsatisfactoriness." Why do we find life unsatisfactory? Because we cling to it as if it were permanent, but it is not. Most of all, we cling to ourselves as if we were permanent, but we are not, or so argued some of the early Buddhist philosophers. (This was actually a matter of lively debate among some of the earliest Buddhist schools.) Rather, the "self" is just the product of five ever-changing processes or aggregates. Thus, there is *an-ātman*—no *Ātman*, soul, or permanent and unchanging "self."

In Sanskrit, these five processes or aggregates are called *skandha*-s, the singular form of which referred to a bundle of sticks, especially as used to make fire.[2] The first *skandha* is that of the physical processes of the body (*rūpa*), while the other four include the mental processes of the mind: feeling (*vedanā*), the "hedonistic" aspect of our experiences as pleasant or painful; perception (*saṃjñā*), our mental representation and classification of external and internal experiences; volitional activities (*saṃskāra*), most of all our will (*cetanā*), especially as it forms our moral character; and consciousness (*vijñāna* or *citta*), our awareness and analysis of our external and internal experiences. Collectively, these five processes are the "self." There is nothing beyond or behind them that is permanent. Who we are changes from moment to moment and day to day. When we "reincarnate," our mental processes merely transmigrate to another body. After we achieve enlightenment (*nirvāṇa*), we are released from transmigration at death.

What are Buddhist "arguments" for the lack of a permanent and unchanging self or soul? We see some of them in an early Buddhist text called the *Milinda Pañha*, which contains a "chariot sermon" that was delivered by an early Buddhist monk named Nāgasena. In response to the question "What is your name?" by King Milinda—possibly Meander, an Indo-Greek king who ruled northeast India in the second century BCE—Nāgasena said that he has many names, each of which "is just a denomination, a designation, a conceptual term, a mere name."[3] In reality, there is no permanent, unchanging self behind these names. Nāgasena went on to illustrate this point by asking about the chariot on which Milinda rode to the discourse. The chariot is not axle, wheels, body, etc. Rather, "chariot" is also "just a denomination, a designation, a conceptual term, a mere name." Put in terms of the five aggregates, the self is not the body, not feeling, not perception, not volition, and not consciousness. The self is nothing but the term that we apply to the aggregate of these functions. We can never perceive or conceive some underlying, unchanging "self" that is not just a part or process that is changing over time. There is no essential, permanent, unchanging "self."

Of course, there are many more positions in South Asian philosophy of religion about what the self is, most of which we will encounter in subsequent chapters. But these two—the *Upaniṣadic* and the early Buddhist—put the fundamental issue in sharp relief. What is the best way to make sense of the self? Is there an enduring, permanent, individual substance that is me? Or am I merely a set of ever-changing processes that do not ultimately exist as anything permanent?

Note that for early Indian philosophy, this issue is not merely academic, for liberation itself rests on it. If, on the one hand, there is some substantial, eternal "soul" (*Ātman*), and if that soul is one with ultimate reality (*Brahman*), then the way of liberation requires coming to understand this over years of ascetic behavior, scriptural study, and meditative practice. If, on the other hand, there is no substantial, individual self, and if this false notion is our biggest impediment to seeing things as they really are, then the way of liberation requires coming to understand this over years of ascetic behavior, scriptural study, and meditative practice.

Philosophy of religion tends to divorce itself from the lived reality of religion. In a sense, it must if it is to analyze and evaluate arguments. Nevertheless, global-critical philosophers of religion should be mindful that arguments have lives in religious traditions and are compelling to the extent that they enable humans to live life well (among other reasons). In the case of religion, this means living in relation to what is ultimately important (among other things).

III. Lakȟóta Philosophy of Religion

In Chapter 3, we explored the Lakȟóta saying "all my relations" (*mitákuye oyásiŋ*) as an epistemological principle (concerning what we know and how); here, we examine it ontologically (with respect to what exists and how). Of course, the primary use of *mitákuye oyásiŋ* is ritual: all Lakȟóta ceremonies end with it. According to the holy man (*wičháša wakȟáŋ*) Archie Fire Lame Deer, the purpose of this ritual utterance is to signify that "we have prayed for *all* our relatives: every human being on this Earth and every living thing—every animal down to the tiniest bug, and every plant down to the tiniest wildflower."[4] As the anthropologist William Powers puts it, "all species—and this would include animals, birds, insects, trees, flowers, and rocks"—are, for the Lakȟóta, considered *oyáte* ("people" or "nation").[5]

For the Lakȟóta philosopher Vine Deloria, Jr., even if "all my relations" is a Lakȟóta ritual utterance and an American Indian epistemological principle, it is grounded in American Indian ontology. This ontology entails that "everything in the natural world has relationships with every other thing and the total set of relationships makes up the natural world as we experience it."[6] For Deloria, it is therefore the covenantal relationship within the community that is key, not a personal relationship between the individual and some God.[7] This is because, on the one hand, there is no salvation except for continuance of the tribe itself, and, on the other hand, there is no concept of an individual alone.

Deloria is quick to add, though, that this does not mean that there is no sense of a personal self in American Indian culture(s). In fact, such a sense is reflected not only in naming customs—in which individuals receive names that reflect their unique qualities, exploits, abilities, physical characteristics, or religious experiences—but also in the vision quest (*haŋbléčeyapi* in

Lakȟóta), which is primarily an individual responsibility, at least in many American Indian tribes. Although Lakȟóta traditions do not abstract the person out of her community context, they do make a place for each person in each community.

Nor do the Lakȟóta abstract the person out of a wider, natural context. As Archie Fire Lame Deer indicates above, "all my relations" applies to relations not only between humans but also with animals, plants, and even inorganic species. Among these relations, the ones with other animals are often most important and sacred. It should come as no surprise, therefore, that Deloria dedicates one entire chapter of his book on traditional religion to "interspecies relations." In that chapter, Deloria itemizes and exemplifies three types of interspecies communications: those in which an animal features prominently in an encounter with the sacred, those in which an animal aids a human who is extremely vulnerable, and those in which an animal offers important commentary on human activities.[8]

These relationships are established and performed through sacred language. According to anthropologist William Powers, the Lakȟóta "employ metaphorical extensions between humans and animals," by which nonhuman species are "treated as if they are human."[9] Writes Powers, "Just as the animals and birds exhibit metaphorically the characteristics of humans, humans may also exhibit the characteristics of animals."[10] Thus, Powers concludes, "All these metaphorical extensions in the sacred language serve to underscore the interdependency of humans and other species, including all animate and inanimate objects. Humans, then, are very much just another part of the universe—nothing less, nothing more."[11]

What we have here appears to be the key premise of this Lakȟóta view of the "self": human beings are not substantially different from the rest of the natural world. There is no person-like God to create humans in "His" image and command humans to rule over the rest of the natural world. The "self," therefore, must be understood in relationship to everything else, not as an individual substance-self.

IV. Yorùbá Philosophy of Religion

According to contemporary scholars and practitioners of *Òrìṣà* religion, the traditional "self" in Yorùbá culture—more precisely, the tradition of Ifá divination—is composed of three parts: *ara*, the physical body; *èmí*, the principle of life; and *orí*, the head, which is the bearer of the destiny (*àyànmọ́*) and the determination of the personality of the self. Next chapter, we will find out that things are a little more complicated than this. But for now, we will stick with these three.

First, the *ara* is constructed. This is a two-step process that occurs in the womb, with the *Òrìṣà* Ògún fashioning the body's skeleton and the *Òrìṣà* Ọbàtálá molding the body's form. Next, the *èmí* or life-breath is breathed into the body by the *Òrìṣà* Olódùmarè, thereby making each human His child; it is for this reason—as well as because the *èmí* survives death—that *èmí* is sometimes translated as "soul." Finally, each person chooses a destiny or lot (*àyànmọ́*) that will determine their character, occupation, success in life, time of death, and so on. This destiny resides within the actual head (*orí*), as an inner or spiritual head (*orí-inu*), which also has a heavenly counterpart (*orí orún*). After the person "chooses" an *orí*, it is affixed to her by Olódùmarè while she kneels before Him.

Although each person chooses her or his own destiny, no one knows what this destiny is, since each person can only see the outside of the heads, which have been formed by the celestial potter Ajàlá. Moreover, Ajàlá is a notoriously sloppy craftsman, so many of the clay heads that he forms have internal imperfections. Nevertheless, one goal of existence is to realize one's destiny, whatever that might be. This is a lifelong process that involves the ritual practice of Ifá divination, by means of which a person learns, over time, aspects of her destiny, usually within the context of seeking answers and remedies for illnesses and misfortunes.

For the Yorùbá philosopher Segun Gbadegesin, Yorùbá belief in destiny expresses a fundamental principle that human existence has meaning: "that human beings are not on a purposeless mission in this world; that they have a mission to fulfill, a message to deliver—which is the meaning of their existence—and that this mission has been fully endorsed by the creator."[12] However, Gbadegesin also believes that the Yorùbá concept of destiny suggests "some anxiety about human helplessness in certain situations."[13] Indeed, the Yorùbá cosmos is replete with evil forces that cause harm and death to humans: so-called witches, sorcerers, and even Anti-gods (*Ajogun*). To help counter these forces, the person's heavenly *orí*—their spiritual self or personal divinity—assists in the realization of that person's destiny, at least so long as it receives sacrifices and offerings through a ritual process called "feeding the head."

The *Òrìṣà* and ancestors also aid humans in repelling evil and realizing destiny. Each person will therefore seek to align herself with an *Òrìṣà* who can serve as her protector. In this sense, writes Judith Gleason, the *Òrìṣà* "are like immense magnifying mirrors in which we behold ourselves as potentialities," "guardians through whom one lives a more intense life vicariously, guides whose excess of energy leads their devotees to a more placid, a more balanced existence."[14] Similarly, the *babaláwo* Philip John Neimark emphasizes that the different personality traits of people make them suitable to different *Òrìṣà*. Thus, "[l]earning to be comfortable with [the *Òrìṣà*'s] characteristics and to tap into them in a meaningful way is an important step toward successfully traveling our paths."[15]

Here, we have yet another concept of the self, one that includes something like a soul (*èmí*), but functionally devalues it to a person's destiny (*orí*), which is located elsewhere in the body (as well as in heaven). What arguments can be provided for why destiny is the key aspect of a person? First, it captures our sense of purpose, meaning, and direction. Second, it explains why we sometimes find ourselves "stuck" with a lot in life that is not to our liking and perhaps even tragic. Third, it therefore helps to explain why bad things happen to good people (or the inverse).

V. East Asian Philosophy of Religion

In Chinese philosophy of religion, humans are fundamentally in relation to and ideally in harmony with the wider social and natural world. In this section, we will look at two early, influential, and long-lasting religio-philosophical understandings of this relationality and harmony: those found in the *Analects* of Confucius—which in Chinese is called the "selected sayings" (*Lúnyǔ*, 論語) of Confucius and some of his disciples—and the *Dàodéjīng* of the mythical sage Lǎozǐ. Each has its beginnings in the later Zhou Dynasty (722–221 BCE), which was a period of increasingly widespread political instability, social upheaval, and human suffering. Each, therefore, advances a solution to this problem. Or to put it in Chinese terms, each proposes a "way" (*dào*) on which humans should walk to restore harmony to the world.

The solution of Confucius (551–479 BCE) was to cultivate personal virtue, observe ritual propriety, and rectify social order. For Confucius, this required returning to the "tried and true" ways of the past, especially those that were studied and taught by a subclass of scholars (*rú*) who were part of a wider knightly class (*shì*, 士) during the early Zhou Dynasty (1027–770). Over time, these "ways" came to involve not only the rituals and ceremonies of the royal court but also the six arts that were necessary for correct knowledge and performance of these rituals and ceremonies: history, poetry, music, astrology, archery, and mathematics. For Confucius and later Confucians, however, this category grew to include all the ways in which humans comport themselves in relationship with one another—everything from state ceremonies and rituals to everyday conventions and mores.

It is crucial for Confucians that all these "rituals" be performed "properly"—thus, one key Confucian virtue is *lǐ* (禮), ritual propriety. These rituals should not, however, be performed blindly; rather, they must be infused with an equally important Confucian virtue: *rén*, which is variously translated as "benevolence," "goodness," "human-heartedness," and "humaneness," among other things. The Chinese character for *rén* is composed of those for "human being" and "two," thereby suggesting that we only become fully human in relation with other humans. In response to the question, "What is *rén*"? Confucius answered, "Love your fellow humans," also offering an inverse variation of the "Golden Rule": Do not do onto others what you would not have them do onto you.[16] *Rén*, however, must flow through *lǐ* (禮), as another passage from the *Analects* maintains: "To return to the observance of the rites [*lǐ*] through overcoming the self constitutes benevolence [*rén*]."[17] Consider, for example, the handshake, kiss, or bow; depending on the society in which one finds oneself, one (or more) of these conventions serves as an indispensable means of greeting someone "properly," thereby conveying one's "human heartedness."

If *lǐ* is the means by which *rén* is expressed, then filial piety (*xiào*, 孝) is the "beginning of *rén*." By obeying and respecting parents one learns how to express *rén* through *lǐ* (禮) in all five of the "Five Constant Relationships" (*wǔlún*, 五倫) that structure society: (1) father/son, (2) older sibling/younger sibling, (3) husband/wife, (4) elder/younger, (5) ruler/subject. Although these relationships are obviously hierarchical, they are also reciprocal—both "superior" and "inferior" have relational responsibilities: (1) father is responsible for the education and moral formation of son, who must be respectful and obedient to father; (2) elder brother must assume responsibility for raising the younger siblings, and younger siblings must be compliant; (3) husband is authoritative protector of wife, who is protected homemaker and mother; (4) elder is responsible to support and develop the character of younger, who must show respect and be open to advice; (5) ruler must assume responsibility and care for his subjects, who must obey their ruler. These relationships took male-centric forms throughout most of Chinese history; nevertheless, they emphasize the importance of being in right relationship with other human beings and therefore have a value beyond their patriarchal applications.

What then is the "self" for Confucius? It is a self that is fundamentally in relation with others, that strives for moral perfection by performing moral cultivation, and that observes social conventions and official rituals to express a "human-heartedness" with other human beings. But it is also a self that in cultivating virtue and ordering society forms a "triad" between Heaven (*Tiān*), earth (*dì*), and humankind. As one recent scholar of Confucius has therefore observed, with Confucius "the secular is sacred."[18]

A second text from early Chinese philosophy of religion gives us a very different picture of what humans are. This text is the elliptic and enigmatic, poetic and mystical *Dàodéjīng*, which is traditionally believed to have been authored by a man called Lǎozǐ, who is purported to have lived in the sixth century BCE, just before the time of Confucius. (In fact, some legends have an elderly Lǎozǐ meeting a youthful Confucius.) Scholars, however, believe that the *Dàodéjīng* is a composite work of many authors, with "Lǎozǐ," which simply means "Old Master," signifying this composite. Whatever the case, the *Dàodéjīng* exerted considerable influence not only on Daoist religious philosophy and religious traditions but also on Chinese thought and behavior more generally.

There is no better place to begin an understanding of the *Dàodéjīng* then with its title: the classic (*jīng*) of the way (*dào*) and its power (*dé*). What is *dào*? Literally meaning "path"—with the Chinese character of a head over a foot—*dào* had begun to take on the meaning of "guiding way" or "guiding discourse" during the time when "100 Schools Contended." There was, for example, the *dào* of the *rú* (Confucians) and the *dào* of the *mò* (Mohists), both of which proposed guiding ways or discourses for restoring harmony in society. In the *Dàodéjīng*, however, *dào* also takes on natural, cosmic, and metaphysical dimensions. This *Dào* is nothing less than the mysterious source of the cosmos and pervading force that patterns its operation. This *Dào* is not a God; rather, it is beyond all qualifications, especially anthropomorphic ones. This *Dào* gives rise to the cosmos, not intentionally or at some moment in time, but spontaneously and continuously. This *Dào* is also the way that the cosmos naturally functions, with opposites harmoniously balanced, usually in cyclical fashion.

What, then, is the power (*dé*) of *Dào*? For starters, it is just what was said above—the power to make all things function in their natural states and processes, with opposites such as winter and summer, night and day, cold and hot, oscillating in an ongoing, harmonious balance. *Dào* therefore flows through all things, humans included. Humans, however, are the one part of the natural world that can act contrary to *Dào*, bringing imbalance and disharmony not only to themselves but also to their societies and the natural world. The key question, then, is how do we function like *Dào*? To answer this question is to speak about the *dé* of humans, a term that includes the power or efficacy of humans as well as their character or virtue.

One frequent "response" to this question in the *Dàodéjīng* is non-action (*wúwéi*, 無爲). Just as *Dào* does not act with effort and in its own interest, so humans also should not act with effort and in their own interest. Rather, humans should act in accordance with what is natural and effortless, navigating their way through life in a manner that is as spontaneous and effortless as possible. Where there is tension and conflict, the Daoist does not "power through"; rather, she steps back and feels how to act naturally and disinterestedly in a manner that reduces tension and conflict, is in accordance with what seems natural, and is achieved in a minimally effortful way. A term that therefore often accompanies *wúwéi* is *zìrán* (自然), which literally means "self-so" or "so-of-itself," but is often translated as "spontaneity" or "naturalness" and associated with metaphors such as an unhewn log, flowing water, infants, and mothers.

This emphasis on non-purposeful, spontaneous, natural action is in contradistinction to the Confucian project of cultivating personal virtue, observing ritual propriety, and rectifying social relations. The *Dàodéjīng* opposes such Confucian endeavors as "cutting, filing, polishing" of what is already perfectly natural, as symbolized by the unhewn log. Moreover, the *Dàodéjīng* contends that when Confucians disturb what is perfectly natural through efforts of cultivation, ritualization, and rectification, they inevitably stir up desire, which breeds competition, in turn causing strife and chaos. Better instead, to return to what is natural and effortless—*Dào*. As chapter 38 of the *Dàodéjīng* reads, "The person of superior integrity [*dé*] takes no action, nor has he a purpose for acting"; only when the way (*Dào*) and virtuous power (*dé*) are lost, do Confucian virtues such as *rén* (human-heartedness), *yì* (moral rightness), and *lǐ* (禮, ritual propriety) arise.[19]

One might be tempted, then, to read the *Dàodéjīng* simply as a mystical guide for sagely individuals; in fact, though, the *Dàodéjīng* appears to be a manual for rulers, making it one more attempt to solve the problem of the chaos and conflict of the latter Zhou Dynasty. Regardless, it offers us one more perspective on what the self is, a perspective that is not unlike the Lakȟóta self, one that sees humans as fundamentally in relation with all the other beings and processes through which *Dào* flows.

VI. Mediterranean/Abrahamic Philosophy of Religion

In contrast to the traditions and thinkers above, Abrahamic philosophy of religion might seem to maintain the concept of an individuated, substantial self—a soul, even. But things are not always as they seem.

We begin with the Hebrew Bible, where we first note that there are at least three different relevant terms.[20] Although the ancient Hebrew terms *nepeš* and *nĕšāmâ* are often translated as "soul," they refer more particularly to breath or life, distinguishing a principle of vitality from the material body or, in the case of *nĕšāmâ*, referring specifically to conscious life. A third term, *rûaḥ*, which is commonly translated as "spirit," instead denotes powers outside the body that operate in or through the body; these powers are a divine gift that offer a mysterious vitality to the material body. None of these terms—*nepeš*, *nĕšāmâ*, *rûaḥ*—originally refers to an immortal, immaterial soul. Rather, the earliest biblical view about what happens to humans after death is that all the dead enter a shadowy underworld called Sheol. It is not until after the Jews returned from Babylonian Captivity (in the sixth century BCE), where they were influenced by Persian religion (Zoroastrianism), that we begin to see a difference between the post-mortem fates of good and bad people, with the former going to a heavenly realm; the latter, to a hellish realm. Still, these are the fates of resurrected bodies, not immaterial souls.

Resurrection of the dead took a while to catch on. At the time that Jesus lived (first century CE), it was a point of contention between two groups of Jews, with the Sadducees holding that the resurrection of the dead was not based in scripture (especially Torah), and the Pharisees and their rabbinic successors claiming otherwise. Given that Jesus and the writers of the New Testament identified more with the latter than the former, resurrection of the dead was not a contested idea in the New Testament itself and was soon enshrined in Christian creeds (as we will see in Chapter 6). Nevertheless, as ancient Greek philosophy (first) and modern European philosophy (later) came to influence Christianity, resurrection of the dead was conjoined with, and sometimes displaced by, immortality of the soul. Indeed, it is the Greek term for "soul" (*psychē*) that was used to translate the Hebrew word *nepeš*, with the Greek term for "spirit" (*pneuma*) being used for *rûaḥ*.

Since the New Testament writers expected the imminent return of Jesus, they did not devote attention to the mechanics of resurrection of dead. The Qur᾽ān, by contrast, did. Here, the relevant distinction is between the Arabic

Table 4.1 Scriptural Terms for "Soul" and "Spirit" in Abrahamic Religions

Scripture	Term	Meanings
Hebrew Bible	*Nepeš*	Hebrew term for an internal principle of vitality; commonly translated as "soul" (or *psychē* in ancient Greek)
	Něšāmâ	Hebrew term for an internal principle of vitality, especially with respect to conscious life; commonly translated as "soul" (or *psychē* in ancient Greek)
	Rûaḥ	Hebrew term for a divine power outside the body that offers vitality to the body; commonly translated as "spirit" (or *pneuma* in ancient Greek)
New Testament	*Psychē*	Ancient Greek term for a principle of vitality; sometimes also denotes the immortal and immaterial essence of the person (e.g., in Plato); used to translate *nepeš*; commonly translated as "soul"
	Pneuma	Ancient Greek term for a divine power outside the body; used to translated *rûaḥ*; sometimes used indistinctively with *psyche*
Qur'ān	*Nafs*	Arabic term for "soul"; leaves the body at death and later rejoins it on the Day of Judgment
	Rūḥ	Arabic term for Allah's spirit; breathed into Adam

terms *nafs*, which is translated as "soul," and *rūḥ*, "spirit." (Note the similarities to the Hebrew words *nepeš* and *ruah.*) *Rūḥ* usually refers to God's spirit, which is breathed into Adam, whereas *nafs* is used of the human soul. With death, the soul leaves the body, rejoining it on the Day of Judgment, after which the righteous go to paradise and the wicked go to hell. Nevertheless, just as in the case of medieval Jewish and Christian philosophy, resurrection of the dead was often conjoined with, and sometimes displaced by, immortality of the soul by some Islamic philosophers (as we will also see in Chapter 6).

As fascinating as these distinctions are—soul versus spirit, resurrection of the dead versus immortality of the soul (see Table 4.1)—they do not really tell us how the self is experienced in the Abrahamic religious traditions. We turn, then, to a representative philosopher of religion for each religion, though with the caveat that these philosophers of religion do not of course speak for their entire traditions.

In the case of Judaism, no idea is more fundamental than that of a covenantal relationship between the Jewish people and their God YHWH, which is consummated in the 613 commandments (*mizvot*) given to Moses by YHWH on Mount Sinai. For the twentieth-century German-Jewish philosopher of religion Martin Buber (1878–1965), this covenantal relationship between the Jewish people and YHWH was understood more widely as a dialogical relationship between a human being and some other. In German, Buber calls this dialogical relationship "*Ich und Du*"—the encounter between some "I" (*Ich*) and some "You" (*Du*), where the "You" can be either natural (plants, animals), human, or spiritual (art, God). In the I–You encounter, the I comes to the You with the whole being, establishing an immediate relationship in the living present. Buber contrasts this I–You encounter with an I–It relationship in which the "It" is possessed as an object. This is the realm of the everyday, of order, of knowledge. Importantly, both relations are necessary, though it is only in the I–You encounter that we are most fully human: Although humans cannot live with "It," writes Buber, "whoever lives only with that is not human."[21] Moreover, there is no pure and solitary "I" for Buber; there is only I in relationship with either "You" or "It."

In the case of Christianity, one dominant understanding of the self is of that which stands sinful before the God of Christianity and is therefore in need of forgiveness. Perhaps no Christian philosopher of religion has better conveyed this sense of sinfulness than Saint Augustine (354–430). For Augustine, humans are "originally sinful" by virtue of inheriting the sin of the first human, Adam. What this means for each and every human being is that, although they can freely desire or choose to do what is right, they are unable to effect or perform this choice since their free will has been damaged through the "Fall" of humankind. This distinction can be put in terms of the preceding discussion of soul/spirit and flesh: "the spirit is strong, but the "flesh is weak" (Matthew 26:41). For Augustine, this was a "monstrous" or "morbid" human condition, according to which "the will to act was not equaled by the power [to act]."[22] Only through acceptance of the forgiveness of sins (through the death and resurrection of Jesus Christ) could the will be healed—able not only to will the good but also to effect the good. As Augustine recounts in his *Confessions*, "Lady Continence" instructed him in a vision to do just this:

> Why are you relying on yourself, only to find yourself unreliable? Cast yourself upon him [God], do not be afraid. He will not withdraw himself so that you fall. Make the leap without anxiety; he will catch you and heal you.[23]

By contrast, there is no such notion of original sin in Islam (nor in Judaism). Rather, there is simply the sin that humans commit. Chief among these sins are those of idolatry/polytheism (Ar. *shirk*)—failing to understand and act in such a way that realizes Allah's unity and singularity (*tawḥīd*), associating other things with Allah, or taking other things as Gods. For many Muslims, every day provides an opportunity to realize and enact Allah's oneness, especially by resisting the temptation of self-sufficiency, the mistaken belief that they are independent of, and can manage life without, Allah. For some mystical Muslims (Sufis), it is the very notion of a self/soul (*nafs*) that is the biggest obstacle to realizing the oneness of God. This is so not only since humans often act in selfish and self-centered ways but also because if one's self/soul is thought to be separate from Allah, then Allah is not absolutely one and entirely all. For such Sufis, the mystical experience was understood as one of *fanā*ʾ, the "passing away" or "annihilation" of the self, after which it subsists (*baqā*ʾ) alone in Allah. In the case of so-called "sober" (*ṣaḥr*) Sufis such as al-Ghazālī (1058–1111), *fanā*ʾ was interpreted as "closeness" (*qurb*) to Allah, but for so-called "drunk" (*sukr*) Sufis such as the ninth-century Bāyazīd Bisṭāmī, *fanā*ʾ was the total annihilation of the self, such that only Allah remains in a state of mystical union. (Of course, "sober" and "drunk" are just metaphors; for more about this, see Chapter 8.) Some of Bisṭāmī's utterances about this self-annihilation were later recorded by the Persian Sufi poet and hagiographer known by his pen names Farīd ud-Dīn and ʿAṭṭār (*c.* 1145–*c.* 1221). For example, ʿAṭṭār tells us that at the culmination of Bisṭāmī's mystical ascension (*mi*ʿ*rāj*) to Allah through the seven spheres of heaven (which was modeled after that of Muḥammad himself; see Figure 4 and Chapters 7 and 12), Bisṭāmī's "attributes were annihilated" in Allah's own attributes, after which Allah bestowed on Bisṭāmī "a name of God's own presence" and addressed Bisṭāmī with Allah's own selfhood. It was then that "[s]ingleness became manifest; duality vanished."[24]

Here, then, we have three more conceptions of the self: that which does not exist on its own but only in relationship with others; that which cannot exist (freely) on its own but only after redeemed by a God; and that which should not exist on its own but only in the oneness of a God. Again, we should be mindful that these three conceptions are not representative of their religious traditions in general (Judaism, Christianity, and Islam, respectively). Nevertheless, they have proved influential conceptions of the self in and for their respective traditions and have also generated significant philosophical interpretation and evaluation beyond those traditions.

Figure 4 Muḥammad's Miʿrāj. Khamseh of Nizami, "Ascent of Muhammad to Heaven," *c.* 1539–43, Public Domain, Wikimedia Commons.

VII. European/Academic Philosophy of Religion

Whence, then, the idea that we are individual, substantial, immaterial, and immortal souls? In addition to the ancient Greek philosopher Plato, the most influential philosophical source of this notion of soul is the modern French philosopher René Descartes (1596–1650). For Descartes, there are two basic substances in the cosmos: *extended substance* or matter/body, which is the substance of things that exist in space, possessing length, breadth, and depth; and *thinking substance* or mind/soul, which is the substance of things that think. Thinking substance is then further divided into *infinite thinking substance*, which is God, and *finite thinking substance*, which is humans. For humans, there are two primary attributes of mind/soul: *intellect* (or perception), the operation of the intellect to perceive sensations, to imagine, and to conceptualize; and *volition*, the ability of the will to desire, make judgments, and assert/deny. Although mind/soul and its attributes are temporarily housed in the body, a person is not their body but their mind/soul. Whereas the body is divisible, material, and mortal, the mind/soul is indivisible, immaterial, and immortal.

Why posit such a view of the self? Several reasons can be found in Descartes' writings, especially his influential *Meditations on First Philosophy* (1641). First, given that knowledge for Descartes consists of that which is clearly and distinctly perceived, he simply maintains that he has "clear and distinct" perceptions of both material bodies in space (that have length, breadth, and depth) and of immaterial minds (that perceive, conceive, desire, and judge). Beyond this, Descartes offers a couple of thought experiments: although he can doubt the existence of his body, he cannot doubt the existence of his mind (since there can be no such doubt without a mind doing the doubting); although he can imagine himself existing without a body, he cannot imagine himself existing without a mind (since, again, there can be no such imagining without a location for it in the mind).[25] To put Descartes' core argument in deductive form:

P1: If something *x* thinks, then *x* exists;
P2: I think (or doubt, or imagine, . . .);
C: I exist.

For Descartes—as for philosophers to follow, right up to the present—this "substance dualism" between the brain/body and mind/soul opened up a philosophical can of worms known as the "interaction problem": if brain/body is material and mind/soul is immaterial, how can the two interact? How can intentions formed by an immaterial mind/soul (e.g., to pick up my cup) cause effects in by material brain/body (e.g., the picking up of my cup)? How can sensations received through my material brain/body (e.g., of the cup in front of me) cause effects in my immaterial mind/soul (e.g., as I now contemplate the essence of cup-ness)? For Descartes, this interaction somehow occurred in the pineal gland. Of course, however, this solution solved nothing (but rather only specified a location for the solution). Nor has anyone since Descartes solved this problem, which is today known as the "hard problem of consciousness."

Although Descartes' view of self has come under increasing philosophical scrutiny in the twentieth century, especially as neuroscience, cognitive science, and evolutionary psychology have come to understand the workings of the brain, it is not without contemporary philosophical support. We will explore the arguments of some of these recent "substance dualists" in Chapter 6. For now, however, we continue with three more philosophically significant views of the self in academic philosophy of religion, the first of which, that of Scottish philosopher David Hume (1711–76), is in direct contrast with that of Descartes.

Whereas Descartes was a rationalist who held that our most foundational pieces of knowledge are innate, preexisting sensory input, Hume was an empiricist who rejected innate ideas. For Hume, all knowledge instead arises through experience, specifically impressions, which can be from an external source in the case of sensation or from an internal source (emotions and mental operations) in the case of reflection. From these "forceful, lively, and direct" impressions, humans later create ideas, chiefly by remembering past impressions and reasoning about them. Ideas are therefore "faint and obscure," especially when contrasted with impressions; thus, humans tend to fall into error about them. To ascertain whether ideas have a basis in reality, we must trace them back to a grounding set of impressions. In the case of the idea of a mountain, we can do just this; for a golden mountain, we cannot.

As you can imagine, however, Hume was not primarily interested in the ideas of mountains, whether golden or not; instead, he trained his sights on some of the core ideas of Western philosophy, especially substance, causality, and (a Western philosophical) God. In none of these cases could he trace the idea back to grounding impressions; moreover, in the case of God, he offered devastating criticisms of philosophical proofs for the existence of God as well as popular arguments from the testimony of miracles. In later chapters, we will consider Hume's critiques of the design proof (Chapter 9) and of miracles (Chapter 12). Here, we focus on Hume's critique of substance, especially self-substance.

Let us begin, however, with material substance, since Hume's argument against it is quite simple: we only ever experience the properties of objects, never the objects-themselves. Consider a coffee cup: we experience its shape, color, size, and solidity (etc.), but not the cup-itself as a material substance that is the bearer of these properties. Certainly, we have the idea of the cup-itself; however, we cannot trace it back to any confirming experience, so it seems to be something that the mind constructs.

As with the material substances of the world, so with the immaterial substance of the self: although we have such an idea, we cannot ground it in any experiential impressions. This was exactly the point of the following thought experiment that Hume conducted in his 1739–40 *Treatise on Human Understanding*:

> For my part, when I enter most intimately into what I call *myself*, I always stumble on some particular perception or other, of heat or cold, light or shade, love or hatred, pain or pleasure. I can never catch *myself* at any time without a perception, and can never observe any thing but the perception.[26]

Try it for yourself. Can you experience yourself? Absent any perception? Or do you only ever experience some sensation, emotion, desire, or thought (etc.)? Whence, then, the idea of a substance-self (that is the bearer of its properties and is unchanging over time)? Hume thought that we invent this idea to "bundle" together our "heap" of impressions and ideas, extending it to cover both past and future perceptions. In actuality, however, there is no such self, not as an underlying, unchanging substance anyway. This self is but a creation of our mind.

Just as with Descartes, Hume's understanding of the self has survived up to the present, undergoing numerous developments, variations, and critiques, some of which we will examine in Chapter 6 when we take up the question of whether we survive death. Here, however, we turn from these two selves that have dominated analytic philosophy to two that are influential in Continental philosophy, where the focus has been on how selves are products of socialization. One classical (Enlightenment) source of such a view is German philosopher Karl Marx (1818–83). We examine this view in the later "post-Marxist" French philosopher Louis Althusser (1918–90), who devoted much of his career to interpreting the political philosophy of Karl Marx, especially Marx's notion of ideology.

Let us begin with some Marxist basics. Every society is constituted by an economic base and the superstructure of the state. The base encompasses "economic modes of production" and "social relations of production." For example, a small, island society whose main form of sustenance is fish will need to produce the means of catching and cooking fish—not to mention everything else that is required to survive—and this will require dividing labor accordingly. Metaphorically resting on top of this economic infrastructure is the superstructure of the state—two types of means by which the state maintains its modes and relations of production. First, there is simply the state itself and its apparatuses: government and its laws, courts, prisons, police, army, and so forth. Second, there is the "ideology" of the state, which includes political, ethical, legal, philosophical, religious, and even aesthetic ideas and practices. To continue the example above, our small, island society will need leaders and means by which they exercise direct control over the fishing economy (e.g., laws and ways of enforcing them), as well as ideas and practices by which they indirectly justify their power and the division of labor (e.g., religious myths and rituals).

It was this latter set of ideas, especially as embedded in practices and institutions, that interested Althusser most, especially as they functioned within capitalistic societies. In offering a list of such "ideological state apparatuses" (ISAs), Althusser included religion, education, family, law, politics, unions, communications (e.g., media, internet, television), and culture (e.g., literature, arts, sports).[27] Although many of these ISAs are "private" and therefore not under direct control of the state, they nevertheless serve the interests of the state by producing "subjects" who understand their relationship to the state to be "naturally given" rather than socially constructed. Take, for example, the institution of the family. Since a capitalist economy requires as many consumers as possible, it values the notion of a nuclear family, in which every member is a unique individual. Humans in such societies understand themselves as such—as unique individuals within nuclear families, which they will one day leave to begin their own nuclear families of unique individuals. Although we might believe that we are "naturally" individual or that families are "really" nuclear, we and they are only so because our ideological state apparatuses have taught us so.

This is Althusser's notion of "ideological interpellation"—the process by which humans become constituted as self-conscious "subjects," understanding what they are, always in relation to the state, usually obliviously so. By means of our educational and political systems, our religions and philosophies, the media and internet, even our families and sports, we come to understand ourselves as unique individuals, as consumers, as free, as equal, and so forth. To put the matter in the terms of this chapter, we are not substantial individuals, at least not naturally; rather, we are "interpellated"—brought into being, given an identity—as such through ideological state apparatuses. There is no self-conscious subject prior to or apart from interpellation; interpellation brings the subject into being and gives it an identity.

Not long after Althusser penned his influential, late-career essay "Ideology and Ideological State Apparatuses" (1970), arguing that subjects in general are socially constructed through ideological state apparatuses, American philosopher Judith Butler (b. 1956) was to publish her equally influential, early-career "Performative Acts and Gender Constitution" (1988), arguing that gender is socially constructed though performative acts. This is Butler's theory of gender performativity: gender is not something given by nature but rather "performed" in society. With respect to the feminine gender in particular (though applicable as well to the male gender), Butler maintained there was no biological essence or core, such that some preexisting substantial identity or locus of agency might simply express or enact it. Rather, feminine gender is performed through bodily action and thereby socially constructed as gender roles that are transmitted from generation to generation. Moreover, subjects do not freely choose to perform gender; rather, they inherit and internalize gender norms, acting in accordance with them, thereby becoming the "object" of their gender performances. Thus, gender performances construct not only the gender of the performer but also the illusion that this gender is somehow natural, substantial, or essential. Nevertheless, Butler hoped that by understanding gender as performed, we might find the possibility of performing it differently.

Two years later, Butler's *Gender Trouble* went further, undermining the distinction between (biological) sex and (social) gender, maintaining that the former is also socially constructed: "If the immutable character of sex is contested, perhaps this construct called 'sex' is as culturally constructed as gender; indeed, perhaps it was always already gender, with the consequence that the distinction between sex and gender turns out to be no distinction at all."[28] For Butler, sexed bodies are themselves socially constructed, not in the sense that there are no independently existing sexed bodies but rather that there is no understanding of sexed bodies apart from social constructions of gender. Moreover, the view that sexed bodies are the biological or natural foundations for socially constructed genders is itself a social construction. The assignment of sex, which Butler views as performative rather than descriptive, is therefore always in some sense oppressive, involving socially instituted power structures. Thus, just as Butler's "Performative Acts and Gender Constitution" sought the possibility of performing gender differently, so Butler's *Gender Trouble* encouraged non-binary, non-hetero-normative understandings of sexed bodies.

Here, in sum, we have four more perspectives about what the self is, all from modern/postmodern "academic" philosophy: an immaterial and immortal substance-soul (Descartes), a "bundling" of a "heap" of impressions (Hume), an ideological interpellation (Althusser), and a performative construction (Butler). Now it is time to "put together" these and other views of the self, philosophizing about "who we are" in comparative perspective.

VIII. Putting it All Together

We have collected a dizzying diversity of views about the self in the some of the philosophies of religion around the globe. How do we philosophize about them?

For starters, recall the three-step method of philosophizing about religion from our last chapter: robust description, formal comparison, and critical evaluation. Above, we described the cultural-historical settings and conceptual meanings of the relevant forms of reason-giving, sometimes also their logical forms or rhetorical-political ends. It is therefore now time to compare and evaluate.

In the way of comparison, we begin with the comparative category of *self*, asking whether and how it biases the contents of comparison. If by *self* we mean that which is absolutely permanent and unchanging over time (substance), that which is radically distinct and separate from everything else (individual) or that which has complete control and power over itself (autonomous), then we will need a different comparative category or a more expansive understanding of *self* since some of the "selves" that we described above are not those of individual autonomous substances. If we take the former route—i.e., a different comparative category—we might try categories like *person* or *human*. Given the dominance of the category of *self* in professional philosophy and public discourse, however, we might take the latter route, understanding *self* more expansively as the locus of human awareness, control, and identity, with the individual autonomous substance self being just one example of this wider category. (But if you would rather employ a different category, feel free to do so.)

Whichever category we employ, we can sort the above understandings of "self" into four ideal types in accordance with how they view the substance and individuality of the self (reserving the issue of autonomy for next chapter).

The first ideal type is precisely that of the self as substantial and individual. These include some variations of contemporary Abrahamic religion, especially as influenced by ancient Greek-Platonic philosophy and modern European-Cartesian philosophy. Here, the self is understood as a substantial, autonomous, and individual soul, usually one that is created by a God and retains its individuality and substance after death.

The second ideal type is that of the self as part of wider cosmic reality. This is exemplified in the Upaniṣadic view of the self as *Ātman-Brahman*, as well as some Abrahamic mysticisms in which the soul returns to and becomes one with this God (e.g., Sufism above). This second ideal type might also include Daoism insofar as it sees all things coming from and returning to *Dào*.

The third ideal type understands the self to be configured or constituted by relationships with other beings. This ideal type includes the Confucian self that is a product of its relationships with other human beings; the Lakȟóta self that is a product of its relationships with all natural things; the Yorùbá self that is and negotiates relationships not only with its own *orí* but also with the *Òrìṣà* and other human beings, both living and dead; and Martin Buber's dialogical self that exists in relation to a "You" or an "It."

Finally, the fourth ideal type reduces the self to underlying processes, whether physical, psychical, or social. This includes the Buddhist view of the self as constituted by "aggregates," the Humean view of the self as a "bundle" of impressions, the Althusserian subject that is produced by "ideological state apparatuses," and the Butlerian self in which gender and sex are constructed and performed. (See Table 4.2 for a summary of all four types.).

Now we are finally ready to evaluate. What reasons can be provided for and against these various selves? We could go back through each of them, working out their argumentative forms and evaluating their premises one by one. However, since we are here dealing with competing sets of theories, we might instead employ our set of epistemic virtues from Chapter 3 (as provided again in Table 4.3), asking in the case of each theory of self, whether is it empirically accurate, externally coherent, practically useful, internally consistent, theoretically simple, and explanatorily productive.

Space prevents us from addressing each virtue with respect to each theory, but that is no reason why you cannot do some of this work yourself. Which

Table 4.2 Four Types of "Selves"

Type	Examples
(1) Self is substantial and individual	Some contemporary Abrahamic religion, especially as influenced by ancient Greek-Platonic philosophy and modern European-Cartesian philosophy
(2) Self is part of wider cosmic reality	Upaniṣadic notion of *Ātman-Brahman*, Abrahamic mysticism where soul returns to a God as ultimate reality, Daoism (and perhaps Chinese religio-philosophy more generally)
(3) Self is fundamentally in relationship	Confucian relationships with other humans, Lakȟóta relationships with all natural things, Yorùbá relationships with ancestors (etc.), Buber's dialogical self in relation to others
(4) Self is reducible to underlying processes	Buddhist "aggregates," Hume's "bundled" self, Althusser's ideologically interpolated self, Butler's socially constructed and performed self

Table 4.3 Epistemic Virtues of True Theories

Name	Central Question
Empirical accuracy	Is the theory accurate with how we experience empirical reality?
External coherence	Does the theory cohere with other forms of knowledge?
Practical usefulness	Is the theory useful to the way we live our lives, whether socially or individually?
Internal consistency	Is the theory internally consistent?
Theoretical simplicity	Is the theory conceptually simple?
Explanatory scope	Does the theory help explain other aspects of natural or social reality?

theories are best supported by relevant scientific theories and findings? Which cohere best with our body of socially constructed knowledge? Which are most "useful" to how we live our lives together in society?

Of course, a set of epistemic virtues is not an algorithm. There is no objective and definitive means of "scoring" a particular theory with respect to a particular virtue or of "ranking" one virtue against one another. Some might say that accuracy with science is what matters most, whereas others will instead privilege personal utility. This does not mean, however, that there are no good reasons at all to prefer one theory to another. Moreover, to draw on another means of evaluation from Chapter 3—experiential intuition and interpretive insight—we should not only be mindful about how our life experiences influence the beliefs we have and the reasons we give about who we are but also make our beliefs and reasons vulnerable to those of others.

Now it is time to end by recognizing that we are only just beginning. As we will soon see, how we answer the question "Who am I?" has profound consequences for how we understand where we come from, where we are going to, how we will get there, and what obstacles we will encounter. Put religiously, if we do not know who we are, then we will not know how to attain salvation, liberation, or attunement (etc.). Put metaphorically, if we do not know who we are, we will not know where we are going and how to get there (etc.).

Questions for Discussion

1. Which conception of the self (above) do you identify with most? What reasons can you give for the meaning, value, and truth of this self with respect to other selves?
2. To what extent do some of the conceptions of the self (above) challenge the modern Western notion that the self is individual and substantial? What reasons do we have for thinking that we are individual and substantial selves?
3. Take one conception of the self (above) and show how it motivates answers to the other four questions about the self.

Primary and Scholarly Sources

East Asia

Confucius. *The Analects* XII. Trans. D. C. Lao, 112–17. New York: Penguin Classics, 1979.

Dàodéjīng, chapters 37–8 (= chapters 81, 1 in Mair's translation). In *Tao Te Ching*, trans. Victor H. Mair, 105, 3. New York: Bantam Books, 1990.

European/Academic

Althusser, Louis. "Ideology and Ideological State Apparatuses," Part V, "Ideology Interpolates Individuals as Subjects." In *On the Reproduction of Capital*. Trans. Ben Brewster, 261–6. New York: Verso, 2014.

Butler, Judith. "Performative Acts and Gender Constitution." *Theatre Journal* 40/4 (December 1988): 519–31.

Descartes, René. *Meditations on First Philosophy*, Meditation 2. Trans. Donald A. Cross, 3rd ed., 63–70. Indianapolis, IN: Hackett, 1993.

Hume, David. *Treatise on Human Nature*, I.4.6. Eds. David Fate Norton and Mary J. Norton, 164–71. New York: Oxford University Press, 2000.

Lakȟóta

Deloria, Vine, Jr., *God is Red: A Native View of Religion: The Classic Work Updated*, 194–8. Golden, CO: Fulcrum Publishing, 1994.

Deloria, Vine, Jr., *The World We Used to Live in: Remembering the Powers of the Medicine Men*, chapter 4. Golden, CO: Fulcrum Publishing, 2006.

Mediterranean/Abrahamic

Attar, Farid al-Din. *Muslim Saints and Mystics: Episodes from the Tadhkirat al-Auliya' (Memorial of the Saints) by Farid al-Din Attar*, "Abu Yazid al-Bestami." Trans. A. J. Arberry, 105–10. Boston, MA: Routledge & Kegan Paul, 1966.

Augustine, *The Confessions*, book VIII.ix (21)–VIII.xii (30). Trans. Henry Chadwick, 147–54. New York: Oxford University Press, 1991.

Buber, Martin. *I and Thou*. Trans. Walter Kaufmann, 3–57. New York: Touchstone, 1996.

South Asia

Bṛhadāraṇyaka Upaniṣad 4.4.22. In *Upaniṣads*, trans. Patrick Olivelle, 67–8. New York: Oxford University Press, 1996.

Milinda Pañha. In *Buddhist Scriptures*, trans. Edward Conze, 146–51. New York: Penguin Classics, 1959.

Yorùbá

Gbadegesin, Segun. *African Philosophy: Traditional Yoruba Philosophy and Contemporary African Realities*, chapter 2. New York: Peter Lang, 1991.

Ray, Benjamin C. *African Religions: Symbol, Ritual, and Community*, 2nd ed., 34–8, Upper Saddle River, NJ: Pearson, 1999.

5

Where Do I Come From?

Learning Objectives

- Understand some of the important and interesting ways in which religious thinkers, texts, and traditions answer the question "What is my original condition"?
- Explain how some of these answers challenge the idea that the self is individual, substantial, and autonomous.
- Compare and evaluate philosophies of religion about original or natural free will, goodness, and enlightenment.

I. Introduction

Now that we have answered the question "Who am I?" let us answer it again. Seriously, though, our pursuit of last chapter's leading question led us to ask whether the self should be understood as an individual substance or as a set of internal processes or a web of external relations. That leaves us with the question of whether the self is autonomous, which takes us into the philosophical terrain of free will, moral goodness, and naturally reliable cognitive capacities. However, since the leading question of this chapter is "Where do I come from?" we investigate these questions through the lens of the self's *origin*. What is my original, natural, or inherent human condition? Am I originally, naturally, or inherently free, good, or enlightened?

Just as our "folk psychology" suggests that we are individual-substantial selves, so it leads us to believe that we are free to choose and do as we please (within limits of course). Let us call this the "folk concept" of free will, which is not unrelated to autonomy—the capacity to make informed, uncoerced decisions. As you can probably see, although the philosophical issue of free will is centrally at play with respect to autonomy, so are questions about whether humans are naturally good and in possession of reliable cognitive capacities. For if we are marred by an original or natural "badness" or "ignorance," then we would seem not to have the original or natural capacity to make informed, uncoerced decisions.

Indeed, this is just what a significant number of traditional philosophers and philosophies of religion assert: that humans are not originally or naturally free or good or enlightened, and that we do not therefore possess the original or natural capacity to make informed, uncoerced decisions, especially about that which matters most—our own religious destinations, goals, or ends. Rather, some of these philosophers and philosophies hold that the original or natural human condition is one of bondage, badness, or benightedness. Not only is this true of a significant number of traditional philosophies of religion; it is also true for a significant number of contemporary philosophical and scientific theories and findings—that humans are not nearly as free, good, and enlightened as our folk psychology would have us believe. This, in short, is what we will investigate in this chapter.

II. Mediterranean/Abrahamic Philosophy of Religion

In Abrahamic philosophy of religion, the question "What is my original human condition?" evokes answers in terms of "the image of God" (Lt. *imago dei*) in which humans are created. What exactly this image is, however, has long been a subject of disagreement, with some understanding it as reason; others, goodness; still others, freedom. A more relevant point of contention, however, has been whether humans actually are originally rational, good, and free. Below, we focus on original freedom, looking at how debates about free will played out in medieval Christian and Islamic philosophy of religion. (Given Judaism's emphasis on maintaining the covenantal relationship with YHWH, free will was not as contentious in Jewish philosophy of religion.) As you know from the introductory section of this chapter, however, debates about free will also involve disagreements about original goodness and knowledge. So, all three issues are in play.

The problem of free will in Christianity is rooted in the writings of the Apostle Paul (5–67), who was himself influenced by the Roman philosophical school of Stoicism. For the ancient Greek founders of Stoicism, the cosmos was believed to oscillate eternally between an expansion from and a return to a set of primordial principles: an active principle identified with God (Gk. *theos*), reason (*logos*), and designing fire or breath (*pneuma*); and passive, inert, unqualified matter.[1] Since this expansion always occurs in accordance with reason, with the designing fire/breath containing the "seminal patterns" (*logoi spermatikoi*) of all things, early Stoics might have held a kind of "compatibilist" view of free will and determinism (which we will return to later in this chapter): although the cosmos always unfolds in the best possible and same exact way, humans are free insofar as they do will to do what occurs nonetheless.

Regardless of how we interpret Stoicism on this issue, what is of primary interest for us is the teachings of the Apostle Paul on free will. For Paul, a Jew who was trained in Jewish Law as a Pharisee, the core issue involved human sinfulness and salvation. Paul came to believe that the Law (as given to Moses on Mount Sinai) could not be freely upheld by humans due to the sin they inherited from the first man and woman, Adam and Eve. Only by the grace of the Christian-Trinitarian God and through faith in Jesus Christ could humans be forgiven from this sin and saved.

It was not until the Christian theologian Augustine of Hippo (354–430), however, that the orthodox Christian position on free will was articulated as such. Although Augustine affirmed the freedom of the will in some of his early writings, notably *On Free Will* (*c.* 394), he later changed his mind and even "retracted" some of these earlier views, arguing in his 427 *Retractions* of *On Free Will*:

> For human beings cannot pick themselves up voluntarily—that is, by their own free choice—as they fell voluntarily. To the misery imposed by this just condemnation belong ignorance and difficulty, which afflict all human beings from the very outset of their lives. And no one is freed from this evil except by the grace of God.[2]

What changed? It seems that as Augustine increasingly wrestled with the New Testament letters of St. Paul, he gradually came to the conclusion that the Christian-Trinitarian God predestines those who are saved without consideration of their worthiness (for otherwise humans could earn their own salvation). As with St. Paul, Augustine's explanation for why humans cannot freely do the good and earn their own salvation involved the "original sin" of Adam and Eve (though, to be clear, St. Paul never used that phrase). Augustine, however, understood the result of this sin not just as a wounding of human freedom and intelligence but also as an irresistible urge for sexual desire and pleasure (concupiscence) that was transmitted through sexual intercourse. Absent infant baptism, even newborns were condemned to hell due to original sin.

About the time that Augustine began articulating this view of original sin, a Christian theologian named Pelagius (360–418) moved from his home in the British Isles to Rome, where he became disturbed by the lax morality of Roman society. Pelagius blamed this promiscuity on theologies such as Augustine's that emphasized divine grace over against human effort, opposing these theologies with a strict moralism that recognized the innate human ability to attain salvation. For Pelagius, everything that the Christian-Trinitarian God created is good, humans included. Humans are not therefore "fallen" and can freely avoid sinning, choosing to obey God's commandments. Although Pelagius recognized that the free performance of good works could only be done by the grace of this God, he nevertheless maintained that such actions could be freely chosen and enacted by humans.

As Pelagius' teachings spread around the Mediterranean world of the late fourth, early fifth century, other Christian theologians entered the fray, most notably St. Jerome on the side of Augustine and Caelestius on the side of Pelagius. Ultimately, the papacy intervened, with one pope condemning and excommunicating Pelagius and Caelestius in 416, and both another pope and the Council of Carthage doing the same in 418. Thirteen years later, the Third Ecumenical Council (in the city of Ephesus in 431) went further, proclaiming Pelagianism a heresy.

Much like this Christian dispute, the Islamic debate about free will was eventually reconciled by stressing divine predetermination over against human free will. Absent in this debate, however, was the notion of original sin. Rather, it was Allah's omnipotence that was centrally at issue.

The debate flared up during the second century of the ʿAbbāsid Caliphate (750–1258), a Persian empire centered in Baghdad, where the arts and sciences flourished unlike any other place on earth at the time.[3] The ʿAbbāsids superseded the first Islamic dynasty, the Umayyad Caliphate (661–750), which was widely seen as corrupt and therefore accused of not being divinely predetermined. This term for predetermination, *qadar* (Ar.), later became influential for the Muʿtazilite school of theology, which defended Allah's justice, human free will, and human culpability vis-à-vis divine *qadar*. The Muʿtazila were known as the school of the "unity and justice of Allah"—the former for emphasizing the unity (*tawḥīd*) of God vis-à-vis the co-eternality of the Qurʾān and the distinct reality of the divine names; the latter for emphasizing the justice (*ʿadl*) of God over against divine omnipotence and predetermination. The Muʿtazila dominated intellectual life in the early ʿAbbāsid Caliphate to such a degree that caliph al-Ma'mūn (r. 813–33) proclaimed a "test" (*mihṇa*) in 833, according to which Islamic judges and scholars were examined to see whether they adhered to Muʿtazilite teaching that the Qurʾān was created, not eternal. Although this *mihṇa* only lasted about fifteen years, it had lasting effects, one of which was that the co-eternality of the Qurʾān with Allah became the orthodox position soon thereafter, another of which was that Muʿtazilite theology began to meet its demise by the early tenth century.

Among the teachings of the Muʿtazila that their critics attacked, we focus here on those related to free will and divine justice. To defend divine justice in a world of evil, Muʿtazila ascribed evil to free will (much like Augustine did in his early writings). Humans freely choose to do wrong acts; Allah does not compel or predetermine such action. Thus, not only is Allah not the source of evil; Allah is also justified in rewarding and punishing humans in accordance with their right and wrong actions. If humans were not free, maintained the Muʿtazila, then Allah's reward and punishment would not be just.

These teachings were not without immediate dissent, both by other Muʿtazila and by Ḥanbali theologians. However, it was not until the early tenth century that the Muʿtazilite school of theology was eclipsed by the newly formed Ashʿarite school of theology. Although the founder of this school, Abū al-Ḥasan al-Ashʿarī (*c.* 874–936), had been trained as a Mu'tazilite theologian, after a series of three dreams in which Prophet Muḥammad told him to "support the traditions," he renounced Mu'tazilite theology for one that was more properly grounded in Qurʾān and *hadīth* (though he still employed philosophical reasoning, which was also commanded to him in his dreams by Muḥammad).

With respect to the problem of free will and divine justice, al-Ashʿarī deployed the notion of "acquisition" (*kasb*), maintaining that even though Allah is the real and ultimate cause of everything, humans "acquire" their intentionally willed actions (insofar as they do so will them), thereby assuming moral responsibility for those actions. This is a subtle distinction, though not an incoherent one: Allah is omnipotent because Allah is the ultimate cause of all events in the world (by rearranging atoms from moment to moment); nevertheless, insofar as a person freely decides to do something wrong (e.g., rob a bank), that person is morally culpable for that choice, despite the fact that Allah is the ultimate cause of those events in the world (e.g., the robbing of the bank). Take for example al-Ashʿarī's distinction between a person "who shakes from palsy or shivers from fever" and one "who goes and comes."[4] Although Allah is the ultimate cause of both sets of actions, in the first case the shaking and shivering occur by "necessity," whereas in the second case the coming and going are "acquired" insofar as the person freely chooses to come and go. Thus, al-Ashʿarī attempted to balance divine omnipotence, human freedom, and moral culpability—no easy task, indeed, though successful in the end, as the Ashʿarite school of theology was to win the day against the Muʿtazila.

III. Yorùbá Philosophy of Religon

The problem of free will that bedeviled Christian and Islamic philosophers of religion shows up much differently in Yorùbá philosophy of religion (and arguably not at all in South Asian, East Asian, and Lakȟóta philosophy of religion). As you remember from last chapter, the Yorùbá understanding of the self includes an *orí* (head), which contains a person's destiny in life (*àyànmọ́*). Although the individual "chooses" this *orí* before birth, she does so solely on the external appearance of the head, without knowledge of the actual destiny that is contained within it. Does this mean that the lives of the Yorùbá are predetermined? That they have no "free will" to do other than what is encoded in their destiny? That reward and punishment are therefore always unmerited?

Yorùbá philosophers of religion have responded to this "problem" in different ways. Kọ́lá Abímbọ́lá, for example, considers it "much ado about nothing," pointing out that *Ifá* poems make a clear distinction between a person's *orí* as a principle of earthy success/failure and two other components of the self: *ẹsẹ̀* (literally, "leg"), the principle of individual effort and struggle; and *lwà*, good character.[5] Since the potentialities of one's *orí* must be actualized by individual effort and struggle (*ẹsẹ̀*), good character (*lwà*) is earned, and reward for good character is merited. Not only does Abímbọ́lá therefore find this problem to be much ado about nothing; he also chalks it up to the failure of "Western Anglo-American philosophy" to make a "distinction between determinism with respect to earthly success and with respect to moral character."[6] Although one's earthly success might be determined by one's choice of an *orí*, one's moral character is instead a product of *ẹsẹ̀*—individual effort and struggle. For example, although you might be predestined for a life of failure in business, you can still freely choose to be honest in business.

A second Yorùbá philosopher of religion, Moses Makinde, stands in basic agreement with Abímbọ́lá's distinction between *orí* and *ẹsẹ̀*, maintaining that "*orí* is *a mere potentiality*" (emphasis his).[7] Even though an *orí* therefore "represents human destiny, it does not do so unconditionally," for "certain things need to be done along with the choice of a good *orí* in order to bring such a potentially good choice into fruition."[8] Importantly, this includes making sacrifices to one's *orí* that not only involve "an element of freedom" but also reshape one's destiny.[9] Even a bad *orí* can be purified by means of such sacrifices, thereby improving a bad destiny. For Makinde, this points to the compatibility of destiny and freedom in a concept he calls "weak Destiny," in which destiny is variable, moral responsibility is applicable, and reward and punishment are merited.[10]

A third Yorùbá philosopher of religion, however, challenges Makinde's notion of "weak Destiny" in particular and Abímbọ́lá's confidence about individual effort and struggle more generally. For Segun Gbadegesin, such solutions do not do justice to the ways that the Yorùbá actually talk and think about destiny, especially "in pathetic cases where a person cannot be wholly blamed for his/her misfortune"; here, "the Yoruba mind makes a final recourse to explanation in terms of destiny: what is the case is what has to be since it has been so predestined."[11] Although Yorùbá philosophers of religion such as Makinde and Abímbọ́lá might stress the notion of *ẹsẹ̀* to relieve Yorùbá philosophy of religion of certain logical and moral difficulties, Gbadegesin points out that this runs the danger of trivializing the importance of the destiny of the *orí*. "Many Yorùbá," writes Gbadegesin, "are not prepared to let go the concept of destiny. For, in the final analysis, neither good character nor dynamism nor industry guarantees a success that is not encased in one's destiny."[12]

What should we make of this disagreement? We need not reconcile it to learn from it: destiny is a key aspect of the Yorùbá understanding of what the self is and where it comes from. There are reasons why things happen as they do, whether good or bad. Not everything is in our control. Perhaps most things are not, in fact, in our control. There will be times of failure and suffering, despite our best efforts and intentions otherwise.

IV. South Asian Philosophy of Religion

Unlike Christian, Islamic, and Yorùbá philosophy of religion, South Asian philosophy of religion has not had much of an issue with free will. You might find this surprising, given how central the principle of *karma* is to South Asian religion and philosophy. But even while *karma* not only determines each life into which one is born but also necessitates that all moral action will eventually bear moral consequences, it does not rule out some measure of freedom within each lifetime. (More on *karma* in Chapters 7 and 13.)

It is instead the issue of enlightenment that preoccupies South Asian philosophy about the original condition of the "self," with most South Asian philosophies of religion understanding humans as (re)born into a condition of ignorance and therefore in need of arduous effort toward liberative knowledge. As we have already seen (and will continue to see), these "selves" can be quite different from one school (*darśana*) to the next. Nevertheless, they are all in need of liberating knowledge.

In our last chapter, you learned about two of these "selves"—the eternal, cosmic self or *Ātman* of the *Upaniṣads* and the "no-self" or *an-ātman* of early Buddhism. What could be more different, right? In the first case the self is ultimately eternal and unchanging, and in the second case it is not. All the same, these "selves" are (re)born into similar conditions of ignorance and must exert meditative effort in similar ways to overcome that ignorance.

As you know from the previous chapter, early Buddhists rejected the notion of an eternal, unchanging *Ātman*, maintaining instead that the "self" is a bundle of five sets of processes: bodily, sensory, perceptual, volitional, and conscious. Humans cannot be (re)born in an originally enlightened condition, for there is no substance self or soul to possess this property. Instead, humans must arduously strive to practice the Eightfold Path to attain *nirvāṇa*, which involves "waking up" to what is really the case. Most of all, this means coming to see that there is "no self," at least not if self is taken as permanent and unchanging.

But how exactly does one "wake up" to the impermanence of the self and world? Within a century of the death of the historical Buddha (*c.* 563–*c.* 483 BCE), Buddhism splintered into a variety of different sects, many disagreeing about monastic rules of practice (*vinaya*), some also about what impermanent "reality" really is. In as many as seven of these sects, "higher doctrines" or "further teachings" called *abhidharma*-s were written to systematize the teachings of the Buddha about the fundamental constituents of reality as experienced. Of these, we focus especially on the *abhidharma* of the Theravāda tradition, as it is the only form of early, pre-Mahāyāna Buddhism still practiced today (primarily in Sri Lanka and Southeast Asia).

All *abhidharma* philosophies are motivated by what Amber Carpenter calls "the chariot principle: all the way down."[13] Remember the Buddhist monk Nāgasena's "Chariot Sermon" from last chapter, the one in which a chariot is compared to the self? Just as "chariot" is only a name for the sum of its chariot parts, so the self is only a name for the sum of its parts (i.e., the five aggregates). But what then about the wheels of the chariot or the sensory perceptions of a person? Are they not also composed of aggregate parts and therefore not really real? Thus begins the search for the fundamental constituents of reality as experienced, those elements out of which our complex experiences are built, and into which our complex experiences can be analyzed and dissolved through meditative discipline.

For all *abhidharma* philosophies, these fundamental elements of experience were called *dharma*-s. Different schools numbered them differently, with the Theravāda positing eight-two total *dharma*-s—fifty-two mental ones that pertain to internal experiences, twenty-eight physical ones that involve external experiences, awareness itself (*citta*), and finally *nirvāṇa*. With the exception of *nirvāṇa*, these *dharma*-s are "conditioned"—mutually interdependent on one another. Moreover, their existence is merely momentary—a brief "flash" of experience in which they first arise, then cause effects, and finally pass away. Nevertheless, each *dharma* possesses a definitive nature or substance (*svabhāva*) and therefore cannot be reduced to, or analyzed by, the others. Each *dharma* therefore serves as a distinct "atom" of experience (e.g., color, solidity, pain, locality), combinations of which constitute the complex things that we experience at an everyday level (e.g., table, hunger).

What does all this have to do with our primary questions of the chapter—what are we "originally," and why are we that way? For starters, Theravāda Buddhism suggests that humans are "originally" ignorant or deluded insofar as they take the things of everyday experience as really real—their own "selves" most of all. This is just how humans "naturally" live. It therefore takes lifetimes of dedicated, meditative practice, at least in Theravāda Buddhism, for monks to "unlearn" their propensities to reify themselves and the things of the world, piercing this veil of illusion and "waking up" to the way things really are—a flow of momentary *dharma*-s, continuously appearing and disappearing.[14]

In at least one sense, things are quite the opposite for the writers of the *Upaniṣads*, for in this case humans tend to confuse themselves for their changing bodies and minds, failing to see that they are an eternal, unchanging, universal *Ātman*. In at least another sense, however, the problem and solution are remarkably similar: we mistake our ordinary perceptions of ourselves and the world as what is really real, and we must therefore exert intensive ascetic and meditative effort to undo this natural inclination. In short, we must overcome the ignorance of the everyday into which we are (re)born.

Here, we look less to the *Upaniṣads* themselves than to the Hindu *darśana* of Vedānta, which took the *Upaniṣads* as the culmination of Vedic (Hindu) scripture. As you may recall from Chapter 1 above, there are several sub-schools of Vedānta, each of which understands differently the relationship between *Ātman* and *Brahman*, three of which are non-dual (*advaita*), qualifiedly non-dual (*viśiṣṭādvaita*), and dual (*dvaita*). We focus below on Advaita Vedānta, not only because it was the first sub-school of Vedānta but also since one of its earliest proponents developed a philosophical theory for why we do not see ourselves as *Ātman* and reality as *Brahman*. (We will look at the other two sub-schools in the next chapter, Chapter 6.)

This Advaita Vedānta philosopher was Śaṅkara (*c.* 788–*c.* 820), who maintained that there is no difference between *Ātman* and *Brahman*; they are one and the same. In fact, there are no real differences at all, not ultimately; everything just is *Ātman/Brahman*, a state of pure consciousness or undifferentiated unity. This is the highest of three orders of existence, absolute existence (*paramārthika sattā*), below which are empirical existence (*vyavahārika sattā*) and illusory existence (*prātibhāsika sattā*). Just as we "cancel" or "negate" (*bādha*) the optical illusions of illusory existence when we see that they are not empirically real, so we cancel or negate our perceptions of plurality in space and change over time when we see what is ultimately real: *Ātman/Brahman*.

But why do we misperceive *Ātman/Brahman* as changing, differentiated empirical reality in the first place? To answer this question, Śaṅkara developed a theory of superimposition (*adhyāsa*), which he defined in his commentary (*bhāṣya*) on the founding *sūtras* of the Vedānta *darśana*—the *Brahma Sūtras* (aka *Vedānta Sūtras*)—as "the apparent presentation, in the form of remembrance, to consciousness of something previously observed, in some other thing."[15] In such cases, perceptual error results from the superimposition of something that was previously experienced (even in former lives) onto something that is presently being perceived. Śaṅkara's classic example is the misperception of a coiled rope as a snake, in which case the prior experience of a snake is remembered and superimposed onto the present perception of a rope. Likewise, we superimpose our empirical experiences of the world onto the ultimate reality of *Ātman/Brahman*, misperceiving that which is undifferentiated and changeless as differentiated and changing.

But why, you might ask, do we do that? Why do we not naturally see *Ātman/Brahman* for what it is? Why are we prone to superimposition?

Śaṅkara's answer to this question involves the concepts of *māyā* (illusion) and *avidyā* (ignorance). Although Śaṅkara himself tended not to differentiate the two, his students did, with *māyā* referring to an ontological-metaphysical state and *avidyā* referring to an epistemological-psychological condition. In the former case, *māyā* is the creative power of *Brahman* to generate the "illusory" multiplicity and change of the cosmos; in the latter case, *avidyā* is the tendency of humans to mistake this empirical world of multiplicity and change for what is really real. Either way, this is our "original condition"—an illusion and ignorance that is simply part of the fabric of the reality in which we find ourselves. Although Śaṅkara's two chief disciples were to disagree whether this condition is only an ignorance (*avidyā*) that is located in the individual self (*jīvātman*) or also a cosmic illusion (*māyā*) that relates to *Brahman*, this condition is nevertheless "original" in the sense that all humans are subject to it.[16]

And so it goes for most South Asian *darśana*-s: humans are (re)born into a state of ignorance insofar as they fail to understand what they really are.

V. East Asian Philosophy of Religion

East Asian philosophy of religion tends not to share the pessimism—or is it a realism?—of South Asian philosophy of religion, at least not with respect to the original condition of the self. Nor does it concern itself with issues of free will as found in Christian, Islamic, and Yorùbá philosophies of religion. Instead, one of the earliest questions of Chinese philosophy of religion concerned the original goodness of humans. To the extent that Chinese philosophers of religion found humans originally good, some later found humans originally enlightened as well.

We again begin the story with Confucius (551–479 BCE), who did not have much to say about whether human beings were originally good. Indeed, this question was wholly impractical to Confucius, who was primarily concerned with restoring personal virtue and social order rather than theorizing them. Not long after Confucius, though, the goodness of human nature became central to questions about how to cultivate personal virtue and rectify social order. For these later Confucians, it was only by giving an account of human nature that one could say why and how the Confucian project should be implemented.

We pick up this story with Mencius, the Latinized form of Mèngzǐ (372–289 BCE), a fourth-generation Confucian, who became so important to later

Song-Dynasty (960–1279) (Neo)Confucians that his writings were included in the Confucian canon alongside Confucius' teachings. Indeed, Song-Dynasty (Neo)Confucians dubbed Mencius the "Second Sage."

Like Confucius, Mencius was a scholar (*rú*) of the knightly class (*shì*, 士), which was increasingly displaced and disenfranchised under the Warring States period (403–221 BCE) as the vassal lords it served were conquered by larger states. Consequently, Mencius spent most of his life travelling from state to state, seeking employment by giving advice about how to rule. In doing so, Mencius no doubt gained familiarity with many of schools and positions that were then competing with Confucianism, most notably Mohism, which criticized Confucian rituals for lacking ethical justification and practical benefit. Consequently, Mencius deemphasized external ritual, turning instead to the human heart-mind (*xīn*, 心) and its original nature (*xìng*, 性) to offer a basis for the Confucian project.

In maintaining that the nature of the heart-mind is good, Mencius did not mean that humans were born "already good" or with fully developed good qualities. Rather, *xìng*, which is commonly translated as "nature," denotes the "natural dispositions" or "characteristic tendencies" of humans.[17] In the words of one scholar, it is "the course on which life completes its development if sufficiently nourished and not obstructed or injured from outside."[18]

Nothing better conveys this understanding of human nature than Mencius's use of the agricultural metaphor "sprouts" (*duān*, 端). Just as there are four Confucian virtues for Mencius—human-heartedness (*rén*), moral rightness (*yì*), ritual propriety (*lǐ*, 禮), and moral wisdom (*zhì*, 智)—so there are four "sprouts" or "beginnings" of these virtues, each of which is present in the human heart (*xīn*) at birth as an original feeling or disposition. The "sprout" of *rén* (human-heartedness) is compassion, which Mencius believed all people spontaneously and uncalculatingly feel, for example with respect to a child who is about to fall into a well:

> When I say that all men have the mind which cannot bear to see the suffering of others, my meaning may by illustrated thus: Now, when men suddenly see a child about to fall into a well, they all have a feeling of alarm and distress, not to gain friendship with the child's parents, nor to seek the praise of the neighbors and friend, nor because they dislike the reputation [of lack of humanity if they did not rescue the child]. From such a case, we see that a man without the feeling of commiseration is not a man.[19]

Likewise for the other three virtues and sprouts: *Yì* (moral rightness) finds its beginning in shame, which is demonstrated in the way we intuitively treat bad behavior or mistreatment as shameful; *lǐ* (ritual propriety), in respect,

Table 5.1 Mencius's Four Sprouts

Confucian Virtue	Mencian Root	Behavioral Exemplification
Human-heartedness (*rén*)	Compassion	Instinctive attempt to save a child who is about to fall into a well
Moral rightness (*yì*)	Shame	Regarding bad behavior or mistreatment as shameful
Ritual propriety (*lǐ*, 禮)	Respect	Respect of children for parents
Moral wisdom (*zhì*)	Approval and disapproval	Judgment about one's own actions via internal reflection

which is exhibited by children who are naturally respectful of their parents; and *zhì* (moral wisdom), in an intuitive approval of right and disapproval of wrong, which is evidenced by the fact that all people make judgments about the rightness and wrongness of their actions by means of internal reflection. See Table 5.1 for a summary of all four.

It is because these "sprouts" are in the nature (*xìng*) of the human heart-mind (*xīn*) that humans are originally good (*shàn*, 善). Nevertheless, as mere "sprouts," the Confucian virtues must be nourished. For this to happen, three things are necessary: first, a physical environment in which basic needs are met; second, a social environment in which Confucian virtues, rituals, and relations are taught; third, individual effort in the tasks of cultivating the virtues, observing the rituals, and rectifying social relations. Thus, if humans "grow up" into something that is not good, the fault does not lie in their nature; it lies in an unsupportive environment or a weak will.

For Mencius, this "nature" is endowed by *Tiān* (Heaven), which is unambiguously good, possessing all the Confucian virtues. It might seem, therefore, that Mencius's *Tiān* is more of a person-like divinity than an impersonal natural force. Not so. Mencius's *Tiān* "does not speak" but rather "simply reveals through deeds and affairs."[20] Thus, although *Tiān* is the source of goodness, humans themselves must enact goodness. And although *Tiān* is the sanction of goodness, good behavior is in fact not always rewarded. This was the existential condition of the Warring States period—one in which the righteous did not always prosper and the wicked were not always punished, one therefore in which it was increasingly untenable to hold that *Tiān* was actively involved in the reward of virtue and punishment of vice. (More on this in Chapter 13.)

This trajectory reached its zenith with the fifth-generation Confucian Xúnzǐ (荀子, 313–238 BCE), who maintained that *Tiān* did not care for human affairs—indeed, *Tiān* could not since *Tiān* was nothing but impersonal natural law. For Xúnzǐ, *Tiān* operates with "constancy" and therefore without concern for the righteous and wicked.[21] Humans cannot control, influence, or even discern the ways of *Tiān*, be it through petition, morality, or divination. Humans, therefore, simply should not concern themselves with *Tiān*.

Not only is Xúnzǐ's *Tiān* not the source or sanction of human goodness; humans are not good at all, at least not originally. On the contrary, Xúnzǐ repeatedly insisted that human nature (*xìng*) is bad (*è*, 惡). Although this claim appears diametrically opposed to Mencius's, their positions might not be as different as they seem. By *xìng*, Xúnzǐ did not mean, as Mencius did, what humans would become if supported by the external environment and nurtured by moral education. In fact, Xúnzǐ criticized Mencius on just this point: if humans require such support and nurture to become good, then humans are not naturally good. Human nature (*xìng*), rather, is what is given by nature in general (aka, *Tiān*)—the inborn faculties, capacities, and desires of humans

Xúnzǐ and Mencius, therefore, agreed that humans can become good; nevertheless, Xúnzǐ insisted that human nature is bad (*è*). What did he mean by this? Although *è* is sometimes translated as "evil," it is closer in meaning to "detestable," "revolting," or "ugly," as represented by the character of a deformed head. For Xúnzǐ, this "ugliness" is a product of our inherent natural desires for profit and pleasure, particularly how in striving to satisfy them we come into conflict and strife with other human beings who are trying to satisfy other desires. Perhaps, then, it is not the case that human nature, for Xúnzǐ, is "evil" or "bad"; rather, humans simply lack an innate conception of morality.

Regardless, Xúnzǐ's Confucian project of moral self-cultivation does require more effort and resolve than Mencius's. For Mencius, the Confucian virtues are already in human nature as "spouts" that are ready to "shoot forth" when nurtured by a Confucian education in a supportive environment. Xúnzǐ, by contrast, employed the metaphors of straightening crooked wood and grinding blunt metal in speaking about the "deliberative action" (*wéi*, 爲)—note the contrast with the "effortless action" (*wúwéi*, 無爲) of the Daoists—that is necessary to bring human behavior into accord with sagely rituals (*lǐ*, 禮):

> Thus, crooked wood must await steaming and straightening on the shaping frame, and only then does it become straight. Blunt metal must await honing and grinding, and only then does it become sharp. Now since people's nature is bad, they must await teachers and proper models, and only then do they

> become correct. They must obtain ritual [*lǐ*] and *yì* [moral rightness], and only then to they become well ordered.[22]

These rituals encompass not only the rites and ceremonies of the early Zhou Dynasty but also the patterns and models of the natural and moral worlds. They are not arbitrarily chosen or functionally expedient; rather, they are the product of scholarly observation of the natural and human orders by generations upon generations of sages. Only through education in and practice of these rituals and principles can humans act in opposition to their innate desires and thereby transform their human nature. Indeed, these rituals are so crucial to social order that even those that are performed for *Tiān* as if *Tiān* were an anthropomorphic deity must be observed.

As you know, it was Mencius who was to win this argument, at least in Confucian philosophy. Song Dynasty (Neo)Confucians included his writings alongside those of Confucius in the "Four Books" of Confucianism, whereas Xúnzǐ was declared a heretic. One significant reason for this outcome involved the long and deep influence of Daoism's understanding of the originally harmonious nature of all things, especially humans. Even Buddhism was to lose its "Indian pessimism" in China, with many Chinese Buddhist sects maintaining that an original Buddha-nature permeates all things, making it easier for humans to recover an original enlightenment rather than overcome an original ignorance. We will pick back up some of these themes in Chapters 7 and 8.

VI. Lakȟóta Philosophy of Religion

If there is an "original" quality of humans in Lakȟóta "religion," it is a fundamental relationality with the rest of nature. This quality is not only one of fundamental relationality but also of sacred, mysterious power, known as *wakȟáŋ*. Everything has *wakȟáŋ* to some degree and therefore is *wakȟáŋ* in some respect—sacred, mysterious, and powerful—since this sacred, mysterious power extends throughout the universe, bestowing power to do *wakȟáŋ* things and to be related to other *wakȟáŋ* things as "fathers and mothers."[23] Although the potential to do and understand *wakȟáŋ* things exists most of all in the "holy man" (*wičháša wakȟáŋ*) or "holy woman" (*wíŋyaŋ wakȟáŋ*), all Lakȟóta can become *wakȟáŋ* by participating in the sacred rites of the sacred pipe (*čhaŋnúŋpa wakȟáŋ*). Thus, the anthropologist Joseph Epes Brown describes *wakȟáŋ* as "an essential and mysterious bond, binding together the people, the animals, the earth, and all that is."[24]

If *wakȟáŋ* is "the animating force of the universe" and "the common denominator of its oneness," it is located most of all in *Wakȟáŋ Tȟáŋka*, the "great incomprehensibility" or "great mystery."[25] Under the influence of Euro-American Christianity, *Wakȟáŋ Tȟáŋka* would come to be thought of as Christian-God-like, at least by some Lakȟóta. But there is evidence to suggest that *Wakȟáŋ Tȟáŋka* was formerly regarded as the sum total of all sacred, mysterious beings, and forces, especially the sixteen *tobtób kiŋ*. Indeed, some Lakȟóta still speak about *Wakȟáŋ Tȟáŋka* this way today.[26] Regardless, *Wakȟáŋ Tȟáŋka* is the sacred, mysterious source and power of the universe—that which creates and maintains all things in a sacred relationality.

It would seem that the Lakȟóta did not think of this sacred relationality as "original" to creation; rather, it comes only after White Buffalo Calf Woman, one of the *Wakȟáŋ Tȟáŋka* (as Wóȟpe), brings the sacred pipe to the Lakȟóta and teaches them its rituals.[27] The myth that tells this story, according to one anthropologist, "narrates what to the Lakȟóta people was the single most important manifestation of the sacred, the one that founded the Lakȟóta world and gave the people their orientation in time and space."[28] Not only did the pipe bring sacred relationality between the Lakȟóta and the buffalo; the pipe also established a relationship with *Wakȟáŋ Tȟáŋka*, its smoke functioning as the means by which prayers were carried upward to *Wakȟáŋ Tȟáŋka*.[29] Thus, for one Lakȟóta, Left Heron, "the people lacked all that was most basic to their human condition" before the pipe; "there was nothing sacred before the pipe came; there was no social organization and the people ran around the prairie like so many wild animals."[30]

What we have, then, seems to be the inverse of the Christian "Fall" narrative. Rather than a *fall from* an original state of goodness and harmony, the Lakȟóta myth narrates an *ascent to* goodness and harmony. Regardless, Lakȟóta philosophy of religion understands all of creation, including humans, to be fundamentally interrelated and sacred.

VII. European/Academic Philosophy of Religion

Of the three "original conditions" explored so far in this chapter, free will has received the most attention in academic philosophy. We therefore begin with a longer examination of it, turning afterwards to shorter explorations of whether humans are innately good or have naturally reliable cognitive capacities.

From the time of the European Enlightenment, philosophers and scientists have been increasingly confident that since human beings are natural organisms and natural organisms are governed by natural laws, then human behavior is law governed. Can human action be law-governed and yet free? Some say no, maintaining that human behavior is either causally determined and therefore not free or not causally determined and therefore free. Others say yes, holding that it is possible to view human behavior as both causally determined and free. These philosophical positions, respectively, are known as determinism, libertarianism, and compatibilism.

Compatibilism boasts the longest and richest history since the European Enlightenment, stretching back to some of the earliest Enlightenment philosophers, many of whom were empiricists with respect to knowledge. In addition to David Hume (1711–76), whose "bundle theory" of self we examined last chapter, "classical compatibilism" includes the early empiricists Thomas Hobbes (1588–1679) and John Locke (1632–1704), the latter of whom defined free will as simply "the freedom to execute what is willed."[31] If you desire to pick up your coffee cup and do so pick up your coffee cup, then we can say that you freely picked up your coffee cup. Nevertheless, your desire to pick up your coffee cup was causally determined by all your prior experiences (by means of the relevant natural laws). Thus, human behavior can be both causally determined and free. Crucial here—as with Abrahamic philosophy of religion above, though in an obviously different way that we will explore in the final section of this chapter—is the distinction between freedom to choose and freedom to effect what is chosen. The choices we make are causally determined by all our prior experiences and the relevant natural laws; nevertheless, we are free insofar as we do enact those choices. Had your dog charged by and knocked over your coffee cup as you were reaching out for it, then you would not have freely enacted what you chose.

But is this really free will if our choices are determined by antecedent experiences and natural laws? Critics of compatibilism on "both sides" say no, with determinists averring that if our decisions are determined then we are not free, and libertarians insisting that our decisions are not determined and therefore that we are free. Compatibilists, however, maintain that only compatibilism recognizes our scientific assumptions and findings about the law-governed nature of reality, while also preserving a sense of free will and moral responsibility.

For a very different kind of compatibilism, one that could also be classified as libertarianism, we turn to another European Enlightenment philosopher, Immanuel Kant (1724–1804). With respect to knowledge in general, Kant was to "split the difference" between rationalists such as René Descartes (1596–1650) and empiricists such as Hume, agreeing with the latter that all knowledge begins with experience and with the former that some *a priori* knowledge is necessary even to have coherent experience at all. Kant argued that without *a priori* "forms of intuition" of space and time, our experiences would not be organized on a spatial field and in a temporal sequence, and that without *a priori* "categories of understanding" such as substance and causality (among others), we would not experience causally related "things" in the world. For Kant, space, time, substance, and causality are not themselves features of the world; rather, they constitute the *a priori* forms and categories by means of which humans necessarily experience things in the world, ourselves and others included—as substances in a spatial field that are causally determined in a temporal sequence.

This at least is the case "phenomenally," with respect to what we experience through our senses and categorize with our mind; as for what really is the case "noumenally," however, Kant saw things differently, maintaining that we must posit a free will (as well as an immortal soul and a God who rewards or punishes that soul after death). Why? Kant argued that we also have moral experiences about what we "ought" to do. And since we have these experiences of the "moral law," we must assume that we are able to act in accordance with it. Free will, therefore, must be postulated, even though it can never be proved.

Should we therefore understand Kant as a compatibilist or a libertarian? Perhaps this matters less than the fact that Kant offers compelling reasons for both free will and causal determinism. On the one hand, moral experience, if not human agency more generally, presupposes free will; on the other hand, human behavior cannot be explained unless understood as caused by antecedent states and natural laws. (Imagine if you willed to dump your coffee on your friend's lap for no reason at all.) But can one "have it both ways," claiming that humans are thoroughly determined with respect to nature/brain yet radically free with respect to will/mind? Or is Kant's solution just a way of avoiding the problem?

Fast forward to the latter half of the twentieth century, when a series of experiments in the newly established field of neuroscience began problematizing the "folk psychology" notion that some non-physical "I" causes the movements of its body.[32] The first such experiment was Benjamin

Libet's groundbreaking 1980s study in which an electro-encephalogram (EEG) was used to measure the brain activity associated with the "readiness potential" for behavior, comparing it to the moment at which a subject reported a decision (to move a finger). The results of the study suggested that the unconscious activity of the brain preceded the subject's conscious decision to act by approximately one-half of a second. Although Libet's conclusions have been robustly criticized on a number of grounds—most notably that the subject's awareness of an intention to move is too ambiguous, and that the measured brain activity was associated with a "gearing up" to decide and not the decision itself—a number of other neuroscientific studies, using different methods and tools (fMRI, electrodes) have produced similar results. Not only does the unconscious brain appear to register certain decisions before people are aware of having made those decisions; neuroscientists can even predict with relative accuracy (60 percent in one study, 80 percent in another) what decision a person will make.

One reason why these studies are so troubling for proponents of free will is that one of the strongest "arguments" for free will has been our own inner sense that we freely and deliberately make our choices. But what if this inner sense is wrong? Although you might believe that your intention to pick up your coffee cup is the cause of you picking up your coffee cup (by means of the appropriate bodily mechanisms), this conscious intention might simply be a "byproduct" of what has already occurred in your brain.

Do studies like this suggest or show that we do not have free will? Philosophers and scientists do increasingly disavow the dualistic "folk" or "Cartesian" notion of free will, according to which some non-material "mind" or "self" causes the material brain/body to do stuff. For reductive materialists, mental states like belief and desire reduce to and are explained by neurological states and processes. Eliminative materialists go further in maintaining that mental states like belief and desire simply do not exist and therefore cannot be reduced to and explained by more basic neurological states and processes (in the same way that crystalline spheres and demons cannot be reduced and explained because they simply do not exist). In both cases, we simply are our brains—nothing more.

Here we again run up against Descartes' "interaction problem" and the so-called "hard problem of consciousness": How can a non-physical mind cause a physical brain to do things? How does consciousness arise from and interact with a physical brain? The easiest solution, of course, is one of the materialist ones above: simply jettison what is non-physical—mind and free will, for starters. In fact, this might be the only plausible scientific solution insofar as science is restricted to the study and explanation of that which is material. Perhaps, however, we still do not know enough about the human brain to say whether and how free will might be explained in terms of the brain's workings. Perhaps, quantum indeterminacy might offer a scientific crack through which free will can slip, so to speak, as some libertarians have claimed. Moreover, there remains our felt sense that we do freely make decisions, as well as our socio-legal assumption that people can only be held accountable for behavior that they do freely enact. And so goes the ongoing debate about free will.

"Original goodness" and "original knowledge" have not been explored by academic philosophers of religion to the degree that free will has. Nevertheless, the theories and findings of a couple of relatively new fields of scientific study are germane to these topics—neo-Darwinian evolutionary theory and cognitive science, respectively.

No recent work in evolutionary theory has exerted more popular philosophical and scientific influence than Richard Dawkins' *The Selfish Gene*. By "selfish gene," Dawkins refers to a gene-centered view of evolution as opposed to an organism- or group-centered one. Here, the "fundamental unit" and "prime mover" of life is the "replicator"—"anything in the universe of which copies are made," i.e., what we call "genes."[33] Although genes come "packaged" in organisms—what Dawkins calls "discrete vehicles" or "survival machines"—organisms are in fact created by genes, if not indirectly controlled by them, at least in some important respects.

Of course, genes are not literally selfish; nevertheless, if a gene's objective is to survive and replicate, especially in the face of competition with other genes, then "ruthless selfishness" must be assumed the "predominant quality" of a gene.[34] This "gene selfishness" will usually manifest itself in selfish behavior in organisms, which act in ways that ensure their own genes are replicated and spread. There are, however, "special circumstances" in which selfish genes best achieve their goals through "limited forms" of altruism between organisms.[35] In the case of "kin-directed altruism," an organism behaves in a way that reduces its own chance of survival for the sake of increasing the chance of survival of kin, whether offspring or close relations, thereby increasing the chances that its genes (and ones like them) are spread. In the case of "reciprocal altruism," an organism behaves in a way that reduces its own chance of survival for the sake of increasing the chance of survival of non-kin, though with the expectation that the favor will be returned, thereby increasing its own chances of survival in the long run. (Examples here include the vampire bat, which offers regurgitated blood to other vampire bats, and the vervet monkey, which signals a predator alarm for other vervet monkeys.)

Some evolutionary theorists and moral philosophers have argued that the putative fact of *biological altruism*—that we do sometimes behave altruistically—provides an evolutionary explanation for *psychological altruism*, our concern for the welfare of others for their own sake. Some are tempted to go further and claim that this *descriptive ethics* of how people do sometimes behave provides philosophical justification for a *normative ethics* of how people ought to behave. For Dawkins, however, altruism is not only "special" and "limited" (in the senses above) but also behavioral, not psychological, since it concerns what the organism does, not what its motives are. Moreover, as Dawkins makes in clear in the first chapter of *The Selfish Gene*, he does not advocate a normative morality based on evolutionary biology; if anything, he does just the opposite. Maintaining that "a human society based simply on the gene's law of universal ruthless selfishness would be a very nasty society in which to live," he suggests that if a moral is to be extracted as his book, it should be that of a warning:

> Be warned that if you wish, as I do, to build a society in which individuals cooperate generously and unselfishly toward a common good, you can expect little help from biological nature. Let us try to *teach* generosity and altruism, because we are born selfish.[36]

Although Dawkins was later to admit that the second half of this second sentence is misleading,[37] we can nevertheless ask about the relevance of neo-Darwinian evolutionary theories such as Dawkins'—which feature both selfishness and altruism—for evaluating age-old philosophical theories about innate human goodness, especially the Confucian ones we looked at above. This, we will get to in the next section. For now, however, we turn to our third and final topic for this section: "original enlightenment" or naturally reliable cognitive capacities.

In this case, cognitive science in general and cognitive science of religion in particular are most relevant. For the latter, evolved cognitive systems and capacities of the brain are used to explain how religious thoughts and practices are acquired and transmitted. For many cognitive scientists of religion, the religious applications of these cognitive systems and capacities are evolutionary byproducts—what are called "non-adaptive traits" or "spandrels." (For more on this, see Chapter 12.) Take, for example, the *hyperactive agent detection device* (HADD), a key concept from cognitive science of religion. The human brain (and those of many other animals too) evolved in such a way to "over-detect" for agents, especially predators. This of course is a survival strategy; if you hear a rustling in the woods, you will instinctively startle and direct your attention to it, assuming it is caused by an animal, perhaps even a predatory animal. For some cognitive scientists of religion, this evolved cognitive capacity helps explain why humans first created and transmitted concepts of "superhuman agents" such as Gods, Spirits, and Ancestors. We "over-detected" for agency, (mis)assuming that some superhuman agent was responsible for some otherwise unexplainable happenings.

What does this have to do with the "originally enlightened" condition of humankind? Given that humans are hyperactive agent detectors, they over-detect for agency since it is much more costly not to detect for an agent that is actually present (especially in the case of a predator) than to detect for agents when none are there. This means that the human brain seems to have evolved in a way that makes it prone to commit mistakes about agency. And this, really, is just the tip of the iceberg, as Pascal Boyer illustrates in his (partial) "menagerie of mental processes" that "lead us away from clear and supported beliefs":

- *Consensus effect*: adjusting one's impression of a scene to how others describe it;
- *False consensus effect*: wrongly judging that one's own impressions are shared by others;
- *Generation effect:* believing that one's own self-generated memories (of what did not occur) are more accurate than the memories of others;
- *Memory illusions*: believing a false memory that has been implanted by another (e.g., an experimental psychologist);
- *Source monitoring defects*: confusion about the source of particular information;
- *Confirmation bias*: detecting and recalling information that confirms one's hypotheses, while overlooking and forgetting information that disconfirms one's hypotheses;
- *Cognitive dissonance reduction*: readjusting memories of previous beliefs and impressions in light of new experience.[38]

Consider also that humans are cognitively predisposed to make mistakes with respect to pattern recognition in at least two ways: *apophenia*, the tendency to perceive meaningful connections where they do not exist (e.g., among numbers with respect to the lottery); and *pareidolia*, the tendency to

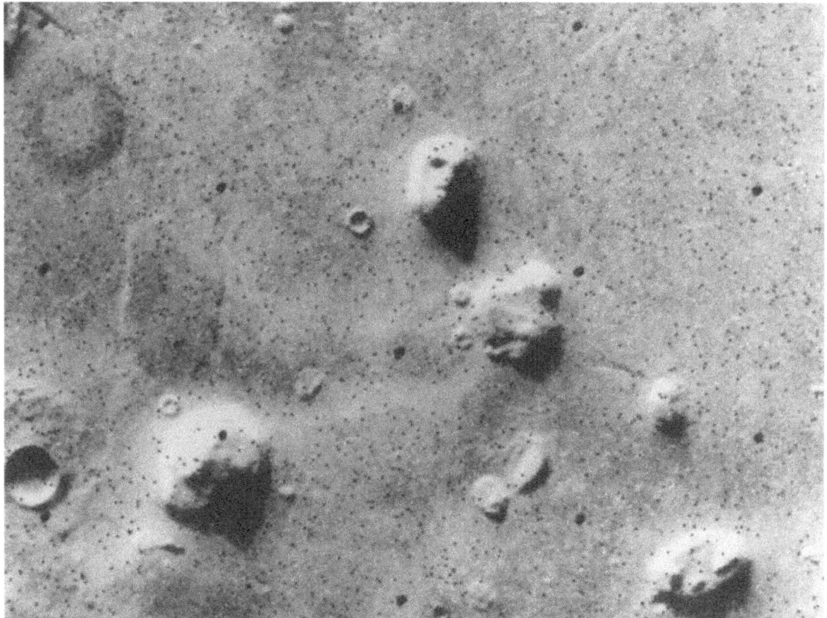

Figure 5 "Face of Mars." Viking 1, NASA, Public domain, Wikimedia Commons.

perceive images, especially faces, where they do not exist (e.g., clouds, or in the case of Figure 5, a rock mesa in the Cydonia region of Mars).

Are we then "originally ignorant"?

VIII. Putting it All Together

Do we have an original human condition, and if so, what is it? Are we naturally or innately free or not? Good or not? Enlightened or not? Do we have natural or innate tendencies or dispositions toward action that is freely chosen, behavior that is morally good, and the acquisition of knowledge and insight that is true and enlightening?

We have encountered a bevy of positions above, the most recent of which come from the natural sciences. How relevant are these sciences to answering age-old questions about human nature? How relevant are neuroscientific studies to determining whether we are free or not? Neo-Darwinianism to deciding whether we are good or not? Cognitive science to figuring out whether we are "enlightened" or not?

Take free will. Above, we have seen religious and philosophies theories that include the following:

1 we are free to choose but cannot freely effect choices (for the good) until we are redeemed by a God (Augustine);
2 we are free to choose, or at least to "acquire" choices that have been predetermined by a God, but that God effects those choices (al-Ashʿarī);
3 we are free to choose, especially with regard to issues of morality, but our destiny will always determine issues of success (Abímbọ́lá);
4 we do not freely choose but do freely effect choices when we enact what has been chosen (Locke);
5 we are radically free from a "noumenal" perspective but entirely determined from a "phenomenal" perspective (Kant).

What relevance are Libet's and subsequent neuroscientific experiments to deciding this issue? To ask this question is again to invoke our list of *epistemic virtues* from Chapter 3, asking if *empirical adequacy* should lead the way in evaluation, or whether *external coherence* or *practical usefulness* are equally or more important.

We can also ask *phenomenological* questions about how we experience ourselves as free—for no matter how many scientific experiments demonstrate that our brain registers that some decision has been made before consciously chosen, we still experience ourselves as free, at least in certain ways. Note, however, that we also experience our thoughts and actions as constrained in certain ways—shaped by our histories, our experiences, our relationships, our parents, even our brain chemistry. In this last case (brain chemistry), it is worth pointing out that some of "us" do increasingly think of ourselves as just our brains and bodies. Whence, then, we might ask, is the conflict between whether our brain fires first or we consciously choose first?—for we are both.

Perhaps we should take a step back from evaluation to comparison, asking whether the same concept of *free will* is in play for all these theories and experiments? What exactly does it mean to freely choose? Do "I" only freely choose if brain chemistry is not involved at all or if the brain does not "fire" prior to an inner sense of choosing? Do we only freely choose if our past experiences, current environment, and genetic code pay no role in our decisions? Or do we freely choose when we are presented with a range of options, one of which we select and enact, no matter how our past experiences, current environment, and genetic code factor into this decision?

To move another step "backwards" in our method, we could scrutinize the descriptions above for contexts in which either the range of choices or the ability to enact choices was absent or restricted for certain members of societies due to race, ethnicity, class, gender, or sexual orientation. We might even find that some religious philosophies of free will were (and still are) deliberately used for such ends—to legitimate the attenuation or abasement of the freedoms of certain members of societies—or that the Western philosophical emphasis on free will is itself deeply patriarchal. The feminist Jewish philosopher Melissa Raphael, for example, points out that "freedom is not, as liberal individualism would have us believe," simply a fundamental quality or goal of human existence, but rather "a privilege of historical and political power" that is very often "a function of alienated power where the powerful have bought freedoms or prevailed upon others so as to be free of ordinary constraints and dependencies" (especially male freedom from relational responsibilities to female partners and their families).[39] Patriarchal freedom "is therefore a function and cause of the alienation of [female] relationality."[40]

As with free will, so with goodness and enlightenment (which, as we have seen above, are often interconnected, especially in the notion of autonomy, the capacity to make informed, uncoerced decisions). We can and should ask about the relevance of contemporary scientific theories for age-old religious philosophies. But we should also ask about the "coherence" and "usefulness" of these theories and philosophies, as well as the ways in which we experience ourselves and others as innately or naturally good (or not) and "enlightened" (or not). We should also examine whether and how original goodness and original enlightenment constitute stable categories for cross-cultural philosophy of religion. If we do have neo-Darwinian "selfish genes," does that mean that we do not have Confucian "sprouts of virtue" or that we are not sacredly interrelated with all of creation, as some Lakȟóta believe? If we do exhibit hyperactive agent detection or confirmation bias, does that mean that we tend toward original ignorance, as many South Asian philosophies of religion hold, and that we could never be "originally" or "suddenly" enlightened, as many forms of East Asian Buddhism maintain? Finally, we should scrutinize cases in which religious philosophies of goodness and enlightenment were (and still are) used to legitimate the attenuation or corruption of the goodness and intelligence of certain peoples, genders, races, and classes—for to do so is to practice philosophy of religion not only globally but also critically.

Questions for Discussion

1 Are humans originally free or not? Good or not? Enlightened or not? Describe, compare, and evaluate some of our philosophies of religion with respect to one of these questions.
2 Are the contemporary sciences of relevance in answering any of the "age-old" questions about original freedom, goodness, or enlightenment? Show why or why not.
3 To what extent do some of these conceptions of the self (above) continue to challenge the modern Western notion that the self is individual, substantial, *and autonomous*?

Primary and Scholarly Sources

East Asia

Mencius, 2A6, 6A6. In *A Source Book in Chinese Philosophy*, ed. Wing-Tsit Chan, 65–6, 53–4. Princeton, NJ: Princeton University Press, 1963.
Xúnzǐ, chapter 23. In *Xunzi: The Complete Text*, trans. Eric L. Hutton, 248–57. Princeton, NJ: Princeton University Press, 2014.

European/Academic

Boyer, Pascal. *Religion Explained: The Evolutionary Origins of Religious Thought*, 144–8, 299–302. New York: Basic Books, 2001.
Dawkins, Richard. *The Selfish Gene*, 30th anniversary ed., chapter 1. New York: Oxford University Press, 2006.
Kant, Immanuel. *Groundwork of the Metaphysics of Morals*, Section III. In *The Cambridge Edition of the Works of Immanuel Kant: Practical Philosophy*, trans May J. Gregor, 94–6. New York: Cambridge University Press, 1996.
Locke, John. *An Essay Concerning Human Understanding*, II.xxi.21–9. Ed. Kenneth P. Winkler, 98–101. Indianapolis, IN: Hackett Publishing, 1996.
Smith, Kerri. "Taking Aim at Free Will." *Nature* 477 (September 2011): 23–5.

Lakȟóta

DeMallie, Raymond J. "Lakota Beliefs and Rituals in the Nineteenth Century." In *Sioux Indian Religion*, eds. Raymond J. DeMallie and Douglas R. Parks, 25–43. Norman, OK: University of Oklahoma Press, 1987.

Sword, George. "Wakan." In *The Sun Dance and Other Ceremonies of the Oglala Division of the Teton Dakota*, ed. J. R. Walker, 137–8. London: Forgotten Books, 2008.

Mediterranean/Abrahamic

al-Ash'arī, Abū al-Ḥasan. *Kitāb al-Luma'*, §§82–95. In *The Theology of al-Ash'arī*, ed. Richard J. McCarthy, 53–62. Beyrouth: Imprimerie Catholique, 1953.

Augustine. *Retractions* I.9.6. In *Augustine: Earlier Writings*, ed. J. H. S. Burleigh, 104–5. Philadelphia, PA: Westminster Press, 1953.

South Asia

Anuruddha. *Abhidhammatthasaṅgaha, with commentary by Sumaṅgala*. In *Buddhist Philosophy: Essential Readings*, eds. William Edelglass and Jay L. Garfield, 19–25. New York: Oxford University Press, 2009.

Śaṅkara. *Brahma Sūtra Bhāṣya*, Preamble. In *A Sourcebook in Indian Philosophy*, eds. Sarvepalli Radhakrishnan and Charles A. Moore, 509–10. Princeton, NJ: Princeton University Press, 1957.

Yorùbá

Abímbọ́lá, Kọ́lá. *Yorùbá Culture: A Philosophical Account*, chapter 3. Birmingham: Iroko Academic Publishers, 2005.

Gbadegesin, Segun. *African Philosophy: Traditional Yoruba Philosophy and Contemporary African Realities*, chapter 2. New York: Peter Lang, 1991.

Makinde, Moses. "An African Concept of Human Personality: The Yorùbá Example." In *African Philosophy: The Demise of a Controversy*, 103–19. Ile-Ife: Obafemi Awolowo University Press, 2007.

6

Where Am I Going To?

Learning Objectives

- Understand some of the important and interesting ways in which religious thinkers, texts, and traditions answer the questions: "Do I survive death, and if so, how?"
- Understand some of the ways in which these answers challenge the notion that the self is individual and substantial.
- Compare and evaluate philosophies of religion about the survival of death.

I. Introduction

This chapter turns from the origins of the self to its destinations. In terms of the journey metaphor, it is titled "Where am I going to?" More precisely, this chapter asks, "Do I survive death?"

Note that these two questions are hardly synonymous, even if put in terms of the *ultimate destinations* of the self. On the one hand, you might view your ultimate destination as your *final* state of being after death. On the other hand, you could think about your ultimate destination as what is most *basic* or *important* to you in life. Put simply, the ultimate religious destinations of humans include both postmortem and this-worldly ends. If, for example, you are a Buddhist, you might understand your ultimate goal as that of leaving the wheel of rebirth after your final death *or* as attaining *nirvāṇa* and "waking up" to the ways things really are in this life. Or if you are a Christian, you might understand your ultimate goal as entering heaven after death *or* as being saved from your sins and living in right relationship with the Trinitarian-Christian God during this life.

Because these are two different topics—postmortem destinations, this-worldly paths and ends—we will cover them over two different chapters, focusing here on the former and in the next chapter on the latter. Do not, however, let this organizational decision mislead you into thinking that post-mortem destinations are the most important destinations for religious philosophies. In fact, this chapter will show how post-mortem destinations are sometimes unimportant or irrelevant for philosophies of religion, some of which are focused solely on how we should live our lives here and now, others of which simply reject life after (final) death.

One final, comparative issue before we get started. This chapter will compare philosophies of *afterlife* rather than philosophies of *immortality*. Why? Whereas *immortality* tends to connote the survival of an individuated soul, *afterlife* does not. Why does this difference matter? Although what survives (final) death in some philosophies of religion is an individuated soul that retains its identity, no such self survives (final) death in many other philosophies of religion. In this later case, the self might instead dissolve into a state of identity-less bliss, or return to and become unified with a cosmic or divine reality, or become part of other living beings with different self-identities. We should not, therefore, presume that in philosophizing about the survival of death we are philosophizing about the survival of an individuated self.

II. South Asian Philosophy of Religion

In the case of South Asian philosophies of religion, we begin by recognizing that most deaths are not final deaths. Rather, the "self" is reborn again and again, only to attain final death and release from rebirth upon the elimination of all *karma*. What happens after this final death, however, varies from philosophy to philosophy, with destinations as different as isolation from everything else, unification with ultimate reality, survival in a heavenly realm, and termination of individual identity.

We pick up the story where we left it last chapter—the non-dual (*advaita*) Vedānta of Śaṅkara (*c.* 788–*c.* 820). What happens to the eternal and universal soul (*Ātman*) after final death in Advaita Vedānta? Stated as such, the question is misleading, for *Ātman* is pure consciousness and ultimate reality, which is never born and never dies. What then happens to the person *qua* body-mind after attaining the meditative insight of *Ātman*/*Brahman*?

Simply put, they no longer mistake themselves as their individual body-mind; rather, they just are *Ātman/Brahman*. This is a state of freedom (*jīvan-mukti*) from ignorance in this life and of absolute freedom (*videha-mukti*) or release (*mokṣa*) from the wheel of rebirth upon death. Since the individuated body-mind self is ultimately unreal, there is no such thing to continue after final death; rather, there is only *Ātman/Brahman*. Drawing on a metaphor from the *Muṇḍaka Upaniṣad* in his commentary (*bhāṣya*) on the *Brahma Sūtras*, Śaṅkara suggested that this experience was like that of rivers disappearing into the sea: "as rivers losing the names and forms abiding in them disappear in the sea, so the individual self also losing the name and form abiding in it becomes united with the highest person [*Ātman*]."[1]

Things are not so different in early (Theravāda) Buddhism. As you know from Chapter 4, the historical Buddha taught that there is no permanent, unchanging self (*an-ātman*); rather, we are an aggregate of five sets of bodily-mental processes called *skandha*-s. And as you know from Chapter 5, the *abhidharma* traditions of early Buddhism maintained that these five aggregates are themselves constituted by momentary, experiential "flashes" called *dharma*-s. Upon attaining meditative enlightenment of this "no-self," one "wakes up" to the way things are, attaining enlightenment (*nirvāṇa*) in this life and final release from rebirth (*parinirvāṇa*) after death. As with Hindu Advaita Vedānta, therefore, there is no-thing—no individuated self-soul—to go anywhere after final death; rather, there is only *parinirvāṇa*. As one contemporary scholar of Buddhism maintains, this need not mean that *parinirvāṇa* is a state of nothingness; rather, it is one "beyond normal comprehension."[2] To support this interpretation, Peter Harvey draws on the Buddha's saying that, "while one would know whether a burning fire had gone out, one could not meaningfully ask what direction the quenched fire had gone in: east, west, south or north." Writes, Harvey, although "to a Western-educated person, an extinct fire goes nowhere because it does not exist, the Buddha's audience in ancient India would generally have thought of an extinguished fire as going back into a non-manifested state as latent heat." So, likewise, for one who has attained *parinirvāṇa*. Nevertheless, it would seem that individual identity and awareness do not continue after final death, just as in Śaṅkara's Advaita Vedānta.

Outside Advaita Vedānta and Theravāda Buddhism, however, South Asian accounts of what happens after final death are different, with self-souls enjoying communion with *Brahman*, entering a heavenly abode, or simply becoming a state of isolated bliss.

We resume the story with two of the other major sub-traditions of Vedānta, the qualified non-dual (*viśiṣṭādvaita*) Vedānta of Rāmānuja (1017–

1137) and the dual (*dvaita*) Vedānta of Madhva (1238–1317). For Rāmānuja, *Ātman*/*Brahman* is everything and ultimately non-dual, just as for Śaṅkara. This non-duality, however, is "qualified" in the sense that there are qualifications or distinctions within *Brahman*. What are these qualifications? They are every finite soul (*jīvātman*) and material thing of the cosmos. These souls and things are the parts (*aṃśa*-s) or modes (*prakāra*-s) of *Brahman*, which is thusly qualified, even while remaining non-dual since there is nothing other than *Brahman*. To use the metaphor of Rāmānuja, conscious souls and material things are the body of *Brahman*, which to them are its soul, the supreme soul (*paramātman*) of the cosmos. Unlike Śaṅkara, individual souls and material things are not ultimately illusory; nevertheless, their existence is dependent on *Brahman*, which both causes them to be (as their efficient cause) and constitutes their existence (as their material cause).[3] What does this mean for the "destination" of humans? In contrast to Śaṅkara, Rāmānuja's liberated soul does not lose self-awareness and identity, for this would mean the "annihilation of the self"; rather, as Rāmānuja writes in his commentary (*bhāṣya*) on the *Brahma Sūtra* it "shines forth in a state of final release" as a "knowing subject."[4] For Rāmānuja, this was a state of proximity to and communion with *Ātman*/*Brahman*, which he understood personally as Lord Viṣṇu (especially in union with his female partner Śrī or Lakṣmī).

As you can imagine, the exponent of dual (*dvaita*) Vedānta, Madhva, takes things one step further. Souls and matter are not merely *Brahman* (as they are for Śaṅkara); nor are they parts of *Brahman* (as for Rāmānuja). Rather, souls and matter are eternally distinct substances that are qualitatively different from *Brahman*. In fact, Madhva itemizes five kinds of fundamental differences: *Brahman* and insentient matter (*prakṛti*), *Brahman* and souls (*jīva*-s), souls and matter, different souls, and different material things. Although individual souls and material things are created by *Brahman* (which for Madhva is understood personally as Lord Viṣṇu), they are created as separate from *Brahman*, not from out of *Brahman* as mere parts of *Brahman* (as with Rāmānuja). *Brahman* is therefore what causes them to be (efficient cause) but not what constitutes them (material cause). What does this mean for the "destination" of humans? Upon death, souls enter a heavenly realm where they retain their distinct individuality rather than returning to or becoming *Brahman*.

These are most of the varieties of the Vedānta school of Hindu philosophy: Śaṅkara's non-dualism, Rāmānuja's qualified-non-dualism, and Madhva's dualism.[5] What about the other schools of Hindu philosophy and Jainism? We begin by going back to the beginning, so to speak.

In the earliest Vedic scriptures, death is not much of an issue; rather, the first two sections of the *Vedas* (*saṃhita*-s, *brāhmaṇa*-s) are preoccupied with the propitiation of the Vedic deities during sacrificial rituals and the ritual words chanted during these sacrifices. To the extent that there was reflection on death and what happened afterwards, it, too, was understood as a sacrifice that returns people to the cosmos or sends them to some heavenly realm.

These early sections of the *Vedas* were later taken as the basis for one of the other schools of Hindu philosophy—Pūrva Mīmāṃsā, which is literally the school of "earlier interpretation," i.e., the school that interprets the earlier (pre-*Upaniṣadic*) sections of the *Vedas*. It should therefore come as no surprise to learn that the founding *sūtras* of Mīmāṃsā represent the afterlife as heavenly reward for those who perform the requisite ritual sacrifices and live according to "duty" (*dharma*). This is not, however, the heaven of any ultimate or creator God, for the school of Mīmāṃsā denies the existence of any such being (even while it recognizes the existence of numerous "lower" Gods).

Perhaps the oldest school of (proto) Hindu philosophy, however, is Sāṁkhya, the earliest texts of which also do not make mention or have need of an ultimate/creator God. The cosmos, rather, is bifurcated into two principles: on the one hand, cosmic consciousness or that which experiences (*Puruṣa*); on the other hand, nature or that which is experienced (*prakṛti*). Although *Puruṣa* is a pure subject and mere witness, it becomes enraptured by that which it experiences—the evolution of *prakṛti*—mistaking itself for the "highest" or "finest" elements of *prakṛti*, which are the intellect (*buddhi*) and ego-identity (*ahaṃkāra*) of the empirical self. Upon realizing what it really is, however, *Puruṣa* enjoys an "isolated" (*kaivalya*) existence of pure bliss, while the play of *prakṛti* returns to its primordial state.

We will learn more on the evolution of *prakṛti* in Chapter 9. For now, the point is that some South Asian philosophies of religion think of the end goal as one of isolation of the soul from everything else. This is true also for Jainism, which understands reality dualistically, dividing substances into living, conscious souls (*jīva*-s) and non-living, insentient objects (*ajīva*-s). The most significant of these *ajīva*-s is matter (*pudgala*), since it binds to souls, causing them to be reborn. Only with liberation from matter, can the soul be freed from rebirth, ascending to the apex of the cosmos, where it enjoys perfect omniscience and bliss. As in the case of Sāṁkhya, this is a state of isolation (*kaivalya*) that does not involve any person-like deity or ultimate reality (neither of which exist, according to Jainism).

Such a state of isolation also serves as an ultimate end in the Hindu philosophical schools for which there is a creator God called *Īśvara* (meaning

Table 6.1 Types of Liberation in South Asian Philosophy of Religion

Ideal Types	Examples
(1) Individuated soul goes to "heaven"	Some *Vedas*; Mīmāṃsā; Dvaita Vedānta
(2) Individuated soul is isolated	Jainism, Sāṁkhya. Nyāya-Vaiśeṣika
(3) Individuated soul returns to some God or ultimate reality (*Brahman*)	Some *Upaniṣads*; Viśiṣṭādvaita Vedānta
(4) Illusion of individuation is removed	Some *Upaniṣads*; Theravāda Buddhism; Advaita Vedānta

"Lord")—Nyāya, and eventually also Vaiśeṣika, the two of which grow together over time, joining in the early second millennium.[6] In fact, neither school is very concerned with what happens after (final) death: the former is preoccupied simply with "getting the knowledge right"; the latter, with understanding reality correctly. That said, Nyāya-Vaiśeṣika do understand the underlying self (*Ātman*) to be a non-physical substance in which mental events inhere. Since all mental events are impermanent, none can be identified with *Ātman*—not even consciousness (which, they argued, is not present during dreamless sleep). Thus, the fully liberated soul no longer possesses consciousness, even though it does retain its own individuality. The liberated Nyāya-Vaiśeṣika soul is therefore isolated, much like liberated souls of Jainism and Sāṁkhya, even though there is a creator God (*Īśvara*) in Nyāya-Vaiśeṣika, unlike Jainism and Sāṁkhya.

Now you see what is meant in saying there are a variety of answers in South Asian philosophy of religion to the question "Do I survive death?" Let us therefore conclude this section with four "ideal types" that help tame this variety: (1) the soul remains individuated and enters a heavenly paradise (sometimes of a God, sometimes not); (2) the soul remains individuated but is isolated from everything else; (3) the soul remains individuated, though as a part of ultimate reality; (4) the illusion of individuation is removed.[7] See Table 6.1 for a tabulated summary of each type.

III. East Asian Philosophy of Religon

Just as with South Asian religious philosophy, there is a diversity of views in East Asian religious philosophy with respect to what happens to humans after death. With few exceptions, these views are not those of particular religious traditions or communities—i.e., there is generally no "Confucian" or "Daoist" or "Buddhist" view of the afterlife. This is true because each of these traditions not only is internally diverse but also mingles together with the others as well as with an assortment of "Chinese" or "folk" philosophies of the afterlife.[8]

One of the earliest relevant views about the afterlife concerns a belief in two kinds of souls: a *hún* (魂) soul, associated with *yáng*, that rises upward to heaven, and a *pò* (魄) soul, associated with *yīn*, that sinks downward to the earth. Upon death, the *hún* soul becomes a spirit (*shén*, 神) that can be invited to reside in an ancestral tablet, where it looks after the well-being and prosperity of the family in return for proper veneration and attention. By contrast, the *pò* soul remains with the body, residing in the grave where it decomposes with the body, while also enjoying its own veneration and attention during the springtime festival of "tomb-sweeping" called Qīngmíng. In the case of untimely deaths, however, the *pò* soul can become a wandering "ghost" (*guǐ*, 鬼), against which the living must perform ritual means of protection. In some cases, this protection ultimately requires transforming the deceased into a deity, whose raw power can be tamed through proper worship.

Another early Chinese view of the afterlife involves a shadowy underworld called the "Yellow Springs," to which the souls of commoners descend upon death. Over time, both this underworld/hell and the celestial-world/heaven came to be structured by the Chinese bureaucratic model and influenced by the Buddhist idea of rebirth, eventually resulting in the following picture. Upon death a preliminary hearing is held for one's spirit by Chénghuángshén, the "God of Walls and Moats." Those found virtuous are allowed to go directly to a Buddhist or Daoist paradisiacal realm, where they reside indefinitely, or to the lowest realm of hell, where they are immediately reborn. Everyone else is required to descend to hell, where they undergo a fixed period of punishment in one or more of its ten levels, after which they drink an elixir of oblivion, climb onto the wheel of transmigration, and are reborn into their next body.

Of the many paradisiacal realms and bureaucratic courts of the celestial world, two of the most influential are the Buddhist "Pure Land" and the realm of the Daoist immortals. In the former case, recall that Pure Land Buddhism (in all its varieties) is by far the most popular form of Buddhism in East Asia. In contrast to Chán/Zen, which involves arduous "self-effort," Pure Land requires simple acts of devotion to or faith in Amitābha, who created a heavenly realm into which his devotees are reborn after death, from which they can attain *nirvāṇa*. In fact, some Pure Land thinkers maintained that it was impossible to attain *nirvāṇa* from this world during its current age of decline and degradation; only by being born into Amitābha's Pure Land could *nirvāṇa* be realized. (More on this in Chapter 11.)

In the case of Daoist realms of immortals, we see traces of a quest for immortality as early as the eighth century BCE. However, it is apparently not until the Qin and Han Dynasties (221–206 BCE, 206 BCE –220 CE) that emperors sent men to search for a "drug of no death" and the realms in which legendary immortals were said to reside (either on the island mountain of Penglai in the eastern sea or in the Kunlun Mountains in the west). Over time, this search for an actual elixir of immortality was taken up by Daoist practitioners, who instead practiced an "internal alchemy" (*nèidān*, 内丹) that involved methods such as breathing exercises, yogic postures, and meditative regimens by which to attain longevity, if not immortality. Through successful practice of these methods during life, Daoist sages could ascend to immortal realms after death (rather than avoiding death altogether).

For some Chinese philosophers, however, death and the afterlife were not only of little concern but also denigrated to the extent that they became the concern of others. This critical attitude begins with Confucius (551–479 BCE), who responded to a student's question about death by saying: "You do not understand even life. How can you ask about death?"[9] Nevertheless, observance of rituals and customs (*lǐ*, 禮) relating to death (e.g., funerary ceremonies and mourning rituals) were of critical importance for Confucius in particular and Confucianism in general. Thus, the fourth-generation Confucian Xúnzǐ (313–238 BCE) counselled absolute adherence to such rituals, even while he maintained that Heaven (*Tiān*) is merely the uncaring forces of nature, questioning popular belief in spirits and ghosts and suggesting there is no postmortem existence for humans. This stance is reflected in Xúnzǐ's use of the term "as if": one venerates ancestors "as if" their spirits could participate, "as if" they survived death, "as if" they are still present.[10] What was crucial for Xúnzǐ was not abstract beliefs about what happens after death, but ritual actions that enable the living to deal with the death of their loved ones.

In the case of Daoism, although aspirations of and techniques for attaining longevity can be found in its classic texts, little sustained attention is paid there to the question of what happens to humans after death. The *Dàodéjīng* simply recognizes that all things come from and return to *Dào*, whereas the

Zhuāngzǐ speaks about death as one of many natural processes of transformation. One of the more striking passages from the *Zhuāngzǐ* recounts Zhuāngzǐ's reaction to his own wife's death, which was ultimately one of joyful celebration rather than doleful mourning (as was expected by Chinese conventions and prescribed by Confucian rituals). When Zhuāngzǐ was chastised by a friend for this behavior, he responded by explaining how, just as there were natural transformations by which his wife was born, so there are natural transformations by which she died:

> In the midst of the jumble or wonder and mystery a change took place and she had a spirit. Another change and she had a body. Another change and she was born. Now there's been another change and she's dead. It's just like the progression of the four seasons, spring, summer, fall, and winter. Now she's going to lie down peacefully in a vast room [the universe]. If I were to follow after her bawling and sobbing, it would show that I don't understand anything about fate [what naturally occurs]. So I stopped.[11]

Given that death is simply a natural transformation, the *Zhuāngzǐ* advises you to be "content" with the time you have and to "dwell" in "this order," for in doing so "neither sorrow nor joy can touch you."[12]

Finally, while Pure Land Buddhists generally strive to be reborn in the Pure Land of Amitābha, this ideal came under criticism insofar as it assumed either that the Pure Land is a permanent heavenly realm or that what is reborn there is a permanent individual soul. The Pure Land, rather, is just one among many "useful means" (Sk. *upāya*; Ch. *fāngbiàn*, 方便) to attain *nirvāṇa* by realizing that nothing is permanent, especially some kind of self/soul. One of the earliest such criticisms is found in the *Platform Sūtra of the Sixth Patriarch* (*Liùzǔ Tánjīng*, 六祖壇經), a text that records the *dharma* teaching from a temple platform by the legendary sixth headmaster of Chán Buddhism in China, Huìnéng (Dàjiàn Huìnéng, 大鑒惠能, 638–713. Although this text is important in many ways, some of which we will look at in Chapter 8, what is important here is its claim that only "deluded people" of "low intelligence" recite the name of Amitābha in hopes of being reborn into the Pure Land.[13] By contrast, those "enlightened" people of "high intelligence" purify their mind and thereby create "pure lands" here and now.

Here, we again see tension between popular concern with what happens after death and philosophical criticism of those concerns, maintaining that it is far more important to concern oneself with the here and now, which can and should be infused with enlightened understanding, effortless action, and sacred ritual.

IV. Lakȟóta Philosophy of Religon

As we have seen already with Lakȟóta philosophy of religion, it is difficult to ascertain the religio-philosophies of the Lakȟóta prior to colonial contact. It would seem, though, that Lakȟóta ideas about death involved some form of reincarnation. To understand how, we must first understand Lakȟóta ideas about "soul(s)."

According to William Powers, an anthropologist who spent decades of research on the Oglala Lakȟóta Reservation of Pine Ridge, one relevant Lakȟóta belief is that all beings pass through four states of individuation, which correspond to four souls or four aspects of one soul: (1) *šičuŋ*, potentiality; (2) *tȟúŋ*, giving birth; (3) *ní*, life or breath; and (4) *nağí*, ghost.[14] Powers relates these four aspects of the soul in the following ways:

> Each individual comes into being as the result of (1) having a potentiality for being [*šičuŋ*], (2) transforming this potentiality through birth into an essence that is independent of the body [*tȟúŋ*], (3) providing continuous evidence that this essence exists [*ní*], and (4) finally providing evidence that the essence independent of the corporeal existence continues after death, therefore freeing its potentiality to inhere in another (potential) organism to begin the process all over, ad infinitum, in what we understand in English to be a system of reincarnation [*nağí*].[15]

Key here is that after death, one's potentiality for being, *šičuŋ*, leaves the body, returning to the sacred, mysterious beings and powers (*Wakȟáŋ Tȟáŋka*), eventually entering a new body. Thus, Powers maintains that the whole life process for the Lakȟóta is "one in which immortality is achieved through reincarnation."[16]

This analysis is shared by another anthropologist, Raymond DeMallie, who availed himself of the early twentieth-century research of James Walker. According to Walker, one Lakȟóta holy man named Finger reported that when a baby is born, its body is animated by Tákuškaŋškaŋ, one of the sixteen, sacred, mysterious powers (*Wakȟáŋ Tȟáŋka*), who gives the body a "guardian spirit" (*šičuŋ*), what Powers refers to above as a "potentiality."[17] Tákuškaŋškaŋ also gives each body both a *niyá* (or *ní*), which DeMallie translates as "ghost" (but Powers translated as "life"), as well as a *nağí*, which DeMallie translates as "spirit" (but Powers translated as "ghost"). Regardless of these differences of translation, what is important is that after death, the *šičuŋ* (guardian/potentiality) escorts the *nağí* (spirit/ghost) beyond the Milky Way (*Wanáği Tȟačháŋku*, literally "Spirit's Trail"), after which, the

Table 6.2 Lakȟóta Terms for What Happens to the "Soul/s" after Death

Lakȟóta Term	Powers Translation	DeMallie Translation	Function
Šičuŋ	Potentiality	Guardian	Given to body at birth, escorts *nağí* beyond the Milky Way at death, returns to enter a new body
Ní/Niyá	Life or breath	Ghost	Given to body at birth, helps *šičuŋ* escort *nağí* beyond the Milky Way at death, returns to enter a new body
Nağí	Ghost	Spirit	Given to body at birth, escorted beyond Milky Way by *šičuŋ* at death

šičuŋ (guardian/potentiality) and the *ní/niyá* (ghost/life) return to the sacred, mysterious powers (*Wakȟáŋ Tȟáŋka*) to await the entry into a new body.[18] Thus, we have a form of reincarnation—since the *šičuŋ* (guardian/potentiality) will eventually enter a new body—while at the same time, there is an aspect of the self/soul (*nağí*: spirit/ghost) that does not reincarnate but instead passes beyond the Milky Way.[19] See Table 6.2 for the different translations of each type or aspect of "soul" in Powers and DeMallie.

Some of this complexity is also registered by Vine Deloria, Jr., albeit in a generalized way. Deloria maintains that for American Indians there is no such thing as salvation *qua* escape from this planet; rather, "Indians see themselves returning to nature, their bodies becoming the dust of Mother Earth, and their souls journeying to another place across the Milky Way or sometimes being reborn in a new generation of the tribe."[20] For Deloria, death is simply a transition to a wider life; thus, there is no fear of death in American Indian traditional ways.[21]

V. Yorùbá Philosophy of Religon

As with South Asian, East Asian, and Lakȟóta philosophy of religion, so too with Yorùbá philosophy of religion—there is not only a diversity of views about death but also an underlying theme of reincarnation after death.

In the case of the tradition of Ifá divination, the life-breath or soul (*èmí*) is said to go before Olódùmarè and receive judgment for its deeds on earth. In some accounts this involves the relaying of reports about these deeds through seven different heavens (*ọrun*), in the last of which resides Olódùmarè, who delivers the final judgment.[22] Regardless, good souls then reincarnate again into human bodies, whereas bad souls are either chained in *ọrun*, never to be reborn again, or reborn into less fortunate human or animal life-forms. In some cases, apparently as influenced by Islam, bad souls are said to pass over into a "bad heaven," a "heaven of potsherds" (*ọrun-apadi*), where they reside forever.[23]

Given that Olódùmarè judges all upon death, it would seem that Olódùmarè determines (at least partially) the subsequent life into which each "good soul" is reborn. It is curious, therefore, that the *èmí* appears to choose a new *orí* and therefore a new destiny before each new life on earth. For Yorùbá philosopher of religion Moses Makinde, this ambiguity suggests that Olódùmarè's determination of "what a soul becomes after life is not absolute, for what a soul becomes in life still depends on his choice of *orí*."[24] Moreover, as you will remember from last chapter, a person not only must actualize the potentialities of her *orí* through individual effort (*ẹsẹ̀*) but also can make sacrifices and offerings to a bad *orí* to change it. Thus, there is a measure of "freedom" that the individual has with regard to her destiny and Olódùmarè's judgment.

One reason for the diversity and ambiguity of views about death and rebirth in the *Ifá* corpus is that they were likely superimposed on an older substratum of beliefs and practices about death and rebirth. As with many other sub-Saharan African religious traditions, these beliefs and practices centrally concern the ancestors. For the Yorùbá, in cases of natural and timely death,[25] the deceased travels from the realm of the living (*ayé*) to the realm of the *Òrìṣà* (*ọrun*), reuniting with ancestors and becoming an ancestor themselves. Although all ancestors eventually reincarnate into new lives on earth, they first enjoy an extended period in "heaven" (*ọrun*), from which they continue to interact with descendants on earth. According to one Yorùbá proverb, therefore, "the human stay in heaven is much longer than the stay on earth."[26] As anthropologist Benjamin C. Ray concludes about Yorùbá views of death, "human life is a fleeting visit to a foreign land, an impersonal place of potential conflict, in contrast to the homelike comfort of heaven, where we return to dwell with our family relations, the ancestors."[27]

Not only are these views held; they are also enacted, especially in the annual festival of *egúngún*, at which recently deceased, family heads are represented by masked *egúngún* dancers.[28] By possessing these dancers, ancestors can revisit the earth, communicate with their descendants, and listen to their requests. According to Ray, the *egúngún* festival therefore demonstrates that "what is of importance is not the afterlife itself but the way in which the dead continue to be involved in this life among the living."[29]

Here, there is little speculation about "last things," "for there are no last things towards which human life is headed; there is no culminating end to individual lives or to human history in general."[30]

VI. Mediterranean/Abrahamic Philosophy of Religon

We might assume that answers to the question of what happens to us after we die in Jewish, Christian, and Muslim philosophies of religion are simple and unequivocal: heaven (or hell). But as you recall from Chapter 4, there is a good bit of difference and disagreement in these traditions with respect to this question.

One set of differences concerns the testimony of the Bible.[31] The earliest dated references to death and the afterlife in the Hebrew Bible consign all the dead (both righteous and wicked) to the shadowy underworld of Sheol, where they exist as a "shade," never to escape, forever cut off from YHWH and the living.[32] Sheol therefore constituted part of the lower tier of the biblical "three-tiered cosmos" (which we will look at further in Chapter 9): Sheol and the waters below, on which float a disk-shaped earth, over which spans a heavenly dome, waters above, and the throne room of YHWH.

In the latter half of the first millennium BCE, apparently as influenced by Persian religion during and after the Babylonian Captivity (586–539 BCE), the righteous dead began to be thought of as entering Paradise (Hb. *pardēs*, literally "garden") rather than Sheol. Even later, perhaps in conjunction with the persecution of the Seleucid ruler Antiochus IV (r. 175–164 BCE), biblical texts started referring to a resurrection of the dead at judgment day (after which good bodies/selves go to Pardēs and bad bodies/selves go to Sheol). By the first century of the Common Era, there was bitter disagreement between two Jewish sects about whether the resurrection of the dead was biblical or extra-biblical, with Pharisees claiming the former, Sadducees, the latter.

Insofar as Jesus was more aligned with the Pharisees than the Sadducees, he, too, taught the resurrection of the dead, with Pardēs either as an intermediate state between death and judgment or as a final state for the righteous, and Gehenna as a pit of fire in which the wicked are burned like trash. (Gehenna was an actual ravine outside of Jerusalem used for trash.) After Jesus' death, the Apostle Paul later taught that it was Jesus' resurrection

Figure 6 Resurrection of the Dead. Luca Signorelli, "Resurrection of the Flesh," *c.* 1500, Chapel of San Brizio (Duomo di Orvieto), Public domain, Wikimedia Commons.

from the dead that made possible human resurrection from the dead. For Paul, everyone who believes in the power of Jesus' resurrection and accepts the gift of salvation from death will rise with Jesus Christ in a body that is like his "glorious" body (Philippians 3:21). (See Figure 6.) However, given the conviction of early, first-century Christians (like Paul) that Jesus' return was imminent, not much attention was devoted to the details of this resurrection and what came afterwards.

At about the same time, the Greek philosophical notion of an immortal soul (*pyschē*) was beginning to influence Jewish and Christian thought. This notion of soul dates at least as far back as the writings of Plato (427–347 BCE), which contain a variety of relevant philosophical and mythological accounts. Most important here is Plato's early dialogue *Phaedo*, which offers several different proofs for the immortality of the soul, the most influential of which can be formalized as follows:

- P1: Knowledge about that which is invisible and unchanging can only be attained by a knower that is invisible and unchanging
- P2: The Forms (e.g., absolute justice, absolute equality) are invisible and unchanging

- P3: The Forms are known by the soul
- C1: The soul is invisible and unchanging
- P4: Only things that are visible and change are composite (made of parts)
- P5: The soul is invisible and unchanging (from C1)
- C2: The soul is a non-composite unity
- P6: Only things that are composite are subject to dissipation and dissolution
- P7: The soul is a non-composite unity (from C2)
- C3: The soul will never dissipate or dissolve (and therefore is immortal).[33]

Of course, not every ancient Greek philosopher thought the same. Plato's own student Aristotle (384–322 BCE) held that since the soul was simply the principle of life in that which lives (which for Aristotle included animals and plants), then things that no longer lived no longer had souls. Epicurus (341–270 BCE), the founder of the Hellenistic school of Epicurean philosophy, went further in arguing that it was not only impossible to survive death (since all things are only atoms) but also irrational to fear death (since we are not conscious of anything after death). Nevertheless, it was Plato's views on the soul that most influenced the late-ancient and early-medieval philosophies of religion of Jews, Christians, and Muslims.

The earliest notable example is Philo of Alexandria (*c.* 25 BCE–*c.* 50 CE), a Jewish philosopher who held that rational and righteous souls are liberated from their bodily prison at death, after which they return to and become one with YHWH. Later, as the notion of the resurrection of dead became established in all Abrahamic theologies, medieval Jewish philosophers like Saadia ben Yosef Gaon (882–942) taught that the soul is separated from the body at death, later to be rejoined to the resurrected body at the final judgment. Even later, as Aristotle's philosophy began to eclipse Plato's, the most renown medieval Jewish philosopher, Moses ben Maimon (Latinized as Maimonides, 1135–1204), maintained that those who acquire intelligence in this life become part of the "active divine intelligence" after death, whereas the souls of the ignorant and wicked simply dissipate with their bodies. In response to criticism that he had neglected biblical teaching about the resurrection of the dead, Maimonides later admitted an additional bodily resurrection of dead, which would occur with the coming of the Messiah. However, he specified that these resurrection bodies would themselves eventually die, with only their souls going on to eternal life.

In the case of Christianity, one of the first notable philosophies of the afterlife, that of the early Church-Father Origen of Alexander (184–253), held that all souls are eventually saved since the love of God ultimately cannot be resisted. It is difficult to know exactly what Origen wrote, for he was posthumously convicted of heresy and most of his writings were destroyed (allegedly for teaching the preexistence and transmigration of souls). It is likely, however, that Origen held a doctrine of *apokatastasis* (Gk.), the eventual restoration of all souls (even the devil's) to the Christian-Trinitarian God. Origen was certainly not alone among early Christians in favoring a Platonic-soul view of the afterlife. Moreover, his ideas were extremely influential on later Christian theologians, especially those who would play a key role in the development of orthodox Trinitarian doctrine at the first Ecumenical Council, most notably the Cappadocian Father Gregory of Nyssa (d. 386), who also held a doctrine of *apokatastasis*.

Plenty of other Church Fathers, however, believed in the resurrection of the body. For the Greek bishop Iraneus (130–202), the Christian-Trinitarian God has the power to reconstitute what was already made (i.e., resurrect the body) just as this God had the power to create bodies in the first place. And for Ignatius of Antioch (d. early second century) and Tertullian of Carthage (155–240) resurrection was of the entire fleshly body, not just some spiritualized version of it. Augustine (354–430) later reconciled the biblical resurrection of the body with the Greek immortality of the soul, teaching that the soul departed from the body at death and entered an intermediary state of peace or misery until the Last Judgment, at which time an incorruptible "spiritual body" (rather than a flesh body) was resurrected, which then went on to eternal reward or punishment. Moreover, it was during Augustine's life that resurrection of the dead was officially enshrined in Christian doctrine at the very end of the Nicene-Constantinople Creed (381): "We look forward to the resurrection of the dead, and to life in the world to come. Amen." Nevertheless, Plato's immortal soul has continued to "elbow out" the Bible's resurrected body over the long history of Christianity, especially during and after the European Enlightenment.

We end with Islamic philosophy of religion, where again we see the most vigorous debate about these matters. Unlike the Bible, the Qur᾽ān is fairly unambiguous about what happens after death—the soul leaves the body at death, rejoining it on Judgment Day when the body is resurrected, after which the righteous go to paradise and the wicked go to hell. Nevertheless, two issues were left unaddressed: Is the resurrected body the same body or a new body? What happens to the soul in between death and Judgment Day? Although these issues were to exercise Islamic theology (Ar. *kalām*), Islamic philosophy (*falsafa*) was more concerned with reconciling the Qurʾān with Greek philosophy. In the case of Islamic philosophers al-Fārābī (*c.* 872–950) and ibn Sīnā (980–1037), that reconciliation occurred with respect to (Neo) Platonic philosophy, which understood all of reality to be an eternal, ongoing process of emanation from a first principle or God. For al-Fārābī, human souls that achieve abstract conceptual thought in this lifetime attain an immaterial status and therefore immortality in the form of reunion with the divine, whereas the majority of souls never attain an immaterial status and therefore cease to exist after death. By contrast, ibn Sīnā maintained that all souls were immortal but that different types of souls had different ends: on the one hand, virtuous-rational souls that live a rational life and control their lower passions, as well as virtuous-non-rational souls that live in accordance with the divine law, achieve the eternal bliss of contemplating the celestial beings and Allah; on the other hand, non-virtuous, non-rational souls are condemned to eternal torment.

For the orthodox (Ashʿarite) theologian, jurist, and Sufi al-Ghazālī (1058–1111), both philosophers were heretical for neglecting the Quranic notion of the resurrection of the body. Al-Ghazālī's *Incoherence of the Philosophers* (*Tahāfut al-Falāsifa*) identified twenty issues of philosophical innovation that were contrary to Quranic teaching and Islamic law, three of which were grounds for declaring philosophers like al-Fārābī and ibn Sīnā to be infidels (Ar. *takfīr*): (1) holding the world to be eternal rather than created (which we will look at in Chapter 10); (2) maintaining that Allah knows universals but not particulars (which will we look at in Chapter 12); and (3) denying the resurrection of the dead (i.e., that the souls of humans will return to their bodies at the Last Judgment). It was not that al-Ghazālī disputed the immortality of the soul; his only disagreement with "the philosophers" on this point was that, whereas they claimed it could be known by reason, he insisted that it could only be known by revelation. Rather, what al-Ghazālī vehemently objected to was the philosophers' denial of "the revivification of bodies," "physical pains and pleasures in hell and paradise," and "the existence of paradise and hell as described in the Qurʾān."[34]

Not less than 100 years later, the Islamic philosopher, jurist, and physician ibn Rushd (1126–98) penned his *Incoherence of the Incoherence* (*Tahāfut al-Tahāfut*) to defend "the philosophers" against al-Ghazālī's attacks, especially the three grounds on which al-Ghazālī proclaimed them infidels. With respect to the resurrection of the body, ibn Rushd protested that the philosophers in fact did not deny it but rather understood it to be "spiritual" in the sense that human souls are given a new, celestial body. What arises from the dead, wrote ibn Rushd, is not the original bodies of the deceased, "for that which has perished does not return individually and a thing can only return as an image of that which has perished, not as a being identical with what has perished."[35]

In short, there is disagreement in Abrahamic philosophy of religion regarding whether postmortem existence is solely that of an immortal soul or also of a resurrected body. To complicate the situation more, all three of the Abrahamic traditions contain mystical sub-traditions, some of which understand the final state of the human as mystical union with an ultimate reality beyond personhood. Recall, for example, the Sufi notions of *fanā*ʾ (annihilation) and *baqā*ʾ (subsistence), which characterize not only the mystical experience in this life but also the state of the "self" after death. In this state, the "self" is annihilated, no longer existing as an individuated being, instead subsisting solely in and as Allah. Similar ideas exist in Jewish and Christian mysticism as well. We will encounter some in future chapters.

VII. European/Academic Philosophy of Religon

Academic philosophy of the afterlife largely revolves around the question of whether souls exist.[36] Those who respond affirmatively typically defend "substance dualism," which posits that human beings are composed of two substances—body and soul. Arguments for substance dualism commonly serve as arguments for immortality, at least insofar as the soul is assumed or demonstrated to be an immaterial substance that is not subject to decomposition.

As you know from Chapter 4, arguments for substance dualism stretch back at least as far as René Descartes (1596–1650). There, you were introduced to two thought experiments that Descartes offered with respect to the existence of the soul/mind. Imagine that you exist but your body does not—insofar as you can imagine such a scenario, the soul/mind must be a separate substance from the body/brain. Now imagine that your soul/mind does not exist—insofar as you try to imagine this, some *thing*, a soul/mind, must be doing this imagining, which must therefore exist. In sum, although it is possible to doubt the existence of the body, it is impossible to doubt the existence of the soul/mind. To put it in terms of the renowned Cartesian proof: I think, therefore I am.

But what kind of soul/mind is this, and how can we know that it is immortal? Here Descartes appeals to what is later known as the "Principle of the Identity of Indiscernibles." Two things can be considered identical, if and only if, they exhaustively share the same attributes. Are the brain/body and mind/soul the same "thing"? According to Descartes, the body is divisible into parts, extended in space, and possesses physical properties, whereas the mind/soul is "simply indivisible," "united to the whole body," without extension in space, and without physical properties. Thus, Descartes concludes not only that the body/brain and mind/soul must be different substances but that the soul must be immortal since it is indivisible (thereby drawing on the classic Platonic argument above).

As you also know from Chapter 4, this view of substance eventually came under criticism by empiricists like David Hume (1711–76), who held that humans never experience substances *per se* but rather only the properties of would-be substances. This is as true for our experiences of external objects as it is for our experiences of ourselves. Neither do I experience the substance of the cup in front of me (but rather only its properties), nor do I experience the substance of my self (but rather only my sensations, perceptions, thoughts, feelings, and so forth). My self is therefore nothing but a "heap of impressions," especially as these impressions are "bundled together" in a way that provides a continuing sense of identity over time. The fact that there is bundling—or thinking, doubting, or imagining, to use the mental operations deployed by Descartes—does not entail that there is a bundler, especially not as a self-substance, let alone an immortal soul-substance.

A third European Enlightenment approach was eventually offered by Immanuel Kant (1724–1804). On the one hand, Kant argued that the immortality of a substance-self cannot be proved: even if the soul could be demonstrated to be non-composite (per the Platonic proof above), that would not entail the soul is immortal since it is conceptually possible for non-composite things eventually to cease to exist (e.g., by slowly fading away). On the other hand, however, Kant maintained that an immortal soul must be postulated by practical reason: otherwise, we would have no reason to hope that our freely chosen and enacted deeds would eventually be rewarded by a God in the afterlife in proportion to their virtue.

By and large, these three Enlightenment positions not only remain in play today but also largely dominate the field. To be sure, substance dualism has fallen on hard times, as it becomes less and less possible and plausible to show how a non-physical soul/mind exists within and interacts with a physical body/brain. Not only are substance dualists therefore faced with the "interaction problem" (see Chapter 4); they also must now confront a growing body of neuroscientific research that correlates mental/psychological states to brain/physical states, thereby suggesting that the former is dependent on the latter and that a mind/soul therefore cannot exist without a body/brain.

Critics of substance dualism have also countered the three Cartesian arguments above. First, psychological imagination is not necessarily a good guide to what is logically possible; indeed, it is possible to imagine illogical scenarios such as a barber who shaves only people who do not shave themselves and therefore ceases to be a barber if he shaves himself (= "Barber Fallacy"). Moreover, it is debatable whether one can in fact imagine oneself existing without a body, for how then, e.g., would we perceive? Second, even if we were able to doubt the existence of the body but not the existence of the mind this would not entail that the mind and the body are different substances, the former of which is immaterial and immortal. Third, there are cases where two things are identical even though not everything that can be predicated of one thing can be predicated of the other; for example, if a masked man robs a bank, a witness would identify the robber as a masked man, though not as her father, even if it were her father who robbed the bank (= "Masked Man Fallacy").

Of course, contemporary substance dualists are not without their own counter-arguments. In the case of the "interaction problem," Christian philosophers such as Richard Swinburne (b. 1934) charge that even if we cannot fully explain how body and soul interact that does not entail that such interaction does not take place at all. For Swinburne, one of the "most obvious phenomena of human experience" is that bodily events cause brain events, which in turn cause perceptions, feelings, thoughts, and so forth. If we cannot explain how this occurs, that does not mean that they do not occur; is just means that "human beings are not omniscient, and cannot understand everything."[37] Substance dualists also maintain that the correlation of brain states and mental states simply shows how the brain is an "instrument" of the soul (rather than that the soul/mind is dependent on the brain/body), with some using the example of a violin that serves as an instrument for a violinist. That there is a correlation between the two does not entail that the violin can be reduced to the violinist, nor that damage to the violin entails damage to the violinist or her talent.

Moral and pragmatic arguments, both for and against the need to posit an immortal soul or compensatory afterlife, also continue down to the present, though usually not in Kantian form. Peter Singer (b. 1946), for example, has argued that the merit and worth of our good acts does not depend on the future, especially our immortality.[38] Singer offers the example of humanitarians who help a rural village in a developing country to free itself of debt and become self-sufficient with respect to food. If their efforts are successful and the villagers are heathier, happier, better educated, and economically secure, then we are not inclined to say that their efforts were wasted or their lives were meaningless, even though the fruits of their efforts and the lives of the villagers might not last a long time and will not last forever.

Christian philosophers William Hasker (b. 1935) and Charles Taliaferro (b. 1952), however, point out that although there is "some wisdom" in Singer's position, we should nevertheless wonder whether the humanitarians truly care about their efforts and the villagers' lives if it does not matter to them whether both last a long time, if not forever. Just imagine that upon leaving the village after completing their work, the humanitarians announce:

> No matter what happens, no matter whether you all are struck by a massive plague in an hour and all die a horrible death or whether a thousand years from now your society will be condemned as deserving of nothing but contempt, what we have done today is our only concern and the value of our act is not diminished regardless of what awaits you![39]

This would be bizarre, claim Hasker and Taliaferro. And if we would wish for the efforts of the humanitarians and lives of the villagers to last for a long time, would we not also wish for the lives of the villagers to last forever in a blessed afterlife?

And so goes the merry-go-round of arguments about the soul.

At this point you might protest—especially since many of the contemporary philosophers who argue for the existence of an immortal soul are Christians—that the Abrahamic religions proclaim the resurrection of the body, not the immortality of the soul. What philosophical sense can we make of this religious idea—that afterlife existence requires a resurrected body? For the most part, this question has turned on that of personal identity—how can a resurrected body/person be identical with the body/person who has died? Three types of answers are possible. First, if it is the case that humans are immortal souls that acquire a new body after death, then there would seem to be no problem for personal identity, though all the above difficulties for the immortal soul would remain. Second, if it is the case that humans simply are their bodies, which resurrect as such after death, then again there would seem to be no problem for personal identity, though these bodies would be in the exact same condition as at the time of death. (Also consider that resurrection would not be possible in cases of cremation, and that it would be necessary to explain why deceased bodies apparently remain in the ground.) The third solution sides both with the first, maintaining that resurrected bodies are new spiritual bodies, and with the second, jettisoning the soul as philosophically and scientifically implausible. What then guarantees continuity of identity between the body/brain that dies and the new resurrected body/brain? One solution, the so-called "re-creation theory" of John Hick (1922–2012), proposes that a God recreates a body/brain with the exact same features as that which died. But which atomic and cellular features exactly from which of countless varieties over a lifetime? And what guarantees that this is the same you and not just a replica? After all, if some God could re-create one such body/brain, then this God could re-create numerous such body/brains. What would make any of them "you" over against the others?

Although most contemporary analytic philosophy of religion limits itself to variations of these two afterlife possibilities—immortality of the soul, resurrection of the body—there is at least one other significant "Western" philosophical position on immortality to consider: the view of some "process" philosophers or theologians that the self lives on as part of a God. Given that the contemporary positions of resurrection of the body and immortality of the soul are products of Abrahamic theology, especially as influenced by Greek and European philosophy, we could think of this process philosophical view of immortality (within/as a God) as the inheritor of the mystical traditions of the Abrahamic religions. Regardless, process philosophy has a rather unique view of who or what God is, one that is commonly characterized as panentheistic ("all-in-God"), with this God fully immanent within, though not simply reduced to, the cosmos (as in pantheism), "luring" each actual event of the cosmos into higher degrees of order while also "prehending" the totality of all such "occasions" to preserve the past. Since this God not only prehends (grasps hold of, holds on to) everything that occurs in the cosmos but also just is everything that occurs in the cosmos, our experiences live on in this God even after we die. Or so argued Charles Hartshorne (1897–2000), one of the most famous process philosophers: immortality is not *subjective*, that of my own individual consciousness, but *objective*, that of the consciousness of this God, which retains everything that ever has been.

As with previous chapters, we can also ask about the relevance of "science," which in this case includes a growing body of evidence related to "cases of the reincarnation type" (CORT) and "near death experience" (NDE).[40] With regard to CORT, Ian Stevenson has collected thousands of cases of past-life memories, in which he sees "four universal features": (1) recollection of a former life at an early age (2–4 years of age); (2) refraining from speaking about a former life at an older age (5–7 years of age); (3) high incidence of violent death in a former life; and (4) frequent mention of the mode of death. There are also ample reports of NDEs,[41] which also display "near-universal features," such as the experience of leaving one's body, travelling through a tunnel toward intense light, and meeting "beings of light" (which are sometimes deceased relatives or friend). In the case of NDEs, however, there are also notable cultural differences, for example a one-life model in the "West" versus a reincarnation model elsewhere, the absence of a "life review" for hunter-gatherer societies, and occasionally "hellish" NDEs in the case of "damnation theologies." For some scholars, these CORTs and NDEs constitute evidence of an afterlife; for others, however, they can be explained through ordinary natural processes (e.g., anoxia, the lack of oxygen). In short, the jury is still out.

VIII. Putting it All Together

Yet again, we have a diversity of responses to our leading question—in this case, do humans survive death and if so how?

Although most South Asian philosophies of religion maintain that humans are reborn after death, they differ considerably about what happens when humans finally win liberation from rebirth, with some holding that a self/soul returns to and becomes one with some ultimate reality; others, that the self/soul attains a state of isolated bliss and knowledge; still others, that the self/soul ascends to a heavenly realm; and yet more others, that the self/soul loses individuated identity yet enjoys ultimate bliss. In the case of East Asian philosophy of religion, there are examples of the self/soul returning to nature in some way, or entering an underworld of tribulation or a heaven of bliss, or ultimately attaining *parinirvāṇa*. In Abrahamic philosophy of religion, we have examples of resurrection of the body, immortality of the soul, and return to a transpersonal, mystical God. Lakȟóta and Yorùbá traditions add to this complexity with cases of apparently dual ends, in which parts of the self/soul reincarnate and other parts reunite with dead ancestors.

With the European Enlightenment, however, the range of philosophically debated positions largely winnows to just one: whether there is a soul that is separate from the body and therefore immortal. And with the increased success of the neurosciences, the plausibility of this soul has steadily decreased. Once again, therefore, we are faced not only with the question of what the global-critical philosopher of religion will "do" with the findings of science but also how these findings affect those philosophies of religion that are not of the "West." (For example, insofar as some of the "souls" of South Asian philosophies do not interact with bodies and minds, there would appear not to be the "interaction problem" that plagues the "Western" notion of mind/soul.) Or maybe you think that science is of no relevance whatsoever to philosophies of the afterlife, and that if evaluation of these philosophies occurs at all, it must employ criteria of external coherence and pragmatic usefulness rather than of empirical adequacy. Should philosophies of the afterlife be evaluated based on whether they provide meaning and comfort to the individual?

It is with respect to the criterion of pragmatic usefulness that we are well advised to pay attention to two final critical perspectives on philosophies of the afterlife, one a more recent feminist critique, the other a classic Marxist critique. The recent feminist critique is that of Grace Jantzen (1948–2006), who accused Western culture of "necrophilia," an obsession with death and violence, masculine concerns that justify men's control over mortality and female bodies; Jantzen therefore argued that this "masculine symbolic" needed to be displaced by a "feminist imaginary" that instead championed natality and flourishing.[42] The classic Marxist critique, by contrast, indicted religious philosophies of the afterlife as "the opiate of the masses," ideologies of control that promise happiness and justice in the afterlife for those who obey the state in this life, especially those who suffer unhappiness and injustice.[43] Might it then be the case that philosophies of the afterlife are *not* pragmatically useful, especially if we understand pragmatic usefulness not to be limited to the selfish needs of the individual but rather to extend to societies more widely? Do philosophies of the afterlife distract from this-worldly issues, from natality and flourishing, from gender and racial justice, from economic and political oppression? Might Confucius have been right in asking whether we should concern ourselves with death if we do not yet understand life?

Questions for Discussion

1 Do humans survive death, and if so, how? Describe, compare, and evaluate some of the philosophies of religion with respect to these questions.
2 Are the natural sciences of relevance in answering the question of whether humans survive death? Even for non-Western philosophies of religion? Show why or why not.
3 To what extent do some of these conceptions of the self continue to challenge the modern Western notion that the self is individual and substantial?
4 Should we philosophize about death if we do not yet understand life (per Confucius)? Are there issues of justice at stake here?

Primary and Scholarly Sources

East Asia

Platform Sūtra of the Sixth Patriarch, §35. In *Philosophical Classics, Volume VI: Asian Philosophy*, eds. Forrest E. Baird and Raeburne S. Heimbeck, 488–9. Upper Saddle River, NJ: Pearson Prentice Hall, 2006.

Xúnzǐ, chapter 19. In *Xunzi: The Complete Text*. Trans. Eric L. Hutton, 206–17. Princeton, NJ: Princeton University Press, 2014.

Zhuāngzǐ, chapters 18.2 and 6.5. In *Wandering on the Way: Early Taoist Tales and Parables of Chuang Tzu*, trans. Victor H. Mair, 168–9, 57–9. New York: Bantam Books, 1994.

European/Academic

Descartes, René. *Meditations on First Philosophy*, Meditation 6. Trans. Donald A. Cross, 3rd ed., 93–105. Indianapolis, IN: Hackett Publishing, 1993.

Hasker, William and Charles Taliaferro, "Afterlife." In *The Stanford Encyclopedia of Philosophy*, ed. Edward N. Zalta, Spring 2019 ed. Available online: https://plato.stanford.edu/archives/spr2019/entries/afterlife/ (March 11, 2022).

Kant, Immanuel. *Critique of Practical Reason*, Book II, Chapter II, Section IV. In *The Cambridge Edition of the Works of Immanuel Kant: Practical Philosophy*, trans May J. Gregor, 238–9. New York: Cambridge University Press, 1996.

Kripal, Jeffrey. *Comparing Religions*, 288–94. New York: Wiley-Blackwell, 2014.
Jantzen, Grace M. *Becoming Divine: Towards a Feminist Philosophy of Religion*, 137–41. Bloomington, IN: Indiana University Press, 1999.
Marx, Karl. "Contribution to the Critique of Hegel's Philosophy of Right." In *The Marx-Engels Reader*, 2nd ed., ed. Robert C. Tucker, 16–25. New York: W. W Norton & Co., 1972.

Lakȟóta

DeMallie, Raymond J. "Lakota Beliefs and Rituals in the Nineteenth Century." In *Sioux Indian Religion*, eds. Raymond J. DeMallie and Douglas R. Parks, 29–30. Norman, OK: University of Oklahoma Press, 1987.
Powers, William K. *Sacred Language: The Nature of Supernatural Discourse in Lakota)*, 134–6. Norman, OK: University of Oklahoma Press, 1986.

Mediterranean/Abrahamic

al-Ghazālī. *Incoherence of the Philosophers (Tahāfut al-Falāsifa)*, "Problem XX." Trans. Sabih Ahmad Kamali, 229–35. Lahore: Pakistan Philosophical Congress, 1963.
Ibn Rushd, "About the Natural Sciences: The Fourth Discussion." In *Averroes' Tahafut al-Tahafut (The Incoherence of the Incoherence)*, reprint ed., vol. 1, trans. Simon Van Den Bergh, 359–64. London: E. J. W. Gibb Memorial Trust, 2008.
Plato. *Phaedo*, 77e–80c. In *Five Dialogues: Euthyphro, Apology, Crito, Meno, Phaedo*, 2nd ed., trans. G. M. A. Grube, ed. John M. Cooper, 116–19. Indianapolis, IN: Hackett Publishing, 2002.

South Asia

"Itivuttaka," §44. In *Buddhist Texts through the Ages*, trans. Edward Conze, 96–7. Rockport, MA: Oneworld Publications, 1995.
Madhva. *Brahma Sūtra Bhāṣya*, II.i.14. In *A Sourcebook in Indian Philosophy*, eds. Sarvepalli Radhakrishnan and Charles A. Moore, 562. Princeton, NJ: Princeton University Press, 1957.
Rāmānuja. *Brahma Sūtra Bhāṣya*, I.i.1. In *A Sourcebook in Indian Philosophy*, eds. Sarvepalli Radhakrishnan and Charles A. Moore, 547–8. Princeton, NJ: Princeton University Press, 1957.
Śaṅkara. *Brahma Sūtra Bhāṣya*, I.iv.21–2. In *A Sourcebook in Indian Philosophy*, eds. Sarvepalli Radhakrishnan and Charles A. Moore, 517–22. Princeton, NJ: Princeton University Press, 1957.

Yorùbá

Makinde, Moses. "Immortality of the Soul and the Yoruba Theory of the Seven Heavens (Ọ̀run Méje)." In *African Philosophy: The Demise of a Controversy*, chapter 7. Ile-Ife: Obafemi Awolowo University Press, 2007.

Ray, Benjamin C. *African Religions: Symbol, Ritual, and Community*, 2nd ed., 102–4. Upper Saddle River, NJ: Pearson, 1999.

7

How Do I Get There?

Learning Objectives

- Understand some of the important and interesting ways in which religious thinkers, texts, and traditions conceptualize religious paths.
- Compare religious paths concerning whether they stress this-worldly or post-mortem destinations, bodily practice or mental belief, self-help or other-help.
- Compare and evaluate philosophies of religion with respect to the question, which path, if any, leads to its destination?

I. Introduction

In Chapter 7, we turn to the paths by which the self reaches its destination. As you know from the last chapter, this-worldly paths are sometimes thought to lead to post-mortem destinations: salvation in Christianity can be viewed as a means of getting into heaven upon death, enlightenment in Buddhism, as a way of achieving final release from rebirth upon death. However, as you also know from last chapter, this is not always the case: for some philosophies of religion, postmortem destinations are not important, knowable, or existent. Even in the cases of Christianity and Buddhism, respectively, salvation might be viewed as living in right relationship with God rather than going to heaven after death, enlightenment, as "waking up" to the way things really are here and now rather than escaping from the wheel of rebirth. In sum, the religious paths that people follow in life are not always, perhaps not even usually, for the sake of reaching religious destinations after life; rather, they are for the sake of religious ends in life.

This is certainly one topic on which we could focus in this chapter—whether religious paths are for this-worldly or post-mortem destinations. Another would be to explore whether religious paths primarily involve the body or the mind. Yet another is to compare "other-help" or "cat-hold" paths in which humans rely on the help of another (usually a God or Gods) and "self-help" or "monkey-hold" paths in which humans do for themselves.[1] Still another could examine whether observance of moral rules and religious duties is an exhaustive component of religious paths or whether such paths sometimes also require going "beyond good and evil."

Although all these foci will be tangentially involved in this chapter and the last one—morality and religion—will be centrally involved in the next chapter, our primary focus here is a question that has been more central to the philosophy of religion over the last fifty years or so: Which path, if any, leads to its destination? One could put this question in terms of truth: Which religion, if any, is true? Or in terms of efficacy: Which religion, if any, is an effective means of bringing about its desired end? Either way, this question has come to be known in philosophy of religion as the "problem of religious pluralism": given that there are so many different religious traditions with so many different paths and destinations, must it be the case that only one, at best, can be true or effective? As we will see in the final section of this chapter, there is more to this question than "meets the eye," at least from the perspective of global-critical philosophy of religion. First, though, let us explore some religious paths.

II. Lakȟóta Philosophy of Religion

As we learned in Chapter 5, it is by means of the sacred pipe (*čhaŋnúŋpa wakȟáŋ*) and its rituals that the Lakȟóta order society and establish relationship with the sacred, mysterious powers (*Wakȟáŋ Tȟáŋka*). This is how the Lakȟóta reach their destination (or one of their destinations, anyway)—a life of sacred relationality, not some postmortem state.

According to Lakȟóta myth, the pipe and its rituals were first given to the Lakȟóta by White Buffalo Calf Woman, who is one of the *Wakȟáŋ Tȟáŋka* (as Wóȟpe). As the story goes, two men were out hunting one day, when White Buffalo Calf Woman appeared on the horizon and began walking toward them. One of the men had lascivious thoughts toward White Buffalo Calf Woman and was therefore reduced to bones, while the other man was told to return to the tribe and prepare for her arrival. Soon afterwards, White

Buffalo Calf Woman appeared in the camp and presented the sacred pipe to chief Standing Hollow Horn, pronouncing:

> Behold this and always love it! It is *lela wakan* [very sacred], and you must treat is as such. No impure man should ever be allowed to see it, for within this bundle there is a sacred pipe. With this you will, during the winters to come, send your voices to *Wakan-Tanka*, your Father and Grandfather.[2]

White Buffalo Calf Woman preceded to teach the first of the sacred rituals, indicating that the other rituals would be revealed in time (Figure 7). Then, she departed, transforming first into a red and brown buffalo, then into a white buffalo, and finally into a black buffalo.

This is by far the most important myth to the Lakȟóta—more so than any of their creation myths[3]—for it tells how the relationship between human beings and *Wakȟáŋ Tȟáŋka* was first established and continues to be enacted through ritual. About it, one anthropologist writes: "This myth narrates what to the Lakȟóta people was the single most important manifestation of the sacred, the one that founded the Lakȟóta world and gave the people their orientation in time and space."[4]

As for the rituals themselves, there are seven, the first of which is the *keeping of the spirit* (*wanáǧi yúhapi*), a rite of keeping and feeding the *náǧi* (ghost or spirit) of the deceased for a period of time (six months or more), after which it is released to travel down the "Spirit Trail" to an afterlife. The second ritual is *making spirit* (*inípi*), now more commonly known as the "sweatlodge," a rite of purification that serves as preparation for other rituals, transitioning participants from the mundane to the sacred, bringing them into a state of harmonious relationality with all things. Third is *crying for a vision* (*haŋbléčeyapi*), otherwise known as the "vision quest," in which a person, often an adolescent male, under the guidance of an elder, often a "holy man" (*wičháša wakȟáŋ*), prays alone in the wilderness for up to four days without food or water for a vision from the spirits; this vision, which must later must be interpreted by the elder, will determine a person's spiritual calling in life. Fourth is the *Sun Dance* (*wiwáŋyaŋg wačhipi*), a ceremony in which men are connected to a pole by a rope that is tied to a skewer or eagle claw that is inserted into their chest, then dance around the pole for four days until they finally break free, offering their pierced flesh to *Wakȟáŋ Tȟáŋka*.[5] The fifth ritual is *making relatives* (*húŋkapi*), the means by which a person is adopted into a new family or a new bond is created between two people who are not related by blood. The sixth ritual, *preparing a girl for womanhood* (*išnáthi awíčhalowaŋpi*), is a coming-of-age ceremony for girls

Figure 7 White Buffalo Calf Woman. Dennis Jarvis, "DSC01043, White Buffalo Calf Woman," August 7, 2018. CC BY-SA 2.0, flickr.com. https://www.flickr.com/photos/22490717@N02/43612608584.

Table 7.1 Seven Sacred Rites of the Lakȟóta

Name	Description
Wanáği yúhapi (keeping of the ghost/spirit)	Rite of mourning
Inípi (making spirit, aka "sweatlodge")	Rite of purification
Haŋbléčeyapi (crying for a vision, aka "vision quest")	Rite of calling (usually for men)
Wiwáŋyaŋg wačhipi (Sun Dance)	Rite of offering
Húŋkapi (making relatives)	Rite of adoption
Išnáthi Awíčhalowaŋpi (preparing a girl for womanhood)	Rite of transition (for women)
Tȟápa Waŋkáyeyapi (throwing the ball)	Rite of symbolic recreation

after their first menstruation. And the seventh and final ritual is a symbolic game called *throwing the ball* (*tȟápa waŋkáyeyapi*) in which a young girl standing in the middle of a field tosses a ball that symbolizes *Wakȟáŋ Tȟáŋka* to the four corners of the field, in each corner of which people attempt to catch the ball, thereby drawing close to the sacred spirits and attaining sacred knowledge.[6] See Table 7.1 for a summary of all seven of these rites.

As you probably already know, participation in these rites is (part of) what it means to be Lakȟóta, at least traditionally. It would not be common for someone who is not Lakȟóta to join in these rites, especially not as a means of attaining some other-worldly ends. In fact, these rites are not undertaken by the Lakȟóta themselves for the sake of reaching some post-mortem destination. Thus, in the case of the Lakȟóta we seem not to have an example of a religious path that can be thought of as true or effective for all exclusively of other such paths.

III. Yorùbá Philosophy of Religion

For Yorùbá religions, Ifá divination is an important means by which practitioners learn not only what their destiny (*àyànmọ́*) is but also how to achieve it, particularly when confronting illness and misfortune or beginning a new venture. Ifá is conducted by a diviner known as a "father of secrets" (*babaláwo*), who is master of a voluminous compendium of sacred scripture known as *Odù Ifá*, which is divided into 256 collections (*odù*), each of which contains a variety of poems about mythical precedents, resolutions, and related sacrifices. Upon consulting a *babaláwo*, the client whispers her issue not to the *babaláwo* but to his divining apparatus and thereby to the *Òrìṣà* of wisdom and destiny—Ọrunmila, who is also known as Ifá. The *babaláwo* then petitions Ọrunmila, establishing a link between Ọrunmila, the client, and the client's *orí*. Next, the *babaláwo* casts sixteen sacred palm nuts or a divining chain to determine which *odù* to consult. The *babaláwo* then reads several poems from the relevant *odù* (all of which are known by memory), from which the client chooses the one most relevant to her issue. Finally, the client and *babaláwo* together determine the next steps for the client to take, most importantly which sacrifice (*ẹbọ*) the client needs to make to which *Òrìṣà*.

This sacrifice, which is made not only to the relevant *Òrìṣà* but also to the client's *orí*, is crucially important to the success of Ifá divination. Only by "feeding" the relevant *Òrìṣà* with the relevant sacrifice (e.g., animal, nut, prayer) will the divination come to pass. In this sense sacrifice is food for the Gods. However, as Kọ́lá Abímbọ́lá writes, the sacrifice has deeper meanings, most notably "a code of communication between the natural and the supernatural realms of the Yorùbá cosmos ... founded on the principle of exchange that in order to bring about positive changes in one's life, s/he—the actor—must give up something."[7] Moreover, sacrifice is not limited to divinatory contexts; devotees traditionally sacrificed to their *Òrìṣà* at home every four days, in a fellowship of devotees every sixteen days, and with the entire community at annual celebrations and other special occasions.[8] Thus, anthropologist J. D. Y. enumerates sacrifice as "one of two principal modes of relationship" that linked humans and *Òrìṣà* in traditional Yorùbá religion.[9]

The other principal mode of relationship between humans and *Òrìṣà* is possession (*gùn*) of a devotee by an *Òrìṣà* in a state of ecstatic trance. It is for this reason, among others, that Yorùbá philosopher Olúfémi Táíwò maintains that questions about which *Òrìṣà* one "worships" make little sense to the Yorùbá.[10] Devotees do not worship *Òrìṣà* as much as they "have," "are," and "make" *Òrìṣà*.[11] By "have," Táíwò means that *Òrìṣà* are inherited by devotees—or, more precisely, *Òrìṣà* inherit their devotees—and that failure to serve them therefore results in dangerous disorder. By "are," Táíwò refers to possession, the "mounting" and "riding" of devotees by *Òrìṣà* during which the devotee "is" the *Òrìṣà* for a brief period of time. "In that state," writes Táíwò, "he or she is a participant in that *mysterium* that defines the religion, and he or she is taken out of the circle of mortal humans, is free from finitude and unshackled from all limits imposed by the human form."[12] Finally, by "make," Táíwò includes the different ways in which devotees relate to *Òrìṣà*: not just through the aforementioned divination, sacrifice, and possession but also through invocation, greeting, song, chant, worship, construction of shrines and icons, observance of taboos, creation of ritual cleanliness, and so forth. Thus, concludes Táíwò, the relationship between humans and *Òrìṣà* is "the core of Yorùbá religious phenomena"; indeed, "it is Yorùbá religion."[13]

Here, again, we seem to have an example of a religious path that is neither for the sake of a post-mortem end nor uniquely true or effective to the exclusion of other religious paths.

IV. South Asian Philosophy of Religion

Our exploration of religious paths in South Asian philosophy of religion has thus far focused primarily on what are called *jñāna yoga*—paths or means of "yoking" (*yoga*) that involve the attainment of knowledge about what is and is not truly real (*jñāna*). Within the traditions of Hindu philosophy that accepted the authority of the *Vedas*, this includes the following six *darśana*-s:

- Nyāya, a school of epistemology that is primarily concerned with "getting the knowledge right," maintaining that upon doing so, the self (*Ātman*) gains release (*mokṣa*) from the cycle of rebirth (*saṃsāra*) and enters a state of conscious-less bliss;
- Vaiśeṣika, a school of (atomistic) metaphysics that looks to "the basic stuff of reality," holding a view of rebirth and release similar to Nyāya (especially after the two merge in the early second millennium);
- Sāṁkhya, a school of (dualistic) metaphysics that posits two fundamental existents, a pure experiencer (*Puruṣa*) and that which it experiences (*prakṛti*), affirming that the former is liberated from rebirth and enjoys an "isolated" (*kaivalya*) state of pure bliss upon realizing that it is not the latter;
- Yoga, a school of practice that adopts the metaphysics of Sāṁkhya, teaching an eight-step path of yogic technique and meditation by which pure consciousness (*Puruṣa*) liberates itself from material nature (*prakṛti*), achieving release from rebirth;
- Mīmāṃsā, a school of scriptural interpretation that focuses on the earlier sections of the *Vedas*, defending the efficacy of Vedic fire rituals for liberation, which consists of a heavenly existence with the many Gods of early Vedic religion;
- Vedānta, a school of scriptural interpretation that instead looks to the final section of the *Vedas*, the *Upaniṣads*, proclaiming that understanding the relationship between the innermost self (*Ātman*) and ultimate reality

> (*Brahman*) brings release from the cycle of rebirth, which in the case of non-dual (*advaita*) Vedānta consists of identity-less, consciousness-less bliss as *Ātman-Brahman*; in the case of qualified non-dual (*viśiṣṭādvaita*) Vedānta, a return to and communion with *Ātman-Brahman* (understood personally as Lord Viṣṇu); and in the case of dual (*dvaita*) Vedānta, a heavenly existence in which distinctions are preserved between different souls and between these souls and *Brahman* (again understood personally as Lord Viṣṇu).

Of course, there are also the two ancient traditions of South Asian philosophy of religion that did not accept the authority of the *Vedas* and that have survived to this day:

- Jainism, which practices a fourteen-stage path involving the "Three Jewels" of deep faith, pure conduct, and right knowledge, at the end of which the soul is isolated (*kevala*) from the body and ascends to the apex of the cosmos where it enjoys perfect knowledge and bliss;
- (Therāvada) Buddhism, which follows the "Noble Eightfold Path," which includes steps pertaining to insight (right view, right intention), ethics (right speech, right action, right livelihood), and meditation (right effort, right mindfulness, right meditation), culminating in *nirvāṇa* in life and release from rebirth (*parinirvāṇa*) after death, after which self-identify disappears.

As even these brief summaries suggest, all these paths require more than just knowledge; for starters, ethical behavior and meditative practice are also usually integral. Nevertheless, these paths came to be categorized as ones of knowledge (*jñāna*) insofar as final release from the cycle of rebirth was incumbent upon attaining "deep knowledge" about how things "really are," especially the "true nature" of the self. Thus, they came to be contrasted with other types of paths, especially ones of action (*karma yoga*) and devotion (*bhakti yoga*).

These three paths were first identified as such in a short, eighteen-chapter, ancient text that has over time become the most popular and famous of all Hindu scriptures: *Bhagavad Gītā*, which translates roughly to "Song of the Lord." Written around the turn of the millennium (200 BCE–200 CE), it is but a sliver of the longest epic poem in the world, the 1.8-million-word *Mahābhārata*, which, according to some Hindus, tells of events that occurred approximately three millennia earlier.

The *Bhagavad Gītā* itself is set on the morning of a great battle between two families of the ruling Kuru clan, the Pāṇḍavas and Kauravas. Arjuna, a prince of the Pāṇḍavas, is distraught as he surveys the battlefield, anticipating the bloodshed that the day will bring. However, Arjuna's charioteer Kṛṣṇa—whom Arjuna does not yet know is actually an incarnation (*avatāra*) of Lord Viṣṇu—tells Arjuna that he must fight, for that is his duty (*dharma*) as a member of the warrior/ruler (*kṣatriya*) caste (*varṇa*).

This is Arjuna's "moral dilemma": whether to obey duty to caste, which requires him to fight, or to heed an arguably universal ethic not to kill. We will return to this dilemma next chapter, where we take up obstacles to religious paths. For now, we turn first to one way in which the *Bhagavad Gītā* resolved this dilemma—by reinventing the concept of *karma* (action)—then we look at the paths of *karma yoga* and *bhakti yoga* more generally.

Prior to the *Bhagavad Gītā*, especially in early portions of the *Vedas*, *karma* had a narrow meaning that pertained to the ritual actions of *brahmin* priests in Vedic fire rituals. By means of correctly performed ritual words and acts, the ritual effected its desired end, usually some material good, though in some cases the creation of an immortal self to survive death. However, in the later *Vedas*, especially some of the *Upaniṣads*, these actions came to be seen as ineffective, resulting only in the creation of *karmic* effect that bound the doer to the wheel or rebirth rather than bringing release from it. Call this the first reinvention of *karma*: from the ritual actions of *brahmin* priests to the moral actions and effects of all people.

With this first reinvention, *karma* became something to be overcome, for insofar as we act, we are create *karmic* "seeds" that must "ripen" (bear effects) at some later date or in some later life, thus requiring us to be reborn. Put succinctly, *karma* binds us to *saṃsāra*. Even if we do only good deeds, we still must be reborn, for all these good deeds will need to produce good *karmic* effects at some future time. What to do?

For some of the writers of some of the *Upaniṣads*, the solution was one of "inaction." Only by denying oneself certain creature comforts (asceticism), removing oneself from certain social processes (renunciation), and stilling oneself in yogic meditation, could one slow and stop the accumulation of *karma*, thereby freeing oneself from the cycle of rebirth. The *Bhagavad Gītā*, however, saw such inaction as impossible:

> He who shirks action does not attain freedom; no one can gain perfection by abstaining from work. Indeed, there is no one who rests for even an instant; every creature is driven to action by his own nature.[14]

Why? The chief reason involves Sāṁkhya metaphysics (which undergirds the *Bhagavad Gītā*), especially its three fundamental "qualities" (*guṇa*-s) that constitute all the experienceable things of reality, the material-mental self included: *sattva* (luminosity, goodness), *rajas* (passion, activity), and *tamas* (ignorance, inertia). Since these *guṇa*-s constitute every material-mental thing, the self included, the self cannot not act. Now what to do?

The solution of the *Bhagavad Gītā* is simple and elegant: act in a way that is without selfish attachment to the "fruits" or "consequences" of one's actions, for in doing so the "real self" (*Ātman*), which does not act, will not accrue *karmic* effects:

> Strive constantly to serve the welfare of the world; by devotion to selfless work one attains the supreme goal of life. Do your work with the welfare of others always in mind. It was by such work that Janaka attained perfection; others, too, have followed this path.[15]

This is the path of *karma yoga*, one of two paths that Kṛṣṇa declared at the beginning of time: "*jnana yoga*, the contemplative path of spiritual wisdom, and *karma yoga*, the active path of selfless service."[16] Thus, the *Bhagavad Gītā* rehabilitates the path of action (*karma*), placing it on equal footing with the path of knowledge (*jñāna*).

However, it is the third path, devotion (*bhakti*), that is most celebrated in the *Bhagavad Gītā*, perhaps because this appears to be its first occurrence as such in a South Asian text. Literally meaning, "attachment" or "participation," *bhakti* is a path of loving devotion to a God or other superhuman being that "yokes" the devotee to the object of devotion. In doing so, the God (etc.) simply cuts the devotee's *karma*.

Although it is not entirely clear whether and how the *Bhagavad Gītā* ranks *bhakti yoga* with respect to *karma yoga* and *jñāna yoga*, there are passages that suggest its superiority. For example, Kṛṣṇa asserts in chapter 12:

> Those who set their hearts on me and worship me with unfailing devotion and faith are more established in yoga [than those who seek the eternal formless Reality].[17]

In fact, though, this path of *bhakti* is not exclusive of those of *karma* and *jñāna*, for in devoting oneself to Kṛṣṇa, one also acts selflessly, devoting the fruits of one's actions to Kṛṣṇa, and attains knowledge, devotionally meditating on entering into Kṛṣṇa:

> But they for whom I am the supreme goal, who do all work renouncing self for me and meditate on me with single-hearted devotion, these I will swiftly rescue from the fragment's cycle of birth and death, for their consciousness has entered into me.[18]

Whatever the case, what is important for us is that the *Bhagavad Gītā* adds two paths, most notably *bhakti*, to the path of *jñāna* (on which we have focused so far in this book). Moreover, the *Bhagavad Gītā* is not alone among early first-millennium South Asian texts that celebrate paths of devotion, as both Jainism and Buddhism, not to mention Hinduism more broadly, increasingly adopt devotional practices during the first millennium (to buddhas and bodhisattvas in the case of Buddhism, and to *tīrthaṅkara*-s in the case of Jainism). Where does this "*bhakti* fever" come from? Although no one knows exactly, one intriguing theory is that it does not come from any of these three ism-ized religions but rather from regional religious practices that had not (yet) been incorporated into them.

Regardless, what is the relevance of this diversity of South Asian paths with respect to our leading question of the chapter: Which path, if any, leads to its destination? Attainment of what knowledge? Devotion to which God? One answer to these questions is simply "all of them." Although there certainly was disagreement and competition at times between different paths of knowledge and devotion, many of them over time came to be regarded simply as "different paths up the same mountain," especially as Indians have come to regard all the religio-philosophies of the Indian subcontinent as part of "Hinduism"—Jainism, Buddhism, and Sikhism included. The question, therefore, does not concern which one is right in general but rather which one is right for you. Moreover, since beings have countless lifetimes to get things right—to cut *karma* and leave *saṃsāra*—there would seem to be no great urgency in any one lifetime.

V. East Asian Philosophy of Religion

Post-mortem goals are not often the primary goals in East Asian philosophy of religion; flourishing and harmony in this life are usually more important. Moreover, over time the Chinese came to see the "three teachings" (*sānjiào*) as interdependently integral to flourishing and harmony, with Confucianism pertaining to harmony in the family and society, Daoism, to harmony in the body and nature, and Buddhism, to harmony in the mind and in rebirth.

We have already looked at the emphasis on ritual-propriety (*lǐ*, 禮) and human-heartedness (*rén*) in early Confucianism, especially the *Analects* of Confucius (551–479 BCE). The Confucian sage scrupulously observed ritual performance in everything from state ceremonies and rites to everyday etiquette and convention, always in a manner that was benevolent toward others.[19] We have also already seen how Mencius (372–289 BCE) understood humans to have an original nature (*xìng*) of goodness: four "spouts" (*duān*), one for each of the four Confucian virtues: compassion for human-heartedness (*rén*), respect for ritual propriety (*lǐ*, 禮), shame for moral rightness (*yì*), and approval/disapproval for moral wisdom (*zhì*).

Here, we turn the other two ancient texts that the Song Dynasty (Neo) Confucian Zhū Xī (朱熹, 1130–1200) placed alongside Confucius's *Analects* and Mencius's *Mencius* as the "Four Books" (Sìshū, 四書) of Confucianism: *The Great Learning* (*Dàxué*, 大學), and *The Doctrine of the Mean* (*Zhōngyōng*, 中庸). Although these works were ascribed to Confucius' disciple Zēngzǐ (曾子, 505–432 BCE) and grandson Zǐsī (子思, 481–402 BCE), respectively, they were amalgamated into the Confucian classic *The Record of Rites* until Zhū Xī extracted them and made them two of the Four Books. Since each has something important to add to our understanding of the Confucian path, we turn to them now.

The Great Learning is known for its eight-step connection between the "investigation of things" and "peace in the world." Only by investigating things can the sage "extend knowledge," "make the will sincere," "rectify the heart-mind," "cultivate character," "regulate the family," "govern the state," and finally achieve "world peace."[20] Several things are important here: if one wants to achieve world peace and govern the state, one must first attend to one's family life; if one wants to cultivate character and rectify the heart-mind, one must first make the will "sincere" or "integrated" (*chéng*, 誠); and if one wants to extend knowledge, one must "liken to oneself" (*shù*, 恕), a reciprocal process whereby one expects of others what one expects of oneself (and vice versa). But what was most crucial for Song Dynasty (Neo) Confucians was the investigation of things (*géwù*, 格物), which involved discerning the natural patterns of Heaven (*Tiān*) and moral patterns of humankind. The rigorous study of these patterns, especially the moral patterns found in classic literature, is one crucial component of the Confucian path as understood during the (Neo)Confucianism of the Song Dynasty (960–1279).

A second component is found in the second book Zhū Xī extracted from *The Record of Rites*—*The Doctrine of the Mean*, which portrays the relationship between human nature and *Tiān* in quasi-mystical terms. Although human nature, which is endowed by *Tiān*, is naturally at equilibrium (*zhōng*, 中), this equilibrium is disturbed by the arousal of feelings in humans, requiring humans to pursue a balance of emotions (*yōng*, 庸). When humans realize this harmony to the highest degree, Heaven

(*Tiān*) and earth (*dì*) attain their proper order, and all things flourish. Key in this process is sincerity/integration (*chéng*), which is an active force of the universe that transforms and completes things, drawing humans and *Tiān* into harmony. According to *The Doctrine of the Mean*, sincerity/integration is nothing less than "the Way [*Dào*] of Heaven [*Tiān*]"; those who are absolutely sincere/integrated "form a trinity with Heaven and earth," assisting in their transforming and nourishing processes.[21] How does one achieve this? For some (Neo)Confucians, it included a second key method, one that was influenced by, yet differentiated from, the meditation practices of Daoists and Buddhists—quiet sitting (*jìngzuò*, 靜坐). For Zhū Xī, *jìngzuò* did not mean "to sit still like a blockhead, with the ear hearing nothing, the eye seeing nothing, and the mind thinking nothing," as he claimed was the case for Daoists and Buddhists.[22] Rather, it involved "holding fast to seriousness" or reverence (*jìng*, 敬) and "making our thoughts sincere" or integrated (*chéng*), which one contemporary scholar interprets as internal reflection on what is learned through the external investigation of things, constituting a "circular journey of tranquility and activity."[23]

Although these two practices—on the one hand, investigating things and extending knowledge; on the other hand, holding fast to seriousness and making thoughts sincere—are important additions to the Confucian project, they nevertheless served traditional Confucian goals of virtue cultivation, ritual performance, and hierarchical ordering. As you know, early Daoist classics challenged this ritual-social way (*dào*) of Confucianism, opposing to it a natural-individual way that is effortless and spontaneous, contextual and perspectival. The *Dàodéjīng* criticized the Confucian path of "cutting, filing, and polishing," offering instead a path of effortless action (*wúwéi*) and natural spontaneity (*zìrán*) that is attuned to natural rhythms of the *Dào*. The *Zhuāngzǐ* chided the Confucian (and Mohist) obsession with determining what is "this" and "not," commending instead an ability to see all things in interdependent relativity and harmony from the perspective of the *Dào*. Although it is not clear whether and how these teachings were practiced, some scholars of Daoism find evidence in these texts of meditation techniques, some of which include "embracing the One" (*bàoyī*, 抱一), "maintaining the One" (*shǒuyī*, 守一), "fasting the heart-mind" (*xīnzhāi*, 心齋), and "sitting-in-forgetfulness" (*zuòwàng*, 坐忘).

In Daoist practice, however, things were different, at least with respect to the critique of Confucian social practices and values. The first large-scale Daoist movement, The Way of the Celestial Masters (Tiānshī Dào 天師道), which was later claimed the origin of the largest Daoist sect today (The Way of

Orthodox Unity, Zhèngyī Dào, 正一道), began in the late Han Dynasty as a theocracy in southwest China. As such, sociopolitical order was paramount; thus, the families of the movement were divided into twenty-four parishes, each led by a "libationer" who recorded the misdeeds of people (among other things), which included violations of Confucian virtues such as human-heartedness (*rén*) and filial piety (*xiào*). As for the second largest Daoist movement today, The Way of Complete Perfection (Quánzhēn Dào, 全眞道), although it does feature an "internal alchemy" (*nèidān*) that draws on meditative techniques from classic Daoist texts, using them to transcend dualistic thoughts, merge with a primordial state of emptiness, and become absorbed into the ineffable *Dào*, it is nevertheless a regimented monastic order in which traditional Confucian virtues of ritual propriety and hierarchical order play key roles.

With some notable exceptions that we will examine next chapter, the same is largely true for East Asian Buddhism in general and Chinese Buddhism in particular: Confucian and other traditional virtues of ritual propriety and hierarchical order are integral to practice. This is just one of several ways in which East Asian/Chinese culture indelibly imprinted East Asian/Chinese Buddhism. Here is another that is critically important for our discussion of paths: East Asian Buddhism generally came to see that all things, especially humans, possess an original Buddha-nature—an innate or natural condition of Buddhahood that is already awakened. The attainment of enlightenment is therefore sudden and spontaneous rather than a long, laborious process.

To some extent, this goes back to a mysterious fifth–sixth-century text named *The Awakening of Faith in Mahāyāna*, which understands enlightenment (Sk. *nirvāṇa*, Ch. *nièpán*, 涅槃) to involve three aspects or steps: an original enlightenment made possible by Buddha-nature (Sk. *tathagātagarbha* or *buddhadhātu*; Ch. *fóxìng*), an initial enlightenment that involves the arousal of an aspiration to enlightenment (Sk. *bodhicitta*, Ch. *pútíxīn*, 菩提心),[24] and actual or "final" enlightenment. (Note how far we have come from traditional South Asian Buddhism, where the individual monk exerts lifetimes of effort to remove ignorance and attain enlightenment.) Whether due to the direct influence of this text or general optimism about human nature in Chinese culture, the idea of original enlightenment was to find its way into every single school of Chinese Buddhism.

In the case of Chán Buddhism, however, the idea of original enlightenment did not go far enough, so to speak, as Chán eventually came to embrace that of sudden enlightenment as well. As legend has it, an illiterate seller of firewood named Huìnéng (638–713) attained sudden enlightenment upon overhearing the recitation of the *Diamond Sūtra*, after which he traveled to the monastery of Hóngrěn (弘忍, 601–674), the fifth patriarch of Chán Buddhism, where he took up a job in the kitchen pounding rice. Before long, it came time for Hóngrěn to retire and pass on his mantle; he therefore designed a poetry contest for his pupils, for which Hóngrěn's chief student, Shénxiù (玉泉神秀, *c.* 601–706), composed a verse about the need to diligently wipe the mirror of the mind:

> The body is the tree of perfect wisdom.
> The mind is the stand of a bright mirror.
> At all times diligently wipe it.
> Do not allow it to become dusty.[25]

Hóngrěn's response to Shénxiù's poem was that although it "arrives at the front door," it "does not enter it," and whereas it is fine for ordinary people, it does not bring supreme wisdom. Later, Huìnéng, who was illiterate, dictated his own verse to another monk to write down. Unlike Shénxiù's verse, Huìnéng's conveyed the original enlightenment of Buddha-nature:

> Fundamentally perfect wisdom has no tree.
> Nor has the bright mirror any stand.
> Buddha-nature is forever clear and pure.
> Where is there any dust?[26]

Recognizing the enlightened understanding of Huìnéng, Hóngrěn conferred the patriarchy on him, albeit secretly to protect his life, then sent him away in the middle of the night. Huìnéng fled south, where he began a southern school of Chán, a school of "sudden enlightenment," which, over time, eclipsed Shénxiù's northern school of "gradual enlightenment."

In fact, it was the Chinese emperor who settled this dispute between these schools, choosing the southern over the northern. Thereafter, "Five Houses" of Chán Buddhism came to populate southern/Chinese Chán Buddhism, with only two surviving to the present: Cáodòng (曹洞), known as Sōtō in Japan, which emphasizes sitting meditation; and Línjì (臨濟), known as Rinzai in Japan, which also makes use of *gōng'àn*-s (公案; Jp. *kōan*-s), records of elliptic and enigmatic questions and exchanges between masters and students that were taken as objects of meditation (e.g., What was my original face before my mother and father were born?). In both cases, meditation is a key path of practice (though by no means the only one). Indeed "Chán" is just the Chinese pronunciation of the Sanskrit word *dhyāna* (meditation), with "Zen" being the Japanese pronunciation of "Chán."

Contrary to Western misconceptions, however, it is not Chán but Pure

Land Buddhism that is most populous in East Asia. In contrast to Chán, which became known as a "hard path" of "self-effort" (*zìlì*, 自力; Jp. *jiriki*), Pure Land offered an "easy path" of "other effort" (*tālì*, 他力; Jp. *tariki*), one that simply required devotion to Amitābha, the Buddha of the Pure Land of Sukhāvatī ("Happy Land"), especially through repetition of the formula *niànfó* (念佛, Jp. *nembutsu*), which translates as "recollection of" or "calling on" Buddha. By means of such devotion and Amitābha's grace, Pure Land practitioners could be reborn in his Pure Land, from which *nirvāṇa* was much easier to attain.

Although Chán and Pure Land might therefore seem like polar opposites, by the sixteenth century they had come to be harmonized, at least to some extent, with Chán monasteries incorporating the repetition of *niànfó* into the daily liturgies, regarding the Buddha-nature "within" and Amitābha "without" as different ways of viewing the same reality.[27] Hence, this section returns to where it began: over time, paths of practice in East Asia that were once opposed to each other—most notably Confucianism, Daoism, and Buddhism—came to be harmonized as mutually interdependent components of one grand, East Asian way.

VI. Mediterranean/Abrahamic Philosophy of Religion

Scholars commonly pattern the paths of the Abrahamic religions on an orthopraxic/orthodoxic continuum. On one end lies the orthopraxic religion of Judaism, for which "correct-practice" is central—observance of God's commandments (Hb. *mitzvot*), especially as codified in Jewish law (*hălākâ*). On the other end of the continuum lies the orthodoxic religion of Christianity, for which "correct-belief" is crucial—faith that the death and resurrection of Jesus Christ saves one from sin, as demonstrated by adherence to Christian doctrine, especially as delineated in the Nicene-Constantinople Creed. In between these two ends is Islam, for which both "correct practice" and "correct belief" are important, with the "Five Pillars" pertaining mostly to practice, the "Six Constituents of Faith," to belief.[28]

This is no doubt a good part of the story. But we would be remiss not to note, on the one hand, that there have been orthodoxic aspects of and voices in Judaism, most notably the Thirteen Principles of Faith enumerated by the medieval Jewish philosopher Maimonides (1138–1204), and, on the other hand, that for at least half of the Christian world, it is bodily participation in the sacraments, especially Eucharist, that effects the salvation of Jesus Christ. With respect to the latter, we can also observe that a faith/works continuum patterns Christianity itself, with many newer Protestant and Restorationist churches proclaiming salvation through the grace of God by faith alone, and the more traditional Orthodox and Catholic churches pointing to the importance of "good works," especially participation in the sacraments.

Despite all these distinctions and disagreements, however, one important difference "jumps out" when we consider Abrahamic paths alongside the other religious paths we have explored so far: the importance of obedience to divine command. There are historical and theological explanations for this, some of which pertain to the influence of Persian religion and Babylonian law on early Judaism, others of which involve the ways in which Abrahamic religions anthropomorphize a single, omnipotent, and omnibenevolent God. Moreover, there are important differences between and within these Abrahamic religions about what their God commands and how, with Jews and Muslims regarding the wide-ranging and all-encompassing laws found in the Torah and Qurʾān, respectively (especially as interpreted and codified in *hălākâ* and *sharīʿa*, respectively), and Christians often looking instead to just ten of the commandments from the Torah, as well as the teachings of Jesus Christ, Saint Paul, and other New Testament writers, all of whom lived under the rule of the Roman Empire, which supplied most of the laws of the land. Still, insofar as the God of these religions was thought of as radically free, entirely powerful, and thoroughly good, a certain question arose for philosophers of these religions: can this God command anything whatsoever to be morally good and legally binding for humans, or can He only command what actually is morally good and rationally true? This is the question that we will pursue for the remainder of this chapter.

In fact, the relevant philosophical stage was set long before Jewish, Christian, and Islamic philosophers of religion came on the scene to philosophize about this question. This stage-setting occurred by means of a simple question posed to a character named Euthyphro by the ancient Greek philosopher Socrates in Plato's dialogue *Euthyphro*: Do the Gods love piety because it is pious, or is piety pious because the Gods love it?[29] Now referred to as the "Euthyphro Dilemma," Socrates' question essentially asks, "What makes pious acts pious?" Are they pious because they accord with some moral norm of piety? Or are they pious because the Gods say they are? Insofar as this is a "dilemma," it offers two less-than-desirable choices: on the one hand, Gods are beholden to "higher" moral norms; on the other hand, Gods arbitrarily set these norms.

When applied to the Abrahamic religions, the Euthyphro Dilemma arguably becomes even thornier, offering two even less desirable choices: on the one hand, God is subject to natural or rational standards and laws (and therefore is not all-powerful); on the other hand, God can command anything to be moral (and therefore can act in apparently unpredictable and capricious ways). These two positions later took shape as two different ethical theories, "natural law" ethics and "divine command" ethics.

We see one early version of debate about this matter in tenth-century Islamic theology (Ar. *kalām*), especially as the "rationalist" school of the Mu'tazila came to be opposed by the school that would assume the status of orthodoxy, the Ash'arītes.[30] As you recall from Chapter 5, the Mu'tazila were known as the school of the "unity and justice of God," the latter of which spells out implications not only for human freedom but also for divine morality: humans freely choose and commit good or bad acts, which Allah justly rewards or punishes since Allah must act in accordance with justice. To put it in terms of the Euthyphro Dilemma, God loves justice because it is just. More accurately, Allah loves justice because Allah is just—justice is not something separate from Allah to which Allah is beholden. And since Allah necessarily is just, humans can use reason to ascertain what Allah does and does not command them to do.

Not so for the dissident Mu'tazilite theologian al-Ash'arī (*c.* 874–936), who would go on to found the Ash'arite school of theology. For al-Ash'arī, not only does Allah predetermine and cause every event in the world; Allah also establishes and commands standards of right and wrong. Thus, al-Ash'arī averred that "if God declared lying to be right, it would be right, and if He commanded it, none could gainsay Him."[31] Again, to put it in terms of the Euthyphro Dilemma, for al-Ash'arī, what is right is right because Allah wills and commands it.

We also find a range of positions on the "Euthyphro Dilemma" in medieval Jewish philosophy of religion, though perhaps none as extreme as the Ash'arite one above. For Saadia Gaon (882–942), a "Jewish Mu'tazilite" who served as head ("*gaon*") of the academy of Jewish (Talmudic) learning in the city of Babylon during the 'Abbāsid Caliphate (750–1258), humans could discover the reasons for some of the commandments (*mitzvot*) of the Torah independently of revelation. These are what Saadia called "laws of reason" (e.g., do not murder, do not steal), which he distinguished from "laws of revelation" (e.g., Sabbath laws, dietary code) about which "reason passes no judgment in the way either of approval or disapproval" (even though Saadia himself provided general and individual reasons as to why even "laws of revelation" were reasonable). By contrast, the most influential of all medieval Jewish philosophers, Maimonides (1138–1204), maintained that although there are reasons for all of YHWH's commandments, none could be known by reason independently of revelation. Nevertheless, Maimonides held an Aristotelian-influenced understanding of the relationship between practical/moral virtue and intellectual/theoretical virtue, one aspect of which was that the more humans are habituated in and practice these commandments, the more humans can come to know their reasons (and therefore want to practice them all the more).

With St. Thomas Aquinas (1224–74), a Dominican (Catholic Christian) monk who lived in the century after Maimonides, we see the most extensive integration of Aristotelian philosophy into Abrahamic religion with respect to ethics in particular and philosophy in general. Although Aquinas believed that the highest happiness or good—the beatific vision of the Christian-Trinitarian God—was not possible until the life hereafter, he nevertheless maintained that happiness in this life was possible through virtuous activity, which included both practical/moral and theoretical/intellectual components. With respect to the former, Aquinas emphasized that humans could not only acquire imperfect natural virtues (e.g., courage, justice, piety) through habituation but also receive perfect theological virtues directly from God (e.g., faith, hope, love). Such practical/moral virtues were surpassed only by the intellectual/theoretical virtue of "contemplation," which Aquinas believed humans could also achieve, enjoying the highest form of happiness in this life. Although a lot more could be said about Aquinas' moral theory, which is quite sophisticated and nuanced, suffice it to point out that Aquinas considered at least some moral virtues and laws "natural" and therefore knowable through experience and reason. Not all Christians agreed. In fact, it was a version of this position—that a person virtuous in Aristotle's terms "is sufficiently disposed for eternal happiness"—that was among the 219 propositions condemned by the Bishop of Paris in 1277, just three years after Aquinas' death. Aquinas, however, was to have the last laugh, albeit postmortem, as he would be canonized in 1323, proclaimed a Doctor of the Church in 1567, and declared the supreme model of the Christian philosopher in 1879.

Among those who disagreed with Aquinas were members of a rival mendicant Christian order, the Franciscans, which unlike Aquinas' Dominican order, tended to reject the philosophy of Aristotle and privilege divine will over divine intellect. Just one generation after Aquinas, we therefore find the Franciscan friar John Duns Scotus (1265/6–1308) differing with Aquinas's Aristotelian-based, reason-centric moral philosophy. Two of these disagreements are especially important for us. First, humans do not naturally aim toward happiness *qua* virtuous rational activity; rather, humans are naturally or originally sinful, requiring salvation from the Christian-Trinitarian God before they can act virtuously. Second, most of this God's moral laws are not naturally or rationally necessary and therefore cannot be known through ordinary experience and moral reflection, with the only two exceptions being the first two of the Ten Commandments: "You shall have no other Gods before me," and "You shall not take the name of the Lord your God in vain." With respect to moral laws that *cannot* be known through ordinary experience and moral reflection, Scotus referenced the "second tablet" of the Ten Commandments (which was said to contain commandments four through ten), especially both the fifth commandment, "Thou shalt not kill," for which God could and did provide exceptions, most notably when he commanded the patriarch Abraham to kill his son Isaac, and the seventh commandment, "Thou shalt not steal," which was contingent, not necessary, applying only to humans with property. Although there is some scholarly disagreement about how to interpret Scotus on this matter, it seems that he held that the good was good simply because God willed it (at least in most cases). This Christian God can will (almost) anything to be good, and humans cannot know why.

In drawing this chapter to a close, let us briefly note one final question concerning religious paths: Do practitioners of these Abrahamic religions understand their paths to be uniquely true or effective to the exclusion of other paths? To a large extent, the question only applies to Christianity and Islam, which, unlike Judaism, are not ethnically bounded, did seek converts, and are concerned with what happens to people after death. Answers to this question in these religions have varied from person to person, place to place, and time to time. Scriptural passages, ecclesiastical pronouncements, and philosophical arguments can be adduced to support any of a variety of positions, the chief of which—exclusivism, inclusivism, pluralism—we will look at in the next section.

VII. European/Academic Philosophy of Religion

For reasons that are not so difficult to understand, a significant amount of scholarly and public discourse about religion since the European Enlightenment in the "West" has been occupied with the question "Which religion, if any, is true?" One reason involves the European Enlightenment's construction of religion as a system of belief, as well as its obsession with ascertaining which beliefs are true. Also relevant is the exclusive monotheism of the Abrahamic religions, especially Christianity and Islam, which have at times maintained that other Gods are unreal or demonic and that other religions are false or inferior. If, finally, we consider that Christian-European countries colonized much of the rest of the world—not only economically but also ideologically—then we begin to understand how widespread the Abrahamic-Enlightenment understanding of "religion" has become. Even in areas where there once were not "religions"—in the sense of mutually exclusive systems of belief—there now often are.

By the latter half of the twentieth century, this question had become known as the "problem of religious pluralism." Why is religious pluralism a "problem"? Well, if religions are thought of as belief-systems, and if these belief-systems are as significantly different and mutually incompatible as they seem to be, then only one of them, at best, can be true—or so said certain scholars.

No recent scholar of religion has spilled more ink on this "problem" than the British philosopher and theologian John Hick (1922–2012). Hick held that there were three basic ways of solving the "problem" of religious pluralism: a "dogmatic hypothesis" that insists that only one religion is true, a "skeptical hypothesis" that protests that no religion is true, and a "pluralistic hypothesis" that recognizes the truth of many different religions. Rejecting the first hypothesis for ignoring the diversity of religious experience and the second hypothesis for dismissing the rationality of living on the basis of one's own religious experiences, Hick claimed that it was necessary to postulate a common ground for the diverse religious experiences of humankind.[32] Hick called this ground "the Real-in-itself," contrasting it to "the Real-as-experienced-and-thought." Although the Real-in-itself cannot be directly thought and experienced, it can be indirectly thought and experienced as the many different personal Gods and impersonal Absolutes of the world's religions. In fact, Hick believed that the cognitive structure of consciousness included these two categories or concepts—personal God, impersonal Absolute—and that when the Real-in-itself was experienced or thought, it was "schematised or made concrete within actual religious experience as a range of particular gods or absolutes."[33] The Real-in-itself, however, remains absolutely unknowable and ineffable; thus, humans simply cannot know which Real-as-experienced-and-thought, if any, actually is the Real-in-itself. Hick maintained that humans could, though, be confident that Reals-as-experienced-and-thought are "authentic manifestations" of the Real-in-itself insofar as they lead to the moral transformation of humans from self-centeredness to Reality-centeredness.[34]

Every scholarly idea of course has its critics. In the case of Hick's "pluralism hypothesis," one of the more trenchant critics has been Keith Yandell (b. 1938), whose essay "How to Sink in Cognitive Quicksand: Nuancing Religious Pluralism" is directed at a version of Hick's religious pluralism (as advocated by Peter Byrne in this case). Yandell maintains that this view of religious pluralism is committed to two fundamental general themes: no religion is true, and everyone will do very well in the long run. Regarding the first, Yandell asserts that, whether this thesis is read metaphysically or epistemologically, it brings "bad news" to the religions of the world, for in the former case it implies that religions are wrong about the diseases they diagnose and the cures they offer, and the latter case it entails that religious believers who think they have gotten things right in fact are wrong.[35] Regarding the second, Yandell argues that it is inconsistent to affirm moral truth by requiring religious believers to meet certain basic moral standards (in order to do very well in the long run), while denying religious truth (about what is really real). This, however, is just the tip of the iceberg for Yandell, who goes on to level many other charges against religious pluralism, the most relevant of which are that religious pluralism is committed to the claim that all religions are epistemologically tied; that its truth claims, whether moral or metaphysical, are in fact part of the religious diversity that it says cannot be true; that it is in fact a second-order religion that explains first-order religions; and that it is a weak explanation at best vis-à-vis purely secularist explanations that simply take all religions to be false. In sum, Yandel avers that religious pluralism "is a tissue of inconsistencies"; the sooner we realize this the better off we will be in advancing toward a "true account of religious plurality."[36]

As you can perhaps tell, Yandell's position is a version of what Hick calls the "dogmatic hypothesis" (a Christian one, to be precise). More generally, this position is known in scholarly literature as "exclusivism," the view that only one religious philosophy can be true. In between this position and the pluralism of Hick lies a third position, inclusivism, which holds that "other" religious traditions can be true by virtue of being (inferior) versions of some other, entirely true religion. A couple of notable examples of inclusivism come from the Hindu and Christian traditions. For some forms of Hinduism, most notably those inspired by Advaita Vedānta, the many different versions of Hinduism in particular and all religions in general are seen as many different ways of attaining a realization of the ultimate, *Brahman*, and therefore of being released from the wheel of rebirth. (See, for example, the nineteenth-century saint Rāmakrishna [1836–86], whom we will look at in the next chapter.) In the case of Christianity, the most famous scholarly example of inclusivism is the Roman Catholic theologian Karl Rahner's (1904–84) notion of "anonymous Christians"—people who, through no fault of their own, do not know about Jesus Christ or the Christian Church, yet "sincerely seek God" and "strive by their deeds to do his will as it is known to them through the dictates of conscience." You might also recognize this idea in the popular *Chronicles of Narnia* series by the British writer and theologian C. S. Lewis (1898–1963), especially the final book, *The Last Battle*, wherein Lewis has Aslan, who is representative of Jesus Christ, tell a commander of the forces of Tash, who is representative of the Devil, that any virtuous act ostensibly done in Tash's name is actually done to Aslan, since Tash can only receive vicious acts, Aslan, only virtuous acts. This commander, Emeth, is therefore "saved" by means of the virtuous acts that he had performed for Tash.

Yet another way in which scholars of religion have tried to solve the "problem" of religious pluralism is by attempting to show that there is something fundamentally common to all religio-philosophical traditions. Known generally as "perennialism," this position comes in two different forms: perennial *philosophy*, which claims that all religio-philosophies share core philosophical teachings; and perennial *psychology*, which looks instead to core religious experiences. Just as gardeners refer to plants that regrow each year as "perennials" (versus annuals which do not survive the winter), scholars refer to philosophies or experiences that recur in many different religio-philosophical traditions as "perennial" philosophies or psychologies.

Huston Smith (1919–2016) is one example of the former, even though his classic perennialist work, *Forgotten Truth: The Primordial Tradition*, rejected the term perennialism for the "less exclusively intellectual" label "primordial tradition." Smith claimed that this primordial tradition is "the way things are"; the "universal testimony of humankind" that gives rise to the different religions of the world; and the "fundamental vision by humankind" of the isomorphic, multi-tiered nature of reality and the self.[37] For Smith, both reality and self are composed of four tiers that are isomorphically interrelated by the "law of inverse analogy" such that higher levels of reality correspond to deeper levels of the self.[38] Thus, the terrestrial tier of reality corresponds to the body; the intermediate tier of reality, to the mind; the celestial tier of reality, to the soul; and the infinite tier of reality, to the spirit. As one moves higher up the tiers of "reality" and deeper into the tiers of the "self," human knowing and speaking increasingly fail, ultimately reaching the "domain of the inexpressible."[39]

Is this true? As always, it is up to you to decide. Note, however, that critics of this perennial philosophy have simply and cogently demonstrated not only how different are the "infinites" and "spirits" of different religio-philosophical traditions but also how differently they are claimed to be inexpressible (if they are even claimed so at all).

In the case of perennial psychology, Robert K. C. Forman (b. 1947) has drawn attention to a special kind of religious or "mystical" experience, which he calls a "pure consciousness event" (PCE), defining it as "wakeful though contentless (nonintentional) consciousness," "a trophotropic state of hypoarousal marked by low levels of cognitive and physiological activity."[40] For Forman, PCEs are not to be confused with non-mystical visionary experiences (e.g., of the Virgin Mary), which are ergotropic states of hyperarousal marked by high levels of cognitive and physiological activity, nor with quasi-pure trophotropic states such as the dualistic mystical state (DMS) and the unitive mystical state (UMS).[41] Why? Simply put, PCEs are "pure" of content. They are in no way constructed or mediated by cognitive-mental categories or cultural-linguistic concepts; therefore they are cross-culturally identical, constituting unimpeachable evidence for a "perennial psychology."[42] As Forman maintains,

> [I]f a Buddhist, Hindu or African forgot every thought, sensation, emotion, etc., then no historically conditioned idea, form, category or even sensory information would remain conscious to differentiate the resultant events from on to another. A formless trance in Buddhism may be experientially indistinguishable from one in Hinduism or Christianity. This model swings the pendulum back towards the perennial philosophy camp, that mysticism is alike from one culture to another.[43]

Is this true? Or do the critiques of perennial philosophy above also apply here: that religio-philosophies in fact do not share such a common experience, that this is therefore "sloppy scholarship," that all experiences are to some degree conceptually mediated and culturally constructed, that apparently "pure" or "ineffable" experiences are in fact experienced and identified differently in different religio-philosophical traditions, and so forth? Who has the better arguments and stronger evidence? Yet again, it is up to you to decide. Speaking of which, let us now try to "put it all together."

VIII. Putting it All Together

Once again, we can begin "putting it all together" by reminding ourselves of the diversity our content—here, types of religious paths for the "self." In some cases, these paths lead to, and are significantly oriented toward post-mortem destinations; in other cases, this-worldly ends. For some paths, cognitive attitudes are most important; for many others, bodily practices (or a combination of the two). Some paths rely on the other-help of some God or super-human being; others, self-help alone.

There is also the leading question of our chapter. Can only one of these paths, at best, be a true and effective means of reaching its destination, or is it possible for several different paths, perhaps all of them, to be true and effective, each in its own way and toward its own end? Are all paths "authentic" insofar as they constitute experiences of and contain ideas about the "Real-in-itself," leading their practitioners from self-centeredness to "Reality-centeredness" (per John Hick)? Are all paths true and efficacious by virtue of being instances of a perennial philosophy, correlating higher levels of reality with deeper levels of the self (per Huston Smith)? Do all paths cultivate the same "pure," contentless experience, one that unites the experiencer within herself and with whatever she considers sacred or divine outside herself (per Robert K. C. Forman)?

It again bears mentioning that the urgency of the question is a product of certain cultural-historical forces and conditions, all dating to the second half of the second millennium: exclusivist forms of Christianity, especially as shaped by the Protestant Reformation; religion as a system of belief, especially as constructed in the European Enlightenment; and world religions as mutually exclusive belief-systems, especially as promulgated through European colonization. Feminist philosophers of religion add that obsession with the justification of religious beliefs and evaluation of religious arguments are typically male, and that exclusivist forms of religion have typically been a tool of patriarchal power. Pamela Sue Anderson, for example, contrasts the exclusivist-inclusivist-pluralist debate about salvation in the afterlife with "a feminist perspective" that allows for "religiously diverse solutions to 'the so-called human problem'" that "expose obstacles to truth in this life," especially those obstacles that "denigrate women and non-privileged men with violence and abuse."[44]

It also bears mentioning that cultural views about these matters not only can change but in fact have already begun to change. Witness, for example, the recent growth of people identifying as "spiritual but not religious," belonging to multiple religious traditions, and innovating new religiosities.

(See Chapter 2.) The philosopher of religion might therefore wonder whether framing the "problem of religious pluralism" as a choice between pluralism, inclusivism, and exclusivism—as well as the "skepticism" that says no religious tradition is true—is a false dilemma, one that limits the range of credible options. Or whether this so-called problem is a problem at all. For what it is worth, this book thinks just this—viz., that the practice of global-critical philosophy of religion need not take up religious traditions as whole entities but rather should look to the ideas and arguments of particular religious texts and thinkers on a topic-by-topic basis, always with a sensitivity to socio-historical context and rhetorical-political ends.

What do you think?

Questions for Discussion

1 Describe and compare some of the philosophies of religion above with respect to whether they stress this-worldly or post-mortem ends, feature practices or beliefs, or rely on self-help or other-help. Which of these issues is most important and interesting to you?
2 Describe, compare, and evaluate philosophies of religion with regards to the question, Which path, if any, leads to its destination?
3 Should the philosopher of religion evaluate entire religious traditions with respect to their truth or efficacy? Compare and evaluate the range of responses to this question.
4 What is the Euthyphro Dilemma? Why has it been of such interest to Abrahamic philosophy of religion? (Why) is it of little interest outside Abrahamic and European philosophy of religion?

Primary and Scholarly Sources

East Asia

The Doctrine of the Mean. In *A Source Book in Chinese Philosophy*, ed. Wing-Tsit Chan, 95–114. Princeton, NJ: Princeton University Press, 1963.

The Great Learning. In *A Source Book in Chinese Philosophy*, ed. Wing-Tsit Chan, 84–94. Princeton, NJ: Princeton University Press, 1963.

Platform Sūtra of the Sixth Patriarch, §§ 1–10. In *Philosophical Classics, Volume VI: Asian Philosophy*, eds. Forrest E. Baird and Raeburne S. Heimbeck, 474–7. Upper Saddle River, NJ: Pearson Prentice Hall, 2006.

Zhuāngzǐ, chapter 6.9. In *Wandering on the Way: Early Taoist Tales and Parables of Chuang Tzu*, trans. Victor H. Mair, 63–4. New York: Bantam Books, 1994.

European/Academic

Forman, Robert K. C. "Introduction: Mysticism, Constructivism, and Forgetting." In *The Problem of Pure Consciousness: Mysticism and Philosophy*, ed. R. Forman, 3–49. New York: Oxford University Press, 1990.

Hick, John. *An Interpretation of Religion: Human Responses to the Transcendent*, 2nd ed., 233–51. New Haven, CT: Yale University Press, 2004.

Smith, Huston. *Forgotten Truth: The Primordial Tradition*, 1–18. New York: Harper Colophon Books, 1976.

Yandell, Keith. "How to Sink in Cognitive Quicksand: Nuancing Religious Pluralism." In *Contemporary Debates in Philosophy of Religion*, eds. Michael L. Peterson and Raymond J. VanArragon, 191–200, 215–17. Malden, MA: Blackwell, 2004.

Lakȟóta

Archie Fire Lame Deer and Richard Erdoes. *Gift of Power: The Life and Teachings of a Lakota Medicine Man*, chapter 14. Santa Fe, NM: Bear & Co. Publishing, 1992.

Elk, Black. *The Sacred Pipe: Black Elk's Account of the Seven Rites of the Oglala Sioux*, recorded and ed. by Joseph Epes Brown, 3–9. Norman, OK: University of Oklahoma Press, 1953.

Powers, William K. *Yuwipi: Vision & Experience in Oglala Religion*, 89–103. Lincoln, NE: Bison Books, 1984.

Mediterranean/Abrahamic

Aquinas, Thomas. *Summa Theologica*, Part Iia, Question 100, Article 3. Available online: https://www.documentacatholicaomnia.eu/03d/1225-1274,_Thomas_Aquinas,_Summa_Theologiae_%5B1%5D,_EN.pdf (accessed March 11, 2022).

Hare, John. "Religion and Morality." In *The Stanford Encyclopedia of Philosophy*, ed. Edward N. Zalta, Fall 2009 ed. Available online: https://plato.stanford.edu/archives/fall2019/entries/religion-morality/ (accessed March 11, 2022).

Plato. *Euthyphro*, 9a–11b. In *Five Dialogues: Euthyphro, Apology, Crito, Meno, Phaedo*, trans. G. M. A. Grube, ed. John M. Cooper, 13–16. Indianapolis, IN: Hackett Publishing, 1981.

Scotus, John Duns. *Ordinatio*, Distinction 44. Available online: https://www.aristotelophile.com/Books/Translations/Ordinatio%20I.pdf (accessed March 11, 2022).

South Asia

Bhagavad Gītā, III, XII. Trans. Eknath Easwaran, 17–22, 66–8. New York: Vintage Spiritual Classics, 1985.

Yorùbá

Makinde, Moses. "*Ifá* as a Repository of Knowledge." *Odu: A Journal of West African Studies* 23 (1983): 161–21.

Táíwò, Olúfẹ́mi. "Òrìsà: A Prolegomenon to a Philosophy of Yorùbá Religion." In *Òrìsà Devotion as World Religion: The Globalization of Yorùbá Religious Culture*, eds. Jacob K. Olupona and Terry Rey, 84–105. Madison, WI: University of Wisconsin Press.

8

What Obstacles are in My Way?

Learning Objectives

- Understand some of the important and interesting ways in which religious thinkers, texts, and traditions conceptualize religious obstacles for the self.
- Compare and evaluate philosophies of religion with regard their obstacles for the self.
- Explain and evaluate the view that religion itself (including religious doctrines, moralities, and institutions) is an obstacle both in contemporary Western philosophy and in traditional religious philosophies.
- Explore the relationship of religious obstacles to religious paths and destinations (as well as to religious "selves" and their "original conditions").

I. Introduction

Our final chapter on the journey of the self looks at the obstacles that prevent us from reaching our destinations. When we originally considered the topic of destinations in Chapter 6, we focused on the question of whether we survive death. Last chapter, we turned to the paths by which we reach both this-worldly and post-mortem destinations. In this chapter, we ask what keeps us from walking these paths and reaching these destinations, whether this-worldly or post-mortem.

As we will soon see, these obstacles are numerous and varied. In some cases, what prevents us from reaching our destinations are "original conditions" that we inherit such as original sinfulness, ignorance, selfishness, or imbalance. In other cases, these obstacles are simply the sinful, ignorant, selfish, or immoral acts we commit. Yet another type of obstacle is our individuated existence itself, which separates us from what is really real and truly true, sometimes due to the concepts and words we use, which delude us about what is really real and truly true. There is also the problem of evil beings—malevolent deities, spirits, or other superhuman agents who cause illness, conflict, or death. Humans, too, thwart one another from living the way they should, whether by failing to create and support nurturing environments for spiritual and moral cultivation, or by instituting and perpetuating social environments that are unjust and oppressive. Slavery and racism certainly fit here. So does patriarchy and sexism. Perhaps also capitalism and classism. Some would even say that what keeps us from living the way we should is religion itself.

Although we will survey examples of all these types of obstacles below, we will focus especially on the last one—religion as obstacle. Why? For one, it is an especially live issue in contemporary philosophy of religion, if not also for contemporary societies more broadly, especially as a variety of atheisms, agnosticisms, and humanisms become more popular and pervasive worldwide. Also, as we will also soon see, religion is sometimes an obstacle in traditional religious philosophies, especially as the path of some religion—its rituals, doctrines, moralities, texts, and institutions—becomes mistaken as its end.

II. Lakȟóta Philosophy of Religion

In Lakȟóta traditional ways, there is no single, philosophically or mythologically prominent and direct answer to the question: what obstacles prevent me from reaching my destination? We therefore take several indirect routes.

Like many other American Indian people, the Lakȟóta do have myths about a trickster deity, who for them is the spider Iktómi. Iktómi is the progeny of Iŋyaŋ the rock, the oldest form of creation, and the Wakiŋyaŋ, "Thunder Beings" who manifest themselves in thunder and lightning. Although Iktómi is a spider, he can take other forms. For example, in the form of a wolf he tricked the Lakȟóta forefathers to leave their subterranean existence for the surface of the earth (through Wind Cave in the Black Hills of South Dakota), where they found themselves without protection from the elements. Iktómi then came to their rescue, teaching them how to make fire, obtain and prepare food, build shelter, and make clothing. It is Iktómi, therefore, who teaches "the original Lakota how to live as cultural beings."[1]

In other stories about Iktómi, he changes form to trick and deceive. In one story, for example, he transforms into a man to marry his mother-in-law, after which he transforms into a young man to marry his oldest daughter.[2] Stories about Iktómi, therefore, serve to teach Lakȟóta children proper conduct in society—one must not act as Iktómi does if one is "to grow up to be a respectable and responsible member of the community."[3] Moreover, since in deceiving Iktómi always ends up being deceived, stories about Iktómi illustrate the trouble and embarrassment that result from socially improper behavior.[4] With respect to this aspect of American Indian tricksters in general, Vine Deloria, Jr., observes that "the primary use of Trickster tales is to demonstrate the uniform nature of the physical world and its laws and to show that disobedience of natural laws produces foolishness and opens a person to ridicule."[5] So, although it is not the case that Iktómi himself is an obstacle to humans reaching their destination, Iktómi reveals what those obstacles are: behavior that goes against what is in accordance with the order of nature and society. Indeed, preventing such behavior is crucial in small, tight-knit communities, where socially deviant behavior can have disastrous effects.

Although there is no evidence that sacred rituals and moral norms were ever violated or transcended for higher "religious" aims, Lakȟóta societies do recognize and celebrate exceptional individuals called *heyókȟa* who receive a vision of the Wakiŋyaŋ and thereafter behave in an "opposite" or "backwards" fashion, flaunting social convention and taboo. Literally meaning "crazy," *heyókȟa* might ride horses or use language backwards, go naked in the freezing cold and bundle up on the hottest days, or, as in the case of one famous *heyókȟa* named "Straighten-Outer," attempt to straighten curved things like bowls, eggs, and wagon wheels.[6] Why? One theory is that a *heyókȟa* simply "makes people laugh" not only at the *heyókȟa* but also at themselves, thereby teaching us "not to take ourselves too seriously" and that "there is laughter among the tears."[7] Another theory is that the violation of social conventions and taboos by *heyókȟa* paradoxically serves to define those conventions and taboos for others. A third theory postulates that, precisely because they are "crazy," *heyókȟa* are able to criticize and challenge those in power, especially when they abuse their power.

We would be woefully remiss, not to mention naively "uncritical," if we did not also point out that a whole new set of "obstacles" has been erected for the Lakȟóta and other American Indians since their "discovery" by Euro-Americans. First and foremost, there is the loss of land, especially the forcible removal from ancestral homelands and violation of treaties to protect those lands. Perhaps more devastating, however, is the loss of tradition, which includes prohibitions of and restrictions on practicing religious ceremonies and rituals. We will examine these issues further when we look at obstacles in the way of the cosmos in Chapter 13.

III. Yorùbá Philosophy of Religion

If the path and destination in Yorùbá philosophy of religion involves learning and living one's destiny, especially when confronting sickness and misfortune, then the obstacles to this path and destination just are these sicknesses and misfortunes. In the tradition of Ifá, however, all such sicknesses and misfortunes are identified with the *Ajogun*, a term that Kọ́lá Abímbọ́lá translates as "Anti-god," though literally means "warrior."

By some accounts, there are 200 primordial *Ajogun*, all creations of Olódùmarè. However, since additional *Ajogun* have come into existence after the creation of the world, their number is represented as 200+1, with the "+1" denoting the set of new *Ajogun*. These 200+1 *Ajogun* are said to reside on the "left-side" of the cosmos, from which they wage continual war on the "right-sided" inhabitants of the cosmos: humans, animals, plants, and the 400+1 primordial *Òrìṣà*. (As with the *Ajogun*, new *Òrìṣà* have come into existence since the creation of the world, thus the "+1" applies to them as well.) This is the "natural state" of the cosmos and therefore also of human life—strife, chaos, and war.

Chief among these 200+1 *Ajogun* are the "eight warlords": Death (Ikú), Disease (Àrùn), Loss (Òfò), Paralysis (Ẹ̀gbà), Big Trouble (Ọ̀ràn), Curse (Èpè), Imprisonment (Ẹ̀wọ̀n), and "All Other Afflictions" (Èṣe).[8] For humans, there is no escaping the *Ajogun* in general and these "eight warlords" in particular. Not only is conflict the natural state of the cosmos; the afflictions with which the *Ajogun* are associated are common human experiences—indeed, necessary ones, at least in the case of death (Ikú).

Humans are not, however, helpless against the *Ajogun*. If they are afflicted by a particular *Ajogun* (e.g., disease), they can make the properly divined sacrifices at the end of an Ifá session, which the *Òrìṣà* Èṣù—who straddles the left/right divide—will deliver to respective *Ajogun*, thereby buying the afflicted human some temporary relief. Nevertheless, affliction will eventually return, as the cosmos always reverts back to its natural state of conflict.

Èṣù himself can also be a source of affliction, sowing confusion and conflict in the affairs of humans if the sacrifice at the end of Ifá divination is not performed at all or is performed incorrectly. In doing so, Èṣù acts in trickster-like ways, causing quarrels between best friends and treachery among royal families.[9] For anthropologist Benjamin C. Ray, these stories about Èṣù "are meant to describe what the Yorùbá perceive to be an active force in the world, a principle of uncertainty and confusion that pervades human affairs."[10] A common moral of Èṣù stories is therefore that "humans should never assume they are in total control of their lives or fully aware of the consequences of their actions."[11]

Yet another obstacle is yet another "left/right straddler"—the *àjẹ́*, a term commonly translated as "witch" but actually meaning "powerful person." From the perspective of the tradition of Ifá, *àjẹ́* are humans (*ènìyàn*) who give up their good human nature to become "negative humans" (*eníyán*), allying themselves with the *Ajogun* in their war against *Òrìṣà* and humans.[12] As we will see in Chapter 13, understandings of *àjẹ́* are a bit more nuanced and complex. Regardless, the perceived threat of the *àjẹ́* also underscores a common set of obstacles in Yorùbá traditions involving sickness and misfortune, uncertainty and confusion, affliction and conflict.

As we will also see in Chapter 13, another major obstacle for Yorùbá, the most enslaved people in all of Africa, is European colonialism and its lasting effects.

IV. South Asian Philosophy of Religion

By now you know that the primary obstacle in South Asian philosophy of religion is ignorance, which we examined in Chapter 6 as an "original condition," especially in the *abhidharma* philosophy of early (Theravāda) Buddhism and the Advaita Vedānta school of Hindu philosophy. In the former case, humans ignorantly take the things of experience—especially themselves—to be fully real, when in fact all our experience (including of our self) reduces to and is constructed out of underlying *dharma*-s—momentary "flashes" of experience that serve as the foundational bits of experience. Only with extensive, intensive meditation can one learn to pierce the veil of everyday illusion and "wake up" to the world and (no)self as they really are. Likewise, Advaita Vedānta holds that our everyday perception of reality and ourselves is at issue. In this case, however, what is really real is *Ātman*/*Brahman*. All perceptions of individuality, multiplicity, and change are the result of erroneous superimposition (*adhyāsa*) and therefore must be overcome by truly understanding of the words of the *Upaniṣads*.

Although the obstacle of ignorance is fairly consistent across the *darśana*-s of South Asian philosophy, we now know from last chapter's exploration of the *Bhagavad Gītā* that paths of knowledge (*jñāna*) are not the only ones in South Asian religion. The first millennium of the Common Era was to witness an explosion of paths of devotion (*bhakti*) to Hindu Gods, Buddhist buddhas and bodhisattvas, and Jain *jina*-s (as well as a variety of "tribal" Gods that were not assimilated into Hinduism, Buddhism, or Jainism). Also, there are paths of "action" (*karma*) that involve adherence to moral norms and social conventions, whether in the form of caste duty or the ethical principles of Buddhism or Jainism.

Of course, each path correlates to a range of obstacles—everything that serves as an impediment to attaining liberating knowledge, expressing loving devotion, and observing social duties and moral prescriptions. What is more philosophically significant, however, is how paths of knowledge and devotion sometimes come into conflict with the path of action, at least as it is understood to require adherence to moral norms and social conventions. In these cases, to attain certain insights or to express certain devotions means behaving in ways that go against or beyond morality and convention.

We begin by returning to the *Bhagavad Gītā*, this time with respect to its "moral dilemma." As you might remember from last chapter, the text opens with the Pāṇḍava warrior-prince Arjuna surveying what will become a battlefield later that day, reluctant to join the conflict and kill his opponents, the Kauravas, who are his first cousins. In response, Arjuna's charioteer, Lord Kṛṣṇa, tells him that he simply must fight, for this is his religious duty (*dharma*) as a member of the warrior/ruler (*kṣatriya*) caste (*varṇa*). Besides, adds Kṛṣṇa, even if Arjuna kills the body of his enemy, he will not kill their *Ātman*, which is what they really are:

> One man believes he is the slayer, another believes he is the slain. Both are ignorant; there is neither slayer nor slain. You were never born; you will never die. You have never changed; you can never change. Unborn, eternal, immutable, immemorial, you do not die when the body dies.[13]

Moreover, since the Kauravas have cheated the Pāṇḍavas out of their kingdom and refused to give it back, thereby breaking their word, the war against the Kauravas is a "just war."

Thus, *Bhagavad Gītā* gives us an example of how religious duty might come into conflict with moral sensibilities: it is the sacred duty of a warrior to kill in battle, even when the opposing army is populated by blood relations. Nevertheless, insofar as sacred (caste) duty just is social (caste) duty in this case, we seem not to have a conflict between what is socially normative and religiously requisite. Nor do we have a conflict between what is religiously normative and religiously transgressive.

This is not to say, however, that there are not such examples in South Asian philosophy of religion. By about the ninth century, a different kind of *gītā* ("song") had been written—one of many *gītā*-s in South Asian literature—the *Avadhūta Gītā*, or song of the "free soul." Who is a "free soul"? Among the several meanings of *avadhūta* (from the root "to shake") is a reference to enlightened persons who behave in apparently "crazy" ways because they have "shaken off" social conventions and norms. The text and term are particularly important to the Nath sect, a Hindu Śaivite sub-tradition known for its esoteric and heterodox practices, especially by members of its monastic movement.

Naths are among several South Asian sects and movements that Western scholars have categorized as "tantric," an allegedly colonial category for what struck nineteenth-century Indologists as esoteric, magical, or odd. Literally meaning "loom," "warp," or "weave," the term *tantra* is used in South Asian texts in a diversity of ways, though especially with respect to texts that "spread out," "put forth," or "extend" a system of religio-philosophical doctrines and practices. These tantric teachings often go beyond what was traditional or typical for the earlier religious systems of the subcontinent—e.g., Vedic religion or Palī Buddhism—including the use of magical utterances (*mantra*-s), geometric patterns (*maṇḍala*-s), and bodily gestures (*mudrā*-s); the mapping of one's own body to a subtle or cosmic body and the awakening of a mysterious serpent power within (*kuṇḍalinī-yoga*); the ritual naming and invocation of a variety of different deities, especially Goddesses; and the enactment of an assortment of bodily and mental techniques of purification and control. What is relevant here is that tantric systems sometimes commend behavior that is unconventional, immoral, sinful, or heterodox, though only for the sake of "higher" religious ends and only within the strictures of that system.

Take, for example, what are called "proto-tantric" passages in the second-century Mahāyāna Buddhist *Vimalakīrti Sūtra*, which maintains:

> Only those guilty of the five deadly sins can conceive the spirit of enlightenment and can attain Buddhahood, which is the full accomplishment of the qualities of the Buddha![14]

Although these five sins—killing one's father, killing one's mother, killing a saint, breaking up the Buddhist monastic community (*saṃgha*), or causing the Buddha to bleed—typically cause immediate rebirth in hell, here they serve as means of achieving *nirvāṇa*. Should we interpret this literally? Or is the *sūtra* simply making the point that in the quest for *nirvāṇa*, one should not be attached to anything, not even Buddhist teachings and moral norms? For good reasons, we probably incline toward the latter interpretation—after all, we seem not to have stories about Buddhist monks actually killing their parents for the sake of achieving *nirvāṇa*. Nevertheless, there are examples of "mad" monks and nuns (*nyönpa*) among the tantric traditions of Buddhism in Tibet, "free spirits"—*nyönpa* is the Tibetan for *avadhūta*—who violate religious and moral conventions and norms, apparently as a sign that they have transcended them, as well as to criticize the religious status quo.

Other examples of transgressive conduct can be found in some of the devotional (*bhakti*) sects of Hinduism, where devotees engage in excessive action out of intense love for a God.[15] Here, we look at just one example, the nineteenth-century saint Rāmakrishna (1836–86). Although Rāmakrishna served as a priest at a temple dedicated to Kālī—the fierce Goddess often depicted with a bloody sword, a bloody tongue, and a neckless strung with the heads of evildoers—he experimented with many other religious traditions: the practice of Tantric Hinduism, devotion to the Vaiṣṇavite God Rāma, the philosophy of Advaita Vedānta, and visions of Muḥammad and Jesus. He believed that all religions were true, though only as situated within a Vedānta framework that held Hinduism to be the eternal religion and Kālī to be the ultimate reality. Rāmakrishna is particularly known for his odd behavior, which included conversing with images of Kālī, singing and dancing with images of Kālī, feeding Kālī, lying in Kālī's bed, eating Kālī's offerings, and playing with his own body waste. Rāmakrishna admitted that this behavior was madness, though maintained it was madness for that which is permanent (Kālī) rather than for the impermanent things of the world that most people pursue in their daily lives.

Thus far, we have looked at how moral norms and social conventions become obstacles for South Asian religious paths. We now end by looking at how religions themselves, religious doctrines in particular, become obstacles, especially when reified and absolutized. This takes us into a new form of

South Asian Buddhism, Mahāyāna, and its first philosophical school, Madhyamaka.

Although there is some uncertainty about the socio-historical origins of Mahāyāna Buddhism, its first signs are *sūtras* that show up in the early first millennium that purport to be the teachings of the historical Buddha (which were allegedly lost or hidden, later to be rediscovered or revealed). These *sūtras* champion a "great path" (= "Mahāyāna") that is superior to the so-called "lesser path" (= "Hīnayāna"), which is a pejorative term that was applied to all preexisting schools of Buddhism (the only surviving one of which is Theravāda). From the perspective of these Mahāyāna *sūtras*, "Hīnayāna" Buddhism was selfish, emphasizing the enlightenment of the individual over and above the needs of others; elitist, privileging the male monk who alone could attain *nirvāṇa*; and negligent of the core Buddhist insight of impermanence, especially as expressed in the doctrine of interdependent arising (*pratītya-samutpāda*): "That being, this comes to be; from the arising of that, this arises; that being absent, this is not; from the cessation of that, this ceases."[16]

For early proponents of Mahāyāna Buddhism, the interdependence of all things is conveyed by the notion of emptiness (*śūnyatā*), which is not sheer nothingness but rather the absence of anything independent, permanent, and ultimate. For the first Mahāyāna Buddhist philosopher, Nāgārjuna (*c.* 150–*c.* 250), who founded the Madhyamaka school of philosophy (and was later regarded as "the second Buddha"), the critique of emptiness was applied first and foremost to the *dharma*-s of *abhidharma* philosophy—even these momentary "flashes" of experience do not have their own independent existence or nature and therefore cannot serve as the ultimate constituents of reality-as-experienced. But in proclaiming that "all *dharma*-s are empty," Nāgārjuna went further, maintaining that all the teachings (*dharma*) of the Buddha are empty—emptiness included—for all of these teachings are merely words or concepts and therefore cannot be ultimately real or true. This critique of emptiness reached a fever pitch in the final two chapters (24–5) of Nāgārjuna's classic philosophical text, *Fundamental Teachings on the Middle Way* (*Mūla Madhyamaka Kārikā*), which concern the Four Noble Truths and *nirvāṇa*, respectively.

In chapter 24, Nāgārjuna deploys his "two truths" doctrine, which maintains that "the Buddha's teaching is based on two truths: a truth of worldly convention and an ultimate truth."[17] Conventional truths are not, in this case, lesser truths—they are the only truths we have, the truths that we come to agree upon through shared human inquiry. The Four Noble Truths are therefore empty—a conventional truth or aid, not an ultimate truth. So too is *nirvāṇa*, asserts Nāgārjuna in the next and final chapter, where he proclaims that *nirvāṇa* is nothing other than *saṃsāra*, the cycle of rebirth and suffering:

> There is not the slightest difference
> Between cyclic existence [*saṃsāra*] and nirvāṇa.
> There is not the slightest difference
> Between nirvāṇa and cyclic existence.[18]

Nirvāṇa, like *saṃsāra*, is but a word or concept. Moreover, since the ultimate truth is just to see that all truths are merely conventional, *nirvāṇa* is just seeing *saṃsāra* for what it is—our conventional reality in which nothing is independently, permanently, essentially, or ultimately real. One might say then, that with Nāgārjuna, Buddhism itself becomes an obstacle insofar as it or its teachings and practices are taken to be ultimately real and true.

V. East Asian Philosophy of Religion

In East Asian philosophy of religion, the greatest obstacle for humans does not involve freedom or knowledge but harmony and balance. This is true for all three of China's "three teachings"—Confucianism, Daoism, and Buddhism—though in different ways for each. Confucianism is primarily concerned about obstacles that affect the balance of the family and society; Daoism, the balance of the body and nature; Buddhism, the balance of the mind and individual (particularly with respect to death and rebirth). Underlying all these religious philosophies is the fundamental conviction that the human heart-mind (*xīn*) is naturally or originally good. What prevents us from living the way we should is what prevents us from seeing, recovering, and nourishing that original goodness.

We begin with Daoism, as its classic texts and teachings are one source of the view that human beings in particular and nature in general are originally and essentially good. In the *Dàodéjīng* we read that the *Dào* gives birth to all things, nurtures them, provides for them, sustains them, and protects them. Those that return to and unite with *Dào*, return to the root and origin, achieving harmony and longevity. If there is an obstacle to this "path," it is simply behavior that is not effortless, spontaneous, and natural, for example, the "cutting, filing, and polishing" of Confucians, which only ends up ruining what is naturally perfect. So, too, for the *Zhuāngzǐ*, in which attitudes that are dogmatic and myopic keep us from being attuned to and aligned with *Dào* (e.g., the judgments of true/false and right/wrong made by Confucians and Mohists). For both texts, we might also say that since everything just is *Dào*, there really are no obstacles at all—we simply must realize what is already so.

Such understandings of human nature came to influence the fourth-generation Confucian Mencius (372–289 BCE), who posited four "sprouts" of human goodness, each of which is original or innate to the nature (*xìng*) of the human heart-mind (*xīn*): compassion, the sprout of human-heartedness (*rén*); shame, of moral rightness (*yì*); respect, of ritual propriety (*lǐ*, 禮); and approval of right and disapproval of wrong, of moral wisdom (*zhì*). As you know from Chapter 5, these sprouts are dispositions or tendencies that do not automatically give rise to their corresponding virtues. Standing in the way of the "path" of their development are three potential "obstacles": physical environments in which basic needs cannot be met; social environments in which Confucian virtues, rituals, and relations are not taught; and the lack of individual effort in the cultivation of virtues, observance of rituals, and rectification of social relations. Here, we focus on the second: the "externals" of society that instill and support behaviors that thwart human nature. Mencius exemplified this with his allegory of Ox Mountain, a mountain that is densely forested and supportive of wildlife until humans cut down all the trees.[19] After that, some shrub grass and other low-lying plants began to grow, at least until humans bring livestock to graze on the vegetation. Eventually, nothing grows anymore on Ox Mountain. This is how it is with corrupt and immoral societies—they "chop down" the natural dispositions and tendencies toward good in humans through repeated efforts at inculcating and rewarding vicious and immoral behavior.

Although the later (Neo)Confucian philosopher Zhū Xī (1130–1200) followed Mencius in holding that the nature of the heart-mind is originally good (as constituted by sprouts of the Confucian virtues), he devoted more attention to the dynamics of this nature, finding the roots of "badness" therein. In this respect Zhū Xī was especially influenced by an early Confucian work that we looked at last chapter, *The Doctrine of the Mean* (*Zhōngyōng*), which in its opening section differentiates a state of equilibrium (*zhōng*), which exists before the feelings (*qíng*, 情) of pleasure, anger, sorrow, and joy are aroused, and a state of harmony (*yōng*), which arises when these feeling attain their balance or "mean."[20] Zhū Xī brought to this differentiation another key distinction, one that he inherited from the (Neo)Confucian philosophers who preceded him: immaterial "pattern-principle" (*lǐ*, 理) and material "vital energy" (*qì*). We will explore *lǐ* and *qì* in more detail in the next chapter; for now, you can think of *lǐ* as both the natural pattern-principles of the cosmos and moral norms of human behavior, *qì*, as the underlying material force and energy of everything. (N.B. there are two different Chinese characters that are transliterated as *lǐ*. You were introduced to the first, "ritual propriety" [禮], in Chapter 1; now you are introduced to the second, "pattern-principle" [理].)

What do *lǐ* and *qì* have to do with human nature prior to the arousal of feelings and after feelings have been harmonized? In the former case, human nature is constituted only by pattern-principle—natural and moral patterns and norms—thus it is wholly good. However, since humans never exist without a material body, and since all material things are constituted by vital energy, the pattern-principle in humans is always intermixed with vital energy. It is in this intermixture of pattern-principle and vital energy that the feelings arise, a process that Zhū Xī metaphorizes as the disturbance of tranquil water or the dirtying of a clean mirror.[21] The Confucian sage must therefore learn to harmonize these feelings (which for Zhū Xī also included love, hate, and desire, totaling seven in all; see Table 8.1). Doing so involved the methods discussed last chapter: the "external" practices of investigating things and extending knowledge, combined with the "internal" practices of holding fast to seriousness and making thoughts sincere. As Zhū Xī writes,

> So long as in one's daily life the effort at seriousness and cultivation is fully extended and there are no selfish human desires to disturb it, then before the feelings are aroused it will be as clear as a mirror and as calm as still water, and after the feelings are aroused it will attain due measure and degree without exception. This is the essential task in everyday life.[22]

Daoism also exerts considerable influence on East Asian Buddhism, particularly with respect to how it understands what humans are, what paths they travel, and what obstacles they encounter. Last chapter we looked at both *The Awakening of Faith in Mahāyāna* and the *Platform Sūtra of the Sixth Patriarch*, the former of which taught that humans are originally enlightened through an innate Buddha-nature, the latter, that

Table 8.1 Four Virtues and Seven Feelings[23]

Four Virtues = the natural, unmixed nature of pattern-principle (*lǐ*, 理) in humans	(1) human-heartedness (*rén*), (2) ritual propriety (*lǐ*, 禮), (3) moral rightness (*yì*), (4) moral wisdom (*zhì*)
Seven Feelings (*qíng*) = what is aroused when *lǐ* (理) is mixed with vital energy (*qì*)	(1) pleasure, (2) anger, (3) sorrow, (4) joy, (5) love, (6) hate, (7) desire

since "Buddha-nature is forever clear and pure," (final) enlightenment can be attained suddenly. Last chapter we also looked (briefly) at the practice of meditation in Chán (Jp. Zen) Buddhism and of chanting the name of Amitābha Buddha (Ch. *niànfó*; Jp. *nembutsu*) in Pure Land Buddhism. Although there are of course obstacles to both—laziness, selfishness, delusion, wickedness—all such obstacles can be overcome through mindful practice, especially as empowered by innate Buddha-nature. Even in the case of Pure Land Buddhism, which understands our own Buddha-realm to be in a period of decline, making it impossible to attain *nirvāṇa* now from here, there is an "easy path" of practice that relies on the "other effort" (Ch. *tālì*; Jp. *tariki*) of the Buddha Amitābha to be reborn in his Pure Land, from which *nirvāṇa* is easy to attain (see Chapter 11).

Once again, we therefore see the "positive" understanding of human nature in East Asian philosophy of religion. Humans are spontaneously natural (in the case of Daoism) or naturally good (in the case of Confucianism) or originally enlightened (in the case of Buddhism). Although some effort is required to recover that original nature, the obstacles are minimal given that one must only recover what originally was, not attain something new.

Nevertheless, it bears mentioning in closing that, as in the case of some South Asian philosophies of religion, words and concepts, on the one hand, and doctrines and moralities, on the other hand, are sometimes viewed as an obstacle to recovery of our original nature in East Asian philosophy of religion. This is particularly the case in Daoism and Buddhism, especially as human words and concepts are mistaken for what is really real—the eternal flow of *Dào*, or the experiential immediacy of Buddha-nature, respectively.

In the case of Daoism, we have already glimpsed this in its classic texts, *Dàodéjīng* and *Zhuāngzǐ*. According to chapter 38 of the *Dàodéjīng*, those of highest virtue do not act virtuously, whereas those who act virtuously are without virtue. Only when the way (*Dào*) is lost, continues chapter 38, do the Confucian virtues of humaneness (*rén*), moral rightness (*yì*), and ritual propriety (*lǐ*, 禮) arise.[24] For the *Zhuāngzǐ*, judgments of right and wrong are "mutually dependent" and "go by circumstance," contra the rigid and absolutistic positions of the Confucians and Mohists, who affirm what each other deny and deny what each other affirm.[25] That which seems wrong, might be right in certain circumstances; that which seems useless, might be useful in certain circumstances. Here, there is a critical distrust of all conventional morality—especially Confucian and Mohist—at least insofar as it is rigidified and reified.

In the case of Buddhism, we have just seen in the previous section how some early Mahāyāna Buddhist texts were keen to emphasize that commitment to the fundamental Buddhist teachings of impermanence and emptiness entailed that no Buddhist path or teaching could be ultimately real or true. Nāgārjuna's *Fundamental Teachings on the Middle Way* (*Mūla Madhyamaka Kārikā*) proclaimed that "all *dharma*-s are empty"—including core Buddhist teachings about the Four Noble Truths, the Eightfold Path, the Three Jewels, and even *nirvāṇa* itself. So too did the *Vimalakīrti Sūtra*, which also commended committing the five deadly sins.[26] These are just some of the many early Mahāyāna Buddhist texts that subject core Buddhist teachings and practices to the critique of emptiness, advancing instead the notion of "useful means" (Sk. *upāya*; Ch. *fāngbiàn*)—that any "means" can be "useful" to attaining *nirvāṇa*, even apparently unconventional, immoral, sinful, and heterodox means.

These Mahāyāna Buddhist texts and ideas took root in East Asia, especially in Chán/Zen Buddhism, which purports to be a direct transmission outside of Buddhist scripture and therefore sometimes takes up a critical attitude to classical Buddhist doctrines and ethics. For example, Línjì Yìxuán (臨濟義玄, d. 866), the founder of Línjǐ school of Chán Buddhism (which is known as the Rinzai school in Japan), is renowned for sayings like the Buddha is a "dried human excrement-removing stick," those who seek the *dharma* "have no need for the Buddha," and you should "kill the Buddha if you happen to meet him."[27] Here, Buddhism itself, especially as reified in doctrines and institutions, becomes an obstacle to the practice of Buddhism.

Although Línjì Yìxuán is also known for beating his students (with a stick used to swat mosquitos)—apparently to jar them out of conventional ways of thinking—we have no record of him enacting immoral or heterodox behavior, at least not in the ways that another Chán/Zen monk did. This "monk," Ikkyū (一休宗純, 1394–1481), was a Japanese Zen monk (of the Rinzai school) who spent most of his life living outside monasteries, having rejected all his masters and adopted a vagabond life, thereby earning the name "Crazy Cloud." Ikkyū was especially known for insisting that enlightenment could be attained and furthered through conventionally immoral acts, especially sex, which he regarded as religious rite. He frequented bars and brothels, often in his black monk robes, eventually developing an open and passionate relationship with a blind singer named Lady Mori. Here we see "in action" the Mahāyāna Buddhist principle that any means—especially love and sex in this case—might be a "useful means" for "waking up." Thus, we again see how some philosophies of religion take religion, morality, and convention as obstacles on the religious path.

VI. Mediterranean/Abrahamic Philosophy of Religion

What keeps us from reaching our destination in Abrahamic philosophy of religion is usually some variation of sin, with notable differences in how sin is understood (and forgiven) in these religions. For Judaism, sins are violations of the 613 commandments (Hb. *mitzvot*) by which Jews stand in covenantal relationship with YHWH.[28] When the Jerusalem Temple existed, sacrifices were offered there for forgiveness of personal and corporate sins; since the destruction of the Second Temple, however, sins are forgiven by "right action"—acts of loving kindness (*gĕmîlût ḥăsādîm*) and repentance (*tĕšûbâ*), as well as "ample apology" in the case of sins between people—with the first ten days of the Jewish calendar (from Rosh Hashanah to Yom Kippur) serving as a special, sacred time when people remember their sins of the year, make restitution with people they have wronged, and seek forgiveness from YHWH. By contrast, the Western Christian church largely adopted the view of St. Paul (5–67), as interpreted by Augustine (354–430) and other early theologians, that sin was an original condition inherited by all humans, rendering them unable to freely enact the good until forgiven through the grace of the Trinitarian God and faith in the death and resurrection of Jesus Christ. Not all, however, agreed with Augustine's interpretation of this original sin as an irresistible inclination toward lustful desire and an overburdening sense of guilt, both inherited through procreation; most notably, Eastern Orthodox Christianity does not take original sin as a state of guilt that prevents humans from entering into communion with the Trinitarian God. With Islam, we flip back to a Jewish model of sin as individual acts rather than universal condition—in this case, anything that goes against the commands of Allah as revealed in Qur'ān (the word of Allah), recorded in *ḥadīth* (the sayings and doings of Prophet Muḥammad), systematized through various schools of Islamic Law (*sharī'a*), and interpreted through the rulings of Islamic jurisprudence (*fiqh*).[29] Although the Qur'ān distinguishes between major sins and minor sins (53:31–2), with sins against Allah as the most severe (especially *shirk*, accepting other deities besides Allah, or associating things that are not Allah with Allah), it also teaches that Allah is merciful and forgives sin for those who genuinely repent (*tawba*), a term that, like the Hebrew term *tĕšûbâ*, means to "turn" or "return" to God.

Arguably more philosophically interesting, however, are the mystical traditions of Abrahamic religions, where the greatest obstacle on the path toward unity with the Abrahamic God is the self. If we think of ourselves as something separate from this God, something needing to journey to this God, then we prevent ourselves from realizing that we already are united with this God in some sense. There is nothing to do and nowhere to go, except to realize what is already the case. In this sense, institutionalized religious paths, especially doctrines and moralities, can also constitute obstacles, for no such path or concept is God in Godself.

Islamic mysticism (Sufism) is again exemplary in this respect, especially since the passionate love of the mystic lover for the divine beloved was a prominent part of Islamic mysticism (Sufism) as far back as the early female Sufi Rābiʿa (718–801), who declared that Allah should be worshipped not from fear of hell or hope of paradise but simply for the love of God alone. Although Rābiʿa is not known for committing or commending any morally or religiously questionable behavior, two Sufis during the next two centuries ran afoul of Islamic orthodoxy for utterances they made during mystical states of union with Allah: Bāyazīd Bisṭāmī (d. 874), for proclaiming "Glory be to me"; and Manṣūr al-Ḥallāj (*c.* 858–922), for uttering "I am the Truth" (*Anā al-Ḥaqq*). In the latter case, al-Ḥallāj, who had moved to Baghdad, where he was viewed as a threat by the ruling ʿAbbāsid Caliphate (for political reasons that went well beyond his mystical utterances), was brutally executed in 922.

Unsurprisingly, the century after al-Ḥallāj's execution saw Sufi practitioners and hagiographers wrestling with Sufism's relationship to orthodox Islam. During this time, the distinction between "drunk" (*sukr*) and "sober" (*ṣaḥr*) Sufism took shape, with the former term indicating a "drunken" state of union between the Sufi and Allah, the latter representing this state more "soberly" as one of calm communion, not ecstatic union. From the perspective of drunk Sufism, it was not al-Ḥallāj but Allah who uttered "I am Truth," since al-Ḥallāj had been "annihilated" (*fanāʾ*) and therefore "subsisted" (*baqāʾ*) only in/as Allah in this mystical state of union. From the perspective of both drunk and sober Sufism, al-Ḥallāj's mystical utterances should never have been conveyed to the masses and authorities, people who simply could not understand and therefore would misinterpret. Nevertheless, "drunk" Sufis would continue speaking not only about the experience of union with Allah but also how passionate love for Allah involved transgressing or transcending moral and religious norms and conventions.

One example comes from the Persian Sufi poet known by the pen-name Farīd ud-Dīn ʿAṭṭār (*c.* 1145–*c.* 1221), whose *Conference of the Birds* narrates an allegorical story about a group of birds that set out on a journey to find a king called the Simorgh. Only thirty birds ultimately have the courage and resolve for the journey, which requires passing through seven valleys representing the seven stages (*maqaamat*) that a Sufi must master to draw close to and become unified with Allah: quest, love, mystery, detachment and serenity, unity, awe, bewilderment, and poverty and nothingness.[30] As the birds reach the final valley/stage of poverty and nothingness, ʿAṭṭār metaphorizes the union of Sufi and Allah in the frequently retold image of the moth burned up in the flame:

> He knows, he knows the truth we seek,
> That hidden truth of which we cannot speak. [. . .]
> No creature's Self can be admitted here,
> Where all identity must disappear.[31]

And when the birds finally reach the Simorgh, ʿAṭṭār explains that these "thirty birds"—which is just the meaning of *simorgh*—see only themselves in the mirror of the Simorgh, their "selves" annihilated, only "Allah" subsisting.

Not only does self disappear in this state of union, according to ʿAṭṭār; "evil" does as well:

> With God both Self and evil disappear.
> When I escape the Self I will arise and be as God.[32]

Indeed, *Conference of the Birds* is chock full of examples of morally and religiously questionable behavior that is undertaken out of love for the beloved. One of the more striking examples is Sheikh Sam'an, a devout Sufi Sheikh, who burns the Qurʾān, drinks wine, gives up Islam, bows before a Christian girl, and becomes a swineherd, all out of passionate love for her. Although the Sheikh later repents for his actions, the moral of the story is nonetheless clear: the Sufi must be willing to do anything, even renounce religion/Islam, out of love for the beloved, Allah.

The history of Christianity is not without its own condemned and executed mystics, not to mention "fools for Christ" who engaged in conventionally and morally questionable behavior for the sake of demonstrating the depth of their devotion and criticizing the status quo. With respect to the executed, one medieval example now commonly celebrated is the female mystic Marguerite Porete (d. 1310). A member of the lay order known as the Beguines, Porete was burned at the stake in 1310 as part of a wider crackdown on the "Free Spirit heresy," more specifically for the views advocated in her work *The Mirror of the Simple Souls Who are*

Annihilated and Remain Only in Will and Desire of Love. Written as a dialogue between the Soul, Love, and Reason, the "Simple Soul" relinquishes Reason, which cannot comprehend the Trinitarian God, for Divine Love. When the Simple Soul is full of Divine Love, it is completely united with this God, having no will other than this God's, transcending reason and the virtues, attaining a beatific state of sinlessness. As Porete avows through the character Love:

> I am God, says Love, for Love is God and God is Love, and this Soul is God by the condition of Love. I am God by divine nature and this Soul is God by righteousness of Love.[33]

Given that Porete's Simple Soul transcended not only moral distinctions but also the church's control—which was of course *male* control—Porete was accused of antinomianism and her book was banned. Then, both her and her book were burned.

Although those possessing a copy of Porete's *The Mirror of the Simple Souls* were required to relinquish it to Dominican authorities (under pain of excommunication), it nevertheless found its way into the hands of other mystics, one of whom may have been the Dominican monk Meister Eckhart (*c.* 1260–*c.* 1328), whose work contains similar themes. Among the most relevant are some of Eckhart's sermons (which he delivered in the German vernacular), one of which, "Sermon 52," takes the biblical beatitude "Blessed Are the Poor in Spirit" as its subject matter, contrasting an inferior external poverty with a superior internal poverty. This internal poverty "wants nothing," "knows nothing," and "has nothing." It "wants nothing" because it does not will or desire anything at all, not even to will to do God's will—it is devoid of will and desire. It "knows nothing" because it is unaware that it does not will anything or live for anything—it is free of all knowledge and understanding. And it "has nothing" because it is nothing—for to be something is to preserve a distinction between itself and the Trinitarian God. Only by being free of the obstacle of the self and its will and understanding can the soul be unified with this God. Even "God" is an obstacle if taken as a particular being or concept that is dualistically contrasted with the self. Thus, Eckhart's sermon later goes on to make the astounding request "I pray to God that he may make me free of 'God.'"[34] Although Eckhart did not meet the same fate as Porete, twenty-eight of his teachings were condemned as heretical in a Papal Bull issued by Pope John XXII in 1329, one year after Eckhart's death.

By contrast to Islam's "drunk Sufis" and Christianity's "fool for Christ," ecstatic and unconventional behavior was not as pronounced in Jewish mysticism since mystical learning and practice were more strictly guarded by older male rabbis and observance of the commandments (Hb. *mitzvot*) and law (*hălākâ*) were a precondition for the practice of mysticism. Nevertheless, medieval Jewish mysticism—Lurianic Kabbalah in particular—offers the fascinating example of "God as obstacle."

Although first-millennium Jewish mystics generally attempted either to undertake mystical journeys up through the realms of heaven to the throne room of YHWH or to plumb the depths of mystical knowledge in the Torah in order to master the secrets of creation, the first few centuries of the second millennium witnessed the birth of a new form of Jewish mysticism in southern France and Spain, which was known as "Kabbalah," literally meaning "tradition." Influenced by Neo-Platonic philosophy, especially as it had influenced Christian and Muslim mysticism, Kabbalah was "theosophical" and "theurgical" in focus—the former in attempting to mystically understand the divine through its manifestations; the latter in attempting to mystically influence the divine through ritual and meditative action.

Even later, after the Jews were expelled in 1492 from Spain (which had become for them a kind of promised land outside the Promised Land), Kabbalah was developed and systematized by Isaac Luria (1534–72), who lived in the town of Safed in the Galilee region of Israel, where many exiled Spanish Jews settled (and which was then under control of the Ottoman Empire). Three teachings form the core of "Lurianic Kabbalah," which over time became the preeminent form of Kabbalah in particular and Jewish mysticism in general. First, *ṣimṣûm* is the act by which *ʾÊn Sôp*—"The Limitless," God prior to manifestation—self-contracts, abandoning space to make room for creation, leaving behind divine residue in the process. Second, *shevirah* involves the emanation of this God into ten *sĕpîrôt* (divine creative powers, metaphorized as lights), each of which is contained in a divine vessel, the lower seven of which are unable to contain the light and therefore shatter (*shevirah*), causing these *sĕpîrôt* to become embedded in evil husks of formless matter, held in captivity by the powers of darkness (Figure 8). Third, *tiqqûn* is the repair of the *sĕpîrôt*, which is the responsibility of humans with respect to the tenth and final *sĕpîrâ*, the only *sĕpîrâ* unable to free itself from captivity, the *Shekinah* (which referred to the "dwelling" or "settling" of the divine presence in the Hebrew Bible and was later understood as the divine feminine in Kabbalah). This "repair," which is accomplished by

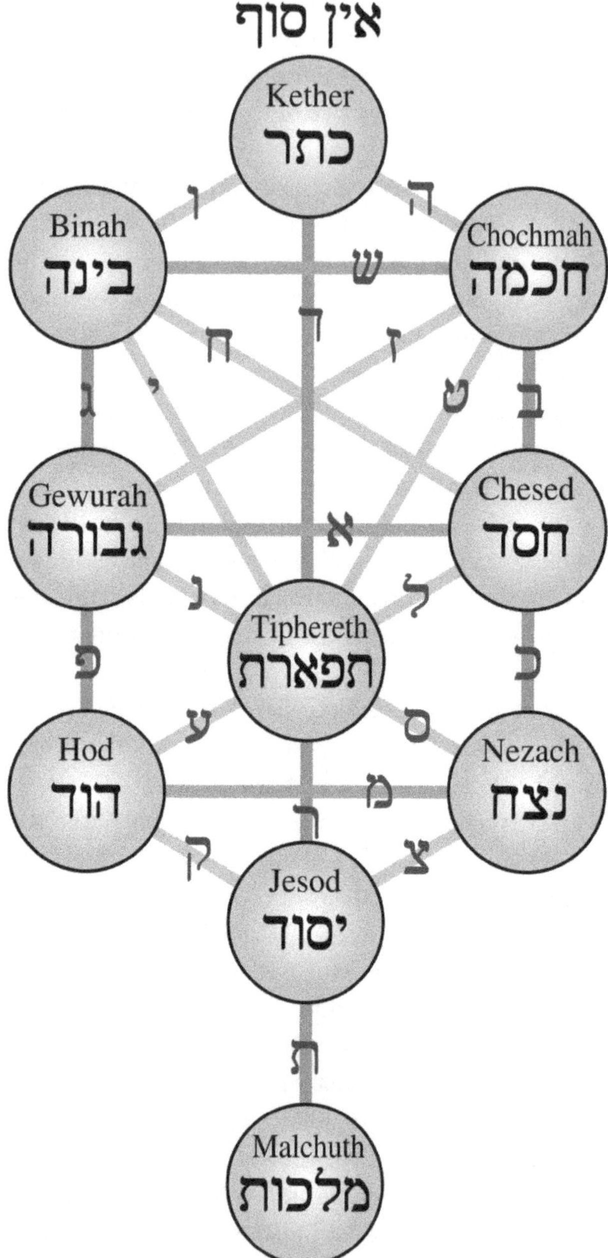

Figure 8 Sěpîrôt of Jewish Kabbalah. AnonMoos, "Kabbalistic 'Tree of Life,'" July 26, 2014, Public Domain, Wikimedia Commons.

Jews through upholding the commandments, especially when accompanied by acts of mystical meditation or intention (*kawwānâ*), ultimately leads to the coming of the Messiah. For this now-predominant form of Jewish mysticism, one might therefore say that the greatest obstacle in the path of the self is the brokenness of YHWH, which humans alone must fix.

VII. European/Academic Philosophy of Religion

One of the more notable features of nineteenth-century philosophy of religion is that religion itself begins showing up as an as an obstacle, perhaps even the chief obstacle, that prevents humans from reaching their destination. We begin with a group of nineteenth-century philosophers who were influenced by, though broke from, the philosophy of German philosopher Georg Wilhelm Hegel (1770–1831). (We will look at Hegel himself in Chapter 11.)

Whereas Hegel looked to a dialectic of ideas for the impelling force of historical development, the subsequent generation of "Young Hegelians" strove to "set Hegel on his feet," arguing that it is nature as concrete facticity that motivates historical progress. One of the first "Young Hegelians," Ludwig Feuerbach (1804–72), set out to show this in the case of religious systems, positing that religion evolved in three broad stages: during the first stage of animism, humans venerated the forces of nature and natural phenomena; with the next stage of polytheism, humans began deifying attributes of themselves, creating an anthropomorphic God for every such attribute; and in the final stage of monotheism, these attributes coalesced in a single transcendent deity who was said to possess all the essential attributes of humankind. Feuerbach therefore maintained that "theology is anthropology"; the study of Gods, but that of humans who create Gods in their own image. In the third stage in particular, humans project onto a single God their own three chief powers in unlimited perfection: omniscience (the power of reason), omnipotence (the power of will), and omnibenevolence (the power of love). In doing so, humans alienate themselves from their own nature. Thus, religion must be overcome (even though it forms an integral stage in the development of human consciousness since humans must objectify their essence before they can become aware of it as such). Instead of creating Gods, humans must learn to "deify" themselves.

Another Hegelian-influenced critic of religion is Karl Marx (1818–83). As you know from Chapter 4 (where we looked at the post-Marxist philosopher Louis Althusser), Marx held that religion is one part of an ideological superstructure that serves to legitimate the state, which itself seeks to perpetuate its economic modes and social classes of production. Just a moment of reflection begins to show how this works in contemporary Western societies: religion—"civil religion" in particular—is not only supportive of working hard and accumulating possessions but also associates economic security and success with moral and spiritual righteousness. Worse, maintained Marx, for those who do not experience such socioeconomic security and success, religion serves as an "opium," numbing them from rising up against socioeconomic oppression and injustice by promising them recompense for their suffering in a blessed afterlife if they remain "good citizens." For Marx, however, it was inadequate simply to understand "religion as obstacle," as he believed Feuerbach had done; one also needed to overcome it, especially in society. Thus, Marx's "Theses Against Feuerbach" was to proclaim: "The philosophers have only *interpreted* the world, in various ways; the point, however is to change it."[35]

Arguably the fiercest nineteenth-century critic of religion, however, was Friedrich Nietzsche (1844–1900), who pronounced through the voices of some of his literary characters that "God is dead." Although it is tempting to interpret this utterance as a simple advocation of the nonexistence of God, its meaning goes far beyond, including what Nietzsche believed to be the implausibility of all absolute truths and values, especially moral truths. Nietzsche's *On the Genealogy of Morals* took up the task of demonstrating the non-objectivity of moral values, especially altruism, presenting a "genealogy of morals" in three broad stages. First there was the "master morality" of the ancient Greeks, where good and bad were applied to people, not actions. The nobility were virtuous or excellent (Gk. *aretē*) simply because they were superior to the commoners. Then there was a "slave revolt" in morality motivated by *ressentiment* of the powers and privileges of the strong, with Jewish and Christian priests inventing morality, redefining good as that which is useful or beneficial to the weak and powerless, extolling virtues such as humility, weakness, and submission. Strong and independent individuals were now regarded as dangerous and therefore evil. Priests had become the new masters, controlling a blindly subservient "herd" of parishioners through a life-denying and instinct-suppressing ethic. In the third and final stage, this ethic became that of the democratic and socialist nation-states of Nietzsche's day and age, which valued equality and mediocrity over individuality and power. For Nietzsche, all such "no-saying" and "life-denying" moralities—especially those of religion—needed to be rejected by an "overman" (*Übermensch*) who instead "wills to power" by affirming his natural moral instincts, creating his own life-promoting and life-preserving values, and thereby rising above the mediocre, "levelled-down" herd. In short, for Nietzsche religion is a "no-saying" to life, an inversion and perversion of the natural instincts and motivations of humans.

Even among some Christian philosophers of religion in the nineteenth century, we see religion becoming an obstacle to authentic human existence. Most notable is the nineteenth-century Danish philosopher Soren Kierkegaard (1813–55), who saw "Christendom"—the reification and normalization of Christianity as a sociopolitical entity, especially in the Danish State Church—as the greatest obstacle to the practice of Christianity, making it safe and easy rather than risky and difficult. For Kierkegaard, no one better embodied this risky and difficult path than the biblical patriarch Abraham, who was the subject of Kierkegaard's pseudonymously authored work *Fear and Trembling*. From the perspective of philosophy, not to mention society more generally, Abraham constitutes a "problem," since Abraham attempted to sacrifice his son Isaac in response to YHWH's command. This is abhorrent from the perspective of ethics, for it is clearly immoral and unethical to sacrifice humans, let alone one's own children, especially a child promised by a God. And yet the Bible—especially the New Testament writer, Saint Paul—calls Abraham a "knight of faith." How can this be? For Kierkegaard, Abraham was beholden to a higher aim or goal (Gk. *telos*) than that of ethical duty to the moral law and other humans—that of "absolute relationship to the absolute."[36] Kierkegaard called this a "teleological suspension of the ethical"—a suspension of our commitments to moral norms and social conventions for the sake of absolute obedience to the Christian-Trinitarian God, which requires going beyond morality, beyond even Christianity.

As we turn to the twentieth century, we see religion increasingly showing up as an obstacle for many feminist philosophers of religion.[37] Here we look at the American philosopher Mary Daly (1928–2010) and the French philosopher Luce Irigaray (b. 1930), who share some significant similarities with each other. Both adopt a (Feuerbachian) projection theory, arguing that the "Father God" of Abrahamic religion in general and Christianity in particular is a projection of male identity. Both therefore deconstruct patriarchal conceptions of God as transcendent, objective, and father/son-like. In lieu of these conceptions, both forward a "female divine" that is fully immanent in the female self, allowing female subjectivity to become more expansive and free. Although neither relegate religion to the category of illusion *per se*, both hold religion to be fully immanent, without any objective, supernatural reality. For Irigaray, this affirmation of immanence is counterbalanced by the elevation of "woman" to the status of the divine—a "feminine divine" that provides a "sensible transcendental." This divine is located in between two people who encounter each other face to face, especially in the recognition of sexual difference.

Finally, we consider the twenty-first century movement known as "New Atheism," especially as manifested in the writings of their so-called "Four Horsemen": Richard Dawkins (b. 1941), Daniel Dennett (b. 1942), Sam Harris (b. 1967), and Christopher Hitchens (1949–2011).[38] Despite their differences, the philosophies of these authors share metaphysical, epistemological, and ethical components. Metaphysically, they believe that there is no supernatural or divine reality; epistemologically, they claim that religious belief is irrational since it not based on empirical/scientific evidence; and ethically, they assume that there is a universal and objective secular moral standard. This objective-secular morality arguably sets the "Four Horsemen" apart from other atheists, playing a pivotal role in their arguments that religion is bad in an assortment of ways. Although religion might be an evolutionary byproduct of certain adaptive traits and abilities, which themselves proved important for survival, religion is no longer beneficial, if it ever was. Indeed, three of the New Atheists (Harris, Dawkins, and Hitchens) are quite explicit in their moral condemnation of religious people on the grounds that religious beliefs and practices have predominately negative consequences (e.g., suicide bombings, Inquisition, religious wars, witch hunts, homophobia). In sum, religion makes people bad, not good. Thus, each of the New Atheists recommends or references a non-religious means of personal fulfillment and collective well-being (involving science, wonder, or secular spirituality).

VIII. Putting it All Together

Once again, we are left with a diversity of philosophies—in this case about what, if anything, are the obstacles that humans must overcome to travel some path to some destination. Those obstacles can be basic conditions of human beings, for example, original sin or tendencies toward sin (in the case of some Abrahamic religious philosophies), original ignorance or tendencies toward ignorance (in the case of some South Asian religious philosophies), original imbalance or tendencies toward imbalance (in the case of some East Asian religious philosophies), or states of separation from personal Gods or impersonal Absolutes (in other Abrahamic and South Asian religious philosophies). Obstacles can also be due to a simple failure of individual effort with respect to sin, ignorance, desire, or other vices. Or obstacles can be the product of the corrupting influence of society on originally good, enlightened, or balanced humans; or of words and concepts that distort our perception of what is really real; or of unjust social institutions created by humans such as colonialism, patriarchy, or religion itself. Obstacles can also be the result of external beings or forces, whether Anti-gods or demons or "witches," who oppose humans in their efforts to attain their goals and destinations. Then again, perhaps our only real "obstacle" is to think that there are obstacles in the first place. Table 8.2 offers one rudimentary attempt to categorize some of the obstacles we have described above.

Which is correct? As in the case of previous chapters, how you answer this question is to great extent a product of the beliefs and values that you bring to this chapter. That is not to say, however, that you cannot take "other" philosophies of religion seriously and that these philosophies of religion cannot challenge your beliefs and values. Moreover, as a philosopher of "global-critical" philosophy of religion, you can set aside your beliefs and values to some extent and ask about the epistemic virtues of these theories. Are there any empirical realities relevant to evaluating these theories? Which theories cohere with other established forms of knowledge? Which theories best explain human behavior? Do any theories suffer from internal contradictions? Which theories are most useful to how we live our lives, both personally and

Table 8.2 Types and Examples of Obstacles

Types of Obstacle	Examples
Obstacles due to an inherited human condition	Original sin, original ignorance, original imbalance, separation from what is ultimately real
Obstacles due to a failure of individual effort	Acts of sin, acts of ignorance, acts of selfish desire, acts of laziness, etc.
Obstacles due to society	Corrupting influence of society, words/concepts, unjust social institutions, religion itself
Obstacles due to other (usually malevolent) beings	Anti-gods, witches, demons, perhaps also tricksters

socially? In answering questions such as these, you can begin to evaluate the truth of these obstacles, at least for yourself and in your context, though also in relation to some of the more influential theories from around the globe.

And what about the claim that religion itself is an obstacle for the paths of humans? In the very least, we now know that variations of this claim are found in religious traditions themselves, especially when institutionalized doctrines, rituals, and moralities are taken as ends in themselves (rather than means to ends). To this, we can add awareness of an increasing number of paths and practices that are not typically thought of as "religious" but nonetheless used by humans to orient themselves to what they believe is ultimately real, true, and good. Whether these paths are called "atheistic," "humanistic," "philosophical," "spiritual," or something else, one significant aspect of them is their claim that one can be "good without God." Indeed, ample sociological research would seem to confirm this, as there is no strong correlation between religiosity and moral behavior, nor between irreligiosity and immoral behavior.[39]

In closing, let us take note of the fact that this is our final chapter about the journey of the self. Consider, therefore, how our investigation of obstacles in this chapter involves our previous explorations of the paths and destinations of the self, as well as its natures and origins. If we are most concerned with what comes after death (whether an afterlife or rebirth or something else), with this serving as our destination or goal, then our obstacles will be whatever prevents us from living in a way to reach that destination. But if our destinations are this-worldly, whether of knowledge, equanimity, well-being, flourishing, peace, or justice, then our obstacles will be whatever prevents us from attaining those ends on earth. Are we inclined to call such this-worldly destinations, paths, and obstacles religious? For some, they clearly are.

Questions for Discussion

1. Describe, compare, and evaluate some of the philosophies of religion above with respect to how they conceptualize religious obstacles for the self.
2. Is religion itself an obstacle for human beings? Explain and evaluate reasons for and against this claim. Include reasons that come from within religious traditions.
3. Explore the relationship between obstacles, paths, and destinations in some of the philosophies of religion in this chapter. Compare them to your own obstacles, paths, and destinations.

Primary and Scholarly Sources

East Asia

Mencius, 6A7–8. In *A Source Book in Chinese Philosophy*, ed. Wing-Tsit Chan, 55–7. Princeton, NJ: Princeton University Press, 1963.

Xī, Zhū. "First Letter to the Gentlemen of Hunan to Equilibrium and Harmony." In *A Source Book in Chinese Philosophy*, ed. Wing-Tsit Chan, 600–2. Princeton, NJ: Princeton University Press, 1963.

Yìxuán, Línjì. "Recorded Conversations." In *A Source Book in Chinese Philosophy*, ed. Wing-Tsit Chan, 444–9. Princeton, NJ: Princeton University Press, 1963.

Zhuāngzǐ, chapter 2.5. In *Wandering on the Way: Early Taoist Tales and Parables of Chuang Tzu*, trans. Victor H. Mair, 14–16. New York: Bantam Books, 1994.

European/Academic

Feuerbach, Ludwig. *The Essence of Christianity*, section 2. Trans. George Eliot, 12–14, 29–32. New York: Harper & Row, Publishers, 1957.

Irigaray, Luce. "Divine Women." In *Sexes and Genealogies*, trans. Gillian C. Gill, 55–72. New York: Columbia University Press, 1993.

Marx, Karl. "A Contribution to the Critique of Hegel's Philosophy of Right." In *The Marx-Engels Reader*, 2nd ed., ed. Robert C. Tucker, 16–25. New York: W. W. Norton & Co., 1972.

Nietzsche, Friedrich. *On the Genealogy of Morals*, Essay 1, §§16–17. In *Basic Writings of Nietzsche*, trans. Walter Kaufmann, 488–91. New York: The Modern Library, 1992.

Kierkegaard, Soren. *Fear and Trembling: Dialectical Lyric by Johannes de Silentio*. Trans. Alastair Hanay, 83–95. New York: Penguin Books, 1985.

Taylor, James E. "New Atheism." *Internet Encyclopedia of Philosophy*. Available online: https://iep.utm.edu/n-atheis/ (accessed March 11, 2022).

Lakȟóta

"Ikto'mi Marries his Daughter." In *Dakota Texts*, trans. Ella Deloria, 11–19. Lincoln, NE: Bison Books, 2006.

Powers, William K. *Yuwipi: Vision & Experience in Oglala Ritual*, 12–13. Lincoln, NE: Bison Books, 1984.

Mediterranean/Abrahamic

Attar, Farid ud-Din. *Muslim Saints and Mystics*. Trans. A. J. Arberry, 264–71. Boston, MA: Routledge & Kegan Paul, 1966.

Attar, Farid al-Din. *The Conference of the Birds*. Trans. Afkham Darbandi and Dick Davis, 56–75, 191–6. New York: Penguin Books, 1984.

Eckhart, Meister. "Sermon 52." In *Meister Eckhart: The Essential Sermons, Commentaries, Treatises, and Defense*, trans. Edmund Colledge and Bernard McGinn, 199–203. Mahwah, NJ: Paulist Press, 1981.

Porete, Marguerite. *The Mirror of Simple Souls*, chapter 21. Trans. Ellen Babinsky, 103–4. Mahwah, NJ: Paulist Press, 1993.

Scholem, Gershom. *Major Trends in Jewish Mysticism*, 260–78. New York: Schocken Books, 1946.

South Asia

Bhagavad Gītā, II. Trans. Eknath Easwara, 8–16. New York: Vintage Spiritual Classics, 1985.

The Holy Teaching of Vimalakīrti: A Mahāyāna Scripture. Trans. Robert A. F. Thurman, chapter 8. University Park, PA: Pennsylvania State University Press, 1976.

Nāgārjuna. *The Fundamental Wisdom of the Middle Way: Nāgārjuna's Mūlamadhyamakakārikā*, chapter XXV. Trans. Jay L. Garfield, 322–34. New York: Oxford University Press, 1995.

Olson, Carl. *The Mysterious Play of Kālī: An Interpretive Study of Rāmakrishna*, chapter 4. Atlanta, GA: Scholars Press, 1990.

Yorùbá

Abímbọ́lá, Kọ́lá. *Yorùbá Culture: A Philosophical Account*, chapters 3–4. Birmingham: Iroko Academic Publishers, 2005.

Ray, Benjamin C. *African Religions: Symbol, Ritual, and Community*, 2nd ed., 13–15. Upper Saddle River, NJ: Pearson, 1999.

Part III

Journeys of the Cosmos

---

9 What Is the Cosmos?
10 Where Does the Cosmos Come From?
11 Where Is the Cosmos Going To?
12 How Does the Cosmos Get There?
13 What Obstacles are in the Way of the Cosmos?

9

What Is the Cosmos?

Learning Objectives

- Describe, compare, and evaluate the diversity of cosmoses in our six traditions of philosophy of religion.
- Explain how different cosmologies serve different religious ends.
- Explain the relationship between contemporary scientific cosmoses and traditional and recent "religious" ends, evaluating whether such cosmoses can provide worlds for religious paths and destinations.

I. Introduction

We now begin the journey of the cosmos. What ever does that mean?

For starters, let us define cosmos as "everything that is, taken as an ordered whole." With respect to the first half of this definition, "everything that is" should be understood in the widest possible sense, including ultimate beings and realities like Allah, *Òrìṣà*, *Brahman*, and *Dào* (even when they are said to be "beyond being") as well as nonphysical principles and processes such as mind, *wakȟáŋ*, *karma*, and *lǐ* (pattern-principle, 理). With respect to the second half of the definition, "taken as an ordered whole" means that a "cosmos" is more than just a "bunch of stuff"; rather, it is "stuff" upon which humans have imposed a certain order, transforming it into a meaningful whole. That "meaningful whole" might simply involve the fact that all that exists is due to a "Big Bang" and destined for a "Big Freeze," or it might be that all that exists is created by Gods or really just *Brahman* or the ceaseless flow of the *Dào*. Whatever the case, everything that is has been ordered as a whole.

As should now be clear, this use of the term "cosmos" is not synonymous with the contemporary scientific meaning of "universe." Certainly, contemporary scientific universes are types of cosmoses. We might even say that scientific understandings of the universe are becoming the most widespread and prominent cosmoses. But other understandings of the cosmos remain, some of which articulate themselves in relation to contemporary scientific paradigms, others of which are unaware of or unconcerned with such paradigms. For some of these "other" cosmoses, there are realities more fundamental or ultimate than physical entities and processes; for others, there are dimensions or realities beyond the scientific universe.

What, though, do we mean in speaking about the *journey* of the cosmos? Of course, the cosmos does not pack its bags and head out the door. Still, the structure of the journey metaphor can be used to generate productive philosophical questions about the cosmos, just as with the self:

- What is the cosmos (if anything)?
- Where did the cosmos come from (if anywhere)?
- Where is the cosmos going to (if anywhere)?
- How does the cosmos get there (if at all)?
- What obstacles lie in the way of the cosmos (if any)?

For each question, the parenthetical phrases are crucial. We do not presume that the cosmos has an origin, destination, and path (etc.)—for to do so would be to favor a teleological view of the cosmos (for which the cosmos has an ultimate end or aim), which is often present in Abrahamic religious traditions but absent elsewhere. Put simply: we do not presume that the cosmos is on a journey, whether literally or metaphorically. Maybe the cosmos has a beginning and end; maybe it does not.

Also note that, as in the case of the self, appearances can be misleading. We might think that the cosmos exists in a manner that is fully independent and real, just as we did with the self. But this chapter will show how some philosophies of religion challenge this view. Perhaps the cosmos is only an illusion, or really some ultimate reality, or undergirded by fundamental material energy, or constituted by numerous universes. Whatever the case, what is especially interesting for philosophy of religion is how these cosmologies relate to the religious practices and goals of humans, for, as we will soon see, religious cosmologies are not for the sake of "doing science" but rather of offering worlds in which to live religiously. This raises an interesting question that we will take up at the end of this chapter: as contemporary scientific cosmologies grow in influence and importance, (how) can religious practices and goals be "enworlded" in them? To put the question in terms of Western philosophy of religion, (how) are scientific cosmoses designed for the religious paths and destinations of humans?

II. Lakȟóta Philosophy of Religion

With respect to Lakȟóta religious philosophy, an answer to the question "What is the cosmos?" could really just replicate the answer to the question "Who Am I?"—The cosmos is a sacred relationality. As the phrase "all my relations" (*mitákuye oyásiŋ*) indicates, especially when performed in a ritual context, all things are interrelated. And as the term *wakȟáŋ* implies, every object is mysteriously sacred, animated by a spiritual power that extends throughout the universe and relates all things together. For the Lakȟóta, this sacred relationality encompasses four traditional types of beings—the "two-legged peoples" (humans), the "four-legged peoples" (animals with legs), the "crawling peoples" (animals without legs), and the "winged" (animals that fly)—as well as plants and even rocks. Also included are the sacred, mysterious beings and powers of *Wakȟáŋ Tȟáŋka*, as well as malevolent beings and powers, the former of whom we will consider in the next chapter, the latter, in the last chapter.

Here, we focus on how one Lakȟóta philosopher of religion, Vine Deloria, Jr., expounds upon the Lakȟóta understanding of the cosmos as sacred relationality, identifying six core components of it. First, the universe is moral, which "is to say, there is a proper way to live in the universe: There is a content to every action, behavior, and belief."[1] Second, the universe is alive, which requires two kinds of mutual respect between humans and other members of the universe: on the one hand, humans and their communities must practice self-discipline and act responsibly toward other forms of life; on the other hand, humans and their communities must seek to establish communications and covenants with other forms of life on a mutually agreeable basis.[2] Third, everything in the universe is related. Here, Deloria refers explicitly to the Lakȟóta ritual utterance "all my relations," emphasizing that the first three characteristics of the cosmos—moral, alive, related—entail that "responsibility for maintaining the harmony of life falls equally on all creatures."[3] Fourth, all relationships are historical. For Deloria, this means that the passage of time affects all beings, species, and relationships, and therefore that right knowledge of the cosmos must continually be updated and right relationships between the species must continually be reestablished. Fifth, the nature of relationships is determined by space, which manifests itself the three major ways in the Lakȟóta universe: (1) the ceremonial directions, which are invoked during rituals to establish the place of the ritual as the center of the cosmos; (2) the sacred places, which are places of special power and significance that define meaning for the life around them; (3) the particular place that each species (including different groups of humans) comes to occupy and live in. Finally (sixth), the meaning of relationships is determined by time, which is thought of in terms of the cycles of the seasons, the lengths of maturation, and the proper times for action. For Deloria, this means that every entity in an ecosystem has a part to play in the creation of the future, with humans having a "special vocation" to initiate new relationships and events. To sum up, the Lakȟóta cosmos is morally normative, thoroughly alive, complexly interrelated, continually renewed, spatially differentiated, and temporally measured.

The Lakȟóta cosmos is not one in which or from which humans need to be "saved." Nevertheless, it is one in which humans can live in correct moral, ritual, and relational comportment with each other, other species, and the sacred, mysterious beings (*Wakȟáŋ Tȟáŋka*). Crucial, therefore, are what Deloria calls the "three major manifestations of space" (under characteristic five above), especially the first and second. With respect to the first (ceremonial directions), each Lakȟóta ritual offered the sacred pipe to the four cardinal directions plus sky (up) and earth (down), thereby representing the entire cosmos, drawing all sacred powers into participation in the ritual, and establishing the ritual itself as a central, seventh dimension—the "here and now." With respect to the second, the Black Hills (Pahá Sápa) of South Dakota are where the Lakȟóta first emerged on the surface of the earth from their previous subterranean life; it is therefore a place of special sacred power, the center of the cosmos, "the heart of everything that is." This, as we will continue to see below, is one recurrent aspect of religious cosmoses: they feature sacred locations at which extraordinary interactions with divine beings and worlds have occurred and still do occur. This, therefore, is one way in which religious cosmologies serve religious practices and ends.

III. Yorùbá Philosophy of Religion

According to some Yorùbá scholars and practitioners, the cosmos is divided into two basic planes of existence: "heaven" (*ọ̀run*), which is the abode of supernatural beings, and earth (*ayé*), the abode of humans, animals, and plants. Heaven—which is not equivalent to heaven in Abrahamic religions—is itself structured into (at least) two further parts: "heaven above" (*ọ̀run ọ̀kè*), and "heaven below" (*ọ̀run odò*).[4]

The point of contact between earth and "heaven above" is the sacred city of Ilé-Ifẹ̀ (in the southwestern region of present-day Nigeria), for it is here that the *Òrìṣà* first descended to earth during creation. After creation, however, only Olódùmarè and *Òrìṣà* associated with meteorological phenomena remained in "heaven above" (e.g., Ṣàngó, an *Òrìṣà* of thunder). All the other *Òrìṣà*—as well as the *Ajogun* (Anti-gods), *àjẹ́* ("powerful people," aka witches), and ancestors—instead came to reside in "heaven below" (which is located inside the earth's crust), out of which they arise to possess their devotees).

Although this "high God" (variously named Olódùmarè or Ọlọ́run) existed before the creation of the world and was involved in its creation, He/It is (probably) not an all-powerful, all-knowing God in the Abrahamic sense.[5] Why? Olódùmarè is not all-powerful since He/It did not independently and entirely create the world, and He/It is not all-knowing since He/It must consult the *Òrìṣà* Ọrunmila to know the future.[6] Nevertheless, Olódùmarè plays several important roles in Yorùbá religions, especially the Ifá tradition: He/It is involved in the creation of the heavens and earth, He/It breathes the life-breath/soul (*èmí*) and bestows the chosen destiny (*orí*) into each living being, and He/It delivers judgment to each life upon death.

Most of the divine action, though, is performed by the other *Òrìṣà*, who are invoked to remediate suffering and misfortune as well as to secure safety and blessing. Only in the last few centuries—most likely due to European colonializing and missionizing, Yorùbá diaspora to the Americas, and the scholarly construction of "Yorùbá religion"—have the *Òrìṣà* come to be systematized into what one might call a pantheon. Nevertheless, the following six *Òrìṣà* enjoyed some measure of distribution across "Yorùbáland" at least as far back as European colonization. First, there is Ọrunmila, the *Òrìṣà* of Ifá divination (who is therefore sometimes called Ifá). As the *Òrìṣà* of divination, Ọrunmila is the *Òrìṣà* of destiny and wisdom. He is the owner of the *Ifá* corpus, as well as one of three *Òrìṣà* who were present with Olódùmarè at creation. Another important *Òrìṣà* who was present with Olódùmarè at creation is Èṣù (aka Ẹlẹ́bára), the divine messenger who delivers sacrifices to the *Òrìṣà* and other spiritual beings, and who brings misfortune to those who do not offer sacrifices at all or offer them improperly.[7]

Table 9.1 Six Pan-Yorùbá *Òrìṣà*

Ọrunmila	*Òrìṣà* of Ifá divination, destiny, and wisdom
Èṣù	*Òrìṣà* of divine messages, including sacrifices
Ọbàtálá	*Òrìṣà* of creation (human beings in particular)
Ọ̀ṣun	*Òrìṣà* of the source, especially rivers and children
Ṣàngó	*Òrìṣà* of thunder and lightning
Ọ̀gún	*Òrìṣà* of iron, war, and hunting

The third and final *Òrìṣà* who was present at creation is Ọbàtálá (aka Òrìṣà-Nlá), the *Òrìṣà* of creation, especially responsible for the creation of human beings (as we will see next chapter). A fourth pan-Yorùbá *Òrìṣà* is Ọ̀ṣun, one of many female *Òrìṣà* associated with rivers; above them all, Ọ̀ṣun is "the goddess of the source," which includes not only flowing water (rivers) but also children (fertility). Fifth, a former king of the Ọ̀yọ́ people named Ṣàngó is the *Òrìṣà* of thunder and lightning, associated with virility, masculinity, fire, lightning, stones, warriors, and magnetism. Finally, Ọ̀gún, a mythological leader of warriors, is the *Òrìṣà* of iron, war, and hunting, also associated today with technology, metal, and transportation. (See Table 9.1.)

According to the *Ifá* corpus, there are 400 of these primordial *Òrìṣà*, which are counterbalanced by 200 primordial "Anti-gods" called *Ajogun*. However, since new *Òrìṣà* and *Ajogun* have been added since the creation of the world, their numbers are represented by 400+1 and 200+1, respectively, where the "+1" designates the set of all recently added *Òrìṣà* or *Ajogun*. The 400+1 *Òrìṣà* reside on the right side of the cosmos, along with Olódùmarè, the ancestor spirits, and humans. The left side of the cosmos is instead populated by the 200+1 *Ajogun*.

This is the Yorùbá cosmos: one of perpetual conflict and war between its right and left sides. For humans, it is also one of ongoing sickness and misfortune, as instigated by the left side, requiring diagnosis, remedy, and protection from the right side. The ultimate means by which this diagnosis, remedy, and protection occurs is a divine energy or ritual power called *àṣẹ*, with Olódùmarè regarded as the supreme essence or source of *àṣẹ* (and the *Òrìṣà* as manifestations of *àṣẹ*). Literally meaning "so be it" or "may it happen," *àṣẹ*" infuses and interconnects all things, empowering change, especially with regard the operation of Ifá divination and healing.[8]

IV. South Asian Philosophy of Religion

In South Asian philosophies of religion, we find a diversity of positions about what the cosmos is. One of the earliest (Vedic) understandings involved ritual sacrifice, with Ṛg Veda's "Hymn to the Cosmic Person" (10.90) portraying the cosmos as a gigantic primordial person, *Puruṣa*, which is ritually sacrificed to bring existence and order to the world. This order, *ṛta*, is the rhythm, balance, and harmony not only of natural phenomena but also in moral and ritual action. Derived from the root word "go," *ṛta* is the ultimate way that things should "go." Correct performance of the Vedic fire ritual not only requires it but also brings it about.

With the later development of the *darśana*-s, fully formed South Asian cosmologies began to appear. One of the oldest was probably that of Sāṁkhya, which we see early traces of in some of the *Upaniṣads* and the *Bhagavad Gītā*, even though it may have not been fully articulated until the fourth–fifth century *Sāṁkhya Kārikā* of Īśvarakṛṣṇa. You have already learned about Sāṁkhya's fundamental dualism between *Puruṣa*, the pure consciousness of the self, and *prakṛti*, the primordial matter of the cosmos. Now we look at how all things evolve from *prakṛti*.

This evolution begins with the *guṇa*-s, three constituent strands of *prakṛti*, which together give *prakṛti* the potential to transform: *sattva*, the subtle matter of pure thought, which is responsible for the self-manifestation and self-maintenance of *prakṛti*; *rajas*, the kinetic matter of energy and movement, which energizes *prakṛti* to transform itself unceasingly; and *tamas*, the reified matter of inertia, which is responsible for the constancy and endurance of *prakṛti*. The actual transformation of *prakṛti* occurs when *Puruṣa* comes close to it, disturbing the equilibrium of the *guṇa*-s and causing them to activate *prakṛti*. This first illumination is intelligence (*buddhi*), which becomes aware of itself as "ego sense" (*ahaṃkāra*). Next come the features of humans—mind (*manas*) plus five organs of sensation and five organs of action. Last to show up are the objects of the world in five subtle forms and five gross forms. Altogether, twenty-three structures (*tattva*-s) evolve, which, added to *Puruṣa* and *prakṛti*, total twenty-five. *Sāṁkhya*, in fact, simply means "number."

What is important here is how this cosmology serves religious ends—for it is in reversing the process of evolution, so to speak, that *Puruṣa* comes to see that it is not any of the things of *prakṛti*—not a body or that body's actions, not sensory perceptions or the mind that brings order to them, not ego, not even intelligence. *Puruṣa* is nothing but pure consciousness, which in witnessing the evolution of *prakṛti*, becomes so enraptured that it forgets what it really is, mistaking itself as body, mind, ego, and intelligence. How does *Puruṣa* remember itself? Īśvarakṛṣṇa's *Sāṁkhya Kārikā* says that it is through "repeated study" of these principles or structures of *prakṛti* that knowledge arises that *Puruṣa* is not any of them, not even the finest elements of intelligence (*buddhi*) and ego-sense (*ahaṃkāra*). Having been seen, which is metaphorized as the spectacle of a dance, *prakṛti* (gendered as female), then ceases "her" evolution, while *Puruṣa* (gendered as male), having seen the dance of *prakṛti*, attains separation from the mind-body and enjoys a state of blissful isolation (*kaivalya*).[9]

Another early South Asian cosmology comes from Jainism. Although Jainism has origins at least as far back as the sixth century BCE (when Mahāvīra lived), it is not until the first millennium that we see Jain cosmology elaborated in texts, one of the most important of which is Umāsvāti's *Tattvārtha Sūtra* (second–fifth century CE). Unlike "Hindu" *darśana*-s that privilege permanence and Buddhist *darśana*-s that emphasize impermanence, the *Tattvārtha Sūtra* maintains that the cosmos and everything in it are characterized by "origin, disappearance, and permanence"—i.e., both permanence and change.

Within this cosmos are five basic categories of substances (*dravyas*-s): souls (*jīva*-s), motion (*dharma*), rest (*adharma*), matter (*pudgala*), and space (*ākāśa*). The basic distinction, however, is between souls, which are animate (*jīva*), and everything else, which is inanimate (*ajīva*). With respect to human practice, the most important inanimate substance is matter (*pudgala*), which sticks to the soul, causing delusion, suffering, and rebirth. Much like Sāṁkhya, therefore, the overall objective of Jainism is the isolation (*kaivalya*) of the soul (*jīva*). If in Sāṁkhya this involves coming to see that the soul (*Puruṣa*) never was involved in matter (*prakṛti*) in the first place, isolation in Jainism requires removing from the soul (*jīva*) the matter (*pudgala*) that sticks to it due to *karma*.

The Jain cosmos (*loka*) is where this goal is pursued. It is eternal and uncreated, with no "God" to generate it. Not only is it referred to as a cosmic person (*Loka Puruṣa*); it is also shaped like and drawn as a cosmic person, with legs spread apart and arms resting on waist (in roughly the shape of a diamond on top of a triangle: narrow at the top, wide below that, narrow in the middle, wide below that). (See Figure 9.)

This cosmos consists of three main realms, each itself called a *loka*, together which constitute a *triloka* or "three-realm" cosmos. The narrow

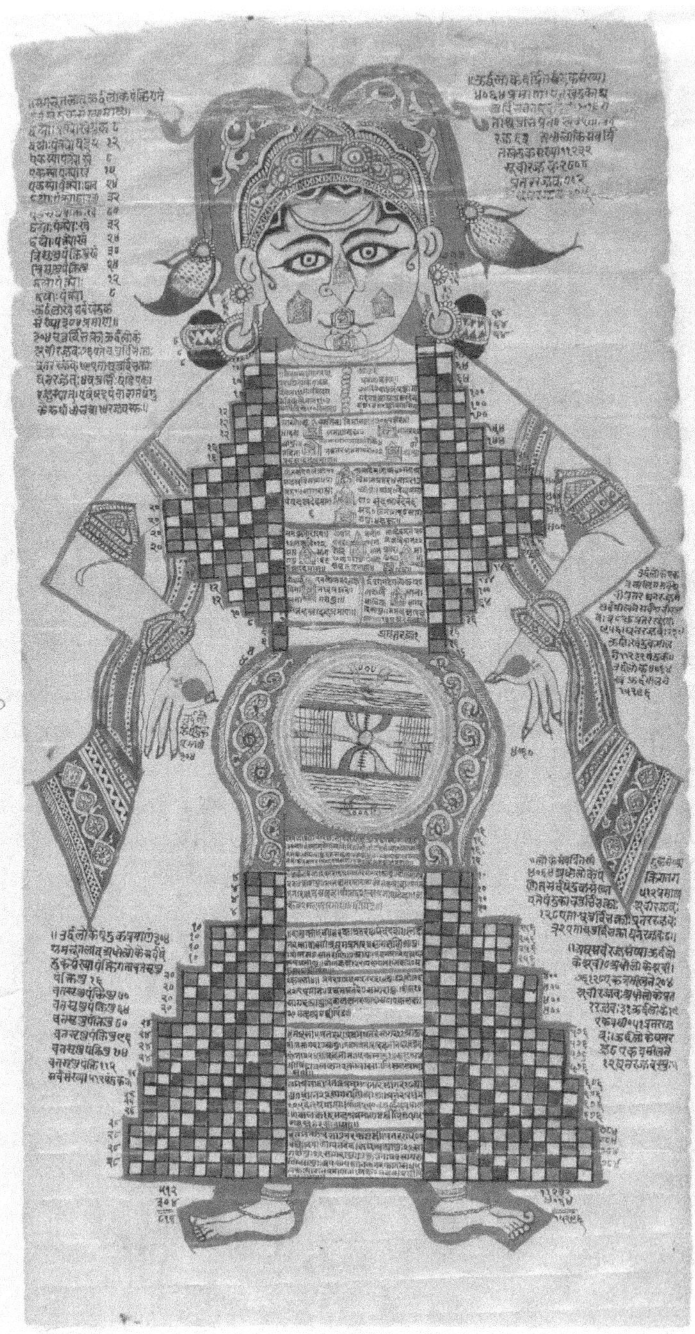

Figure 9 Jain Cosmic Person (*Loka Puruṣa*). Wellcome Collection, "Sanskrit Delta 82," sixteenth century, CC BY 4.0. https://wellcomecollection.org/works/bt4wcdrf.

region where the "diamond" and "triangle" meet is the Middle Realm (*Madhya Loka*), which is the abode for humans, animals, and plants. On either side of this Middle Realm lie much larger regions—the Lower or Hell Realm (*Adho Loka* or *Naraka*) of demons and hellish beings, and the Upper or Deity Realm (*Ūrdhva* or *Dev Loka*) of demi-gods and heavenly beings. Beyond this Upper Realm is a fourth *loka*, the abode of liberated beings (*Siddhaloka*), which some Jains locate outside the entire *triloka*.

The Middle Realm is the smallest *loka*; nevertheless, it is most important, for it is the only *loka* from which liberation can be attained. Although it is possible for human souls to be reborn into the Upper Realm (or the Lower Realm), that type of rebirth, while immensely pleasurable, is ultimately unsatisfactory since it cannot lead to liberation (but rather only to rebirth in the human realm). What happens when humans finally do attain liberation in the "Middle Realm"? In the words of the *Tattvārtha Sūtra*, "the soul soars upwards to the border of cosmic space," i.e., the abode of liberated beings (*Siddhaloka*), permanently isolated from matter, enjoying perfect omniscience and bliss.[10]

Yet another notable South Asian cosmology comes from the Hindu *darśana* of Vaiśeṣika, which dates at least as far back as its foundational *sūtra*, the *Vaiśeṣika Sūtras* of Kaṇāda (*c.* 200 BCE). For Vaiśeṣika, there are nine fundamental substances, four of which are the atomic building blocks out of which ordinary objects are composed: earth, water, fire, and air. Although ordinary objects can be created and destroyed, atoms cannot, for they are eternal and indestructible. Thus, although Vaiśeṣika was later to include a God (*Īśvara*) in its cosmology, especially as it merged with Nyāya in the early second millennium, that God does not create *ex nihilo* ("out of nothing") but rather is the source of motion for pre-existing atoms (setting in motion their combinatorial possibilities). (We will look at this in detail in the next chapter.)

In addition to these first four substances, Vaiśeṣika includes a fifth material substance (ether) and four non-material substances: time, space, soul (*Ātman*), and mind (*manas*). Whereas mind (*manas*) is the organ of knowing, which receives and organizes perceptions, soul (*Ātman*) is the locus of consciousness. Although the category of soul originally only included individual human souls, it later came to include the "supreme soul" (*paramātmān*) of *Īśvara* (Lord), especially as Vaiśeṣika was influenced by and merged with Nyāya.

In additional to substance (which comes in the nine forms above), Vaiśeṣika posits five more fundamental categories (*padārtha*-s): quality, action/motion, universal, particularity, and inherence (with "negation" or "absence" later added as a seventh overall category). These details need not detain us here. Instead, let us turn back to the relationship between cosmology and religious paths and ends, asking how the Vaiśeṣika cosmos is "designed for enlightenment." The answer to this question is quite simple: it by "getting the knowledge right" (about the cosmos) that the soul becomes liberated, freed from the pain and suffering of embodied existence. Thus, the very first line of the *Vaiśeṣika Sūtras* reads: "Now, therefore, we shall explain *dharma*," which in the second line is identified as that through which "one achieves exaltation and the supreme good," which in the fourth line is said to arise from the knowledge of the fundamental categories and substances (etc.) of the cosmos.[11]

Whereas Vaiśeṣika, Jainism, and Sāṁkhya offer us realist cosmologies in which the cosmos is in some way how we experience it, the Advaita Vedānta cosmology of Śaṅkara (*c.* 788–*c.* 820) is thoroughly non-realist: everything that is just is *Ātman-Brahman*; all appearances otherwise are ultimately illusory. The Viśiṣṭādvaita Vedānta of Rāmānuja (1017–1137) also maintains that *Brahman* is everything (non-dual), while simultaneously recognizing that finite souls and material things are "real" parts or qualifications of Brahman. By contrast, the Dvaita Vedānta of Madhva (1238–1317) holds that *Brahman*, individual souls, and material things are all fully real and eternally distinct from one another. Despite these differences, however, understanding and enacting the right relationship between self and cosmos is crucial to attaining release from rebirth (*mokṣa*).

We end this section on South Asian cosmologies with a word of modesty from the historical Buddha. According to early Buddhist scripture, there were a number of questions about which the Buddha refused to give answers, two sets of which are cosmological:

- Is the world eternal, or not eternal, or both eternal and not eternal, or neither eternal nor not eternal?
- Is the world finite, or infinite, or both finite and infinite, or neither finite nor infinite?

Why did the Buddha refuse to answer these questions? Because they were not conducive to what humans should really be doing—working toward enlightenment. Nevertheless, early (Theravāda) Indian Buddhists were to divide our cosmos into six realms (Gods, demi-gods, humans, animals, hungry ghosts, and hells), and later (Mahāyāna) Buddhists were to add that our cosmos is just one of an infinite number of "Buddha-worlds," each of

Table 9.2 South Asian Cosmologies

School	Cosmology
Sāṁkhya	*Puruṣa*, *prakṛti*, and the 23 constituents that emerge from *prakṛti*
Jainism	*Triloka* (Upper Realm, Middle Realm, Lower Realm)
Vaiśeṣika	6 categories; 9 substances; atoms of fire, water, air, and earth
Advaita Vedānta	Everything is *Ātman-Brahman*
Viśiṣṭādvaita Vedānta	Individual souls and material things are parts of *Brahman*
Dvaita Vedānta	*Brahman*, souls, and things are eternally distinct from one another
Theravāda Buddhism	Six realms: Gods, demi-gods, humans, animals, hungry ghosts, hells
Mahāyāna Buddhism	Innumerable Buddha-worlds

which offers different paths of enlightenment for its inhabitants. Once again, therefore, we see how South Asian cosmologies are designed for the pursuit of enlightenment. See Table 9.2 for a summary of all of these South Asian cosmologies.

V. East Asian Philosophy of Religion

One significant root of Chinese cosmology is an ancient text called the *Yìjīng* (*Classic of Changes*), which was originally used for divination rituals during the Zhou Dynasty (1122–256 BCE) and later recognized as one of the "Five Classics" (*Sìshū Wǔjīng*, 五經) of Confucianism during the Han Dynasty (206 BCE –220 CE). The heart of the text contains a series of sixty-four six-lined "hexagrams," each a combination of two three-lined "trigrams," which are themselves constituted by combinations of unbroken (*yīn*) and broken (*yáng*) lines, with eight possible trigram combinations (e.g., *yáng-yáng-yáng*, *yáng-yīn-yáng*, *yīn-yīn-yáng*, etc.). Each of the sixty-four hexagrams is associated with a judgment and interpretation of future "changes," one of which would be randomly selected through a process such as choosing stalks or casting coins. Over time, however, philosophers understood these changes less in terms of personal destiny and more as the functioning of the cosmos—the way (*dào*) of *yīn* and *yáng*, with *yīn* as that which causes things to pass out of being, and *yáng* as that which causes things to come into being. (Originally, these terms just referred to the shady and sunny sides of a hill.)

By the time of the Han Dynasty, the "School of Yīn and Yáng" had combined this understanding of *yīn* and *yáng* with a theory about the "five material phases" (*wǔxíng*): wood (minor *yáng*), the process of bending and straightening; fire (major *yáng*), the process of flaming and rising; metal (minor *yīn*), the process of yielding and molding; water (major *yīn*), the process of wetting and sinking; and earth (balance/transition of *yīn* and *yáng*), the process of growth and fructification. These changes were associated not only with material processes, seasons, and directions but also with parts of body, positive virtues, and negative emotions. All changes in the cosmos, both physical/natural and moral/social, were thereby understood as the result of how *yīn* and *yáng* manifested the five elements.

During the Han Dynasty, this "correlative cosmology" of *yīn/yáng* and the five material processes became associated with yet another fundamental cosmological concept—*qì*, a term whose application extends from the vital breath of the body to the material energy of the cosmos. For example, the Confucian scholar Dǒng Zhòngshū (董仲舒, 176–104 BCE)—who was also instrumental in establishing the Five Classics of Confucianism as the foundation for state education—saw *qì* as the all-pervading and radiating nature of everything. As the polar forces of *yīn* and *yáng*, through the five material processes, *qì* caused all "changes" in the cosmos, both natural and social.

Although *qì*, *yīn/yáng*, and *wǔxíng* form the bedrock of Chinese cosmology in general, each of the "three teachings" (Confucianism, Daoism, Buddhism) is not without its own distinctive cosmological contributions. For Daoism, it is the *Dào* that is all things, both as their ultimate source and as their transformative force. As early as the classic texts *Dàodéjīng* and *Zhuāngzǐ*, the cosmological operations of the *Dào* were understood with regard to *qì* and *yīn/yáng*. *Dào* just is or essentially is related to primordial *qì*, the polar forces of which are *yīn* and *yáng*. Thus, when the *Dàodéjīng* speaks of *Dào* giving birth to unity, which then gives birth to duality, then to trinity, then to the myriad (10,000) creatures, "unity" was understood as *qì*, "duality," as *yīn/yáng*.[12] (More on this next chapter.)

In the case of Chinese Buddhism, it is the school of Huáyán that makes the most notable cosmological contribution. The school's founding *sūtra*, *Avataṃsaka Sūtra* speaks of a "unity in totality," the interrelation and interpenetration of each and every part of reality (Sk. *dharma*; Ch. *shì*, 事), in which are contained and reflected each and every other part of reality. For Chinese Huáyán philosophers such as Fǎzàng (法藏, 643–712), this makes all of reality the expression of fundamental Buddha-nature, which just is emptiness (*śūnyatā*), interdependent arising (*pratītya-samutpāda*), or pattern-principle (*lǐ*, 理)—the last of which, as we will soon see, was to become a crucially important concept for (Neo)Confucian philosophy of religion. One of Fǎzàng's creative means of illustrating this interpenetration involved the metaphor of a golden lion. Although the lion appears to have different parts such as teeth, claws, and eyes, the entire lion is in fact composed of the same substance—gold, which represents emptiness, Buddha-nature, and pattern-principal. In each part or phenomenon of the cosmos, therefore, there is every other part or phenomenon of the cosmos. "In this way," writes Fǎzàng, "the geometric progression is infinite, like the jewels of Celestial Lord Indra's net,"[13] thereby drawing on a common Buddhist metaphor about the jewels on the hairnet of Indra—an important deity in pre-Hindu, Vedic religion in India—each jewel of which reflected all the other jewels. Similarly, every aspect of reality reflects and is reflected in every other aspect of reality. The cosmos is one grand harmony of interrelations and interpenetrations.

Over time, these ideas were to influence Confucianism, which during the Song Dynasty (960–1279) saw the development of a distinctly (Neo) Confucian cosmology. For some of these (Neo)Confucian philosophers, the central concept was the pattern-principle (*lǐ*) of Huáyán Buddhism. In the case of the brothers Chéng Hào (程顥, 1032–85) and Chéng Yí (程頤, 1033–1107), pattern-principle is that which gives specific form and function to *qì*, which itself is the underlying material force of the cosmos. Everything that is, therefore, is a combination of *lǐ* and *qì*. This is as true for the physical things of the universe as it is for us moral beings (humans), for whom pattern-principle is the fundamental Confucian virtue of human-heartedness (*rén*). Thus, there is a union between humans and the cosmos with regard to pattern-principle.

Not much later, the Neo-Confucian philosopher Zhū Xī (1130–1200) drew together the philosophy of the Chéng brothers and other (Neo) Confucian philosophers into a complete systematic philosophy of nature and morality. For this, Zhū Xī is considered the third most important Confucian thinker, ranking behind only Confucius and Mencius.

Like the Chéng brothers, Zhū Xī held that everything that exists is a combination of *qì* and *lǐ*: "Humans and things are all endowed with the principle [*lǐ*] of the universe as their nature, and receive the material force [*qì*] of the universe as their physical form."[14] According to one contemporary scholar, pattern-principle therefore establishes natural patterns in three different ways.[15] In its "universal mode," it "establishes the patterns or rules that all natural and human processes obey"; in its "particular mode," it "exists in each thing as its defining nature, impelling material force to fashion itself into particular things by means of its patterns"; and in its "normative mode," it "sets the standards that measure correctness or deviancy, fulfillment or deficiency, goodness or badness, right or wrong, virtue or vice." In sum, therefore, you can think of pattern-principal as providing the general laws of nature, the particular forms and functions of natural entities, and the standards of moral behavior for humans.

Although pattern-principle (*lǐ*) therefore has "priority" over vital energy (*qì*), it does not exist without vital energy. About this, Zhū Xī was to write:

> Fundamentally principle [*lǐ*] and material force [*qì*] cannot be spoken of as prior or posterior. But if we must trace their origin, we are obliged to say that principle is prior. However, principle is not a separate entity. It exists right in material force. Without material force, principle would have nothing to adhere to. As material force, there are the Agents (or Elements [*wǔxíng*]) of Metal, Wood, Water, and Fire. As principle, there are humanity [*rén*], righteousness [*yì*], propriety [*lǐ*], and wisdom [*zhì*].[16]

How should we understand this priority? Pattern-principle (*lǐ*) is certainly epistemologically "prior" to vital energy (*qì*) since it can be abstracted from material force and studied as such; indeed, this is one major aim of (Neo) Confucian practice: to study pattern-principle through the "examination of things" and "extension of knowledge." We might also say that pattern-principle has ontological priority over vital energy since pattern-principle constitutes the "permanent possibilities of *qì* formation," meaning that *qì* can only be formed into the patterns made possible by *lǐ*.[17] But what about temporal priority? Here, things are less clear. Although Zhū Xī does say that "[b]efore heaven [*Tiān*] and earth [*dì*] existed, there was after all only principle," Chinese cosmological processes are generally regarded as eternally ongoing rather than originating at some point in time. We will return to this matter next chapter, where we will learn about a couple more key principles in Zhū Xī's cosmogony—*Tàijí*, the Supreme Polarity/Ultimate, and *Wújí* (無極), the Non-Polarity/Ultimate—for it is these principles that are the ultimate sources of everything that is.

Before drawing this section to a close, we should note that Zhū Xī's system was subsequently and repeatedly criticized by other (Neo)Confucian philosophers as being too dualistic insofar as neither pattern-principle (*lǐ*) nor vital energy (*qì*) reduce to or originate from the other. One (Neo)

Confucian contemporary of Zhū Xī, Lù Xiàngshān (陸象山, 1139–93), instead maintained that pattern-principle is only the heart-mind (*xīn*), which Heaven (*Tiān*) gives to every person, and from which everything in the universe originates. The path to becoming a Confucian sage, therefore, involves investigating only the mind, not external things. Three centuries later, Lù Xiàngshān's critique was reinvigorated by another Neo-Confucian philosopher, Wáng Yángmíng (王陽明, 1472–1523), who also held that pattern-principle is only of the heart-mind (*xīn*). Wáng Yángmíng is renowned for his claim that there are neither pattern-principles nor things outside the mind. For this, he (along with Lù Xiàngshān) is known as a proponent of the "School of Mind" (*xīnxué*, 心學), whereas Zhū Xī (along with the Chéng brothers) is known as a proponent of the "School of Pattern-Principle" (*lǐxué*, 理學).

Regardless of how pattern-principle was conceived, its investigation—whether internal and external, or only internal—became crucial to (Neo) Confucian practice. Once again, we therefore see how cosmologies have implications for the paths and destinations of the self.

VI. Mediterranean/Abrahamic Philosophy of Religion

One might be inclined to think that cosmological pictures are less diverse and complicated in Abrahamic religious traditions. This is not the case.

The earliest view of the cosmos in the Hebrew Bible is that of a "three-tiered universe," with a flat, disk-shaped earth floating on water, below which resides the underworld of Sheol, over which spans a heavenly dome or "firmament" (on which the celestial bodies are located and above which there is water that falls to the earth when it rains). Perhaps this is the only truly biblical view about what the cosmos is. Regardless, the three-tiered universe was a cosmology for religious practice, with YHWH's throne sitting on top of the firmament and the dead residing in a shadowy underworld. To be on the earth, therefore, was to be as close as possible to YHWH, especially at sacred places where special contact with the divine was possible like Mount Sinai and the Jerusalem Temple.

Under Hellenistic and Roman rule (beginning in the fourth century BCE), this three-tiered universe began to be replaced by Greek cosmologies in which a spherical earth was surrounded by concentric heavens. This cosmic architecture enabled mystical journeys to these heavens, a common theme in first-millennium Jewish, Christian, and Islamic scripture and literature. A rational principle of creation was also introduced to explain the process of creation and types of things created—a female-gendered "Wisdom" (Hb. *Ḥokmâ*; Gk. *Sophia*) in the case of some of the later additions to the Hebrew Bible (notably some passages in Proverbs and the Wisdom of Solomon), and a male-gendered "Reason" (Gk. *Logos*) in the case of some later New Testament writings (notably Revelations and the Gospel of John, which identify Jesus as *Logos*). This borrowing of cosmological theories and principles from Greek and Roman philosophies lasted up until the scientific revolution, at which time an increasing number of Abrahamic philosophers of religion turned to the cosmologies of modern science.

Before the scientific revolution, however, Abrahamic cosmologies were usually Platonic or Aristotelian in nature, with most of the early influence coming from Platonism. Platonic philosophy did not end with Plato but rather was preserved, interpreted, and elaborated at Plato's Academy for nearly a millennium by philosophers who are now classified under the headings of "Old Academy" (from Plato's death in 347 BCE through the first century BCE), "Middle-Platonism" (from the first century BCE through the third century CE) and "Neo-Platonism" (from the third century CE through 529 when Plato's Academy was closed). For much of this time, Platonic cosmologies featured a series of emanations or processions from an ultimate principle called the One or the Good, through a realm of intelligible principles (Platonic Forms) that serve as patterns for the material world, and eventually to the realm of material beings, especially humans, who have material bodies but also immaterial souls and minds. It was by virtue of reversing this process of procession, therefore, that humans could "return" to the One/Good, unifying their soul and mind through contemplative and ritual techniques.

For Abrahamic philosophers and theologians influenced by Platonic philosophy, it was usually God's "divine names" that served as the principles or powers of creation and therefore assumed the role of the rational causal principles in Platonic philosophy (which were usually called *logoi* in Greek, the plural of *logos*). God's divine name "Being," for example, was thought of as the source of existence in all things; "Life," the source of life for living things; "Wisdom" or "Reason" as the source of intelligence for intelligent things. This is exactly how "procession" works in the case of the extremely influential Christian Neo-Platonist who is known now as Pseudo-Dionysius the Areopagite (sixth century CE) but was believed then to have been the first-century convert of St. Paul (as referred to in Acts 17:34). Dionysius envisioned the cosmos as a hierarchy of beings (and *hyper*-beings) extending from God/Good/One, out through the causal powers of God's divine names, down to the nine ranks of celestial beings (angels), and finally into the realm of things that are embodied, especially the ecclesiastical ranks of the Christian Church. By contemplative performance of the sacraments of the Christian Church, communion in particular, humans could unify their souls and minds and become (more) like God.

Not only does divine procession or emanation move out from this Trinitarian God down to creation; it also occurs within the Godhead itself. For Dionysius, the members of the Trinity (Father, Son, Spirit) are processions within the Godhead, whereas the divine names (Being, Life, Wisdom) are processions out from this "hyper-essential Trinity." Even the Christian (Nicene-Constantinopolitan) Creed itself speaks of the Son and the Holy Spirit as *generations* or *processions* from God the Father:

> We believe in one God,
> the Father almighty,
> maker of heaven and earth,
> of all things visible and invisible;
> And in one Lord, Jesus Christ,
> the only begotten [Gk. *monogenē*] Son of God,
> begotten [*genēthenta*] from the Father before all ages,
> light from light,
> true God from true God,
> begotten [*genēthenta*] not made,
> of one substance with the Father,
> through Whom all things came into existence,
> . . .
> And in the Holy Spirit, the Lord and life-giver,
> Who proceeds [*ekporeuomenon*] from the Father,
> . . . .[18]

In the case of Jewish philosophy of religion, this emanation within the Godhead is one of the most prominent features of Medieval Jewish mysticism (Kabbalah). As you learned last chapter (and saw in Figure 8), Kabbalists thought of YHWH as emanating through a series of ten creative powers (Hb. *sĕpîrôt*), metaphorized as lights (among other ways). Here, we begin by noting the names for these *sĕpîrôt* (in Hebrew)—*Keter* (will), *Ḥokmâ* (wisdom), *Binah* (intellect), *Ḥesed* (love), *Gĕbûrâ* (justice), *Tip'eret* (beauty), *Neṣaḥ* (victory), *Hôd* (majesty), *Yĕsôd* (foundation), and *Malkût* (sovereignty, receptivity, also known as the *Shekhinah*). You can again see, therefore, how the emanations within an Abrahamic God are associated with divine names or attributes. As stated by the *Zōhar*, a book believed to contain the mystical secrets conveyed by YHWH to Moses on Mt. Sinai (though in fact dating to thirteenth-century Spain), it is through these "spheres on high" (*sĕpîrôt*) that humans come to know and commune with the "Blessed Holy One":

> Through these gates, these spheres on high,
> the Blessed Holy One becomes known.
> Were it not so, no one could commune with Him.[19]

Each of these *sĕpîrâ* is also gendered and identified with a part of the body and a biblical character; thus, the nature of the cosmos has profound implications for how women and men live in it.[20] This is all the more true in later Lurianic Kabbalah, where humans become responsible for repairing the tenth *sĕpîrâ*, the female *Malkût* or *Shekhinah*, and therefore "fixing God."

Within Islamic philosophy, there are a number of early advocates of Platonist-emanationist cosmologies, most notably al-Fārābī (*c.* 872–950) and ibn Sīnā (980–1037). Here, however, we focus on the mystical cosmology of ibn al-ʿArabī (1165–1240), who lived in Andalusia on the Iberian Peninsula during a time of rich exchange between Jewish, Christian, and Islamic philosophers, theologians, and mystics.[21] For ibn al-ʿArabī, Allah is the one absolute reality from which all other things derive. The entire universe, humans in particular, is the self-manifestation of Allah, who is, on the one hand, the transcendent, immutable creator and absolutely unified truth (*Ḥaqq*) and, on the other, the immanent, mutable created and constantly refreshed. Although Allah is unknown in His essence, He reveals Himself to humans through His divine names (*ʾasmā*), of which there are ninety-nine in Islam. As with the Christian Dionysius and Jewish Kabbalah, these names are not merely conventional or arbitrary human symbols but rather the very way that Allah reveals Himself in creation. They are divine realities (at least in Allah's relation to creation), the universal features of the cosmos (e.g., life, knowledge, desire, power, speech, generosity, justice—the "seven leaders" among the names), and the very image of Allah in which humans are created. They are therefore the means by which humans come to know Allah, both as what Allah is (as the source of the names) and what Allah is not (as transcendent of the names). Insofar as humans come to be characterized by these divine names—to know them, to live by them, to realize them—they return to Allah, becoming "deiformed" (formed as or like God). In this sense the divine names serve as the Sufi stations or stages (*maqaamat*) in the return to Allah. By means of the divine names humans achieve through effort ("voluntary return") what the rest of creation effects automatically ("compulsory return"), for the entire cosmos continually unfolds from and returns to Allah in every single moment, as Allah (re)creates the cosmos in each instant through divine speech.

We would be remiss if we did not quickly mention two final Abrahamic cosmologies, the first of which was influenced not by Plato but by Aristotle. For Aristotle, everything that exists—with two exceptions below—is a combination of matter and form. Forms inform material stuff, making it into the things of the universe. In the case of natural entities—humans, dogs, trees—these forms are passed on through "seeds," which tell matter how to develop into the type of thing that is encoded in the form. Human seeds "tell" matter how to develop into humans; dog seeds, into dogs; tree seeds, into trees. The only two "things" that are not a combination of matter and form are Prime Matter and the Unmoved Mover, the former of which is simply unformed matter—matter apart from some particular form—the latter, pure, matter-less form. This pure, matter-less form is Aristotle's version of God—not a creator *ex nihilo*, since Aristotle's cosmos is eternal, but rather the first cause and first mover of chains of causation and motion, as well as the eternal mind that forever thinks the basic truths and natural laws of the cosmos. There is of course much more to Aristotle's cosmos and its physical properties, laws, and principles. But this is enough for our purpose here, which is simply to acknowledge that many notable Jewish philosophers (e.g., Maimonides, 1138–1204), Christian philosophers (e.g., Aquinas, 1225–74), and Islamic philosophers (e.g., ibn Rushd, 1126–98) adopted aspects of this Aristotelian cosmos, albeit with Gods that were less like Aristotle's Unmoved Mover and more like the God(s) of the Abrahamic religions. Nevertheless, it was by means of imitating this God via intellect that humans could achieve a state most like Him in this life and most near to Him in the afterlife.

Finally, Islamic theology (*kalām*) largely opted for an atomistic-occasionalistic cosmos in lieu of Aristotle's cosmos. For such a cosmos, Allah creates each and every arrangement of atoms at each and every moment. (Note the similarities with ibn al-ʿArabī above.) Thus, Allah is the actual cause of every event. The apparent natural and human causes of events are only the "occasions" by which Allah carries out causation. We will examine this cosmos in more detail in Chapter 12 under the topic of miracles. But as you already know from Chapter 5, this cosmos provided the means by which orthodox Ashʿarite theology resolved the problem of divine omnipotence

Table 9.3 Abrahamic Cosmologies

Type	Description
Scriptural (early)	Three-tiered universe: heavenly dome above, earth in between, underworld below
Scriptural (later)	Earth surrounded by concentric circles, on each of which is one or more celestial bodies
Platonist	Emanation within God, then from out of God, first into a realm of incorporeal beings (e.g., angels), then into a realm of corporeal beings (e.g., humans)
Aristotelian	Most of what exists is a combination of matter and form; "God" is pure, matter-less form, i.e., intellect
Islamic Atomism-Occasionalism	Cosmos is composed of atoms, the positions of which are re-created every moment (occasion) by Allah

and human freedom in opposition to Muʿtazilite theologians that stressed human freedom. For Ashʿarites, Allah is entirely omnipotent and sovereign, the cause of every event (by virtue of the repositioning of atoms), even while humans are able to freely choose to do what Allah causes, thereby acquiring moral culpability for their actions.

Table 9.3 sums up these Abrahamic cosmologies. In each case, it is not difficult to see how they serve religious paths and goals.

VII. European/Academic Philosophy of Religion

When we ask the question "What is the cosmos?" in today's day and age, many appeal to scientific cosmology for an answer, usually in terms of the large-scale properties and dynamics of the universe as a whole.[22] For some time now, scientific cosmology has been dominated by the Big Bang Theory, which is undergirded by two other theories. The first is Albert Einstein's (1879–1955) General Theory of Relativity, which not only generalizes Isaac Newton's (1643–1727) theory of gravity to all bodies, even those moving incredibly fast, but also reconceives gravitation as a distortion of space and time. The second is the Cosmological Principle, which assumes that the contents of the universe are homogeneous and isotropic when averaged over very large scales—more or less the same everywhere and in every direction. As astronomers learn more and more about our own galaxy and some of the other 100–200 billion galaxies in the cosmos, both theories continue to receive significant empirical support. Not long ago (December 1, 2014), a gathering of astronomers in Ferrara, Italy reported that the universe is 13.8 billion years old and composed of 4.9 percent atomic matter, 26.6 percent dark matter, and 68.5 percent dark energy. This "dark matter" and "dark energy" are two of the topics that occupy contemporary cosmologists and astronomers; some of the others include String Theory, whether there is just one universe or many "multiverses," and whether the universe is infinite or finite in size.

Big Bang Theory has been of interest to philosophers of religion, too, especially insofar as it seems "friendly" to the existence of a divine cause of the Big Bang. Nowhere was this hope captured better than in the famous line by astronomer and planetary physicist Robert Jastrow (1925–2008):

> For the scientist who has lived by his faith in the power of reason, the story ends like a bad dream. He has scaled the mountains of ignorance, he is about to conquer the highest peak; as he pulls himself over the final rock, he is greeted by a band of theologians who have been sitting there for centuries.[23]

Many cosmologists are quick to point out that the question of what gave rise to the Big Bang is beyond the realm of the Big Bang Theory, especially if the cosmos is enclosed and finite and if space and time began with the Big Bang. There are, though, several speculative theories about this topic, including Steven Hawking's (1942–2018) theory that there is no boundary condition to the cosmos; rather, the arrow of time shrinks infinitely as the universe becomes smaller and smaller, never reaching a clear starting point. Other cosmologists have challenged the "Genesis-like" view of cosmology that Big Bang suggests, hypothesizing that the universe generates and regenerates itself in an endless cycle of creation, a process that might occur not just in our universe but in a "multiverse"—a multitude of universes, each with its own laws of physics and life story.

There is also the issue of what happens on the "other end" of the Big Bang. Recent evidence shows that the universe is expanding at an ever-increasing speed and therefore will not return to its original singularity in a "Big Crunch"; this certainly adds a complication to the (Christian) theologian's hope that, if the Big Bang was God's creation of the cosmos, then the Big Crunch was God's final end to the cosmos. We will consider this and other "ends" to the cosmos in Chapter 11, and in Chapter 10 we will look at arguments for the existence of creator Gods from the existence of the cosmos. For now, however, we can bring our discussion of Big Bang cosmology to a close by suggesting that it seems way too premature to draw any conclusions about the existence of creator Gods from Big Bang Theory. Finally, we can examine another way in which scientific cosmology has been of interest to contemporary philosophy of religion: the Anthropic Principle and its relationship to the so-called "fine-tuning" of the cosmos.

The term "Anthropic Principle" dates back to 1973, when Brandon Carter used it in contrast to the Copernican Principle, arguing that, although humans are not "central" to the universe—as the Copernican, heliocentric solar-system revealed—they do occupy a "necessarily privileged" position since there was not (human) life earlier in the history of the cosmos and there will not be (human) life later in the history of the cosmos.[24] Carter went on to define two forms of the Anthropic Principle, a weak form (WAP) that referred only to this privileged location as observers of the cosmos and a strong form (SAP) that asserted "the Universe (and hence the fundamental parameters on which it depends) must be such as to admit within it the creation of observers within it at some stage."[25] For Carter, SAP merely entailed that for there to be observers of a cosmos, there must be some cosmos in which there are observers. However, with the 1986 publication of John Barrow and Frank Tipler's *The Anthropic Cosmological Principle*, SAP was interpreted differently—as if it were necessary for there to have been a cosmos fine-tuned for life: "The Universe must have those properties which allow life to develop within it at some stage in its history."[26] In this case, the "must" has a teleological sense, as evinced by another sentence from Barrow and Tipler's book: "There exists one possible Universe 'designed' with the goal of generating and sustaining 'observers.'"[27]

The Anthropic Principle in general and Barrow and Tipler's interpretation of SAP in particular has bolstered recent forms of the design argument for the existence of a designer God, such as we find in the Abrahamic traditions, especially as philosophically rarefied. The design argument, quite simply, argues from the alleged design of the cosmos to the existence of a cosmic designer by way of analogy: if the cosmos demonstrates design that is analogous to the design of things we know, then it probably was designed by a designer analogous to the to the designers we know. Within the Western philosophical tradition, the most famous example of the argument is William Paley's (1743–1805): if you stumbled upon a wristwatch while walking on the beach, you would assume that it had been produced by an intelligent watchmaker, not the ocean; likewise with the cosmos, which resembles a cosmic watch and therefore evinces the existence of a cosmic watchmaker. Such arguments were quite common during the European Enlightenment, when many scientists believed they were discovering the handiwork of their God. However, the Enlightenment also saw the most devastating critique of these arguments, as penned in David Hume's (1711–76) posthumously published *Dialogues Concerning Natural Religion* (1779), which predates Paley's design argument by over twenty years. Among Hume's critiques are:

1 that we have observed no other cosmoses and therefore have no grounds for an argument by analogy;
2 that since we can only infer about a cause what is in the effect, the existence of an allegedly well-designed cosmos could also be used to infer the existence of multiple designers (rather than one), designers who use preexisting materials (rather than creating *ex nihilo*), or designers that are more like the principle of life in a body (rather than an intelligent, separately existing mind);
3 that if the cosmos is eternally re-generated, then it will demonstrate apparent design in one of its generations; and
4 that the cosmos is in fact not well designed but rather full of needless, random suffering.

We will return to this last argument in Chapter 13 when we consider the "problem of evil." For now, we remain with the Anthropic Principle and how it has been used to support variations of the proof from design.

First, there is the use of fine-tuning in new design arguments that draw on Bayesian probability theory. As you may remember from Chapter 3, Bayes' Theorem stipulates that the probability of some hypothesis given the evidence (P [H/E]) is a function of the probability of the evidence given the hypothesis (P [E/H]), multiplied by the prior probability of the hypothesis before or without the evidence (P [H]), divided by the probability of the evidence apart from the hypothesis (P [E]).

$$P(H/E) = \frac{P\,(E/H) * P\,(H)}{P(E)}$$

According to proponents of the fine-tuning argument, the probability of the existence of a (usually Christian) God given the fine-tuning of the cosmos (P [H/E]) is high, since the probability of fine-tuning given the existence of such a God (P [E/H]) is very high, and the prior probability of fine-tuning (P [E]) by itself is very low, much lower than the prior probability of the existence of this God (P [H]). Opponents, however, counter that the probability of the fine-tuning of the cosmos given the rival "maximal-multiverse hypothesis" is exactly one: if there are an infinite number of cosmoses, then one cosmos just is our (fine-tuned) cosmos. Other opponents simply point out that there is nothing at all remarkable about the fine-tuning of the cosmos given the fact that we could not remark about it if it were not fine-tuned. Still other opponents maintain it makes no sense to ask about the probability of these supposedly fine-tuned laws, constants, and conditions since there simply would not be a universe without them.

In addition to the fine-tuning argument, there have been recent attempts to defend what is called "Intelligent Design," two versions of which are William Dembski's (b. 1960) notion of "specified complexity" and Michael Behe's (b. 1952) notion of "irreducible complexity." For Dembski, a mathematician, a *specified* pattern is one that admits short descriptions, whereas a *complex* pattern is one that is unlikely to occur by chance. When a pattern is both specified and complex—as is the case with living things—Dembski argues that it must be guided by intelligent processes, for it is extremely improbable that evolutionary algorithms could select or generate living things with specified complexity. Behe, by contrast, is a biologist who maintains that natural selection, in which change is slight and successive, is not able to produce "irreducibly complex" systems that cannot function if they are missing a part. One example is the bombardier beetle, which has a defense mechanism that involves the production of secretory cells, a reservoir that contains such cells and opens into a reaction chamber, the contents of which, when combined with the secretory cells, produces a noxious gas that is expelled through an opening at the tip of the abdomen of the beetle. None of these parts is evolutionarily adaptive on its own, contends Behe; only when they are all present does the "irreducibly complex" system work.

Some of criticisms of Dembski and Behe have focused on the particularities of their theories. In the case of Dembski, complex specified information has been called mathematically unsound as well as tautological, simply a matter of definition, with no real evidence that it exists in nature. And in the case of Behe, not only have potentially viable evolutionary pathways been proposed for allegedly irreducibly complex systems, but such systems have also been shown to arise naturally and spontaneously as the result of self-organizing chemical processes. Still other criticisms take the form of Hume's second and third critiques of the design argument above: first, even if there is "complex specificity" and "irreducible complexity," they do not prove the existence of a creator *ex nihilo* (as in the Christian traditions to which both Dembski and Behe belong); second, given enough time and chance, "complex specificity" and "irreducible complexity" will arise. Both

Dembski's and Behe's theories have also been accused of being "arguments from ignorance" (i.e., arguments from what we do not [yet] know). Moreover, there is the lurking "problem of evil," yet another of Hume's criticisms of the design argument—if the universe was designed for life, it is a shockingly inefficient and therefore an apparently unintelligent or uncompassionate design.

VIII. Putting it Together

So, what "really" is the cosmos? On the one hand, more and more of us seem more and more inclined to let science answer this question. Are scientific and religious answers as exclusive of one another as they seem? Can the cosmos be exactly what science says and also "really" be some ultimate reality or the creation or emanation of some God? Can the cosmos be a sacred relationality, an ongoing battle of good and evil, or a continuous flux of *yīn* and *yáng*, and also be "nothing but" vibrating strings? Can science be true, while the cosmos is still "really" the biblical three-tiered universe, a cosmic man, one of many Buddha-worlds, or the atomic arrangements of Allah from moment to moment?

On the other hand, there is the apparent fact that scientific answers about what the cosmos really is have gotten increasingly counter-intuitive—vibrating strings, dark matter and energy, space-time warping, multiverses. Moreover, scientific cosmoses feel less and less hospitable to humans—vast, dark, and devoid of meaning and purpose. One might think that such inhospitality began during the European Enlightenment, with the reduction of the cosmos to scientific "laws" and the removal of divine mystery and miracle from it. But even this cosmos served a religious worldview and praxis—the prefect creation of a perfect God, who, even if removed from creation, "wanted" humans to approximate perfection in their moral actions, political systems, and scientific practices.

As we have seen above, the same is true even of contemporary scientific cosmologies, which have been used by contemporary Christian theists to demonstrate how their God patiently and faithfully guides cosmological and evolutionary processes. Contemporary scientific cosmologies have also inspired new modes of religiosity, most notably religious naturalisms that reject supernatural beings and forces yet cultivate attitudes of sacred wonder for a mysterious cosmos. Is this, in a sense, just what Lakȟóta philosophy of religion says with *wakȟáŋ*? Ifá divination with *àṣẹ*"? South Asian philosophies of religion with cosmic consciousness? Chinese cosmologies with pattern-principle (*lǐ*) and vital energy (*qì*)? Abrahamic cosmologies with emanation from and return to God?

We might also ask whether and how traditional religious cosmoses constitute worlds for the oppressed and marginalized. Take women, for example. Not only are most of the "high Gods" of most of the religions of the world male (more on this next chapter); the cosmos itself is often gendered in ways that privilege men. In South Asia, there is the "cosmic man" (*Loka Puruṣa*) of Vedic religion and Jainism as well as Sāṁkhya's account of a male consciousness (*Puruṣa*) that becomes distracted by and loses "Himself" in the dance of a female materiality (*prakṛti*). In East Asia, the feminine *yīn*, which is identified with earth (*dì*) and characterized as passive, receptive, and yielding, is inferior to the masculine *yáng*, which is identified with Heaven (*Tiān*). And Abrahamic religions and European philosophies usually gender the earth as female, conflating and justifying the subjugation of nature and women. Of course, there are exceptions—female deities of cosmic importance (note especially Ọ̀ṣun above and White Buffalo Calf Woman elsewhere) and female-gendered cosmic principles (note especially *Ḥokmâ*/*Sophia* above and *Dào* elsewhere)—but one might wonder whether they suffice for the (re)imagination of cosmoses that offer religious paths for the oppressed and marginalized.

As always, it is up to you to decide, both about this matter and the others above.

Questions for Discussion

1. Describe, compare, and evaluate several of the cosmologies above. Given that these cosmologies provide religious worlds in which to live and practice, how should they be evaluated? (How) can they be of truth, value, or meaning for you?
2. What is the relationship between religious cosmologies and religious practices? When have changing practices caused changes to cosmologies? When have changing cosmologies caused changes to practices? Does the "chicken" or the "egg" come first?
3. Explore the relationship between contemporary scientific cosmologies and both traditional and recent religious worldviews. Does "science" create less hospitable cosmoses for "religion"? Or can any cosmos be religiously salutary?

Primary and Scholarly Sources

East Asia

Fǎzàng. "Treatise on the Golden Lion." In *A Source Book in Chinese Philosophy*, ed. Wing-Tsit Chan, 409–14. Princeton, NJ: Princeton University Press, 1963.

Xī, Zhū. "The Complete Works of Chu Hsi," 49:1–8. In *A Source Book in Chinese Philosophy*, ed. Wing-Tsit Chan, 634–8. Princeton, NJ: Princeton University Press, 1963.

European/Academic

Hume, David. *Dialogues Concerning Natural Religion*, Parts IV–V. Ed. Richard H. Popkin, 28–38. Indianapolis, IN: Hackett Publishing, 1980.

Manson, Neil A. "The Fine-Tuning Argument." *Philosophy Compass* 4/1 (2009): 271–86.

Paley, William. *Natural Theology*, chapter 1. Eds. Matthew D. Eddy and David Knight, reprint ed., 7–10. New York: Oxford University Press, 2008.

Lakȟóta

Archie Fire Lame Deer and Richard Erdoes. *Gift of Power: The Life and Teachings of a Lakota Medicine Man*, 132–49. Santa Fe, NM: Bear & Co. Publishing, 1992.

Deloria, Vine, Jr. "If You Think about it, You Will See that it is True." In *Spirit and Reason*, 46–58. Golden, CO: Fulcrum Publishing, 1999.

Mediterranean/Abrahamic

ibn al-ʿArabī. *Kitāb Al-Futūḥāt al-Makkiyya*, chapter 558. In *The Meccan Revelations*, vol. 1, trans. William C. Chittick and James W. Morris, 57–64. New York: Pir Press, 2004.

Pseudo-Dionysius. *Divine Names*, chapter 2. In *Pseudo-Dionysius: The Complete Works*, trans. Colm Luibheid. Mahwah, NJ: Paulist Press, 1987.

Zōhar. "Openings." In *Zohar: The Book of Enlightenment*, trans. Daniel Chanan Matt, 65–8. Mahwah, NJ: Paulist Press, 1983.

South Asia

Īśvarakṛṣṇa. *Sāṁkhya Kārikā*, I.1–73. In *A Sourcebook in Asian Philosophy*, eds. John M. Koller and Patricia Koller, 52–9. New York: Macmillan Publishing Co., 1981.

Kaṇāda. *Vaiśeṣika Sūtras*, I.1.1–31. In *An Introduction to Indian Philosophy: Perspectives on Reality, Knowledge, and Freedom*, ed. Bina Gupta, 196–8. New York: Routledge, 2012.

Umāsvāti. *That Which Is: Tattvārtha Sūtra*, 3.1, 10.5–8. Eds. Kerry Brown and Sima Sharma, 69–70, 255–6. San Francisco, CA: HarperCollins Publishers, 1994.

Yorùbá

Abímbọ́lá, Kọ́lá. *Yorùbá Culture A Philosophical Account*, chapter 3. Birmingham: Iroko Academic Publishers, 2005.

Gbadegesin, Segun. *African Philosophy: Traditional Yoruba Philosophy and Contemporary African Realities*, chapter 4. New York: Peter Lang, 1991.

10

Where Does the Cosmos Come From?

Learning Objectives

- Describe, compare, and evaluate the cosmogonies of our six traditions of philosophy of religion.
- Explain why proofs for the existence of a God "matter" in some cultural-historical contexts while being absent from, or insignificant in, others.
- Critically examine the different uses or ends of proofs for the existence of a God.

I. Introduction

In this chapter, we turn to some of the central questions of contemporary philosophy of religion, especially in its analytic or theistic mode: Does the cosmos have a divine origin, and if so, what is its nature? Ever since the European Enlightenment, if not earlier, philosophy of religion in the "West" has been centrally concerned with these questions. So much so, that it is just natural for some people to assume these are core questions of philosophy of religion for everyone. As we will see, however, this is not the case.

In fact, outside of the Mediterranean/Abrahamic and European/Academic traditions of philosophizing about religion, there is only one religio-philosophical school (within the four remaining traditions) that offers proofs for the existence of a God—the South Asian Hindu *darśana* of Nyāya. Moreover, many religio-philosophical "schools" do not hold that the cosmos was created at all, let alone by a person-like deity. Thus, the question "Where does the cosmos comes from?" does not reduce to "Can the existence of a God be proved from the existence or design of the cosmos"?—at least not for *global-critical* philosophy of religion.

Rather, we might first ask whether the cosmos is created or generated at all. (This is what is meant by *cosmogony*, a theory about the generation [Gk. *gonos*] of the cosmos [*kosmos*].) If we find that it is created or generated, we might next ask whether it is created by a person-like God or Gods or generated through an impersonal principle, force, or ground. If we find that it is created by a person-like God or Gods, we might then ask whether by a single God or multiple Gods, whether from preexistent materials or out of nothing, whether at some point in time or eternally, and so forth. Drawing in feminist and intersectional perspectives, we might also scrutinize why creator Gods are usually personified as paternal male, and whether creator Gods and cosmic forces might more appropriately be sexed as maternal female, non-binary, or other.

Given the general absence of proofs for the existence of Gods throughout "non-Western" religious philosophies, we should also ask why "Western" philosophers have been so concerned with them at various stages of Western philosophy. As we will soon see, there are different reasons for this concern at different points of this history: medieval Abrahamic philosophy and theology, early European Enlightenment philosophy, and post-Second World War Anglo-American philosophy of religion. In the first case, concern with proofs involved whether Abrahamic religion could be harmonized with Greek philosophy in general and Aristotelian philosophy in particular; in the middle case, whether "lowest common denominator" religion could be given religiously independent philosophical grounds (and therefore rest on foundations as secure as science); in the last case, whether Christianity in particular and "theism" more generally can be defended from philosophical and cultural critique.[1]

Take all this as a reminder that when we "robustly describe" religious reason-giving, we do so with respect to not only logical form and conceptual meanings but also cultural-historical context and rhetorical-political ends. Simply put, there is a lot more "going on" with proofs for the existence of a God than just "whether they work." Also take all this as a reminder that when we "formally compare" religious reason-giving, we look for stable, cross-cultural categories under which all the relevant content can be included. Proofs for the existence of Gods, obviously, is not such a category, at least not if we are comparing diverse philosophies of religion with respect to the question "Where does the cosmos come from?" Finally, take all of this as reminder that when we critically evaluate religious reason-giving, we draw on a variety of tools, some of the most important of which bring critical awareness of our own biases and worldviews, especially as they are not shared by other peoples and cultures.

II. East Asian Philosophy of Religion

As you already know, East Asian philosophies of religion tend not to think of a highest being, force, or principle as humanlike. Moreover, East Asian philosophies of religion tend to think of the cosmos as without beginning (at least temporally). In a sense, then, our answer to this chapter's question will resemble our answer to last chapter's question, involving a first principle such as *Dào* or *Tàijí*; core cosmological components such as *qì*, *yīn* and *yáng*, and *wǔxíng*; and an ongoing process by which the cosmos flows from lesser to greater degrees of differentiation then back again.

You have seen already how this works in the cases of Daoism and (Neo) Confucianism, especially as both incorporate ideas that had their origins in philosophical interpretations of the *Yìjīng* and in the School of Yīn and Yáng. (In spite of the fact that the Chinese Buddhist school of Huáyán made important contributions to Chinese cosmology with its understanding of a fundamental pattern-principle [*lǐ*, 理] that underlies all interdependent phenomena [*shì*, 事], Buddhism tended not to advance cosmogonies, or in this case accounts of how differentiation proceeds from and returns to non-differentiation.)

In the case of Daoism, the Daoist classic *Dàodéjīng* speaks of *Dào* as the origin of everything and the way of nature. *Dào* eternally gives rise to all things—first to "one," which is often taken as *qì*; then to "two," the polar forces of *yīn* and *yáng*; then to "three," which is sometimes interpreted as Heaven (*Tiān*), earth (*dì*), and humankind; and finally to the myriad or 10,000 things.

> The Way [*Dào*] gave birth to unity,
> Unity gave birth to duality,
> Duality gave birth to trinity,
> Trinity gave birth to the myriad creatures.[2]

Later, the five material phases (*wǔxíng*) and eight trigrams (from the *Yìjīng*) were added to this process, the "one" (primordial *qì*) was identified as *Tàijí* (Supreme Polarity/Ultimate), and the *Dào* was understood to have a non-differentiated form called *Wújí*, the "Non-Polarity" or "Non-Ultimate," sometimes even a form prior to non-differentiation called *Wú Wújí*, the

Table 10.1 Daoist Cosmogony/Cosmology

(--) Non-non-differentiated Dào (*Wú Wújí*, Non-Non-Polarity/Ultimate) →
(-) Non-differentiated Dào (*Wújí*, Non-Polarity/Ultimate) →
(1) Material force (*qì*), which is identified with the Supreme Polarity/Ultimate (*Tàijí*) →
(2) *Yīn* and *yáng* →
(3) Heaven (*Tiān*), Earth (*dì*), and humans (at least according to some interpretations) →
(5) Five material phases (*wǔxíng*) →
(8) Eight trigrams →
(10,000) The myriad things

"Non-Non-Polarity" or "Non-Non-Ultimate." When you put this all together, you get a "cosmogonical" picture something like Table 10.1.

Note, however, that this process occurs eternally and continually, not at some temporal beginning in time, and that it happens in reverse order in the cases of death (after which our bodies return to undifferentiation) and meditation (in which our heart-minds attain states of undifferentiation).

With Confucianism, it was not until Song Dynasty (Neo)Confucianism in general and Zhū Xī (1130–1200) in particular that a robust cosmology was articulated and systematized. This story is told in a way that has Zhū Xī drawing from five preceding (Neo)Confucian philosophers, referred to as the "Five Masters of the Northern Song Dynasty." From Shào Yōng (邵雍, 1011–77) and especially Zhōu Dūnyí (周敦頤, 1017–73), Zhū Xī borrowed the Daoist cosmological picture above: a first principle that exists in undifferentiated and differentiated form (*Wújí* and *Tàijí*), and a process by which the first principle generates the polar forces of *qì* (*yīn* and *yáng*), then the five material phases (*wǔxíng*), and finally the 10,000 things. (See Figure 10, Zhōu Dūnyí's "Diagram of the Supreme Polarity/Ultimate [*Tàijítú*, 太極圖].")

From Zhāng Zài (張載, 1020–77), Zhū Xī recognized the importance of *qì*, which Zhāng Zài identified with the function of the "Supreme Polarity/Ultimate." And from the Chéng brothers, Chéng Hào (1032–85) and Chéng Yí (1033–1107)—who were the nephews of Zhāng Zài and the students of Zhōu Dūnyí—Zhū Xī drew the notion of *lǐ* (理, pattern-principle), as a cosmological source, force, and form that acts upon *qì* to pattern it into the particular things of the cosmos.

Zhū Xī's special brilliance was in bringing all these ideas together, "correlating" opposites together in dyads, tracing a cosmogonical process from non-differentiation to differentiation, and revealing the underlying human-moral importance of these correlations and processes. As for the

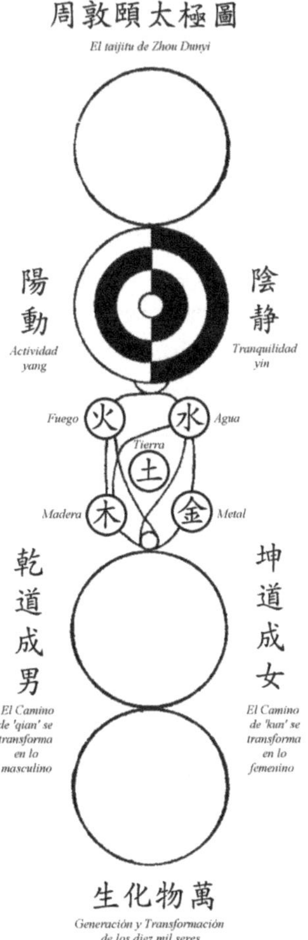

Figure 10 Zhōu Dūnyí's "Diagram of the Supreme Polarity/Ultimate (*Tàijítú*)." Edescas2, "El taijitu," July 2, 2006, Public domain, Wikimedia Commons.

correlations, last chapter we looked at how Zhū Xī correlated pattern-principle (*lǐ*, 理) and vital energy (*qì*), with pattern-principle serving as the patterns for how vital energy forms into the stuff of the cosmos. But this is just half the picture since Zhū Xī identified both *lǐ* and *qì* with more primordial forms, which were themselves correlated with one another—in the case of *lǐ*, the Supreme Polarity/Ultimate (*Tàijí*), which Zhū Xī called "the most primitive and original form of *lǐ*," likening it to "the top of a house or the zenith of the sky, beyond which point there is no more";[3] and in the case of *qì*, the "Non-Polarity/Ultimate," which is "unformed primal *qì*" or "pure potentiality."[4] Both feature in Zhū Xī's cosmogonical process, which involves the primordial stimulation of *Wújí* by *Tàijí* causing the *yīn/yáng* polarity of *qì* to arise, with *Tàijí* serving as both a principle of movement that generates *yáng* and a principle of tranquility that generates *yīn*.[5] From here, the *yīn/yáng* polarities of *qì* give rise to the five material forces, which then generate the cosmos itself: Heaven (*Tiān*), earth (*dì*), and the myriad (or 10,000) things.

Despite these correlations (*Tàijí/Wújí*, *lǐ/qì*) as well as the apparent fact that neither *Tàijí* nor *lǐ* (理) exist apart from *Wújí* and *qì*, *Tàijí* and *lǐ* have epistemological and ontological priority over *Wújí* and *qì*, as we learned last chapter. To restate, this means, epistemologically, that *lǐ* can be abstracted from *qì* and studied and, ontologically, that *lǐ* constitutes the permanent possibilities for *qì*-formations. Here, we can add another obvious priority (which goes back to Chapter 8): ethical. Whereas *lǐ* constitutes the moral standards and norms for human behavior, *qì* is the source of "feelings" (*qíng*)—pleasure, anger, sorrow, joy, love, hate, desire—that the Confucian sage must learn to control and balance. For Zhū Xī, then, understanding what the cosmos is and where it comes from is crucially important for knowing what humans are and how they should live. And what, finally, about temporal priority? Here, we return to Zhū Xī's assertion that neither *Tàijí* nor *lǐ* (理) exist apart from *Wújí* and *qì*, respectively. It would seem that Zhū Xī's cosmos—and the Chinese cosmos more generally—is without beginning or end, constituted by the eternal oscilllation of differentiation and undifferentiation.

III. Lakȟóta Philosophy of Religion

In the case of Lakȟóta philosophy of religion the cosmos is created by, or perhaps just comprised of, the creative force of *Wakȟáŋ Tȟáŋka*, which means something like great incomprehensibility, great mystery, or great sacred. *Wakȟáŋ*, as you learned in Chapter 6, encompasses several different meanings—that which is difficult to understand, that which is sacred, that which is powerful, and that which pervades and unifies all things. These sacred, mysterious, powerful beings and forces are collectively known as *Wakȟáŋ Tȟáŋka*.[6]

After colonial contact, *Wakȟáŋ Tȟáŋka* became more and more like the God of Christianity.[7] Evidence suggests, however, that *Wakȟáŋ Tȟáŋka* was originally conceived of as plural (and is still conceived as such by some). According to at least one early account, *Wakȟáŋ Tȟáŋka* refers to a group of sixteen benevolent spirits or powers known as the *tobtób kiŋ*, "the four times four."[8] (Additionally, there are a number of malevolent *wakȟáŋ* that we will consider in Chapter 13.) Many of these *wakȟáŋ* were personified, natural phenomena with human characteristics.

As for creation myths, the Lakȟóta do have one that involves some of the *tobtób kiŋ* of *Wakȟáŋ Tȟáŋka*.[9] In the beginning, there was no time or space, only Iŋyaŋ, the rock, surrounded by Haŋhépi, the darkness. Iŋyaŋ wanted something to rule over, so he let out his blood, the source of his power, and created a circle out of himself, forming it around himself and naming it Makȟá, the earth and the waters on it. The powers of earth and water could not get along, so part of these powers departed forming the sky, Tákuškaŋškaŋ, who became supreme. When Haŋhépi and Makȟá later got into a quarrel, Tákuškaŋškaŋ banished Haŋhépi to the underworld and created Aŋpétu, the daylight. When Makȟá complained that she was cold, Haŋhépi then created Wí, the sun, to warm Makȟá. And when Makȟá complained that she was too hot, Tákuškaŋškaŋ decided to alternate daylight and darkness, with Wí, sun, following Haŋhépi, moon, around Makȟá. Finally, Tákuškaŋškaŋ created the first two two-leggeds—Wazíya, "Old Man Wizard," and his wife, Wakáŋka, "Old Woman Witch"—who were servants of the *Wakȟáŋ Tȟáŋka*, dwelling in the underworld. (You read in Chapter 8 about how the Lakȟóta eventually emerged from under the ground to live on the surface of the earth, and you will read in Chapter 13 about how a certain "evil" came into the world through the deeds of Wazíya, Wakáŋka, and others.)

However, as Vine Deloria, Jr., maintains: "The beginning and end of time are of no apparent concern for many tribal religions"; thus, at no point "does any tribal religion insist that its particular version of the creation is an absolute historical recording of the creation event."[10] And as Elaine Jahner points out, it is the myth about the sacred pipe (see Chapter 7) that is most important to the Lakȟóta, not creation myths: "This myth [about the sacred pipe] narrates what to the Lakota people was the single most important manifestation of the sacred, the one that founded the Lakota world and gave the people their orientation in time and space."[11] Jahner therefore concludes that "stories that explain how the world first came into being and then achieved its current form held a less important place than those that tell how a particular, definite relationship between human beings and spirits came about and is perpetuated through ritual."[12] In other words, "Lakota emphasis was far less on an original genesis than it was on the ongoing genesis which is the basis of sacred history."[13]

IV. Yorùbá Philosophy of Religion

Yorùbá creation myths are fairly straightforward, at least in the versions in which they have been codified for scholarship (which trace back to the *Ifá* corpus). What is interesting about them, as with Lakhóta creation myths, is that the creation of the cosmos is carried out by multiple Gods—one "high God" (Olódùmarè) and three primordial *Òrìṣà* (Ọrunmila, Èṣù, and Ọbàtálá). These Gods first created "heaven above" (*ọrun ọkè*), eventually populating it with a total of 400 *Òrìṣà*. Olódùmarè then called on Ọbàtálá to descend from the heavens to the primordial waters below, where he was to spread some earth over the waters to create dry land in between the mountain peaks that poked through the waters. Ọbàtálá, however, got drunk on palm wine and forgot his task. Olódùmarè therefore asked Ọbàtálá's younger brother Odùduwà to finish the job.[14] Odùduwà descended by means of iron chains (fashioned by Ọ̀gún), along with a snail shell filled with earth and a chicken to spread out this earth. After the chicken scratched the earth in all directions, Odùduwà put a chameleon on the ground to test its strength. After two passes over the earth, the chameleon reported that the earth was "wide enough." Thus, the capital city was named Ilé-Ifẹ̀—with *Ilé* meaning "home," and *Ifẹ̀* meaning "that which is wide."

In time, the other *Òrìṣà* descended from *ọrun ọkè* on Ọ̀gún's iron chain, settling first in Ilé-Ifẹ̀ and later spreading out from there to establish other cities and towns. Ọbàtálá was given a second chance, tasked by Olódùmarè to create the first human beings by shaping them out of clay. Olódùmarè then breathed the life-breath (*èmí*) into them. As you know from Chapter 5, this is still the case: Ọbàtálá creates the bodies (*ara*) of humans (along with Ọ̀gún, who fashions the spine), after which Olódùmarè breathes in their soul (*èmí*).

As with Lakȟóta philosophy of religion (not to mention many other creation myths), there would appear to be minimal concern for matters of cosmogony. If the creation of the cosmos is important, it is so mostly for the sake of establishing the origins of the Yorùbá people. Also interesting is the fact the multiple Gods take part in the creation of the cosmos, with Olódùmarè needing (or at least getting) assistance. As we mentioned in Chapter 9, this suggests, according to Kọ́lá Abímbọ́lá and other Yorùbá philosophers of religion, that Olódùmarè is (probably) not an all-powerful, all-knowing God. As we have seen and will continue to see, however, this is also the case for many other creation accounts and theologies, as other agents, principles, and materials—be they subservient deities, angelic beings, divine emanations, rational principles, or preexistent matter—are generally introduced to explain the mechanics of creation and the types of things created.

V. South Asian Philosophy of Religion

South Asian accounts of where the cosmos comes from are as old as the *Vedas*. You learned last chapter about the *Puruṣa-Sūkta* (Ṛg Veda 10.90), according to which the cosmos was created out of the ritual sacrifice and dismembering of a primordial cosmic human (*Puruṣa*). Although *Puruṣa* is sacrificed by the Gods, the Gods also arise from this sacrifice, as do the four castes, the four collections of *Vedas*, animals, and other celestial and terrestrial phenomena. Another hymn (Ṛg Veda 10.121) ascribes creation to an apparently unknown God—perhaps Prājapati ("Lord of creation")—who is referred to simply as a "golden embryo" (*hiraṇyagarbha*). Paradoxically, this embryo both impregnates and is impregnated, bringing forth creation. Yet another creation myth, *Nāsadīya* (Ṛg Veda 10.129), wonders whether anyone really knows how the cosmos was created. Perhaps the one who looks down on it from highest heaven alone knows; perhaps he does not.

The source of the cosmos is later understood to be *Brahman* in (some of) the *Upaniṣads*, as well as in the founding *sūtras* of the philosophical *darśana* that is rooted in the *Upaniṣads*—the *Brahma Sūtras* of Vedānta. For the Viśiṣṭādvaita (qualified non-dual) school of Vedānta, *Brahman* is both the efficient cause (*nimitta kāraṇa*) and the material cause (*upādāna kāraṇa*) of the cosmos—i.e., that which causes the cosmos to exist (efficient cause) and that out of which the cosmos comes to exist (material cause). The Dvaita (dual) school of Vedānta, by contrast, makes *Brahman* only the efficient cause of the cosmos, as the cosmos is created apart from *Brahman*, not out of *Brahman*.

By contrast to the Vedānta *darśana*, especially in its Viśiṣṭādvaita and Dvaita forms, most medieval South Asian philosophical traditions did not think that the cosmos was generated by or from anything resembling a divine being. This includes the "Hindu" *darśana*-s Sāṁkhya and Mīmāṃsā, as well as the Buddhist and Jain philosophical schools. The most notable exception is the Hindu *darśana* Nyāya, especially as it was influenced by and merged with Vaiśeṣika in the late first and early second millennium. Not only did Nyāya philosophers at this time hold that a divine being called

Īśvara ("Lord") was involved in the (partial) creation of the cosmos; they also offered proofs for the existence of *Īśvara* that became fiercely contested by other South Asian philosophical schools. We turn to this now.[15]

For Nyāya philosophers, *Īśvara* is the means by which each cosmic cycle is set into motion, as well as the creator of the *Vedas*, the establisher of the relationships between words and their meanings, and the guarantor of the operations of karmic justice, among other things. *Īśvara* is not, however, a creator "out of nothing" since the basic substances of the cosmos—earth, air, fire, water, ether, time, space, minds, souls—are eternal. (Note that these are the basic substances of the Vaiśeṣika *darśana*, with which Nyāya merged in the early second century.)

Naiyāyika proofs for the existence of *Īśvara* circulated in the latter half of the first millennium, finally to be collected, systematized, and elaborated by the tenth-eleventh century Nyāya philosopher Udayana in a text called the *Nyāyakusumāñjali*, which means something like "bouquet of arguments offered to God."[16] In the fifth and final chapter—or "cluster" of "flower blossoms"—Udayana begins by offering the following nine arguments for the existence of *Īśvara* (which double into eighteen later in the chapter).[17] Table 10.2 summarizes all nine.

Although some of these proofs are particular to South Asian philosophy of religion, others bear resemblance to the cosmological and teleological-design proofs in Abrahamic and Academic philosophy of religion, the former of which argue from the existence of the cosmos to its creator or cause, the latter, from features of the cosmos such as purposiveness or design to a designer of the cosmos. For Roy Perrett, the most central of Udayana's proofs combines both cosmological and teleological arguments into a "cosmoteleological" proof, which Perrett renders in the following five steps of South Asian inferential logic (see Chapter 3):

1 Hypothesis: earth and the like have an intelligent maker as an instrumental cause.
2 Ground or reason: because they are effects.
3 Corroboration: whatever is an effect has an intelligent maker as an instrumental cause, like a pot (which has an intelligent maker as an instrumental cause), and unlike an atom (which is not an effect).
4 Application: earth and the like, since they are effects, have an intelligent maker as an instrumental cause (i.e., they fall under the general rule of pervasion in (3)).
5 Conclusion: therefore, each and the like have an intelligent maker as an instrumental cause.[18]

Table 10.2 Udayana's Nine Arguments for the Existence of *Īśvara*

1. Since the world is an effect and all effects have efficient causes, the world must have an efficient cause, which is *Īśvara*.
2. Since atoms are inactive and require motion in order to combine to form substances, they must be moved by some intelligent source, which is *Īśvara*.
3. Since something must sustain and destroy the world, and since the unintelligent cannot do this, there must be an intelligent sustainer and destroyer, which is *Īśvara*.
4. Since each word has a meaning and represents an object, there must be a cause of the representational power of words, which is *Īśvara*.
5. Since the *Vedas* are infallible, they must have been authored by an infallible author, which is *Īśvara*.
6. Since the infallible *Vedas* testify to the existence of *Īśvara*, *Īśvara* must exist.
7. Since the *Vedas* contain divine moral laws, they must have a divine creator of these laws, which is *Īśvara*.
8. Since humans possess the ability to infer and form numerically perfect concepts [as is evinced by the ability to infer numerical concepts beyond one, which is the only number that is directly experienced], there must be a divine consciousness, which is *Īśvara*.
9. Since everybody reaps the fruits of their actions (through *karma*), there must be a balance sheet of merit and demerit that is kept by an intelligent guide, which is *Īśvara*.

Note, again, that atoms for Nyāya-Vaiśeṣika are eternal; they are not therefore "effects" that require an intelligent maker. Only combinations of atoms (such as trees and mountains) are "effects" that require an intelligent maker. This proof therefore rests on a distinction between things that are known to be made and therefore are effects (e.g., pots), things that are known not to be made and therefore are not effects (e.g., atoms), and things that are in question with respect to whether they are made and therefore effects (e.g., trees and mountains). Since trees and mountains are composite things like pots, they are inferred to be effects that are made (though unlike pots, not by humans). Or so said Udayana and other Nyāya philosophers.

Other philosophers were to say differently. For the eleventh-century Buddhist logician Ratnakīrti, there were clear cases of things that were effects but were not intelligently made—growing grass, for example. Nyāya philosophers like Udayana could not, therefore, infer from "being an effect" to "being intelligently made." Although pots and mountains might both be in the class of "things that are effects," that does not necessitate them both being in the class of "things that are intelligently made."

Nyāya proofs were also criticized by some of the "Hindu" *darśana*-s, especially those for which there was no "creator God." For the Mīmāṃsā philosopher Kumārila Bhaṭṭa, just as the *Vedas* are authorless (*apauruṣeya*), so the cosmos is without an author. In the case of the *Vedas*, *Īśvara* cannot be their author since, on the one hand, if He were without a body He could not speak (and therefore author the *Vedas*), and on the other hand, if He were with a body, He could not author the *Vedas* (since bodies are imperfect and the *Vedas* are perfect). In the case of the cosmos, *Īśvara* cannot be its creator since *Īśvara* would first need to form a desire to create, but desire to bring about some state of affairs implies lack or imperfection, which is incompatible with the nature of *Īśvara*.

In the case of the Sāṁkhya *darśana*, Aniruddha, a fifteenth-century commentator on the *Sāṁkhya Sūtra*, maintained that *karma* is to be preferred over *Īśvara* as the cause of the cosmos. If *karma* exists as a fundamental law of the cosmos, then *Īśvara*'s existence is unnecessary. And if *Īśvara* were to create (without *karma*), he would have to do so out of self-interest or other-interest; but he cannot create out of self-interest since this is incompatible with his nature; and he evidently did not create out of other-interest since there is so much suffering in the world. *Karma* alone is therefore the cause of the cosmos.

Perhaps the most interesting "Hindu" critique of proofs for the existence of a God—whether *Īśvara* (above) or *Brahman* (below)—comes from a philosopher who believed in the existence of a God: Rāmānuja, the founder of Viśiṣṭādvaita Vedānta. In opposition to Śaṅkara, the founder of Advaita Vedānta, Rāmānuja argued that the existence of *Brahman* cannot be proved by inference (*anumāna*) but rather can only be known through the testimony (*śabda*) of the *Vedas*. At issue was the single word in the third verse of the first book and chapter of the *Brahma Sūtras*: *śāstryonitvāt*, which can be translated either as "because it [*Brahman*] is the source of scriptures" or "because the scriptures are the source [of all knowledge of *Brahman*]." Śaṅkara's commentary maintained the former: the existence of the *Vedas* is proof of the existence of *Brahman* as the source of the *Vedas*. Rāmānuja, by contrast, argued for the latter: only through the revelation of the *Vedas* can we know that *Brahman* exists.

Even more interesting, however, is how Rāmānuja next provided three arguments against the human ability to infer the existence of *Brahman* by reason. (See Table 10.3.) We already encountered variations of the first two of these arguments last chapter, when we looked at the eighteenth-century Scottish philosopher David Hume's (1711–76) critique of the design argument for an Abrahamic God. Remarkably, Rāmānuja's arguments anticipate Hume's by a good 700 years. Even more remarkable, though, is

Table 10.3 Rāmānuja's Refutations of Proofs for the Existence of *Brahman*

1. Although we can infer that the world was created, we cannot know by reason that it was created at one time and by one being.
2. Since some of the things we observe in the cosmos appear as artifacts and others as organisms, we cannot know by reason whether the world is a manufactured product (using the artisan-artifact model) or whether it is the embodiment of a supreme soul (using the soul-body model).
3. According to the *Upaniṣads*, *Brahman* can only be known from the *Upaniṣads*.

that Rāmānuja's arguments were not intended as a means of discrediting belief in the existence of "God" (as Hume's seemed to be). Rather, Rāmānuja critiqued arguments for the existence of "God" so that people might believe based on the testimony of Vedic scripture alone. Proofs for the existence of a God, it seems, are sometimes an obstacle to belief in that God.

VI. Mediterranean/Abrahamic Philosophy of Religion

As in the case of other religious traditions, Abrahamic religious traditions are not without their creation myths. Notably, the first chapter of Genesis (the first book of the Bible) provides the myth of a God referred to as ʾĔlohîm, who creates the cosmos by remotely speaking it into existence in six days, creating man and woman at the same time after creating the animals, while the second chapter of Genesis offers a myth of the God YHWH physically forming a man called Adam from dust and blowing the breath of life into him, then creating animals in an effort to find a companion for Adam, and finally removing a rib from Adam to create the first woman, Eve. Like Genesis 2, the Qurʾān describes Allah forming Adam from clay and blowing Allah's spirit into him. When Allah later commands the angels to bow before his creation, Adam, Iblīs (Satan) refuses, saying he will only bow before Allah. (This make Iblīs a model of sorts for some Sufis, since Iblīs understands best the absolute unity and singularity [*tawḥīd*] of Allah, refusing to bow before Adam.)

Our focus here, however, is on *proofs* for the existence of a God, of which there is certainly no shortage in Abrahamic philosophy of religion. Unlike South Asian philosophy of religion, there was no disagreement in

Abrahamic philosophy of religion about whether a God exists and creates the cosmos—not until the late European Enlightenment, anyway. One might then wonder why so many Abrahamic philosophers of religion forwarded proofs for the existence of a God, many of which turned on this God's relationship to the cosmos.

One reason concerns Aristotle's philosophy of the cosmos. Since Aristotle's philosophy was taken as science by many late medieval Abrahamic philosophers of religion, and since Aristotle not only held that the cosmos was eternal but also provided proofs for the existence of an Unmoved Mover or First Cause of an eternal cosmos, Aristotle's cosmos and proofs needed to be confronted by Abrahamic philosophers of religion.[19] Tables 10.4 and 10.5 summarize these Aristotelian proofs as later adapted by the Medieval Christian philosopher Thomas Aquinas (whom we will get to in a bit).

Confrontation of Aristotle's cosmos and proofs is most evident in medieval Islamic philosophy of religion, where Islamic theology (*kalām*) adopted a proof for the existence of a creator of the cosmos, while Islamic philosophy (*falsafa*) offered proofs that were thought to work regardless of whether the cosmos was temporally created or eternally generated. The Islamic philosopher ibn Sīnā (980–1137), for example, advanced a proof of necessary existence that came to be known as the "Proof of the Truthful." This proof distinguished between contingent things that need external causes to exist and a necessary existent that exists on its own due to its intrinsic nature. If everything that exists were contingent, argued ibn Sīnā, there would be an infinite regress of

Table 10.4 Aristotle's Proof from Motion (as adapted by Aquinas)

P1: There are things that change (from a state of potentiality to a state of actuality);
P2: Things in the process of change cannot cause their own change (i.e., they cannot be at the same time both actually *x* and potentially *x*);
P3: There cannot be an infinite regress of change (since if there were no first change, there would be no change at all);
C: Thus, there must be a first cause of change (or first mover), God, a pure actuality, the origin of motion/change.

Table 10.5 Aristotle's Proof from Causation (as adapted by Aquinas)

P1: There are ordered series of causes;
P2: Things cannot cause themselves (for if they did, they would have to precede themselves);
P3: A series of causes cannot regress indefinitely (since if there is no first cause, there can be no effects at all);
C: Thus, there must be a first cause, God, the origin of all causal series.

contingent things, which would itself as a collection be either contingent or necessary. If this collection were necessary, then the existence of a necessary existent would be proved. If this collection were contingent, then it would require something outside itself to exist, which itself would have to be either a necessary existent or just another member of the collection. Either way, a necessary existent would have been proved to exist. From there, ibn Sīnā provided arguments to show that this necessary existent must possess the attributes of a philosophically rarefied Abrahamic God: uniqueness, simplicity, and therefore oneness (*tawḥīd*), as well as immateriality, intelligence, power, generosity, goodness, will, sufficiency, and self-subsistence. Table 10.6 summarizes ibn Sīnā's "Proof of the Truthful."

Importantly, if ibn Sīnā's argument works, then it works regardless of whether the cosmos is eternally generated or temporally created: either way a series of contingent things requires a necessary existent. This vexed the theologian, mystic, and jurist al-Ghazālī (1058–1111), who declared Islamic philosophers such as ibn Sīnā infidels (*takfīr*) on three grounds: (1) declaring the cosmos eternal, (2) maintaining that God only knows universal truths (not particular beings), (3) and denying bodily resurrection. Not only did al-Ghazālī denounce the eternality of the cosmos as un-Islamic, but he also forwarded his own proof for the existence of a temporal creator of the cosmos. This proof, which has roots in the traditions of Islamic theology (*kalām*), is known simply as the *kalām* argument. Table 10.7 summarizes it.

Table 10.6 Ibn Sīnā's "Proof of the Truthful"[20]

P1: If everything that exists is contingent, then there would be an infinite regress of contingent things, which itself, as a collection, is either contingent or necessary;
P2: If this collection is necessary, then the existence of a necessary existent has been proved;
P3: If this collection is contingent, then it requires something outside itself to exist, which itself must be either a necessary existent or just another member of the collection;
C: Either way, a necessary existent has been proved to exist.

Table 10.7 Al-Ghazālī's *Kalām* Cosmological Argument[21]

P1: Every being that begins has a cause for its beginning;
P2: The world is a being that begins;
C: Therefore, the world possesses a cause for its beginning.

In our own day and age, this *kalām* argument is used to try to prove the existence of a (Christian) God, as we will soon see. But what about al-Ghazālī's day and age—a day and age when no one, apparently, doubted the existence of some kind of Abrahamic God? If al-Ghazālī's proof was not actually trying to prove the existence of such a God, then what was it doing? For starters, it was clearly arguing for the creation of the cosmos out of nothing (Lt. *ex nihilo*) vis-à-vis Aristotelian-influenced Islamic philosophers like ibn Sīnā who maintained, or at least permitted the possibility, that the cosmos was somehow eternal. More intriguing, however, is that fact that one instance of al-Ghazālī's proof was written into his "Jerusalem Letter" to the Muslims in Jerusalem who were then besieged by Christian Crusaders. Apparently, proofs for the existence of a God also served consolatory and edificatory ends in medieval Abrahamic philosophy of religion.

Not much later, the Islamic philosopher ibn Rushd (1126–98) rebutted al-Ghazālī's attacks on Islamic philosophy by maintaining that philosophers in fact do not believe the cosmos to be really eternal or really temporal but rather "generated from eternity." However, since reason itself cannot prove this claim, ibn Rushd contended that Islamic philosophy must offer proofs for the existence of a God that work regardless of whether the cosmos is temporally created or generated from eternity. Ibn Rushd offered two such proofs, both of which are versions of arguments from design (which we considered last chapter).[22]

The next step in the history of these philosophical proofs involved a Jewish rabbi and physician named Moses ben Maimon (Maimonides, 1135–1204), whose *Guide for the Perplexed* forwarded four proofs for the existence of God.[23] Before offering these proofs, however, Maimonides criticized the *kalām* proof (of al-Ghazālī and other "theologians") as resting on "shaky ground" in two respects: the question of whether the cosmos has been created or is eternal cannot be answered "with mathematical certainty," and the atomist-occasionalist metaphysics on which the *kalām* proof depends (see Chapter 9) is "questionable." It is better, therefore, maintained Maimonides, to provide proofs that work regardless of whether the cosmos is eternal or temporal. Two of these proofs, for Maimonides, were Aristotle's proofs from motion and causation. In both cases, the impossibility of an infinite regress of motions or causes, necessitates the existence of an Unmoved Mover or First Cause. (Note, once again, that this mover/cause is not a temporal creator.) Maimonides also included ibn Sīnā's argument from contingent things to a necessary existent. Finally, Maimonides offered a proof from the notion of logical symmetry, from which we can infer that if there are objects that are moved and move (others) as well as objects that are moved but do not move (others), there must be something that moves (others) but is not itself moved.

When it finally came time for the Christian (Dominican) monk Thomas Aquinas (1225–74) to offer his now celebrated "Five Ways" of proving the existence of a God, so many proofs abounded that he could simply recycle. His first two proofs were the aforementioned Aristotelian arguments from motion and causation; his third proof, ibn Sīnā's argument from contingency; and his fifth proof, a variant of ibn Rushd's arguments from purpose and design. The only proof of Aquinas' that we have not yet learned is his fourth, a proof with antecedents in Plato (427–347 BCE) and Augustine (354–430) that argues from the gradation of perfections in things to an ultimate standard of perfection (since a standard of perfection is necessary to judge a gradation of perfections). Table 10.8 lists all of these "Five Ways."

We might at this point again wonder why all these philosophers of religion devoted so much time and energy to proofs of the existence of a creator God in cultural-historical contexts that were apparently without unbelievers in such a God. One answer, again, concerns the rivalries between proponents of proofs for the creation of a temporal universe and proponents of proofs that work regardless of whether the universe is temporal or eternal. The real issue therefore appears to concern the degree to which an Abrahamic philosopher attempted to reconcile religious revelation with Aristotelian philosophy. Additionally, (at least) two more issues were at play for Aquinas: first, how his proofs could be used as a means to evangelize Jews and Muslims, both of whom he believed were proving the existence of the wrong God, so to speak; second, how his *a posteriori* proofs from the existence and nature of the cosmos could be used to refute those of the rival Franciscan order, which offered *a priori* proofs for the existence of God based on the mere concept of God.

These *a priori* proofs, our last ones of this section, were those of the Benedictine monk Saint Anselm (1033–1109), whose *Proslogion* forwarded

Table 10.8 Aquinas' Five Ways[24]

Argument	Predecessor/s of Argument
1. Proof from motion to a first mover	Aristotle
2. Proof from causation to a first cause	Aristotle
3. Proof from contingency to necessity	ibn Sīnā
4. Proof from gradated series to ultimate standard	Plato, Augustine
5. Proof from design to a designer	ibn Rushd

two such proofs.[25] The first began by defining God as "that thing than which nothing greater can be thought," then rejected the possibility that this concept exists only in the mind, for if it did, something greater than this concept could be thought. Only if this concept exists in reality (and not just in the mind) is it truly the concept of "that than which nothing greater can be thought." The second proof began by stating that there are two ways of thinking the non-existence of this God: one can think about the word that signifies the thing or the thing itself. But whereas it is possible to think the non-existence of this God in the first way, it is not possible to think the non-existence of this God in the second way since the nature of this God is that of necessary existence (as that thing than which nothing greater can be thought).

Interestingly, the motivation for Anselm's proofs appears to have involved prayer and veneration of his God. As a Benedictine monk, Anselm would have encountered the biblical phrase "the fool says in his heart there is no God" two times every week during Matins.[26] But there were no actual "fools" in Anselm's day and age. Perhaps, then, this phrase became a sort of theological puzzle for Anselm, which he solved by showing how, if the fool really thought about the definition of this God, the fool would have recognized that this God must necessarily exist. Regardless, what is especially relevant here is that the Franciscan order adopted Anselm's proofs (especially as filtered through St. Bonaventure, 1221–74), contrasting them to the "ineffective" Five Ways of Aquinas, which were adopted by his Dominican order. Franciscans and Dominicans were to continue this debate for hundreds of years, eventually provoking doubt in laypeople who were beginning to attend universities (like Oxford or Paris) about the ability to prove the existence of any God at all, perhaps even about whether any God existed at all. In this sense, one recent philosopher of religion has called European Enlightenment atheism an "own goal."[27]

VII. European/Academic Philosophy of Religion

Just as Dominicans and Franciscans pattered the intellectual scene in European universities in late medieval period, so Rationalists and Empiricists patterned the intellectual scene in European philosophy in the early-mid-Enlightenment period, with Rationalists holding that our most foundational pieces of knowledge are innate, preexisting sensory input, and Empiricists rejecting all innate ideas, instead maintaining that all knowledge arises through sense experience. These different epistemological positions generated different approaches to proving the existence of an Abrahamic-European God, as Rationalists tended to argue from the existence or nature of the idea of this God (without recourse to any sense experience, i.e., *a priori*), while Empiricists looked to the existence or nature of the cosmos (or other contents of sense experience, i.e., *a posteriori*). Thus, René Descartes (1596–1650), a paradigmatic Rationalist, offered two (quasi-Platonic/Anselmian) proofs from the existence of (innate) ideas, which are listed in Tables 10.9 and 10.10.

By contrast, John Locke (1632–1704), an Empiricist who argued against innate ideas, opted for a (quasi-Aristotelian/Thomistic) proof from the existence of certain experiences and principles established through experience, which is listed in Table 10.11.

Although few philosophers challenged proofs altogether at this early stage of the European Enlightenment, cracks had begun to show by the time of David Hume's (1711–76) posthumously published *Dialogues Concerning Natural Religion*, which itself voiced trenchant critiques of both the *a priori* and *a posteriori* proofs above, as well as a newly popular *a posteriori* proof

Table 10.9 Descartes' First Proof[28]

P1: We have an idea of infinite perfection;
P2: The idea we have of ourselves entails finitude and imperfection;
P3: There must be as much reality in the cause of any idea as in the idea itself;
C: Therefore, the idea of infinite substance must have originated from a being with infinite substance.

Table 10.10 Descartes' Second Proof[29]

P1: The idea of God is that of a supremely perfect being;
P2: Existence is a perfection;
C: Therefore, God must possess the perfection of existence.

Table 10.11 Locke's Proof[30]

P1: Humans have a clear perception of their own (finite) being;
P2: Humans know that something cannot come from nothing;
C1: Therefore, humans know that something had to have existed from eternity;
P3: There must be in the cause what is in the effect;
C2: Therefore, what exists from eternity must be omnipotent (the source of all power), omniscient (the source of all knowledge), and immaterial (the source of immaterial souls).

that argued from the design of the cosmos to an intelligent designer (the latter of which we learned about last chapter). One generation later, Hume's writings were to awaken a youthful Immanuel Kant (1724–1804) from his "dogmatic slumber," after which he penned incisive critiques of the proofs, organizing them into their three contemporary categories in the process: ontological, cosmological, and "physico-theological" (aka, design or teleological). For Kant, the latter two proofs rested on the ontological proof, for only the ontological proof could show that the concept of an "intelligent designer," "first cause," or "necessary being" was instantiated as an actually existing being. However, not only was the ontological proof irreparably flawed for holding existence to be a predicate, but the cosmological and physico/design/teleological proofs had their own independent issues (some of which we will look at below or have already looked at last chapter).

By the early/mid-nineteenth century, proofs for (and against) the existence of an Abrahamic-European God had largely fallen into disuse among Western philosophers, whether due to the force of Kant's critiques, the rise of intellectual atheism, or a shift to history and politics as the "hot" philosophical topics. Although there were some notable exceptions along the way, it was not really until the 1970s that the proofs began experiencing a revival, one that has lasted up to the present, most commonly in a form of philosophy of religion known as "Christian," "Anglo-American," "analytic," or "theistic" (since this form of philosophy of religion is usually practiced by Christians or post-Christians, who are largely from English-speaking countries, who use tools of linguistic-logical analysis, and who evaluate the concept of a theistic God). What changed? Perhaps the fear of "godless communism," or the end of colonial rule, or the growing "culture wars," or the "clash of civilizations" between the "West" and Islam, or simply a perceived threat to traditional Christianity and its values. No matter—what is most important for us is that proofs for the existence of this God once again began to bear significant weight with respect to the rationality of religion, at least for these philosophers.

We have already examined design proofs in Chapter 9, and in Chapter 12 we will look at religious experiences and miracles, two topics that are of philosophical and popular interest with respect to providing evidence for the rationality of belief. Here, we therefore focus on cosmological and ontological proofs in recent Christian-theistic-analytic philosophy of religion.

Given that the focus of this chapter is "Where does the cosmos come from?" we begin with the cosmological proof, which argues from the sheer existence of the cosmos to the existence of a cause or creator of the cosmos. No contemporary philosopher of religion is associated more with the

Table 10.12 William Lane Craig's Kalām-Cosmological Proof[32]

P1:	Everything that begins to exist has a cause of its existence;
P2:	The universe began to exist;
C:	Therefore, the universe has a cause of its existence.

cosmological argument than William Lane Craig, a Christian philosopher, theologian, and apologist.[31] Interestingly, Craig's cosmological argument takes the form of the Islamic *kalām* argument that was preferred by medieval theologians, not the Aristotelian cosmological arguments that were favored by medieval philosophers. In fact, Craig's cosmological argument looks a lot like al-Ghazālī's above, as indicated in Table 10.12. Using this cosmological argument to conclude that the universe has a cause of its existence, Craig goes on show how that cause must be an uncaused, beginningless, changeless, timeless, spaceless, immaterial being of enormous power.

You will remember that medieval philosophers like ibn-Rushd, Maimonides, and Aquinas accused the *kalām* argument of resting on an unprovable premise that could only be held by faith—viz., that the cosmos has a beginning (and is not therefore eternal). Craig therefore provides two arguments and also adduces evidence from astrophysics to show that time is finite. First, he maintains that the existence of an actual infinite is metaphysically impossible due to absurdities that arise from it. Craig illustrates this point by using the example of Hilbert's paradox of the Grant Hotel, in which one can add an additional guest to a fully occupied hotel with infinitely many rooms by moving the guest in room 1 to room 2, the guest in room 2 into room 3, and so on to infinity. But, claims Craig, it is absurd to add an additional guest to a fully occupied hotel, which will have the same number of guests (infinity) both before and after adding the additional guest. Craig concludes therefore that finitism is most plausibly true, which means that the series of past events in the universe must be finite, so the cosmos must have had a beginning. Second, Craig shows how forming an actual infinite through successive addition is metaphysically impossible. Not only is it metaphysically impossible to count up to or down from infinity, but also if the universe were eternal, an infinite number of events would have occurred before the present moment, which Craig says is impossible. Craig also draws on Big Bang theory to support his argument that the universe has a beginning, maintaining that it predicts a cosmic singularity, which marks the origin of the universe in the finite past. Given recent discoveries about the expansion of the universe after the Big Bang,

Craig also maintains that thermodynamic properties of the universe show it is not eternal. Of course, no argument for the existence of a God is without its critics, which in the case of cosmological proofs in general have usually taken the form of arguments (1) that the universe just is (and therefore does not require a creator, cause, or explanation), (2) that there is no need to explain the universe as a whole if one can explain its individual constituents, and (3) that it cannot be established that everything requires a cause or explanation.

Turning now to the ontological proof, it is first notable that its lead proponent is again a Christian philosopher, in this case Alvin Plantinga.[33] Unlike Anselm's and Descartes' "ontological" proofs, Plantinga's ontological proof explicitly utilizes modal logic, which deals with the logic of possibility and necessity, usually in conjunction with the imagination of possible worlds. Table 10.13 offers Plantinga's proof in a series of steps.

Let us dig in a bit. Steps one and two are definitions that establish the premise of step three. *Maximal excellence* in some possible world is defined as possession of omnipotence, omniscience, and omnibenevolence; and *maximal greatness* is defined as possession of these properties in all possible worlds. Given these definitions, step three premises that it is possible for a being of maximal greatness to exist. Note that Plantinga argued that, although this premise is not rationally demonstrated, it is not contrary to reason; others (e.g., Michael Martin), however, have disputed this: if certain components of perfection are contradictory, such as omnipotence and omniscience, then premise 3 is contrary to reason. Regardless, steps 4 and 5 draw on an established principle of modal logic (called "Axiom S5") to argue that if is it possible that it is necessary for an omniscient, omnipotent, and omnibenevolent being to exist (4), then it is necessary for an omniscient,

Table 10.13 Alvin Plantinga's Modal Version of the Ontological Proof[34]

1. A being has *maximal excellence* in a given possible world *W* if and only if it is omnipotent, omniscient and perfectly good in *W*; (Definition 1)
2. A being has *maximal greatness* if it has maximal excellence in every possible world; (Definition 2)
3. It is possible that there is a being that has maximal greatness; (Premise)
4. Therefore, possibly, it is necessarily true that an omniscient, omnipotent, and perfectly good being exists;
5. Therefore, it is necessarily true that an omniscient, omnipotent and perfectly good being exists;
6. Therefore, an omniscient, omnipotent and perfectly good being exists.

omnipotent, and omnibenevolent being to exist (5). Here, other critics (e.g., Richard Gale) have maintained that the phrase "possibly necessarily" (Axiom S5) is problematic, since it is effectively the same as "necessarily" and therefore begs the question. Still other critics (e.g., A. C. Grayling) have pointed out that just as one can premise that there is a possible world containing a maximally great entity, so one can premise that there is no possible world in which anything is maximally great. For most people, however, the ontological argument from the nature/definition of a God to the existence of a God just fails to convince in the way that arguments from the existence and order of the cosmos do.

Before we draw this section to a close, we examine one more kind of proof for the existence of a God—a "cumulative case" argument that the Christian philosopher and apologist Richard Swinburne developed in the late 1970s. Swinburne does not believe that any one argument for the existence of a God suffices. Most, though, raise the probability of the existence of a God, so that, taken together, they make it more probable than not that a God exists. More precisely, Swinburne assesses several arguments for the existence of a God in terms of whether their premises make their conclusions more probable. Swinburne calls this their "C-inductive strength," which he puts in terms of Bayesian probability theory as follows: the probability (P) of the hypothesis (h), given the evidence derived from experience (e) and tautological background evidence (k), is greater than the probability of the hypothesis given only the background evidence: P(h/e.k) > P(h/k). Swinburne finds this to be the case in terms of arguments that involve (1) the existence of the cosmos, (2) the order of the cosmos, (3) the existence of consciousness, (4) human opportunities to do good (morality), (5) the pattern of history (providence), (6) the evidence of miracles, and (7) the occurrence of religious experience.[35] Swinburne then assesses all seven of these arguments, taken together, in terms of their "P-inductive strength," in which the probability (P) of the hypothesis (h) given the evidence ($e_1 \ldots e_7$) and background evidence (k) must be greater than .5: $P(h/e_1 \ldots e_7.k) > .5$.

In conclusion, Swinburne claims that although the intrinsic probability (P [h/k]) of theism is low (since it provides no good argument for why there is anything at all since this God freely chooses to create), it is very high given the relevant evidence. In other words, given the existence and nature of the universe (P [e/h.k]), there are good reasons why a creator God brought about such a universe, i.e., that the probability that *this* universe was brought about by *this* God is strong. And when the evidence of religious experience is thrown into the mix, the combined arguments make a good P-inductive argument. Of course, this argument too is not without its critics, one of whom accuses Swinburne of wildly over-estimating the prior probability of (Christian) theism given (1) the variety of Christian theological positions, especially non-theistic ones, about the nature of a God; (2) the preponderance of non-theistic religious philosophies throughout the world; and (3) the naturalistic explanations of theistic belief provided by cognitive psychology and evolutionary biology.[36]

VIII. Putting it All Together

Once again, we are confronted with the question of how we put all this together. Above we have cultural-historical contexts for which the concept of some kind of creator God is not present, not important, simply assumed, and hotly contested. In the very least, a philosophy of religion that is "global," not to mention "critical," should not assume that belief in some kind of creator God is a normative and central component of religious traditions and communities. Rather, a global-critical philosophy of religion should seek to explain why belief in the existence of some kind of creator God matters in some cultural-historical contexts but not in others. Most importantly, such an explanation should investigate the political and rhetorical ends that proofs (and disproofs) serve in different cultural-historical contexts, especially the contemporary contexts in which we now find them. If proofs arguably make very little difference with respect to whether a person believes in the existence of a God, what then are they used to do? Perhaps they still serve the ends that they did in medieval Abrahamic philosophy of religion: to show to oneself and others that one's religious beliefs are "rational" given what wider societies or intellectual circles take as knowledge, to combat perceived deviances and deficiencies in the beliefs of others, to support and encourage others who believe similarly, and to work out theological and philosophical puzzles for oneself. Proofs for the existence of a God also now function as Christian or theistic apologetics, defending belief in the existence of a (usually Christian) creator God against the perceived onslaught of scientific-philosophical atheism and relativistic-cultural liberalism.

A philosophy of religion that is both global and critical should also examine the nature and variety of Gods both in these proofs and in religio-philosophies more generally. As argued in the Introduction of this book, the increasingly widespread use of the English-term "God" for different Gods obscures the fact that these different Gods are . . . well, different. Moreover, deployments of the singular noun "God" not only usually imply that there really is only one God but also often assume that this one God is in fact one's own God. (For these reasons, I have tried my best always to specify *which God* is under discussion and to capitalize the terms for all Gods; see my Introduction.) Feminist philosophers of religion would also have us scrutinize the gendering of Gods, who are almost always male, at least with respect to the "high" ones. Not only male but also white, Grace Jantzen adds, especially with respect to the traditional philosophy of religion:

> The philosophy of religion in the west has largely assumed a male, "omni-everything" God: as a bishop wrote in *Church Times* a few years ago, "God is a relatively genderless male deity": we need only add that he is also white. It is of course always immediately added that God does not have a body, and therefore has neither colour nor gender; and that God loves all people equally. But lurking behind the denial is the imaginary: the body that God does not have is male and white.[37]

(Why) are the Gods of the West often assumed to be male and white? (Why) are Gods more generally often male? (Why) is it the case, as Mary Daly once maintained, that "if God is male, then the male is God?"[38] This would seem to be a problem for more than just the terms and images we employ.

As philosophers of religion, we should also of course evaluate theories about where the cosmos comes from in general and proofs for the existence of a God in particular. Regarding these theories, first note the diversity. Above we have seen (1) religio-philosophies for which the cosmos does not have an origin, (2) religio-philosophies for which the origin of the cosmos is of little religio-philosophical interest, (3) religio-philosophies for which the origin of the cosmos involves a plurality of Gods, (4) religio-philosophies for which the cosmos originates from an impersonal force or principle, whether at some point in time or eternally, (5) religio-philosophies for which the cosmos is created by some personal God out of preexisting material stuff, and (6) religio-philosophies for which the cosmos is created by some personal God out of nothing. How, if at all, might we evaluate which is true?

As you know, this textbook's approach to (global-critical) philosophy of religion advocates evaluating in a way that remains aware of one's own biases and worldview, is situated in one's own search for meaning, value, and truth, and asks not only about whether religio-philosophical theories are empirically adequate but also how they cohere with other socially rooted theories, how they are useful to how we live our lives socially and individually, and whether they meet any of the other of the epistemic criteria we looked at in Chapter 3. What this means, at least in part, is that you should begin by asking what arguments *you* can provide for why the cosmogonies and cosmologies above might be meaningful, valuable, and truthful *to you*. What reasons do *you* have regarding whether the cosmos is created by a person-like God or Gods, continually emerges from and returns to a cosmic force or principle, or is a brute fact requiring no explanation other than what scientific cosmologies can provide?

Questions for Discussion

1. Describe, compare, and evaluate some of the cosmogonies of our six traditions of philosophy of religion. What arguments can be provided for and against them? Which cosmogonies do you find true? Why?
2. Why did proofs for the existence of a God "matter" in some cultural-historical contexts but not in others? Do they "matter" in your cultural-historical context? What is to be learned more generally about the relationship between such Gods and religion?
3. Critically examine the different uses or ends of proofs for the existence of a God. Which uses or ends are most striking to you? (Why) Do proofs for the existence of a God rarely seem to be reasons motivating belief in the existence of a God?

Primary and Scholarly Sources

East Asia

Dàodéjīng, chapters 42, 52 (= chapters 5, 14 in Mair's translation). In *Tao Te Ching*, trans. Victor H. Mair, 9, 20. New York: Bantam Books, 1990.

Dūnyí, Zhōu. "Explanation of the Diagram of the Great Ultimate." In *A Source Book in Chinese Philosophy*, ed. Wing-Tsit Chan, 463–4. Princeton, NJ: Princeton University Press, 1963.

Xī, Zhū. "The Complete Works of Chu Hsi," 49:8–16. In *A Source Book in Chinese Philosophy*, ed. Wing-Tsit Chan, 638–41. Princeton, NJ: Princeton University Press, 1963.

European/Academic

Craig, William Lane. *The Kalām Cosmological Argument*, 63–5. Eugene, OR: Wipf & Stock, 2000.

Descartes, René. *Meditations on First Philosophy*, Meditation 3. Trans. Donald A. Cross, 3rd ed., 76–7. Indianapolis, IN: Hackett Publishing, 1993.

Descartes, René. *Meditations on First Philosophy*, Meditation 5. Trans. Donald A. Cross, 3rd ed., 90–1. Indianapolis, IN: Hackett Publishing, 1993.

Locke, John. *An Essay Concerning Human Understanding*, IV.x.1–6. Ed. Kenneth P. Winkler, 275–83. Indianapolis, IN: Hackett Publishing, 1996.

Plantinga, Alvin. *The Nature of Necessity*, 213–17. New York: Oxford University Press, 1974.

Swinburne, Richard. *The Existence of God*, 2nd ed., 328–42. New York: Clarendon Press, 2004.

Lakȟóta

Archie Fire Lame Deer and Richard Erdoes. *Gift of Power: The Life and Teachings of a Lakota Medicine Man*, 251–65. Santa Fe, NM: Bear & Co. Publishing, 1992.

Dooling, D. M., ed. *The Sons of the Wind: The Sacred Stories of the Lakota*, 3–20. Norman, OK: University of Oklahoma Press, 1985.

Powers, William K. *Sacred Language: The Nature of Supernatural Discourse in Lakota*, 118–26. Norman, OK: University of Oklahoma Press, 1986.

Mediterranean/Abrahamic

al-Ghazālī. *Incoherence of the Philosophers* (*Tahāfut al-Falāsifa*), Problem IV. Trans. Sabih Ahmad Kamali, 90–1. Lahore: Pakistan Philosophical Congress, 1963.

Anselm, *Proslogion*, chapters 1–4. In *The Prayers and Meditations of Saint Anselm with the Proslogion*, trans. Sister Benedicta Ward, S.L.G., 239–46. New York: Penguin Books, 1973.

Aquinas, Thomas. *Summa Theologica*, Part I, Question 2, Article 3. Available online: https://www.documentacatholicaomnia.eu/03d/1225-1274,_Thomas_Aquinas,_Summa_Theologiae_%5B1%5D,_EN.pdf (accessed March 11, 2022).

South Asia

Clayton, John. *Religions, Reasons and Gods: Essays in Cross-Cultural Philosophy of Religion*, 121–8, 143–55. New York: Cambridge University Press, 2006.

Joshi, Hem Chandra. *Nyāyakusumāñjali of Udayanacāryā: A Critical Study*, 217–65. Delhi: Vidyanidhi Prakashan, 2002.

Perrett, Roy W. *An Introduction to Indian Philosophy*, 170–3. New York: Cambridge University Press, 2016.
Rāmānuja. *Śrībhāṣya*, I.1.3. In *Brahma-Sūtras according to Śrī Rāmānuja*, 7th reprint, trans. Swami Vireswarananda and Swami Adidevananda, 85–6. Calcutta: Advaita Ashrama, 2012.

Yorùbá

Abímbọ́lá, Kọ́lá. *Yorùbá Culture: A Philosophical Account*, chapter 3. Birmingham: Iroko Academic Publishers, 2005.
Gbadegesin, Segun. *African Philosophy: Traditional Yoruba Philosophy and Contemporary African Realities*, chapter 4. New York: Peter Lang, 1991.

11

Where Is the Cosmos Going To?

Learning Objectives

- Describe, compare, and evaluate philosophies about the end of the cosmos (eschatologies), or the absence thereof, in our six traditions of philosophy of religion.
- Explain the relationship between philosophies about the end of the cosmos and socio-historical contexts of suffering, asking about the relevance the latter for evaluating the former.
- Evaluate how, if at all, contemporary scientific and philosophical eschatologies affect traditional religious eschatologies.

I. Introduction

Chapter 11 turns from the origins of the cosmos to its ends. In terms of the journey metaphor, our primary question concerns the "destination" of the cosmos. We articulate this philosophically by asking whether the cosmos has an end and, if so, what happens after that, if anything. To do so we employ the comparative category of *eschatology*, however, not without first critically scrutinizing and broadening it.

An ancient Greek term with currency in the Abrahamic religions, *eschatology* is a rational account of the end of the cosmos (also often of the ultimate, post-cosmos destination of humans). For Abrahamic religions in general, as well as for some Academic philosophies of religion influenced by Abrahamic religions (or scientific eschatologies), this is the end of the cosmos as we know it, after which there is a usually "new and improved" cosmos (e.g., a "new heaven and new earth"). Elsewhere, however, it is uncommon to find the cosmos itself coming to a complete and final end. Rather, it might be the case that the cosmos routinely cycles through periods of ascendance and descendance (as we find for some South Asian and East Asian philosophies of religion), or that the cosmos is in a state of perpetual struggle (as we find with Yorùbá philosophy of religion, possibly also Lakȟóta philosophy of religion), or that the cosmos is an ongoing oscillation between non-differentiation and differentiation (as with some East Asian philosophies of religion), or that the human realm of the cosmos "progresses" into some ideal state (as with some Academic philosophies of religion, possibly also Lakȟóta philosophy of religion). We can therefore only use *eschatology* as a category of comparison if we not only broaden it to include a variety of cosmic ends but also bear in mind the power of the "null result" (see Chapter 1)—i.e., that one answer to the question "What is the cosmos' destination?" is simply that the cosmos has no destination or end.

In expanding the category of *eschatology* to include a variety of cosmic ends, we see that eschatologies are often deployed in times of suffering. Maybe there is a prolonged drought or flood, or an invasion by and domination under oppressive foreign rule, or a natural disaster that significantly alters the practices and structures of a society, or a rapid change of customs and values that threaten age-old traditions—it is during such times that we tend to see the flourishing of eschatological and apocalyptic religious ideas and practices. Why? Such ideas and practices provide relief in at least three ways: first, they predict an imminent end to the trouble and a future state without troubles; second, they promise a reward for those who have suffered unfairly and a punishment for those who have caused this suffering; third, they maintain that everything is really okay with the cosmos, its superhuman beings and forces, its sacred orders and truths. In all these ways, we might say that "eschatology performs theodicy," the justification of "God" given the presence of "evil." To do so, however we again need to broaden our categories, including all Gods, forces, and orders in the first case ("God"), and all suffering, injustice, and disorder in the second case ("evil").

Does this connection between eschatology and theodicy mean that eschatologies are merely human inventions and therefore untrue? Not necessarily. Just because the idea of some future or other world arose during a time of trouble as a means of remediating that trouble does not entail that idea is untrue. We still need to do the philosophical work of evaluating the idea on its own with respect to its truth and value. This we will do at the end of this chapter. First, though, let us look at some "eschatologies."

II. Mediterranean/Abrahamic Philosophy of Religion

The Abrahamic emphasis on eschatology began with some of the Jewish prophets, who, living through the invasions of the Assyrians and Babylonians in the eighth through sixth centuries BCE, declared the "Day of the Lord [YHWH]" as a future day of judgment when YHWH would punish the wicked and reward the righteous.[1] Given that early Jewish eschatology focused on the entire Jewish nation rather than individuals, this Day of YHWH was usually seen as a time when the enemies of Israel would be punished and Israel itself would be delivered in final victory. However, for some of the later prophets, the Day of the Lord brought punishment even to the wicked among Israel. Regardless, eschatology functioned as theodicy: the fact that the wicked (usually foreign powers) prospered while the righteous (some or all members of Israel) suffered would eventually be rectified by YHWH.

Eventually, the idea of *the resurrection of the dead* came to accompany the Day of YHWH, especially after the Jews were released from captivity in Babylon, where they were influenced by Persian religious ideas. During this "Second Temple" period of Judaism, some began maintaining that after the righteous and wicked were judged (during the Day of the Lord), both would be resurrected from the dead, with the wicked suffering eternal punishment, and the righteous (Israel) enjoying a golden age of paradisiacal bliss. YHWH would redeem Israel from captivity and foreign rule, return the ten "lost tribes" of Israel to the Promised Land, restore the Davidic monarchy and the Jerusalem Temple, create a Messiah to lead the people and usher in an age of justice and peace, restore the angelic state of humankind before sin, bring all the people of the world into recognition that the God of Israel is the only true God, and create a new heaven and new earth. In accordance with influential Persian and Greek ideas at the time, some of the later prophets also envisioned a time of distress and catastrophe preceding the Day of the Lord. As these apocalyptic ideas increasingly influenced Jewish thought just prior to the first century CE, this time of distress was associated with a series of plagues and a final war against the Gentile armies.

Given the close connection between eschatology and theodicy, it is not surprising that Messianic fervor and apocalyptic expectation spiked for Jews during times of suffering. Several such spikes happened under Hellenistic and Roman rule and persecution (third century BCE through second century

CE). Later spikes were to occur instead under Christian rule and persecution (e.g., the expulsion of the Jews from the Iberian Peninsula in 1492, pogroms against Jews throughout Europe, and of course also the Holocaust). Most illustrative and relevant for us is the first of these: the expulsion of the Jews from Spain in 1492 and the form of Jewish mysticism subsequently innovated by Isaac Luria (1534–72). As you already learned in Chapters 8 and 9, three teachings form the core of this "Lurianic Kabbalah": (1) the self-contraction of "The Limitless" (*ʾÊn Sôp*) prior to creation (*ṣimṣûm*); (2) the emanation of The Limitless into ten *sĕpîrôt*, each of which is contained in a divine vessel, the lower seven of which cannot contain their divine light and shatter (*shevirah*); and (3) the need for humans to repair (*tiqqûn*) the tenth *sĕpîrâ*, the *Shekinah*, the only emanation unable to mend itself. Only after the *Shekhinah* is repaired will the Messiah come, Israel be redeemed from oppression, and a new heaven and earth be created. Thus, humans play a key role in repairing their God, redeeming suffering, and bringing about the end of this world and the beginning of a new, peaceful, and just world.

With the rise of less supernaturally oriented forms of Judaism, the flourishing of Zionism, and the eventual establishment of the State of Israel, Messianic fervor and apocalyptic expectation has waned for Jews over the last century. Nevertheless, it remained strong in some mystical-orthodox forms of Judaism, with some Chabad-Lubavitch Hasidic Jews continuing to believe that the Rebbe, Menachem Mendel Schneerson (1902–94), did not die in 1994 but rather will soon reveal himself to be the Messiah.

Christians believe Jesus to be the Messiah, reinterpreting the notion of the Messiah from someone who redeems Israel from foreign oppression and rule to someone who offers religious salvation to the world. Nevertheless, Christians have traditionally expected the return of their Messiah in the same way that Jews have expected the coming of their Messiah. In fact, the first generation of Christians were so certain that Jesus would return during their lifetime, that they did not develop a detailed eschatology about end times. Only after these hopes were dashed, especially after the Roman army re-conquered Israel and destroyed the Second Temple in 66–70, did eschatological endeavors begin in earnest. Nevertheless, the basic contours of these eschatologies reflected Jewish ones, albeit as enhanced by the contents of the book of Revelation, the last book of the Christian New Testament: a great tribulation during which an "Antichrist" will rule, the second coming of Jesus Christ and defeat of the Antichrist, a day of judgment, a resurrection of the dead, a reign of peace, and the creation of a new heaven and new earth. Just as with Jewish eschatology, Christian Messianic fervor and apocalyptic expectation has spiked during times of trouble, e.g., the Plague during the Middle Ages, as well as our own age of rapid globalization, upheaval of social values and mores, mind-boggling scientific and technological advances, pending environmental disaster, and perennial war and conflict.

Since we are all too well acquainted with our own troubles, let us look instead at those of the Black/Bubonic Plague, which was the deadliest pandemic of human history, killing between 30–60 percent of Europeans and 100–200 million people overall in Eurasia and North Africa between 1347 and 1350.[2] As you can imagine, many Christians took the plague as a sign of the end of the world, a tribulation to be followed by the reign of the Antichrist, the return of the Messiah, and the Last Judgment. One of the more sensational responses were flagellants, processions of hordes who flagellated themselves and others, probably to punish themselves for sin and prepare the way for the coming of the kingdom of God. Thousands of Jews were also massacred during these years, as Christians blamed Jews for the suffering.

How did Christians interpret this suffering? One surviving manuscript, the unpublished *Liber secretorum eventuum* (1349) of a Franciscan visionary named John of Rupescissa, gives us one such account. John predicted that the Antichrist would soon appear and reign for 3.5 years up until 1370, at which time he would be defeated by the second coming of Jesus, who would establish a 1,000-year reign of peace on earth ("Millennium") before the Day of Judgment, resurrection of the dead, and creation of a new heaven and new earth. This idea of a "Millennium" is alluded to in the New Testament book of Revelations (20:4–6), with some interpreting it as occurring after the reign of an Antichrist ("Post-millennialism"), others, as coming before ("Pre-millennialism") this reign. Whereas early Medieval theologians apparently "abhorred" it, the notion of a Millennium became quite popular among theologians and laity in the thirteenth century, especially in interpreting the Plague, which was read as one of many disastrous signs to precede the coming of this 1,000-year reign of peace (regardless of whether it occurred after or before the coming of the Antichrist). It should again be clear, therefore, how eschatology serves to justify pain and suffering, offering comfort and inspiring perseverance, bringing assurance that pain and suffering is part of a divine plan.

Islamic eschatology too resembles Jewish eschatology in its basic contours: at the end of time, there will be a period of chaos and catastrophe, followed by the appearance of a Messianic figure called al-Mahdī ("the guided one"), who will establish a seven-year rule in Medina, after which Jesus will descend from heaven and, with al-Mahdī, battle al-Masīḥ ad-Dajjāl ("the false Messiah, the liar, the deceiver"), ridding the world of evil and injustice. This will be followed by an era of peace and life in accordance with religious values, which will be ruled over by Jesus. After that, there will be a resurrection from the dead and a final tribulation and battle, followed by the Day of Judgment, at which the righteous will be rewarded with paradise and the wicked will be punished in hell.

In Shīʿa Islam—or at least the largest of its sects, the "Twelvers"—al-Mahdī is believed to be a human who has already been born and is in fact still living.[3] All Shīʿa sects trace a lineage of "imams"—literally "leaders of the community," though with special significance for Shīʿa Islam—beginning with ʿAlī, the cousin and son-in-law of Prophet Muḥammad (whose daughter, Fāṭimah, ʿAlī married). According to all Shīʿa, the first three "rightly guided caliphs," who were appointed sequentially after Muḥammad—first Abū Bakr (r. 632–4), then ʿUmar (r. 634–44), then ʿUthmān (r. 644–56)—were all usurpers of the caliphate, for it should have been ʿAlī, a blood relative of Muḥammad, to have been named successor to Muḥammad. Eventually ʿAlī (r. 656–61) was appointed caliph, becoming the fourth and final of the "rightly guided caliphs" (at least according to Sunni Islam). By this point in time, however, the unity of Islam was fracturing, with ʿUthmān's followers from the Umayyad clan accusing ʿAlī's followers of having murdered ʿUthmān. ʿAlī was forced to leave the Arabian Peninsula for the Persian city of Kufa (in present-day Iraq), after which a short war broke out between ʿAlī's followers and the Umayyads that both sides claimed to have won. Shortly thereafter, the Umayyad ruler Muʿāwiya proclaimed himself the next caliph in 660. A year later ʿAlī was assassinated.

After ʿAlī's death, the fledgling Shīʿa community in Kufa invited ʿAlī's eldest son (to Fāṭimah), Ḥasan, to come to Kufa and serve as imam, but Ḥasan abdicated his rule in the face of pressure from the Umayyads (who were now firmly in control of the caliphate, with their capital in Damascus). Later, the Shīʿa community in Kufa had more success with ʿAlī's second son (to Fāṭimah), Ḥusayn, who agreed to leave his home on the Arabian Peninsula for Kufa. Before he arrived, however, the local governor, an Umayyad official, learned of Ḥusayn's journey, blocked his route to Kufa, and eventually dispatched an army of 4000 troops, which killed Ḥusayn and most of his party of fifty relatives and friends at the town of Karbala in 680. This event was to transform Shīʿa Islam from a political movement to a religious community, as the Shīʿa community in Kufa held themselves personally responsible for Ḥusayn's death, having failed to prevent the massacre of his party by the Umayyad army. Soon thereafter, the Shīʿa developed both a distinctive set of practices, one of which was flagellating one's body with a whip and beating one's brow with a sword to punish oneself and repent for Ḥusayn's death, and a distinctive set of beliefs, one of which was that Ḥusayn's death in particular and the martyrdom of all the imams in general functions as "surrogate suffering," mediating between Allah and humans, sparing the followers of the imams from experiencing Allah's full judgment.[4]

ʿAlī, Ḥasan, and Ḥusayn constitute the first three imams. After them, come nine more, at least for the majority sect of "Twelvers." In the case of many of the latter imams, especially numbers seven through eleven, the newly established ʿAbbāsid Caliphate (which overthrew the Umayyads in 750) held them under "house arrest" in or nearby the newly established capital of Baghdad, fearing an uprising of the growing Shīʿa community. Twelver Shīʿa maintain that each of these imams was assassinated, with the lone exception of the twelfth and final imam, Muḥammad al-Mahdī, whom is believed to have gone into hiding in 873 at the age of four, later to enter a state of long-term "occultation" on earth in 940. Just as some Jews and Christians look for signs of the coming or return of the Messiah, respectively, so do Twelver Shīʿa look for signs of the reappearance of al-Mahdī, for when that occurs, the end of the cosmos is nigh—injustices will be righted, the wicked will be punished, and peace will reign.[5]

III. Lakȟóta Philosophy of Religion

Unlike the Abrahamic religions (though like most of the other religious traditions considered below), Lakȟóta religious thought does not posit that the cosmos "goes anywhere." As Vine Deloria, Jr., has contended, American Indians tend to think more spatially than temporally; thus, the end of time, like the beginning of time, is "of no apparent concern for many tribal religions."[6] This is certainly true for the Lakȟóta view of the cosmos, in which sacred spaces are more detailed and significant than sacred times. Moreover, insofar as "time determines the meaning of relationships"—as we learned from Vine Deloria, Jr., in Chapter 9—it is thought of in terms of the cycles of the seasons, the lengths of maturation, and the proper times for action, not in terms of the ultimate destinations or ends of the cosmos.

Be that as it may, American Indian religion in general and Lakȟóta religion in particular provide us with a very interesting example of eschatology in times of trouble—the Ghost Dance of the late 1800s. Although evidence suggests that the Ghost Dance was first practiced in 1870 under leadership of Northern Paiute prophet Wodziwob (aka Fish Lake Joe), it did not become widespread until the revelation of another Northern Paiute prophet popularly named Wovoka (with the Paitue name Quoitze Ow and the Euro-American name Jack Wilson). In fact, it was during the solar eclipse of New Year's Day, 1889 that Wovoka reported the following revelation:

> When the sun died, I went up to heaven and saw God and all the people who had died a long time ago. God told me to come back and tell my people they must be good and love one another, and not fight, or steal or lie. He gave me this dance to give to my people.[7]

After this revelation, Wovoka began teaching this "Ghost Dance" to his fellow Paiutes, encouraging them to renew their connection to the land, ancestors, and spirits, as well as to bond together as a means of responding to the collective stresses that accompanied Euro-American expansion. The Ghost Dance itself typically lasted five days. Participants gathered in a circle in a cleared, flat, ceremonial site. They then performed a series of side steps or shuffling movements while chanting songs that were given to Wovoka in his visionary state.

It did not take long for the Ghost Dance to spread to the other tribes west of the Mississippi, in part due to the miracles that Wovoka performed to substantiate the truth of his prophecy and the efficacy of the dance. The Lakȟóta in particular sent a delegation to Wovoka, which returned with a prophecy that a major catastrophe would annihilate all the whites in the Spring of 1891, after which the spirits of the deceased American Indians would return to the earth. For reasons that are not entirely clear, Lakȟóta performances of the Ghost Dance were accompanied with the belief that Ghost Dancers would be immune to the bullets of the Euro-Americans if they wore a special "Ghost Shirt" while dancing. This conviction met tragic ends when the Seventh Calvary massacred 290 of 370 unarmed Lakȟóta near the creek of Wounded Knee on the morning of December 29, 1890, pursuing men, women, and children for miles to hunt them down in a frozen riverbed.

Despite its tragic end, the Ghost Dance performed a vision of a world to come—a world that restored balance to the earth, native people, and ancestors who died prematurely. Not only was the Ghost Dance a collective response aimed at healing the natural environment and its indigenous people; it was also a ritual of collectivization and resistance that empowered its participants, even as it intensified tensions with Euro-Americans. Writes James Mooney, an anthropologist who researched the Ghost Dance for the Bureau of American Ethnology at the Smithsonian not long after the Wounded Knee massacre: "The great underlying principle of the Ghost dance doctrine is that the time will come when the whole Indian race, living and dead, will be reunited upon a regenerated earth, to live a life of aboriginal happiness, forever free from death, disease, and misery."[8]

For some American Indians, this "dream" remains in place, as Vine Deloria, Jr. notes in his writing about the "eschatological visions" of the American Indian Movement (AIM) of the late twentieth century: "Rather than seeking a new social order or a new system of economic distribution and management, Indians are seeking no less than the restoration of the continent and the destruction, if necessary, of the white invaders who have stolen and raped their lands. As fantastic as such an aim may sound, it has deep roots in Indian consciousness."[9]

Once again, it should be clear how suffering and injustice inspires eschatological and apocalyptic ideas and ideals.

IV. Yorùbá Philosophy of Religion

Much like the Lakȟóta, "traditional," precolonial Yorùbá religions do not think of the cosmos as going anywhere, i.e., as in having an end, whether final or intermediary. Nor does recorded history of the Yorùbá people include any significant, widespread apocalyptic or millennial prophecies or movements, at least not within the context of what we have been calling Yorùbá religions. Rather, the Yorùbá cosmos is one of conflict in perpetuity, an ongoing battle of 400+1 *Òrìṣà* (Gods) and 200+1 *Ajogun* ("Anti-gods"). There is no escaping the *Ajogun*, at least some of them. Everybody will meet death (Ikú); everyone faces disease (Àrùn) and loss (Òfò). Stretches of health and happiness are of course possible, largely through the efforts of the *Òrìṣà* Èṣù, who delivers portions of sacrifices to the *Ajogun*, thereby mitigating the evil they cause. Nevertheless, the cosmos always returns to its natural order of conflict and strife since the struggle between the *Òrìṣà* and *Ajogun* is without end. In other words, the Yorùbá cosmos does not "go" anywhere.[10]

By contrast, Yorùbá religion has gone somewhere, nearly everywhere really, due at first to the fact that the Yorùbá were the most enslaved people during the Atlantic slave trade of the eighteenth and nineteenth centuries.[11]

Most of this enslavement occurred after the collapse of the mighty Ọ̀yọ́ Empire in the early nineteenth century. Although Great Britain and France were soon to outlaw slavery in their colonies (in the 1830s), slavery endured until the late nineteenth century in Spanish and Portuguese colonies like Cuba and Brazil (where slavery was abolished in 1886 and 1888, respectively). As Yorùbá slaves were taken to these colonies, they continued practicing their religious traditions, first by disguising Yorùbá *Òrìṣà* as Catholic saints, eventually by developing distinctly hybridized religions that combined Yorùbá, Catholic, and indigenous traditions. These religions subsequently came to be known as Santería (or Regla de Ocha or Lucumí) in Cuba and as Candomblé in Brazil.

As you can imagine, Yorùbá traditional religion—which was never just one thing—changed in this process. Notably, the *Òrìṣà* were reduced in number and organized into a pantheon. Practices also became systematized and formal institutions were developed. Thus, as one anthropologist of Yorùbá religion contends, just as the first Christian missionaries to Yorùbáland in the early nineteenth century created the notion of "Yorùbá traditional religion" (which prior to that was a diversity of partly overlapping practices and beliefs in different villages and towns), it was Yorùbá slaves in the Americas and their descendants that first created the reality of a single, systematized Yorùbá religion.[12] To follow this story forward, the Cuban diaspora carried Yorùbá religion in the form of Cuban Santería to the US (and elsewhere), where some African Americans were attracted to it as the most authentically African form of religion. As one example, the present-day village of Oyotunji ("Oyo Returns") in South Carolina observes an entire ritual cycle of festivals for major *Òrìṣà* and also offers a "roots divination" where clients can learn their Yorùbá ancestry.

By contrast, religion in Yorùbáland has become less "traditional" and more Christian and Muslim over the course of the twentieth century. (This is true of most of sub-Saharan Africa, Nigeria included.) At this time and in this context, we see the rise of the most significant form of Yorùbá millennialism—a complex of "Aladura" Christian churches that now boast millions of members worldwide.

It is difficult to pinpoint an origin for the Aladura churches.[13] One crucial, early set of events, however, are the visions and revelations of Josiah Ositelu (d. 1966). Having experienced recurring, frightening visions of a great "eye" of the Christian God in 1925, Ositelu, who was at the time a catechist of the Christian Missionary Society (CMS), first resorted to traditional medicine, then consulted a Christian healer, who informed him that he had been called by this God, then bathed him in holy water. Thereafter, Ositelu began receiving revelations from this God, who called him to begin a new church, with new rules (no pork), new names of God (Kadujah, Taroja), and other new practices and symbols. Ositelu was summarily dismissed from the CMS for "erroneous beliefs and teachings," after which he began preaching from village to village, establishing his own church, the Church of the Lord (Aladura).

This was a time of illness and upheaval in Nigeria—the influenza epidemic of 1918, an outbreak of the bubonic plague in the 1920s, the slow demise of traditional Yorùbá religions, the increased spread of Christianity, and the instability of a recently established cash economy. Ositelu read such "signs" as indications that the "pagan world" would imminently be replaced by a new, Christian age. To counter physical illnesses and navigate social vicissitudes, he preached the miraculous power of prayer, fasting, and other means of healing and prophecy, as well as a fierce opposition to traditional medicine, divination, and deities. In fact, the term *aladura* just means "those who pray," as it is Christian prayer—not Ifá divination and *Òrìṣà* sacrifice—that constitutes the preeminent means by which to cure illness and misfortune and to combat "witches" and other evil forces.

Yet again, we see a connection between suffering and eschatology, as well as the deployment of Christian eschatological ideas by missionized and colonized peoples.

V. East Asian Philosophy of Religion

The cosmos also does not go anywhere in Chinese religious philosophy. Put in terms of traditional Chinese cosmology, the cosmos just is the flow of *qì* in its *yīn* and *yáng* polarities and five material phases (*wǔxíng*). For Daoism, this is the transformative power of the *Dào*; for (Neo)Confucianism, the imprinting of pattern-principle (*lǐ*, 理) on vital energy (*qì*). In the case of East Asian Buddhism, however, an additional theory is involved, one with South Asian roots, which maps the stages of decline that the cosmos suffers after the appearance of each Buddha. Since this theory is of eschatological significance, we focus on it here, especially in its Japanese Buddhist form.

Known as the "Three Periods of the Dharma" (Ch. *Sān Shí*, 三時), this theory holds that the cosmos passes through three stages after the appearance of each Buddha. In the first, the "Former Day of the Law" or "Age of Right Dharma," the Buddha's disciples are able to uphold his teachings; on some accounts, this stage lasts for 1,000 years; on others, 500. In the second stage, the "Middle Day of the Law" or "Age of Semblance Dharma," the upholding of the Buddha's teachings is only one of resemblance; this stage also lasts for either 1,000 or 500 years. In the third and final stage, the "Latter Day of the Law" or "Degenerate Age," the teachings of the Buddha (*dharma*) decline, with people no longer able to uphold them; this stage, which is commonly known as the "Degenerate Dharma" (*Mappō Dharma*), lasts for 10,000 years.

This "Three Periods of the Dharma" theory was particularly influential with the Japanese Buddhist school of Tendai, which emphasized the South Asian Buddhist scripture in which the theory is expounded, the *Lotus Sūtra*. Although Tendai Buddhism was the Japanese transplant of Chinese Tiāntāi Buddhism, it underwent some notable changes through its founder, Saichō (767–822). First, Tendai emphasized the general East Asian Buddhist understanding of original enlightenment—all beings possess Buddha-nature and therefore are inherently enlightened. Second, Tendai added the view of the Huáyán (Ch.) / Kegon (Jp.) school of Buddhism that all things interpenetrate each other, as encapsulated in the phrase "3,000 worlds in each thought." Third, Tendai underscored the unity of the ultimate and the conventional. To realize this unity of the ultimate and the conventional, to see "3,000 worlds in each thought," and therefore to awaken one's original Buddha-nature, Saichō encouraged a synthesis of practices—everything from sitting meditation, to scripture study, to esoteric practices, to devotional chanting, to social action. But it was Tendai's devotional chanting, especially to Amitābha, that was to exert the most influence, serving to give rise to new forms of Buddhism in Japan.

The first is known simply as the "Pure Land School" (Jōdo-shū, 淨土宗), which was established in 1175, when a Tendai monk named Hōnen (法然, 1133–1212) left the Tendai monastic center of Mt. Hiei and began teaching that devotional recitation of the name of Amitābha was sufficient for enlightenment. Citing the recent occurrence of natural disasters and civil war, Hōnen maintained that the world had entered the third stage of *Mappō Dharma*. He claimed, therefore, that the esoteric and meditative practices of Tendai and other Japanese Buddhist schools were no longer efficacious for enlightenment. What was needed instead was a path that relied on the saving grace of Amitābha, to whom people could entrust themselves by means of recitation of Amitābha's name as *nembutsu* ("remembrance of the Buddha"; Ch. *niànfó*). Doing so guaranteed forgiveness of all past sins and rebirth into Amitābha's Pure Land, from which it was then possible to attain enlightenment. Thus, Hōnen proclaimed the "other power" (*tariki*; Ch. *tālì*) of Amitābha superior to the "self-power" (*jiriki*; Ch. *zìlì*) of Tendai and other schools of Buddhism like Zen (Ch. Chán). In fact, Hōnen maintained that "[t]he path to liberation from the cycle of birth-and-death at the present time is none other than birth in the Pure Land of Amida Buddha," and "the practice for birth in the Pure Land is none other than *nenbutsu*."[14]

Hōnen's school of Pure Land proved very attractive to the lower classes of Japanese society—those who did not have the time or means to practice Buddhism in a monastery, those who engaged in professions that violated the Five Precepts (e.g., fishing or hunting), and those monks and nuns who had violated other Buddhist precepts. One of Hōnen's "converts" was another Tendai priest named Shrinan (親鸞, 1173–1262), who left Mt. Hiei in 1201 to become Hōnen's disciple. Six years later, Tendai opposition to Hōnen's movement led to the exile of both men, though to different locations. Thus, although Shrinan never intended to start his own movement, that was in fact what happened: after his death, his disciples established the "True Pure Land" school (Jōdo Shinshū, 浄土真宗), naming Shinran as its founder.

For Shinran, the *Mappō Dharma* was more than simply an "age"; it was a basic existential condition similar to the wheel of rebirth/suffering (*saṃsāra*) in Buddhism, perhaps not unlike "original sin" in Christianity. *Mappō Dharma* could not therefore be relieved by any form of self-effort, not even through the recitation of *nembutsu*. Only faith (*shinjin*, 信心) in Amitābha's saving grace could ensure birth in the Pure Land (Figure 11). Thus, Shinran declared that the very utterance of *nembutsu* "springs entirely from the power of the *Other*, quite apart from the power that lies within oneself."[15]

Figure 11 Amitābha. Tịnh Tông Học Viện, "Amitabha 013," May 4, 2017, CC BY-NC-SA 2.0, flickr.com. https://www.flickr.com/photos/154345899@N03/33629271933.

Table 11.1 Japanese Buddhist Teachings during the *Mappō Dharma*

School	Founder	Teachings
Pure Land (Jōdo-shū)	Hōnen (1133–1212)	Recitation of Amida's name (*nembutsu*) grants rebirth in Pure Land
True Pure Land (Jōdo Shinshū, or Shin)	Shrinan (1173–1262)	Faith (*shinjin*) in Amida's saving grace makes possible the recitation of *nembutsu*
Nichiren	Nichiren (1222–82)	Recitation of "Homage to the wonderful *Lotus Sūtra*" ensures enlightenment

The third school influenced by Tendai was also begun by a Tendai monk—Zeshobo, who later adopted the name Nichiren (日蓮, 1222–82). For Nichiren, it was recitation not of Amitābha but of the *Lotus Sūtra* that was key to enlightenment, for only this teaching was effective during *Mappō Dharma*. Moreover, Nichiren held that the entire *sūtra* was present in one single line: "Homage to the wonderful *Lotus Sūtra*" (Jp. *namu myōhō renge kyō*). He therefore encouraged his followers simply to chant this line, which alone could ensure their enlightenment during the *Mappō Dharma* (of which Nichiren saw signs in the unusual number of natural calamities at this time). Not only was *namu myōhō renge kyō* the only way to attain enlightenment; it also served as an effective means of social and political reform.

Once again, we see how theories of the end, so to speak, emerge from and speak to times of suffering. See Table 11.1.

VI. South Asian Philosophy of Religion

There is less apprehension and concern about "end times" and apocalyptic cataclysm in South Asian philosophy of religion.[16] South Asian cosmologies generally think of the cosmos as cycling through extremely long periods of time, in some cases eternally. Because the cosmos either never ends at all or ends very far off in the future, its end is not of much philosophical interest. Nevertheless, we will see that theories about the end of the cosmos again have important consequences for religious behavior and thought.

Traditional Hindu "eschatology" began to take shape in the longest epic poem known to humankind, the *Mahābhārata* (which was probably written between 200 BCE and 200 CE), later to be elaborated in some of the *Purāṇa*-s, myths and legends of the Hindu Gods (which were mostly written in the latter half of the first millennium). In these texts the length of the cosmos is measured in terms of *yuga*-s and *kalpa*-s (as well as *manvantara*-s, but we will not get into that). Each cycle of the cosmos precedes through four *yuga*-s, which are named for the four throws of the dice: *kṛta* (four), *tretā* (three), *dvāpara* (two), and *kali* (one). During this time, the cosmos devolves from the truth and virtue of the *kṛta yuga*—which is also called the *satya* or "truth" *yuga*—to the ignorance and vice of the *kali yuga*. Perhaps it comes as no surprise to learn that we currently inhabit the *kali yuga*, which began in 3102 BCE with the end of the war described in the *Mahābhārata* (which you were introduced to in Chapters 7 and 8, and which you will learn more about in Chapter 12.) By some accounts, there are over 400,000 years left in our *kali yuga*.

At the end of each four-*yuga* cycle—aka "*mahāyuga*"—the cosmos is (partially) destroyed, then recreated again. It takes 1,000 of these *mahāyugas* to make one *kalpa*, which is calculated to be 4.32 billion years, and which is said to be just one day in the life of the Lord Brahmā, who creates the cosmos each day at dawn. This cycle of creation and destruction continues every day of Brahmā's 100-year life, after which the entire cosmos is reabsorbed into Brahmā, who alone remains. By some accounts, we are currently in the fifty-first day of Brahmā's life, so the cosmos has quite a long way still to go. To restate what should now be obvious, this Hindu cosmos lasts for a very long time.

As mentioned above, we currently reside in the *kali yuga* of our cosmic cycle (*mahāyuga*), a *yuga* characterized by ever increasing spiritual ignorance, moral degeneracy, and social injustice, as well as by natural disasters, environmental ruin, and widespread disease. Only with the appearance of Kalki, the tenth and final "descent" (*avatāra*) of Lord Viṣṇu, and his eventual defeat of the demon Kali—who is not to be confused with the Goddess Kālī—will this current *yuga* come to an end (and with it this entire *mahāyuga*). First, all evil, then the cosmos itself will be (partially) destroyed by Lord Śiva, after which Lord Brahmā will recreate the cosmos, initiating the first *yuga* (*kṛta* or *satya*) of the next *mahāyuga*.

Much like Vaiṣṇavite Hinduism, for which there are ten "descents" (*avatāra*-s) of Lord Viṣṇu to earth during times of need, the last of whom is yet to come, South(east) Asian Theravāda Buddhism recognizes that

Buddhas recurringly appear on earth during such times. Unlike Vaiṣṇavite Hinduism, however, Theravāda Buddhism does not associate the coming of the future Buddha—Maitreya—with the end of a cosmic cycle and the destruction of the cosmos. Rather, Maitreya will come at a time when the teachings (*dharma*) of the historical Buddha, Gautama, are no longer practiced by humans and therefore need to be renewed. (Unsurprisingly, many have claimed or been claimed to be Maitreya; most of this, however, has happened in East Asia, not South Asia.)

Like Hindu eschatology, therefore, South(east) Asian Theravāda Buddhist eschatology—indeed, East Asian Buddhist eschatology too, as we saw above—understands the cosmos to oscillate between periods of increased and decreased knowledge and virtue. Theravāda Buddhism also sees the cosmos cycling through periods of evolution and contraction, with periodic partial destructions of the cosmos (at the end of each *kalpa*). Unlike the Hindu eschatology above, however, there is no "last day of Brahmā" for Buddhism, i.e., no final end to the cosmos.

The same is true for the Jain cosmos, which is shaped like a primordial human and therefore finite in space. With respect to time, however, the Jain cosmos is eternal, just like the Theravāda Buddhist cosmos. Time is represented as a twelve-spoked wheel, each spoke of which corresponds with an age. During the first six spokes or ages, there is a progressive "descending" (*avasarpiṇī*) of human stature, knowledge, and virtue, after which there are six spokes or ages of progressive ascending (*utsarpiṇī*). There is no beginning or end to this process, which continues indefinitely like a spinning wheel. Neither is there any periodic destruction/contraction and recreation/evolution in this process, as in the Hindu and Theravāda Buddhist cosmoses above.

What about the other *darśana*-s, especially the Hindu *darśana*-s with cosmologies or metaphysics that did not originally articulate their cosmologies in terms of the *yuga-kalpa* cosmology above? In the case of Sāṁkhya, the periodic creation and destruction of the cosmos in *yuga-kalpa* cosmology simply corresponds to the evolution and contraction of *prakṛti* (with the three *guṇas* coming to a state of equilibrium and rest in the period in between destruction and creation); in fact, the *Mahābhārata* itself draws on Sāṁkhya metaphysics to articulate its *yuga-kalpa* cosmology. Most forms of Vedānta also work in tandem with *yuga-kalpa* cosmology, with the exception that it is really *Brahman*, not Brahmā, who is the ultimate cause and creator. By contrast, Advaita Vedānta regards time and space to be ultimately illusory; thus, there can be no real creation/destruction or evolution/dissolution since everything is really just *Ātman-Brahman*. For Mīmāṃsā, the cosmos is real, though eternal, with no beginning or end. And for Vaiśeṣika, time is an eternal substance, the basis for all movement and change in space. Finally, in the case of South Asian Mahāyāna Buddhist philosophies—Madhyamaka and Yogācāra—time either does not really exist (Madhyamaka) or is just the succession of moments of awareness (Yogācāra).

Suffice it to say, yet again, that there is quite a lot of diversity among South Asian philosophies of religion. One common thread, however, is that either there is not an end to the cosmos or that end is a long way away.

VII. European/Academic Philosophy of Religion

If we date the origins of academic philosophy of religion to the European Enlightenment, then the first significant philosophical reflection about the "end of the cosmos" was really about the "end of history." In fact, history was one of the chief topics of philosophical reflection in Europe in the nineteenth century. One reason why pertains to European colonialism, which was at its apex in the nineteenth century. By then, some religio-philosophical texts from India, China, and Japan had been translated into European languages, the ideas therein stirring European thought. For some European philosophers, the "problem" then became how to account for the "enlightenment" of Europe given evidence of sophisticated philosophical and religious ideas elsewhere in the world. No longer could this story be told simply in terms of the history of the West: from ancient Greece and Rome to the rise of Christianity to a descent into the "Dark Ages" to the Enlightenment of Europe. Now it had to include the rest of the world. Could one give an account of the progress of ideas in temporal succession throughout the world?

The first significant solution to the problem, proffered by the German philosopher Georg Wilhelm Friedrich Hegel (1770–1831), goes by the name "dialectical idealism." The "idealism" part of this phrase refers to the claim of Hegel and other "German Idealists" that reality was ultimately or fundamentally constituted by *Geist*, a German word with a range of meanings including ghost, spirit, mind, and consciousness. *Geist* unfolds in history according to a dialectical logic of ideas called *aufheben*, whereby the dominant idea or spirit of some age is "*aufheben*-ed"—negated yet preserved and transcended—by the dominant idea or spirit of the subsequent age. In broad strokes, this unfolding occurs in two stages, a realm of nature in which *Geist* is alienated from itself (in the sub-stages of mechanics, chemics, and organics), and a realm of spirit in which *Geist* returns to itself (through the sub-stages of subjective spirit, objective spirit, and absolute spirit). In this second stage of human history, humans gradually become aware of themselves as conscious and free, eventually enshrining into law the abstract right of every person as free and autonomous. For Hegel, this story moves "from East to West," with the "Oriental" *Zeitgeist* ("spirit of the age") recognizing only one person as free (the emperor), the "Greco-Roman" *Zeitgeist* regarding some persons as free (non-barbarians, non-slaves), and the Germanic *Zeitgeist* finally decreeing that all persons are free. Thus, Hegel claimed that history had reached its "end" with the constitutional monarchy of the Prussian State, which recognized and protected the freedom and dignity of all people. More recently the neoconservative political philosopher Francis Fukuyama (b. 1952) has drawn on Hegel's work in proclaiming that liberal democracy is the "end of history" since it cannot be improved upon, at least not in principle.

Not so for another nineteenth-century German philosopher, Karl Marx (1818–83), who saw communism as the end of history. You already know some of the basics of Marxism from Chapter 5: the primary force motivating human history is "material," not ideal; humans use material forces of production to satisfy their needs; these forces of production determine social relations of production; over time, this division of labor hardens into a class structure where some people rule and others are ruled; rulers use not only the state but also "ideology" (political, religious, philosophical, aesthetic) to maintain the social relations of production; nevertheless, revolutions occur from time to time as new material forces of production confound existing social relations of production and an oppressed, rising social class overthrows its rulers. This is "dialectical materialism": human history is the dialectical interaction between material forces of production and social relations of production. Not unlike Hegel's "dialectical idealism," Marx told the story of human history in broad stages, in this case from tribal ownership ("Asiatic"), to ancient communal ownership (Greece and Rome), to feudal or estate ownership (Europe), then to capitalism and eventually communism. Although Marx saw capitalism as a necessary and even progressive stage of development, he believed it would eventually be overthrown since it alienated humans from their nature as "makers" (*homo faber*), from the products of their labor (which are taken from them), from their productive activity (since they are told what to make), and from other people (through competition). Capitalism also extracts a "surplus value" from workers since it does not pay them fairly for what their labor is worth. Marx therefore believed that the working class would eventually rise up against their bourgeois rulers, overthrow capitalism (whether by revolution or vote), and institute a classless society that brings true equality, freedom, and happiness for all.

Not only have Marx's ideas proved very influential in world history; they have also exerted considerable impact on academic philosophy of religion, especially on what is now known as "Continental philosophy of religion"—philosophy of religion that occurred on, or was inspired by philosophers from, the "continent" of Europe, especially France and Germany (as distinguished from the British Isles). No idea has been more important to the relationship between Marxism and Continental philosophy of religion, if not to Continental philosophy of religion in general, than that of *messiah*. This story traces back to the thought of the Jewish-German philosopher Walter Benjamin (1892–1940), especially Benjamin's 1940 essay "On the Concept of History," which speaks of a "weak messianic power," associating it with "now-time" (*Jetzzeit*), which is "a model of Messianic time," "shot through with chips of Messianic time," constituting "the strait gate through which Messiah might enter." What exactly Benjamin meant by this is by no means clear; early reception stressed either a Marxist-materialist or a Jewish-mystical interpretation. (Benjamin himself worried about the "enthusiastic misunderstanding" his essay would provoke.) It seems, however, that both meanings were in play: on the one hand, in order to undermine the ruling class, be it Nazi Fascists or Social Democrats, one had to disrupt the notions of linear time and historical progress used to justify the ruling class; on the other hand, the means of disruption is a "messianic" redemption of the past that recalls to the present the failed revolutions of the oppressed classes in the past, re-presenting them in a "now-time" that "blasts open" the ruling class's ideology of historical progress "in a flash."[17] Benjamin's messianism is therefore "inverted"—redemption lies in our relationship to the past, not in the some future event yet to come.

Over fifty years later, Jacques Derrida's (1930–2004) notion of messianicity looked to the opposite direction—the future. First delivered as a series of lectures for a "Whither Marxism?" conference (1993) that was held not long after the fall of the Berlin Wall (1989), Derrida's *Specters of Marx* maintained that even after the demise of communism, Marx's specter still haunted Western society, especially now that neoconservatives such as Francis Fukuyama had proclaimed the triumph of liberal democracy as the "end of history." In fact, Derrida maintained that economic disparity and oppression were worse than ever, decrying that "no degree of progress allows one to ignore that never before, in absolute figures, have so many men, women and children been subjugated, starved or exterminated on the earth."[18] By contrast, Derrida demanded that we remain open to the future, to what is not yet and therefore radically other, to what can never be coopted into a linear narrative of progress by any religious, political, or philosophical ideology. Indeed, Derrida saw this openness to the "irreducibly heterogenous otherness" of the "future-to-come" as a "universal structure of experience," which he called "messianicity." Such "messianicity" is the "messianic without messianism"; it is not some specific event of some particular historical narrative, be it Marxist, Hegelian, communist, neoliberal, neoconservative, Jewish, Christian, or Islamic. Rather, it is the "site of justice"—an openness, respect, and responsibility to the other (person) that does not reduce the other to one's own ideological framework, biases, prejudices, preconceptions, expectations, etc. Here lies one key similarity between Derrida's messianicity and Benjamin's messianism, not to mention the general significance of these concepts for this chapter: there is no "end of history" if by that we mean some future utopian state that is the culmination of historical progress.

In stark contrast to Continental philosophy of religion's focus on human history and historical progress, a growing number of analytic, "Anglo-American" philosophers of religion have taken up questions of "the end" with respect to scientific cosmology. We therefore turn first to scientific theories about the end of the cosmos, then to how some philosophers of religion have engaged these theories.

Although several scientific theories have been proposed about the end of the cosmos, they are all variations on two possibilities: either space collapses back in upon itself or it expands into an endless void.[19] Which possibility is actualized depends in part on the density of the cosmos—whether it is above or below the "critical density" calculated by scientists. If the cosmos' true density is greater than this critical density, then the expansion of the universe will eventually stop and reverse; but if true density is less than critical density, then the cosmos will continue to expand forever. This is due to the gravitational force exerted by matter—the more matter, the more gravitational force exerted on it. If enough gravitational force is exerted on enough matter, it will cause the expansion of the universe from the Big Bang to stop and reverse, as matter is increasingly drawn together.

Another factor in these calculations involves a mysterious entity called "dark energy," which was originally discovered in 2011 when scientists set out to ascertain how much the expansion of the universe was slowing down. What three Nobel-prize-winning astrophysicists instead found is that the expansion of the universe is accelerating due to the force of dark energy, which counteracts gravity, pulling the universe apart. If dark energy continues to exert the same force on the universe in the future, then space will continue to expand, with the distance between galaxies stretching wider and wider and at a faster and faster pace. Eventually we will not be able to see anything beyond the Milky Way because everything will be so far away. This scenario is sometimes called the "Big Freeze," because the universe will end up cold, dark, and empty.

Given the discovery that the expansion of the universe is accelerating, the "Big Freeze" currently seems the most likely scenario for the end of the cosmos. However, whether this likely scenario comes to pass depends in part on the hypothesis that the strength of dark energy has remained steady throughout time. Not only does the evidence currently support this hypothesis, but if dark energy is in fact what Einstein called the "cosmological constant"—which some cosmologists currently hold—then, as the name suggests, it would remain constant over time. But if dark energy is not a constant and instead increases over time, we could be facing what scientists call a "Big Rip." In this case, dark energy would eventually be able to counteract gravity and expand into not only the space between galaxies but also the space within them. Galaxies would then become "ripped apart," perhaps solar systems, too.

The third and final theory for the end of the cosmos—Big Crunch"—was in fact the original theory proposed by twentieth-century scientists (though later discredited in the 2011 discovery of dark energy, per above). In this scenario the strength of dark energy diminishes over time, allowing gravitation to exert more and more attraction between planets, solar systems, and galaxies. Eventually the rate of expansion therefore slows and stops, after which it reverses, with gravitation winning the "tug of war" with dark energy and the density of the universe beginning to increase. At first, this change would be small and harmless, but eventually the collapse of the cosmos would produce a state similar in density and size to the Big Bang—an infinitely dense singularity. What happens next is anyone's guess—the "crunch" could stop once it gets down to its smallest, densest state, or some kind of repellant force could kick in, forcing space back outward, beginning the cycle all over again. (See Table 11.2 for a summary of all three theories.)

Whatever the case, this Big Crunch or Rip or Freeze is billions or trillions of years away, leading some Christian philosophers of religion simply to

Table 11.2 Scientific Eschatologies

Names	Theory
Big Freeze	Dark energy remains the same, and expansion of the universe continues to increase; distance between galaxies grows wider and wider, faster and faster
Big Rip	Dark energy increases, eventually counteracting gravity; distance between and within galaxies increases; galaxies become "ripped apart"
Big Crunch	Dark energy decreases, eventually counteracted by gravity; rate of expansion slows, stops, and reverses, perhaps returning to a singularity

ignore it in favor of traditional Christian eschatology. Surely, these philosophers of religion argue, Jesus will return and God will create a "new heaven and new earth" before a Big Crunch, Rip, or Freeze. Why then should we worry about scientific eschatologies?

A very different approach is to reinterpret traditional Christian eschatology in light of scientific cosmology. One early example is New Testament scholar Rudolf Bultmann (1884–1976), who in 1941 called for a "demythologization" of the New Testament since its "mythological," first-century worldview was implausible in the twentieth-century world of science and technology. What mattered was the existential meaning of Jesus' teachings, not any supernatural elements or feats in the New Testament. In the case of the *eschaton* (Gk. end), Bultmann argued it should be understood as already realized in the present. As Bultmann proclaimed in his 1955 Gifford Lectures: "In every moment slumbers the possibility of being the eschatological moment. You must awaken it."[20]

"Liberation theologies" (including feminist and postcolonial ones) have also emphasized the "here and now" of eschatology, though not as what has already been realized existentially but as what must be realized politically. For such theologians, the "Kingdom of God" is not some far-off time and faraway place; rather, it is "preferential option for the poor" (and oppressed), which must be enacted in the present against all systems of oppression. In the words of one liberation theologian, this is not a "longitudinal eschatology" but a "latitudinal eschatology," where "what is to be expected lies already here, nearby or adjacently, instead of being perennially deferred to an impending future or already realized in the past."[21] This eschatology is not concerned with "the last things" but with "those things in our midst"—the poor, marginalized, and oppressed, for whom the "Kingdom of God" brings good news.

Finally, a growing number of analytic, Christian philosophers of religion have concerned themselves with the relationship between traditional, Christian eschatology and modern, scientific cosmology. One notable example is John Polkinghorne (b. 1930), who employs the notion of *ex vetere* ("out of the old")—in contradistinction to *ex nihilo* ("out of nothing")—to speak about God's creation of a "new heaven and new earth" at the end of time as a transformation "out of the old" cosmos rather than a brand new creation "out of nothing."[22] For Polkinghorne, this requires us to think about the ways in which this transformed cosmos will be both continuous and discontinuous with the current cosmos. We can therefore look to science for "elements of continuity," as well as for what might be "discontinued" when the cosmos is transformed. For another Christian philosopher of religion, Robert John Russell (b. 1946), these discontinuities include "those physical and biological processes which underlie disease, suffering, and death; temporality marred by the loss of the past and the unavailability of the future; and ontological determinism, which undercuts genuine personhood and relationality."[23]

VIII. Putting it All Together

Do these scientific eschatologies matter for traditional religious eschatologies?

One thing we can point out for starters is that some religious cosmologies appear to be linear; others, cyclical; still others, neither or both. In the first case (Abrahamic philosophy of religion for the most part), the cosmos has a clear beginning and end, or at least a point at which the current order or age ends and a new order or age begins. In the second case (South Asian philosophy of religion for the most part, as well as some East Asian philosophy of religion), the cosmos goes through periodic cycles of creation and destruction or ascension and descension. And in the third case (some East Asian philosophy of religion, Yorùbá philosophy of religion, possibly also Lakȟóta philosophy of religion), there is neither a linear trajectory nor a cyclical repetition of the cosmos writ large; instead, there are just ongoing "mini-cycles" (e.g., the oscillation of *yīn* and *yáng*, the struggle between the *Òrìṣà* and *Ajogun*, the cycles of nature).

Given that the "Big Crunch" scenario of the end allows for at least the conceptual possibility of a re-creation of the cosmos (through another Big Bang), it has proved most friendly to religious thinkers, especially Hindu philosophers and Abrahamic mystics. Whether this is scientifically possible is another matter altogether. Moreover, the actual "Crunch" would be preceded by billions to trillions of years during which no life could survive in the cosmos, especially human life on planet Earth (as would also be the case after a subsequent "Big Bang").

Of course, the Messiah or *Mahdī* could appear or return before this or any of the other scientific scenarios play out. If so, we would seem to have a different cosmological problem on our hands. Where exactly would a new heaven and new earth be created? More basically, where exactly do heaven and hell exist in cosmological space? The traditional scriptural view thought of heaven as up and hell as down. Scientific cosmologies, however, render this view untenable.

Additionally, there is the problem of "progress" in academic philosophy (of religion). Are we humans in this cosmos "going anywhere" in terms of achieving an optimal political-legal order, socioeconomic arrangement, moral-philosophical enlightenment, or scientific-epistemic totality? It would appear that no religious tradition (at least in this book) forecasts human beings and communities progressing in these ways. In fact, most say quite the opposite. What about the related notions of messianism and messianicity in Continental philosophy of religion, which instead encourage redeeming the past or opening to the future as a means of disrupting secular ideals of progress? Where does "preferential treatment for the poor," oppressed, and marginalized fit into all this: as a step on the road of "progress," or as a disruption of neoliberal capitalism?

Finally, there is the issue of the relationship between eschatology and suffering. As we mentioned in the introductory section to this chapter, many eschatologies, especially those that involve apocalyptic events, are products of cultural-historical contexts of intense suffering or unexpected tragedy. Eschatologies, therefore, seem as if they are "invented" for the sake of comforting those living through suffering or tragedy, providing the promise of future reward and restitution. If true, does this historical fact make these eschatologies false? Not exactly, for as we mentioned in the introduction to this chapter, an idea is not true or false based on when, why, or from whom it originated. Nevertheless, this historical fact would seem to decrease the plausibility of these eschatologies. Moreover, it would appear that what science continues to discover about the cosmos continues to decrease the plausibility of an afterlife in some heavenly realm.

Then again, if science has taught us anything, it is that science continually changes. What do you think?

Questions for Discussion

1 Describe, compare, and evaluate eschatologies in our six traditions of philosophy of religion. Can religious eschatologies be evaluated with respect to the empirical adequacy, conceptual coherence, pragmatic usefulness, or some other criterion?
2 Explain the relationship between eschatology and suffering. If it is the case that religious eschatologies generally arise from and flourish in times of intense suffering and unexpected tragedy, does this diminish their plausibility?
3 Evaluate how, if at all, contemporary scientific eschatologies affect traditional religious eschatologies. Do scientific eschatologies decrease the plausibility of traditional religious eschatologies?

Primary and Scholarly Sources

East Asia

Hōnen. "The Philosophy of *Nenbutsu*." In *Japanese Philosophy: A Sourcebook*, eds. James W. Heisig, Thomas P. Kasulis, and John C. Maraldo, 243–4. Honolulu, HI: University of Hawaiʻi Press, 2011.

Nichiren. "Historical Consciousness and Liberation." In *Japanese Philosophy: A Sourcebook*, eds. James W. Heisig, Thomas P. Kasulis, and John C. Maraldo, 89–90. Honolulu, HI: University of Hawaiʻi Press, 2011.

Shinran. "*Nenbutsu*: The Will of No-Will." In *Japanese Philosophy: A Sourcebook*, eds. James W. Heisig, Thomas P. Kasulis, and John C. Maraldo, 253. Honolulu, HI: University of Hawaiʻi Press, 2011.

European/Academic

Benjamin, Walter. "On the Concept of History." Available online: https://www.sfu.ca/~andrewf/CONCEPT2.html (accessed March 11, 2022).

Bultmann, Rudolf. *The Presence of Eternity: History and Eschatology: The Gifford Lectures 1955*, 138–55. New York: Harper, 1957.

Derrida, Jacques. *Specters of Marx: The State of the Debt, the Work of Mourning and the New International*. Trans. Peggy Kamuf, 165–76. New York: Routledge, 1994.

Hegel, G. W. F. *Introduction to the Philosophy of History*, chapter 6. Trans. Leo Rauch, 92–8. Indianapolis, IN: Hackett Publishing, 1988.

Marx, Karl. *The German Ideology*, Part I, Section D. Moscow: Marx-Engels Institute, 1932, originally written in 1845–6. Available online: https://www.

marxists.org/archive/marx/works/1845/german-ideology/ch01d.htm (accessed March 11, 2022).

Russell, Robert John. "Cosmology and Eschatology." In *The Oxford Handbook of Eschatology*, ed. Jerry L. Walls, 563–75. New York: Oxford University Press, 2007.

Lakȟóta

Deloria, Vine, Jr. "Religion and Revolutions Among American Indians." In *For this Land: Writings on Religion in America*, ed. James Treat, 36–43. New York: Routledge, 1999.

Mooney, James. *The Ghost-Dance Religion and Wounded Knee*, 777–91. New York: Dover Publications, 1973.

Mediterranean/Abrahamic

Halm, Heinz. *Shi'a Islam: From Religion to Revolution*. Trans. Allison Brown. Princeton, NJ: Markus Wiener Publishers, 1997.

Lerner, Robert E. "The Black Death and Western European Eschatological Mentalities." *American Historical Review* 86/3 (1981): 533–52.

Scholem, Gershom. *Major Trends in Jewish Mysticism*, 244–86. New York: Schocken Books, 1946.

South Asia

The Bhāgavata Purāṇa, 3.11. Trans. Makarand Joshi, 278–8. Delhi: Motilal Banasirdass Publishers, 1950. Available online: https://archive.org/details/bhagavatapuranaeng011950ocrmotilalbanasirdass/page/n35/mode/2up (accessed March 11, 2022).

Buddhaghosa. *The Path of Purification: Visuddhimagga*, Book XIII, §§29–71. Trans. Bhikkhu Ñáóamolibook, 3rd online edition, 407–15. Buddhist Publication Society, 2011.

Yorùbá

Abímbọ́lá, Kọ́lá. *Yorùbá Culture: A Philosophical Account*, chapter 3. Birmingham: Iroko Academic Publishers, 2005.

Peel, J. D. Y. *Christianity, Islam, and* Oriṣa *Religion: Three Traditions in Comparison and Interaction*, chapter 11. Oakland, CA: University of California Press, 2015.

Ray, Benjamin C. *African Religions: Symbol, Ritual, and Community*, 2nd ed., 184–95. Upper Saddle River, NJ: Pearson, 1999.

12

How Does the Cosmos Get There?

Learning Objectives

- Describe, compare, and evaluate anomalous events and extraordinary experiences in our six traditions of philosophy of religion.
- Explain how the categories *natural law* and *miracle* offer challenges to comparative philosophy of religion and evaluate solutions to these challenges.
- Evaluate the use of the natural and social sciences for explaining and evaluating anomalous events and extraordinary experiences.

I. Introduction

Up next is our fourth question about the cosmos: What is its path? It scarcely needs said that we are not asking about the literal path of the cosmos; rather, we are using the metaphor of *path* to generate interesting and important philosophical questions about how the cosmos operates or functions between its beginning (or lack thereof) and end (or lack thereof).

Such questions would seem to be increasingly handled by science: the cosmos operates according to natural laws. Yet religious traditions tend to affirm and value the occurrence of phenomena that run contrary to how science says the cosmos operates—miracles and other extraordinary events, manifestations of what is sacred or divine, exceptional religious and mystical experiences. This category is vast, including physical events in the natural world (e.g., making the sun stand still), sensory appearances of divine beings (e.g., angelic appearances), mental manifestations of divine beings (e.g., hearing the voice of a God in one's head), journeys of the mind or body to alternate realities (e.g., mystical journeys), possession of body or mind by divine beings (e.g., spirit possession), healing of body or mind (e.g., miraculous healing), and other extraordinary religious experiences (e.g., achieving a sense of union with some ultimate reality). Are these all violations of natural law? Are they all miracles?

Here we confront several critical issues. For starters, the term *miracle* typically denotes the intervention of a God in the workings of the cosmos in a manner that violates a natural law. But as we already know, some religious traditions do not have such a God or do not think of Them/Her/Him/It as intentionally acting in person-like ways, let alone intervening in the cosmos. Equally problematic is the term *natural law*. Not only do philosophers of science and scientists disagree about whether laws of nature "really exist" or are merely statistical regularities, but the global-critical philosopher of religion must also take up the question "natural law for whom"?

Consider this example: if I am a shaman who, upon ingesting some psychotropic substance or chanting some hypnotic mantra, am enabled to journey to some other dimension of reality, is this a miracle? What if my culture or community expects this very result since it happens every time? Here is another example: if I am a meditator who, upon attaining complete detachment from my body and mind, attains an intensely blissful state of equanimity, is this a miracle or otherwise extraordinary? Again, what if my culture or community expects this very result since it happens every time?

On the one hand, we might say that what is contrary to natural law is relative to the natural regularities and patterns for some culture or tradition. On the other hand, shamans and mystics who achieve the states described above are generally thought of as exceptional or extraordinary in their cultures and traditions. So even if the results of their methods are expected, these results are not ordinary. Moreover, "Western science" (both natural and social) not only has proved more and more successful at explaining and predicting how the world works but also has penetrated wider and wider into the societies of the world.

All this is to say that, for the global-critical philosopher of religion, there is some value in considering anomalous and extraordinary religious phenomena from the perspective of the natural sciences since they are increasingly the *lingua franca* about how the natural world works. But the global-critical philosopher of religion must also be aware that the category of the *miraculous* is largely an Abrahamic-Western one. If we think of miracles solely as violations of natural laws by means of divine intervention, then we will not appreciate that some anomalous and extraordinary phenomena are expected to occur naturally or are caused by human agents.

We will return to the category of *miracle* in the conclusion of this chapter. For now, though, let us look at some "data," employing the broader categories of *anomalous events* and *extraordinary experiences* to do so.

II. Mediterranean/Abrahamic Philosophy of Religion

In the case of the Hebrew Bible, some of the most significant anomalous events and extraordinary experiences occurred during the life of the legendary patriarch Moses (who purportedly lived sometime around the fifteenth century BCE). Moses was born in the land of Egypt, during a time when the Jewish (Hebrew) people were enslaved to the Pharaoh, the ruler of Egypt. As the story goes, a God one day manifested himself to Moses in a burning bush on the sacred mountain of Sinai, revealing His true name as "YHWH" and calling Moses to lead the people out of Egypt and back to the promised land of present-day Israel. After Pharaoh refused Moses' request to "let God's people go," Moses was empowered by YHWH to inflict the Egyptians with ten plagues: turning the Nile to blood; infestations of frogs, gnats, and flies; death of Egyptian livestock; boils on people and animals; damaging hail; infestation of locusts; three days of darkness; killing of firstborn sons of the Egyptians.[1] Finally, Pharaoh relented, permitting the Hebrews to leave; however, he then changed his mind, commanding his army to pursue the Hebrews. At this point in the narrative YHWH enabled Moses to create a path of dry land in the middle of the sea so that the Jews could pass to safety (after which the Pharaoh's army was swallowed by the sea).

Later, during the Jews forty-year wandering through the Arabian wilderness, they encamped at the base of YHWH's sacred mountain, Mt. Sinai, which Moses ascended to "see" YHWH and to receive the 613 commandments (Hb. *mizvot*), which became the basis of the covenantal relationship between YHWH and the Jewish people. Moses' ascent of Sinai later became a biblical model for Jewish (and Christian) mystics, as they attempted to "see" YHWH (or the Trinitarian God) by mystically ascending to heaven. Just as important, though, were the visions that were recorded by the Jewish prophets Isaiah and Ezekiel, especially Ezekiel's vision of the "chariot-throne" of YHWH on top of the heavenly firmament above the earth. First millennium Jewish mystics attempted to recreate these experiences, ascending through the palaces or levels of heaven (*hêkālôt*) to reach the chariot-throne (*merkābâ*) of God and gain a vision of YHWH.[2] This literature apparently culminated in an enigmatic, elliptical text called the *Šî ʿûr Qômâ*—literally the "Dimensions of the Body"—which purports to give the measurements of YHWH's body. These measurements, however, are so mind-bogglingly astronomical that the text might instead point toward the indescribability and incomprehensibility of YHWH.

In the Christian tradition, the anomalous events par excellence concern the birth, career, death, and resurrection of Jesus Christ. Christians generally believe Jesus to be the incarnation of God, i.e., God in the person of the Son of God, who is one member of the Trinity, along with God the Father and the Holy Spirit. Although Jesus is reported to have performed numerous miracles during his three-year preaching career (most of the healing and exorcising variety), none is as important as the miracle of his resurrection from the dead, which many Christians think of as atoning for their sin and therefore effecting their salvation.

Jesus's life also serves as a model for Christians, in this case for Christian mystics who seek to experience communion or union with their Trinitarian God. For some of these mystics, the story of the Jesus's "transfiguration" on Mt. Tabor was key to their spiritual and mystical journeys. In this New Testament story, the three disciples who went with Jesus to the top of Mt. Tabor to pray (Peter, James, John) saw Jesus, accompanied by Moses and the Prophet Elijah, "transfigured before them; his face shining as the sun, and his garments . . . white as the light" (Matthew 17:2). For Christian mystics like Symeon the New Theologian (949–1022), this experience became a goal for their own spiritual practice, as they sought to experience the same light as seen by Jesus's disciples on Mt. Tabor, the "infinite and incomprehensible" light of God. For other Christian mystics, most notably the influential sixth-century author referred to as "Pseudo-Dionysius the Areopagite," Moses's ascent up and experience on Mt. Sinai remained the preeminent model for Christian mystics who enter into the "divine darkness" of God (just as Moses entered into the beclouded darkness at the top of Mt. Sinai), becoming united with the Trinitarian God in a state of "not knowing" the incomprehensible and ineffable mystery of this God.

Like Christianity, Islam in general recognizes the miracles of the Hebrew Bible and New Testament. Jesus, however, is not regarded as having died and resurrected from the dead. Rather, Allah removed him from the cross before death (or before even being nailed to the cross) and raised him bodily to heaven. With respect to the Prophet Muḥammad, the two chief miracles were the revelation of the Qurʾān to him and his night journey to Jerusalem and ascent to heaven. The former is a miracle not only because the angel Gabriel spoke the words of the Qurʾān to Muḥammad but also because Muḥammad was illiterate. The latter is a miracle since Muḥammad was taken from Mecca to Jerusalem by a magical steed called a *burāq*, after which he ascended into heaven to speak to God and receive instruction about the daily prayers.

Much in the way that Moses' mountaintop experience became a model for Jewish mystics and both Moses' and Jesus' mountaintop experiences became models for Christian mystics, Muḥammad's mystical ascent (*miʿrāj*) to Allah through the spheres of heaven served as a model for Muslim mystics. This Islamic mystical journey, like the first-millennium *hêkālôt-merkābâ* mysticism of Judaism as well as the Christian Apostle Paul's report of being "caught up" to a "third heaven" (2 Corinthians 12:2–4), is situated in an ancient Greek cosmos that thinks of the Earth as surrounded by a series of concentric spheres of celestial bodies or heavens (rather than the earlier biblical model of a heavenly firmament over the earth). To ascend or journey to this God required passing through these spheres or "palaces" (Hb. *hêkālôt*), each of which was typically occupied by angels and/or a scriptural patriarch (e.g., Abraham, Moses). In the case of Islamic mysticism (Sufism), these spheres were also sometimes associated with the stages of the Sufi path (Ar. *maqaamat*) or with a series of trials and temptations. The latter is the case for the famed ninth-century Sufi known as Bāyazīd Bisṭāmī (d. 874–5 or 848–9), who was tempted in each of the seven spheres with various rewards. Bisṭāmī, however, refused all of them, ultimately reaching the throne of Allah, where he was allowed to look on Allah's splendor and light, after which he was "brought so close" to Allah that he was nearer to Him "than the spirit is to the body."[3]

By now it should be clear how scriptural stories serve as practical models for Abrahamic mystics. (Table 12.1 provides a tabulated recap.) In what remains of this section, we turn back to the subject of miracles, this time with respect to Islamic philosophy of religion, where yet another contentious issue played out between Islamic theologians and philosophers.[4] As you know from earlier chapters (especially Chapter 9), the theologically orthodox view of the cosmos in Islam is the atomistic-occasionalistic cosmology of Ashʿarite theology, one chief representative of which is the theologian, jurist, and mystic al-Ghazālī (1058–1111). According to this cosmology, Allah is

Table 12.1 Abrahamic Exemplars and Experiences for Mystical Re-enactment

Role Model and Experience	Mystical Re-enactments
Moses' Ascent up Mt. Sinai	Jewish and Christian mystics
Isaiah's and Ezekiel's Visions of the Divine Throne Room	Jewish mystics
Jesus' Transfiguration	Christian mystics
Muḥammad's Night-journey and Ascension to Heaven	Islamic mystics

the ultimate cause of the positions of all the atoms in the cosmos from moment to moment; their apparent this-worldly causes are only the "occasions" by which Allah effects causation.

What does this mean for "miracles"? Just as Allah is the cause of events that are expected and routine such as making the sun rise every morning, so Allah is the cause of events that are not expected and routine including events that humans come to think of as "miraculous." There are not, therefore, laws of nature that are independent of Allah; everything that humans experience as behaving in a uniform, law-governed manner is the result of Allah causing those things to happen in a uniform, law-governed manner. So, it is incorrect to think of miracles as "violations" of "laws of nature." Nevertheless, when Allah acts in ways that runs counter to the natural regularities perceived by humans, then humans can say that a "miracle" has happened. Moreover, for al-Ghazālī, the everyday regularity of nature is as much a "gift" from God as its apparent interruption in the cases of "miracles."[5]

By contrast, the Islamic philosopher ibn Rushd (1126–98), accepted the Aristotelian view that for there to be scientific knowledge of the world, there must be natural order. Necessary causation within nature is a demonstrative truth based on empirical facts. We see things affect, cause, produce, and influence other things (contra al-Ghazālī who claimed that we never actually see the causal connection between things). Ibn Rushd, therefore, accused al-Ghazālī's theory of miracles as counter-productive to scientific knowledge and contrary to commonsense. Moreover, ibn Rushd maintained that the miracles stories in the Qur᾽ān should not be read literally, at least not by philosophers, while also recognizing that miracle accounts are beneficial for ordinary people, the naïve beliefs of whom should not be publicly questioned by philosophers.[6] Might this distinction still be of use today?

III. South Asian Philosophy of Religion

South Asian philosophy of religion is not unlike Abrahamic philosophy of religion with respect to the "path of the cosmos," at least insofar as anomalous and extraordinary events and experiences are often important features of this path. There are, though, some important differences between the two (meta)traditions, especially with respect to how such phenomena are usually caused.

First and foremost, for those traditions of South Asian philosophy of religion that stress meditation, "religious experience" is generally seen as the "automatic" result of meditative discipline and practice, not as what is "freely" given by some God. This is especially true for the Yoga *darśana*, which has roots that may stretch back as far as the Indus Valley Civilization (fl. 2600–1900 BCE), and which is first textually witnessed in some of the early *Upaniṣads* (700–500 BCE), even though its founding *sūtras*, *Yoga Sūtras*, did not appear until about the third century of the Common Era. Allegedly written (or perhaps only compiled) by Patañjali, the *Yoga Sūtras* itemizes "Eight Limbs" of Yoga, which ultimately culminate in the isolation (*kaivalya*) of pure consciousness (*Puruṣa*) from material nature (*prakṛti*) and its release (*mokṣa*) from the cycle of rebirth (*saṃsāra*). (Again note, therefore, what we have earlier observed—viz., that the practice of Yoga draws on the metaphysics of Sāṁkhya.) To achieve this end, one must pacify the mind, stopping the "fluctuations of consciousness" (*cittavṛtti*-s), especially as they are triggered by prior karmic actions that cause one to misidentify *Puruṣa* with *prakṛti*. This state of pacified, blissful consciousness—*samādhi*—is the eighth and final step of the "eight-limbs" of Yoga. See Table 12.2.

Only by following these steps does one attain an experience of *samādhi*, which although transient at first, can be stabilized through practice, eventually leading to the elimination of all karmic seeds, the complete pacification of consciousness, the liberating knowledge of the self (*Puruṣa*), the isolation of the self from material nature (*prakṛti*), and the release of the self from rebirth.

Although the sequence of these "Eight Limbs" is unique to the Yoga *darśana*, the meditative techniques of Yoga are common to other South Asian philosophies of religion. Theravāda Buddhism, most notably, also itemizes an "Eightfold Path," the last three "spokes" of which pertain to meditative practices, the eighth and final, "right *samādhi*." Early Buddhist

Table 12.2 Eight-Limbs of Yoga[7]

No.	Name	Description
1	Restraint (*yama*)	Five rules of outer control: non-violence, truthfulness, non-stealing, celibacy, non-possession
2	Self-discipline (*niyama*)	Five rules of inner control: moral, mental, and physical purity; contentment; ascetic practice; self-analysis; contemplative devotion to the Lord (*Īśvara*)[8]
3	Posture (*āsana*)	Right bodily postures, especially sitting in lotus position
4	Control of breath (*prāṇāyāma*)	Rhythmic breathing that circulates vital energy (*prāṇa*) throughout the body
5	Withdraw of senses (*pratyāhāra*)	Withdrawing attention from the senses to the self
6	Concentration (*dhāraṇā*)	Beginning to concentrate the mind on an object of meditation to achieve one-pointedness (*ekāgratā*) of mind
7	Meditation (*dhyāna*)	Achievement of continuous meditation on the object of meditation
8	Absorption (*samādhi*)	Two kinds: first, the object of contemplation alone remains (as the mind is absent any fluctuations); second, the object is also transcended (as the pure self is only aware of itself)

scriptures (Pāli canon) associate *samādhi* with the practice of one-pointed meditation, which proceeds through stages of deepening concentration or meditation (*dhyāna*-s), some "with form," others "without form." Early Buddhist scriptures also associate *samādhi* with the term *śamatha*, meaning "calm abiding" or "pacification." For some Theravāda Buddhists, this *śamatha* or "stopping/calming" meditation is taken as preliminary to *vipaśyana* or "seeing/insight" meditation, which penetrates ordinary reality (including the self) down to its underlying characteristics of impermanence (*anitya*), unsatisfactoriness (*duḥkha*), and no-self (*an-ātman*).

If you are now thinking that we have so far been talking about the path of the self rather than the path of the cosmos, you are right. These "religious experiences" are not "given by the Gods" but rather the product of meditative discipline and practice, which is one key path by which the self attains its ultimate end of release from rebirth in South Asian philosophies of religion. There are, however, examples of religious experiences given by Gods in South Asian religions. We will turn to a classic example of this soon, looking also at anomalous events as we do so. First, though we note the role that "miracles" play in Yoga.

Patañjali's *Yoga Sūtras* not only itemize the "Eight Limbs" by which a yogi can attain isolation of the soul from the body and therefore release from rebirth; it also details the miraculous powers or "attainments" (*siddhi*-s) that a yogi achieves through yogic practice. These powers include:

> knowledge of previous lives, knowledge of other minds, power to become invisible, knowledge of the time of death by insight into the duration of karmic effects, understanding the languages of animals, appropriation of the powers of animals (strength of an elephant, flight of birds), clairvoyance, knowledge of heavenly bodies and the astral regions (including realms of the gods), control of the body (including autonomous functions), vision of heavenly beings, entry into other bodies, levitation, mastery over fire, translocation at will, and the power to determine the characteristics of physical objects.[9]

For David Weddle, a contemporary scholar of miracles in comparative perspective, these powers are possible because the yogi can act in the present in a way that is free from the effects of *karma*, as determined by the past.[10] Nevertheless, as Patañjali himself recognized, these powers can be a distraction to the end goal of yoga—attaining *samādhi*, isolating the soul, escaping rebirth.

Although the attainment of such miraculous powers is common to other South Asian meditative traditions, most notably Buddhism, they are not without their critics.[11] For the seventh-century Mīmāṃsā philosopher Kumārila Bhaṭṭa, the issue was not about yogic powers or perceptions as such but whether they could serve as the source of knowledge claims. Nevertheless, given an assumption about the constancy of human behavior over time—that people in the past were "like people nowadays" (*adyatanavat*)—Kumārila also held that we have little reason to believe that past yogis such as the historical Buddha or Lord Śiva possessed extraordinary yogic powers. The laws of *karma* simply are not suspended until one is released from rebirth. Moreover, since the yogic perceptions of yogis differed considerably, contradicting one another, none of them could be trusted.

We now pivot to religious experiences given by the Gods and, with it, manifestations of, and miracles performed by, the Gods. In the main case we examine below, all three categories coincide: the manifestation of a God constitutes not only a miraculous event but also a religious experience for the human observer. (Compare Moses' experience of the burning bush.) This phenomenon is the classic theophany of Lord Kṛṣṇa in the Hindu epic *Mahābhārata*.

As you already know from Chapter 7, the *Gītā* is set on the morning of a great battle between two families of the ruling Kuru clan, the Pāṇḍavas and Kauravas. Arjuna, a prince of the Pāṇḍavas, is distraught as he surveys the battlefield, anticipating the bloodshed that the day will bring. However, Arjuna's charioteer Kṛṣṇa—whom Arjuna does not yet know is actually an incarnation (*avatāra*) of Lord Viṣṇu—tells Arjuna that he must fight, for that is his duty (*dharma*) as a member of the warrior/ruler (*kṣatriya*) caste (*varṇa*). Moreover, even if Arjuna kills the body of his enemy, he will not kill their *Ātman*, which is what they really are.

Kṛṣṇa then turns to the different means by which the self can realize its true nature as *Ātman*; these are the three disciplines (*yoga*-s) of knowledge (*jñāna*), action (*karma*), and devotion (*bhakti*). Here, as we mentioned in Chapter 7, we seem to have the first mention of the path of *bhakti* as such. Perhaps for this reason Arjuna asks to know more about it, specifically requesting that Kṛṣṇa reveal to him his true form. Kṛṣṇa grants this request, bestowing Arjuna with "spiritual vision" since his physical eyes are inadequate. Arjuna then sees all the Gods and living creatures within Kṛṣṇa, who is described as the Lord of all creation and the body of the cosmos; the supreme, changeless Reality (*Brahman*) without beginning, middle, and end; time, the destroyer of all things. (See Figure 12.) Finally, the theophany ends with Kṛṣṇa telling Arjuna that through Kṛṣṇa's grace, Arjuna has been united with him, and through Arjuna's unfailing devotion to Kṛṣṇa, Arjuna can know him, see him, and attain union with him.

> It is extremely difficult to obtain the vision you have had; even the gods long always to see me in this aspect. Neither knowledge of the *Vedas*, nor austerity, nor charity, nor sacrifice can bring the vision you have seen. But through unfailing devotion, Arjuna, you can know me, see me, and attain union with me.[12]

This is the way of devotion (*bhakti*). For us, it is also an example of a miraculous divine manifestation and religious experience in South Asian religious philosophy, among which there are countless others. In fact, the God Viṣṇu makes ten incarnations or descents (*avatāra*-s) to earth in times of need, only one of whom (the eighth) is Kṛṣṇa, all of whom performed miraculous deeds (except of course the tenth *avatāra*, Kalki, who is yet to come). Moreover, not only were miraculous deeds performed in the "mythic past" by *avatāra*-s of Viṣṇu and other Hindu deities; they continue to be enacted up to the present by humans who are devotees and manifestations of these deities. One recent example is Sathya Sai Baba (1926–2011), who

Figure 12 Kṛṣṇa in Universal Form (*viśvarūpa*). The Picture Art Collection, "Vishvarupa1910: M A Joshi and company," *c.* 1910, Alamy Stock Photo.

was reported to have performed many miraculous deeds, most notably "materializations" of objects and healings of the sick, and is believed by his many followers to have been an *avatāra* (incarnation) of Śiva.

IV. East Asian Philosophy of Religion

In East Asian philosophy of religion, the cosmos is generally not seen as going anywhere and therefore does not have a path so to speak. Rather, the cosmos continually transforms yet eternally abides through the flow of *qì* as expressed in the polarities of *yīn* and *yáng*. Nevertheless, there are plenty of occurrences of anomalous events and extraordinary and experiences in East Asian philosophy of religion.

With respect to anomalous events, we turn first to East Asian Buddhism, especially its "Three Bodies" (Sk. *trikāya*; Ch. *sānshēn*, 三身) theory. Not long after the death of the historical Buddha, his disciples and followers began to wonder, who or what exactly is the Buddha? (Compare perplexity and disagreement about who Jesus was in early Christianity.) In some early Indian Buddhist schools, this question was answered by positing that the Buddha has two bodies: a form body (Sk. *rūpakāya*), which was his actual physical body, and a *dharma* body (Sk. *nirmāṇakāya*), which represented his celestial, enlightened state. For some of these schools, the form body of Buddha was said to be no more than a projection of his eternal, omniscient, and omnipotent dharma body. In Mahāyāna Buddhism, especially as expressed in East Asia, this twofold understanding of the Buddha's body eventually expanded to three, as the *dharma* body of the Buddha was transformed into reality itself *qua* empty, interdependent, and nirvanic. The celestial body of the Buddha, then, became his "enjoyment body" (Sk. *saṃbhogakāya*), which was a result of the merit that the Buddha gained both before and after becoming enlightened. This merit not only endowed the Buddha with superhuman "powers" but also enabled him to create and occupy a celestial buddha-land (Sk. *buddhakṣetra*) from which to enact his superhuman powers for the sake of the enlightenment of all sentient beings. By contrast, the "manifestation body" (Sk. *nirmāṇakāya*) was thought of as the way the Buddha appeared to human beings on earth, an apparition or manifestation for the sake of the enlightenment of sentient beings. See Table 12.3.

We have been using the term "the Buddha" above; in fact, though, there are countless buddhas in Mahāyāna Buddhism, at least in theory, each inhabiting a buddha-land and using superhuman powers and manifestations for the sake of the enlightenment of sentient beings. You have already been introduced to Amitābha, who created a celestial Pure Land so that sentient beings could be reborn into it and attain enlightenment from it (especially in

Table 12.3 Three Bodies Theory

Dharmakāya	"Truth body": enlightened reality as "empty," interdependent, and nirvanic
Saṃbhogakāya	"Enjoyment body": celestial body of the Buddha in a heavenly realm with superhuman powers
Nirmāṇakāya	"Manifestation body": apparitional appearance of the Buddha on earth

the "Age of Mappō," when enlightenment is otherwise impossible). Other important celestial buddhas include Akṣobhya, who aids people to attain enlightenment in his buddha-land of Abhirati, and Vairocana, whose rays of knowledge help others overcome the darkness of ignorance.

In Mahāyāna Buddhism there are also celestial bodhisattvas, which are buddhas-in-the-making, each of whom takes a vow to strive endlessly for the enlightenment of others. Advanced bodhisattvas, much like buddhas, possess superhuman powers to achieve this goal. The most popular bodhisattva is Avalokiteśvara, who is usually said to reside in the Pure Land Buddha-realm of Amitābha, looking down on the suffering of sentient beings in our Buddha-realm with compassion, ready to assist all in need. In East Asia, for reasons that are not entirely known, Avalokiteśvara takes female form as Guānyīn (觀音) in China and Kannon in Japan (or encompasses both genders, or transcends gender altogether).[13]

By now, the message should be clear: in East Asian Mahāyāna Buddhism, buddhas and bodhisattvas are able to manifest themselves into our buddha-land or others by means of extraordinary powers in ways that are anomalous, even "miraculous." Indeed, Mahāyāna scriptures are often chockfull of such manifestations and miracles.

One delightful example comes from the Mahāyāna *sūtra Vimalakīrti Nirdeśa*, a second-century Indian-Sanskrit text that purported to take place during the life of the Buddha and later became very influential and popular in East Asian Buddhism. Here, a bodhisattva named Vimalakīrti, who appears to be a mere householder, manifests himself as sick to teach *dharma* (truth), one means of which involves the performance of apparent miracles. To list only three: Vimalakīrti's house is first emptied of everything then furnitured with 3,200,000 towering thrones from another buddha-land so his guests have somewhere to sit; a Goddess who lives in Vimalakīrti's house first manifests herself in physical form, then changes that form from female to male and back again; and the entire assembly in Vimalakīrti's house (thrones and all) are reduced to the palm of Vimalakīrti's hand so he can transport them into the presence of the Buddha.[14] Why? An answer is provided in the text itself when the Buddha asks one of his disciples whether he has seen the miraculous performances of the bodhisattvas and, if so, what concept he has produced toward them. To this, the monk Śāriputra responds:

> Lord, I produced the concept of inconceivability toward them. Their activities appeared inconceivable to me to the point that I was unable to think of them, to judge them, or even to imagine them.[15]

What is the point? First, that the power of Mahāyāna bodhisattvas far surpasses that of the pre-Mahāyāna disciples of the Buddha (who are stigmatized as belonging to the tradition of "Hīnayāna," the "lesser path," in contrast to Mahāyāna, the "great path"). Second, that the Buddhist *dharma* is itself inconceivable, surpassing everything that humans can think or say about it. Indeed, one of the alternate titles the *Vimalakīrti Sūtra* is "inconceivable liberation" (*acintyavimokṣa*). Both enlightenment itself and any teaching about it are inconceivable and indescribable.[16]

Are these miracles real? That all depends on what is meant by "miracle" and "real." Certainly, it would seem that buddhas and bodhisattvas are able to perform extraordinary deeds. Nevertheless, these deeds—indeed, everything humans experience—are part of an ever-changing, interdependently existing reality that is ultimately "empty" in the sense of lacking substantial, permanent, independent existence.

We wrap up this section by turning to extraordinary experiences, first noting that such experiences are often not caused by some God but rather the result of meditative discipline and practice, at least in the case of many Confucian, Daoist, and Buddhist philosophies of religion. Also, especially for Chán/Zen Buddhism, such experiences are not usually of divine objects or unitive states but rather of ordinary, everyday reality seen for what it really is—empty, yet nirvanic. In other words, these experiences are not extraordinary at all, at least not in terms of their contents.

We focus on the figure who is commonly taken to be most representative of Japanese Zen Buddhism in the Sōtō tradition, Dōgen (道元, 1200–53). For Dōgen, Zen Buddhism just is the practice of *zazen* (Jp. 座禅), "sitting meditation," more particularly *shikantaza*, "just sitting," which is a form of meditation that neither focuses on a meditational object nor attempts to clear the mind of content but rather stays in the present moment and refrains from fixating on any mental content. For Dōgen, the practice of *zazen* is not a means of attaining enlightenment; it just is enlightenment. This is what Dōgen called the "oneness of practice-enlightenment" (Jp. *shushō-ittō* or *shushō-ichinyo*): "To practice the Way singleheartedly is, in itself, enlightenment. There is no gap between practice and enlightenment or zazen and daily life."[17] To practice *zazen* is to realize the fullness of being in each moment, which just is Buddha-nature, the interconnectedness of all things and all moments, which Dōgen conveyed in his innovative concept of "time-being" (Jp. *uji*).

Here, "extraordinary, religious experience" is neither extraordinary nor religious; rather, it is just awareness of what really is without the conceptual reifications of ordinary perception. As one Chinese Zen (Chán) master was to put it, "Before the practice, mountains are mountains, during the practice, mountains are not mountains, and after the realization, mountains are [truly] mountains [again]."[18]

V. Lakȟóta Philosophy of Religion

As in the case of East Asian philosophy of religion, Lakȟóta philosophy of religion does not see the cosmos as going anywhere and therefore as having a path. Still, it contains plenty of occurrences of anomalous events and extraordinary experiences.

We have already witnessed some examples of these phenomena in the preceding chapters. We have seen examples of sacred manifestations and miraculous interventions in the myth about White Buffalo Calf Woman giving the sacred pipe to the Lakȟóta, as well as the myth about the trickster Iktómi leading the Lakȟóta from their subterranean existence to the surface of the earth. Last chapter we learned about Wovoka's ascension to heaven, reception of a revelation, and performance of miracles. And in Chapter 7, we read about the ritual of "crying for a vision" (*haŋbléčeyapi*), in which one waits for a vision from *Wakȟáŋ Tȟáŋka* for up to four days, without company, food, or water.

In the remainder of this chapter, we turn to something we have not yet studied: the "holy man" (*wičȟáša wakȟáŋ*) or "holy woman" (*wíŋyaŋ wakȟáŋ*), especially their ability to receive revelations, perform miracles, and otherwise communicate with the spiritual world.[19] To do so, we look to Vine Deloria, Jr., who has dedicated an entire book to the "remembering the powers of the medicine man."

Deloria begins by recognizing two paths by which American Indians made sense of their world: empirical observation and the "sporadic intrusion of higher powers in their lives, manifested in unusual events and dreams."[20] The second of these paths especially involves the holy men/women, who receive powers and knowledge through dreams and visions. Among these powers are the ability to control the weather, heal, predict the future, communicate with spirits, communicate with other species, locate lost objects, resist bullets, animate, and become invisible. In the remainder of this section, we focus first on the Lakȟóta *yuwípi* ritual, then on the ability of holy men/women to control the weather.

According to Deloria the *yuwípi* ("binding with ropes") ritual serves to provide the Lakȟóta with a "continuing source of information that is relevant to the immediate situation in which they find themselves" rather than a general message "that is supposed to cover all future contingencies," as is usually the case in Christianity.[21] For this ritual, a holy man is tightly bound with ropes and blankets or hides, then placed on the floor of a tipi or lodge in which all light has been sealed out and around which 405 small tobacco pouches have been distributed. The holy man then begins to sing *yuwípi* power songs, after which the spirits enter the area in the form of blue lights. After this, the holy man enters a trance state, in which he is able to heal people, find lost objects, and predict the future, both by reading the minds of those who are present at the ritual and by transacting with the spirit world. At the end of the ritual, after all the answers have been given and the spirits have left, lights are lit, revealing that the *yuwípi* holy man is now free of his binding and that the pouches have been emptied of their tobacco.

Another power of the holy man/woman involves the ability to produce rain and control weather. Here, Deloria delineates three types, with power residing differently in different types.[22] First, holy men/women can be directly asked to produce rain; for this type, the power resides in the special songs and dances given to the holy men/women in visions or dreams. Second, holy men/women can be asked to change the course of a storm; in this case, the spirits control the rainmaking, which holy men/women know how to manipulate through their own actions. Third, holy men/women sometimes engage in contests to demonstrate their power; for this type, the weather becomes an arena through which spiritual powers give relief to people. In sum, Deloria maintains that these events generally "give testimony to the presence of a larger universe that supersedes our physical world yet imposes certain limits on us as we pursue our daily lives."[23]

VI. Yorùbá Philosophy of Religion

At the risk of sounding repetitive, Yorùbá philosophy of religion gives us one more example of a cosmos that does not have a path, at least not one that goes anywhere, yet includes abundant examples of anomalous events and extraordinary experiences.

We turn first to the latter, extraordinary experience, since it reexamines material to which you have already been introduced: spirit possession. In investigating the "path of the self" in Chapter 7, we explored Olúfémi Táíwò's assertion that devotees of Yorùbá *Òrìṣà* "have," "are," and "make" *Òrìṣà*. "Are" is most relevant here, for it concerns spirit possession, the process by which

Òrìṣà possess devotees by "mounting" them and "riding" them. In this state, says Táíwò, the devotee simply "is" the *Òrìṣà*—"taken out of the circle of mortal humans," "free from finitude," and "unshackled from all limits imposed by the human form."[24]

One important context for Yorùbá spirit possession is communal dances for *Òrìṣà* led by drummers.[25] For different *Òrìṣà* there are different consecrated drums, rhythms, and dance steps.[26] Once the beat gets going fast enough, altered states of consciousness are induced in which the *Òrìṣà* "climbs" up out of the heaven that lies below the crust of the earth, mounts the dancers, and rides them. Through this process, the dancer—if not the entire community—benefits from the sacred energy (*àṣẹ*) that comes from the *Òrìṣà*. This, as you recall from Chapter 7, is one of two principal ways in which humans and Gods interrelate in Yorùbá religion, the other of which, sacrifice, is also relevant in this chapter, as we will soon see.[27]

Under the category of anomalous events, we could include all the legendary, miraculous actions of all the *Òrìṣà*. As is generally true, extraordinary beings perform extraordinary deeds. This is no less true in Yorùbá religion than in, e.g., Christianity or Buddhism. Consider the *Òrìṣà* Ọ̀ṣun, who is sometimes listed as one of the three *Òrìṣà* present with Olódùmarè from the very beginning of the cosmos and always ranked among the "first batch" of seventeen *Òrìṣà* to descend to earth, the only female *Òrìṣà* in the group. Because she was excluded from the activities of the other sixteen *Òrìṣà*, rain ceased to fall and famine engulfed the city of Ilé-Ifẹ̀ Only after the other these male *Òrìṣà* bowed before her and begged for forgiveness did the rain again fall. Later in life, barren, she was miraculously granted her first child, a boon that she now miraculously grants to other barren women who devote themselves to her.[28]

Given the importance of healing in Yorùbá religion, we now turn our attention to it for the rest of this section. As might already be clear, the name of each of the major "Anti-gods" (*Ajogun*) refers both to a "supernatural" God and a "natural" affliction: Death (Ikú), Disease (Àrùn), Loss (Òfò), Paralysis (Ẹ́gbà), Big Trouble (Ọ̀ràn), Curse (Èpè), Imprisonment (Ẹ̀wọ̀n), and "All Other Afflictions" (Èṣe). (Following the convention of Kọ́lá Abimbọ́lá, we disambiguate the two through capitalization: *Disease/Àrùn* refers to the deity (*Ajogun*); *disease/àrùn*, to the affliction.[29]) Thus, there is usually both a supernatural and natural cause of affliction as well as both a supernatural and natural remedy for affliction. Take, for example, Disease/disease (Àrùn/*àrùn*). Upon learning the cause of one's disease from a divinatory priest (*babaláwo*) in an Ifá session, one might not only sacrifice to the appropriate Gods but also consult a "medicine maker" (*oníṣègùn*) for herbs and medicines. (Sometimes, but not always, the *babaláwo* is also an *oníṣègùn*.) Insofar as the disease is "supernatural," it is the sacrifice that effects the healing, especially as the client's *orí* pleads with the *Òrìṣà* Èṣù to intercede with Àrùn. Insofar as the disease is only "natural," it is the herbs and medicines that bring healing (by restoring balance to the body through a form of homeopathic medicine that treats "like with like").

Might we therefore say that healing is "miraculous" in the former case but not the latter—i.e., only when supernatural causes and beings are involved? Or is there always a "miraculous" element to Yorùbá healing insofar as the causes of affliction are ascertained in Ifá divination by means of the *Òrìṣà* Ọrunmila? No matter how we answer these questions, Yorùbá religion presents us with yet more interesting and important material to consider in philosophizing about anomalous events and extraordinary experiences.

VII. European/Academic Philosophy of Religion

For at least a couple of reasons, religious and mystical experience have been topics of intense investigation for twentieth- and twenty-first-century academic philosophy of religion. One reason involves the flourishing of scientific methods by which to study religious experience, especially in the fields of psychology, neuroscience, cognitive science, and the evolutionary sciences. Another reason, which we began exploring in Chapter 7, is a bit more complex, concerning the ways in which philosophers of religion used mystical experience to attempt to demonstrate a common core to the religio-philosophical traditions of the world. For these philosophers of religion, mystical experiences of union were cross-culturally identical and therefore served as a common ground for all religions. Moreover, these experiences were believed to be conceptually immediate and linguistically ineffable and therefore immune to reduction to and explanation by the natural and social sciences.

We begin with William James (1842–1910), whose 1901–2 Gifford Lectures—subsequently published as *The Varieties of Religious Experience*—defined religion both personally and experientially as "the feelings, acts and experiences of individual men in their solitude, so far as they apprehend themselves to stand in relation to whatever they may consider the divine."[30]

For James, the "root and centre" of these religious experiences are "mystical experiences," which display four traits: (1) they are ineffable, defying linguistic expression; (2) they possess a noetic quality, providing insight into depths of truth; (3) they are transient, lasting for only a brief period of time; and (4) they are received passively, as the will is grasped and held by a superior power.[31] James maintained that these mystical experiences, which he thought occurred in many different religious traditions as well as outside formal religion altogether, are not only authoritative for the "mystics" who have them but also challenge the assumption that "normal," non-mystical states are the sole and ultimate dictators of what humans may believe. Moreover, he asserted that mystical experiences in particular and religious experiences in general produce both a "zest for life" and an "assurance of safety, a temper of peace, and, in relation to others, a preponderance of loving affections."[32] James therefore claimed that, contra psychological and biological reductions of religion, religious experience serves one of the "most important biological functions of humankind."[33]

James' view of religious experience was later taken as one example of perennial philosophy or psychology, which, as you know from Chapter 7, holds that a core set of philosophical ideas or a common type of mystical experience shows up "perennially" in all the religio-philosophical traditions of the world, giving these diverse traditions a shared foundation. In the latter half of the twentieth century, perennialism was increasingly criticized by a position that came to be known as "contextualism," which countered that since all experience is mediated by concepts and preconceptions, mystical experiences cannot be precisely the same between religious traditions and are always somehow expressible. One of the first and most notable contextualist critiques was delivered by Steven Katz (b. 1944), whose epistemological assumption was quite simple: "There are NO pure (i.e., unmediated) experiences."[34] Given this assumption, Katz maintained that "the forms of consciousness which the mystic brings to experience set structured and limiting parameters on what the experience will be, i.e. on what will be experienced, and rule out in advance what is 'inexperienceable' in the particular given, concrete context."[35] Thus, the mystical experiences of, e.g., Buddhists can never be the same as those of Jews: Buddhist will have Buddhist experiences, and Jews will have Jewish experiences. For Katz and other "contextualists," it is therefore impossible for mystical experience to serve as the cross-culturally identical, conceptually unmediated, and linguistically ineffable core of religion.

To this, feminist philosophers of religion such as Grace Jantzen (1948–2006) have added that scholarly emphasis on the *ineffability* of mystical experience in the nineteenth and twentieth centuries coincided with a loosening of male ecclesiastical control over the legitimation of female mystical experiences (at least with respect to some Christian traditions). In other words, at very same time that women were given full access to mysticism, mysticism was declared radically private and utterly ineffable: "the alleged inexpressibility of mystical experience correlates neatly with the silencing of women in the public arena of the secular world: women may be mystics, but mysticism is a private intense experience not communicable in everyday language and not of political importance."[36]

Cognitive scientists have also subjected religious experience to critical analysis, showing how it is a non-adaptive, evolutionary byproduct of more fundamental cognitive functions. In 1979 Stephen Jay Gould and Richard Lewontin first used the architectural term *spandrel*—the triangular spaces between adjacent pillars and the dome they support—to refer to those byproducts of evolution that were not initially selected for their own adaptive advantage.[37] Just as architectural spandrels were not originally designed for the purposes for which they were later used—decorative carving and painting of religious subject matter, for example at the famous Basilica of Saint Marco in Venice—so religious behaviors and beliefs were not naturally selected for their own evolutionary advantage; rather, they are byproducts of other evolutionary adaptations. Cognitive scientists such as Pascal Boyer (b. 1965) have proposed some of these more basic cognitive functions, one of which is an inference system governing moral intuition, the violation of which evokes strong emotions. For Boyer, this is one reason why humans create and believe in concepts of "full access agents" like Gods, Spirits, or Ancestors: since our moral intuitions suggest to us that behaviors are right or wrong by themselves, not depending on who considers them or from what point of view, and since we are generally ignorant about where these moral intuitions come from and precisely what they say, we gravitate toward concepts of Gods, Spirits, or Ancestors that have access to all the relevant information about moral situations and therefore know the rightness or wrongness of the relevant behavior. Chapter 5 explored other such cognitive tools, most relevantly "hyperactive agent detection," by means of which we over-detect for agents that might cause us harm. Here, we can add another, "etiology," by which we project causal narratives and other explanations for natural events. According to some cognitive scientists of religion, these evolutionarily adaptive, cognitive functions were co-opted by religion, used to create supernatural beings and cosmic myths.[38] Religious experience, in short, is the product of errant cognition.

While we are at it, let us add one more perspective to the mix—an academic perspective that takes issue with academic perspectives about religious experience. This perspective is that of Jeffrey Kripal (whose work was noted in Chapter 7 with respect to "near-death experiences" (NDE) and "cases of the reincarnation type" (CORT). For Kripal, extraordinary and anomalous experiences are not only quite common in general but also increasingly occur either outside the strictures of organized religious traditions or in newer religious movements that are not very institutionalized. It is not possible therefore to explain these experiences simply by virtue of what someone might expect given their religious context (per the contextualists). Nor is it plausible to reduce these experiences to the misapplication of evolutionarily evolved cognitive systems, for in some cases these experiences reveal details about events yet to happen that actually do so happen (e.g., crashed airplanes).[39] Kripal honestly admits not to know what to make of such experiences, except that they challenge prominent explanatory frameworks in the academic study of religion. For us, his work also serves as awareness that "religious experience" need not occur and increasingly does not occur under the auspices of organized religious traditions.

Turning now to "miracles," we begin by noting that contemporary scholarship is not quite as active and contentious. One reason, of course, is that unlike religious experiences, miracles cannot be performed or received at will and therefore cannot be subjected to systematic study. Another important reason seems to involve a shrinking of scientific processes by which miracles could conceivably happen. If everything that occurs in the natural world does so by means of some natural process (whether in the body or in nature itself), then contemporary accounts of miracles in particular and divine action in general would need to show how these processes could be utilized by supernatural beings or forces. Projects like this, however, smack of "God of the gaps"—attempts to plug "God" into the "gaps" of our current scientific knowledge, which when closed by future growth of our scientific knowledge, leave this God "high and dry." "God of the gaps" projects are as old as Aristotle's Unmoved Mover (which was needed to explain how the celestial bodies move in perpetual circular motion), but they became especially notorious during the scientific revolution. Newton, for example, invoked God's active intervention to prevent the stars from falling in on each other and to counteract the motion in the universe from decaying due to viscosity and friction.

Note that "God of the gaps" accounts are not explanations of miracles per se. In fact, Enlightenment scientists like Newton were "deists," who believed that, although a deistic God created the universe with all of its simple and elegant laws of nature, this God did not act or intervene in those laws. Nevertheless, miracles continued to play an important role for many others (as they still do today). It is for this reason that David Hume (1711–76) wrote a scathing critique of miracles in his 1748 *Enquiry Concerning Human Understanding*. Together with his devastating critiques of the proofs for the existence of God, this critique of miracles aimed to cut the legs out from under all argumentative support for the existence of the philosophical and popular Gods of the European Enlightenment.

Although Hume defined miracles as violations of the laws of nature, he believed that laws of nature could never be proved since the regularity of nature upon which laws of nature depend could never be proved. Rather, laws of nature were only ever inductively probable, never deductively true. Nevertheless, insofar as we have never experienced phenomena in violation of laws of nature, we never have good reasons to believe that laws of nature can be violated. Put differently, if miracles are violations of laws of nature, then it is never reasonable to believe that a miracle has occurred, for our evidence for the regularity of nature is much stronger than the testimonial evidence for a miracle. Testimonial evidence, moreover, is generally dubious. Witnesses lack integrity; their testimonies not only tend to sensationalize but also originate in "barbarous nations"; and they support rival religious systems. Testimonies for miracles, therefore, are only "weak probabilities," whereas the laws of nature are very strong probabilities. Or so claimed Hume.[40]

As a result of Enlightenment science and philosophy, appreciative theories of miracles in Western religious contexts were left with two basic alternatives: either a theistic God really does intervene in the laws of nature and does so by suspending those laws, or a deistic God cannot intervene in the laws of nature and therefore has instead created a cosmos that can be subjectively appreciated by God's creation as "miraculous." However, for contemporary philosophers of religion such as Robert John Russell (b. 1946), these alternatives reflect both bad science and bad (Christian) theology. On the one hand, quantum mechanics has showed us that the universe is fundamentally indeterminate, so there is no need to appeal to an interventionist God who intrudes into a completely determined, causally-closed system of natural laws—for there is no such system. On the other hand, appeal to an interventionist God acknowledges this God's transcendence but devalues immanence, picturing this God as standing outside the cosmos and its "laws" rather than within them. Russell opts instead for a theory of *non-interventionist, objective divine action* (NIODA). It is "non-interventionist" since God does not have to suspend natural laws in order to act, and it is "objective" in the sense that divine action is not just a figment of human imagination. How then does this God act within natural law? To answer this question, Russell looks to quantum indeterminacy, championing a God who acts through the collapsing of wave functions.

VIII. Putting it All Together

Once again, we are left with a whole lot to put together. However, in this case the phenomena do bear resemblance from tradition to tradition, at least insofar as each tradition includes cases of anomalous events and extraordinary experiences. How can we compare and evaluate them?

The first thing of note is that such phenomena tend to influence religiosity more than arguments for the existence of Gods that we examined in Chapters 9 and 10. The "reasons" people give on behalf of their religious beliefs and practices often employ allegedly anomalous events and extradordinary experiences of personal significance. What shall a philosopher do with such "reasons"?

Regarding anomalous events, if the philosopher of religion is to practice *globally*, then she must be mindful of the issue we raised in the introduction—what counts as "natural law" and its violation will sometimes differ from culture to culture. *Miracle* is not a stable cross-cultural category for cross-cultural philosophy of religion, at least not if it connotes a violation of natural law through the invention of a God. This is why we have been using the category of *anomalous event*, which retains the sense of being contrary to law/order (*a-nomos*) yet recognizes that what constitutes law/order can be different from context to context.

Regardless, if the philosopher of religion is to practice *critically*, she should include the theories and tools of the natural and social sciences in explaining and evaluating anomalous events that are religiously significant. If so, then even if some anomalous event is ordinarily expected in some particular context, the fact that it cannot be explained from a scientific perspective will itself need to be explained by the global-*critical* philosopher of religion. This said, we quickly add that the theories of the natural sciences have gotten less and less intuitive. Moreover, the sciences very well could one day provide plausible explanations for at least some apparently anomalous events, at least in cases where interventions from Gods "outside" the natural world are not involved. One has to wonder, though, whether the ability to provide scientific explanations of ostensibly anomalous events and experiences would ultimately serve to bolster or undermine them with respect to their religious significance and utility.

Regarding extraordinary experiences, the sciences in question are both cognitive-evolutionary and social-psychological. Perhaps religiously significant extraordinary experiences are nothing more than the illusory products of evolutionarily developed cognitive systems misapplied beyond their domain (e.g., humans projecting agency onto superhuman beings or needing to justify their own moral intuitions). Perhaps religiously significant extraordinary experiences reduce to and are explained by the ways in which human minds are differently wired in different cultural-historical settings (e.g., Catholics expecting visions of Mary, Buddhists, of Guānyīn). Or perhaps neither explanatory paradigm suffices given the preponderance of non-traditional extraordinary experiences that appear not to reduce to socio-historical contexts or cognitive-evolutionary operations? And maybe, as some postcolonial philosophers of religion have maintained, paradigms of explanation should come from discourses besides or in addition to the natural and social sciences—discourses of marginalized, non-Western religious traditions that are generally treated as "data" to be explained by Western scientific discourses rather than as "theories" that are capable of explaining in their own right.[41]

Suffice it to say for now that anomalous events and extraordinary experiences are as widespread and impactful as ever, despite the ways in which the sciences appear to exhaust all explanations of how the cosmos functions in a law-governed way.

Questions for Discussion

1 Describe, compare, and evaluate some of the anomalous events and extraordinary experiences above from different traditions of philosophy of religion. What does the pervasiveness of these phenomena suggest about their reality? Why are they ostensibly present in so many different cultural-historical contexts?

2 How would you define "miracle" in a manner that is suitable for cross-cultural comparison? Or would you propose a different category instead?

3 What is the role of the natural and social sciences in explaining and evaluating allegedly miraculous/anomalous events and mystical/extraordinary experiences? Should the global-critical philosopher of religion employ the sciences to "reduce" people's experiences of the divine or sacred?

Primary and Scholarly Sources

East Asia

Dōgen. "On the Endeavor of the Way." In *Moon in a Dewdrop: Writings of Zen Master Dōgen*, ed. Kazuaki Tanahashi, 143–7. New York: North Point Press, 1985.

The Holy Teaching of Vimalakīrti: A Mahāyāna Scripture, chapter 11. Trans. Robert A. F. Thurman, 84–90. University Park, PA: Pennsylvania State University Press, 1976.

European/Academic

Gould, Stephen Jay and Richard Lewontin. "The Spandrels of San Marco and the Panglossian Paradigm: A Critique of the Adaptationist Programme." *Proceedings of the Royal Society B* 205/1161 (1979): 581–98.

Hume, David *Enquiry Concerning Human Understanding*, "Section X: Of Miracles." Ed. Eric Steinber, 2nd ed. Indianapolis, IN: Hackett Publishing, 1993.

James, William. *The Varieties of Religious Experience: A Study in Human Nature*, ed. Matthew Bradley, 368–93. New York: Oxford University Press, 2012.

Jantzen, Grace M. *Power, Gender and Christian Mysticism*, 322–8. New York: Cambridge University Press, 1995.

Katz, Steven. "Language, Epistemology, and Mysticism." In *Mysticism and Philosophical Analysis*, ed. Steven Katz, 22–74. New York: Oxford University Press, 1978.

Kripal, Jeffrey and Elizabeth G. Krohn. *Changed in a Flash: One Woman's Near-Death Experience and Why a Scholar Thinks It Empowers Us All*. Berkeley, CA: North Atlantic Books, 2018.

Russell, Robert John. *Cosmology: From Alpha to Omega* chapter 4. Philadelphia, PA: Fortress Press, 2008.

Lakȟóta

Archie Fire Lame Deer and Richard Erdoes. *Gift of Power: The Life and Teachings of a Lakota Medicine Man*, 150–61. Santa Fe, NM: Bear & Co. Publishing, 1992.

Deloria, Vine, Jr. *The World We Used to Live in: Remembering the Powers of the Medicine Me*, 43–81. Golden, CO: Fulcrum Publishing, 2006.

Feraca, Stephen E. *Wakinyan: Lakota Religion in the Twentieth Century*, 30–44. Lincoln, NE: University of Nebraska Press, 1998.

Mediterranean/Abrahamic

al-Ghazālī. *Incoherence of the Philosophers (Tahāfut al-Falāsifa)*. Trans. Sabih Ahmad Kamali, 188–93. Lahore: Pakistan Philosophical Congress, 1963.

ibn Rushd. "About the Natural Sciences: The First Discussion." In *Averroes' Tahafut al-Tahafut (Incoherence of the Incoherence)*, reprint ed., vol. 1, trans. Simon Van Den Bergh, 316–32. London: E. J. W. Gibb Memorial Trust, 2008.

"The Miʿrāj of Bistami." In *Early Islamic Mysticism: Sufi, Qurʾān, Miʿrāj and Theological Writings*, trans. Michael A. Sells, 242–50. Mahwah, NY: Paulist Press, 1996.

South Asia

Bhagavad Gītā, XI. Trans. Eknath Easwaran, 58–65. New York: Vintage Spiritual Classics, 1985.

Patañjali. *Yoga Sūtras*. In *An Introduction to Indian Philosophy: Perspectives on Reality, Knowledge, and Freedom*, ed. Bina Gupta, 194–6. New York: Routledge, 2012.

Yorùbá

Abímbọ́lá, Kọ́lá. *Yorùbá Culture: A Philosophical Account*, chapter 4. Birmingham: Iroko Academic Publishers, 2005.

Olúfẹ́mi Táíwò, "Òrìsà: A Prolegomenon to a Philosophy of Yorùbá Religion," in *Òrìsà Devotion as World Religion: The Globalization of Yorùbá Religious Culture*, eds. Jacob K. Olupona and Terry Rey, 84–105. Madison, WI: University of Wisconsin Press, 2008.

13

What Obstacles are in the Way of the Cosmos?

Learning Objectives

- Describe, compare, and evaluate cosmic obstacles in our six traditions of philosophy of religion.
- Evaluate some of the theodicies proposed to the problem of evil in Abrahamic and Academic philosophy of religion.
- Explain the limitations of the traditional problem of evil, particularly with respect to philosophies of religion that are not Abrahamic or Academic.

I. Introduction

Our final chapter examines "obstacles" for the "journey" of the cosmos. If the "journey" of the cosmos involves its functioning and order, then its "obstacles" are that which stands in the way of that functioning and order. Our question is therefore something like this: what prevents the cosmos from working the way it should?

Note that this question is always asked from the perspective of some human. It is we who have ideas about how the cosmos should work and want to know why it is not working the way we think it should. Sometimes this misfunctioning or disorder is strictly individual: Why does the cosmos not work for me? Why do I suffer? More often, though, misfunctioning and disorder applies to a wider community, perhaps an entire people, or even humankind in general: Why does the cosmos not work for us? Why do we suffer?

Whatever the case, what might seem entirely theoretical is often very practical. We want to know why we suffer and how to make it stop. This is true even in the case of the classical "problem of evil," which is usually put in terms of the following dilemma: If some God is all-powerful and all-loving, why does evil exist? Solutions to the dilemma, therefore, typically address either of these two attributes of this God or the nature of evil itself: Either this God is not all-powerful and cannot prevent evil, or this God is not all-loving and does not care to prevent evil, or evil is not really evil. Insofar as the solutions to this problem attempt to defend some God's justice vis-à-vis evil, they are called "theodicies" (from the Greek word *theodicy*, with *theos* meaning God, and *dikē* meaning justice).

What makes these apparently theoretical theodicies practical? For starters, they are usually asked and answered in times of suffering. Jews, for example, have asked this question throughout their history: Why have the Babylonians destroyed YHWH's temple and taken us into captivity? Why have the Spanish expelled us from our homes in Spain? Why have the Germans exterminated us in gas chambers? Answers to these questions have ranged from "we have sinned," to "we are an example for the world," to "God is broken," to "God is dead."

No matter which answer is provided, the act of giving answers can be comforting insofar as it gives reassurance that things will somehow be okay and forges solidarity with other sufferers. Even if the answer is "we don't know," the act of giving such an answer offers some measure of understanding and security. Consider, for example, the explanations that you might hear at the funerals of someone who has died in an unexpected and untimely manner: We do not know why this has happened, but we trust that it is somehow for the best and that the deceased is in a better place.

Two final terminological issues and a caveat before we turn to our content: First, theodicies are traditionally divided into those pertaining to "moral evil" or "natural evil": moral evil concerns what *humans* do (e.g., genocide); natural evil, what *nature* does (e.g., earthquakes). Second, "evil" includes a range of phenomena from physical pain and emotional suffering to social disorder and injustice, to natural disasters and environmental catastrophes, to natural imbalances and disharmonies, to evil beings and forces, to human finitude. Both terminological issues—the theoretical types and actual varieties of "evil"—will be important as we explore the diversity of "obstacles" to the "journey" of the cosmos below, many of which cannot be classified under the traditional problem of evil.

Please bear this in mind as you read. Theodicy is traditionally a "Western" project that centrally involves two concepts: on the one hand, an omnipotent, omniscient, and omnibenevolent God (which we will call the "O^3 God" below); on the other hand, evil. In this chapter, however, we broaden the meaning of *theodicy* to include any religio-philosophical attempt to explain why the cosmos does not function or operate as it should. Since most philosophies of religion do not have an O^3 God, most philosophies of religion have no need to justify such a God. Rather, they might attribute "evil" to cosmic law, the workings of nature, destiny, malevolent beings, oppressive foreign rule, structures of injustice, and so forth. All the same, explanations are offered of that which is misfunctioning, disordered, or painful. Arguably, therefore, we can compare and evaluate these disparate "theodicies." First, though, let us describe them.

II. South Asian Philosophy of Religion

If there is something comparable to "evil" in South Asian religious philosophy, it is ultimately attributable to human behavior, which is rewarded or punished through the law of *karma*. At its simplest, *karma* is a moral law of cause and effect: for every moral act, there is a moral effect, whether positive or negative. In fact, however, every mental event—action, perception, intention, emotion, thought—leaves behind a mental seed or imprint (*saṃskāra*) deep in the person's psyche, which later "ripens" or manifests as tendencies and dispositions toward future actions and general habits. As these tendencies and dispositions are enacted, they create even more seeds or imprints, thereby further deepening these tendencies and dispositions, determining to ever greater degrees the future actions, perceptions, intentions, emotions, and thoughts of the person.

Generally speaking, there is always some room for "free will." The future actions of a person are never completely determined. One may always choose for the best, even in the worst situation, even if only in some small way. And if the person does choose for the best, even in the worst situation, even if in some small way, this choice will in turn create tendencies and dispositions toward positive actions and habits. Nevertheless, the doctrine of *karma* constitutes an explanation for why "bad things" happen: they are the manifestations of imprints caused by wrong bodily or mental behavior in the past. For every evil that befalls humans, it is caused by some prior *karmic* act.

For the non-theistic/a-theistic religious philosophies of South Asia (Buddhism, Jainism, Sāṃkhya, Mīmāṃsā), *karma* more or less suffices as an explanation of "evil." But for South Asian religious philosophies with a God that somehow causes this cosmos to be—*Brahman* or *Īśvara*—it was necessary to explain the relationship between this God and *karma*. In these cases, we have what one contemporary philosopher has called a "theo-karma-dicy"—a justification of "God" given the fundamental law of *karma*. We now turn to three such theo-karma-dicies, one from the Nyāya school, the other two from the Vedānta school.[1]

In Chapter 10 you learned about Nyāya proofs for the existence of *Īśvara*. Nyāya "theodicy" is an extension of these proofs and their conception of *Īśvara*. For classical Nyāya philosophers, *Īśvara* was thought to possess divine attributes such as being an intelligent maker, omnipotence, omniscience, and goodness. Although *Īśvara* did not create the cosmos "out of nothing" (but rather put preexisting atoms into motion), a certain "problem of evil" remained: Why did *Īśvara* fashion the cosmos *this way*, i.e., with so much suffering due to *karmic* acts?

The response of classical Nyāya philosophers is that *Īśvara* oversees yet respects the law of *karma*, allowing humans to create and destroy their own *karma* as they progress toward release from rebirth. *Īśvara* does not intervene, permitting *karma* to operate by its own inexorable laws. *Īśvara* does, however, ensure that karmic reward and punishment are distributed in proportion with good and bad moral action. Moreover, *Īśvara*'s original cosmic design ensures that all beings can, by their own efforts, strive toward release (*mokṣa*) from the cycle of rebirth (*saṃsāra*) and the law of *karma*.

This defense of the justice of *Īśvara* was not without its critics, many of whom have already been mentioned in Chapter 10. Sāṁkhya philosophers (among others) maintained that the existence of *karma* as a fundamental law of the cosmos made the existence of *Īśvara* unnecessary as a guarantor of *karma*. Mīmāṃsā philosophers drew attention to the apparent defects in the cosmos, questioning why *Īśvara* could not do something about all the bad *karma* in the cosmos, wondering then whether *Īśvara* really cared. Jain and Buddhist philosophers summed up both responses in averring that God's existence was "superfluous at best, sinister at worst."[2] Contemporary philosopher Purushottama Bilimoria has also invoked the Anglo-European philosophical distinction between "moral evil" and "natural evil," pointing out that Nyāya theodicy does not address the latter:

> Are earthquakes, tsunamis, bushfires, hurricanes, and other devastating natural turbulences of necessity causally linked to people's *karma*, especially

> that of the hundreds and thousands of victims, particularly innocent children, animals, and plant life, affected by such disasters?[3]

Despite all these criticisms, however, Nyāya offers us one example of a South Asian theodicy that attempts to reconcile the operation of the law of *karma* with the goodness and power of a God. We turn now to two more examples, both from the school of Vedānta.

Vedānta's concern with "evil" goes all the way back to its founding *sūtras*, the *Brahma Sūtras*, which are attributed to Bādarāyaṇa (fifth century of the Common Era). Here, in verses II.1.34–6, Bādarāyaṇa responds to an imaginary interlocutor who raises the charge that if *Brahman* is the cause of the world, then inequality between humans (with respect to the amount of *karma* they begin with) and cruelty in the world reflect a flaw in *Brahman*. Bādarāyaṇa's response is succinct and elliptic: "there is no beginning" to the world; thus, "*karma* is not differentiated" amongst humans at this imaginary beginning.

Śaṅkara (*c.* 788–*c.* 820), the founder of the "non-dual" (*advaita*) school of Vedānta, gives us the first extant commentary on these verses.[4] As with Nyāya's *Īśvara*, Vedānta's *Brahman* is not the cause of suffering and evil; rather, *Brahman* responds to human activity, rewarding the good and punishing the evil. *Brahman* is therefore the guarantor of the universal law of *karma*, which Śaṅkara compared to the rain that falls everywhere, yet allows different things to grow differently in accordance with their own capacities. Unlike *Īśvara*, however, *Brahman* is not the creator of the cosmos. In fact, Śaṅkara held that a loving and good *Īśvara* could not have created a universe full of suffering. Rather, the cosmos is beginningless (*anādi*). There is no initial state of unequal *karmic* distinctions between humans that is arbitrarily assigned by *Brahman*; therefore, *Brahman* is not the original cause of the *karma* that *Brahman* subsequently rewards and punishes.

In the case of the next major commentator on the *Brahma Sūtras*, things were a bit different due in part to a different conception of *Brahman*.[5] Whereas Śaṅkara held that *Brahman* just is the cosmos,[6] Rāmānuja, the founder of the "qualifiedly non-dual" (Viśiṣṭādvaita) school of Vedānta, argued that *Brahman* was also the cause of the cosmos, which exists in relationship to *Brahman* as a body does to a soul. Moreover, Rāmānuja's *Brahman* is Lord Viṣṇu, more exactly, Viṣṇu-Nārāyaṇa, whom Rāmānuja refers to as *Īśvara* (Lord). This means that while *karma* remains an inexorable law of the cosmos, it is also measured in terms of what is pleasing and displeasing to *Īśvara*. It also means that *Īśvara* can personally reward good deeds and even help humans eradicate their negative *karma*, thereby enabling them to achieve liberation from rebirth. In both cases, we might say that a "personal touch" had been added to the problem of reconciling *karma* with "God." Nevertheless, things are similar "in the end": persons act freely and therefore are blameworthy for their immoral actions.[7]

Of course, one might again wonder about "natural evil," especially since all things constitute the body of *Brahman*. One might also question whether *Īśvara* is truly faultless of the immoral actions of humans since, as the "inner self" (*antarātman*), "inner controller" (*antaryāmin*), or "existential support" (*ādhāra*) of every person, *Brahman* permits and enables all actions to be realized. Moreover, one might ask why this *Brahman*/*Īśvara* seems to help some humans more than others in the eradication of negative *karma* and attainment of release from rebirth.

Needless to say, theo-karma-dicy is not easy. But as we shall see, it is no less difficult than theo-dicy. In both cases, there is a "givenness" or "facticity" to suffering that is not easily explained or dismissed if there is a divinity powerful enough to remove it and good enough to want it removed.

III. East Asian Philosophy of Religion

In the case of East Asian philosophy of religion, we end where we began—the period of the later Zhou Dynasty later referred to as "100 Schools Contend" (which lasted from the sixth to the third century BCE). One of the matters about which these schools contended was whether "Heaven" (*Tiān*) cared about the affairs of humans and, if so, whether He/It could do anything about them.[8]

As you remember, the meaning of *Tiān* in early Chinese philosophy ranged from a person-like deity to an impersonal natural force. In fact, over the course of the entire Zhou Dynasty (1122–256 BCE), especially during the period known as Warring States (453–221 BCE), the meaning of *Tiān* shifted from the former to the latter, at least for some philosophers. One reason for this change involved a certain problem of "evil." In the midst of social chaos and upheaval, civil warfare and destruction, and widespread pain and suffering, the person-like, caring, and efficacious nature of *Tiān* could no longer be plausibly maintained. Slowly by slowly, *Tiān* was regarded as nothing more than the impersonal, orderly operation of nature, which the sage could learn and live in accordance with.

We begin this philosophical story with those who defended the goodness and reliability of *Tiān*—Mohists. As you might remember from Chapter 3, Mohists were the chief rival to Confucians during this time: against the Confucian defense of hierarchical social roles, Mohists maintained that "everyone is equal before *Tiān*" and should therefore practice "inclusive care" (*jiān ài*) without respect to kinship or status; against the Confucian emphasis on traditional rituals and conventions (*lǐ*, 禮), Mohists argued that the proper measure of human action is whether it benefits "all under *Tiān*," not whether it accords with tradition. Grounding these emphases on inclusive care and practical benefits was a model of *Tiān* as caring and rewarding. *Tiān* Himself/Itself was said to practice "inclusive care" and therefore was commended as imitable. Moreover, the "will" of *Tiān* favored inclusive caring, rewarding such behavior in humans and punishing the opposite. "If I do what Heaven desires, Heaven will also do what I desire," maintained Mòzǐ; but if I "do what Heaven does not desire, I will lead the ordinary people of the world to land themselves in misfortune and calamity in the conduct of their affairs."[9]

For Mohists, everyone who questioned the goodness and power of *Tiān* was a threat to human virtue and social order. The greatest such threat came from the Confucians, whom the Mohists accused of advocating four policies that could destroy the world: (1) denying that *Tiān* and spirits are discerning or numinous; (2) affirming that fate/destiny (*mìng*, 命) exists and therefore that failure/success and order/disorder are outside human control; (3) holding long funerals; and (4) performing extravagant musical performances.[10] For us, the first two accusations are key: that *Tiān* is indifferent and therefore cannot be counted on to reward the good and punish the wicked, and that there is a "fate" or "destiny" that acts on human affairs irrespective of human value and worth. Since we have already discussed the first (*Tiān*), we turn now to the second (*mìng*).

Although early Zhou-Dynasty usage of *mìng* in the phrase *Tiān-mìng* pertained to the "command of *Tiān*," especially as it brought about the demise of the (immoral) Shang Dynasty and rise of the (moral) Zhou Dynasty, the meaning of *mìng* shifted over the course of the Zhou Dynasty to refer to unfortunate events that were outside human control—something like "blind fate." For Confucians, the relationship between *mìng* (as blind fate) and *Tiān* (as quasi-personal, quasi-natural force) was somewhat ambiguous; in fact, *mìng* was increasingly identified with *Tiān* as those aspects of nature that were outside human control and understanding, that acted without respect for the moral character of those humans affected, and that therefore must simply be accepted.

Not so for Mohists, who sought to drive a wedge between *Tiān*, which was unambiguously good, and *mìng*, which was amoral. Mohists believed that *Tiān* would ultimately reward the good and punish the bad *in this life* (since there are no other-worldly rewards and punishments in this cosmology) regardless of what *mìng* might bring. In defense of this claim, Mohists provided two arguments: first, hard work and moral behavior indeed did bring worldly success as a matter of fact; second, belief in *mìng* was dangerous to social order and human virtue.[11]

It was not until the fifth generation Confucian Xúnzǐ (310–235 BCE) that we see a direct critique of this Mohist position, combined with a robust account of how virtue is rewarded without the help of *Tiān*. Before then, however, another Confucian philosopher and two Daoist texts anticipate Xúnzǐ's view.

In the case of the first Daoist text, *Dàodéjīng*, neither *Tiān* nor *Dào*—the latter of which is the source of the former—are "humane" or good (*rén*); moreover, neither *Tiān* nor *Dào* care for or reward the behaviors of humans. Nevertheless, sages should attune their lives to the patterns of *Dào* for their actions to succeed, since only action that is in accordance with the natural way comes to fruition. In the case of the Confucian philosopher, Mencius (372–289 BCE), there is a turn away from a *Tiān* that is "above humans" toward one that is "in humans"—the originally good dispositions and tendencies of nature (*xìng*). Here, the *Tiān* that is above merges with fate (*mìng*), collectively encompassing naturally occurring events that cause humans harm and ruin and that cannot be explained or resisted and so must be accepted. Finally, in the case of the second Daoist text, *Zhuāngzǐ*, we see the rejection not only of a caring and efficacious *Tiān* but also of an objective human perspective by which judgments of right and wrong can be made. The result is that there simply is no "problem of evil," for evil is only a problem if humans can objectively establish that some things are not as they should be and that some superhuman agent or power cares and is able to do something about it.

This trajectory reaches its culmination in Xúnzǐ who, like Zhuāngzǐ, severs the connection between Heaven and humans, yet like the Mohists, maintains that virtue is rewarded and vice is punished. How? For Xúnzǐ, *Tiān* is merely nature. It does not know or care about the affairs of humans, is not an agent that can reward or punish, and is not identified in any way with what is morally good. If you take care of your health and finances, *Tiān* cannot make you sick or poor; and if you do not take care of your health and finances, *Tiān* cannot make you healthy or poor, writes Xúnzǐ, concluding:

"You must not complain against Heaven; its way is simply thus [i.e., of natural regularity]."[12] Moreover, although *Tiān* does give humans their nature (as with Mencius), that nature is not good (unlike Mencius) since each human naturally strives to fulfill her own desires, thereby coming into conflict with other humans who are striving to fulfill other desires. It is up to humans, therefore, to check these desires, overcome this nature, and cultivate their virtues.

Crucial in this process are the traditional rituals and conventions (*lǐ*, 禮) of the ancient sage kings, which are neither given by Heaven nor written into nature. Rather, they are the result of scholarly observation and experimentation by generations of sages. They are therefore what has been proved to "work." People who follow these traditions will flourish; those that flaunt them, founder. Writes Xúnzǐ,

> Those who cross waters mark out the deep places, but if the markers are not clear, people will fall in. Those who order the people mark out the Way [*Dào*], but if the markers are not clear, there will be chaos. The rituals [*lǐ*, 禮] are those markers. To reject ritual is to bemuddle the world, and to bemuddle the world is to create great chaos.[13]

Here, therefore, we see a certain problem of "evil" addressed not by limiting the power or goodness of an omnipotent and omnibenevolent God, nor by denying the existence of evil, but by jettisoning such a God altogether. The occurrence of "evil" is reason to believe that such a God does not exist. What remains of the problem of evil is therefore a human problem—to be "solved" by deliberative action (*wei*) in accordance with rituals and conventions (*lǐ*, 禮) that are conducive to harmony and order.

IV. Lakȟóta Philosophy of Religion

With Lakȟóta philosophy, we move even further away from the classical Western "problem of evil."[14] For starters, there are so-called *Wakȟáŋ Tȟáŋka Šíča*, destructive or malevolent deities, which are often itemized as two-fold or three-fold: Íya, a giant who eats people and who serves as the "chief" of the other *Wakȟáŋ Tȟáŋka Šíča*; Ibom, who causes evil through destructive cyclones and is sometimes said just to be Íya in cyclone form; and Gnaški, aka "Crazy Buffalo," who uses cunning and deceit to incite crime and cruelty.[15]

Other arguably less malevolent yet still deceitful deities and humans feature in a particular story from Lakȟóta creation myths. The first humans,

Old Man Wizard (Wazíya) and Old Woman Witch (Wakáŋka), gave birth to a daughter called Ité, meaning "Face," since she had the most beautiful face in the world. Seeing that Wazíya and Wakáŋka desired a place among the sixteen *Wakȟáŋ Tȟáŋka*, the trickster Iktómi suggested to them that they send Ité to tempt Wí (Sun) to leave His wife Haŋwí (Moon) for Ité. Impassioned by Uŋk—the source of passion, contention, and "evil," according to Archie Fire Lame Deer—Wí succumbed to Ité, who gave birth to a son, shaming Haŋwí. When the other *Wakȟáŋ Tȟáŋka* discovered what had happened, the wrongdoers were punished: Wazíya and Wakáŋka were banished to the end of the world; Ité's face was disfigured on one side, after which she was known as Anúgite, the "Two-Faced Woman"; Iktómi was chastised and despised by the other *Wakȟáŋ Tȟáŋka* (though it is said that he did not care); Uŋk was thrown into the water, transmogrifying into terrifying monsters of the water and land; and Wí (Sun) had Haŋwí (Moon) taken from him so that they now had to alternate ruling each 24-hour cycle. Although Uŋk still sows contention, Iktómi still tricks, and Anúgite still tempts, none of them arguably constitute an obstacle for the "journey of the cosmos." Moreover, since the *Wakȟáŋ Tȟáŋka* are not conceptualized as all-powerful, all-loving, and actively involved in the happenings of the cosmos, "evil" seems to be no "problem" for them.

Instead, when American Indian philosophers of religion speak about "obstacles" to the flourishing of themselves and their cosmos, they usually single out the actions and ideas of Euro-Americans. We first saw signs of this in Chapter 8, when we briefly looked at the forcible removal of American Indians from their ancestral homelands, the violation of treaties with the US government that putatively protected those lands, the prohibition or restriction of the practice of religious ceremonies and rituals, and the conversion of American Indians to European culture and religion—all perpetrated by Christians in accordance with the principles and practices of Christianity. We also saw in Chapter 12 how Wovoka's Ghost Dance vision in the late nineteenth century, especially as later interpreted by the Lakȟóta, included the prediction of a catastrophe that would remove all whites from the land. Moreover, we heard about how the "eschatological vision" of some members of the American Indian Movement (AIM) of the late twentieth century involved a restoration of the land and destruction of the white invaders who had stolen and devastated those lands.

Here, we turn again to Vine Deloria, Jr., who has written more on this topic than most, perhaps all. In many of Deloria's books and essays about religion, he places the blame squarely on Christianity, which is the preeminent obstacle of the cosmos. In one essay, Deloria calls Christianity "the chief evil ever to have been loosed on the planet."[16] In another, he avers that the "[e]ducational, economic, social, and legal problems of Indian peoples stem almost directly from Protestant theology and a misapplication of basic biblical ideas in the arena of political thought."[17] Through misunderstanding and misuse of the biblical concepts of *covenant*, *go forth and multiply*, and *have dominion over all the other species of creation*, Christians "have perpetuated massacres and theft unparalleled in the history of mankind" and justified slavery as "God's rightful contribution to the well-being of the Americans, God's chosen people."[18] Deloria therefore concludes:

> The case of the American Indian is clear and uncomplicated. American Indians suffer because the non-Indians have devised ways and means of not keeping their word. Non-Indians have violated their covenants with Indian tribes.[19]

Thus, in another essay, "Open Letter to the Heads of the Christian Churches in America," Deloria admonishes the heads of Christian churches in the US:

> At each point an in every aspect, you refused to confront our ideas but chose instead to force your opinions, myths, and superstitions on us. You have never chosen to know us. You have only come to confront and conquer us.[20]

And in his book on Christianity and American Indian religion, *God is Red*, Deloria rebuts the excuse that those Christians who committed these acts were not "really Christians":

> In point of fact they really were Christians. In their day they enjoyed all the benefits and prestige Christendom could confer. They were cheered as heroes of the faith, enduring hardships that a Christian society might be built on the ruins of pagan villages. They were featured in Sunday school lessons as saints of the Christian church. Cities, rivers, mountains, and seas were named after them.
>
> And if the exploiters of old were not Christians, why did not the true Christians rise up in defiance of the derogation of their religious heritage and faith?[21]

In this last case, Deloria draws in Christian emphasis on a "life hereafter" as a means of actively justifying or passively ignoring the "most dastardly deeds" committed by the followers of Christianity.[22] Deloria therefore concludes that Christianity must be rejected wholesale, not merely piecemeal: it was "misdirected from its inception," having arisen "out of a Near Eastern milieu in which control of populations was the important value," using its institutions to "exercise control over the beliefs, values, and behaviors of large masses of people."[23]

In short and in sum, Christianity is for some American Indians the chief obstacle for the cosmos. We will return to this again at the end of this chapter.

V. Yorùbá Philosophy of Religion

Since there is not really a destiny and path for the cosmos in Yorùbá philosophy of religion, there are not really obstacles for the cosmos either—at least not obstacles that prevent the cosmos from achieving some end or goal. There are, though, beings and forces that prevent the cosmos and humans from flourishing. In the *Ifá* corpus, they are known as *Ajogun*, which Kọ́lá Abimbọ́lá, translates as "Anti-god," though literally means "warrior."

The total number of *Ajogun* is said to be 200—half the number of the 400 *Òrìṣà*. However, just like the *Òrìṣà*, new *Ajogun* continue to come into existence. Thus, the number of *Ajogun* is conventionally numbered at 200+1 (and the *Òrìṣà* at 400+1). *Ajogun* inhabit the "left-hand" of the cosmos; *Òrìṣà*, the "right-hand." The cosmos is therefore an arena of perpetual conflict and war, with the *Ajogun* continually seeking the complete destruction of the *Òrìṣà*, as well as all human, animal, and plant life.

Eight *Ajogun* are chief in this war: Death (Ikú), Disease (Àrùn), Loss (Òfò), Paralysis (Ẹ́gbà), Big Trouble (Ọ̀ràn), Curse (Èpè), Imprisonment (Ẹ́wọ̀n), and "All Other Afflictions" (Èṣe). It is they, along with the other 192+1 *Ajogun*, who are responsible for most "evil," especially "natural evil" Only by divining the nature of an affliction and sacrificing to the appropriate *Òrìṣà* and *Ajogun* can that affliction be remedied for a period of time. Eventually, though, the cosmos returns to its natural state—conflict, strife, pain, suffering. This is simply the way things are; *Ajogun* are part of the fabric of reality, both as evil beings and as natural afflictions. In fact, the *Ajogun* are said to have been created by Olódùmarè, just as the *Òrìṣà* were.[24]

Having created the *Ajogun*, Olódùmarè feared they might desolate the cosmos. According to the *Ifá* corpus, he therefore charged one of the primordial *Òrìṣà*, Èṣù, with mitigating their power. Thus, Èṣù plays an indispensable role in the sacrifices that humans make for the Gods, ensuring that they are delivered to the appropriate *Òrìṣà* and *Ajogun*. For this reason, Èṣù is portrayed as "straddling the left/right divide" even though he is technically a "right-handed" *Òrìṣà*. Moreover, Èṣù himself can bring confusion and disorder to people when they fail to sacrifice to him or sacrifice incorrectly.

Yet another "straddler" of the left/right divide are *àjẹ́*, a term that is sometimes translated as "witches" but more accurately means "powerful people." According to some, the *àjẹ́* are allies of the *Ajogun* in their war against *Òrìṣà* and humans. From this perspective, *àjẹ́* function through the agency of humans (*ènìyàn*) who give up good human nature to become "negative humans" (*eníyán*).[25] From other perspectives, however, *àjẹ́* are simply "powerful people," who can use this power either creatively or destructively.[26] In this sense, all diviners (*babaláwo*) and herbalists (*oníṣègùn*) are *àjẹ́*. Regardless, the term is now often reserved (especially by Christians and Muslims) for those with a purportedly evil character, usually female, who are believed to work their evil at night, flying unseen through the air like birds (and are therefore also referred to as *ẹlẹyẹ*, "bird people").[27] Traditionally referred to euphemistically as "Mothers," the power of these "witches" was customarily kept in check (by men) through rituals such as *egúngún* and *gèlèdé* (see Chapter 6).[28]

Finally, as in the case of the Lakȟóta, there is the "evil" of Western colonialism, especially enslavement in the Americas. As mentioned in Chapters 1 and 11, the mighty Ọ̀yọ́ Empire was particularly weak in the early nineteenth century due to infighting and civil wars. This made them an easy target for slave raiders. Indeed, more Yorùbá were enslaved than any other ethnic group in Africa. Nevertheless, Yorùbá culture and religion persisted in the Americas, even while it was overwhelmed by Christianity and Islam in West Africa (as you also know from Chapter 11). Perhaps, then, an even greater obstacle for the Yorùbá cosmos involves the legacy of colonialism: Western ideologies of racial and cultural superiority, Western practices of political and economic hegemony, and the Western depletion of natural and social resources.

VI. Mediterranean/Abrahamic Philosophy of Religion

Abrahamic philosophy of religion inherits the problem of evil in its philosophical form from Greek and Roman philosophy, particularly the Hellenistic schools of philosophy during the Roman Empire: Stoicism, Epicureanism, and Skepticism. Since Stoics held that the cosmos not only was *theos* (God) but also unfolded in accordance with *logos* (reason), they were compelled to give justifications of the apparent existence of evil, especially when challenged by the rival philosophical schools of Epicureanism and Skepticism. For Skeptics, this challenge took the form of the classic problem of evil: either this God cannot remove evil and is therefore not all-powerful, or this God will not remove evil and is therefore not all-loving, or evil is not really evil. Thus was born the field of *theodicy*—an attempt to demonstrate the justice (Gk. *dikē*) of a God (*theos*) given the existence of evil.

It is important to acknowledge, however, that there are precursors to the Greco-Roman field of theodicy within the Abrahamic religions themselves, the most notable of which take up the problem of the "righteous sufferer." Although there are versions of this problem in Egyptian and Mesopotamian literature, it is the biblical version that is generally best known. In it, the patriarch Job is accused by "the satan" (Hb. *haṣṣāṭān*)—which here means "the adversary" or "the accuser," an intermediary between YHWH and the world—of worshipping YHWH only because YHWH has blessed him. As a sort of contest, YHWH allows *haṣṣāṭān* to take Job's wealth, kill Job's children and servants, and inflict Job with boils. Job, however, does not curse YHWH despite his three companions' insistence that his suffering must be deserved, given the common assumption the wicked suffer and the righteous prosper. Instead, Job responds by demanding an attorney to plead his case before YHWH. In the end, however, Job and his attorney receive no answer as to why he suffers. Rather, YHWH appears to Job in a whirlwind and shows him his creative might and power, after which Job "repents in dust and ashes" for his lack of knowledge:

> "I know that you can do all things,
> and that no purpose of yours can be thwarted.
> 'Who is this that hides counsel without knowledge?'
> Therefore I have uttered what I did not understand,
> things too wonderful for me, which I did not know.
> 'Hear, and I will speak;
> I will question you, and you declare to me.'
> I had heard of you by the hearing of the ear,
> but now my eye sees you;
> therefore I despise myself,
> and repent in dust and ashes."[29]

This problem would return many times throughout the history of Judaism: Why do YHWH's chosen people suffer? After the First Temple was destroyed by the Babylonians in 586 BCE, biblical prophets proclaimed that suffering was deserved because of the sins of the people, with the prophet Isaiah adding that Israel had been called by YHWH to be a "suffering servant" that would demonstrate YHWH's might and power to the nations of the world through its suffering. As time wore on and suffering compounded, however, attempts to "blame the victim" became less and less plausible. As you know from Chapter 8's investigation of the obstacles of the self, one popular (Kabbalistic) explanation for the expulsion of the Jews from Spain in 1492 placed blame on squarely on YHWH and the cosmos, maintaining that YHWH's tenth and final emanation, the *Shekhinah*, had fallen into matter and needed to be repaired by Jews and returned to YHWH. Centuries later, innovative Jewish and non-Jewish theological responses to the unparalleled genocide of the Holocaust included: (1) that a new, 614th commandment had been added to the Mosaic covenant, thou shalt not hand Hitler posthumous victories; (2) that the covenant with YHWH had been broken and was no longer binding; (3) that although suffering along with the victims, YHWH was powerless to stop their suffering; (4) that YHWH was simply dead; (5) that theodicy was impossible and undesirable in this case; and (6) that a silence of unknowing and struggle with YHWH were the only appropriate responses.[30]

In the case of Christianity, notable justifications of evil were not always so closely tied to actual occurrences of suffering, instead often functioning as theological puzzles to be solved. This seems to have been the case for St. Augustine (354–430), who advanced a number of different theodicies influenced by Platonic and Stoic philosophy as well as the New Testament letters of the Apostle Paul (5–67). Drawing on a common trope in Neo-Platonic philosophy, Augustine first held that since the Good is equated with Being, a complete absence of good has no being; evil is a privation of the Good and therefore does not actually exist. Looking again to Neo-Platonic philosophy (as well as Stoic philosophy), Augustine claimed that evil could not be part of the initial creation of the Trinitarian God, who is purely good and therefore cannot be responsible for evil. Turning to the Apostle Paul, Augustine maintained that evil entered the world as a punishment for Adam's (original) sin, after which it was disseminated from person to person through sex. Remaining with the Apostle Paul, Augustine contended that original sin prevented humans from freely doing the good until their wills were redeemed by the Trinitarian God. Turning back another standard Neo-Platonic and Stoic trope, Augustine finally claimed that everything that appears "evil" to humans from their limited finite perspectives is actually part of a much larger harmonious and beautiful mosaic, which can only be seen from the infinite perspective of the Trinitarian God.[31]

Contemporary (Christian) philosophers of religion such as John Hick (1922–2012) have contrasted this Augustinian theodicy with the "soul-making theodicy" of the second-century Christian bishop and martyr Irenaeus (130–202).[32] In contrast to Augustine, Irenaeus taught that evil is necessary for the moral development of humans. In this sense, creation is incomplete, requiring humans to utilize their free will to make good moral decisions. Moral evil is necessary to this process, as is natural evil, which offers a context in which humans make moral decisions. Only because of evil can humans progress from a spiritual state of immaturity and self-centeredness to one of maturity and other-centeredness. This is what it means for humans who are created in the "image of God" to become transformed into the "likeness of God."

Finally, with respect to Islamic philosophy of religion, we can first observe that theodicy is one of few domains in which Islamic theology and philosophy is not as robust as Christian and Jewish theology and philosophy. Perhaps one reason for this is that Aristotle never engaged in theodicy, so theodicy never registered as a major point of contention between Islamic theologians (especially al-Ghazālī) and their Aristotelian-influenced philosophical opponents (especially ibn Rushd). Rather, theodicy only shows up as a significant point of contention within the dispute about human freedom and divine omnipotence between the rival Muʿtazilite and Ashʿarite schools of theology. As you recall from Chapter 5, the Muʿtazila defended Allah's justice by attributing evil to the free acts of humans (thereby limiting Allah's omnipotence). Not only was Allah not the source of evil; Allah also justly rewarded and punished virtue and vice, providing ample rewards in the afterlife for those who unjustly suffered. By contrast, Ashʿarites maintained that Allah was entirely omnipotent, predetermining and causing every event in the cosmos, human actions included. Humans, however, did freely choose to do what Allah effected and therefore "acquired" moral culpability. As for why Allah predetermined and caused the world as He did with the evil that it has, humans simply could not know and therefore had to accept "without asking how."

VII. European/Academic Philosophy of Religion

For understandable reasons, the problem of evil has been "all the rage" in twentieth-century philosophy of religion. One primary reason is the apparently unprecedented suffering of the twentieth century, chiefly through the hands of human agents, though also as caused by nature. (One can only imagine how the problem of natural evil might eclipse the problem of moral evil in the twenty-first century given rapidly worsening climate change and environmental disasters.) For a century that was supposed to have been "enlightened" like none before, this came as quite a shock. How could human beings enact such evils on one another? How could a God who is all-loving and all-powerful allow such evils to happen, sitting idly by while the Nazis murdered and exterminated six-million Jews (as well as during the many other genocides and horrors of the twentieth century)? It is therefore of little surprise that the problem of evil haunts not only contemporary philosophy of religion and related academic disciplines but also human endeavors far afield, be they literary, artistic, musical, or architectural. One particularly interesting and relevant example is Archibald MacLeish's 1958 play "J.B.," a modern retelling of the story of Job in which the main character (J.B./Job) spurns the advice of the characters that assume the roles of YHWH and "the satan," instead finding his only solace in his wife, with whom he rebuilds a life without any God.

In the case of analytic philosophy of religion, however, the problem of evil has become linked to the rationality of theism like never before. For many analytic philosophers of religion, belief in an omnipotent, omniscient, omnibenevolent creator God (O^3 God) is only rationally justified if the problem of evil can somehow be neutralized or defeated. Let us put this in a little context.

Although the problem of evil has roots in ancient Western philosophy (as you know from the preceding section), it received new life during the European Enlightenment by philosophers such as Voltaire (1694–1778) and David Hume (1711–76), each of whom directed it against the common philosophical-scientific view that the universe was perfectly designed by perfect God. Among the many provocations for its revival was the 1755 Lisbon earthquake, which struck on the morning of Saturday, November 1, when many of the residents were in the churches and cathedrals celebrating the Feast of All Saints. First, the earthquake toppled the buildings, killing many inside; then those who took refuge at the harbor were washed away by a tsunami triggered by the earthquake (Figure 13). In the city alone, 10,000–30,000 people were killed, making the earthquake one of the deadliest in history. Why would an O^3 God allow this to happen, especially since this God had designed a perfect cosmos? Voltaire's satire *Candide* ridiculed the fictional character Professor Pangloss (and by association the actual philosopher Leibniz), who insists throughout the narrative that this is "the best of all

Figure 13 Lisbon Earthquake and Tsunami, 1755. Science History Images, May 4, 2016, Alamy Stock Photo.

Table 13.1 Logical Problem of Evil[34]

P1:	If an omnipotent, omniscient, and omnibenevolent God exists, then evil does not;
P2:	There is evil in the world;
C:	Therefore, an omnipotent, omniscient, and omnibenevolent God does not exist.

possible worlds," even in the face of apparently pointless, horrific suffering. Hume's posthumously published *Dialogues Concerning Natural Religion* did the same with respect to the fictional character Cleanthes (named after one of the first Stoic philosophers who engaged in theodicy), who maintains that the perfect design of the cosmos bespeaks the existence of a perfect designer.

Not until the latter half of the twentieth century, however, was the problem of evil again revived, this time with rigor and precision.[33] Both a "logical" and "evidential" form of the argument were developed, debated, refined, and re-debated, *ad infinitum*. This all began, however, with a simple form of the logical problem of evil that resembled its ancient philosophical roots (Skepticism, Epicureanism) and modern philosophical articulations (Voltaire, Hume), as in Table 13.1.

As you should be able to tell, this argument is logically valid in form. But are its premises true? The first premise is usually the one in question: Is the existence of an O^3 God incompatible with the existence of evil? Those who say yes, point out that an omnibenevolent being would want to prevent all evils, that an omniscient being knows every way in which evils can come into existence and be prevented, and that an omnipotent being has the power to prevent that evil from coming into existence. Those who say no, argue that evil is necessary for an O^3 God to achieve greater goods. Why? The answer, in short, is free will.

Although the freewill defense also has a long arc in Western philosophy (with Augustine as one its most notable ancient-medieval exponents), it was revived in the 1970s by the Christian philosopher Alvin Plantinga (b. 1932). For Plantinga, an O^3 God is compatible with evil because (1) an O^3 God creates a world containing evil and has a good reason for doing so and (2) it was not within an O^3 God's power to create a world containing moral good but no moral evil. Why? In short, an O^3 God creates at least some creatures (e.g., humans) who are free, and these creatures can and do misuse freedom for evil ends. This God cannot stop these creatures from misusing their freedom for evil ends since they would not then be free. Moreover, a creation in which some beings have free will is better than one in which no beings have free will.

Critics of the freewill defense have wondered why an O^3 God could not create a world in which free persons never misuse their freedom for evil ends, especially evil ends with far-reaching, devasting consequences. Some (notably Marilyn McCord Adams[35]) have maintained that although the value of free will might be sufficient to counterbalance minor evils, it does not outweigh the negative attributes of "horrendous evils" such as rape and murder. Take for example the case of a father who accidentally runs over his child, or of a psychopath who tortures his victim for months before she dies—Is the "good" of free will worth this cost? Could not an O^3 God create free will in a way that precludes its use for these horrendous evils? Another related argument is that those actions of free beings that bring about evil very often diminish the freedom of those who suffer the evil. For example, the murder of a young child prevents that child from exercising free will. In such a case in which the freedom of an innocent child is pitted against the freedom of an evil-doer, it is not clear why an O^3 God could not have done better. These issues become even more thorny in the case of a God who intervenes in the cosmos, for then we can ask why this God intervenes in apparently trivial cases (e.g., to save a pet, to win the Super Bowl) but not in apparently momentous cases (e.g., to prevent genocides or natural disasters).

Nevertheless, the freewill defense has been taken by many as a compelling rebuttal of the logical argument. As a result, the debate has tended to shift toward the evidential argument of evil, which does not seek to show that the existence of evil is logically incompatible with an O^3 God, but that evil counts against or lowers the probability of the existence of an O^3 God. Especially relevant for the evidential problem of evil are the amounts, kinds, and distributions of evil, not the sheer existence of evil. Thus, many of the issues raised in the previous paragraph are still in play.

The evidential problem of evil divides into so-called "absolute" and "relative" versions. In the case of the classic, absolute version of the evidential problem of evil, William Rowe (1931–2015) argued from the existence of "intense suffering," as in Table 13.2.

This argument is also logically valid in form, so we must look to the truth of the premises. Both theists and atheists generally accept P2.[37] In the case of P1, however, it is arguable whether there are instances of intense suffering that an all-powerful and all-knowing God could have prevented without losing some greater good or permitting some evil equally bad or worse. Rowe famously defended P1 with two examples of intense suffering, one involving humans and moral evil, the other involving animals and natural evil:

1 A little girl, Sue, is brutally beaten, raped, and murdered by her mother's drunken boyfriend.
2 A fawn suffers helplessly for days and then dies in a forest fire.

In both cases, the suffering is not only intense but also apparently pointless. Could not an O^3 God have prevented such cases of "horrendous" and "gratuitous" evil without thereby losing some greater good or permitting some evil equally bad or worse?

The second version of the evidential argument is "relative" since it argues that the existence and nature of evil makes the existence of an O^3 God *less likely*, or that the best explanation for the existence and nature of evil is not such a God but rather no God or an indifferent God. William Rowe's student Paul Draper provided one of the more notable examples of a relative version

Table 13.2 Evidential Problem of Evil 1: Absolute Version (Rowe)[36]

P1:	There exist instances of intense suffering which an omnipotent, omniscient being could have prevented without thereby losing some greater good or permitting some evil equally bad or worse;
P2:	An omniscient, wholly good being would prevent the occurrence of any intense suffering it could, unless it could not do so without thereby losing some greater good or permitting some evil equally bad or worse;
C:	Therefore, there does not exist an omnipotent, omniscient, wholly good being.

Table 13.3 Evidential Problem of Evil 2: Relative Version (Draper)[38]

P1: Gratuitous evils exist;
P2: The hypothesis of indifference, *i.e.*, that if there are supernatural beings they are indifferent to gratuitous evils, is a better explanation for (P1) than theism;
C: Therefore, evidence prefers that no God, as commonly understood by theists, exists.

of the evidential problem of evil, one that draws on the existence of "gratuitous evils," as in Table 13.3.

How would one know whether the hypothesis of indifference is a better explanation for gratuitous evils than the existence of an O^3 God? Here, we can again employ probability theory (Bayes' Theorem) to attempt to measure the probability of the hypotheses of *indifference* (H1) v. *O3 God* (H2) given the existence of gratuitous evil. As you remember from Chapter 3, the probability of H1 or H2 given the existence of gratuitous evil (P [H/E]) is a function of the probability of gratuitous evil given H1 or H2 (P [E/H]), multiplied by the prior probability of H1 or H2 before or without the evidence (P [H]), divided by the probability of the evidence apart from H1 or H2 (P [E]).

$$P\ (H/E) = \frac{P\ (E/H) * P\ (H)}{P(E)}$$

If the probability of gratuitous evil given an indifferent or absent God is high (>50%), and if the prior probability of an indifferent or absent God is 50/50, and if the prior probability of gratuitous evil is also 50/50, then the probability of H1 (indifference) is greater than 50%. And if the probability of gratuitous evil given an O^3 God is low (<50%), and if the prior probabilities of an O^3 God and gratuitous evil are again both 50/50, then we have a probability of H2 (O^3 God) that is less than 50 percent. So, it would seem that *indifference* (H1) is a better explanation of gratuitous evil than *O3 God* (H2). But perhaps you might calculate these figures differently.

In response to these evidential forms of the problem of evil (especially Rowe's "absolute" version), some recent proponents of an O^3 God vis-à-vis evil have developed what is called the "Skeptical Theist Defense." Quite simply, this defense contends with Rowe's first premise above, maintaining that humans cannot know whether there are goods for the sake of which an O^3 God permits evils. Although it might *seem* to humans that many evils are pointless, humans cannot know that these evils *actually* are pointless. If an O^3 God does exist, then this God knows the reasons why evils are allowed, the ends they serve, and the goods they achieve. Humans do not and cannot. Rowe's response to this was twofold.[39] First, he maintained that his evidential argument was concerned only with what he called "Restricted Standard Theism" (RST), not the "Expanded Standard Theism" (EST)—involving a finite/infinite gap between God and humans—that was smuggled into the Skeptical Theist Defense. More damningly, Rowe turned the Skeptical Theist Defense against itself, maintaining that we are hard pressed to claim that an O^3 God is all-loving if this God knows the goods that justify apparently pointless suffering yet does not reveal them to humans and, worse, leaves suffering humans without the comfort of divine love. Regardless of which side of this debate one winds up on, it would seem that we are back at the beginning so to speak—human ignorance and divine inscrutability.

There is also the issue of "natural evil," which the freewill defense would seem not to counter, for it is not human free will that causes earthquakes, tornadoes, hurricanes, meteors, and so forth. Nevertheless, one of the most notable recent defenses of natural evil does in fact appeal to free will, with Alvin Plantinga arguing that natural evils are caused by the free choices of supernatural beings such as demons, who cause natural phenomena such as earthquakes, floods, and virulent diseases. Others contend that natural evils are the result of the "Fall" of humankind, which corrupted the perfect world created by God. Still others maintain that natural evils are the byproduct of natural laws, which are themselves requisite for rational human action, or that the observation of natural evils by humans gives them knowledge of moral evil, making their free choices more significant than they would otherwise be. Do any of these suffice to explain the event with which we began this section—the Lisbon Earthquake of 1755?

VIII. Putting it All Together

As in case of proofs for the existence of God, we are again faced with a topic from "Western" philosophy of religion that appears not to fit most philosophies of religion elsewhere. We come closest in the case of South Asian philosophy of religion, where the Nyāya and Vedānta schools engage in attempts to reconcile the existence of a benevolent and powerful God with suffering due to the law of *karma*. Even in South Asia, however, most philosophies of religion are not concerned about this problem, save to point out the deficiencies of Nyāya and Vedānta "karma-theo-dicies." Moreover, there is little to no trace of the classical Western problem of evil in East

Asian, Lakȟóta, and Yorùbá philosophy of religion, except for the unique way that it comes up in early East Asian philosophy of religion with regard to *Tiān* and fate. How then can we philosophize about religion globally and critically with respect to the problem of evil?

Let us begin with our insight from the chapter on proofs for the existence of God (Chapter 10)—something that seems quite natural and obvious in Abrahamic and contemporary philosophy of religion is not so elsewhere. In this case, the issue is in large part the result of the concept of God in Abrahamic and Academic philosophy of religion. You only get the problem of evil per se when you have an all-loving and all-powerful, person-like God who creates and intervenes in the cosmos. Such a God is "in charge of" the cosmos, so to speak. So, if the cosmos contains apparently horrendous and gratuitous suffering, responsibility for this suffering ultimately rests with this God. In other philosophies of religion, quite different things are "in charge of" the cosmos—*karma*, *Dào*, principle (*lǐ*, 理) and vital energy (*qì*), *Òrìṣà* and *Ajogun*, *Wakȟáŋ Tȟáŋka*, and so forth. Since none of these things, arguably, is an all-loving and all-powerful, person-like creator and intervener in the cosmos, none can be held personally responsible. "Evil," rather, is just part and parcel of the cosmos.

Given that we are practicing global-*critical* philosophy of religion, a second insight concerns the relationship between "Western" philosophy of religion—both Abrahamic and Academic—and colonialism. Arguably, few things have caused more suffering to the cosmos and its inhabitants than colonialism. And since very few places in the world were not colonized by European powers from the fifteenth to twentieth centuries, this suffering was widespread. For all these (formerly) colonized peoples, one significant obstacle in the way of their and their cosmos' path is the deprivation of land, resources, ways of life, systems of meaning, human dignity, and life itself. How, if at all, can this practical problem of evil be reconciled with the theoretical problem of evil?

A third insight is available to us by looking outside philosophy to other relevant disciplines—in this case cognitive science. Remember Pascal Boyer's theory from last chapter? For Boyer, one reason why humans first created and continue to believe in Gods, Spirits, or Ancestors is that they are "full access agents" who can see all the relevant information about moral situations and therefore know the rightness or wrongness of the relevant behavior. In cases where someone apparently "gets away with" an immoral, unjust, or unfair behavior, humans can therefore take solace in the belief that Gods, Spirits, or Ancestors have "full access" to this situation, are aware of the inequity, and will somehow redress it in the future. If true, this flips classic theodicy on its head—humans do not need to justify Gods, Spirits, and Ancestors because of evil; rather, we justify evil by appealing to Gods, Spirits, and Ancestors.

Of course, the global-critical philosopher of religion should also take up the traditional-theoretical problem of evil. Is free will an adequate response to moral evil? Is natural law an adequate response to natural evil? Does an O^3 God who gives free will to humans become less than all-powerful? Should an O^3 God be removed from the cosmos to avoid thorny questions about why this God intervenes in some apparently trivial cases but not in other more momentous ones? Or is the absence of an O^3 God a better explanation for gratuitous and horrendous evil? Or is there really no horrendous and gratuitous evil at all insofar as every "evil" works to the greater good from the divine perspective? Maybe the only adequate explanation, in the end, is human ignorance and divine inscrutability?

Nevertheless, the limitations of this endeavor should be obvious, for it only engages mostly Western philosophies of religion. Moreover, one is still left at the end of the day with the arguable fact that Western colonialism has not only perpetrated many horrendous and gratuitous "evils" in our cosmos but also represented those they colonized as "evil," as An Yountae contends, drawing on the work of the Martinican postcolonialist philosopher Franz Fanon:

> Colonial metaphysics offers an answer to the problem of theodicy by reinforcing the theological difference between the colonizer and the colonized, thus endorsing the existing social order as just. The former represents the good, while the latter embodies absolute evil.[40]

Perhaps, then, academic theodicies are themselves part of the problem of evil insofar as they not only "paper over" suffering and evil, making it a merely theoretical philosophical-theological puzzle rather than one to respond to bodily, but also divest themselves and their God of responsibility, as if figuring out a solution to the problem of evil would somehow absolve the sins of this God and His followers.[41]

Such evils of course include patriarchal ones, too—the sins of violence against women. And as feminist philosopher of religion Morny Joy maintains, "the ongoing scandal of violence against women" is never referred to in mainstream philosophy of religion.[42] What if it were to be? For feminist philosopher of religion Grace Jantzen, a feminist approach to violence against women and the "problem of evil" more broadly would first be one of "outrage and bewilderment":

> how *can* the world be like this? How *dare* some people make others suffer in the way that they do? What sort of divinity could we possibly be talking about if such suffering is allowed to continue?[43]

Next, it would be one of action, "transforming outrage into solidarity and compassionate action for love of the world, recognizing and accepting the solidarity and compassion of another also in our own suffering."[44]

But is this philosophy of religion? Or should philosophy of religion stick to the theoretical problem of evil? With respect to questions such as these, Jantzen leads us back to our point of departure in this book—what philosophy of religion is and how it should be practiced:

> Why is it not at least important to ask who is committing the evil, and against whom? If the reply is that these are, of course, important issues, but they do not belong to the philosophy of religion, then we are back again to the question of how the boundaries of the discipline are drawn up, and by whom.[45]

Indeed, this book has tried to do just this—to redraw the boundaries of philosophy of religion more globally and critically, here in this final chapter with respect to the "problem of evil."

Yet again, though, it is up to you to decide. Does solving the problem of theoretical evil distract and insulate one from addressing issues of practical evil? Does justifying some God vis-à-vis evil constitute a justification of evil itself? Or does this justification remain one of the chief tasks of philosophy of religion?

In answering questions such as these, the future of (global-critical) philosophy of religion lies.

Questions for Discussion

1. Describe, compare, and evaluate the obstacles in the way of the cosmos in our six traditions of philosophy of religion. What is to be learned about the diversity of such obstacles?
2. Evaluate some of the theodicies proposed to the problem of evil in Abrahamic and academic philosophy of religion. Which aspects of the traditional problem of evil do you find most difficult to "solve"?
3. Explain the limitations of the traditional problem of evil, and explore the relationship between it and the evils of colonialism. Is the problem of evil itself, and the theodicies proposed to it, part of the problem?

Primary and Scholarly Sources

East Asia

Mòzǐ, chapters 26 and 37. In *Mo Zi: The Book of Master Mo*, trans. Ian Johnston, 125–30, 182–7. New York: Penguin Books, 2010.

Xúnzǐ, chapter 17. In *Xunzi: The Complete Text*, trans. Eric L. Hutton, 175–82. Princeton, NJ: Princeton University Press, 2014.

European/Academic

Draper, Paul. "Pain and Pleasure: An Evidential Problem for Theists." *Nous* 23 (1989): 331–50.

Jantzen, Grace. *Becoming Divine: Towards a Feminist Philosophy of Religion*, 259–64. Bloomington, IN: Indiana University Press, 1999.

Mackie, J. L. "Evil and Omnipotence." *Mind* 64 (1955): 200–12.

Plantinga, Alvin. *The Nature of Necessity*, 164–96. New York: Oxford University Press, 1974.

Rowe, William L. "The Problem of Evil and Some Varieties of Atheism." *American Philosophical Quarterly* 16 (1979): 335–41.

Lakȟóta

Archie Fire Lame Deer and Richard Erdoes. *Gift of Power: The Life and Teachings of a Lakota Medicine Man*, 261–3. Santa Fe, NM: Bear & Co. Publishing, 1992.

Deloria, Vine, Jr. *God is Red: A Native View of Religion: The Classic Work Updated*, 261–6. Golden, CO: Fulcrum Publishing, 1994.

Deloria, Vine, Jr. "A Violated Covenant." In *For this Land: Writings on Religion in America*, ed. James Treat, 72–6. New York: Routledge, 1999.

Deloria, Vine, Jr. "An Open Letter to the Heads of the Christian Churches in America." In *For this Land: Writings on Religion in America*, ed. James Treat, 77–83. New York: Routledge, 1999.

Mediterranean/Abrahamic

Augustine. *The Confessions*, VII.ii (3)–v (7), xii (18)–xiii (19). Trans. Henry Chadwick, 113–16, 124–5. New York: Oxford University Press, 1991.

Job 38–42.

South Asia

Bilimoria, Purushottama. "Toward an Indian Theodicy." In *The Blackwell Companion to the Problem of Evil*, eds. Justin P. McBrayer and Daniel Howard-Synder, 302–17. Malden, MA: Wiley-Blackwell, 2013.

Rāmānuja, *Śrībhāṣya*, II.i.34–6. In *Brahma-Sūtras according to Śrī Rāmānuja*, 7th reprint ed., trans. Swami Vireswarananda and Swami Adidevananda, 237–40. Calcutta: Advaita Ashrama, 2012.

Śaṅkara. *Brahma Sūtra Bhāṣya*, II.i.34–6. In *A Sourcebook in Indian Philosophy*, eds. Sarvepalli Radhakrishnan and Charles A. Moore, 362–5. Princeton, NJ: Princeton University Press, 1957.

Yorùbá

Abímbọ́lá, Kọ́lá. *Yorùbá Culture: A Philosophical Account*, chapter 4. Birmingham: Iroko Academic Publishers, 2005.

Isichei, Eilzabeth. *The Religious Traditions of Africa: A History*, 259–61, 311–13. Westport, CT: Praeger, 2004.

Glossary

a posteriori Latin term for reasoning that is undertaken or knowledge that is produced with recourse to empirical observation or experience.

a priori Latin term for reasoning that is undertaken or knowledge that is produced without recourse to empirical observation or experience.

abhidharma Sanskrit term meaning "about the teachings [of the Buddha]"; third-century bce Buddhist texts that systematize the teachings of earlier Buddhist *sūtras*; one of the "three baskets" in the Pāli canon of Theravāda Buddhism.

Abímbọ́lá, Kọ́lá Contemporary Yorùbá philosopher; engages in research on artificial intelligence, forensic science, evidence and proof, and Africana philosophy; regards his "philosophical account" of traditional Yorùbá culture as an exercise in "cultural philosophy."

Abraham (early second millennium bce) Regarded as a common forefather or "patriarch" by the Abrahamic religions; responded to a call from YHWH to leave his home in Mesopotamia and resettle in what is now Israel.

adhyāsa Sanskrit term meaning "superimposition"; defined by Vedānta philosopher Śaṅkara as "the apparent presentation of something previously observed in some other thing," specifically the superimposition of everyday experience onto the ultimate reality of *Ātman/Brahman*.

àjẹ́ Yorùbá term meaning "powerful person"; commonly used to refer to witches.

Ajogun Yorùbá term literally meaning "warrior"; applied in the Ifá tradition to the 200+1 "Anti-gods" who wage war on humans, animals, plants, and the *Òrìṣà*.

al-Ashʿarī (Abū al-Ḥasan al-Ashʿarī, *c.* 874–936) Persian Islamic theologian who was trained as a Mu'tazilite though later broke with them and founded his own Ashʿarite school of theology.

al-Fārābī (Abū Naṣr al-Fārābī, *c.* 872–950) Islamic philosopher known as "the Second Teacher" (with Aristotle as the first); credited with preserving the Aristotelian corpus through his commentaries on it; influential for later Abrahamic philosophers including ibn Sīnā and Maimonides.

al-Ghazālī (Abū Ḥāmid Muḥammad ibn Muḥammad aṭ-Ṭūsiyy al-Ġazālī, 1058–1111) Islamic philosopher, theologian, jurist, and mystic (Sufi); especially known with respect to philosophy of religion for his condemnation of Islamic philosophy in the *Incoherence of the Philosophers*

(*Tahāfut al-Falāsifa*) and for his cosmological-*kalām* proof for the existence of Allah.

al-Ḥallāj (Abū al-Muġīth al-Ḥusayn bin Manṣūr al-Ḥallāj, *c.* 858–922) Persian Islamic mystic (Sufi); known for exclaiming "I am the Truth" (*Anā al-Ḥaqq*) during a state of mystical union with Allah (for which he was later brutally executed).

al-Mahdī Islamic term meaning "the guided one"; refers to a messianic-eschatological figure who will appear at the end of time to establish a seven-year rule in Medina and battle al-Masīḥ ad-Dajjāl.

ʿAlī (ʿAlī ibn Abī Ṭālib, *c.* 600–61) Cousin and son-in-law of the Islamic prophet Muḥammad; ruled as the fourth rightly guided *caliph* from 656–61; regarded by Shīʿa Muslims as first in the line of *imams*, all of whom were blood relatives of Prophet Muḥammad.

Allah Arabic term meaning "God"; probably derived from Hebrew words for God(s) such as *ʾĒl*, *ʾĔlôah* (sing.), and *ʾĔlohîm* (pl).

Althusser, Louis (1918–90) French post-Marxist philosopher; known for developing Karl Marx's notion of ideology through the concepts of *ideological state apparatuses* and *ideological interpolation*.

Amitābha (Ch. Ēmítuófó, 阿彌陀佛) Sanskrit term meaning "infinite light"; the name of the buddha of measureless light and life (who is also known as *Amitāyus*, meaning infinite life); the central buddha in Pure Land Buddhist teachings and sects.

an-ātman Sanskrit term for "no-self" or "no-soul" (literally no *Ātman*); a key teaching of many early Buddhist schools and Buddhism more generally.

Analects (*Lúnyǔ*, 論語) English term for the "selected sayings" of Confucius and his disciples, which were collected and recorded after his life.

analytic philosophy of religion (aka, Anglo-American philosophy of religion) English term for the dominant form of philosophy of religion in the world today; originates in English-speaking countries, especially England and the United States; privileges analysis and logic, aspires for rigor and clarity, usually limits itself to theistic forms of religion.

Anderson, Pamela Sue (1955–2017) American feminist philosopher of religion known especially for her creative deployment of standpoint epistemology.

anekāntavāda Sanskrit term referring to the Jain "doctrine of non-one-sidedness," according to which reality consists of innumerable things or substances, each of which possesses innumerable essential qualities and non-essential modes.

Anselm (1033–1109) Christian Benedictine monk, theologian, and philosopher; known in philosophy of religion for his ontological proofs for the existence of God.

anthropic principle English term for the apparently privileged position of human observers of the cosmos as well as the fundamental parameters of the cosmos on which the existence of human observers depends; comes in two basic forms, "strong" and "weak."

anumāna Sanskrit term referring to inferential reasoning that draws a conclusion from premises; generally itemized by the *darśana*-s as the second means by which reliable knowledge can be attained (*pramāṇa*).

apocalyptic English term referring to prophecies and movements that prophesy about an imminent cataclysm or final destruction of the world; from the Greek word *apokaluptikos* (uncovering).

apokatastasis Greek term used by the Christian philosopher and theologian Origen of Alexander (184–253) for the idea that all beings, even the devil, are eventually restored to the Trinitarian-Christian God and the contemplation of the divine mysteries.

appeal to authority English term for the appeal to some authority—whether a person, institution, or other—for evidence to support an argument.

Aquinas, Thomas (1225–74) Christian Dominican monk and theologian; known in philosophy of religion for his "Five Ways" of proving the existence of an Abrahamic-Christian God as well as his Aristotelian-influenced account of morality.

Aristotle (384–322 bce) Ancient Greek philosopher who was a student of Plato; arguably exerted more influence on Medieval Western philosophy and theology than any other philosopher; known in philosophy of religion especially for his cosmological proofs for the existence of an Unmoved Mover.

àṣẹ Yorùbá term for the fundamental power of the cosmos to make things happen and change; underlies and empowers all things, the *Òrìṣà* included.

āstika Sanskrit term for "affirmer"; usually gets translated as "orthodox," serving to pick out those South Asian *darśana*-s that accept the authority of the *Vedas*.

Ātman Sanskrit term meaning "essence" or "breath," usually denoting the innermost or universal self or "soul" in Hindu philosophies; for some of these philosophies, *paramātman* is the universal or eternal self, which is never born and never dies, whereas *jīvātman* is the individual self, which is embodied and reincarnates.

ʿAṭṭār, Farīd ud-Dīn (Abū Ḥamīd bin Abū Bakr Ibrāhīm, *c.* 1145–*c.* 1221) pen names of a Persian poet and Sufi mystic who wrote several influential works about Sufi philosophy and hagiography including *Conference of the Birds* (*Manṭiq-uṭ-Ṭayr*) and *Memorial of the Saints* (*Tadhkirat al-Auliyaʾ*).

Augustine of Hippo (354–430) Christian bishop and theologian; known especially in philosophy of religion for his doctrines of original sin and predestination, as well as for his philosophical theories about free will and evil.

Avalokiteśvara Sanskrit term for the bodhisattva of compassion; takes female forms in East Asian countries, most notably Guānyīn in China.

avatāra Sanskrit term for "descent"; applies especially to the descents (or "incarnations") of the Hindu God Viṣṇu into human or animal form.

avidyā Sanskrit term for ignorance, misconception, or misunderstanding; the common religio-philosophical "problem" to be overcome in many South Asian philosophies of religion.

axiology English term for the study of what is good or valuable; a collective term for ethics (the study of what is right and good), aesthetics (the study of what is beautiful), and political philosophy; from the Greek words *axia* (value) and *logos* (rational account).

àyànmọ́ Yorùbá term meaning "that which is affixed"; refers to the destiny that is affixed to each person's *orí* (inner head) before birth.

babaláwo Yorùbá term meaning "father of secrets"; applies to a male diviner in the tradition of Ifá.

baptism English term for one of two chief rites for most Christian churches; can involve the full immersion of the entire body in water or the sprinkling of water on the head; symbolizes the cleansing of sins and entry into the Christian church; from the Greek word *baptismos*.

***baqā*'** Arabic term for "subsistence"; used in some Sufi traditions to refer to the state in which the Sufi is mystically unified with and subsists entirely in Allah.

Bāyazīd Bisṭāmī (Abū Yazīd Ṭayfūr bin 'Īsā bin Surūshān al-Bisṭāmī, d. 874–5 or 848–9) Persian Sufi known for developing the notion of *fanā'* (annihilation the self/soul in union with Allah) and for being a "drunken" (*sukr*) Sufi on account of his ecstatic utterances.

Bayes' Theorem English term for a theorem named after Thomas Bayes (1701–61); used to calculate the probability of a hypothesis given evidence that bears on its probability.

Behe, Michael (b. 1952) American biochemist; known especially for his defense of intelligent design and his theory of "irreducible complexity."

Benjamin, Walter (1892–1940) German-Jewish philosopher; known especially in philosophy of religion for his notion of messianism in "On the Concept of History."

Bhagavad Gītā Sanskrit term meaning "Song of the Lord"; a short, eighteen-chapter section within the 1.8-million-word epic *Mahābhārata*; one of the most popular and sacred scriptures for Hindus.

bhakti Sanskrit term literally meaning "attachment"; applies to South Indian religious traditions and movements that emphasize devotional worship of some God.

bhāṣya Sanskrit word for commentary; refers especially to the commentaries written to expound on the *sūtras* of South Asian schools of philosophy.

Big Crunch, Freeze, Rip English terms for three different theories about how the cosmos will "end," whether by returning to a singularity ("crunch") or expanding indefinitely, in the latter case either only between galaxies ("freeze") or also within galaxies ("rip").

bodhicitta (Ch. *pútíxīn* 菩提心) Sanskrit term composed of the words *bodhi*, meaning "enlightened," and *citta*, meaning "mind"; a Mahāyāna Buddhist concept referring to a wish or motivation to attain enlightenment, especially to help other sentient beings attain enlightenment.

Boyer, Pascal (b. 1965) French-American cognitive anthropologist and evolutionary psychologist; known especially for his cognitive scientific accounts of the creation and transmission of religious ideas.

Brahmā Sanskrit term for the God who is commonly held to be a creator or involved in the creation of the cosmos; held to be a creation of Viṣṇu, Śiva, or the Mother Goddess (Mahādevī) in Vaiṣṇavite, Śaivite, or Śaktite Hindu traditions, respectively.

Brahman Sanskrit term for "that which makes great"; understood in some of the *Upaniṣads* and the Vedānta *darśana* as the ultimate reality and source of the cosmos.

brahmin Sanskrit term for those of the priestly caste, the highest of the four castes in Vedic religion and, subsequently, Hinduism.

Buber, Martin (1878–1965) German-Jewish philosopher and mystic known for his "dialogical philosophy" of relationship between an I (*Ich*) and a You (*Du*).

buddha Sanskrit term meaning "one who has awakened"; refers to the historical Buddha (Gautama, *c.* 563–*c.* 483 bce) as well many other buddhas, e.g., the Buddha of the Pure Land, Amitābha.

buddha-land (Sk. *buddhakṣetra*; Ch. *jìngtǔ*, 淨土) English term for the celestial "field" or "realm" of a buddha in which that buddha exerts superhuman activity and influence; especially important in Mahāyāna Buddhism, which recognizes an infinite number of buddha-lands, some "pure lands," other impure (e.g., our own).

buddha-nature (Sk. *tathāgatagarbha* or *buddhadhātu*; Ch. *fóxìng*, 佛性) English term used for different Sanskrit terms, especially *tathāgatagarbha* (womb or embryo [*garbha*] of one who has "thus-gone" [*tathāgata*], i.e., a buddha) and *buddhadhātu* (the realm or substrate of a buddha); a key concept in many forms of East Asian Buddhism that refers to the innate potential of all sentient beings to attain enlightenment.

buddhadhātu see "Buddha-nature"

Buddhism English term for a South Asian religion that spread throughout Southeast and East Asia in its first 500 years, eventually coming to be known as "Theravāda" ("the way of the elders") in most South and Southeast Asian regions, "Mahāyāna" ("the great path") in most East Asian regions, and "Vajrayāna" ("the thunderbolt path") in Tibet.

Bultmann, Rudolf (1884–1976) German scholar of the New Testament; known especially for advocating an existentialist interpretation and "demythologization" of the Bible.

Butler, Judith (b. 1956) American philosopher known especially for her theory of gender performativity in "Performative Acts and Gender Constitution" (1988).

Cārvāka (aka Lokāyata) Sanskrit term for a materialistic and skeptic school of South Asian philosophy known for rejecting the existence of an immaterial soul and the reliability of inferential reasoning.

Chán (禪) Chinese character literally meaning "meditation"; a form of Mahāyāna Buddhism that dates to the sixth century ce in China; emphasizes direct realization of Buddha-nature through meditative and other means; known in Japan as Zen.

čhaŋnúŋpa wakȟáŋ Lakȟóta term for the "sacred pipe," which was given to the Lakȟóta by White Buffalo Calf Woman and plays an important role in the seven sacred rituals of the Lakȟóta.

chéng (誠) Chinese character for "sincere" or "integrated"; a central concept in the Confucian *Doctrine of the Mean*; a means by which and a state in which the Confucian sage is harmonized or unified with with Heaven (*Tiān*) and earth (*dì*).

Christianity English term for a religion based on the life and teachings of Jesus of Nazareth; divided into four main branches: Orthodox, Catholic, Protestant, and Restorationist; a "soft monotheism" that regards the Trinity—God the Father, God the Son (Jesus Christ), and the Holy Spirit—to be one essence (Gk. *homoousious*) in three substances or persons (*hypostases*).

communion English term for one of two chief rites for most Christian churches; involves drinking wine, juice, or water and eating bread of some kind, the former of which is or symbolizes the blood of Jesus Christ; the latter, his body.

compatibilism English term for a range of philosophical positions that attempt to reconcile causal determinism and free will, arguing (in its classical form) that even while our choices are causally determined we are nevertheless free insofar as we enact our choices.

Confucianism English term for the religio-philosophy that is referred to in China as *rújiā*, the tradition or school (*jiā*) of the scholars (*rú*); as European missionaries and scholars translated "Confucian" texts into European languages during the European Enlightenment, they Latinized the name of Kǒng Fūzǐ ("Master Kong," 551–479 bce) as "Confucius" and created the religio-philosophy of "Confucianism."

Confucius (551–479 bce) Commonly credited as the founder of "Confucianism," even though he thought of himself simply as restoring the traditions and teachings of scholars (*rú*) who had come before him; the Latinized form of Kǒng Fūzǐ (Kǒngzǐ for short), meaning "Master Kong."

Continental philosophy of religion a contemporary, Western style of philosophizing about religion that rivals "analytic" or "Anglo-American" philosophy of religion; known as "continental" since it draws upon philosophers from the Continent of Europe; employs tools from the twentieth-century philosophical movements of *phenomenology* and *hermeneutics*, seeking experiential intuition and interpretive insight.

cosmogony English term for a theory about the origin of the cosmos; from the Greek words *kosmos* (cosmos) and *gonos* (offspring).

cosmological proofs English term for a variety of proofs that argue from the existence of the cosmos or the most basic features of it (e.g., causation, motion, contingency) to the existence of a divine cause or creator of the cosmos.

cosmology English term for a theory about the nature of the cosmos, including its fundamental constituents, forces, and laws; from the Greek words *kosmos* (cosmos) and *logos* (rational account).

Craig, William Lane (b. 1949) American-Christian philosopher, theologian, and apologist; known in the philosophy of religion for his cosmological "*kalām*" proof for the existence of God.

creatio ex nihilo Latin term for "creation out of nothing"; the doctrine that God created the cosmos from out of nothing, i.e., not from preexisting materials or chaos; a common teaching in the Abrahamic religions, especially Christian theology.

Daly, Mary (1928–2010) American feminist philosopher and theologian; known especially for her critiques of androcentrism in Western religion and for her constructive feminist theologies and philosophies.

Dào*/*dào (道) Chinese character for "path" or "way"; in general, a *dào* is a "guiding way" or "guiding discourse" for some school of philosophy (e.g., the *dào* of *rú* for Confucians, and the *dào* of *mò* for Mohists); for Daoists, *Dào* is the mysterious source of the cosmos and pervading force that patterns its operation.

Dàodéjīng (道德經) Chinese characters meaning "the classic [*jīng*] of the way [*Dào*] and its power/virtue [*dé*]"; traditionally ascribed to the mythical sage Lǎozǐ (sixth century bce), though more likely a composite work of many authors (dated to around the third century bce); regarded as one of the core, classic "scriptures" of Daoism.

Daoism English term for the religio-philosophy that is known in China as *Dàojiā* or *Dàojiào*, the "school" (*jiā*) or "teachings" (*jiào*) of the *Dào*; arguable origins in the individuals and communities who wrote the classic Daoist texts *Dàodéjīng* and *Zhuāngzǐ*; consists now of two main institutionalized sects, the Way of Orthodox Unity (Zhèngyī Dào), which is prominent in the south, and The Way of Complete Perfection (Quánzhēn Dào), which is prominent in the north.

darśana Sanskrit term used for the auspicious seeing of a deity in the form of a statue (*mūrti*); also applies to South Asian "schools" of religion/philosophy that have different "views" or "perspectives" about what is real, true, and good.

Dawkins, Richard (b. 1941) British evolutionary biologist; known for his gene-centered view of evolution, critique of intelligent design, and atheistic philosophy.

Day of the Lord [YHWH] English term for an Abrahamic theological concept; the eschatological time during which cataclysmic events will occur, the dead will be resurrected, and all people will be judged and consigned to their ultimate fate.

dé (德) Chinese character frequently translated as "power" or "virtue"; the power of virtue and virtuous people to realize effects in the world; with respect to the *Dàodéjīng*, *dé* is the power of *Dào* to make all things function in their natural forms and functions as well as the power of humans to act in accordance with the rhythms and patterns of *Dào*.

deductive argument English term for an argumentative form in which the conclusion of the argument is necessarily true if the premises of the argument are true (e.g., if all humans are mortal, and if Socrates is a human, then Socrates is mortal).

deism English term for the philosophical position that holds that although a God creates and designs the cosmos (usually as perfectly orderly), that God does not intervene in it (e.g., through miracles).

Deloria, Vine, Jr. (1933–2005) Lakȟóta philosopher, historian, and activist; known especially for his exposition of Native American philosophy, defense of Native American rights, and critique of Euro-American religio-philosophies and political policies.

Dembski, William (b. 1960) American mathematician, philosopher, and Christian apologist; known for his defense of intelligent design, especially his theory of "specified complexity."

Demiurge English term from the Greek *dēmiurgos*; used by the ancient Greek philosopher Plato (427–347 bce) to refer to a God-like being who creates the cosmos out of preexisting materials.

Derrida, Jacques (1930–2004) French philosopher commonly characterized as "postmodern" or "poststructural"; known in general for his deconstructive analysis of language and in the philosophy of religion for his notion of messianicity.

Descartes, René (1596–1650) French Enlightenment philosopher, mathematician, and scientist; best known with respect to the philosophy of religion for his defense of mind/body dualism and ontological proofs for the existence of God.

design proofs see teleological proofs.

determinism English term for a range of philosophical positions that maintain that human behavior is either entirely determined by laws of nature ("hard" or "causal" determinism) or partially or probabilistically determined by laws of nature ("soft" determinism).

dharma Sanskrit term with a wide range of meanings, including sacred duty (especially as determined by caste), reality as it truly is, and teachings or truth; used over the last few centuries to translate the English term *religion*.

***dharma*-s** Sanskrit term used in the Buddhist *Abhidharma* to refer to the underlying constituents of experience; in the Chinese Buddhist school of Huáyán, reality is understood as a grand harmony of interdependent and interpenetrative *dharma*-s (Ch. *shì*, 事).

dì (地) Chinese character for "earth"; one goal of Confucian practice, especially as expounded in *The Doctrine of the Mean*, is to form a harmonious trinity between humans, Heaven (*Tiān*) and earth.

Dialectical idealism English term for a philosophical concept attributed to Georg Wilhelm Friedrich Hegel; understands development in human history to occur due to the "negation" of one idea by another and the "preservation" and "transcendence" of these ideas in a higher-order idea.

Dialectical materialism English term for a philosophical-political theory attributed to Karl Marx and Friedrich Engels; understands development in human history to occur due to irreconcilable "contradictions" between material forces of production and social relations of production.

Dionysius the Areopagite (*c.* sixth century ce) unknown author(s) of texts purportedly written by a first-century Greek convert of the Apostle Paul; exponent of a "negative theology" in which "divine names" are negated of a transcendent God.

Doctrine of the Mean (*Zhōngyōng*, 中庸) one of the "Four Books" of Confucianism; traditionally ascribed to Confucius' grandson Zǐsī; portrays the relationship between humans and Heaven (*Tiān*) in quasi-mystical terms.

Dōgen (道元, 1200–53) Japanese Zen Buddhist in the Sōtō tradition; known for holding that the practice of *zazen* just is enlightenment, as well as for his innovative concept of "time-being" (Jp. *uji*), the interconnectedness of all things and all moments.

Dominican Order English term for an order of the Catholic Church founded in 1216 to preach, teach, and combat heresy; renowned for producing many leading Catholic theologians and philosophers, most notably Thomas Aquinas.

Draper, Paul (b. 1957) American philosopher of religion; known especially for his evidential argument from evil.

dualism English term referring to the conceptual division of something into two opposed aspects; two philosophical forms of dualism include *metaphysical dualism*, which divides the most fundamental aspects of reality into two (e.g., a cosmic mind and primordial matter), and *mind–body* *dualism*, which understands humans to be composed of two different substances, mind/soul and body/brain.

duḥkha Sanskrit term for "suffering," "painfulness," or "unsatisfactoriness"; the "First Noble Truth of Buddhism."

è (惡) Chinese character meaning "bad," "detestable," "revolting," or "ugly"; used by the fifth-generation Confucian Xúnzǐ (313–238 bce) in his argument that human nature (*xìng*) is naturally inclined toward selfish desire.

ẹbọ Yorùbá term meaning "sacrifice"; applies to the sacrifices that are made to the *Òrìṣà*, including at the conclusion of Ifá divination.

Eckhart, Meister (Eckhart von Hochheim, *c.* 1260–*c.* 1328) Christian Catholic (Dominican) philosopher, theologian, and mystic; known for advocating the "birthing of God's Son" (Jesus Christ) in the human soul; accused and tried as a heretic late in life.

egúngún Yorùbá term for an annual festival at which recently deceased family heads are represented by masked dancers, through whom ancestors can revisit the earth, communicate with descendants, and listen to their requests; also used to refer to ancestors, especially those of family heads.

Eight Limbs English term for the eight-step path employed in the Hindu *darśana* of Yoga (restraint, self-discipline, posture, breath-control, sense-withdrawal, concentration, meditation, and absorption).

Eightfold Path English term for the eight-step path that is employed in schools of Buddhism (Right View, Right Intention, Right Speech, Right Action, Right Livelihood, Right Effort, Right Mindfulness, and Right Meditation).

èmí Yorùbá term for the life-breath that is breathed into the human body by Olódùmarè before birth and that survives the death of the body, reincarnating to another body; sometimes translated as "soul."

empiricism English term for the philosophical theory that all knowledge is the product of sense-experience.

'Ên Sôp Hebrew term meaning "without end," "without limit," or "infinite"; used in Jewish Kabbalah to refer to YHWH prior to self-manifestation and creation.

Epicureanism English term for a Greco-Roman school of philosophy founded in the late fourth century bce by the ancient Greek philosopher Epicurus (341–270 bce); Epicureans were metaphysical atomists who pursued lives of simple, sustained pleasure through an absence of bodily pain and a freedom from fear (especially about death and divine punishment).

epistemic virtues English term that is deployed in a variety of ways, here for the range of virtues or properties that humans take true theories to possess (e.g., empirical accuracy, external coherence, practical usefulness, internal consistency, theoretical simplicity, and explanatory scope).

epistemology English term for the study of what is true; includes the nature, sources, limits, justification, and structure of knowledge; traditionally included logic as well; from the Greek words *epistemē* (knowledge) and *logos* (rational account).

eschatology English term for a theory about the end of the cosmos or the ultimate destiny of humans; from the Greek words *eschatos* (end) and *logos* (rational account).

ẹsẹ̀ Yorùbá term literally meaning "leg"; applied to the principle of individual effort and struggle by which the potentialities and destinies of one's *orí* are actualized.

Èṣù Yorùbá term for one of the "primordial" *Òrìṣà* present with Olódùmarè before the creation of the cosmos; straddles the "left/right" divide between the *Òrìṣà* and *Ajogun*, delivering sacrifices to both at the conclusion of Ifá divination; sows confusion and conflict when sacrifices are performed incorrectly or not at all.

ethnophilosophy English term used to refer to the indigenous philosophical worldview of some ethnic group, usually from sub-Saharan Africa; coined by the Beninese philosopher Paulin Hountondji in criticism of the Belgian missionary Placide Tempels's study of the ethnophilosophy of the Bantu people of central and southern Africa.

Euthyphro Dilemma English term for a theological and moral dilemma first posed by the character Socrates in Plato's dialogue *Euthyphro*; the dilemma asks whether the (ancient Greek) Gods love piety because it is pious, or whether piety is pious because the Gods love it.

fà (法) Chinese character used by Mohists to refer to a model, paradigm, or standard that serves as a tool or aid for guiding an action or making a judgment; includes rules or definitions, prototypes or pictures, actual tools or measuring devices, concepts, and role models.

falsafa Arabic word for "philosophy"; applies especially to Islamic philosophy, particularly in contradistinction to Islamic theology (*kalām*).

fanā' Arabic word for "annihilation"; used in some Sufi traditions to refer to the annihilation or passing away of an individual self that is separate from Allah.

Fǎzàng (法藏, 643–712) Third patriarch of Huáyán Buddhism in China; very influential for the philosophical articulation of Huáyán, especially the understanding of reality as a grand harmony of interdependent and interpenetrative *dharma*-s (*shì*).

fēi (非) Chinese character for "not" or "wrong"; debates between Confucians and Mohists attempted to distinguish what is "this" or "right" (*shì*) from what is "not" or "wrong" (*fēi*).

feminist philosophy of religion English term for philosophies that both apply feminist critiques to religion or philosophy, especially patriarchal conceptions of God(s) and rationality, and develop feminist theories and methods of philosophizing about religion, especially ones that decenter male-dominant perspectives and biases.

Feuerbach, Ludwig (1804–72) German anthropologist and philosopher; an atheist and materialist "Left Hegelian" known for his assertion that "theology is anthropology."

Five Constant Relationships (Ch. *wǔlún*, 五倫) Chinese characters for the five sets of hierarchical and reciprocal human relationships that structure society: (1) father/son, (2) older sibling/younger sibling, (3) husband/wife, (4) elder/younger, (5) ruler/subject; in each case, superior takes responsibility for inferior, and inferior respects superior.

Five Great Vows English term for the five cardinal virtues of Jainism (which apply to both monastics and lay practitioners): non-hurting (*ahiṃsā*), truthfulness (*satya*), non-stealing (*asteya*), sexual purity (*brahmacarya*), and non-grasping (*aparigraha*).

Five Pillars of Islam (Ar. *Arkān al-Islām*) English term for the five core practices of Islam: *shahādah* (profession of faith), *ṣalāh* (five daily prayers), *zakāt* (giving of alms), *ṣawm* (fasting during Ramadan), and *ḥajj* (pilgrimage to Mecca).

Forman, Robert K. C. (b. 1947) American philosopher and mystic; known for his advocation of a "pure consciousness event" that is cross-culturally identical, conceptually un-mediated, and linguistically inexpressible.

Four Books (*sìshū*, 四書) Chinese characters for the four Confucian books that were selected, edited, and commented on by (Neo)Confucian philosopher Zhū Xī in the Song Dynasty and later become the curriculum for civil service exams in China (from 1313–1905); they include Confucius's *Analects* and Mencius's *Mencius* as well as *The Great Learning* and *The Doctrine of the Mean.*

Four Causes English term for Aristotle's four means of explaining the nature and function of individual substances; every substance has a material explanation (what it is made of); a formal explanation (its shape, which is determined by the particular kind of thing it is); an efficient explanation (how it was caused to come to be); and a final explanation (what its ideal function is).

Four Noble Truths English term for the four core teachings or truths of the historical Buddha and Buddhism in general: suffering (*duḥkha*) exists, suffering is caused by our clinging to and ignorance about impermanent things, suffering has a solution, and that solution is the Eightfold Noble Path.

Four Sprouts (*duān*, 端) English term for the teaching of the fourth-generation Confucian philosopher Mencius that there is an innate "sprout" or "beginning" in the human heart-mind (*xīn*) for each of the four Confucian virtues; compassion is the "sprout" of *rén* (human-heartedness); shame, of *yì* (moral rightness); respect, of *lǐ* (ritual propriety); and approval of right and disapproval of wrong, of *zhì* (moral wisdom).

Franciscans English term for a group of related mendicant orders of the Catholic Church founded in 1209 by Saint Francis of Assisi (1181/1182–1226); among the more notable Franciscan philosophers or theologians are Bonaventure (1221–74) and John Duns Scotus (1265/6–1308).

Gautama Buddha (*c.* 563–*c.* 483 bce) "Gautama" was the given name of the man commonly referred to as the (historical) Buddha, who lived and taught in what is now northern India and Nepal and is recognized as the founder of Buddhism; other traditional names for him include Siddhārtha (one who has attained his goal), Śākyamuni (sage from the Śākya clan), and Tathāgata (one who has thus gone).

Gbadegesin, Segun (b. 1945) Yorùbá philosopher; known for devoting philosophical attention both to substantive issues in traditional African and Yorùbá philosophy (including the person and individuality, community and morality, and religiosity and causality) and to "contemporary African social, political, and economic realities."

Geist German term meaning "ghost," "spirit," "mind," and "consciousness"; employed by Georg Wilhelm Friedrich Hegel for the spirit/mind of the world (*Weltgeist*), which dialectically and progressively unfolds in history through the minds/spirits of different nations (*Volksgeister*), all of whom are utilized by *Geist* itself as "absolute spirit."

géwù (格物) Chinese characters for the "investigation of things"; the means by which many (Neo)Confucian philosophers strove to see the natural patterns of Heaven (*Tiān*) and moral patterns of humankind; identified in the *Great Learning* as the key means of bringing about "peace in the world"; later made prominent by the twelfth-century Song Dynasty Confucian Zhū Xī (1130–1200).

Ghost Dance English term for a dance ritual revealed by the Paiute prophet Wovoka and practiced by many Native American tribes during the late nineteenth century; Wovoka taught that the dance would bring dead Native Americans back to life, remove European Americans from the continent, and restore peace and harmony to Native American peoples.

gōng'àn (公案; Jp. *kōan*) Chinese characters literally meaning "public case"; records of elliptic and enigmatic questions and exchanges between masters and students that were used to test progress or taken as objects of meditation in Chán/Zen Buddhism.

Great Learning (*Dàxué*, 大學) one of the "Four Books" of Confucianism; traditionally ascribed to Confucius' disciple Zēngzǐ; amalgamated into the Confucian classic *The Record of Rites*; later extracted by Zhū Xī; known for its eight-step connection between the "investigation of things" and "peace in the world."

Guānyīn (觀音) see Avalokiteśvara

guǐ 鬼 (ghost) Chinese character for "ghost"; according to some "folk Chinese" beliefs, the *pò* soul becomes a wandering ghost in the case of untimely and tragic deaths.

gùn Yorùbá term for "riding" or "mounting," the process in which an *Òrìṣà* possesses their devotee, usually during rhythmic dance.

guṇa Sanskrit term for quality, attribute, or property; in the Sāṁkhya school of philosophy, three primordial *guṇa*-s disturb the equilibrium of *prakṛti* at the beginning of every cosmic cycle, causing it to evolve; in the Vedānta school of philosophy, it is common to differentiate between *Brahman* without or before qualities (*nirguṇa*) and *Brahman* with qualities (*saguṇa*).

ḥadīth Arabic term literally meaning "tradition"; refers to collections of sayings and doings of Prophet Muḥammad, each authenticated by a transmission chain; often consulted in matters of Islamic jurisprudence (*fiqh*), ranking second in authority after Qur᾽ān.

hălākâ Hebrew term literally meaning "the way to behave"; refers to the body of Jewish laws that were derived from the 613 commandments (*mitzvot*) in the Torah and the interpretation of these commandments in the Talmud.

haŋbléčeyapi Lakȟóta term meaning "crying for a vision"; more commonly known as a "vision quest"; a four-day period of solitary fasting and prayer during which a person receives a vision from the spirits; one of the seven sacred rituals of the Lakȟóta.

ḥaqq Arabic terms meaning "real" or "true"; one of the ninety-nine names of Allah; some Sufis (e.g., al-Ḥallāj) claimed that they were "the true/real" during mystical experience because their own self (*nafs*) was annihilated (*fanā᾽*) and they subsisted only in God (*baqā᾽*).

hard problem of consciousness English term for the philosophical and scientific problem of explaining how and why conscious, first-person awareness is a product of brain states; distinguished from "easy problems of consciousness" that merely identify the brain mechanisms and functions involved; for some philosophers and scientists, there is no hard problem of consciousness since consciousness simply reduces to or is eliminated by brain mechanisms and functions.

Haribhadra (*c.* eighth-century) Jain philosopher known for propounding the "doctrine of non-one-sidedness" (*anekāntavāda*) in his *Victory Banner of the Many Pointed Doctrine* (*Anekāntajayapatākā*).

Hartshorne, Charles (1897–2000) American philosopher who developed the process philosophy of Alfred North Whitehead into a process theology.

Hegel, Georg Wilhelm Friedrich (1770–1831) German philosopher; arguably the single most important and influential "German Idealist"; known in the philosophy of religion for giving lectures on the "philosophy of religion" as such, and for a dialectical-historical account of the unfolding of *Geist* in different religio-philosophies through time from East to West.

hermeneutics English term for the philosophy of interpretation, especially textual interpretation; began in the early European Enlightenment with biblical and legal interpretation; later became a philosophical movement that explored the interpretation of experience more broadly.

heyókȟa Lakȟóta term literally meaning "crazy" that applies to people who have had visions of the Wakiŋyaŋ ("Thunder Beings") and thereafter behave in an "opposite" or "backwards" fashion, flaunting social convention and taboo.

Hick, John (1922–2012) British philosopher of religion; best known for his defense of a religious pluralism that postulates a common ground ("the Real-in-itself") for the diverse religious experiences and ideas of humankind ("the Real-as-experienced-and-thought").

Hinduism English term for a South Asian religion or family of related religions; taken widely, the label includes all Indians and all religio-philosophies that have their origin on the Indian subcontinent (including Jainism, Buddhism, and Sikhism); taken more narrowly, the label applies to a certain form of modern Hinduism that prioritizes acceptance of *Vedas* as revealed scripture, recognizes the many Gods as facets of one underlying divine reality (usually called *Brahman*), and engages in devotional worship of one or more of these Gods.

Hōnen (法然, 1133–1212) Japanese Buddhist monk who left the Tendai order to teach that devotional recitation of the name of Amitābha was sufficient for enlightenment; regarded as the founder of Jōdo-shū (Pure Land) Buddhism in Japan.

Huáyán (華嚴) Chinese characters literally meaning "flower garland"; the name of a school of East Asian (Mahāyāna) Buddhism that was founded in the latter-half of the first millennium; one of its more notable teachings interprets emptiness as the interdependence and interpenetration of all things in a grand harmony; known in Japan as Kegon.

Huìnéng (Dàjiàn Huìnéng, 大鑒惠能, 638–713) Legendary "Sixth Patriarch" of Chán Buddhism in China; regarded as the founder of the "Sudden Enlightenment" Southern school of Chán; known for delivering the *Platform Sūtra of the Sixth Patriarch* (*Liùzǔ Tánjīng*).

Hume, David (1711–76) Scottish Enlightenment philosopher best known for his radical empiricism, critique of substance-self and causality, and arguments against proofs for the existence of God and the rationality of belief in miracles.

hún (魂) Chinese character for one of two kinds of souls; associated with *yáng*; rises upward to heaven upon death, becoming a spirit (*shén*) that can be invited to reside in an ancestral tablet, where it looks after the well-being and prosperity of the family in return for proper veneration and attention.

hyperactive agent detection device hypothesized cognitive module of humans (and other animals) that "detects" for and ascribes agency even when none is involved; some cognitive scientists of religion maintain that the creation of and belief in ideas of superhuman agents such as Gods, Spirits, and Ancestors is the result of such "hyperactivity."

ibn ʻArabī (Abū ʿAbd Allāh Muḥammad ibn ʿAlī ibn Muḥammad ibnʿArabī al-Ḥātimī aṭ-Ṭāʾī, 1165–1240) Andalusian Muslim philosopher and mystic known for his unparalleled articulation of Sufi metaphysics; later known in Sufi traditions as "the Greatest Master."

ibn Rushd (Abū l-Walīd Muḥammad ibn ʾAḥmad ibn Rušd, 1126–98) Andalusian Muslim philosopher, jurist, and physician; best known for his defense of "the philosophers" against the attacks of al-Ghazālī in ibn Rushd's *Incoherence of the Incoherence* (*Tahāfut al-Tahāfut*).

ibn Sīnā (Abū ʿAlī al-Ḥusayn bin ʿAbdullāh ibn al-Ḥasan bin ʿAlī bin Sīnā al-Balkhi al-Bukhari, 980–1037) Persian philosopher and physician; known in the philosophy of religion for his "Proof of the Truthful" as well as for being one of the targets of al-Ghazālī's condemnation of Islamic philosophy.

ideology English term used in Marxist philosophy to refer to the ideas and practices deployed by the state to legitimate itself and the economic modes of production and social relations of production that it maintains; understood by the post-Marxist philosopher Louis Althusser (1918–90) as *ideological state apparatuses* that included even private means not under the direct control of the state.

Ifá Yorùbá term that applies to a divination method, a set of scriptures, and an *Òrìṣà*; the divination method is used to generate a number that corresponds to a chapter in the scriptures that offers insight about the client's problem or question; the *Òrìṣà* (also known as Ọrunmila or Ọrúnla, the *Òrìṣà* of divination, destiny, and wisdom) is the ultimate source of these scriptures and guarantor of this divination method.

Ikkyū (Ikkyū Sōjun, 一休宗純, 1394–1481) Japanese Zen Buddhist monk and poet; known for insisting that enlightenment could be attained and furthered through conventionally immoral acts, especially sex, which he regarded as a religious rite.

Iktómi Lakȟóta name for a trickster God who usually takes the form of a spider; tricks the Lakȟóta into leaving their subterranean home for the Black Hills; also teaches them how to make fire, obtain and prepare food, build shelter, and make clothing.

Ilé-Ifẹ̀ Yorùbá term for the city of Ife, which is located in the southwestern region of present-day Nigeria; according to the Ifá tradition and Yorùbá culture more widely, Ifẹ̀ is where the *Òrìṣà* first descended to earth; it therefore constitutes the sacred city and center for Yorùbá religion.

inductive argument English term for an argumentative form in which the conclusion is only ever strong or probable (never true) given the truth of the premises (e.g., if this raven is black and that raven is black [and so forth], then all ravens are black).

inípi Lakȟóta term meaning "they make spirit"; more commonly known as a "sweat lodge"; one of the seven sacred rites of the Lakȟóta; a rite of purification that serves as preparation for other rituals, transitioning participants from the mundane to the sacred, bringing them into a state of peaceful relationality with all things.

Intelligent Design English term for the theory that that certain features or organisms of the universe could not have evolved through natural selection alone and therefore must have been "intelligently designed" by some God; commonly regarded as "pseudoscience."

interaction problem English term for the philosophical problem of how a material body and immaterial mind interact.

Irigaray, Luce (b. 1930) French feminist philosopher and cultural theorist; known in the philosophy of religion for her deconstruction of patriarchal conceptions of God(s) and her advocation of a "feminine divine" that is fully immanent in the female self.

Isaac Luria (1534–72) Jewish rabbi and mystic; developed Jewish Kabbalah into what is now called "Lurianic Kabbalah," particularly with respect to the notions of *ṣimṣûm*, *shevirah*, and *tiqqûn*.

Islam Arabic term meaning "submission [to Allah]," also connoting peace and wholeness; an Abrahamic religion commonly said to have been founded by Prophet Muḥammad in the seventh century, though claimed by Muḥammad and Muslims to be the original religion dating back to Abraham (if not Adam); the second largest religion of the world; comprised of two main branches, Sunni and Shīʿa.

Īśvara Sanskrit term meaning "Lord"; used in some Hindu philosophies, most notably Nyāya, for a cosmic creator/designer.

Īśvara Kṛṣṇa (*c.* fourth century ce) South Asian philosopher who authored the *Sāṁkhya Kārikā*, the earliest surviving authoritative text of Sāṁkhya philosophy.

Jainism English term for a South Asian religion that teaches a dualistic theory of reality, in which everything is composed of souls (*jīva*-s) that are entrapped in and deluded by matter (*pudgala*); constituted by two main branches, Śvētāmbara, meaning "white-clad," the monks of which wear only a loin cloth, and Digambara, meaning "sky-clad," the monks of which go naked.

James, William (1842–1910) American philosopher and psychologist; known as the founder of American psychology and a founder of American pragmatism; important to the philosophy of religion for his studies of and theories about religious experience; commonly regarded as a "perennialist."

Jantzen, Grace (1948–2006) Canadian feminist philosopher of religion; known in philosophy of religion both for her critique of philosophy of religion as "necrophiliac," obsessed with death and violence, and for her development of a feminist philosophy, centered on the notions of natality and flourishing.

Jesus of Nazareth (*c.* 5 bce–*c.* 33 ce) Jewish religious teacher and miracle worker; crucified by the ruling Romans for blasphemy and sedition; believed by Christians to have risen from the dead three days later and to have ascended into heaven forty days after that; for (most) Christians, Jesus' death and resurrection makes possible their salvation from sin and reconciliation with God.

jina Sanskrit term meaning "conqueror"; applied by Jains to one who not only attains liberation and therefore release from rebirth but also teaches others this way of liberation; used in reference to Mahāvīra (599–527 bce) and the twenty-three *jina*-s (aka *tīrthaṅkara*-s) to proceed him.

jìngzuò (靜坐) Chinese characters for "quiet sitting"; a meditative practice advocated by some (Neo)Confucians that was influenced by, but distinct from, Buddhist and Daoist meditation practices in medieval China.

jīva Sanskrit term used for "soul," especially in Jainism, for which everything is a combination of soul (*jīva*) and not-soul (*ajīva*).

jñāna Sanskrit term meaning "knowledge"; in Hinduism *jñāna* is often categorized as one of three paths or *yoga*-s by which to attain release from rebirth (the other two of which are *karma*/action and *bhakti*/devotion.

Judaism English term for the oldest of the Abrahamic religions; commonly divided into three periods: Israelite religion during the First Temple in Jerusalem, which largely revolved around temple offering and sacrifice (*c.* 957–*c.* 586 bce); Second Temple Judaism (*c.* 515 bce–70 ce), at which time temple worship was gradually accompanied by Torah study and observance; and Rabbinic Judaism (70–present), for which there is no longer temple worship.

jūnzǐ (君子) Chinese characters for "profound person," "gentlemen," or "person of virtue"; sometimes understood to be the middle stage in the development of the Confucian sage (*shèngrén*), the first of which is the scholar (*shì*).

Kabbalah Hebrew word literally meaning "tradition" or "reception"; used to refer to a form of Jewish mysticism with historical origins in twelfth-century Europe (though traditionally believed to be the mystical secrets revealed to Moses by YHWH on Mount Sinai).

kaivalya Sanskrit word meaning isolation, detachment, or solitude; for Jainism (in which *kaivalya* is also known as *kevala*), the ultimate goal is the isolation of the soul (*jīva*) from matter (*pudgala*); for Sāṁkhya-Yoga, it is the isolation of pure consciousness (*Puruṣa*) from matter-mind (*prakṛti*).

kalām Arabic word for "speech" or "word" (among other things); applies to Islamic theology, especially in contradistinction to Islamic philosophy (*falsafa*).

kalpa see *yuga*

Kaṇāda (*c.* 200 bce) South Asian philosopher; founder of the Vaiśeṣika school of philosophy and author of the *Vaiśeṣika Sūtras*.

Kant, Immanuel (1724–1804) German philosopher; arguably the most important philosopher in "modern" European philosophy; known in the philosophy of religion for his critiques of the ontological, cosmological, and teleological-design proofs for the existence of God, and for his argument that free will, immortality, and a rewarding/punishing God must be presupposed due to the existence and nature of moral experience.

karma Sanskrit word meaning action or deed; generally viewed by South Asian religio-philosophies as a principle according to which all moral action necessarily generates moral effects, whether good or bad, whether in this life or a future life; insofar as a person has *karmic* effects still to take effect, that person is trapped in the cycle of rebirth (*saṃsāra*).

kasb Arabic word for "acquisition"; according to the Ashʿarite school of Islamic theology, humans "acquire" their actions and responsibility for them insofar as they will them, even though Allah causes these actions to be realized in the world.

Katz, Steven (b. 1944) American Jewish philosopher and historian; known in the philosophy of religion for his defense of a "contextualist" understanding of mystical experience over against perennialism.

kevala see *kaivalya*

Kripal, Jeffrey (b. 1962) American scholar of religion; known especially for his studies of paranormal phenomena, esotericism, gnosticism, New Age religion, and comparative religion more generally.

kōan see *gōng'àn*

Lakȟóta Lakȟóta term for a Native American "nation" or "tribe" belonging to the "Seven Fireplaces" (Očhéthi Šakówiŋ), which is more commonly known since Western colonization as the "Sioux" and divided into three linguistic groups: Lakȟóta (or Teton), Dakȟóta (or Yankton), and Nakȟóta (or Santee).

Lǎozǐ (老子, *c.* sixth century bce) Chinese title meaning "Old Master"; applied to the quasi-historical Chinese sage Lǐ Ěr or Lǐ Dān; traditionally held to be the author of the *Dàodéjīng*.

lǐ (禮) Chinese character for rites, ceremonies, rituals, customs, and etiquette; for Confucius and other Confucians, proper performance of *lǐ* is one of the four cardinal Confucian virtues (along with *rén*, *yì*, and *zhì*).

lǐ (理) Chinese character for pattern-principle; used by Huáyán Buddhism to refer to a cosmic pattern-principle that harmonizes all phenomena (*shì*, 事) in mutual interrelation and interpenetration; used by Song Dynasty (Neo)Confucianism to refer to cosmic pattern-principle that informs vital energy (*qì*).

liberation theology English term for a theological approach, typically Christian, with roots in the later twentieth century, that emphasizes liberation of the oppressed from structures of oppression.

libertarianism English term for a range of philosophical positions that maintain that humans are not causally determined and therefore are free (both to choose and to enact that choice).

Línjì Yìxuán (臨濟義玄, d. 866) Chinese Buddhist monk; the founder of the Línjì school of Chán Buddhism.

Locke, John (1632–1704) British philosopher and physician; one of the first and most famous empiricists; known with respect to the philosophy of religion for his cosmological proof of the existence of God and his argument that reason should regulate claims of faith.

logos Greek word for "word" or "reason" (among other things); plays a role in the creation of the cosmos, especially with respect to the types of beings in it, in some ancient Greco-Roman and Abrahamic philosophies; held to be Jesus Christ in the New Testament books of John and Revelations.

Lotus Sūtra one of the most influential Mahāyāna Buddhist *sūtras*; especially important for the Tiāntāi/Tendai, Chán/Zen, and Nichiren schools of Buddhism.

Madhva (1238–1317) Hindu philosopher and chief proponent of Dvatia (dual) Vedānta; held that there were five kinds of fundamental differences: *Brahman* and insentient matter (*prakṛti*), *Brahman* and souls (*jīva*-s), souls and matter, different souls, and different material things.

Madhyamaka Sanskrit term meaning "middle way"; name of the first Mahāyāna Buddhist school of philosophy; founded by the philosopher Nāgārjuna in the second–third century; teaches the emptiness (*śūnyatā*) of all *dharma*-s with respect to their inherent and permanent nature or essence (*svabhāva*).

Mahāvīra Sanskrit term meaning "great hero"; applied to the twenty-fourth and final "conqueror" (*jina*) or "ford-maker" (*tīrthaṅkara*) of Jainism, who is traditionally believed to have lived from 599 to 527 bce.

Mahāyāna see Buddhism

Maimonides (Latinized form of Moses ben Maimon, 1135–1204) Jewish philosopher, rabbi, and physician; known especially for his reconciliation of Judaism with Aristotelian philosophy as well as his codification of Jewish Law (*hălākâ*).

Maitreya Sanskrit term for a bodhisattva who will succeed Gautama Buddha as the next buddha of our buddha-land.

Makinde, Moses Akin (1938–2018) Yorùbá philosopher trained as an analytic philosopher; taught at the University of Ifẹ̀ in Nigeria (among other institutions); argued that Africans should blend Western practices and philosophies with indigenous African elements.

maqaam (pl. = *maqaamat*) Arabic word for "place of residence" or "station"; the *maqaamat* were a series of stations or stages (usually seven) in Sufi practice, which culminated in a state of oneness or closeness with Allah.

Marx, Karl (1818–83) German philosopher, political theorist, and social revolutionary; known in the philosophy of religion for his analysis of religion as one component of an ideological superstructure that serves to legitimate politico-economic orders and realities, especially when religion serves as "the opiate of the masses."

māyā Sanskrit word literally meaning "magic" or "illusion"; in the Hindu *darśana* of Advaita Vedānta, *māyā* is the creative power of *Brahman* to generate the "illusory" multiplicity and change of the cosmos, which humans tend to mistake as really real due to ignorance (*avidyā*).

Mencius (Latinized form of Mèngzǐ, "Master Meng," 孟子, 372–289 bce) Fourth-generation Confucian philosopher; taught that humans are naturally good by virtue of innately possessing four "sprouts" or "beginnings," one for each of the four cardinal Confucian virtues.

***merkābâ-hêkālôt* mysticism** English term for Jewish mystical texts and practices from the first millennium that involve mystical journeys through the spheres or palaces (*hêkālôt*) of heaven to the chariot throne (*merkābâ*) of YHWH.

messiah English term translating the Hebrew *māšîaḥ*, meaning "anointed one"; originally (during First Temple Judaism) applied to a king or priest who was anointed with oil; later (Second Temple Judaism and beyond) came to refer to a figure who would usher in a golden age of justice and peace and create a new heaven and new earth; in Christianity, Jesus Christ is recognized to be the messiah (with the Greek *kristos* translating the Hebrew *māšîaḥ*).

metaphysics English term for the study of what is real, especially that which goes beyond physical reality; its topics include the most general features of reality itself (time, space, substance, generality, causality, numbers), the nature of the self or soul (including free will and determinism), and the existence of God.

Millennialism English term for the Christian belief that there will be a 1,000-year reign of peace prior to the final judgment and the end of this cosmos; applies more broadly to religious or political movements that foretell a future age of peace; from the Latin term *millennium*, meaning "1,000 years."

Mīmāṃsā Sanskrit term for the "Hindu" *darśana* that focuses on the earlier sections of the *Vedas*, maintaining the efficacy of sacrificial fire rituals (*yajña*) for liberation.

mìng (命) Chinese character that originally applied to the "mandate" that the Zhou Dynasty maintained it had received from Heaven (*Tiān*); during the time of Confucius and after, it came to refer to unfortunate "fated" events that were outside human control.

mitákuye oyásiŋ Lakȟóta term meaning "all my relations"; pronounced at the end of every Lakȟóta ceremony to pray for all living things (even rocks) in recognition of a web of relationships that binds all these things together; also serves as an epistemological principle for Lakȟóta philosopher Vine Deloria, Jr.

mitzvot (sing. = mitzvah) Hebrew word for "commandment," 613 of which were revealed by YHWH to Moses on Mt. Sinai; observance of is the means by which Jews maintain their covenantal relationship with YHWH.

Mohism (*Mòjiā*, 墨家) Chinese characters referring to the ancient Chinese philosophical school that followed the teachings of Mòzǐ (*c.* 470–*c.* 391 bce); Mohists were the main rivals to Confucians during the Warring States period (475–221 bce); among their teachings are that all people are "equal before Heaven" and should therefore practice "inclusive care" for each other without respect to kinship or status.

mokṣa Sanskrit term for release from the cycle of rebirth (*saṃsāra*); different Hindu *darśana*-s and religious traditions understand the attainment and state of *mokṣa* differently.

Moses (middle second millennium bce) legendary biblical patriarch; believed to have led the enslaved Hebrews from Egypt to the "Promised Land" of present-day Israel and, in route, to have received the 613 commandments from YHWH on Mount Sinai.

Mòzǐ see Mohism

Mu'tazila Arabic term for an early school of Islamic theology (*kalām*) that flourished during the 'Abbāsid Caliphate in the eighth to tenth centuries; defended the "justice" and "unity" of Allah, the former by holding free will responsible for evil, the latter by denying that Qur'ān is coeternal with Allah.

Muḥammad (Muḥammad ibn 'Abd Allāh, 570–632) Arabian religious, social, and political leader regarded by Muslims as the final prophet from Allah; received the revelation of Qur'ān from the angel Gabriel (Ar. Jibrīl); traditionally regard as the founder of Islam.

mutakallimūn (sing. = *mutakallim*) Arabic term for those who "speak or argue dialectically"; used to refer to Islamic theologians who practice *kalām* (in contradistinction to Islamic philosophers who practice *falsafa*).

mysticism English term that usually refers to the experiential encounter of or union with some God or Ultimate Reality; was also once used to refer to special, esoteric insight or knowledge attained during such experiences or through textual interpretation; etymologically related to the ancient Greek word *muō*, meaning to close or conceal (particularly with respect to the secrets of the Greek "mystery cults," about which initiates should not speak).

nafs Arabic word translated as "soul" or "self"; believed to leave the body at death and later rejoin it on the Day of Judgment; for some Sufi Muslims *nafs* is an obstacle to realizing the oneness of Allah.

Nāgārjuna (*c.* 150–*c.* 250) South Asian Mahāyāna Buddhist philosopher held to be the founder of the Madhyamaka school of Buddhist philosophy.

Nāgasena (*c.* second century bce) South Asian Buddhist monk known for his discourse with King Milinda (which was subsequently titled *Milinda Pañha*, "Questions of Milinda").

nağí Lakȟóta term translated as "spirit" or "ghost"; given to the body at birth and escorted beyond the Milky Way after death to dwell with the ancestors.

nāstika Sanskrit term for "denier"; usually translated as "heterodox," applying to those South Asian *darśana*-s that did not accept the authority of the *Vedas* (especially Buddhists and Jains).

nayavāda Sanskrit term referring to the Jain doctrine of standpoints, according to which the things of reality can only be known from a variety of perspectives (*naya*-*s*).

nèidān (内丹) Chinese characters for "internal alchemy," a variety of ritual, dietary, and meditative means by which Daoists attempt to prolong life or achieve immortality; "internal alchemy" is contrasted with "external alchemy" (*waidan*, 外丹), a means of achieving immortality by partaking of an elixir of immortality.

nepeš Hebrew term often translated as "soul"; refers more particularly to breath or life, distinguishing a principle of vitality from the material body.

něšāmâ Hebrew term often translated as "soul"; refers more particularly to breath or life, especially conscious life.

New Testament The second half of the Christian Bible; contains accounts of the life and teachings of Jesus (Gospels), a history of the early Christian church (Acts), letters written to early Christian churches (Epistles), and a prophecy of the end of time (Revelations); canonized in the late fourth century.

ní (or *niyá*) Lakȟóta term translated as "life," "breath," or "ghost"; given to the body at birth; returns to the *Wakȟáŋ Tȟáŋka* after death to await entry into a new body.

niànfó (念佛, Jp. *nembutsu*) Chinese term translating the Sanskrit term *buddhānusmṛti*, meaning "recollection of the buddha"; refers to the practice of repeating the name of Amitābha, the buddha of infinite light and life.

Nichiren (日蓮, 1222–82) Japanese Buddhist monk; left the Tendai order to begin what would late be called "Nichiren Buddhism"; taught that only the recitation of the *Lotus Sūtra* was effective (during the *Mappō Dharma*) and that the entire *sūtra* was present in one single line: "Homage to the wonderful *Lotus Sūtra*" (Jp. *namu myōhō renge kyō*).

Nietzsche, Friedrich (1844–1900) German philosopher and philologist; known especially in the philosophy of religion for his proclamation that "God is dead," his claim that religion is a "no-saying" to life, and his genealogical account of morality.

nirvāṇa (Ch. *nièpán*, 涅槃) Sanskrit term meaning "to blow out"; refers to the elimination of suffering (*duḥkha*) in a particular lifetime as well as the release from rebirth (*parinirvāṇa*) upon death after *nirvāṇa* has been realized in a particular lifetime.

Nyāya Sanskrit term for the Hindu *darśana* that focuses on the valid means of attaining knowledge (*pramāṇa*) and the logic of inferential reasoning (*anumāna*); merges with Vaiśeṣika in the second millennium; also known for propounding proofs for the existence of *Īśvara*.

Ọbàtálá Yorùbá term for the *Òrìṣà* who creates the physical form of humans; one of the four *Òrìṣà* (including *Olódùmarè*) present at the creation of the cosmos.

Odù Ifá Yorùbá term for a collection of sacred poems and mythical precedents that are organized into 256 collections and was traditionally passed down orally and memorized by Ifá diviners (*babaláwo*-s).

Ògún Yorùbá term for the *Òrìṣà* of iron, war, and hunting; associated today with technology, metal, and transportation.

Olódùmarè (also known as Ọlọ́run) Yorùbá term for the *Òrìṣà* commonly thought of as the "high God," especially in Ifá traditions; one of the primordial *Òrìṣà* who created the cosmos; also breathes life-breath (*èmí*) into humans, affixes their "inner head" (*orí*), and judges them upon death.

oṃ Sanskrit term that constitutes a sacred syllable and symbol for many forms of Hinduism; three phonemes (A-U-M) are symbolic of the creation, maintenance, and destruction of the cosmos, together which constitute the essence of universal consciousness and ultimate reality (*Ātman/Brahman*).

omnibenevolence English term for unlimited or perfect goodness; usually applied to or questioned about the God of Abrahamic religious or European philosophical traditions.

omnipotence English term for unlimited or perfect power; usually applied to or questioned about the God of Abrahamic religious or European philosophical traditions.

omniscience English term for unlimited or perfect knowledge; usually applied to or questioned about the God of Abrahamic religious or European philosophical traditions.

oníṣègùn Yorùbá term for a "medicine maker" who prescribes and prepares herbal and other medicines for clients.

ontological proofs English term for *a priori* proofs for the existence of an Abrahamic religious or European philosophical God based on the concept or meaning of such a God.

ontology English term for the philosophical study of being, the most basic categories of being, the basic kinds of beings, and the ways in which beings "be"; from the Greek words *ontos* (being, that which is) and *logos* (rational account).

orí Yorùbá term literally meaning "head" but often applied to the "inner head" or "spiritual head" (*orí-inu*), which contains a person's destiny (*àyànmọ́*), and which has a heavenly counterpart (*orí orún*).

Origen of Alexander (184–253) Early Christian theologian; known for reconciling Christian theology with Platonic philosophy; was posthumously convicted of heresy and had most of his writings destroyed (allegedly for teaching the preexistence and transmigration of souls).

Òrìṣà Yorùbá term sometimes translated as "deity"; applies to Yorùbá Gods that personify natural phenomena (rivers, thunder) or human activities (ironworking, childbearing) and are often associated with legendary ancestors.

ọ̀run Yorùbá term translated as "heaven"; divided between "heaven above" (*ọ̀run ọ̀kè*), where Olódùmarè and *Òrìṣà* associated with meteorological phenomena reside, and "heaven below" (*ọ̀run odò*), where the majority of the *Òrìṣà* as well as the "Anti-gods" (*Ajogun*) and ancestors reside.

Ọrunmila Yorùbá term for the *Òrìṣà* of wisdom, destiny, and divination (especially Ifá); one of the four *Òrìṣà* (including Olódùmarè) present at the creation of the cosmos.

Ọ̀ṣun Yorùbá term for a female *Òrìṣà* known as "the goddess of the source," which includes both flowing water (rivers) and children (fertility).

other-effort/power (Ch. *tali*; Jp. *tariki*) Chinese term for the need to rely on others, usually buddhas, to achieve enlightenment; used in Japanese to distinguish the "other-effort" of Pure Land Buddhism from the "self-effort" of Zen Buddhism.

Paley, William (1743–1805) British philosopher and Christian apologist; known for his articulation of a design-teleological argument for the existence of God, using the analogy of a watchmaker.

Pāli Canon English term for the scriptures of Theravāda Buddhism; organized into three collections or "baskets" (and therefore also called the *Tripiṭaka* [Sk.], meaning "three baskets"): the first of teachings (*sūtras*) of the historical Buddha, the second of monastic rules (*vinaya*), the third of "higher teachings" (*abhidharma*).

panentheism English term for the philosophical position that holds that a God is immanent in the cosmos (not transcendent "above" it) without being merely reduced to the cosmos (as in *pantheism*); from the Greek words *pan* ("all"), *en* ("in"), and *theos* ("God").

pantheism English term for the philosophical position that holds that the cosmos just is a God or a manifestation of a God (and that this God does not exist apart from the cosmos); from the Greek words *pan* ("all") and *theos* ("God").

Patañjali (*c.* second century bce to fourth century ce) South Asian philosopher; probably one of (at least) two by this name; in this case, the author of the *Yoga Sūtras* and a scholar of Sāṁkhya philosophy.

Paul the Apostle (*c.* 5–*c.* 67) Jewish Pharisee who converted to Christianity after receiving a vision of Jesus; established churches throughout the eastern Mediterranean region to which he wrote letters that became canonized in the New Testament.

Pelagius (360–418) Christian theologian and monk from the British Isles who opposed Augustine's teachings on original sin, maintaining that humans could freely avoid sinning and obey God's commandments; was later condemned and excommunicated and Pelagianism was proclaimed a heresy.

perennialism English term for the view that all religio-philosophies share a common core, whether of a set of philosophical teachings in the case of perennial *philosophy* or of a set of psychological experiences in the case of perennial *psychology*.

phenomenology English term for a field of Western philosophy that studies the "lived experience" or "life world" of people, especially as "phenomena" show up to consciousness prior to reflection and categorization.

Philo of Alexandria (*c.* 25 bce–*c.* 50 ce) Jewish philosopher known for harmonizing Jewish scripture (especially the Torah) and Greek philosophy (especially Plato).

Plantinga, Alvin (b. 1932) American philosopher of religion and Christian apologist; known especially for his modal ontological proof for the existence of God and his free-will defense of the justice of God vis-à-vis evil.

Plato (427–347 bce) Ancient Greek philosopher who was the student of Socrates; best known in the philosophy of religion for his theory of Forms, a God-like Good that is "beyond being," and a God-like Demiurge who fashions the cosmos out of preexisting materials.

Platonism English term for philosophies that are rooted in and inspired by the writings of the ancient Greek philosopher Plato; scholars classify its varieties under the headings of "Old Academy" (from Plato's death in 347 bce through the first century bce), "Middle-Platonism" (from the first century bce through the third century ce) and "Neo-Platonism" (from the third century ce through 529 when Plato's Academy was closed).

pneuma Greek term meaning "breath" or "spirit"; used by New Testament writers to translate the Hebrew term *rûaḥ*, a divine gift that offers a mysterious vitality to the material body.

pò (魄) Chinese character for one of two kinds of souls; associated with *yīn*; sinks downward to the earth upon death, remaining with the body in the grave, where it decomposes with the body, while also enjoying veneration and attention, especially during the springtime festival of "tomb-sweeping" (Qīngmíng).

Porete, Marguerite (d. 1310) French mystic and member of the lay Catholic order of Beguines; was burned at the stake for refusing to recant or remove her book *The Mirror of Simple Souls*.

postcolonialism English term for a critical academic theory used to analyze and critique the political, economic, and cultural (including religious and philosophical) manifestations and effects of colonialism and imperialism.

pramāṇa Sanskrit term for "proof" or "means of knowledge"; the various means by which humans can attain reliable knowledge (e.g., perception, inference, analogy, testimony, not all of which are accepted by all schools of philosophy).

pratītya-samutpāda Sanskrit term for "interdependent arising," the Buddhist principle that all things are interdependent and nothing exists independently; conceived of as a chain of twelve interdependent links.

problem of evil see "theodicy"

Process Philosophy/Theology English term for philosophies and theologies that view reality and beings as fundamentally processive and dynamic rather than substantive and static.

psychē Greek term commonly translated as "soul"; under the influence of Greek philosophy, especially Platonism, increasingly comes to mean the immortal essence of a human rather than the principle of life in that which lives.

pudgala Sanskrit term for "matter"; one of five aspects of *ajīva* (non-soul) in Jainism; traps and deludes souls (*jīva*-s) through the force of *karma*.

Pure Land Buddhism (Ch. *jìngtǔzōng*, 淨土宗) English term for a group of Mahāyāna Buddhist teachings and sects that practice devotion to Amitābha, the Buddha of infinite light and life, with the aim of being reborn in his "Pure Land"; although Pure Land Buddhism originated in South Asia (as early as the first century of the Common Era), it was developed and popularized in East Asia (as early as the second century of the Common Era); in Japan, two of the major forms of Pure Land Buddhism are Jōdo-shū (Pure Land School) and Jōdo Shinshū (True Pure Land School).

qì (氣) Chinese character that is variously translated as vital or material energy or force; flows through all things, animating bodies in particular, the health of which depends on its unimpeded flow.

qíng (情) Chinee character for "feeling"; for (Neo)Confucian philosophers in particular the interaction of material "vital energy" (*qì*) with immaterial "pattern-principle" (*lǐ*, 理) in the human body caused the arousal of seven feelings—pleasure, anger, sorrow, joy, love, hate, and desire—that drowned out immaterial pattern-principle and therefore needed to be controlled and balanced.

Qur'ān Arabic term literally meaning "the recitation"; core scripture for Islam, the eternal and literal word of Allah revealed to Prophet Muḥammad through the Angel Gabriel (Ar. Jibrīl) from 610 to 632; believed to have been written down and codified during the reign of the third Rightly Guided Caliph, ʿUthmān (r. 644–56).

Rābiʿa al-ʿAdawiyya al-Qaysiyya (718–801) Female Arab Muslim saint and Sufi mystic; credited with infusing Sufism in particular and Islam more generally with the passionate love of the mystic lover for the divine beloved.

Rāmakrishna (1836–86) Indian Hindu mystic and saint; devotee of the Goddess Kālī known for his transgressive conduct, which he maintained was madness for that which is permanent (Kālī) rather than madness for the impermanent things of the world.

Rāmānuja (1017–1137) Hindu philosopher and founder of Viśiṣṭādvaita ("qualifiedly non-dual") Vedānta; held that although *Ātman/Brahman* is ultimately non-dual, finite souls and material things exist as qualifications of *Brahman*.

rationalism English term for an epistemological position that maintains, usually in contradistinction to empiricism, that some foundational ideas and truths are innate to the mind and not arrived at or justified through sense experience.

rén (仁) Chinese character composed of the characters for "human being" and "two"; variously translated as "human-heartedness," "benevolence," and "love"; one of the four cardinal virtues for Confucianism (along with *lǐ* [禮], *yì*, and *zhì*).

resurrection of the dead English term for the Abrahamic belief that the dead will be resurrected, usually at the end of time (e.g., the Day of the Lord), with the righteous going to a heavenly realm, the wicked, to hellish realm.

Rowe, William (1931–2015) American philosopher of religion; best known fro his contributions to the evidential argument from evil.

rú (儒) Chinese character for a class of scholars during the early Zhou Dynasty (1027–770 bce) who studied and taught the rituals and ceremonies of the royal court; later applied to what is called "Confucianism" in the West (*rújiā*), which is more accurately rendered as *rú*-ism in China—the tradition or school (*jiā*) of the scholars (*rú*).

rûaḥ Hebrew term translated as "spirit"; denotes powers outside the body that operate in or through the body; a divine gift that offer a mysterious vitality to the material body.

rūḥ Arabic term translated as "spirit"; usually refers to Allah's spirit, which is breathed into Adam.

Russell, Robert John (b. 1946) American philosopher and Christian theologian; best known for his theory of "non-interventionist, objective divine action" (NIODA).

Saadia ben Yosef Gaon (882–942) Jewish rabbi who served as head (*gaon*) of the academy of Jewish (Talmudic) learning Babylon during the ʿAbbāsid Caliphate; practiced a kind of Mu'tazilite theology.

śabda Sanskrit term meaning "speech sound" or "utterance"; employed in South Asian philosophy for verbal testimony or authority, which is one of the possible means of knowledge (*pramāṇa*).

saḥr Arabic term meaning "sober"; used to characterize Sufis who aspire for states of calm communion with Allah rather than ecstatic union.

Śaivite Sanskrit term for a Hindu who worships the God Śiva as the supreme Lord.

Śaktite Sanskrit term for a Hindu who worships the Mother Goddess (*Mahādevī*) as the supreme power or energy (*Śakti*) in the cosmos.

samādhi Sanskrit term for a state of meditative consciousness; the eighth and final step of both the Eightfold Path in Buddhism and the Eight Limbs of Yoga.

saṃgha Sanskrit term meaning "assembly," "association," or "community"; one of the "Three Refuges" in Buddhism, referring to the monastic community of monks and nuns and sometimes also lay Buddhist practitioners.

Sāṁkhya Sanskrit term for the "Hindu" *darśana* that forwards a dualistic metaphysics, showing how the entire cosmos evolves from two fundamental existents.

saṃsāra Sanskrit term for the cycle of rebirth in South Asian religio-philosophies; all beings (including Gods) are bound to the cycle of rebirth due to *karma*; South Asian religio-philosophies therefore generally take release (*mokṣa*) from *saṃsāra* as their ultimate goal.

Ṣàngó Yorùbá term for the *Òrìṣà* of thunder and lightning; associated with virility, masculinity, fire, lightning, stones, warriors, and magnetism.

sānjiào (三教) Chinese characters meaning "three teachings"; refers to the three teachings of Confucianism (*rújiào*), Daoism (*dàojiào*), and Buddhism (*fójiào*), especially as regarded as complementary to one another.

Śaṅkara (*c.* 788–*c.* 820) South Asian Hindu philosopher from the Vedānta school of philosophy; the primary exponent of Advaita (non-dual) Vedānta.

Scotus, John Duns (1265/6–1308) Scottish Catholic philosopher, priest, and friar (Franciscan); known for several unique philosophical contributions as well as his critique of Thomistic ethics.

self-effort/power (Ch. *zili*; Jp. *jiriki*) Chinese term for the ability to achieve enlightenment through one's own effort; used in Japanese to distinguish the "self-effort" of Zen Buddhism from the "other-effort" of Pure Land Buddhism.

sĕpîrôt (sing = *sĕpîrâ*) Hebrew term meaning "emanations"; refers to the ten emanations from YHWH (as *ʾÊn Sôp*, the Infinite) in Jewish Kabbalistic mysticism.

shàn (善) Chinese character meaning "good"; the fourth-generation Confucian philosopher Mencius (372–289 bce) held that the original nature (*xìng*) of the human heart-mind (*xīn*) has good natural dispositions or characteristic tendencies.

sharī'a Arabic word literally meaning "a well-trodden path [to water]"; refers to Islamic law, as grounded in Qur'ān and *ḥadīth* (though also sometimes including juridical consensus and analogical reasoning).

Shekhinah Hebrew word meaning "dwelling" or "settling" (of the presence of YHWH); used in Jewish Kabbalah to refer to the tenth and final *sěpîrâ* to emanate from *'Ên Sôp*.

shén (神) Chinese character with a range of meanings including divine spirits and the human spirit or source of agency and potential; one of the Chinese characters that is used to translate the term "God."

shèngrén (聖人) Chinese character for a Confucian sage; considered by some to be the highest stage of moral development, requiring mastery of all the Confucian virtues.

sheol Hebrew term for a shadowy underworld to which the dead go; one of the first understandings of the "afterlife" in Judaism.

shevirah Hebrew term referring in Lurianic Kabbalah to the "shattering" of the divine vessels containing the lower seven divine emanations (*sěpîrôt*).

shì (事) Chinese character meaning phenomena; in the Chinese Buddhist school of Huáyán, reality is understood as a grand harmony of interdependent and interpenetrative *dharma*-s; see *dharma*-s.

shì (是) Chinese character meaning right/correct or be/exist; debates between Confucians and Mohists attempted to distinguish what is "this" or "right" from what is "not" or "wrong" (*fēi*).

Shī'a English transliteration of the Arabic term meaning "party," referring to the party that followed 'Alī ibn Abī Ṭālib (*c.* 600–61), the cousin and son-in-law of Prophet Muḥammad; the second largest branch of Islam, constituting approximately 10–15 percent of all Muslims in the world today.

shirk Arabic term literally meaning "association"; the preeminent sin in Islam of identifying with or as Allah what is other than Allah; idolatry or polytheism.

Shriran (親鸞, 1173–1263) Japanese Buddhist priest who left the Tendai order, following Hōnen; later regarded as the founder of "True Pure Land School" (Jōdo Shinshū) of Pure Land Buddhism.

shù (恕) Chinese character meaning "liken to oneself" or "self-reflect" in the Confucian classics; a reciprocal process whereby one expects of others what one expects of oneself and vice versa.

šičuŋ Lakȟóta term translated as "potentiality" or "guardian"; given to the body at birth; escorts the *naǧí* beyond the Milky Way after death, then returns to the *Wakȟáŋ Tȟáŋka* to await entry into a new body.

ṣimṣûm Hebrew term meaning "contraction"; used in the Kabbalistic Judaism of Isaac Luria to refer to the process by which God as *'Ên Sôp* ("The

Limitless") contracts to provide space into which the divine emanations (*Sĕpîrôt*) can unfold and, later, creation can occur.

sin English word for an act that violates divine law, or for an original human condition that estranges people from a God, marring their ability to will or enact what is good.

Śiva Sanskrit term for the Hindu God associated with the destruction of the cosmos in modern Hinduism; *Śaivite* Hindus worship *Śiva* also as the creator and preserver of the cosmos.

skandha Sanskrit term referring to a bundle of firewood; often translated as "aggregate" with respect to South Asian Buddhism, which understands the "self" to be the product of five ever-changing aggregates, processes, or bundles.

Skepticism English term for a Greco-Roman school of philosophy with origins in the fourth–third century bce, as well as for a philosophical position more generally; Skeptics/skeptics generally deny that knowledge is possible altogether, or that anything can be known with certainty, or that most or all metaphysical claims can be known.

Smith, Huston (1919–2016) American scholar of religion; known especially for advocating a perennial philosophy called the "primordial tradition."

soteriology English word for a theory or doctrine of salvation; from the Greek words *sōtēria* (salvation) and *logos* (rational account); for some contemporary scholars, soteriology is broadly interpreted to include religious goals or ends other than salvation (e.g., enlightenment, harmony).

spandrel English term originally used in architecture to refer to the triangular spaces between adjacent pillars and the dome they supported; used in evolutionary psychology to refer to byproducts of evolution, especially ones with religious meaning or function, that were not selected for their own adaptive advantage.

Stoicism English term for a Greco-Roman school of philosophy founded in the early fourth century bce by the ancient Greek philosopher Zeno of Citium; Stoics were known for teaching that "virtue is the only good," a necessary and sufficient means of attaining "happiness" (*eudaimonia*), and that humans should live "in accordance with nature," especially as physical reality unfolded according to a divine logic.

Sufism English word for Islamic mysticism, inclusive of individuals, orders, teachings, and practices; probably derived from the Arabic word *ṣūf*, meaning "one who wears wool," due to the coarse woolen garments worn by Sufi ascetics.

sukr Arabic term meaning "intoxicated" or "drunk"; used to characterize Sufis who aspired to states of ecstatic union with Allah rather than calm communion.

Sunni English transliteration of the Arabic term meaning "traditions" or "practices"; refers to the largest branch of Islam, which constitutes approximately 85–90 percent of all Muslims in the world today; regards Abū Bakr (r. 632–4) as the rightfully elected successor (*caliph*) to Prophet Muḥammad.

śūnyatā (Ch. *kōng*, 空) Sanskrit term meaning "emptiness"; for South Asian Mahāyāna Buddhism in general and Madhyamaka philosophy in particular, the view that all things are without an independent, permanent, or intrinsic existence or nature; for East Asian Buddhism, *śūnyatā* is sometimes identified with the interdependent totality of existence or an innate Buddha-nature.

sūtra Sanskrit term literally meaning "thread"; applies in the case of Hindu *darśana*-s to short collections of aphorisms that serve to found or ground the *darśana*; also applies in the cases of Buddhism and Jainism to longer scriptures that record sermons/teachings of the historical Buddha or Mahāvīra.

svabhāva (Ch. *zixing*, 自性) Sanskrit term literally meaning "own-being"; the intrinsic or essential nature of beings; whereas Abhidharma Buddhist philosophies posited that *dharma*-s had *svabhāva*, Mahāyāna Buddhist philosophies such as Madhyamaka maintained that nothing had *svabhāva* but rather everything was empty (*śūnyatā*).

Swinburne, Richard (b. 1934) British analytic philosopher of religion; known especially for his arguments for the existence of God and the rationality of theism, Christianity in particular.

syādvāda Sanskrit term that refers to the Jain doctrine of conditional assertion, according to which assertions about reality are only correct from a certain perspective or in a certain sense.

Tàijí (太極) Chinese characters literally meaning "great pole"; often translated as "great ultimate" or "supreme polarity"; in (Neo)Confucian and Daoist philosophy of religion, *Tàijí* is often held to be a state of non-differentiated potential and unity from which the duality of *yīn* and *yáng* emerges.

tantra Sanskrit term literally meaning "weave," "warp," or "loom"; applies to South Asian texts and traditions that "spread out," "put forth," or "extend" a system of religio-philosophical doctrines and practices that go beyond what was traditional or typical for the earlier religious systems of the subcontinent (e.g., Vedic religion or Palī Buddhism), sometimes commending behavior that is unconventional, immoral, sinful, or heterodox.

tathāgatagarbha see Buddha-nature

tathātā Sanskrit term translated as "suchness" or "thusness"; sometimes used in Mahāyāna Buddhism to refer to the nature of things "such" or "thus" as they are beyond all concepts and words.

Tattvārthasūtra c. second century ce Jain *sūtra* authored by Umāsvāti; the first extant systemization of Jain philosophy.

tawḥīd Arabic term referring to the singularity, unity, or oneness of Allah; for some Sufi Muslims, *tawḥīd* entailed that humans were not separate from Allah and therefore that the self/soul (*nafs*) should be "annihilated" (*fanāʾ*) such that humans "subsisted" (*baqāʾ*) only in Allah.

teleological (and design) proofs English term for proofs for the existence of God based on the purposiveness or design of nature.

teleology English term for the philosophical study of, or for religio-philosophical and scientific theories of, the end, aim, or goal of some thing or species in particular or the cosmos in general; from the Greek words *tēlos* (end, aim, goal) and *logos* (rational account).

theism English term for the view or theory that God or Gods exist; often implies the existence of a single God that is omnipotent, omniscient, and omnipresent, that creates the cosmos, and that intervenes in the cosmos and personally interacts with its creatures, especially humans.

theodicy English term for a philosophical theory that attempts to explain why evil exists given the existence of an omnipotent, omniscient, and omnibenevolent God; from the Greek words *theos* (God) and *dikē* (justice).

Theravāda see Buddhism

Three Periods of the Dharma (Ch. *Sān Shí*, 三時) Chinese term for a Buddhist theory that holds that the world goes through three stages of moral decline after the appearance of each Buddha: first a "Former Day of the Law" or "Age of Right Dharma," then a "Middle Day of the Law" or "Age of Semblance Dharma," and finally a "Latter Day of the Law" or "Degenerate Age" (aka Mappō Dharma).

Three Pillars of Sikhism English term for the three central practices of Sikhism: *nām japō*, to meditate on Wahegugu ("God") and recite the names of Waheguru; *kirat karō*, to honestly earn; and *vaṇḍ chhakō*, to share and consume together.

Tiān (天) Chinese character meaning "Heaven"; regarded by some Chinese philosophers as a person-like supreme God, by others as the impersonal workings of nature.

Tiāntāi (天台) Chinese characters literally meaning "platform in the sky"; the name of a school of East Asian (Mahāyāna) Buddhism that was founded in the sixth century; some of its teachings include seeing all things as both empty of self-existence and provisionally existent, as possessing Buddha-nature and therefore originally enlightened, and as present in every moment of thought; known in Japan as Tendai.

tiqqûn Hebrew term meaning "repair"; refers in Lurianic Kabbalah to the repair of the tenth and final *sĕpîrâ* (Shekinah) through observance of the commandments (*mitzvot*), especially when accompanied by acts of mystical meditation or intention (*kawwānâ*).

tīrthaṅkara Sanskrit term meaning "ford-maker"; applied by Jains to one who not only attains liberation and therefore release from rebirth (thereby fording the "river" of *saṃsāra*) but also teaches this path of liberation to others; used in reference to Mahāvīra (599–527 bce) and the twenty-three *tīrthaṅkara*-s (or *jina*-s) to proceed him.

Torah Hebrew word meaning "instruction," "teaching," or "law"; refers to the first five books of the Jewish and Christian bibles, especially the 613 commandments contained within those books.

trikāya (Ch. *sānshēn*, 三身) Sanskrit term literally meaning "three bodies"; the Mahāyāna Buddhist concept that buddhas have three bodies, a dharma body (*dharmakāya*), which is just is reality "such as it is" (*tathātā*) as empty, interdependent, and nirvanic; an enjoyment body (*saṃbhogakāya*), which is the celestial form of a buddha that dwells in a heavenly realm from which superhuman power can be exerted for the enlightenment of sentient beings; and a manifestation body (*nimāṅakāya*), which is the physical apparition or manifestation of a buddha in an earthly realm.

Trinity English word used to denote the God of Christianity, especially as defined in the Nicene-Constantinople creed (of the first and second Ecumenical Councils) as one in being or essence (*ousious*) and three in underlying substances or persons (*hypostases*).

Udayana (tenth–eleventh century) Nyāya philosopher; author of the *Nyāyakusumāñjali*, which contains proofs for the existence of *Īśvara*; known as one of the foremost Nyāya philosophers.

Umāsvāti (*c.* second–fifth century ce) South Asian Jain philosopher known especially for authoring the *Tattvārthasūtra*, the first extant systemization of Jain philosophy.

Unmoved Mover English term for the "God" of Aristotle; does not create the cosmos but rather guarantees the perpetual motion of celestial bodies and the eternal existence of biological species and metaphysical principles.

Upaniṣads Sanskrit term for the fourth and final section of the *Vedas*; includes a focus on meditative understanding of the universal self (*Ātman*) or ultimate reality (*Brahman*) as the key to obtaining release (*mokṣa*) from the cycle of rebirth (*saṃsāra*).

upāya (Ch. *fāngbiàn*, 方便) Sanskrit term for "useful means" or "expedient means"; a Buddhist concept used in some Mahāyāna texts to connote both the usefulness of any means to attain *nirvāṇa* and the understanding that all means are only means.

vāda Sanskrit term for one of three kinds of public philosophical debate (*katha*); unlike the debates of disputation (*jalpa*) and refutation (*vitaṇḍā*), where the objective was victory, the goal of *vāda* ("discussion") was truth.

Vaiśeṣika Sanskrit term for the "Hindu" *darśana* that posits an atomistic theory of reality including nine types of substances and six kinds of objects of experience; merges with Nyāya in the second millennium.

Vaiṣṇavite Sanskrit term for a Hindu who worships the God Viṣṇu as the supreme Lord.

varṇa Sanskrit term meaning "order" or "color"; applies to the four main caste groups in South Asia: *brahmin* (priest), *kṣatriya* (ruler, warrior), *vaiśya* (merchant, trader, farmer, artisan), and *śūdra* (servant, menial worker).

Vedānta Sanskrit term for the "Hindu" *darśana* that engages in interpretation of *Upaniṣads*, the fourth and final section of the *Vedas*, especially with respect to understanding the relationship between the innermost self (*Ātman*) and ultimate reality (*Brahman*); different schools of Vedānta understand this relationship differently, notably as "non-dual" (*advaita*) "qualifiedly non-dual" (*viśiṣṭādvaita*), or "dual" (*dvaita*).

Vedānta Sūtras (aka *Brahma Sūtras*) Sanskrit text probably written in the fifth century ce by the sage Bādarāyaṇa; attempts to systematize the *Upaniṣads*; constitutes the founding *sūtras* for the Hindu philosophical school of Vedānta.

Vedas Sanskrit term for the sacred scriptures of "Vedic religion," a precursor of modern Hinduism; arranged into four main collections, each with four main sections; probably written down over a period of at least 1,000 years (*c.* 1500–500 bce).

Vedic religion (aka *Brahmanism*) English term for the religious practices and beliefs of the Vedic peoples of the northwest region of the Indian subcontinent from 1500–500 bce; a precursor of modern Hinduism.

Vimalakīrti Nirdeśa (aka *Vimalakīrti Sūtra*) South Asian Buddhist Mahāyāna text composed around 100 ce; includes teachings about non-dualism, useful means, and the miraculous powers of buddhas and bodhisattvas; very influential for East Asian Buddhism.

Viṣṇu Sanskrit term for the Hindu God associated with the preservation of the cosmos in modern Hinduism; makes ten "descents" (*avatāra*-s) into bodily form during times of need, the last of which (Kalki) will occur at the end of this cosmic era (*mahāyuga*).

wakȟáŋ Lakȟóta term meaning sacred or powerful; a sacred power that extends throughout the universe; applies especially to the *Wakȟáŋ Tȟáŋka* (great mysterious sacred), *čhaŋnúŋpa wakȟáŋ* (sacred pipe), and *wičháša wakȟáŋ* and *wíŋyaŋ wakȟáŋ* (holy men, holy women).

Wakȟáŋ Tȟáŋka Lakȟóta term meaning "great mysterious sacred"; original meaning probably referred to a group of sixteen, sacred, mysterious forces; often also used today for a singular, God-like creator.

Wakiŋyaŋ Lakota term for the "Thunder Beings," deities that are among the sixteen *Wakȟáŋ Tȟáŋka*; Iktómi is the progeny of the Wakiŋyaŋ and Iŋyaŋ (the rock); *heyókȟa* (sacred clowns) have visions of the Wakiŋyaŋ.

wanáǧi yúhapi Lakȟóta term meaning the "keeping of the spirit," one of the seven sacred rites of the Lakȟóta; involves keeping and feeding the *náǧi* (ghost or spirit) of the deceased for a period of time (six months or more), after which it is released to travel down the "Spirit Trail" to an afterlife.

wéi shì (為是) Chinese characters translated as a "that's it which deems" (among other ways); criticized by the classical Daoist sage Zhuāngzǐ as the means by which Confucians and Mohists attempted to distinguish what is "this" (*shì*) from what is "not" (*fēi*) with respect to some model, paradigm, or standard (*fà*).

White Buffalo Calf Woman Lakȟóta term for one of the *Wakȟáŋ Tȟáŋka* (as Wóȟpe); gives the sacred pipe to the Lakȟóta and teaches them the seven sacred rituals associated with it.

wičháša wakȟáŋ (and ***wíŋyaŋ wakȟáŋ***) Lakȟóta term for "holy man" (and "holy woman"); sometimes also translated as "medicine man" (or "medicine woman"); has the power to receive revelations, to perform extraordinary deeds including miracles, and to communicate with the spirit world through dreams and visions.

wiwáŋyaŋg wačhipi Lakȟóta term commonly translated as the "Sun Dance," one of the seven sacred rites of the Lakȟóta; a four-day ritual in which men dance around a pole until they break free from the rope that attaches their chest to the pole, thereby offering their pierced flesh to *Wakȟáŋ Tȟáŋka*.

Wovoka (*c.* 1856–1932) Northern Paiute prophet Wodziwob (aka Fish Lake Joe); received the revelation of the Ghost Dance in 1889; subsequently practiced and taught the Ghost Dance to other Native American tribes.

wúwéi (無爲) Chinese characters often translated as "non-action" or "effortless action"; a key concept in Daoism; action that is in accord with the natural patterns or way (*dào*) of the cosmos.

wǔxíng (五行) Chinese characters translated as the five material phases; these phases—fire, water, wood, metal, and earth—are used to explain the patterning of many different natural phenomena such as the seasons, natural elements, and the operations of the body.

xīn (心) Chinese character literally meaning "heart" but often translated as "heart-mind" (since the ancient Chinese believed that the heart was responsible for cognition); early Confucian philosophers Mencius and Xúnzǐ differed about whether the heart-mind was originally good (*shàn*) or bad (*è*).

xìng (性) Chinese character translated as "original nature" or "human nature"; for the fourth-generation Confucian philosopher Mencius, *xìng* was the "natural dispositions" or "characteristic tendencies" of humans, which he believed were good (*shàn*); for fifth-generation Confucian philosopher Xúnzǐ, the original nature of humans was bad (*è*).

Xúnzǐ (荀子, 313–238 bce) Ancient Confucian philosopher known for holding that human nature is originally "bad"; declared heretical by Song Dynasty

(Neo)Confucians; now recognized as one of the most important and original early Confucian philosophers alongside Confucius and Mencius.

yajña Sanskrit word for "sacrifice," "worship," or "offering"; an ancient Vedic fire ritual in which oblations or offerings were poured or placed into a fire, usually while chanting mantras from the *Vedas*.

yáng (陽) Chinese character for active energy, which is complementary with its opposite (*yīn*); traditional Chinese cosmology and medicine understand all change to be the result of the interaction of these complementary aspects of *qì*.

YHWH Hebrew letters designating the proper name of the God of the Jews; believed to have been pronounced *yah-way*; Latinized as "Jehovah"; usually translated in English-language Bibles as "LORD"; no longer pronounced (or written) by observant Jews who commonly replace it with "Adonai" (My Lord) or "HaShem" (The Name).

yì (義) Chinese character for "moral rightness," a moral disposition to do the good combined with a moral sensibility about how to do the good in particular contexts; one of the four cardinal Confucian virtues (along with *lǐ* [禮], *rén*, and *zhì*).

Yìjīng (易經) "The Classic of Changes"; an ancient Chinese divination manual that was later also interpreted cosmologically.

yīn (陰) Chinese character for receptive energy, which is complementary with its opposite (*yáng*); traditional Chinese cosmology and medicine understand all change to the result of the interaction of these complementary aspects of *qì*.

yīn shì (因是) Chinese characters for a "that's it that goes by circumstance" (also translated as "that's it that is mutually dependent," "this that is dependent," "this according to what you go by," or "relying on 'so'"); the classical Daoist sage Zhuāngzǐ advocated a context-dependent *yīn shì* over against a "that's it which deems" (*wéi shì*).

Yoga/yoga Sanskrit term literally meaning "yoke," "join," or "attach"; has at least three distinct applications with regard to philosophy of religion: (1) a set of physical and mental practices by which humans apprehend or unite with divine or cosmic reality or truth; (2) the three "Hindu" religious paths by which to attain release from rebirth (*karma*, *jñāna*, *bhakti*); (3) the "Hindu" *darśana* that focuses on the use of yogic techniques to liberate the innermost self.

Yorùbá Yorùbá term that now refers to an ethnic group located in the West African countries of Nigeria, Benin, Togo, and Ghana; first used by the Hausa people of Northern Nigeria to refer to residents of the city of Ọ̀yọ́; later used in the nineteenth century by the Anglican Church Missionary Society to refer to all the people in the region who spoke similar languages, shared common cultures, and believed in a common descent from the city of Ifẹ̀.

yuga Sanskrit term for a cosmic unit of time; Hindu cosmology views each cosmic cycle as involving four *yuga*-s of descending knowledge and virtue, each named for a throw of the dice: *kṛta* (four), *tretā* (three), *dvāpara* (two), and *kali* (one); these four *yuga*-s constitute one *mahāyuga*, at the end of each of which the cosmos is (partially) destroyed, then recreated again; 1,000 *mahāyugas* constitute one *kalpa*, a 4.32-billion-year period that is said to be just one day in the life of the Lord Brahmā, who creates the cosmos each day at dawn.

yuwípi Lakȟóta term literally meaning "binding with ropes"; refers to a ritual in which a holy man who is bound with robes and blankets performs healing, finds lost objects, and predicts the future.

zazen (Jp. 座禅; from the Ch. *zuòchán*, 坐禪) Japanese characters literally meaning "seated meditation"; a meditative practice that is common to Zen Buddhism.

Zen See "Chán."

zhì (智) Chinese character meaning "knowledge" or "wisdom"; applies not only to having knowledge but also to the ability to use knowledge to make correct judgments and decisions, especially about right and wrong; one of the four cardinal Confucian virtues (along with *lǐ* [禮], *rén*, and *yì*).

Zhōu Dūnyí (周敦頤, 1017–73) Song Dynasty (Neo)Confucian philosopher; one of the "Five Masters of the Northern Song"; known for his development of (Neo)Confucian cosmology as depicted in his "Diagram of the Supreme Polarity/Ultimate (*Tàijítú*).

Zhū Xī (朱熹, 1130–1200) Song Dynasty (Neo)Confucian philosopher; commonly regarded as the greatest such philosopher; synthesized and systematized the teachings of the other Song Dynasty (Neo)Confucian philosophers; edited and commented on the "Four Books," leading to their establishment as the curriculum for civil service exams from 1313–1905.

Zhuāngzǐ (莊子, *c.* 368–*c.* 286 bce) Refers to both an ancient Chinese philosopher and the text purportedly written by him (of which only the first seven "inner chapters" are believed by scholars actually to have been written by him); both the person and the text are commonly classified as "Daoist."

zìrán (自然) Chinese characters literally meaning "self-so" or "so-of-itself"; often translated as "spontaneity" or "naturalness"; applied in Daoism to the way of the *Dào* and that which is naturally, spontaneously, or effortlessly in harmony with it.

Zōhar Hebrew term literally meaning "splendor" or "radiance"; the central and foundational text for Jewish Kabbalah; traditionally ascribed to Shimon bar Yochai, a first-century rabbi and mystic; generally believed by scholars to have been written by Moses de León in the thirteenth century.

zōngjiào (宗教) Chinese characters meaning "religion"; from the Japanese *shūkyō*, which was coined in the late nineteenth century to translate European terms for "religion"; under the People's Republic of China, five *zōngjiào* are state recognized: Buddhism, Catholicism, Daoism, Islam, and Protestantism.

Notes

Introduction

1. I am indebted to those who have paved the way: Gary E. Kessler, *Philosophy of Religion: Toward a Global Perspective* (Belmont, CA: Cengage Learning, 1998); Keith E. Yandell, *Philosophy of Religion: A Contemporary Introduction* (New York: Routledge, 1999); Joseph Runzo, *Global Philosophy of Religion: A Short Introduction* (Oxford: Oneworld Publications, 2001); Gwen Griffith-Dickson, *Philosophy of Religion* (London: SCM Press, 2005); Hendrik M. Vroom, *A Spectrum of Worldviews: An Introduction to Philosophy of Religion in a Pluralistic World*, trans. Morris and Alice Greidanus (Amsterdam: Editions Rodopi BV, 2006); Andrew Eshleman, *Readings in the Philosophy of Religion: East Meets West* (Malden, MA: Blackwell Publishing Ltd, 2008); Mikel Burley, *A Radical Pluralist Philosophy of Religion: Cross-Cultural, Multireligious, Interdisciplinary* (New York: Bloomsbury, 2020).

1 The Traditions of Philosophy of Religion

1. Because this is an introductory textbook of limited size, and because I wanted to cover traditions in adequate depth for cross-cultural philosophizing, only so many traditions could be included. Of those I omitted, I draw especial attention to Australasia, the Malay Archipelago, and Latin America, as well as peoples other than the Yorùbá from sub-Saharan Africa and other than the Lakȟóta from North America. If the publisher will permit a textbook of double the size, perhaps *Philosophies of Religion* 2.0 can also include these traditions.
2. For the purposes of philosophy of religion, I take the European Enlightenment period as running from René Descartes (1596–1650) to Georg Wilhelm Hegel (1770–1831). Descartes' formative *Meditations on First Philosophy* was published in 1641, and Hegel gave his equally formative "lectures on philosophy of religion" in 1821, 1824, 1827, and

1831. (If I am not mistaken, Hegel's lectures are the first notable occurrence of the phrase, "The Philosophy of Religion [*Die Philosophie der Religion*].") Perhaps the most influential philosophers of religion who lived during this time, however, were David Hume (1711–76) and Immanuel Kant (1724–1804). All four of these Enlightenment philosophers of religion will be covered in this book.

3. I am indebted here to Dirk Baltzly's entry on "Stoicism" in the Spring 2018 edition of *The Stanford Encyclopedia of Philosophy*, ed. Edward N. Zalta (available online: https://plato.stanford.edu/archives/spr2019/entries/stoicism/, accessed March 11, 2022), especially in its reconstruction of the "physical theory" of early Greek Stoics (rather than later Roman Stoics).
4. As Richard King (among others) notes, the terms *āstika* and *nāstika* were deployed quite variably until the modern era, at which time they came to differentiate South Asian schools of philosophy that did and did not recognize the *Vedas* as authoritative (and therefore were and were not considered "Hindu"); see *Indian Philosophy: An Introduction to Hindu and Buddhist Thought* (Washington, DC: Georgetown University Press, 1999), 43–5.
5. Mīmāṃsā is therefore called Pūrva Mīmāṃsā, the school of "prior exegesis," whereas Vedānta is called Uttara Mīmāṃsā, the school of "later exegesis."
6. Also note the more pedestrian reasons for what was and was not included in this book in the first note of this chapter.
7. Here, I draw especially on the work of J. D. Y. Peel. See both *Christianity, Islam, and* Oriṣa *Religion: Three Traditions in Comparison and Interaction* (Oakland, CA: University of California Press, 2015), and *Religious Encounters and the Making of the Yoruba* (Bloomington, IN: Indiana University Press, 2001).
8. Peel, *Religious Encounters*, 114. Although traditionally uncommon, diviners can also be a female.
9. Although traditionally uncommon, a Lakȟóta "holy person" can be a female "holy woman" (*wíŋyaŋ wakȟáŋ*). Holy men and women are in a class of religious specialist that is distinct from and "higher than" the "medicine man" (*pȟežúta wičháša*) or "medicine woman" (*pȟežúta wiŋyaŋ*). For typologies of Lakȟóta religious specialists, see Chapter 12.
10. Here are some examples: in the case of South Asian religious philosophy, the use of path and step metaphors in Buddhism, Jainism, and Yoga (among other Hindu *darśana*-s); in the case of East Asian religious philosophy, the ubiquity of "way" (*dào*) language in the *sānjiào*; in the case of Abrahamic religious philosophy, the trope of mystical journey/ascent and the importance of pilgrimage more generally; in the case of African (Yorùbá) religious philosophy, the destiny of the *orí* as journey; in the case of Native American (Lakȟóta) religious philosophy, the journey by which the *šičun* escorts the *nağí*, upon death, beyond the Milky Way.

11. This is the cognitive metaphor theory of George Lakoff and Mark Johnson, which provides an account of how human thinking is structured by metaphors, especially those drawn from concrete bodily experience. At the heart of this account are two claims: humans draw on concrete bodily experience in understanding and expressing abstract concepts, and humans do so by systematically structuring abstract concepts in accordance with bodily experiences. See especially *Philosophy in the Flesh: The Embodied Mind and its Challenge to Western Thought* (New York: Basic Books, 1999).
12. See, for example, two of my papers about the application of this metaphor in global-critical philosophy of religion: (1) "Philosophy of Religion as Journey," *Palgrave Communications* 5/43 (2019): https://doi.org/10.1057/s41599-019-0252-7 (accessed March 11, 2022); and (2) "How To Philosophize About Religion Globally and Critically . . . with Undergraduates," *Religious Studies* 56/1 (2020): 49–63.

2 What Is Religion?

1. *Wakȟáŋ Tȟáŋka* is also commonly referred to as "Tȟuŋkášila," meaning "Grandfather," sometimes in the plural as "Grandfathers." See especially Chapter 10, for more about *Wakȟáŋ Tȟáŋka.*
2. Some scholars believe that Islam was influential to, if not singularly responsible for, the Yorùbá practice of Ifá divination. See, for example, chapter 11 of Peel's *Christianity, Islam, and* Orișa *Religion.*
3. My itemization of these reasons is influenced by Kevin Schilbrack's "Religions: Are there Any?" *Journal of the American Academy of Religion* 78/4 (2010): 1112–38.
4. These are the famed "seven dimensions" of religion posited by Ninian Smart. See, for example, *Dimensions of the Sacred: An Anatomy of the World's Beliefs* (Berkeley, CA: University of California Press, 1999).
5. Although I am influenced by Paul Tillich's notion of "ultimate concern," I think beyond its existential aspects (especially in the directions of community and ritual). See, for example, *Dynamics of Faith* (New York: Harper, 1957).

3 What Is Philosophy?

1. Pierre Hadot, *Philosophy as a Way of Life* (New York: Wiley-Blackwell, 1995).

2. Jean-François Lyotard, *The Postmodern Condition: A Report on Knowledge*, trans. Geoff Bennington and Brian Massumi (Manchester: Manchester University Press, 1984).
3. As, however, an anonymous reviewer has pointed out, feminist and postcolonial philosophy is not always aligned with postmodernism in its rejection of capital-T Truth about capital-R Reality. See, for example, "standpoint epistemology" in Sandra Harding, "Rethinking Standpoint Epistemology: What is 'Strong Objectivity'?" in *Feminist Epistemologies*, ed. Linda Alcoff and Elizabeth Potter (New York: Routledge, 1992), 49–83, and Pamela Sue Anderson, "'Standpoint': Its Rightful Place in a Realist Epistemology," *Journal of Philosophical Research* 26 (2001): 131–53.
4. Although this doctrine was first propounded as such by the eighth-century Jain philosopher Haribhadra (in his "Victory Banner of the Many Pointed Doctrine"), it has roots that go back to depictions of Mahāvīra in the Jain scriptures of the Śvētāmbara tradition (in the "Exposition of Explanations"). Therein Mahāvīra converts a (proto-Hindu) *brahmin* priest by showing how the world and soul (among other things) could be understood as finite or infinite depending on the perspective from which they are viewed. I am indebted here and in the next two notes to Jeffrey D. Long, *Jainism: An Introduction* (New York: I.B. Tauris, 2009).
5. This doctrine dates at least as far back as the second–fifth-century *Tattvārthasūtra* by Umāsvāti, which contrasts the ways in which things can be viewed from perspectives of permanence or change. Later, the fifth–sixth-century Jain philosopher Mallāvadin itemized these perspectives as the following seven:

    1 common standpoint, which does not properly distinguish the general and specific properties of things;
    2 practical standpoint, which understands things only in terms of their specific properties;
    3 general standpoint, which understands things only in terms of their general properties;
    4 manifest standpoint, which understands things only in their present state;
    5 verbal standpoint, which understands things only in terms of their relationship to their names;
    6 etymological standpoint, which understands things only in terms of the nuanced meanings of their names;
    7 meaning standpoint, which understands things only in terms of the ways in which their names are used.

    At the very same time, another fifth-century Jain philosopher, Siddhasena, was to recognize that the list of perspectives on reality (*naya*-s) is potentially limitless.

6. This doctrine also has roots in early Śvētāmbara scripture ("Exposition of Explanations"), in this case in the insistence that all statements be prefixed with the term *syāt*, which literally means "may be" but more precisely denotes the perspective from which an assertion is conditionally true (not probably true). Again, however, it was not until later—in this case the fifth-century philosopher Samantabhadra—that this doctrine was fully developed as a system of "seven parallelogisms" (*saptabhaṅgī-naya*), according to which truth-claims about objects can be asserted and evaluated in seven different ways:

   1 there is a perspective from which some judgment *p* is true;
   2 there is a perspective from which *p* is false;
   3 there is a perspective from which *p* is both true and false (= the combination of 1 and 2);
   4 there is a perspective from which *p* is inexpressible (= the result of 3);
   5 there is a perspective from which *p* is both true and inexpressible (= the combination of 1 and 4);
   6 there is a perspective from which *p* is both false and inexpressible (= the combination of 2 and 4);
   7 there is a perspective from which *p* is true, false, and inexpressible (= the combination of 3 and 4).

   I am indebted here also to Bina Gupta's exposition of *syādvāda* in *An Introduction to Indian Philosophy: Perspectives on Reality, Knowledge, and Freedom* (New York: Routledge, 2012), 70–2.
7. This exposition is also dependent upon Gupta's in *An Introduction to Indian Philosophy*.
8. Cārvāka thereby anticipates the Scottish philosopher David Hume's devastating eighteenth-century critique of induction by over a millennium.
9. In cases of actual debate, the necessary concomitance in step 3 (above) was illustrated by the example provided in step 4. Both parties needed to agree that this exemplified the necessary concomitance. Of course, though, a Cārvākan interlocutor would not grant this.
10. In this and the following paragraph, I draw on Chris Fraser's entry on "Mohism" in the Spring 2022 edition of *The Stanford Encyclopedia of Philosophy*, ed. Edward N. Zalta, available online: https://plato.stanford.edu/archives/spr2022/entries/mohism/ (accessed March 11, 2022).
11. These are the respective translations of A. C. Graham, Victor Mair, Chad Hansen, A. C. Graham (again), and Franklin Perkins.
12. The following draws on Chad Hansen's entry on "Zhuangzi" in the Spring 2017 edition of *The Stanford Encyclopedia of Philosophy*, ed. Edward N.

Zalta, available online: https://plato.stanford.edu/archives/spr2017/entries/zhuangzi/ (accessed March 11, 2022).

13. In addition to Hansen, see Franklin Perkins, *Heaven and Earth Are Not Humane: The Problem of Evil in Classical Chinese Philosophy* (Bloomington, IL: Indiana University Press, 2014), 168.
14. Hansen, "Zhuangzi."
15. The following exposition draws heavily from Vine Deloria, Jr., "Relativity, Relatedness, and Reality," in *Spirit and Reason* (Golden, CO: Fulcrum Publishing, 1999), 32–9.
16. Vine Deloria, Jr., "If You Think about It, You Will See That It is True," in *Spirit and Reason* (Golden, CO: Fulcrum Publishing, 1999), 44.
17. The following exposition draws from Barry Hallen, "Contemporary Anglophone African Philosophy: A Survey," in *A Companion to African Philosophy*, ed. Kwasi Wiredu (New York: Wiley-Blackwell, 2006), 99–148.
18. Note, however, that Tempels himself does not use the term *ethnophilosophy*; rather, the term was coined by the Beninese philosopher Paulin Hountondji in his critique of Tempels.
19. Kọ́lá Abímbọ́lá, *Yorùbá Culture: A Philosophical Account* (Birmingham: Iroko Academic Publishers, 2005), xviii.
20. Segun Gbadegesin, *African Philosophy: Traditional Yoruba Philosophy and Contemporary African Realities* (New York: Peter Lang, 1991), 22.
21. Some philosophers of science (e.g., Karl Popper) have argued that inductive generalization can never have probable strength insofar as a finite number of observations is always divided by an infinite number of possible observations.
22. Richard King, *Indian Philosophy: An Introduction to Hindu and Buddhist Thought* (Washington, DC: Georgetown University Press, 1999), 135. King is here indebted to John Clayton, who championed *vāda* debates for respecting "particularity and difference in a decidedly pluralistic context" rather than aspiring for the "spurious" goals of neutrality and consensus (ibid., 234). See John Clayton, *Religions, Reasons and Gods: Essays in Cross-Cultural Philosophy of Religion* (New York: Cambridge University Press, 2006), 16–57.

4 Who Am I?

1. *Bṛhadāraṇyaka Upaniṣad* 4.4.22, in *Upaniṣads*, trans. Patrick Olivelle (New York: Oxford University Press, 1996), 67–8.
2. This paragraph draws from chapter 3 in Peter Harvey's *An Introduction to Buddhism*, 2nd ed. (New York: Cambridge University Press, 2012).

3. *Milinda Pañha*, in Edward Conze, trans., *Buddhist Scriptures* (New York: Penguin Classics, 1959), 146–51.
4. Archie Fire Lame Deer and Richard Erdoes, *Gift of Power: The Life and Teachings of a Lakota Medicine Man* (Santa Fe, NM: Bear & Co. Publishing, 1992), 132.
5. William K. Powers, *Sacred Language: The Nature of Supernatural Discourse in Lakota* (Norman, OK: University of Oklahoma Press, 1986), 151.
6. Vine Deloria, Jr., "Relativity, Relatedness, and Reality," in *Spirit and Reason* (Golden, CO: Fulcrum Publishing, 1999), 34.
7. Vine Deloria, Jr., *God Is Red: A Native View of Religion: The Classic Work Updated* (Golden, CO: Fulcrum Publishing, 1994), 194. The rest of this paragraph and the following paragraph draw on pp. 194–7.
8. Vine Deloria, Jr., *The World We Used to Live In: Remembering the Powers of the Medicine Men* (Golden, CO: Fulcrum Publishing, 2006), 108.
9. Powers, *Sacred Language*, 151.
10. Ibid., 152.
11. Ibid.
12. Gbadegesin, *African Philosophy: Traditional Yoruba Philosophy and Contemporary African Realities* (New York: Peter Lang, 1991), 46.
13. Ibid.
14. Judith Gleason, in Benjamin C. Ray, *African Religions: Symbol, Ritual, and Community*, 2nd ed. (Upper Saddle River, NJ: Pearson, 1999), 37.
15. Philip John Neimark, in Ray, *African Religions*, 2nd ed., 37.
16. Confucius, *The Analects*, XII.22, XII.2, trans. D. C. Lao (New York: Penguin Classics, 1979), 116, 112.
17. Ibid., XII.1, p. 112.
18. Herbert Fingarette, *Confucius: The Secular as Sacred* (New York: Harper & Row, 1972).
19. *Dàodéjīng*, chapter 38 (= chapter 1 in Mair's translation), in *Tao Te Ching*, trans. Victor H. Mair (New York: Bantam Books, 1990), 3.
20. This paragraph draws from Jack Bemporad's entry on "Soul: Jewish Concept" in the first edition of the *Encyclopedia of Religion*, eds. Mircea Eliade and Charles J. Adams (New York: Macmillan Publishing, 1987).
21. Martin Buber, *I and Thou*, trans. Walter Kaufmann (New York: Touchstone, 1996), 85.
22. Augustine, *Confessions* VIII.ix (21), trans. Henry Chadwick (New York: Oxford University Press, 1991), 147–48.
23. Ibid., VIII.xi (27), pp. 151–2.
24. Farid al-Din Attar, *Muslim Saints and Mystics: Episodes from the Tadhkirat al-Auliya' (Memorial of the Saints) by Farid al-Din Attar*, trans. A. J. Arberry (Boston, MA: Routledge & Kegan Paul, 1966), 108.

25. See especially the second meditation, "Concerning the Nature of the Human Mind: That It is Better Known than the Body," in René Descartes, *Meditations on First Philosophy*, trans. Donald A. Cross, 3rd ed. (Indianapolis, IN: Hackett Publishing, 1993), 63–70.
26. David Hume, *Treatise on Human Understanding* I.4.6, eds. David Fate Norton and Mary J. Norton (New York: Oxford University Press, 2000), 165.
27. Louis Althusser, "Ideology and Ideological State Apparatuses," in *On the Reproduction of Capital*, trans. Ben Brewster (New York: Verso, 2014), 243.
28. Judith Butler, *Gender Trouble*, 2nd ed. (New York: Routledge, 1999), 10–11. The following exposition of *Gender Trouble* is indebted to Mari Mikkola's entry on "Feminist Perspectives on Sex and Gender" in the Fall 2019 edition of *The Stanford Encyclopedia of Philosophy*, ed. Edward N. Zalta, available online: https://plato.stanford.edu/archives/fall2019/entries/feminism-gender/ (accessed March 11, 2022).

5 Where Do I Come From?

1. My exposition of Stoicism is again indebted to Dirk Baltzly's entry on "Stoicism" in in the Spring 2018 edition of *The Stanford Encyclopedia of Philosophy*, ed. Edward N. Zalta (available online: https://plato.stanford.edu/archives/spr2019/entries/stoicism/, accessed March 11, 2022).
2. Augustine, *Retractions* I.9.6, in *Augustine: Earlier Writings*, ed. J. H. S. Burleigh (Philadelphia, PA: Westminster Press, 1953), 104.
3. This and the following three paragraphs are indebted to Peter Adamson's chapter on "Arabic Philosophy and Theology before Avicenna," in *The Oxford Handbook of Medieval Philosophy*, ed. John Marenbon (New York: Oxford University Press, 2013), 58–82.
4. Abū al-Ḥasan al-Ashʿarī, *Kitāb al-Lumaʿ*, §92, in *The Theology of al-Ashʿarī*, ed. Richard J. McCarthy (Beyrouth: Imprimerie Catholique, 1953), 59.
5. Kọ́lá Abímbọ́lá, *Yorùbá Culture: A Philosophical Account* (Birmingham: Iroko Academic Publishers, 2005), 73.
6. Ibid.
7. Moses Makinde, "An African Concept of Human Personality: The Yorùbá Example," in *African Philosophy: The Demise of a Controversy* (Ile-Ife: Obafemi Awolowo University Press, 2007), 114.
8. Ibid.
9. Ibid.
10. Ibid., 121, 132–6.

11. Segun Gbadegesin, *African Philosophy: Traditional Yoruba Philosophy and Contemporary African Realities* (New York: Peter Lang, 1991), 54.
12. Ibid., 56.
13. Amber Carpenter, *Indian Buddhist Philosophy* (New York: Routledge, 2014), 43–7.
14. But why, you might ask, are we "originally" ignorant in such a way? Why do we "naturally" tend to reify the stuff of the world, ourselves included. Theravāda Buddhism seems not to have an answer to this question. In fact, the historical Buddha resisted such "speculative" questions, maintaining that we should instead focus ourselves entirely on the task at hand—waking up, seeing things the way they are, attaining enlightenment.
15. Śaṅkara, *Brahma Sūtra Bhāṣya*, Preamble, in *A Sourcebook in Indian Philosophy*, eds. Sarvepalli Radhakrishnan and Charles A. Moore (Princeton, NJ: Princeton University Press, 1957), 509–10. As with all (Hindu) *darśana*-s, one basis of the Vedānta *darśana* is a foundational set of *sūtras*, in this case the *Brahma Sūtras* (aka *Vedānta Sūtras*), which were probably written in the fifth century CE by a man named Bādarāyana.
16. The former is Sureśvara and the Bhāmatī school that follows; the latter is Padmapāda and the Vivaraṇa school that follows; see Richard King, *Indian Philosophy: An Introduction to Hindu and Buddhist Thought* (Washington, DC: Georgetown University Press, 1999), 56.
17. Franklin Perkins, *Heaven and Earth Are Not Humane: The Problem of Evil in Classical Chinese Philosophy* (Bloomington, IL: Indiana University Press, 2014), 129.
18. Graham, *Disputers of the Tao*, 124.
19. Mencius, *Mencius* 2A6, in *A Source Book in Chinese Philosophy*, ed. Wing-Tsit Chan (Princeton, NJ: Princeton University Press, 1963), 65.
20. Ibid., 5A5, p. 77.
21. *Xúnzǐ*, chapter 17, in *Xunzi: The Complete Text*, trans. Eric L. Hutton (Princeton, NJ: Princeton University Press, 2014), 175.
22. *Xúnzǐ*, chapter 23, in *Xunzi*, 248.
23. Raymond J. DeMallie, "Lakota Beliefs and Rituals in the Nineteenth Century," in *Sioux Indian Religion*, eds. Raymond J. DeMallie and Douglas R. Parks (Norman, OK: University of Oklahoma Press, 1987), 31.
24. Joseph Epes Brown, *Animals of the Soul: Sacred Animals of the Oglala Sioux* (Rockport, MA: Element, 1992), 60.
25. DeMallie, "Lakota Beliefs," 28.
26. Ibid., 28–9. See Chapter 10 for much more about *Wakȟáŋ Tȟáŋka*.
27. DeMallie, "Lakota Beliefs," 31. For more on this myth and these rituals, see Chapter 8.
28. Elaine A. Jahner, "Lakota Genesis: The Oral Tradition," in *Sioux Indian Religion*, eds. Raymond J. DeMallie and Douglas R. Parks (Norman, OK: University of Oklahoma Press, 1987), 52.

29. DeMallie, "Lakota Beliefs," 31.
30. Left Heron, in Jahner, "Lakota Genesis," 52.
31. John Locke, *An Essay Concerning Human Understanding*, ed. Kenneth P. Winkler (Indianapolis, IN: Hackett Publishing, 1996), II.xxi.24.
32. This paragraph draws on Kerri Smith, "Taking Aim at Free Will," *Nature* 477 (September 2011): 23–5.
33. Richard Dawkins, *The Selfish Gene*, 30th anniversary ed. (Oxford: Oxford University Press, 2006), 264.
34. Ibid., 2.
35. Ibid.
36. Ibid., 3 (Dawkins' emphasis). Also relevant is Dawkins' chapter on memes, units of replication at the cultural level. Near the end of the chapter, he writes: "It is possible that yet another unique quality of man is a capacity for genuine, disinterested, true altruism. I hope so, but I am not going to argue the case one way or the other, nor to speculate over its possible memic evolution" (200).
37. Ibid., ix.
38. Pascal Boyer, *Religion Explained: The Evolutionary Origins of Religious Thought* (New York: Basic Books, 2001), 300–1.
39. Melissa Raphael, "The Price of (Masculine) Freedom and Becoming: A Jewish Feminist Response to Eliezer Berkovits's Post-Holocaust Free-Will Defence of God's Non-intervention in Auschwitz," in *Feminist Philosophy of Religion*, eds. Pamela Sue Anderson and Beverly Clack (New York: Routledge, 2004), 144.
40. Ibid.

6 Where Am I Going To?

1. Śaṅkara, *Brahma Sūtra Bhāṣya*, I.iv.21, in *A Sourcebook in Indian Philosophy*, eds. Sarvepalli Radhakrishnan and Charles A. Moore (Princeton, NJ: Princeton University Press, 1957), 517.
2. Peter Harvey, *An Introduction to Buddhism*, 2nd ed. (New York: Cambridge University Press, 2012), 79.
3. See the Glossary entry "four causes."
4. Rāmānuja, *Brahma Sūtra Bhāṣya*, I.i.1, in *A Sourcebook in Indian Philosophy*, 547–8.
5. As with philosophies of religion that take Viṣṇu to be supreme (like Rāmānuja's and Madhva's), philosophies of religion that take Śiva to be supreme are patterned on a non-dual/dual spectrum. Some Śaivite sects, notably Śaiva Siddhānta, think of Śiva and the soul as distinct, even though Śiva lives in the soul. Other Śaivite sects like Kashmir (aka "Trika")

Śaivism posit that Śiva and the soul are both different and non-different (*bhedābheda*); here, there is no difference between Śiva and the soul at the highest level of consciousness, even though the soul must ascend to this state in seven stages, beginning with dualistic reality.

6. This paragraph draws on Roy W. Perrett's *An Introduction to Indian Philosophy* (New York: Cambridge University Press, 2016), 170–3.
7. Of course, there is also the Cārvāka position that there simply is no survival of death.
8. The next four paragraphs draw from the following two sources: Amy Weigand, "The Chinese Experience of Death: Continuity in Transition," in *Death and Dying in World Religions*, ed. Lucy Bregman (Dubuque, IA: Kendall Hunt, 2009), 119–35, and chapter 9 of Angela Sumegi's *Understanding Death: An Introduction to Ideas of Self and the Afterlife in World Religions* (New York: Wiley-Blackwell, 2014).
9. Confucius, *The Analects* XI.12, trans. D. C. Lao (New York: Penguin Classics, 1979), 107.
10. *Xúnzǐ*, chapter 19, in *Xunzi: The Complete Text*, trans. Eric L. Hutton (Princeton, NJ: Princeton University Press, 2014), 211, 217.
11. Zhuāngzǐ, chapter 18.2, in *Wandering on the Way: Early Taoist Tales and Parables of Chuang Tzu*, trans. Victor H. Mair (New York: Bantam Books, 1994), 169.
12. Ibid., chapter 6.5, p. 58.
13. Huìnéng, *Platform Sūtra of the Sixth Patriarch*, in *Philosophical Classics Volume VI: Asian Philosophy*, eds. Forrest E. Baird and Raeburne S. Heimbeck (Upper Saddle River, NJ: Pearson Prentice Hall, 2006), 488.
14. William K. Powers, *Sacred Language: The Nature of Supernatural Discourse in Lakota* (Norman, OK: University of Oklahoma Press, 1986), 134–6. According to Powers, the Lakȟóta have no general name for soul, save for conventions translated by missionaries (e.g., *wóniya* = that which makes breath or life, from "*wó*" = noun marker, "*ni*" = life/breath, "*ya*" = to create/make) (136).
15. Ibid., 134–5.
16. Ibid., 136.
17. Raymond J. DeMallie, "Lakota Beliefs, and Rituals in the Nineteenth Century," in *Sioux Indian Religion*, eds. Raymond J. DeMallie and Douglas R. Parks (Norman, OK: University of Oklahoma Press, 1987), 30. Elsewhere, DeMallie calls *šičuŋ* the potency of *Wakȟáŋ Tȟáŋka* that is embodied in a human being (30).
18. Ibid.
19. According to some accounts, each *nağí* has its life deeds judged by an old woman, after which the good go to lush, green plains where the buffalo roam, while the bad are pushd over a cliff and left to roam the earth and endanger

the living; see William K. Powers, *Oglala Religion* (Lincoln, NE: University of Nebraska Press, 1977), 53. One of the seven sacred rites (which we will look at in the next chapter) involves "releasing" the *naǧí* one year after death. During that year, it is kept and fed to prevent it from enticing others to join it.

20. Vine Deloria, Jr., *God is Red: A Native View of Religion: The Classic Work Updated* (Golden, CO: Fulcrum Publishing, 1994), 155.
21. Ibid., 171, 170.
22. Moses Akin Makinde conjoins this theory of seven heavens with a theory of sixteen reincarnations. See "Immortality of the Soul and the Yoruba Theory of the Seven Heavens (Ọ̀run Méje)," in *African Philosophy: The Demise of a Controversy* (Ile-Ife: Obafemi Awolowo University Press, 2007), 140–68.
23. For these various views, see the following: Makinde, "Immortality," 153, 157; J. D. Y. Peel, *Religious Encounters and the Making of the Yoruba* (Bloomington, IN: Indiana University Press, 2001), 173; Ray, *African Religions*, 2nd ed., 104; and Kọ́lá Abímbọ́lá, *Yorùbá Culture: A Philosophical Account* (Birmingham: Iroko Academic Publishers, 2005), 53.
24. Makinde, "Immortality," 153.
25. In the case of death prior to forty years of age or by unnatural causes, witchcraft is suspected and the deceased is therefore condemned to wander forever in the forests, mountains, and rivers (Ray, *African Religions*, 2nd ed., 102–3).
26. Ibid., 102.
27. Ibid.
28. Also notable is *gèlèdé*, a harvest festival honoring the "Great Mother" (Ìyá Nlá) or "Mother of All Water" (Yemọ́ja) and thereby the creative and destructive powers of all feminine forces, including female ancestors (as well as elderly women, female *Òrìṣà*, and witches or "powerful people" [*àjẹ́*], the latter of which could be placated and harnessed for good through the festival). See Eilzabeth Isichei, *The Religious Traditions of Africa: A History* (Westport, CT: Praeger, 2004), 259–61.
29. Benjamin C. Ray, *African Religions: Symbol, Ritual, and Community*, 1st ed. (Englewood Cliffs, NJ: Prentice-Hall, 1976), 140.
30. Ibid.
31. This and the following five paragraphs draw on Angela Sumegi's chapters on Judaism and Christianity in *Understanding Death: An Introduction to Ideas of Self and the Afterlife in World Religions* (New York: Wiley-Blackwell, 2014).
32. See, for example, Job 10:21, 7:9; Psalms 88:3–7, 115:16–18; Isaiah 38:18–19.
33. Plato, *Phaedo*, 77e–80c, in *Five Dialogues: Euthyphro, Apology, Crito, Meno, Phaedo*, 2nd ed., trans. G. M. A. Grube, ed. John M. Cooper (Indianapolis, IN: Hackett Publishing, 2002), 116–19.

34. Al-Ghazālī, *Incoherence of the Philosophers* (*Tahāfut al-Falāsifa*), trans. Sabih Ahmad Kamali (Lahore: Pakistan Philosophical Congress, 1963), 235.
35. Ibn Rushd, "About the Natural Sciences: The Fourth Discussion," in *Averroes' Tahafut al-Tahafut (The Incoherence of the Incoherence)*, reprint ed., vol. 1, trans. Simon Van Den Bergh (London: E. J. W. Gibb Memorial Trust, 2008), 359–64.
36. My discussion below in indebted to both Gabriel Andrade's entry on "Immortality" in the *Internet Encyclopedia of Philosophy* (https://iep.utm.edu/immortal/, accessed March 11, 2022) and William Hasker and Charles Taliaferro's entry on "Afterlife" in the *Stanford Encyclopedia of Philosophy* (https://plato.stanford.edu/archives/spr2019/entries/afterlife/, accessed March 11, 2022).
37. Richard Swinburne, *The Evolution of the Soul* (Oxford: Oxford University Press, 1997), xii.
38. Peter Singer, *How Are We to Live?* (New South Wales: Random House Australia, 1993), 274.
39. William Hasker and Charles Taliaferro, "Afterlife," *The Stanford Encyclopedia of Philosophy* (Spring 2019 ed.), Edward N. Zalta (ed.), available online: https://plato.stanford.edu/archives/spr2019/entries/afterlife/ (accessed March 11, 2022).
40. This paragraph draws on Jeffrey Kripal's discussion of CORTs and NDEs in *Comparing Religions* (New York: Wiley-Blackwell, 2014), 288–94.
41. The first notable attempt to collect accounts of NDEs was Raymond A. Moody's 1975 book *Life after Life* (New York: Bantam Books).
42. See especially chapters six and seven of Grace M. Jantzen, *Becoming Divine: Towards a Feminist Philosophy of Religion* (Bloomington, IN: Indiana University Press, 1999).
43. See especially Karl Marx's "Contribution to the Critique of Hegel's Philosophy of Right," in *The Marx–Engels Reader*, 2nd ed., ed. Robert C. Tucker (New York: W. W. Norton and Co., 1972), 16–25.

7 How Do I Get There?

1. This distinction, which goes back to medieval Hinduism, analogizes the difference between religious paths that stress deity-dependence and self-dependence. In the case of deity-dependence, the religious practitioner behaves like a baby kitten that is held and carried by its mother's mouth, in the case of self-dependence, like a baby monkey that actively clings to mama monkey. For more about cat-hold theory (*mārjāra-nyāya*) and monkey-hold theory (*markaṭa-nyāya*) in Hinduism, see Richard King's *Indian Philosophy: An Introduction to Hindu and*

Buddhist Thought (Washington, DC: Georgetown University Press, 1999), 224. For the distinction between "self-power" or "self-effort" (Ch. *zìlì*; Jp. *jiriki*) and "other-power" or "other-effort" (Ch. *tālì*; Jp. *tariki*) in Chinese and Japanese Buddhism, see chapter 7 of Peter Harvey's *An Introduction to Buddhism*, 2nd ed. (New York: Cambridge University Press, 2012), especially 216–17, 229–30, 235–6.

2. Black Elk, *The Sacred Pipe: Black Elk's Account of the Seven Rites of the Oglala Sioux*, recorded and edited by Joseph Epes Brown (Norman, OK: University of Oklahoma Press, 1953), 5. According to Julian Rice, "Black Elk consciously tried to make Lakota religion expressive of the same truths of Christianity" (*Black Elk's Story: Distinguishing Its Lakota Purpose* [Albuquerque, NM: University of New Mexico Press, 1991], 6). Rice finds *The Sacred Pipe* to be the "most consistently Christian of Black Elk's works" (8).
3. As Elaine A. Jahner relates, James Walker, the first Euro-American to do intensive "anthropological" research (even though he himself was a physician) with the Lakȟóta (in the late 1800s and early 1900s), "puzzled" that the Lakȟóta "had no single story that compelled belief [about creation/origins] in the way that the first chapters of Genesis function for Christians"; see "Lakota Genesis: The Oral Tradition," in *Sioux Indian Religion*, eds. Raymond J. DeMallie and Douglas R. Parks (Norman, OK: University of Oklahoma Press, 1987), 46.
4. Ibid., 52.
5. According to Archie Fire Lame Deer, the Sun Dance is also performed to renew life, to honor women (who suffer in bringing life), and to help others; see Archie Fire Lame Deer and Richard Erdoes, *Gift of Power: The Life and Teachings of a Lakota Medicine Man* (Santa Fe, NM: Bear & Co. Publishing, 1992), 226–7.
6. According to Beatrice Medicine, the *tȟápa waŋkáyeyapi* was a coming-of-age ceremony for young women (161); she laments that neither this ceremony nor the *išnáthi awíčhalowaŋpi* were practiced at the time she wrote "Indian Women and Traditional Religion," in *Sioux Indian Religion*, eds. Raymond J. DeMallie and Douglas R. Parks (Norman, OK: University of Oklahoma Press, 1987), 168–9. Leonard Crow Dog says the same in Leonard Crow Dog and Richard Erdoes, *Crow Dog: Four Generations of Sioux Medicine Men* (New York: Harper Perennial, 1995), 142, 147–52.
7. Kọlá Abímbọlá, *Yorùbá Culture, Yorùbá Culture: A Philosophical Account* (Birmingham: Iroko Academic Publishers, 2005), 62.
8. J. D. Y. Peel, *Religious Encounters and the Making of the Yoruba* (Bloomington, IN: Indiana University Press, 2001), 101.
9. J. D. Y. Peel, *Christianity, Islam, and* Orișa *Religion: Three Traditions in Comparison and Interaction* (Oakland, CA: University of California Press, 2015), 217.

10. Olúfẹ́mi Táíwò, "Òrìsà: A Prolegomenon to a Philosophy of Yorùbá Religion," in *Òrìsà Devotion as World Religion: The Globalization of Yorùbá Religious Culture*, eds. Jacob K. Olupona and Terry Rey (Madison, WI: University of Wisconsin Press, 2008), 95.
11. Here, Táíwò draws on the work of Ulli Beier in *The Return of the Gods: The Sacred Art of Susanne Wenger* (New York: Cambridge University Press, 1975).
12. Táíwò, "Òrìsà," 98.
13. Ibid., 103, 99.
14. *Bhagavad Gītā* III.4–5, trans. Eknath Easwaran (New York: Vintage Spiritual Classics, 1985), 17.
15. Ibid., III.19–20, p. 19.
16. Ibid., III.3, p. 17.
17. Ibid., XII.2, p. 66.
18. Ibid., XII.6–7, p. 66.
19. According to the fourth-generation Confucian Xúnzǐ, there were in fact three basic stages for someone who undertook this "path": scholar (*shì*), "person of virtue" (*jūnzǐ*), and sage (*shèngrén*). The scholar has taken first steps, the *jūnzǐ* has acquired a good deal of learning but still must think about what is the right thing to do in a situation, and the *shèngrén* has wholly internalized the principles of ritual and morality so that his action flows spontaneously without the need for thought. See David Elstein's entry on Xúnzǐ in the *Internet Encyclopedia of Philosophy*, available online: https://www.iep.utm.edu/Xúnzǐ/ (accessed March 11, 2022).
20. *The Great Learning*, in *A Source Book in Chinese Philosophy*, ed. Wing-Tsit Chan (Princeton, NJ: Princeton University Press, 1963), 86–7.
21. *Doctrine of the Mean*, in *A Source Book in Chinese Philosophy*, ed. Chan, 95–114, at 107–8.
22. Zhū Xī, "The Complete Works of Chu Hsi," 2:22, in *A Source Book in Chinese Philosophy*, ed. Chan, 605–53, at 607.
23. Xinzhong Yao, *An Introduction to Confucianism* (New York: Cambridge University Press, 2000), 220.
24. Hence the emphasis on the "awakening of faith" in the title of this work.
25. Huìnéng, *Platform Sūtra of the Sixth Patriarch*, in *Philosophical Classics Volume VI: Asian Philosophy*, eds. Forrest E. Baird and Raeburne S. Heimbeck (Upper Saddle River, NJ: Pearson Prentice Hall, 2006), 476.
26. Ibid., 477.
27. Harvey, *An Introduction to Buddhism*, 2nd ed., 222.
28. These "Six Constituents of Faith" include belief in the existence and oneness of Allah, in angels, in divinely authored books, in prophets, in the Day of Judgment, and in divine predestination.

29. Plato, *Euthyphro*, 10a, in *Five Dialogues: Euthyphro, Apology, Crito, Meno, Phaedo*, trans. G. M. A. Grube, ed. John M. Cooper (Indianapolis, IN: Hackett Publishing, 1981), 14.
30. The next six paragraphs are particularly indebted to John Hare's entry on "Religion and Morality," in *The Stanford Encyclopedia of Philosophy*, ed. Edward N. Zalta, Fall 2019 ed., available online: https://plato.stanford.edu/archives/fall2019/entries/religion-morality/ (accessed March 11, 2022), as well as both *Medieval Philosophy: An Historical and Philosophical Introduction* (London: Routledge, 2007) and *The Oxford Handbook of Medieval Philosophy* (New York: Oxford University Press, 2013) by John Marenbon.
31. Abū al-Ḥasan al-Ashʿarī, *The Theology of al-Ashʿari*, ed. Richard J. McCarthy, 3–116 (Beyrouth: Imprimerie Catholique, 1953), 169–70.
32. John Hick, *An Interpretation of Religion: Human Responses to the Transcendent*, 2nd ed. (New Haven, CT: Yale University Press, 2004), 249, 279.
33. Ibid., 245.
34. Ibid., 242, 162, 246–7.
35. Keith Yandell, "How to Sink in Cognitive Quicksand: Nuancing Religious Pluralism," in *Contemporary Debates in Philosophy of Religion*, eds. Michael L. Peterson and Raymond J. VanArragon (Malden, MA: Blackwell, 2004), 191–200, 215–17, at 193.
36. Ibid., 200–1.
37. Huston Smith, *Forgotten Truth: The Primordial Tradition* (New York: Harper Colophon Books, 1976), x, 18.
38. Ibid., 20–1.
39. Ibid., 109.
40. Robert K. C. Forman, "Introduction: Mysticism, Constructivism, and Forgetting," in *The Problem of Pure Consciousness: Mysticism and Philosophy*, ed. R. Forman (New York: Oxford University Press, 1990), 5–6, 8. Forman referred to his perennialism as a "psychology" rather than a "philosophy" since he believed that "psychological structures" not "philosophical claims" are cross-culturally identical; see Robert K. C. Forman, "Of Heapers, Splitters and Academic Woodpiles in the Study of Intense Religious Experiences," *Sophia* 35 (1996): 81; Robert K. C. Forman, "Introduction: Mystical Consciousness, the Innate Capacity, and the Perennial Philosophy," in *The Innate Capacity: Mysticism, Psychology, and Philosophy*, ed. R. Forman (New York: Oxford University Press, 1998), 28.
41. Forman, "Introduction: Mysticism, Constructivism, and Forgetting," 8.
42. Ibid., 40, 41, 24, 39.
43. Robert K. C. Forman, "The Construction of Mystical Experience," *Faith and Philosophy* 5 (1988): 264.

44. Pamela Sue Anderson, *Revisioning Gender in Philosophy of Religion: Reason, Love, and Epistemic Locatedness* (New York: Routledge, 2012), 222.

8 What Obstacles are in My Way?

1. William K. Powers, *Yuwipi: Vision & Experience in Oglala Ritual* (Lincoln, NE: Bison Books, 1984), 12.
2. Vine Deloria, Jr., "Ikto'mi Marries His Daughter," in *Dakota Texts*, trans. Ella Deloria (Lincoln, NE: Bison Books, 2006), 11–19.
3. Ibid.
4. Powers, *Sacred Language: The Nature of Supernatural Discourse in Lakota* (Norman, OK: University of Oklahoma Press, 1986), 155.
5. Vine Deloria, Jr., "The Trickster and the Messiah," in *Spirit and Reason: The Vine Deloria, Jr., Reader*, eds. Barbara Deloria, Dristen Foehner, and Sam Scinta (Golden, CO: Fulcrum Publishing, 1999), 28.
6. John (Fire) Lame Deer and Richard Erdoes, *Lame Deer, Seeker of Visions* (New York: Simon & Schuster, 1994), 250.
7. Archie Fire Lame Deer and Richard Erdoes, *Gift of Power: The Life and Teachings of a Lakota Medicine Man* (Santa Fe, NM: Bear & Co. Publishing, 1992), 171, 165.
8. Kọlá Abímbọlá, *Yorùbá Culture: A Philosophical Account* (Birmingham: Iroko Academic Publishers, 2005), 61–2.
9. Yorùbá storytelling also features a trickster in animal form, Àjàpá the tortoise.
10. Ray, *African Religion: Symbol, Ritual, and Community*, 2nd ed. (Upper Saddle River, NJ: Pearson, 1999), 14–15.
11. Ibid., 14.
12. Abímbọlá, *Yorùbá Culture*, 70–1.
13. *Bhagavad Gītā* II.19–21, trans. Eknath Easwaran (New York: Vintage Spiritual Classics, 1985), 10.
14. *The Holy Teaching of Vimalakīrti: A Mahāyāna Scripture*, trans. Robert A. F. Thurman (University Park, PA: Pennsylvania State University Press, 1976), 66.
15. This paragraph draws on pp. 296–8 of Carl Olson's *The Many Colors of Hinduism: A Thematic-Historical Introduction* (New Brunswick, NJ: Rutgers University Press, 2007). For more on divine madness and Rāmakrishna, see Olson's *The Mysterious Play of Kālī: An Interpretive Study of Rāmakrishna* (Atlanta, GA: Scholars Press, 1990).
16. *Saṃyutta Nikāya* ii.28, in *The Connected Discourses of the Buddha*, vol. 1, trans. Bhikkhu Bodhi (Boston, MA: Wisdom Publications, 2005).

17. Nāgārjuna, *The Fundamental Wisdom of the Middle Way: Nāgārjuna's Mūlamadhyamakakārikā*, trans. Jay L. Garfield (New York: Oxford University Press, 1995), XXIV.8, p. 296.
18. Ibid., XXV.19, p. 331.
19. *Mencius* 6A8, in *A Source Book in Chinese Philosophy*, ed. Wing-Tsit Chan (Princeton, NJ: Princeton University Press, 1963), 56–7.
20. "The Doctrine of the Mean," in *A Source Book in Chinese Philosophy*, ed. Wing-Tsit Chan (Princeton, NJ: Princeton University Press, 1963), 98.
21. Zhū Xī, "First Letter to the Gentlemen of Hunan on Equilibrium and Harmony," in *A Source Book in Chinese Philosophy*, ed. Wing-Tsit Chan, 600–2 (Princeton, NJ: Princeton University Press, 1963), 601.
22. Ibid.
23. In Zhū Xī's system, the four virtues arise from *lǐ* (理), whereas the four feelings come from *qì*. For Korean (Neo)Confucianism, this "dualism" was to become a problem, inspiring the famous "Four-Seven Debate" of the sixteenth century. At the heart of the debate was the relationship between *lǐ* and *qì*: if *lǐ* was merely a formal principle or pattern, how could it be primary to the vital processes of material force (*qì*). The problem was metaphorized in terms of the following sentence from Zhū Xī: "Principle attaches itself to yin and yang as a man sits astride a horse" ("The Complete Works of Chu Hsi," 49.14a, p. 641). In response, some Korean (Neo)Confucians wondered, "How can a dead rider (*lǐ*) guide a living horse (*qì*)?" Beyond this, the debate was motivated by a need to ground moral theory in metaphysical theory: only if the metaphysical relationships between *lǐ*, *qì*, the four virtues, and the seven feelings were clear, could the Confucian moral project be possible.
24. *Dàodéjīng*, chapter 38 (= chapter 1 in Mair's translation), in *Tao Te Ching*, trans. Victor H. Mair (New York: Bantam Books, 1990), 3–4.
25. Zhuāngzǐ, chapter 2.5, in *Wandering on the Way: Early Taoist Tales and Parables of Chuang Tzu. Trans. Victor H. Mair* (New York: Bantam Books, 1994), 14–16.
26. *The Holy Teaching of Vimalakīrti: A Mahāyāna Scripture*, trans. Robert A. F. Thurman (University Park, PA: Pennsylvania State University Press, 1976), 50, 45.
27. Línjì Yìxuán, "Recorded Conversations," in *A Source Book in Chinese Philosophy*, ed. Wing-Tsit Chan (Princeton, NJ: Princeton University Press, 1963), 445, 447.
28. This sentence and the next draws on the entry on "Sin" by Joseph Jacobs and Judah David Eisenstein in the *Jewish Encyclopedia*, available online: http://www.jewishencyclopedia.com/articles/13761-sin (accessed March 11, 2022).

29. This sentence and the next draws on the entry on "Sin" in *The New Encyclopedia of Islam*, 3rd ed., ed. Cyril Glassé (New York: Rowman & Littlefield Publishers, 2007), 494.
30. A more common Sufi enumeration of the *maqāmat* is as follows: (1) repentance, (2) watchfulness, (3) renunciation, (4) poverty, (5) patience, (6) trust, (7) satisfaction.
31. Farid ud-Din Attar, *The Conference of the Birds*, trans. Afkham Darbandi and Dick Davis (New York: Penguin Books, 1984), 206.
32. Ibid., 220.
33. Marguerite Porete, *The Mirror of Simple Souls*, chapter 21, trans. Ellen Babinsky (Mahwah, NJ: Paulist Press, 1993), 103–4.
34. Meister Eckhart, Sermon 52, in *Meister Eckhart: The Essential Sermons, Commentaries, Treatises, and Defense*, trans. Edmund Colledge and Bernard McGinn (Mahwah, NJ: Paulist Press, 1981), 202.
35. Karl Marx, "Theses on Feuerbach," in *The Marx-Engels Reader*, 2nd ed., ed. Robert C. Tucker (New York: W. W. Norton & Co., 1978), 145.
36. Soren Kierkegaard, *Fear and Trembling: Dialectical Lyric by Johannes de Silentio*, trans. Alastair Hanay (New York: Penguin Books, 1985), 85.
37. The following exposition is indebted to Nancy Frankenberry's entry on "Feminist Philosophy of Religion" in *The Stanford Encyclopedia of Philosophy*, Edward N. Zalta (ed.), Summer 2018 ed., available online: https://plato.stanford.edu/archives/sum2018/entries/feminist-religion/ (accessed March 11, 2022).
38. This paragraph draws on James E. Taylor's entry on "New Atheism" in the *Internet Encyclopedia of Philosophy*, available online: https://iep.utm.edu/n-atheis/ (accessed March 11, 2022).
39. For example, see some of the essays in *The Oxford Handbook of Atheism*, especially Erik J. Wielenberg's "Atheism and Morality," Miguel Farias's "The Psychology of Atheism," and Phil Zuckerman's "Atheism and Societal Health."

9 What Is the Cosmos?

1. Vine Deloria, Jr., "If You Think About It, You Will See That It is True," in *Spirit and Reason* (Golden, CO: Fulcrum Publishing, 1999), 46.
2. Ibid., 51.
3. Ibid., 52.
4. In those portions of the *Ifá* corpus that are especially influenced by Islam, there is also mention of an *ọrun* that is comparable to hell, *ọrun-àpáàdì*, the "heaven-of-broken-pots." See Kọ́lá Abímbọ́lá, *Yorùbá Culture: A Philosophical Account* (Birmingham: Iroko Academic Publishers, 2005), 53;

J. D. Y. Peel, *Religious Encounters and the Making of the Yoruba* (Bloomington, IN: Indiana University Press, 2001), 173.

5. Why "He/It"? According to Abímbọ́lá, Olódùmarè exists only in spiritual form and therefore is not male (*Yorùbá Culture*, 51). Why "probably"? There is disagreement about the extent to which contemporary understandings of Olódùmarè as capital-G "God-like" are the products of Christian and Islamic influence.
6. Nor does Olódùmarè have any temples or priests. Olódùmarè is, however, invoked at end of offerings to the *Òrìṣà* as well as outside ritual contexts (e.g., in time of personal crisis).
7. According to Abímbọ́lá, Èṣù straddles the left/right divide between the *Òrìṣà* and the *Ajogun* (*Yorùbá Culture*, 69). Thus, people inflicted by the *Ajogun* can sacrifice to Èṣù, who will bring the sacrifice to the appropriate *Ajogun* or *Òrìṣà*, thereby gaining temporary order for the person, at least until the cosmos returns to its natural state of disorder and strife (62). Without Èṣù, claims Abímbọ́lá, the cosmos would be in perpetual state of conflict (69).
8. See Emmanuel Chukwudi Eze, "The Problem of Knowledge in 'Divination': The Example of Ifa," in *African Philosophy: An Anthology*, ed. Emmanuel Chukwudi Eze (Malden, MA: Wiley-Blackwell, 1998), 173–5.
9. Īśvara Kṛṣṇa, *Sāṁkhya Kārikā* I.64–8, in *A Sourcebook in Asian Philosophy*, eds. John M. Koller and Patricia Koller (New York: Macmillan Publishing, 1981), 58–9.
10. Umāsvāti, *That Which Is: Tattvārtha Sūtra*, §10.5, ed. Kerry Brown and Sima Sharma (San Francisco, CA: HarperCollins Publishers, 1994), 255.
11. Kaṇāda, *Vaiśeṣika Sūtras*, in *An Introduction to Indian Philosophy: Perspectives on Reality, Knowledge, and Freedom*, ed. Bina Gupta (New York: Routledge, 2012), 196.
12. *Dàodéjīng* chapter 42 (= chapter 5 in Mair's translation), in *Tao Te Ching*, trans. Victor H. Mair (New York: Bantam Books, 1990), 9.
13. Fǎzàng, "Treatise on the Golden Lion," in *A Source Book in Chinese Philosophy*, ed. Wing-Tsit Chan (Princeton, NJ: Princeton University Press, 1963), 412.
14. Zhū Xī, "The Complete Works of Chu Hsi," 42:26, in *A Source Book in Chinese Philosophy*, ed. Wing-Tsit Chan, 620.
15. Forrest E. Baird and Raeburne S. Heimbeck, "Neo-Confucian Syntheses," in *Philosophical Classics Volume VI: Asian Philosophy* (Upper Saddle River, NJ: Pearson Prentice Hall, 2006), 500.
16. Zhū Xī, "The Complete Works of Chu Hsi," 49:1, in *A Source Book in Chinese Philosophy*, 634.
17. Kirill Thompson, "Zhu Xi," in *The Stanford Encyclopedia of Philosophy*, ed. Edward N. Zalta, Summer 2021 ed., available online: https://plato.stanford.edu/archives/sum2021/entries/zhu-xi/ (accessed March 11, 2022).

18. Later, the Western ("Catholic") Church added the word *filioque* (Lt.) to signify that the Holy Spirit proceeds "also from the Son." The Eastern ("Orthodox") Church, however, rejected this innovation.
19. *Zōhar*, "Openings," in *Zohar: The Book of Enlightenment*, trans. Daniel Chanan Matt (Mahwah, NJ: Paulist Press, 1983), 66.
20. With regard to gendering, note that (1) the left-side, female *sĕpîrôt* of *Bīnâ* (intellect), *Gĕbûrâ* (justice), and *Hôd* (majesty) receive light from the male *sĕpîrôt* above them, nurture it, and birth the *sĕpîrôt* below them; (2) the tenth *sĕpîrôt*, *Malkût* or *Shekhinah*, which in Lurianic Kabbalah falls into and remains embedded in matter, is metaphorized as a (female) vagina, whereas the *sĕpîrôt* just above her, *Yĕsôd*, is metaphorized as a (male) penis; and (3) all the *sĕpîrôt* are said to emanate out from a primordial man (*ʾĀdām Qadmōn*).
21. The following exposition draws on Roy Jackson's monograph *What is Islamic Philosophy?* (New York: Routledge, 2014) as well as William Chittick's entry on "Ibn ʿArabî" for the *Stanford Encyclopedia of Philosophy* (ed. Edward N. Zalta, Spring 2020 ed., available online: https://plato.stanford.edu/archives/spr2020/entries/ibn-arabi/, accessed March 11, 2022).
22. The following exposition of scientific cosmology is informed by the website of the National Aeronautics and Space Administration (NASA), available online: https://map.gsfc.nasa.gov/universe/ (accessed March 11, 2022).
23. Robert Jastrow, *God and the Astronomers* (New York: W. W. Norton & Co., 1978), 116.
24. The following exposition draws on Simon Friederich's entry on "Fine-Tuning" for *The Stanford Encyclopedia of Philosophy*, ed. Edward N. Zalta, Winter 2018 ed., available online: https://plato.stanford.edu/archives/win2018/entries/fine-tuning/ (accessed March 11, 2022).
25. Brandon Carter, "Large Number Coincidences and the Anthropic Principle in Cosmology," in *Confrontation of Cosmological Theory with Observational Data*, ed. M. S. Longair (Dordrecht: Reidel, 1994), 294. Some of these parameters include the following: the gravitational constant, the density parameter, the mass of the proton, the ratio of the strength of electromagnetism to the strength of gravity, the strength of strong nuclear force. Friederich's entry on "Fine-Tuning" for *The Stanford Encyclopedia of Philosophy* divides evidence of fine-tuning into those pertaining to laws of nature, values of constants, and boundary conditions of the universe.
26. John D. Barrow and Frank J. Tipler, *The Anthropic Cosmological Principle* (New York: Oxford University Press, 1986). 21.
27. Ibid., 22.

10 Where Does the Cosmos Come From?

1. *Theism* is defined in this book's glossary as follows: "English term for the view or theory that God or Gods exist; often implies the existence of a single God that is omnipotent, omniscient, and omnipresent, that creates the cosmos, and that intervenes in the cosmos and personally interacts with its creatures, especially humans."
2. *Dàodéjīng*, chapter 42 (= chapter 5 in Mair's translation), in *Tao Te Ching*, trans. Victor H. Mair (New York: Bantam Books, 1990), 9.
3. Zhū Xī, "The Complete Works of Chu Hsi," 49:14, in *A Source Book in Chinese Philosophy*, ed. Wing-Tsit Chan (Princeton, NJ: Princeton University Press, 1963), 641. Elsewhere, Zhū Xī uses the Buddhist/Huáyán metaphor of the moon illuminating objects to speak about the relationship between *Tàijí* and things: "Fundamentally there is only one Great Ultimate, yet each of the myriad things has been endowed with it and each in itself possesses the Great Ultimate in its entirety. This is similar to the fact that there is only one moon in the sky but when its light is scattered upon rivers and lakes, it can be seen everywhere" (ibid., 49:11, p. 638).
4. Kirill Thompson, "Zhu Xi," in *The Stanford Encyclopedia of Philosophy*, ed. Edward N. Zalta, Summer 2021 ed., available online: https://plato.stanford.edu/archives/sum2021/entries/zhu-xi/ (accessed March 11, 2022).
5. Zhū Xī, "The Complete Works of Chu Hsi," 49:9, in *A Source Book in Chinese Philosophy*, 638. Elsewhere, Zhū Xī makes clear that "[t]he Great Ultimate exists only in the yin and yang, and cannot be separated from them" (ibid., 45:1, p. 630).
6. Raymond J. DeMallie, "Lakota Beliefs and Rituals in the Nineteenth Century," in *Sioux Indian Religion*, eds. Raymond J. DeMallie and Douglas R. Parks (Norman, OK: University of Oklahoma Press, 1987), 28.
7. Note that *Wakȟáŋ Tȟáŋka* is also referred to as *Tȟuŋkášila*, meaning "Grandfather Spirit," though sometimes rendered in the plural as "Grandfather Spirits."
8. William K. Powers, *Sacred Language: The Nature of Supernatural Discourse in Lakota* (Norman, OK: University of Oklahoma Press, 1986), 118–26. One of James Walker's informants, George Sword, divided the *Wakȟáŋ Tȟáŋka* into two kinds: *wakȟáŋ kiŋ*, which exist prior to the creation of the world, and *táku wakȟáŋ*, which exist as result of creation of world. The *wakȟáŋ kiŋ* were then subdivided into *wakȟáŋ ankatu*, the "superior *wakȟáŋ*" (which includes Wí [Sun], Tákuškaŋškaŋ [Sky], Makȟá [Earth], and Iŋyaŋ [Rock]), and the *wakȟáŋ kȟoláya*, the "kindred *wakȟáŋ*" (which includes Haŋwí [Moon], Tȟaté [Wind], Wóȟpe [White Buffalo Calf Woman], Wakiŋyaŋ ["Thunder Beings"]),

while the *táku wakȟáŋ* were subdivided into the *wakȟáŋ khúya*, the "subordinate *wakȟáŋ*" (which includes Ťhatȟáŋka [Buffalo], Hunúŋpa [Bear], Ťhatetób [Four Winds], and Yumní [Whirlwind]), and the *wakȟáŋlapi*, the "*wakȟáŋ-like*" (which includes Nağí, Niyá, Nağila, and Šičuŋ—see Chapter 5). Note that Powers doubts the reliability of this classification, which comes from Walker's research with the Lakȟóta (especially in this case, George Sword) in the early twentieth century. Also note that Powers recognizes that this classification has become standard for contemporary Lakȟóta. For a slightly different classification, see Archie Fire Lame Deer Richard Erdoes's, *Gift of Power: The Life and Teachings of a Lakota Medicine Man* (Santa Fe, NM: Bear & Co. Publishing, 1992), 251–65.

9. This myth was apparently the creation of James Walker, who synthesized bits and pieces of myths and stories that he had collected during his time as a physician at Pine Ridge in the late nineteenth and early twentieth centuries. See Elaine Jahner's introduction to James R. Walker, *Lakota Myth*, ed. Elaine A. Jahner (Lincoln, NE: University of Nebraska Press, 1983). For the myth itself, see pp. 206–45. See also the creation myths in *The Sons of the Wind: The Sacred Stories of the Lakota*, ed. D. M. Dooling (Norman, OK: University of Oklahoma Press, 1985), 3–20, as well as Archie Fire Lame Deer and Richard Erdoes's *Gift of Power*, 251–65.
10. Vine Deloria, Jr., *God is Red: A Native View of Religion: The Classic Work Updated* (Golden, CO: Fulcrum Publishing, 1994), 78, 88.
11. Elaine A. Jahner, "Lakota Genesis: The Oral Tradition," in *Sioux Indian Religion*, eds. Raymond J. DeMallie and Douglas R. Parks (Norman, OK: University of Oklahoma Press, 1987), 52.
12. Ibid.
13. Ibid.
14. There are several ways of explaining the mythic relationship between Ọbàtálá and Odùduwà in terms of the political dynamics of the area. One has Ọbàtálá representing the last of the rulers of a confederation of village polities during the "Early Formative" period (500–800 CE), which was supplanted in the "Late Formative" period (800–1100 CE) by centralized polities with a central capital at Ifẹ̀, first ruled over by Odùduwà. Odùduwà therefore finishes the "creation" that Ọbàtálá began. See Aribidesi Usman, *The Yoruba Frontier: A Regional History of Community Formation, Experience, and Changes in West Africa* (Durham, NC: Carolina Academic Press, 2012), 52–5.
15. The following paragraphs of this chapter draw primarily from John Clayton's *Religions, Reasons and Gods: Essays in Cross-Cultural Philosophy of Religion* (New York: Cambridge University Press, 2006), 121–8, 143–55, and from Roy W. Perrett's *An Introduction to Indian Philosophy* (New York: Cambridge University Press, 2016), 200–20.

16. Clayton, *Religions*, 153.
17. Through what Clayton calls a "linguistic conjuring trick," each of these blossoms turns out to be a "double blossom," doubling the number of proofs to eighteen. Writes Clayton: "The resulting display of colour is such as to bring joy to the faithful and pause for thought to the unbeliever" (*Religions*, 154). For an itemization and explication of all eighteen arguments, see Chapter VI of Hem Chandra Joshi's *Nyāyakusumāñjali of Udayanacārya: A Critical Study* (Delhi: Vidyanidhi Prakashan, 2002), 217–65.
18. Perrett, *An Introduction*, 204.
19. See Aristotle's *Metaphysics* XII.6 (in *The Complete Works of Aristotle*, vol. 2, ed. Jonathan Barnes [Princeton, NJ: Princeton University Press, 1984], 1692–4) and Aristotle's *Physics* VIII.5–6 (in *The Complete Works of Aristotle*, vol. 1, ed. Jonathan Barnes [Princeton, NJ: Princeton University Press, 1984], 427–35). For Thomas Aquinas' adaptation, see *Summa Theologica*, Part I, Question 2, Article 3, https://www.documentacatholicaomnia.eu/03d/1225-1274,_Thomas_Aquinas,_Summa_Theologiae_%5B1%5D,_EN.pdf (accessed March 11, 2022).
20. Ibn Sīnā, *Remarks and Admonitions* (*Al-Isharat wal-Tanbihat*), Fourth Class, in *Ibn Sina's Remarks and Admonitions: Physics and Metaphysics: An Analysis and Annotated Translation*, trans. Shams C. Inati (New York: Columbia University Press, 2014).
21. Al-Ghazālī, *Incoherence of the Philosophers* (*Tahāfut al-Falāsifa*), Problem IV, trans. Sabih Ahmad Kamali (Lahore: Pakistan Philosophical Congress, 1963), 90–1.
22. Both are found in ibn Rushd's *Exposition of the Methods of Proof Concerning the Beliefs of the Community* (*al-Kashf ʿan manāhij al-adilla fī ʿaqāʾid al-milla*), see *Faith and Reason in Islam: Averroes' Exposition of Religious Arguments*, trans. Ibrahim Y. Najjar (Oxford: Oneworld, 2001).
23. Maimonides, *The Guide of the Perplexed*, II.1, trans. S. Pines (Chicago, IL: University of Chicago Press, 1963), 149–54.
24. Aquinas, *Summa Theologica*, Part I, Question 2, Article 3.
25. See chapters 1–4 of Anselm's *Proslogion*, in *The Prayers and Meditations of Saint Anselm with the Proslogion*, trans. Sister Benedicta Ward, S.L.G. (New York: Penguin Books, 1973), 239–46.
26. Benedictines read through the Psalms every week during Matins. "The fool says in his heart there is no God" is located in Psalms 14:1 and 53:1. This interpretation of Anselm's proofs is that of Clayton; see his *Religions, Reasons and Gods*.
27. Personal correspondence with John Clayton.
28. René Descartes, *Meditations on First Philosophy*, 3rd ed., trans. Donald A. Cross (Indianapolis, IN: Hackett Publishing, 1993), 76–7.

29. Ibid., 90–1.
30. Locke, *An Essay Concerning Human Understanding*, ed. Kenneth P. Winkler (Indianapolis, IN: Hackett Publishing, 1996), IV.x.1–6.
31. The following exposition of cosmological arguments in general and William Lane Craig's in particular draws on Bruce Reichenbach's entry on "Cosmological Argument" in *The Stanford Encyclopedia of Philosophy*, ed. Edward N. Zalta, Fall 2019 ed., available online: https://plato.stanford.edu/archives/fall2019/entries/cosmological-argument/ (accessed March 11, 2022).
32. William Lane Craig, *The Kalām Cosmological Argument* (Eugene, OR: Wipf & Stock, 2000), 63–5.
33. The following exposition draws on Graham Oppy's entry on "Ontological Arguments" in *The Stanford Encyclopedia of Philosophy*, ed. Edward N. Zalta, Spring 2020 ed., available online: https://plato.stanford.edu/archives/spr2020/entries/ontological-arguments/ (accessed March 11, 2022).
34. Alvin Plantinga, *The Nature of Necessity* (New York: Oxford University Press, 1974), 213–17.
35. For Swinburne, all the arguments above are strong C-inductive arguments for the existence of God with the exceptions of the arguments from morality, miracles, and religious experience.
36. See chapter 4 of Wesley Wildman's *Religious Philosophy as Multidisciplinary Comparative Inquiry: Envisioning a Future for the Philosophy of Religion* (Albany, NY: State University of New York Press, 2010).
37. Grace Jantzen, "'Uneasy Intersections': Postcolonialism, Feminism, and the Study of Religion," in *Postcolonial Philosophy of Religion*, eds. Purushottama Bilimoria and Andrew B. Irvine (Cham: Springer, 2009), 300.
38. Mary Daly, *Beyond God the Father: Toward a Philosophy of Women's Liberation* (Boston, MA: Beacon Press, 1973), 19.

11 Where Is the Cosmos Going To?

1. The following exposition draws from Kaufmann Kohler's entry on "Eschatology" in the *Jewish Encyclopedia*: http://www.jewishencyclopedia.com/articles/5849-eschatology (accessed March 11, 2022).
2. I draw here upon Robert E. Lerner's "The Black Death and Western European Eschatological Mentalities," *American Historical Review* 86/3 (1981): 533–52.
3. My exposition of Shīʿa Islam in this paragraph and the next two is indebted to Heinz Halm's *Shiʿa Islam: From Religion to Revolution*, trans. Allison Brown (Princeton, NJ: Markus Wiener Publishers, 1997).
4. Twelver Shīʿa believe all of the imams to have been martyred, to have been sinless, and to have voluntarily sacrificed themselves.

5. Throughout history, several humans have claimed to be al-Mahdī. In fact, the world religion of Bahá'í owes its origin to a man later named the Báb (d. 1850), who was believed by his followers to be the return of al-Mahdī (along with his follower, Bahá'u'lláh, who was believed to be the return of Jesus).
6. Vine Deloria, Jr., *God is Red: A Native View of Religion: The Classic Work Updated* (Golden, CO: Fulcrum Publishing, 1994), 62–3, 78.
7. James Mooney, *The Ghost-Dance Religion and Wounded Knee* (New York: Dover Publications, 1973), 764.
8. Ibid., 777.
9. Vine Deloria, Jr., "Religion and Revolutions among American Indians," in *For this Land: Writings on Religion in America*, ed. James Treat (New York: Routledge, 1999), 38.
10. According to J. D. Y. Peel, in contrast to a Christian "teleological" view (that is oriented toward a transcendent end), "the normal Yoruba pattern was 'archeological' in that the end was nothing more than a return to the *origins*," which were what received cultural elaboration and social emphasis (*Religious Encounters and the Making of the Yoruba* (Bloomington, IN: Indiana University Press, 2001), 171, Peel's emphasis). In fact, the Yorùbá term *lailai* denotes both the "once upon a time" of the past and the "for ever and ever" of the future (ibid., 172).
11. Here I draw on Peel's *Christianity, Islam, and* Orịṣa *Religion*.
12. Peel, *Christianity, Islam, and* Orịṣa *Religion: Three Traditions in Comparison and Interaction* (Oakland, CA: University of California Press, 2015), 225.
13. The next two paragraphs are indebted to Benjamin C. Ray's section on Aladura Churches in *African Religions: Symbol, Ritual, and Community*, 2nd ed. (Upper Saddle River, NJ: Pearson, 1999), 184–95.
14. Hōnen, "The Philosophy of *Nenbutsu*," in *Japanese Philosophy: A Sourcebook*, eds. James W. Heisig, Thomas P. Kasulis, and John C. Maraldo (Honolulu, HI: University of Hawai'i Press, 2011), 243.
15. Shinran, "*Nenbutsu*: The Will of No-Will," in *Japanese Philosophy: A Sourcebook*, eds. Heisig, Kasulis, and Maraldo, 253.
16. This section is indebted to R. F. Gombrich's entry on "Ancient Indian Cosmology," in *Ancient Cosmologies*, eds. Carmen Blacker and Michael Loewe (London: Allen and Unwin, 1975), 110–42.
17. I am influenced here by Owen Ware's "Dialectic of the Past / Disjuncture of the Future: Derrida and Benjamin on the Concept of Messianism," *Journal for Cultural and Religious Theory* 5/2 (2004): 99–114.
18. Jacques Derrida, *Specters of Marx: The State of the Debt, the Work of Mourning and the New International*, trans. Peggy Kamuf (New York: Routlege, 1994), 106.

19. The following exposition draws on Clara Moskowitz's entry on "Endless Void or Big Crunch: How Will the Universe End?" on Space.com (October 26, 2011), available online: https://www.space.com/13393-universe-endless-void-big-crunch.html (accessed March 11, 2022).
20. Rudolf Bultmann, *The Presence of Eternity: History and Eschatology: The Gifford Lectures 1955* (New York: Harper, 1957), 155.
21. Vítor Westhelle, "Liberation Theology: A Latitudinal Perspective," in *The Oxford Handbook of Eschatology*, ed. Jerry L. Walls (New York: Oxford University Press, 2007), 318.
22. Robert John Russell, "Cosmology and Eschatology," in *The Oxford Handbook of Eschatology*, ed. Walls, 574.
23. Ibid., 574.

12 How Does the Cosmos Get There?

1. Note that in some cases the Pharaoh's magicians perform competing miraculous deeds "by means of their secret arts" (Exodus 7:11, 22; 8:7).
2. As you probably can tell, Ezekiel's mystical journey is situated in the older cosmos of the Hebrew Bible—a firmament above the Earth, on which God's throne is perched. First millennium *hêkālôt-merkābâ* mysticism, by contrast, occupied the newer, ancient Greek cosmos in which concentric spheres of celestial bodies surrounded the Earth. See Chapter 10 for more about this subject.
3. "The Mi'raj of Bistami," in *Early Islamic Mysticism: Sufi, Qur'an, Mi'raj and Theological Writings*, trans. Michael A. Sells (Mahwah, NY: Paulist Press, 1996), 249.
4. The following analysis is indebted to Isra Yazicioglu's "Redefining the Miraculous: al-Ghazālī, ibn Rushd and Said Nursi on Qur'anic Miracle," *Journal of Qur'anic Studies* 13/2 (2011): 86–108.
5. Al-Ghazālī, *Incoherence of the Philosophers* (*Tahāfut al-Falāsifa*), trans. Sabih Ahmad Kamali (Lahore: Pakistan Philosophical Congress, 1963), 188–93.
6. Ibn Rushd, "About the Natural Sciences: The First Discussion," *Averroes' Tahafut al-Tahafut (The Incoherence of the Incoherence)*, reprint ed., vol. 1, trans. Simon Van Den Bergh (London: E. J. W. Gibb Memorial Trust, 2008), 316–32.
7. Patañjali, *Yoga Sūtras*, in *An Introduction to Indian Philosophy: Perspectives on Reality, Knowledge, and Freedom*, ed. Bina Gupta (New York: Routledge, 2012), 194–6.

8. Note that this is not devotion to a deity but rather meditation upon the divine form, most of all the sacred syllable *Oṃ*, which is said to be the name of the Lord (*Īśvara*).
9. David L. Weddle, *Miracles: Wonder and Meaning in World Religions* (New York: New York University Press, 2010), 48.
10. Ibid., 49.
11. Ibid., 63–8. Also see, Larry McCrea, "Just Like Us, Just Like Now: The Tactical Implications of the Mīmāṃsā Rejection of Yogic Perception," in *Yogic Perception, Meditation and Altered States of Consciousness*, ed. Eli Franco (Vienna: Verlag der Österreichischen Akademie der Wissenschaften, 2009), 55–70.
12. *Bhagavad Gītā* XI.52–4, trans. Eknath Easwaran (New York: Vintage Spiritual Classics, 1985), 65.
13. Other important celestial bodhisattvas include Maitreya, the next Buddha to come in our Buddha-realm, and Mañjuśrī, who offers protection and wisdom to those in need.
14. *The Holy Teaching of Vimalakīrti: A Mahāyāna Scripture*, trans. Robert A. F. Thurman (University Park, PA: Pennsylvania State University Press, 1976), 43, 45; 58–9, 61–2, 84.
15. Ibid., 85.
16. Ibid., 52–5.
17. Dōgen, "Recommending Zazen to All People" (*Fukan Zazengi*), in *Zen Master Dōgen: An Introduction with Selected Writings*, trans. Yūhō Yokoi and Daizen Victoria (New York: Weatherhill, 1976).
18. Qīngyuán Xíngsī (青原行思), in D. T. Suzuki, *Essays in Zen Buddhism (First Series)* (London: Rider & Co., 1926), 24.
19. For the sake of simplicity and economy, I treat the *wičháša wakȟáŋ* and the *wíŋyaŋ wakȟáŋ* each as a single type. Be aware, though, that there are numerous subcategories within this type. Anthropologist William Powers posits three major types for both the *wičháša wakȟáŋ* and the *wíŋyaŋ wakȟáŋ*—(1) *wapíyapi* = curers; (2) *wakȟáŋ káǧa* = performers; (3) *wičhaȟmúŋǧa*/*wíȟmuŋǧa* = wizards/witches—as well as a fourth major type for only the *wíŋyaŋ wakȟáŋ*: (4) *wíŋkte* = transvestites (*Sacred Language*, 181, 190). Although Archie Fire Lame Deer does not provide an exhausting typology, he mentions several different important types of "medicine men"—(a) *wičháša wakȟáŋ*, the "all-around shaman"; (b) *pȟežúta wičháša*, one who cures the sick with herbs (for Powers, this is a subclass of the "curers"); (c) the *yuwípi* (for Powers, this is also a subclass of "curers"); (d) the *waáyatan*, a prophet who can see into the future (this is not registered on Powers' typology); (e) the *heyókȟa*, the "sacred clown" who does everything backwards (for Powers, this is a subclass of the "performers"); and (f) the *wapíya*, a conjurer and magician (which seems

to have the properties both of Powers' "bone curer," a subclass of "curers," and of Powers' *wičhaȟmúŋǧa*, which are evil "wizards"); see Archie Fire Lame Deer and Richard Erdoes, *Gift of Power: The Life and Teachings of a Lakota Medicine Man* (Santa Fe, NM: Bear & Co. Publishing, 1992), 150–1.

20. Vine Deloria, Jr., *The World We Used to Live in: Remembering the Powers of the Medicine Men* (Golden, CO: Fulcrum Publishing, 2006), xxiv.
21. Ibid., 83–4.
22. Ibid., 136.
23. Ibid.
24. Táíwò, "Òrìsà," 98.
25. Note that spirit possession is not a common feature of Ifá divination.
26. José Antonio Lammoglia, "Divination and Spirit Possession in the Americas," in *Encyclopedia of African-American Culture and History*, through *Encyclopedia.com*, available oline: https://www.encyclopedia.com/history/encyclopedias-almanacs-transcripts-and-maps/divination-and-spirit-possession-americas (accessed January 24, 2022).
27. J. D. Y. Peel, *Christianity, Islam, and* Oriṣa *Religion: Three Traditions in Comparison and Interaction* (Oakland, CA: University of California Press, 2015), 217.
28. Kọlá Abímbọ́lá, *Yorùbá Culture: A Philosophical Account* (Birmingham: Iroko Academic Publishers, 2005), 126–7; Deidre L. Badejo, "The Pathways of Ọ̀ṣun as Cultural Synergy," in *Òrìsà Devotion as World Religion: The Globalization of Yorùbá Religious Culture*, eds. Jacob K. Olupona and Terry Rey (Madison: University of Wisconsin Press, 2008), 191–201; Benjamin C. Ray, *African Religions: Symbol, Ritual, and Community*, 2nd ed. (Upper Saddle River, NJ: Pearson, 1999), 35–8. Also consider that some of the deeds of some of the Yorùbá *Òrìṣà* are instrumental to "the path of the cosmos" insofar as they involve the establishment of a kingdom and the propagation of the first rulers at the sacred city of Ilé-Ifẹ̀. Recall from Chapter 10, that although Ọbàtálá was tasked by Olódùmarè with descending from the heavens to the primordial waters below, where he was to spread some earth over the waters to create dry land in between the mountain peaks that poked through the waters, he got drunk on palm wine and forgot his task. Olódùmarè therefore asked Ọbàtálá's younger brother Odùduwà to finish the job, which he did with a snail shell filled with earth and a chicken that spread out this earth, thereby creating the city of Ilé-Ifẹ̀, meaning "a home that is wide." For Aribidesi Usman, this mythic relationship between Ọbàtálá and Odùduwà can be understood in terms of the political dynamics of Yorùbáland, with Ọbàtálá representing the last of the rulers of a confederation of village polities during the "Early Formative" period (500–800 CE), which was supplanted in the "Late Formative" period (800–1100 CE) by centralized polities with a central capital at Ifẹ̀, first ruled over by Odùduwà. See

Aribidesi Usman, *The Yoruba Frontier: A Regional History of Community Formation, Experience, and Changes in West Africa* (Durham, NC: Carolina Academic Press, 2012), 52–5.

29. Abímbọ́lá, *Yorùbá Culture*, 61–2, 78–82.
30. William James, *The Varieties of Religious Experience: A Study in Human Nature*, ed. Matthew Bradley (Oxford: Oxford University Press, 2012), 32.
31. Ibid., 290–2.
32. Ibid., 368–9.
33. Ibid., 383.
34. Steven Katz, "Language, Epistemology, and Mysticism," in *Mysticism and Philosophical Analysis*, ed. Steven Katz (New York: Oxford University Press, 1978), 26.
35. Ibid., 26–7.
36. Grace M. Jantzen, *Power, Gender and Christian Mysticism* (New York: Cambridge University Press, 1995), 326.
37. Stephen Jay Gould, and Richard Lewontin, "The Spandrels of San Marco and the Panglossian Paradigm: A Critique of the Adaptationist Programme," *Proceedings of the Royal Society B* 205/1161 (1979): 581–98.
38. Also relevant are the numerous, recent studies of religious experience that draw on brain-imagining research. In some cases, this research has been used to discredit religion, e.g., by showing how the brain states of those having religious experiences are similar to those undergoing temporal-lobe epilepsy; in other cases, this research has been used to bolster religion, e.g., by showing how the brain is optimally wired for religious experiences.
39. See especially Kripal and Elizabeth G. Krohn's co-authored *Changed in a Flash: One Woman's Near-Death Experience and Why a Scholar Thinks It Empowers Us All* (Berkeley, CA: North Atlantic Books, 2018).
40. David Hume, *Enquiry Concerning Human Understanding*, 2nd ed., ed. Eric Steinberg (Indianapolis, IN: Hackett Publishing, 1993), "Section X: Of Miracles."
41. See for example, Oludamani Ogunnaike's soon-to-be-published paper "From Theory to *Theoria* and Back Again and Beyond: Decolonizing the Study of Africana Religions."

13 What Obstacles are in the Way of the Cosmos?

1. This exposition relies heavily on Purushottama Bilimoria's "Toward an Indian Theodicy," in *A Companion to the Problem of Evil*, eds. Justin P. McBryer and Daniel Howard-Synder (Malden, MA, and Oxford: John Wiley & Sons, 2013), 302–17.

2. This is one of the section headings of Anne Valley's chapter on Jainism for the *Oxford Handbook of Atheism*, ed. Stephen Bullivant and Michael Ruse, 351–66 (New York: Oxford University Press, 2013). Peter Harvey makes similar claims about early Buddhist views of a creator God in *An Introduction to Buddhism*, 2nd ed. (New York: Cambridge University Press, 2012), 36–8.
3. Bilimoria, "Toward and Indian Theodicy," 309.
4. Śaṅkara, *Brahma Sūtra Bhāṣya*, II.i.34–6, in *A Sourcebook in Indian Philosophy*, eds. Sarvepalli Radhakrishnan and Charles A. Moore (Princeton, NJ: Princeton University Press, 1957), 362–5.
5. Rāmānuja, *Śrībhāṣya*, II.i.34–6, in *Brahma-Sūtras according to Śrī Rāmānuja*, 7th reprint ed. trans. Swami Vireswarananda and Swami Adidevananda (Calcutta: Advaita Ashrama, 2012), 237–40.
6. As you know from Chapter 5, Śaṅkara believes that humans are prone to misidentify the cosmos as something other than *Brahman* due to both their own ignorance (*avidyā*) and the creative power of *Brahman* to generate the cosmic illusion (*māyā*) of multiplicity and change. Nevertheless, these misidentifications in particular and bad behavior in general are always the responsibility of humans.
7. As with Śaṅkara, Rāmānuja also holds that the souls of persons are eternal, preexisting the creation of any particular cosmos. *Īśvara* is therefore not the cause of immoral actions; nor is there any evil at all in *Īśvara*.
8. The following exposition is influenced by Franklin Perkins' masterful *Heaven and Earth Are Not Humane: The Problem of Evil in Classical Chinese Philosophy* (Bloomington, IL: Indiana University Press, 2014).
9. *Mòzǐ*, chapter 26.2, in *Mo Zi: The Book of Master Mo*, trans. Ian Johnston (New York: Penguin Books, 2010), 126.
10. Ibid., chapter 48.14, p. 323.
11. See *Mòzǐ*, chapters. 37.2, 7–8, in *Mo Zi*, 182–3, 185–6.
12. *Xúnzǐ*, chapter 17, in *Xunzi: The Complete Text*, trans. Eric L. Hutton (Princeton, NJ: Princeton University Press, 2014), 175.
13. Ibid., 181.
14. The following comes from Archie Fire Lame Deer and Richard Erdoes's *Gift of Power: The Life and Teachings of a Lakota Medicine Man* (Santa Fe, NM: Bear & Co. Publishing, 1992), 261–3.
15. I thank Fritz Detwiler for calling my attention to this list (which originates in the research of James Walker).
16. Vine Deloria, Jr., "Christianity and Indigenous Religion: Friends or Enemies?" in *For this Land: Writings on Religion in America*, ed. James Treat (New York: Routledge, 1999), 146.
17. Vine Deloria, Jr., "A Violated Covenant," in *For this Land*, 72.
18. Ibid., 72, 74.
19. Ibid., 76.

20. Ibid., 79.
21. Vine Deloria, Jr., *God is Red: A Native View of Religion: The Classic Work Updated* (Golden, CO: Fulcrum Publishing, 1994), 261–2.
22. Ibid., 264.
23. Ibid., 265.
24. Remember, though, that three of the *Òrìṣà* are primordial, therefore not created by Olódùmarè: Ọrunmila, Èṣù, and Ọbàtálá.
25. Kọ́lá Abímbọ́lá, *Yorùbá Culture: A Philosophical Account* (Birmingham: Iroko Academic Publishers, 2005), 70–1.
26. Benjamin C. Ray, *African Religions: Symbol, Ritual, and Community*, 2nd ed. (Upper Saddle River, NJ: Pearson, 1999), 35, 108–10.
27. According to Jacob Olupọna, the term *oṣó* is used of male "sorcerers", see *African Religions: A Very Short Introduction* (New York: Oxford University Press), 51.
28. See Elizabeth Isichei, *The Religious Traditions of Africa: A History* (Westport, CT: Praeger, 2004), 259–61, 311–13.
29. Job 42:2–6.
30. These are some of the responses featured in Part III of *Wrestling with God: Jewish Theological Responses during and after the Holocaust*, eds. Steven T. Katz, Shlomo Biderman, and Gershon Greenberg (New York: Oxford University Press, 2007).
31. Many of these theodicies appear in Book VII of Augustine's *The Confessions*, trans. Henry Chadwick (New York: Oxford University Press, 1991), see especially, VII.ii (3)–v (7) and Vii.xii (18)–xiii (19).
32. See especially John Hick's *Evil and the God of Love*, 2nd ed. (New York: Palgrave Macmillan, 2007).
33. The following draws from James R. Beebe's entry on the "Logical Problem of Evil" (https://www.iep.utm.edu/evil-log/, accessed March 11, 2022), from Nick Trakakis' entry on the "Evidential Problem of Evil" (https://www.iep.utm.edu/evil-evi/, accessed March 11, 2022) on the *Internet Encyclopedia of Philosophy*, and from Michael L. Peterson's entry on "The Problem of Evil" in *The Oxford Handbook of Atheism*, eds. Stephen Bullivant and Michael Ruse, 71–88 (New York: Oxford, 2013).
34. For a twentieth-century proponent, see J. L. Mackie, "Evil and Omnipotence," *Mind*, 64 (1955): 200–12.
35. Marilyn McCord Adams, *Horrendous Evils and the Goodness of God* (Ithaca, NY: Cornell University Press, 2000).
36. William L. Rowe, "The Problem of Evil and Some Varieties of Atheism," *American Philosophical Quarterly*, 16 (1979): 335–41.
37. Open Theism is an imaginative exception, one that holds that the future is "open" and not under God's control. Process Theology, which stresses the immanence of God in moments, is another exception.

38. Paul Draper, "Pain and Pleasure: An Evidential Problem for Theists," *Nous* 23 (1989): 331–50.
39. William L. Rowe, "Evil and the Theistic Hypothesis: A Response to Wykstra," *International Journal for Philosophy of Religion* 16/2 (1984): 95–100.
40. An Yountae, "On Violence and Redemption: Fanon and Colonial Theodicy," in *Beyond Man: Race, Coloniality, and Philosophy of Religion*, eds. An Yountae and Eleanor Craig (Durham, NC: Duke University Press, 2021), 208.
41. As Kenneth Surin has argued, attempts to justify God vis-à-vis evil all too often fall into attempts to justify evil itself; see his *Theology and the Problem of Evil* (Eugene: Wipf & Stock, 2004).
42. Morny Joy, "Rethinking the 'Problem of Evil' with Hannah Arendt and Grace Jantzen," in *New Topics in Feminist Philosophy of Religion: Contestations and Transcendence Incarnate*, ed. Pamela Sue Anderson (New York: Springer, 2010), 18.
43. Grace M. Jantzen, *Becoming Divine: Towards a Feminist Philosophy of Religion* (Bloomington, IN: Indiana University Press, 1999), 263 (Jantzen's emphases).
44. Ibid.
45. Ibid., 262.

Select Bibliography

Abímbọ́lá, Kọ́lá. *Yorùbá Culture: A Philosophical Account*. Birmingham: Iroko Academic Publishers, 2005.

Adams, Marilyn McCord. *Horrendous Evils and the Goodness of God*. Ithaca, NY: Cornell University Press, 2000.

Adamson, Peter. "Arabic Philosophy and Theology before Avicenna." In *The Oxford Handbook of Medieval Philosophy*, ed. John Marenbon, 58–82. New York: Oxford University Press, 2013.

Adler, Joseph A. "Chinese Religions." In *Encyclopedia of Religion*, 2nd ed., ed. Lindsay Jones. Detroit, MI: Macmillan Reference USA, 2005.

al-Ashʿarī, Abū al-Ḥasan. *Kitāb al-Lumaʿ*. In *The Theology of al-Ashʿarī*, ed. Richard J. McCarthy, 3–116. Beyrouth: Imprimerie Catholique, 1953.

al-Ghazālī. *Incoherence of the Philosophers* (*Tahāfut al-Falāsifa*). Trans. Sabih Ahmad Kamali. Lahore: Pakistan Philosophical Congress, 1963.

Althusser, Louis. "Ideology and Ideological State Apparatuses." In *On the Reproduction of Capital*, trans. Ben Brewster, 232–72. New York: Verso, 2014.

Anderson, Pamela Sue. *Revisioning Gender in Philosophy of Religion: Reason, Love, and Epistemic Locatedness*. New York: Routledge, 2012.

Andrade, Gabriel. "Immortality." In *Internet Encyclopedia of Philosophy*. Available online: https://iep.utm.edu/immortal/ (accessed March 11, 2022).

Anselm. *Proslogion*. In *The Prayers and Meditations of Saint Anselm with the Proslogion*. Trans. Sister Benedicta Ward, S.L.G. New York: Penguin Books, 1973.

Anuruddha. *Abhidhammatthasaṅgaha, with commentary by Sumaṅgala*. In *Buddhist Philosophy: Essential Readings*, eds. William Edelglass and Jay L. Garfield, 19–25. New York: Oxford University Press, 2009.

Aquinas, Thomas. *Summa Theologica*. Trans. Fathers of the English Dominican Province. Available online: https://www.documentacatholicaomnia.eu/03d/1225-1274,_Thomas_Aquinas,_Summa_Theologiae_%5B1%5D,_EN.pdf (accessed March 11, 2022).

Aristotle. *Physics*. In *The Complete Works of Aristotle*, vol. 1, ed. Jonathan Barnes, 315–446. Princeton, NJ: Princeton University Press, 1984.

Aristotle. *Metaphysics*. In *The Complete Works of Aristotle*, vol. 2, ed. Jonathan Barnes, 1552–1728. Princeton, NJ: Princeton University Press, 1984.

Attar, Farid al-Din. *Muslim Saints and Mystics*. Trans. A. J. Arberry. Boston, MA: Routledge & Kegan Paul, 1966.

Attar, Farid ud-Din. *The Conference of the Birds*. Trans. Afkham Darbandi and Dick Davis. New York: Penguin Books, 1984.

Augustine. *Augustine: Earlier Writings*. Ed. J. H. S. Burleigh. Philadelphia, PA: Westminster Press, 1953.

Augustine. *The Confessions*. Trans. Henry Chadwick. New York: Oxford University Press, 1991.

Baltzly, Dirk. "Stoicism." In *The Stanford Encyclopedia of Philosophy*, ed. Edward N. Zalta, Spring 2018 ed. Available online: https://plato.stanford.edu/archives/spr2019/entries/stoicism/ (accessed March 11, 2022).

Barrow, John D., and Frank J. Tipler. *The Anthropic Cosmological Principle*. New York: Oxford University Press, 1986.

Beebe, James R. "Logical Problem of Evil." *Internet Encyclopedia of Philosophy*. Available online: https://www.iep.utm.edu/evil-log/ (accessed March 11, 2022).

Bemporad, Jack. "Soul: Jewish Concept." In *Encyclopedia of Religion*, 1st ed., eds. Mircea Eliade and Charles J. Adams. New York: Macmillan Publishing, 1987.

Benjamin, Walter. "On the Concept of History." Available online: https://www.sfu.ca/~andrewf/CONCEPT2.html (accessed March 11, 2022).

Bhagavad Gītā. Trans. Eknath Easwaran. New York: Vintage Spiritual Classics, 1985.

The Bhāgavata Purāṇa. 5 vols. Trans. Makarand Joshi. Delhi: Motilal Banasirdass Publishers, 1950. Available online: https://archive.org/details/bhagavatapuranaeng011950ocrmotilalbanasirdass/page/n35/mode/2up (accessed March 11, 2022).

Bilimoria, Purushottama. "Toward an Indian Theodicy." In *The Blackwell Companion to the Problem of Evil*, eds. Justin P. McBrayer and Daniel Howard-Synder, 302–17. Malden, MA: Wiley-Blackwell, 2013.

Boyer, Pascal Boyer. *Religion Explained: The Evolutionary Origins of Religious Thought*. New York: Basic Books, 2001.

Brown, Joseph Epes. *Animals of the Soul: Sacred Animals of the Oglala Sioux*. Rockport, MA: Element, 1992.

Buber, Martin. *I and Thou*. Trans. Walter Kaufmann. New York: Charles Scribner's Sons, 1970.

Buddhaghosa. *The Path of Purification: Visuddhimagga*, 3rd online ed. Trans. Bhikkhu Ñáóamolibook. Buddhist Publication Society, 2011.

Bultmann, Rudolf. *The Presence of Eternity: History and Eschatology: The Gifford Lectures 1955*. New York: Harper, 1957.

Butler, Judith. "Performative Acts and Gender Constitution: An Essay in Phenomenology and Feminist Theory." *Theatre Journal* 40/4 (December 1988): 519–31.

Bṛhadāraṇyaka Upaniṣad. In *Upaniṣads*, trans. Patrick Olivelle. New York: Oxford University Press, 1996.

Carpenter, Amber. *Indian Buddhist Philosophy*. New York: Routledge, 2014.

Chittick, William. "Ibn 'Arabî." In *Stanford Encyclopedia of Philosophy*, ed. Edward N. Zalta, Spring 2020 ed. Available online: https://plato.stanford.edu/archives/spr2020/entries/ibn-arabi/ (accessed March 11, 2022).

Clayton, John. *Religions, Reasons and Gods: Essays in Cross-Cultural Philosophy of Religion* New York: Cambridge University Press, 2006.

Clothey, Fred. *Religions of India: A Historical Introduction*. New York: Routledge, 2007.

Collins, James. *The Emergence of Philosophy of Religion*. New Haven, CT: Yale University Press, 1969.

Confucius. *The Analects*. Trans. D. C. Lao. New York: Penguin Classics, 1979.

Conze, Edward, trans. *Buddhist Texts through the Ages*. Rockport, MA: Oneworld Publications, 1995.

Craig, William Lane. *The Kalām Cosmological Argument*. Eugene, OR: Wipf & Stock, 2000.

Daly, Mary. *Beyond God the Father: Toward a Philosophy of Women's Liberation*. Boston, MA: Beacon Press, 1973.

Dàodéjīng. In *Tao Te Ching*. Trans. Victor H. Mair. New York: Bantam Books, 1990.

Dawkins, Richard. *The Selfish Gene*, 30th anniversary ed. New York: Oxford University Press, 2006.

DeMallie, Raymond J. "Lakota Beliefs and Rituals in the Nineteenth Century." In *Sioux Indian Religion*, eds. Raymond J. DeMallie and Douglas R. Parks, 25–43. Norman, OK: University of Oklahoma Press, 1987.

Deloria, Ella, trans. *Dakota Texts*. Lincoln, NE: Bison Books, 2006.

Deloria, Jr., Vine. *God is Red: A Native View of Religion: The Classic Work Updated*. Golden, CO: Fulcrum Publishing, 1994.

Deloria, Jr., Vine. "A Violated Covenant." In *For this Land: Writings on Religion in America*, ed. James Treat, 72–6. New York: Routledge, 1999.

Deloria, Jr., Vine. "An Open Letter to the Heads of the Christian Churches in America." In *For this Land: Writings on Religion in America*, ed. James Treat, 77–83. New York: Routledge, 1999.

Deloria, Jr., Vine. "If You Think about It, You Will See that It is True." In *Spirit and Reason*, 40–60. Golden, CO: Fulcrum Publishing, 1999.

Deloria, Jr., Vine. "Relativity, Relatedness, and Reality." In *Spirit and Reason*, 32–9. Golden, CO: Fulcrum Publishing, 1999.

Deloria, Jr., Vine. "Religion and Revolutions among American Indians." In *For this Land: Writings on Religion in America*, ed. James Treat, 36–43. New York: Routledge, 1999.

Deloria, Jr., Vine. "The Trickster and the Messiah." In *Spirit and Reason: The Vine Deloria, Jr., Reader*, eds. Barbara Deloria, Dristen Foehner, and Sam Scinta, 17–31. Golden, CO: Fulcrum Publishing, 1999.

Deloria, Jr., Vine. *The World We Used to Live in: Remembering the Powers of the Medicine Men*. Golden, CO: Fulcrum Publishing, 2006.

Derrida, Jacques. *Specters of Marx: The State of the Debt, the Work of Mourning and the New International*. Trans. Peggy Kamuf. New York: Routledge, 1994.

Descartes, René. *Meditations on First Philosophy*. 3rd ed. Trans. Donald A. Cross. Indianapolis, IN: Hackett Publishing, 1993.

Doctrine of the Mean. In *A Source Book in Chinese Philosophy*, ed. Wing-Tsit Chan, 95–114. Princeton, NJ: Princeton University Press, 1963.

Dōgen. *Moon in a Dewdrop: Writings of Zen Master Dōgen*, ed. Kazuaki Tanahashi. New York: North Point Press, 1985.

Dooling, D. M. *The Sons of the Wind: The Sacred Stories of the Lakota*. Norman, OK: University of Oklahoma Press, 1985.

Draper, Paul. "Pain and Pleasure: An Evidential Problem for Theists." *Nous* 23 (1989): 331–50.

Eckhart, Meister. *Meister Eckhart: The Essential Sermons, Commentaries, Treatises, and Defense*. Trans. Edmund Colledge and Bernard McGinn. Mahwah, NJ: Paulist Press, 1981.

Elk, Black. *The Sacred Pipe: Black Elk's Account of the Seven Rites of the Oglala Sioux*. Recorded and ed. by Joseph Epes Brown. Norman, OK: University of Oklahoma Press, 1953.

Făzàng. "Treatise on the Golden Lion." In *A Source Book in Chinese Philosophy*, ed. Wing-Tsit Chan, 409–14. Princeton, NJ: Princeton University Press, 1963.

Feraca, Stephen E. Feraca, *Wakinyan: Lakota Religion in the Twentieth Century*. Lincoln, NE: University of Nebraska Press, 1998.

Feuerbach, Ludwig. *The Essence of Christianity*. Trans. George Eliot. New York: Harper & Row, 1957.

Fitzgerald, Timothy. *The Ideology of Religious Studies*. New York: Oxford University Press, 2003.

Forman, Robert K. C. "Introduction: Mysticism, Constructivism, and Forgetting." In *The Problem of Pure Consciousness: Mysticism and Philosophy*, ed. R. Forman, 3–49. New York: Oxford University Press, 1990.

Frankenberry, Nancy. "Feminist Philosophy of Religion." In *The Stanford Encyclopedia of Philosophy*, ed. Edward N. Zalta. Summer 2018 ed. Available online: https://plato.stanford.edu/archives/sum2018/entries/feminist-religion/ (accessed March 11, 2022).

Fraser, Chris. "Mohism." In *The Stanford Encyclopedia of Philosophy*, ed. Edward N. Zalta. Winter 2015 ed. Available online: https://plato.stanford.edu/archives/win2015/entries/mohism/ (accessed March 11, 2022).

Friederich, Simon. "Fine-Tuning." In *The Stanford Encyclopedia of Philosophy*, ed. Edward N. Zalta. Winter 2018 ed. Available online: https://plato.stanford.edu/archives/win2018/entries/fine-tuning/ (accessed March 11, 2022).

Gautama, Akṣapāda. *Nyāya Sūtras*. In *A Sourcebook in Indian Philosophy*, eds. Sarvepalli Radhakrishnan and Charles A. Moore, 358–63. Princeton, NJ: Princeton University Press, 1957.

Gbadegesin, Segun. *African Philosophy: Traditional Yoruba Philosophy and Contemporary African Realities*. New York: Peter Lang, 1991.

Gombrich, R. F. "Ancient Indian Cosmology." In *Ancient Cosmologies*, eds. Carmen Blacker and Michael Loewe, 110–42. London: Allen and Unwin, 1975.

Gould, Stephen Jay, and Richard Lewontin. "The Spandrels of San Marco and the Panglossian Paradigm: A Critique of the Adaptationist Programme." *Proceedings of the Royal Society B* 205/1161 (1979): 581–98.

Graham, A. C. *Disputers of the Tao: Philosophical Argument in Ancient China*. La Salle, IL: Open Court, 1989.

Great Learning. In *A Source Book in Chinese Philosophy*, ed. Wing-Tsit Chan, 86–7 Princeton, NJ: Princeton University Press, 1963.

Gupta, Bina. *An Introduction to Indian Philosophy: Perspectives on Reality, Knowledge, and Freedom*. New York: Routledge, 2012.

Hadot, Pierre. *Philosophy as a Way of Life*. New York: Wiley-Blackwell, 1995.

Hallen, Barry. "Contemporary Anglophone African Philosophy: A Survey." In *A Companion to African Philosophy*, ed. Kwasi Wiredu, 99–148. New York: Wiley-Blackwell, 2006.

Hallen, Barry. *A Short History of African Philosophy*, 2nd ed. Bloomington, IN: Indiana University Press, 2009.

Halm, Heinz. *Shī'a Islam: From Religion to Revolution*. Trans. Allison Brown. Princeton, NJ: Markus Wiener Publishers, 1997.

Hansen, Chad. "Zhuangzi." In *The Stanford Encyclopedia of Philosophy*, ed. Edward N. Zalta. Spring 2017 ed. Available online: https://plato.stanford.edu/archives/spr2017/entries/zhuangzi/ (accessed March 11, 2022).

Hare, John. "Religion and Morality." In *The Stanford Encyclopedia of Philosophy*, ed. Edward N. Zalta, Fall 2019 ed. Available online: https://plato.stanford.edu/archives/fall2019/entries/religion-morality/ (accessed March 11, 2022).

Hasker, William, and Charles Taliaferro. "Afterlife." In *The Stanford Encyclopedia of Philosophy*, ed. Edward N. Zalta. Spring 2019 ed. Available online: https://plato.stanford.edu/archives/spr2019/entries/afterlife/ (accessed March 11, 2022).

Hegel, George Wilhelm Friedrich. *Introduction to the Philosophy of History*. Trans. Leo Rauch. Indianapolis, IN: Hackett Publishing, 1988.

Hick, John. *An Interpretation of Religion: Human Responses to the Transcendent*, 2nd ed. New Haven, CT: Yale University Press, 2004.

The Holy Teaching of Vimalakīrti: A Mahāyāna Scripture. Trans. Robert A. F. Thurman. University Park, PA: Pennsylvania State University Press, 1976.

Hōnen. "The Philosophy of *Nenbutsu*." In *Japanese Philosophy: A Sourcebook*, eds. James W. Heisig, Thomas P. Kasulis, and John C. Maraldo, 243–4. Honolulu, HI: University of Hawai'i Press, 2011.

Huìnéng, *Platform Sūtra of the Sixth Patriarch*. In *Philosophical Classics, Volume VI: Asian Philosophy*, eds. Forrest E. Baird and Raeburne S. Heimbeck, 474–91. Upper Saddle River, NJ: Pearson Prentice Hall, 2006.

Hume, David. *Dialogues Concerning Natural Religion*. Ed. Richard H. Popkin. Indianapolis, IN: Hackett Publishing, 1980.

Hume, David. *Enquiry Concerning Human Understanding*, 2nd ed. Ed. Eric Steinberg. Indianapolis, IN: Hackett Publishing, 1993.

Hume, David. *Treatise on Human Nature*. Eds. David Fate Norton and Mary J. Norton. New York: Oxford University Press, 2000.

ibn al-ʿArabī. *Kitāb Al-Futūḥāt al-Makkiyya*. In *The Meccan Revelations*. Vol. 1. Trans. William C. Chittick and James W. Morris. New York: Pir Press, 2004.

ibn Rushd. *Exposition of the Methods of Proof Concerning the Beliefs of the Community (al-Kashf ʿan manāhij al-adilla fī ʿaqāʾid al-milla)*. In *Faith and Reason in Islam: Averroes' Exposition of Religious Arguments*, trans. Ibrahim Y. Najjar. Oxford: Oneworld, 2001.

ibn Rushd. *Averroes' Tahafut al-Tahafut (Incoherence of the Incoherence)*, reprint ed. vol. 1. Trans. Simon Van Den Bergh. London: E. J. W. Gibb Memorial Trust, 2008.

ibn Sīnā. *Remarks and Admonitions (Al-Isharat wal-Tanbihat)*. In *Ibn Sina's Remarks and Admonitions: Physics and Metaphysics: An Analysis and Annotated Translation*, trans. Shams C. Inati. New York: Columbia University Press, 2014.

Irigaray, Luce. "Divine Women." In *Sexes and Genealogies*, trans. Gillian C. Gill, 55–72. New York: Columbia University Press, 1993.

Isichei, Eilzabeth. *The Religious Traditions of Africa: A History*. Westport, CT: Praeger, 2004.

Īśvara Kṛṣṇa. *Sāṁkhya Kārikā*. In *A Sourcebook in Asian Philosophy*, eds. John M. Koller and Patricia Koller, 52–9. New York: Macmillan Publishing, 1981.

Jackson, Roy. *What is Islamic Philosophy?* New York: Routledge, 2014.

Jahner, Elaine A. "Lakota Genesis: The Oral Tradition." In *Sioux Indian Religion*, eds. Raymond J. DeMallie and Douglas R. Parks, 45–65. Norman, OK: University of Oklahoma Press, 1987.

James, William. *The Varieties of Religious Experience: A Study in Human Nature*. Ed. Matthew Bradley. New York: Oxford University Press, 2012.

Jantzen, Grace M. *Power, Gender and Christian Mysticism*. New York: Cambridge University Press, 1995.

Jantzen, Grace M. *Becoming Divine: Towards a Feminist Philosophy of Religion*. Bloomington, IN: Indiana University Press, 1999.

Jantzen, Grace M. "'Uneasy Intersections': Postcolonialism, Feminism, and the Study of Religion." In *Postcolonial Philosophy of Religion*, eds. Purushottama Bilimoria and Andrew B. Irvine, 295–301. Cham: Springer, 2009.

Joy, Morny. "Rethinking the 'Problem of Evil' with Hannah Arendt and Grace Jantzen." In *New Topics in Feminist Philosophy of Religion: Contestations and Transcendence Incarnate*, ed. Pamela Sue Anderson, 17–32. New York: Springer, 2010.

Kaṇāda. *Vaiśeṣika Sūtras*. In Bina Gupta, *An Introduction to Indian Philosophy: Perspectives on Reality, Knowledge, and Freedom*, 196–8. New York: Routledge, 2012.

Kant, Immanuel. *Critique of Practical Reason*. In *The Cambridge Edition of the Works of Immanuel Kant: Practical Philosophy*, trans. May J. Gregor, 133–272. New York: Cambridge University Press, 1996.

Kant, Immanuel. *Groundwork of the Metaphysics of Morals*. In *The Cambridge Edition of the Works of Immanuel Kant: Practical Philosophy*, trans. Mary J. Gregor, 37–108. New York: Cambridge University Press, 1996.

Katz, Steven T. "Language, Epistemology, and Mysticism." In *Mysticism and Philosophical Analysis*, ed. Steven Katz, 22–74. New York: Oxford University Press, 1978.

Katz, Steven T., Shlomo Biderman, and Gershon Greenberg. *Wrestling with God: Jewish Theological Responses during and after the Holocaust*. New York: Oxford University Press, 2007.

Kierkegaard, Soren. *Fear and Trembling: Dialectical Lyric by Johannes de Silentio*. Trans. Alastair Hanay. New York: Penguin Books, 1985.

King, Richard. *Indian Philosophy: An Introduction to Hindu and Buddhist Thought*. Washington, DC: Georgetown University Press, 1999.

Knepper, Timothy D. "Philosophy of Religion as Journey." *Palgrave Communications* 5/43 (2019). Available online: https://doi.org/10.1057/s41599-019-0252-7 (accessed March 11, 2022).

Knepper, Timothy D. "How To Philosophize about Religion Globally and Critically . . . with Undergraduates." *Religious Studies* 56/1 (2020): 49–63.

Koller, John. *The Indian Way: An Introduction to the Philosophies and Religions of India*, 2nd ed. New York: Prentice Hall, 2006.

Kripal, Jeffrey. *Comparing Religions*. New York: Wiley-Blackwell, 2014.

Kripal, Jeffrey, and Elizabeth G. Krohn. *Changed in a Flash: One Woman's Near-Death Experience and Why a Scholar Thinks It Empowers Us All*. Berkeley, CA: North Atlantic Books, 2018.

Lakoff, George, and Mark Johnson. *Philosophy in the Flesh: The Embodied Mind and Its Challenge to Western Thought*. New York: Basic Books, 1999.

Lame Deer, Archie Fire, and Richard Erdoes. *Gift of Power: The Life and Teachings of a Lakota Medicine Man*. Santa Fe, NM: Bear & Co. Publishing, 1992.

Lame Deer, John (Fire), and Richard Erdoes. *Lame Deer, Seeker of Visions*. New York: Simon & Schuster, 1994.

Lerner, Robert E. "The Black Death and Western European Eschatological Mentalities." *American Historical Review* 86/3 (1981): 533–52.

Línjì Yìxuán. "Recorded Conversations." In *A Source Book in Chinese Philosophy*, ed. Wing-Tsit Chan, 444–9. Princeton, NJ: Princeton University Press, 1963.

Locke, John. *An Essay Concerning Human Understanding*. Ed. Kenneth P. Winkler. Indianapolis, IN: Hackett Publishing, 1996.

Long, Jeffrey D. *Jainism: An Introduction*. New York: I.B. Tauris, 2009.

Lyotard, Hean-François. *The Postmodern Condition: A Report on Knowledge*. Trans. Geoff Bennington and Brian Massumi. Manchester: Manchester University Press, 1984.

Mackie, J. L. "Evil and Omnipotence." *Mind* 64 (1955): 200–12.

Madhva. *Brahma Sūtra Bhāṣya*. In *A Sourcebook in Indian Philosophy*, eds. Sarvepalli Radhakrishnan and Charles A. Moore, 555–72. Princeton, NJ: Princeton University Press, 1957.

Maimonides. *The Guide of the Perplexed*. Trans. S. Pines. Chicago, IL: University of Chicago Press, 1963.

Makinde, Moses. *African Philosophy: The Demise of a Controversy*. Ile-Ife: Obafemi Awolowo University Press, 2007.

Malliṣeṇa. *Syādvādamañjarī*. In *A Sourcebook in Indian Philosophy*, eds. Sarvepalli Radhakrishnan and Charles A. Moore, 262–5. Princeton, NJ: Princeton University Press, 1957.

Manson, Neil A. "The Fine-Tuning Argument." *Philosophy Compass* 4/1 (2009): 271–86.

Marenbon, John. *Medieval Philosophy: An Historical and Philosophical Introduction*. London: Routledge, 2007.

Marenbon, John, ed. *The Oxford Handbook of Medieval Philosophy*. New York: Oxford University Press, 2013.

Marx, Karl. "Contribution to the Critique of Hegel's Philosophy of Right." In *The Marx-Engels Reader*, 2nd ed., ed. Robert C. Tucker, 16–25. New York: W. W. Norton & Co., 1972.

Marx, Karl, with Friedrich Engels. *The German Ideology*. Moscow: Marx-Engels Institute, 1932, originally written in 1845–6. Available online: https://www.marxists.org/archive/marx/works/1845/german-ideology/ch01d.htm. (accessed March 11, 2022).

Matilal, Bimal Krishna. *The Character of Logic in India*, eds. Jonardon Ganeri and Heeraman Tiwari. Albany, NY: State University of New York Press, 1998.

McCrea, Larry. "Just Like Us, Just Like Now: The Tactical Implications of the Mīmāṃsā Rejection of Yogic Perception." In *Yogic Perception, Meditation and Altered States of Consciousness*, ed. Eli Franco, 55–70. Vienna: Verlag der Österreichischen Akademie der Wissenschaften, 2009.

Mencius. *Mencius*. In *A Source Book in Chinese Philosophy*, ed. Wing-Tsit Chan, 51–83. Princeton, NJ: Princeton University Press, 1963.

Mikkola, Mari. "Feminist Perspectives on Sex and Gender." In *The Stanford Encyclopedia of Philosophy*, ed. Edward N. Zalta, Fall 2019 ed. Available online: https://plato.stanford.edu/archives/fall2019/entries/feminism-gender/ (accessed March 11, 2022).

Milinda Pañha. In *Buddhist Scriptures*. Trans. Edward Conze, 146–51. New York: Penguin Classics, 1959.

Mo Zi: The Book of Master Mo. Trans. Ian Johnston. New York: Penguin Books, 2010.

Moody, Raymond A. *Life After Life*. New York: Bantam Books, 1975.

Mooney, James. *The Ghost-Dance Religion and Wounded Knee*. New York: Dover Publications, 1973.

Moskowitz, Clara. "Endless Void or Big Crunch: How Will the Universe End?" *Space.com*. October 26, 2011. Available online: https://www.space.com/13393-universe-endless-void-big-crunch.html (accessed March 11, 2022).

Nāgārjuna. *The Fundamental Wisdom of the Middle Way: Nāgārjuna's Mūlamadhyamakakārikā*. Trans. Jay L. Garfield. New York: Oxford University Press, 1995.

Nichiren. "Historical Consciousness and Liberation." In *Japanese Philosophy: A Sourcebook*, eds. James W. Heisig, Thomas P. Kasulis, and John C. Maraldo, 89–90. Honolulu, HI: University of Hawai'i Press, 2011.

Nietzsche, Friedrich. *On the Genealogy of Morals*. In *Basic Writings of Nietzsche*, trans. Walter Kaufmann, 451–599. New York: The Modern Library, 1992.

Olivelle, Patrick, trans. *Upaniṣads*. New York: Oxford University Press, 1996.

Olson, Carl. *The Mysterious Play of Kālī: An Interpretive Study of Rāmakrishna*. Atlanta, GA: Scholars Press, 1990.

Olson, Carl. *The Many Colors of Hinduism: A Thematic-Historical Introduction*. New Brunswick, NJ: Rutgers University Press, 2007.

Oppy, Graham, and Nick Trakakis. *The History of Western Philosophy of Religion*. 5 vols. New York: Oxford University Press, 1999.

Oppy, Graham. "Ontological Arguments." In *The Stanford Encyclopedia of Philosophy*, ed. Edward N. Zalta. Spring 2020 ed. Available online: https://plato.stanford.edu/archives/spr2020/entries/ontological-arguments/ (accessed March 11, 2022).

Paley, William. *Natural Theology*, reprint ed. Eds. Matthew D. Eddy and David Knight. New York: Oxford University Press, 2008.

Patañjali. *Yoga Sūtras*. In Bina Gupta, *An Introduction to Indian Philosophy: Perspectives on Reality, Knowledge, and Freedom*, 194–6. New York: Routledge, 2012.

Peel, J. Y. D. *Religious Encounters and the Making of the Yoruba*. Bloomington, IN: Indiana University Press, 2001.

Peel, J. D. Y. *Christianity, Islam, and* Orișa *Religion: Three Traditions in Comparison and Interaction*. Oakland, CA: University of California Press, 2015.

Perkins, Franklin. *Heaven and Earth Are Not Humane: The Problem of Evil in Classical Chinese Philosophy*. Bloomington, IN: Indiana University Press, 2014.

Perrett, Roy W. *An Introduction to Indian Philosophy*. New York: Cambridge University Press, 2016.

Peterson, Michael L. "The Problem of Evil." In *The Oxford Handbook of Atheism*, eds. Stephen Bullivant and Michael Ruse, 71–88. New York: Oxford, 2013.

Plantinga, Alvin Plantinga, *The Nature of Necessity*. New York: Oxford University Press, 1974.

Plato. *Euthyphro*. In *Five Dialogues: Euthyphro, Apology, Crito, Meno, Phaedo*, trans. G. M. A. Grube, ed. John M. Cooper, 5–22. Indianapolis, IN: Hackett Publishing, 1981.

Plato. *Phaedo*. In *Five Dialogues: Euthyphro, Apology, Crito, Meno, Phaedo*, trans. G. M. A. Grube, ed. John M. Cooper, 93–155. Indianapolis, IN: Hackett Publishing, 1981.

Poceski, Mario. *Introducing Chinese Religions*. New York: Routledge, 2009.

Porete, Marguerite. *The Mirror of Simple Souls*. Trans. Ellen Babinsky. Mahwah, NJ: Paulist Press, 1993.

Powers, William K. *Oglala Religion*. Lincoln, NE: University of Nebraska Press, 1977.

Powers, William K. *Yuwipi: Vision & Experience in Oglala Ritual*. Lincoln, NE: Bison Books, 1984.

Powers, William K. *Sacred Language: The Nature of Supernatural Discourse in Lakota*. Norman, OK: University of Oklahoma Press, 1986.

Pseudo-Dionysius: The Complete Works. Trans. Paul Rorem. Mahwah, NJ: Paulist Press, 1987.

Rāmānuja. *Brahma Sūtra Bhāṣya*. In *A Sourcebook in Indian Philosophy*, eds. Sarvepalli Radhakrishnan and Charles A. Moore, 543–52. Princeton, NJ: Princeton University Press, 1957.

Rāmānuja. *Śrībhāṣya*. In *Brahma-Sūtras according to Śrī Rāmānuja*, 7th reprint ed. Trans. Swami Vireswarananda and Swami Adidevananda. Calcutta: Advaita Ashrama, 2012.

Raphael, Melissa. "The Price of (Masculine) Freedom and Becoming: A Jewish Feminist Response to Eliezer Berkovits's Post-Holocaust Free-Will Defence of God's Non-intervention in Auschwitz." In *Feminist Philosophy of Religion*, eds. Pamela Sue Anderson and Beverly Clack, 136–50. New York: Routledge, 2004.

Ray, Benjamin C. *African Religions: Symbol, Ritual, and Community*, 1st ed. Englewood Cliffs, NJ: Prentice-Hall, 1976.

Ray, Benjamin C. *African Religions: Symbol, Ritual, and Community*, 2nd ed. Upper Saddle River, NJ: Pearson, 1999.

Reichenbach, Bruce. "Cosmological Argument." In *The Stanford Encyclopedia of Philosophy*, ed. Edward N. Zalta. Fall 2019 ed. Available online: https://plato.stanford.edu/archives/fall2019/entries/cosmological-argument/ (accessed March 11, 2022).

Rowe, William L. "The Problem of Evil and Some Varieties of Atheism." *American Philosophical Quarterly* 16 (1979): 335–41.

Rowe, William L. "Evil and the Theistic Hypothesis: A Response to Wykstra." *International Journal for Philosophy of Religion* 16/2 (1984): 95–100.

Russell, Robert John. "Cosmology and Eschatology." In *The Oxford Handbook of Eschatology*, ed. Jerry L. Walls, 563–75. New York: Oxford University Press, 2007.

Russell, Robert John. *Cosmology: From Alpha to Omega*. Philadelphia, PA: Fortress Press, 2008.

Śaṅkara. *Brahma Sūtra Bhāṣya*. In *A Sourcebook in Indian Philosophy*, eds. Sarvepalli Radhakrishnan and Charles A. Moore, 509–43. Princeton, NJ: Princeton University Press, 1957.

Schilbrack, Kevin. "Religions: Are there Any?" *Journal of the American Academy of Religion* 78/4 (2010): 1112–38.

Scholem, Gershom. *Major Trends in Jewish Mysticism*. New York: Schocken Books, 1946.

Schwartz, Benjamin I. *The World of Thought in Ancient China*. Cambridge, MA: Belknap Press of Harvard University, 1985.

Scotus, John Duns. *Ordinatio*. Available online: https://www.aristotelophile.com/Books/Translations/Ordinatio%20I.pdf (accessed March 11, 2022).

Sells, Michael A., trans. *Early Islamic Mysticism: Sufi, Qurʾān, Miʿrāj and Theological Writings*. Mahwah, NY: Paulist Press, 1996.

Shinran. "*Nenbutsu*: The Will of No-Will." In *Japanese Philosophy: A Sourcebook*, eds. James W. Heisig, Thomas P. Kasulis, and John C. Maraldo, 253. Honolulu, HI: University of Hawaiʻi Press, 2011.

Singer, Peter. *How Are We to Live?* New South Wales: Random House Australia, 1993.

Smart, Ninian. *Dimensions of the Sacred: An Anatomy of the World's Beliefs*. Berkeley, CA: University of California Press, 1999.

Smith, Huston. *Forgotten Truth: The Primordial Tradition*. New York: Harper Colophon Books, 1976.

Smith, Kerri. "Taking Aim at Free Will." *Nature* 477 (September 2011): 23–5.

Sumegi, Angela. *Understanding Death: An Introduction to Ideas of Self and the Afterlife in World Religions*. New York: Wiley-Blackwell, 2014.

Surin, Kenneth. *Theology and the Problem of Evil*. Eugene, OR: Wipf & Stock, 2004.

Swinburne, Richard. *The Evolution of the Soul*. New York: Oxford University Press, 1997.

Swinburne, Richard. *The Existence of God*, 2nd ed. New York: Clarendon Press, 2004.

Táíwò, Olúfẹ́mi. "Òrìsà: A Prolegomenon to a Philosophy of Yorùbá Religion." In *Òrìsà Devotion as World Religion: The Globalization of Yorùbá Religious Culture*, eds. Jacob K. Olupona and Terry Rey, 84–105. Madison, WI: University of Wisconsin Press, 2008.

Taylor, James E. "New Atheism." *Internet Encyclopedia of Philosophy*. Available online: https://iep.utm.edu/n-atheis/ (accessed March 11, 2022).

Thompson, Kirill. "Zhu Xi." In *The Stanford Encyclopedia of Philosophy*, ed. Edward N. Zalta. Summer 2021 ed. Available online: https://plato.stanford.edu/archives/sum2021/entries/zhu-xi/ (accessed March 11, 2022).

Tillich, Paul. *Dynamics of Faith*. New York: Harper, 1957.

Trakakis, Nick. "Evidential Problem of Evil." *Internet Encyclopedia of Philosophy*. Available online: https://www.iep.utm.edu/evil-evi/ (accessed March 11, 2022).

Udayana. *Nyāyakusumāñjali*. In Hem Chandra Joshi, *Nyāyakusumāñjali of Udayanacārya: A Critical Study*. Delhi: Vidyanidhi Prakashan, 2002.

Umāsvāti. *That Which Is: Tattvārtha Sūtra*. Eds. Kerry Brown and Sima Sharma. San Francisco, CA: HarperCollins Publishers, 1994.

Usman, Aribidesi. *The Yoruba Frontier: A Regional History of Community Formation, Experience, and Changes in West Africa*. Durham, NC: Carolina Academic Press, 2012.

Walker, James R. *Lakota Myth*. Ed. Elaine A. Jahner. Lincoln, NE: University of Nebraska Press, 1983.

Walker, James R. *The Sun Dance and Other Ceremonies of the Oglala Division of the Teton Dakota*. London: Forgotten Books, 2008.

Ware, Owen. "Dialectic of the Past / Disjuncture of the Future: Derrida and Benjamin on the Concept of Messianism." *Journal for Cultural and Religious Theory* 5/2 (2004): 99–114.

Weddle, David L. *Miracles: Wonder and Meaning in World Religions*. New York: New York University Press, 2010.

Weigand, Amy. "The Chinese Experience of Death: Continuity in Transition." In *Death and Dying in World Religions*, ed. Lucy Bregman, 119–35. Dubuque, IA: Kendall Hunt, 2009.

Westhelle, Vítor. "Liberation Theology: A Latitudinal Perspective." In *The Oxford Handbook of Eschatology*, ed. Jerry L. Walls, 31–27. New York: Oxford University Press, 2007.

Westphal, Merold. "The Emergence of Modern Philosophy of Religion." In the *Blackwell Companion to Philosophy of Religion*, eds. Philip L. Quinn and Charles Taliaferro, 111–17. Malden, MA: Blackwell Publishers, 1997.

Wildman, Wesley J. *Religious Philosophy as Multidisciplinary Comparative Inquiry: Envisioning a Future for the Philosophy of Religion*. Albany, NY: State University of New York Press, 2010.

Xúnzǐ, *Xunzi: The Complete Text*. Trans. Eric L. Hutton. Princeton, NJ: Princeton University Press, 2014.

Yandell, Keith. "How to Sink in Cognitive Quicksand: Nuancing Religious Pluralism." In *Contemporary Debates in Philosophy of Religion*, eds. Michael L. Peterson and Raymond J. VanArragon, 191–200, 215–17. Malden, MA: Blackwell, 2004.

Yao, Xinzhong. *An Introduction to Confucianism*. New York: Cambridge University Press, 2000.

Yazicioglu, Isra. "Redefining the Miraculous: al-Ghazālī, ibn Rushd and Said Nursi on Qur'anic Miracle," *Journal of Qur'anic Studies* 13/2 (2011): 86–108.

Yountae, An. "On Violence and Redemption: Fanon and Colonial Theodicy." In *Beyond Man: Race, Coloniality, and Philosophy of Religion*, eds. An Yountae and Eleanor Craig, 204–25. Durham, NC: Duke University Press, 2021.

Zhōu Dūnyí. "Explanation of the Diagram of the Great Ultimate." In *A Source Book in Chinese Philosophy*, ed. Wing-Tsit Chan, 463–4. Princeton, NJ: Princeton University Press, 1963.

Zhū Xī. "The Complete Works of Chu Hsi." In *A Source Book in Chinese Philosophy*, ed. Wing-Tsit Chan, 605–53. Princeton, NJ: Princeton University Press, 1963.

Zhū Xī. "First Letter to the Gentlemen of Hunan on Equilibrium and Harmony." In *A Source Book in Chinese Philosophy*, ed. Wing-Tsit Chan, 600–2. Princeton, NJ: Princeton University Press, 1963.

Zhuāngzǐ. In *Wandering on the Way: Early Taoist Tales and Parables of Chuang Tzu*, trans. Victor H. Mair. New York: Bantam Books, 1994.

Zohar: The Book of Enlightenment. Trans. Daniel Chanan Matt. Mahwah, NJ: Paulist Press, 1983.

Index

a posteriori 283, 285, 375
a priori 140, 283, 285, 375, 398
abhidharma 130–1, 153, 211, 215, 375, 383, 399, 406
Abímbọ́lá, Kọ́lá 77, 128–9, 146, 184, 210, 274, 337, 358, 375, 434 n.5, 7
Abraham 41, 43–4, 229, 325, 375
absolute freedom, *videha-mukti* 153
Adams, Marilyn McCord 365
adhyāsa, superimposition 132, 212, 375
African Philosophy: Myth and Reality 76–7
see also Hountondji
ahaṃkāra, ego-identity 155, 243–4
Ajàlá, celestial potter 103
àjẹ́, powerful person or "witch" 211, 241, 359, 375, 426 n.28
Ajogun, Anti-Gods 103, 210–11, 241–2, 303, 317, 337, 358–9, 369, 375, 434 n.7
al-Ashʿarī (Abū al-Ḥasan al-Ashʿarī) 127–8, 146, 196, 375
al-Fārābī (Abū Naṣr al-Fārābī) 167, 255
al-Ghazālī (Abū Ḥāmid Muḥammad ibn Muḥammad aṭ-Ṭūsiyy al-Ġazālī) 111, 167, 281–2, 287, 325–6, 362, 375–6, 390
al-Ḥallāj (Abū al-Muġīth al-Ḥusayn bin Manṣūr al-Ḥallāj) 222, 376
al-Mahdī, the guided one 299–301, 376, 440 n.5
Alexander the Great 66
ʿAlī (ʿAlī ibn Abī Ṭālib) 44, 300–1, 376
Allah 22, 44–5, 109, 111, 126–8, 167–8, 196, 221–3, 237, 255–7, 262, 279, 324–6, 362, 376, 378, 385, 388, 391, 393–4, 396, 401–5, 407, 429 n.28
Althusser, Louis 115–20, 228, 376, 390
Amitābha, Ch. Ēmítuófó, 阿彌陀佛, infinite light and life buddha 51, 157–9, 194, 219, 306–8, 332–3, 376
an-ātman, no-self or no-soul 99, 130, 153, 328, 376
Analects 104–6, 189–90, 376, 386
analytic philosophy of religion 18–20, 115, 128, 172, 268, 286–90, 314, 317, 363, 376
Anderson, Pamela Sue 203, 418 n.3
anekāntavāda, doctrine of non-onesidedness 70–1, 376, 388
Anselm 21, 283–5, 286, 288, 376, 438 n.26
see also ontological proofs; *a priori*
anthropic principle 259–60, 376
anumāna 24–5, 71–2, 90, 276–8, 377, 380, 398, 401
apocalyptic 296–9, 303, 308, 318, 377
apokatastasis, eventual restoration of all souls to God 166, 377
see also Origen of Alexander
appeal to authority 18, 72, 89, 377
Aquinas, Thomas 21, 197–8, 256, 280, 283–4, 287, 377, 383, 438 n.19
Archie Fire Lame Deer 101–2, 356, 428 n.5, 442 n.19
arguments from analogy 83
Aristotle 20–1, 66, 165, 197–8, 253, 256–7, 268, 280, 282–3, 285, 287, 326, 341, 362, 375, 377, 386, 408, 438 n.19
Arjuna 186–7, 212, 330
see also Bhagavad Gītā

àṣẹ, fundamental power of the cosmos to make things happen and change 242, 262, 377
āstika, affirmer, orthodox 24–6, 47, 377, 416 n.4
Ātman, self or soul 24, 45, 90, 98–100, 119–20, 130–3, 152–4, 156, 185–6, 188, 212, 246–8, 311, 330, 351–2, 375, 377, 398, 402, 408–9
ʿAṭṭār, Farīd ud-Dīn 111, 222–3, 377
Augustine of Hippo 21, 110, 125–7, 146, 166, 221, 283, 361–2, 365, 377, 400
Avadhūta Gītā 213–14
Avalokiteśvara, the bodhisattva of compassion 333, 377, 387
see also Guānyīn
Avataṃsaka Sūtra 249
avatāra, descent or incarnation of God 47–8, 187, 309, 330–1, 377, 409
avidyā, ignorance, misconception, or misunderstanding 130–3, 153, 212, 231, 378, 395, 445 n.6
axiology 67, 378
àyànmọ́, destiny 31–2, 54, 102–3, 128–9, 183, 378, 399

babaláwo 31, 53, 104, 183–4, 337–8, 359, 378, 398, 416 n.8
Bakr Ibrāhīm 111, 222–3, 377
Bantu Philosophy, 76
see also Tempels
baptism 42, 125–6, 378
baqā, subsistence 111, 168, 222, 378, 388, 407
Barrow, John 259
Bāyazīd Bisṭāmī 111, 222, 325, 378
Bayes' Theorem 86–7, 260–1, 289–90, 366–7, 378
Behe, Michael 261–2, 378
Benjamin, Walter 313–14, 378
Bhagavad Gītā 186–9, 212–3, 243, 378
bhakti, devotion 47–8, 186–9, 212, 214, 330, 378, 392, 411
bhāṣya, commentary 132, 153–4, 278, 351, 378
Bible 41, 89, 108–9, 163, 166, 225, 229, 252–3, 279, 323–4, 379, 397, 408, 411, 441 n.2
Big Bang Theory 237, 257–8, 287–8, 314–15, 317–18
Big Crunch, Freeze, Rip 237, 258, 315–18, 378
Bilimoria, Purushottama 350–1
Black Elk 75, 428 n.2
bodhicitta, Ch. *pútíxīn*, 菩提心, a wish or motivation to attain enlightenment 192, 379
bodhisattva 189, 212, 333–4, 377, 394, 409, 442 n.13
see also Avalokiteśvara, Maitreya
Bodunrin, Peter 76
Bonaventure 284, 387
Boyer, Pascal 144, 340, 369, 379
Brahmā, creator God in Hinduism 309–10, 379, 412
Brahma Sūtras (aka *Vedānta Sūtras*) 132, 153–4, 275, 278, 351, 409, 423 n.15
brahmacarya, sexual purity 46, 389
see also Five Great Vows
Brahman, ultimate reality 24–5, 45, 61, 98–100, 119–20, 132–3, 152–4, 156, 185–6, 201, 212, 237, 247–8, 275, 278–9, 310–11, 330, 350–2, 375, 379, 388–9, 394–5, 398, 402, 408–9
brāhmaṇa-s 155
brahmin, priestly caste 187, 379, 409, 418
see also varṇa
Buber, Martin 110, 119–20, 379
buddha 46, 61, 99, 130, 153, 194, 214–15, 220, 247–8, 262, 305–7, 309–10, 329, 332–4, 375–6, 379, 386–7, 394, 397, 399, 401, 406–9, 423 n.14, 442 n.13
buddha-land, Sk. *buddhakṣetra*; Ch. *jìngtǔ*, 淨土 332–3, 379, 394
buddha-nature, Sk. *tathāgatagarbha*

or *buddhadhātu*, Ch. *fóxìng*, 佛性 29, 51, 61, 137, 192–4, 212, 214, 218–19, 250, 334, 379–80, 406–7
buddhadhātu, the realm or substrate of a buddha 51, 192; *see also* Buddha-nature
Buddhism 4, 14–15, 25–7, 29, 45, 47–8, 51, 55–6, 130–1, 137, 147, 153, 156, 179, 189, 192, 202, 212, 215–16, 218–20, 249–50, 269, 305–7, 329, 332, 337, 350, 376, 379, 384, 386–7, 394, 397, 403, 405, 406, 413, 416 n.10
Chán/Zen Buddhism, 禪 51, 157, 159, 192–4, 219–20, 306–7, 334–5, 380, 383, 387, 389–90, 394, 399, 403, 412
Hīnayāna Buddhism 215, 334; *see also* Theravāda Buddhism
Huáyán Buddhism 51, 249–50, 269, 306, 383, 385, 389, 393, 401, 404, 436 n.1
Mahāyāna Buddhism 130, 192, 213–15, 218, 220, 247–8, 311, 332–4, 379–80, 394, 406–7, 409
Pure Land Buddhism 51, 157–9, 194, 219, 306–8, 332–3, 376, 379, 389, 399, 401, 403–4
Theravāda Buddhism 153, 156, 186, 211, 215, 248, 309–10, 327, 375, 379, 399, 407, 423 n.14
Vajrayāna Buddhism 379
Bultmann, Rudolf 316, 379
Butler, Judith 117–20, 380

Candide, 363–4
see also Voltaire
Carpenter, Amber 130
Carter, Brandon 259, 435 n.25
Cārvāka, or Lokāyata 24–5, 45–7, 72, 380, 419 nn.8–9, 425 n.7
causality 7, 20–1, 26, 36, 67, 79, 114, 139–40, 253–4, 256, 280, 282–3, 326, 340, 342, 350–1, 380–3, 387, 389, 394–5
cause 3, 20, 22, 25–6, 45–6, 103, 114, 127–8, 131, 140–1, 144, 147, 154, 170, 196, 208, 214, 248–9, 256–8, 260, 275–8, 280–3, 285–8, 296, 303, 310, 314, 323, 326–7, 334, 337–8, 340, 349–51, 354–5, 362–3, 368–9, 381, 386, 393, 401, 426 n.25, 445 n.7
čhaŋnúŋpa wakȟáŋ, sacred pipe 52, 75, 137–8, 138, 180–1, 240, 273, 335, 380, 409–10
Charaka Saṃhitā 23–4
Chariot Sermon 85, 100, 130–1
see also Nāgasena
chéng, 誠, sincere or integrated 190–1, 380
Chéng Hào 250, 270
Chéng Yí 250, 270
Chénghuángshén, God of Walls and Moats 49, 157
Christianity 4, 14–15, 17–18, 20–2, 27, 30, 41–3, 45, 52–3, 55, 58, 90, 108–11, 124–6, 128–9, 133, 138, 151, 163–6, 168, 170–2, 179, 194–203, 221–5, 228–9, 252–4, 255–6, 260–2, 268, 272, 280, 282–3, 286–30, 298–9, 301, 304–5, 307, 311, 314–17, 323–6, 332, 336–7, 340, 342, 356–9, 361–2, 365, 376–8, 380–2, 384, 392–3, 395, 397, 399, 400, 402, 406, 408, 416, 426 n.31, 428 n.2, 434 n.5, 440 n.10
Cleanthes 364
communion 42–3, 153–4, 186, 221–2, 254, 324, 380, 403, 406
compatibilism 139–40, 380
Conference of the Birds 222–3, 377
see also ʿAṭṭār
Confucianism 4, 15, 27, 29, 48, 50–1, 55–6, 134–7, 158–9, 189–92, 194, 216–19, 248–52, 269–72, 305, 380, 383, 387, 393, 402–3, 432 n.23

Confucius, Kǒngzǐ, 孔子 21, 28, 104–6, 133–4, 137, 158, 174–5, 189–90, 250, 376, 380, 383, 386–7, 393, 395, 411
consciousness, 88, 99–100, 114, 132, 141, 152, 155–6, 172, 185–6, 188, 199, 202, 227, 243–4, 246, 263, 277, 289, 303, 311, 327, 337, 339, 386–8, 392, 398, 400, 403, 424–5 n.5
vijñāna or *citta* 100, 131
Continental philosophy of religion 18–19, 87–9, 313–14, 318, 380
Copernican Principle 259
cosmogony 251, 268–6, 274, 381
cosmological proofs 268–9, 276–7, 279–92, 375–6, 377, 381, 381, 393–4, 439 n.31
cosmology 50–1, 237–63, 269–318, 325–6, 354, 381, 411, 412, 435 n.22
Craig, William Lane 286–8, 38, 439 n.31
creatio ex nihilo 246, 256, 260–1, 282, 317, 381

Daly, Mary 229–30, 291, 381
Dào/dào, 道 28–9, 49, 51, 61, 104–7, 119, 158, 191, 216–17, 219, 237, 248–9, 263, 269, 269–70, 305, 354–5, 369, 381–2, 412, 416
Dàodéjīng, 道德經 28, 104–7, 191–2, 216, 219, 249, 269, 354, 381–2, 393
Daoism 15, 27–9, 48–51, 55–6, 74, 84, 106–7, 119–20, 136–7, 157–8, 189–92, 194, 216–19, 249, 269–70, 305, 334, 354, 381, 392, 397, 403, 406, 410, 411–13
darśana, philosophy 23–5, 47, 72, 130, 132–3, 185, 212, 243–6, 267, 275–8, 310, 327, 416 n.10, 423 n.15
Dawkins, Richard 142–3, 230, 382, 424 n.36
Day of the Lord 297, 382, 402
dé, 德, power or virtue 106–7, 382
deductive argument 59, 67, 82–4, 382
deism 341–2, 382
Deloria, Vine, Jr. 75, 84, 101–2, 161, 209, 239–40, 273, 301, 303, 335–6, 356–8, 382, 396, 420 n.15
Dembski, William 261–2, 382
Demiurge 20, 382, 400
Dennett, Daniel 230
Derrida, Jacques 313–14, 382
Descartes, René 84–7, 113–15, 118–20, 140–1, 168, 170, 285, 288, 382, 415 n.2
design proofs 114–15, 247–8, 259–62, 268, 276, 278, 282–3, 285–6, 350, 363–4, 382, 393, 407
see also teleological proofs
determinism 67, 125, 128, 139–40, 317, 380, 382–3, 395
dharma 4, 23, 155, 159, 187, 212, 220, 242, 247, 249, 305–8, 310, 330, 332–4, 383, 397, 407, 408
dharma-s, phenomena, Ch. *shì*, 事 51, 131, 153, 211, 215, 220, 383, 385, 394, 404, 406
dì, 地, earth 28, 106, 191, 251, 263, 269–70, 272, 380, 383
Diagram of the Supreme Polarity/ Ultimate, Tàijítú, 太極圖 270–1, 412
see also Zhōu Dūnyí
Dialectical idealism 311–12, 383
Dialectical materialism 312–13, 383
Dialogues Concerning Natural Religion 260, 285–6, 364
see also Hume
Diamond Sūtra 193
Dionysius the Areopagite 253–5, 324, 383
Doctrine of the Mean, Zhōngyōng, 中庸 190–1, 217, 380, 383, 386
Dōgen 334, 383
Dominican Order 197–8, 284, 383
Dǒng Zhòngshū, 董仲舒 249
Draper, Paul 366–7, 383
dualism 113–14, 154, 168–70, 243–4, 382–4, 409, 432 n.23

duḥkha, suffering 29, 36, 46, 79, 99, 216, 244, 247, 278, 307–8, 333, 350–2, 368–9, 384, 386–7
Durgā 47–8

è, 惡, bad, detestable 136, 384
ẹbọ, sacrifice 53, 184, 384
Eckhart, Meister 224, 384
egúngún, ancestors 162, 359, 384
Eight Limbs 327–9, 384, 403
Eightfold Path 46, 48, 130, 186, 220, 327–8, 403
Einstein, Albert 257, 315
èmí, life-breath 54, 102, 104, 161–2, 241, 274, 384, 398
empiricism 114, 139–40, 169, 284–5, 384, 389, 402
ènìyàn, humans 211, 359
eníyán, negative humans 211, 359
Enquiry Concerning Human Understanding 342
see also Hume
Epicureanism 165, 359, 364, 384
epistemic virtues 85–6, 119–21, 146, 231, 384
epistemology 24, 26, 67–8, 70, 73, 75, 185, 384, 418 n.3
eschatology 295–300, 302, 305, 309–10, 316–18, 385, 439 n.1
ẹsẹ̀, individual effort and struggle 128–9, 385
Èṣù 54, 210–11, 241–2, 274, 303, 338, 358, 385, 434 n.7, 446 n.24
ethnophilosophy 76–7, 385, 420 n.18
European Enlightenment 4, 15, 17–20, 22, 26, 34, 39, 56, 115, 139–40, 166, 169–70, 173–4, 198–9, 203, 259–60, 262, 267, 285, 311, 341–2, 363, 380, 382, 389, 415–16 n.2
see also Descartes; Kant; Hegel; Hume
Euthyphro Dilemma 195–7, 385
'Ên Sôp, the Limitless 225, 298, 384

fà, 法, model, paradigm 73–4, 385, 410
falsafa, philosophy 21, 167, 280, 385, 392, 396
fanā, annihilation 111, 168, 222, 378, 385, 388, 407
Fǎzàng, 法藏 249–50, 385
Fear and Trembling 229
see also Kierkegaard
fēi, 非 73, 385, 404, 410
feminist philosophy of religion 19, 68–9, 147, 174, 203, 229, 268, 291, 316, 339–40, 370–1, 381, 391, 385, 385, 418 n.3
Feuerbach, Ludwig 227–30, 386
Five Constant Relationships, Ch. *wǔlún*, 五倫 105, 386
Five Great Vows 46, 386
Five Pillars of Islam, Ar. *Arkān al-Islām* 44, 386
Five Ways 21, 283–4, 377
see also Aquinas
Forman, Robert K. C. 202–3, 386, 430 n.40
Four Books, *sìshū*, 四書 137, 190, 383, 386–7, 412
Four Causes 154, 424, 386
Four Noble Truths 99, 386
Four Sprouts, *duān*, 端 134–5, 386
Franciscans 21, 197–8, 284, 387
Fukuyama, Francis 312–13

Gadamer, Hans Georg 88
Gale, Richard 289
Gautama Buddha 46, 99, 130, 153, 215, 247, 310, 329, 332, 379, 386–7, 399, 406, 423 n.14.
Gbadegesin, Segun 77, 103, 129, 387
Geist, ghost, spirit, mind, consciousness 311–12, 387–8
géwù, 格物, investigation of things 190–1, 387
Ghost Dance 302–3, 356, 387, 410
Gleason, Judith 103–4

global-critical philosophy of religion 1–10, 15, 19, 30, 34, 48, 57–62, 65, 69–72, 74, 77, 79, 81, 88–91, 101, 204, 231, 290–1, 322, 370
God (some particular one) 2–4, 15–21, 45, 47–9, 52, 56–7, 61, 101–2, 111, 114, 119–20, 125–6, 146, 165–9, 172–3, 179, 188–9, 194–8, 214, 221–5, 227–9, 246, 253–63, 267–8, 272, 275–92, 296–7, 302–5, 322–7, 341–3, 348–52, 355, 357, 359–71
creator God 4, 15, 17, 34, 39–40, 56, 155–6, 277, 283, 289–90, 363, 445
Gods 3–4, 7–8, 19, 36, 39, 45, 56, 61, 66, 79, 111, 144, 155, 184–5, 189, 195–6, 198–9, 212, 227, 231, 237, 241–2, 246–8, 256, 258, 263, 268, 273–5, 290–2, 296, 303, 309, 328–30, 337–8, 340, 342–4, 358, 369–70, 375, 385, 389–90, 399, 403, 407, 436 n.1
Golden Rule 105
gong'an, 公案, Jp. kōan 193, 387, 393
Gould, Stephen Jay 340
Great Learning, Dàxué, 大學 190, 386–7
see also Four Books
Guānyīn, 觀音, *see* Avalokiteśvara
guǐ, 鬼, ghost 157, 388
Guide for the Perplexed 282–3
see also Maimonides
gùn, possession 54, 184, 388
guṇa 70, 243, 310, 388

ḥadīth, tradition 44, 127, 221, 388
hălākâ, the way to behave 194–5, 225, 388, 394
Hallen, Barry 77
haŋbléčeyapi, vision quest 52, 101–2, 181, 183, 335, 388
ḥaqq, true/real 222, 255, 376, 388
hard problem of consciousness 114, 140, 388
Haribhadra 70–1, 84–5, 388
Harris, Sam 230
Hartshorne, Charles 172, 388
Hawking, Steven 258
Hegel, Georg Wilhelm Friedrich 227–8, 311–12, 314, 383, 386, 387, 388, 415–16 n.2
see also Dialectical Idealism; *Geist*
hermeneutics 19, 77, 88, 380–1, 389
heyókȟa 209, 398, 409
Hick, John 172, 199–200, 203, 361–2, 389
Hinduism 14–15, 24, 45–8, 56–7, 98–9, 189, 200–2, 212, 214, 309–11, 379, 389, 392, 398, 405, 409, 427 n.1
Hitchens, Christopher 230
Hōnen, 法然 306–7, 389
Hóngren, 弘忍 193
Hountondji, Paulin 76–7, 420 n.18
How Not to Compare African Traditional Thought with Western Thought 76
see also Wiredu
Huáyán, 華嚴, school of Buddhism 51, 249–50, 269, 306, 383, 385, 389, 393, 404, 436 n.3
Huìnéng 159, 193, 193, 389
Hume, David 114–15, 118–20, 139–40, 169, 259–62, 278–9, 285–6, 342, 363–5, 389, 415–16 n.2, 419 n.8
hún, 魂, one kind of soul 157, 389
hyperactive agent detection device 143–4, 147, 389–90

ibn ʿArabī 255–6, 390, 435 n.21
ibn Rushd 167–8, 256, 282–3, 287, 326, 362, 390
ibn Sīnā 167, 255, 280–3, 375, 390
ideology 115–17, 312–14, 376, 390
Ifá, divination 32, 53–4, 77, 102–4, 128, 161–3, 183–5, 210–11, 241–2, 262–3, 274–5, 305, 337–8, 358–9, 378, 384–5, 390, 398–9, 417 n.2, 433–4 n.4, 443 n.25
Ikkyū Sōjun, 一休宗純 220, 390
Iktómi, trickster God 208–9, 335, 356, 390, 409

Ilé-Ifẹ̀ 241, 274, 337, 390, 443 n.28
inductive argument 67, 72, 83, 390, 439 n.35
inductive generalization 83
ineffable 192, 199–200, 202, 324, 338–40
inference to the best explanation 83–4
inípi, making spirit 52, 181, 183, 391
Intelligent Design 261, 285–6, 378, 382, 391
see also Behe; design proofs
interaction problem 113–14, 141–2, 169–70, 174, 391
Irenaeus 361–2
Irigaray, Luce 229–30, 391
Isaac Luria 225, 298, 391, 404–5
Islam 4, 14–15, 21–2, 27, 30, 41, 43–5, 53, 55, 58, 109, 111–12, 124, 126–29, 130, 133, 162, 166–8, 194–99, 221–3, 225, 252, 255–7, 280–3, 286–7, 299–301, 314, 324–6, 359, 362, 375–6, 385–6, 388, 390–3, 396, 401–2, 404–6, 413, 417 n.2, 433–4 n.4, 434 n.5, 439 n.3
Īśvara 155–6, 246, 275–8, 328, 350–2, 391, 445 n.7
Īśvara Kṛṣṇa 243–4, 391

Jade Emperor, Yù Huáng, 玉皇 49–50
Jahner, Elaine A. 273, 428 n.3
Jainism 14–15, 24–6, 45–8, 56, 70–1, 84–5, 154–6, 186, 189, 212, 244–8, 263, 275, 310, 350, 376, 386, 388–9, 391–2, 394, 397, 401, 406–8, 416 n.10, 418 n.4, 5, 419 n.6, 445 n.2
James, William 338–9, 391
Jantzen, Grace 174, 291, 339–40, 370–1, 391
Jastrow, Robert 258
J.B., 363
see also MacLeish
Jerusalem 41, 163, 221, 252, 282, 297, 325, 392
Jerusalem Letter 282
see also al-Ghazālī
Jesus of Nazareth 17, 42–3, 108, 110, 125, 163–4, 194–5, 201, 214, 221, 253–4, 298–300, 316, 324–6, 332, 376, 380, 384, 392, 394–5, 397, 400, 440 n.5
jina 46, 212, 392, 394, 408
jìngzuò, 靜坐, quiet sitting 191, 392
jīva, soul 25, 46, 133, 153, 154–5, 244
jñāna, knowledge 47, 185–6, 188–9, 212, 330, 392
Job 360, 363
John of Rupescissa 299
Josiah Ositelu 304–5
journey metaphor 6–7, 13, 34–6, 79, 97, 238
Joy, Morny 370
Judaism 109–11, 124, 194–5, 198, 221, 297–8, 325, 360–1, 392, 394–5, 404–5, 426 n.31
jūnzǐ, 君子, gentleman, profound person 28, 392, 429 n.19

Kabbalah 225–7, 254–5, 298, 361, 384, 391–2, 403–4, 407, 412, 435 n.20
kaivalya, isolation 46, 152–3, 155–6, 173, 185–6, 244, 327, 329, 392–3
kalām 21, 166–8, 196, 256–7, 280–3, 287, 375–6, 381, 385, 392, 396, 439 n.32
Kālī 47, 214, 309, 412
Kalki 309, 330, 409
kalpa 309–10
see also yuga
Kaṇāda 246, 392
Kant, Immanuel 140, 146, 169–70, 286, 393, 415–16 n.2
karma 4, 45–7, 130, 152, 186–9, 212, 237, 244, 277–8, 329–30, 349–52, 368–9, 392, 393, 401, 403, 411
kasb, acquisition 22, 127, 393
kathā, debate 24, 408
see also vāda
Katz, Steven 339, 393

kevala, isolation 45, 152, 156, 186, 244, 246, 393
Kierkegaard, Soren 229
King Milinda 100, 397
kōan, *see gong'an*
Kripal, Jeffrey 341, 393, 427 n.40
Kṛṣṇa 47–8, 188, 212, 329–32

Lakȟóta 9, 14, 32–3, 52, 61, 74–5, 84–5, 88, 101–2, 107, 119–20, 137–8, 147, 160–1, 173, 180–3, 208–10, 239–40, 262, 272–4, 296, 301–3, 335–6, 355–58, 380, 382, 388–91, 393, 395–7, 404, 409–10, 412, 416 n.9, 10, 425 n.14, 428 n.3, 436–7 n.8, 437 n.9
Lǎozǐ, 老子 28, 104, 106–7, 381, 393
see also Dàodéjīng
Leibniz 363–4
Lewontin, Richard 340
lǐ, 理, pattern-principle 51, 217–18, 237, 250, 269–72, 305, 369, 393, 401, 432
lǐ, 禮, rites, ceremonies, rituals, customs, and etiquette 28, 73, 105, 107, 134–7, 158, 189–90, 217–19, 353, 355, 393, 402, 411–12
Liber secretorum eventuum 299
see also John of Rupescissa
liberation theology 393
libertarianism 139–40, 394
Línjì Yìxuán, 臨濟義玄 193, 220, 394
Locke, John 139, 146, 285, 394
logos 21, 125, 253, 359, 378, 381, 384–5, 394, 398, 405, 407
Loka Puruṣa, cosmic man 244–6, 263
Lotus Sūtra 306, 308, 394, 397
Lù Xiàngshān, 陸象山 252

MacLeish, Archibald 363
Madhva 25, 154, 247
Madhyamaka 214–16, 220, 311, 394, 396, 406
see also Nāgārjuna
Mahābhārata 186, 309–10, 329, 378
Mahādevī, Mother Goddess 47, 379, 403
Mahāvīra 46, 244, 392, 394, 408, 418 n.4
Mahāyāna, *see* Buddhism
Maimonides 21, 165, 194–5, 197, 256, 282–3, 287, 375, 394
Maitreya 310, 394, 442 n.13
Makinde, Moses Akin 77, 128–9, 162, 394, 426 n.22
Mappō Dharma 306–8, 332–3, 397, 407
maqaam (pl. = *maqaamat*), seven stages 223, 255–6, 325, 394
Martin, Michael 288
Marx, Karl 14, 115–16, 174, 228, 312–14, 376, 383, 390, 395
see also Dialectical materialism
māyā, illusion 132–3, 156, 211–12, 395, 445 n.6
Meander 100
Mecca 43–4, 325, 386
meditation 46, 51, 185–7, 191, 193, 212, 219, 227, 270, 306, 327, 328, 334, 380, 384, 387, 392, 408, 412, 442 n.8
Meditations on First Philosophy 113, 415 n.2
Mencius, 孟子 28, 133–7, 190, 217, 250, 354–5, 386, 395, 403, 410–11
merkābâ-hêkālôt 324–5, 395, 441 n.2
Merriam-Webster 13
messiah 165, 227, 297–301, 313, 318, 376, 395
metaphysics 24, 51, 67, 185, 187, 282, 310–11, 327, 370, 390, 395, 403
Milinda Pañha 100, 397
see also Nāgasena
Millennialism 299, 304, 395
Mīmāṃsā 24, 47, 155, 185, 275, 277–8, 311, 329, 350, 395, 416 n.5
mìng, 命, fate/destiny 353–4, 395
miracle 8, 33, 114–15, 262, 286, 289, 302, 321–6, 329, 333–5, 341–3, 382, 389, 392, 410, 439 n.35

mitákuye oyásiŋ, all my relations 75, 101, 239, 395–6
mitzvot (sing. = mitzvah), commandments 41, 194, 196, 221, 225, 388, 396, 407–8
Mohism, *mòjiā*, 墨家 28, 73–4, 106, 134, 191, 217, 219, 353–4, 381, 385, 396, 404, 410, 419 n.10
mokṣa, release 24–6, 29, 45, 47, 66, 71, 99–100, 152–4, 179, 185–7, 201, 247, 327–9, 334, 350, 352, 392, 396–8, 403, 408, 411
monastic rules, *vinaya* 130, 399
Moses 255, 323–6, 329, 392, 396
Mòzǐ, 353, 369
  see also Mohism
Muḥammad 43–4, 111–12, 214, 221, 325–6, 376, 388, 391, 396, 401–2, 404, 406
Mūla Madhyamaka Kārikā, Fundamental Teachings on the Middle Way 215–16, 220
  see also Nāgārjuna
Muṇḍaka Upaniṣad 153
mūrti, statue 23, 381–2
mutakallimūn (sing = *mutakallim*) 396
Muʿtazila 126–8, 196, 362, 396
mysticism 8, 119–20, 168, 202, 222, 225–7, 254, 298, 325, 340, 392, 395–6, 403, 405, 441 n.2

nafs, soul 108–9, 111, 388, 399, 407
Nāgārjuna 215–16, 220, 394, 396
Nāgasena 85–7, 100, 130–1, 397
nağí, ghost 160–1, 181, 397, 404, 410, 416 n.10, 425–6 n.19, 436–7 n.8
Nāsadīya-Sūkta 275
nāstika, denier, heterodox 25–6, 46, 397, 416 n.4
nayavāda, doctrine of standpoints 70, 397, 418 n.5
nèidān, 内丹, inner alchemy 158, 192, 397
Neimark, Philip John 104
nepeš, soul 108–9, 397
nĕšāmâ, soul 108–9, 397
New Atheism 230, 433 n.38
New Testament 90, 108–10, 125, 195, 229, 253, 298, 299, 316, 324, 361, 379, 394, 397, 400
Newton, Isaac 257, 314–15
ní (or *niyá*), ghost or life 160–1, 397, 436–7 n.8
niànfó, 念佛, Jp. *nembutsu* 194, 291, 306, 397
Nichiren, 日蓮 308, 394, 397
Nietzsche, Friedrich 228–9, 397
nirvāṇa, enlightenment 29, 46, 51, 71, 100, 123, 130–1, 133, 137, 151, 153, 157–9, 173, 179, 192–3, 213–15, 218–20, 247–8, 306, 308, 332–4, 379, 383, 389–90, 399, 403, 408, 423 n.14
  see also bodhicitta; buddha-nature
Nyāya 24, 47, 71–2, 155–6, 185, 246, 267, 275–7, 350–1, 268
Nyāya Sūtras 24

Ọbàtálá 54, 103, 242, 274, 398, 437 n.14, 443 n.28
Odù Ifá 31, 53–4, 77, 183–4, 398
Ògún 103, 242, 274, 398
Olódùmarè, also known as Ọlọ́run, high God 54, 103, 161–2, 210, 241–2, 274, 337, 358, 384–5, 398–9, 434 nn.5–6, 443–4 n.28, 446 n.24
oṃ 99, 398, 442 n.8
omnibenevolence 227, 288, 398
omnipotence 22, 126–8, 227, 256, 288, 350, 362, 398
omniscience 25, 46, 155, 227, 246, 288, 350, 398
On Free Will 125
  see also Augustine
On the Genealogy of Morals 228
  see also Nietzsche
oníṣègùn, medicine maker 337–8, 398

ontological proofs 21, 286, 288–9, 376, 382, 393, 398, 400
 see also Anselm; Plantinga
ontology 101, 133, 251, 272, 317, 398
orí, inner self or head 31, 54, 102–4, 119, 128–9, 162, 183–4, 241, 338, 378, 385, 398–9, 416 n.10
Origen of Alexander 166, 377, 399
 see also apokatastasis
Òrìṣà 31, 53–4, 102–4, 119, 162–3, 183–5, 210–11, 237, 241–2, 274, 303–5, 317, 336–8, 358–9, 375, 377, 384–5, 388, 390, 398–9, 403, 426 n.28, 434 n.6, 7, 443 n.28, 446 n.24
Oruka, H. Odera 77
ọrun 161–2, 240–1, 274, 399, 433 n.4
Ọrunmila 54, 183–4, 241–2, 274, 338, 390, 399
Ọ̀ṣun 242, 263, 337, 399
other-effort/power, Ch. *tālì*, 他力, Jp. *tariki* 194, 219, 399, 403, 427–8 n.1

Paley, William 259, 260, 399
Pāli Canon 89–90, 327–8, 375, 399
panentheism 399
pantheism 172, 399
paryāya, modes 70
Patañjali 327–9, 399
Paul the Apostle 21, 124–5, 163–4, 195, 221, 229, 253, 325, 361, 383, 400
Pelagius 126, 400
perennialism 201–2, 339, 393, 400, 430 n.40
Pharaoh 323, 441 n.1
phenomenology 19, 88, 380–1, 400
Philo of Alexandria 165, 400
Plantinga, Alvin 288, 365, 368, 400
Platform Sūtra of the Sixth Patriarch, 159, 218–19, 388–9
 see also Huìnéng
Plato 20, 66, 109, 113, 119–20, 164–7, 169, 195, 225, 253, 255–6, 283, 285, 361, 377, 382, 385, 399, 400–1
Platonism 253–4, 400–1
pneuma, breath, spirit 108–9, 124–5, 400
pò, 魄, soul 157, 400
Polkinghorne, John 317
Pope John XXII 224
Porete, Marguerite 223–4, 401
post-colonialism 14, 19, 401
Powers, William 101–2, 160–1, 436–7 n.8, 442–3 n.19
prakṛti, matter-mind 154–5, 185, 243–4, 248, 263, 310, 327, 388, 392, 394
 see also Puruṣa; *kaivalya*; Sāṁkhya
pramāṇa, means of attaining knowledge 24, 71–2, 90, 377, 398, 401, 403
pratītya-samutpāda 215, 250, 401
problem of evil 4, 7–9, 15–16, 18, 34–6, 79, 87, 125, 127–8, 208, 260, 262, 273, 296, 300, 309, 347–71, 376–7, 383, 396, 400–2, 407, 443 n.7, 447 n.41
 see also theodicy
Process Philosophy/Theology 172, 388, 401
Proof of the Truthful 280–1, 390
 see also ibn Sīnā
Proslogion, 283–4
 see also Anselm
psychē 14, 108–9, 401
pudgala, matter 25, 46, 155, 244, 391–2, 401
Pure Land Buddhism, Ch. *jìngtǔ*, 淨土宗 159, 194, 219, 306–8, 332–3, 376, 379, 389, 399, 401, 403–4
Puruṣa-Sūkta, *Hymn to the Cosmic Person* 243, 275
Puruṣa, pure consciousness 155, 185, 243–4, 248, 263, 327, 392
 see also prakṛti; *kaivalya*; Sāṁkhya

qì, 氣, vital energy 218, 249–51, 263, 269–72, 305, 331, 369, 393, 401, 411, 432 n.23
qíng, 情, feelings 217–18, 272, 401
Qīngmíng, 清明, festival of sweeping ancestor's graves 49, 157

Qur'ān 44, 108–9, 126–7, 166–7, 195, 221, 223, 279, 325–6, 388, 396, 401–2, 404

Rābi'a 222, 402
Rāma 47, 214
Ramadan 44, 386
Rāmakrishna 201, 214
Rāmānuja 24–5, 153–4, 247, 278–9, 351–2, 424–5 n.5, 445 n.7
rationalism 114, 140, 196, 284–5, 402
Ray, Benjamin C. 162–3, 211, 440 n.13
rén, 仁, benevolence, human-heartedness 28, 105, 107, 134–5, 189–90, 192, 217–19, 250–1, 354, 386, 393, 402, 411–12
Republic 20
  see also Plato
resurrection of the dead 42, 108–10, 163–7, 171–4, 221, 281, 297–300, 324, 392, 402
Retractions 125
  see also Augustine
Ṛg Veda 243, 275
Rowe, William 366–8, 402
ṛta, order 243
rú, 儒 27–8, 73, 104, 106, 134, 380, 402
rûaḥ 108–9, 400, 402
rūḥ 109, 402
rūpa, body 99
Russell, Robert John 317, 342–3, 402

Saadia ben Yosef Gaon 165, 196–7, 402
śabda, testimony 71–2, 278, 403
saḥr, sober 111, 222, 403
Sai Baba, Sathya 330–1
Saichō 306
Śaivite 48, 213, 379, 403, 425 n.5
Śaktite 47–8, 379, 403
samādhi 327–9, 403
Samantabhadra 419 n.6
saṃgha, monastic community 214, 403
saṃhita-s 155
saṃjñā, perception 99
Sāṁkhya 24–5, 47, 155–6, 185, 187–8, 243–4, 247, 263, 275, 278, 310, 327, 350, 403
  see also Īśvara Kṛṣṇa
saṃsāra, rebirth 24, 45, 187, 189, 216, 327, 350, 393, 396, 403, 408
saṃskāra, volitional activities 99, 349
Ṣàngó 241–2, 403
sānjiào, 三教 27, 48, 189, 403, 416 n.10
Śaṅkara 24, 132–3, 152–4, 247–8, 278, 351–2, 375, 403, 445 n.6, 7
Śāriputra 333–4
Schneerson, Menachem Mendel 298
Scotus, John Duns 198, 387, 403
self-effort/power, Ch. *zili*, Jp. *jiriki* 157–8, 194, 307, 399, 403, 427–8 n.1
sěpîrôt, sing = *sěpîrâ*, emanations 225–6, 254–5, 403–4, 435 n.20
Sermon 52
  see also Meister Eckhart
shàn, 善, good 135, 403, 410
Shàngdì, Lord on High, 上帝 49
Shào Yong, 邵雍 270
sharī'a, law 44, 195, 221, 404
Shekhinah 254–5, 298, 361, 404, 435 n.20
shén, 神, spirit 157, 389, 404
shèngrén, 聖人 392, 404, 429 n.19
Shénxiù 193, 404
sheol, underworld 108, 163, 252, 404
shevirah 225, 298, 391, 404
shì, 事, phenomena 51, 249, 269, 383, 385, 392–3, 404
shì, 是, right/correct, be/exist 73–4, 404
shirk, 111, 187, 221, 404
Shī'a 44, 300–1, 376, 404, 439 n.3, 4
Shriran, 親鸞 307, 404
shù, 恕, liken to oneself, self-reflect 158, 190, 404
shūkyō, 宗教 26–7
  see also zōngjiào
šičuŋ 160–1, 404, 425 n.17, 436–7 n.8
Sikhism 14–15, 47–8, 56, 189, 389, 407
ṣimṣûm 225, 298, 391, 404–5

sin 21–2, 42, 110–11, 125–6, 151, 194, 213–14, 220–1, 230–1, 297, 299, 306–7, 324, 361, 377–8, 392, 400, 404–5, 432 n.28, 433 n.29
Śiva 47–8, 309, 329, 331, 379, 403, 405, 424–5 n.5
skandha 99, 153, 405
Skepticism 24, 45, 199, 204, 359–60, 364, 367–8, 380, 405
Smith, Huston 201–3, 303, 405
Sodipo, J. Olubi 77
soteriology 405
spandrel 143, 340, 405
Specters of Mar, 313
  see also Derrida
Stoicism 21, 124–5, 359, 405, 416 n.3, 422 n.1
Sufism 44–5, 111, 119, 167–8, 222–3, 225, 255, 279, 325, 375–8, 390, 394, 396, 402–3, 405, 407, 433 n.30
Sukr 111, 222, 378, 405
Sunni 44, 300, 391, 406
śūnyatā; Ch. *kong* 空, emptiness 51, 192, 215, 220, 250, 389, 394, 406
sūtra 406
svabhāva, Ch. zìxìng, 自性 51, 131, 394, 406
Swinburne, Richard 170, 289–90, 406, 439 n.35
syādvāda, doctrine of conditional assertion 70, 406, 419 n.6

Tàijí, 太極, Supreme Polarity/Ultimate 49, 251, 269–72, 406, 436 n.3
tantra 213–14, 406
tathāgatagarbha 51, 192, 379, 406
  see also Buddha-nature
tathātā, suchness or thusness 406, 408
Tattvārthasūtra 244–6, 407, 418 n.5
tawḥīd 407
teleological (and design) proofs 276–7, 286, 382, 393, 399, 407, 440 n.10
  see also Paley
teleology 407
Tempels, Placide 76, 385, 420 n.18
  see also ethnophilosophy
The Awakening of Faith in Mahāyāna 192, 218, 429 n.24
The Mirror of the Simple Souls 223–4, 401
  see also Porete
The Question of African Philosophy 76
  see also Bodunrin.
The Varieties of Religious Experience 338–9
  see also James
theism 21, 87, 262–3, 267–8, 286–90, 342, 363–7, 376, 406–7
theodicy 296–8, 348–51, 360–8, 370, 401, 407
Theravāda 407
  see also Buddhism: Theravāda Buddhism
Theses Against Feuerbach, 228
  see also Marx
Three Periods of the Dharma, Ch. *sān shí*, 三時 305–8, 407
Three Pillars of Sikhism 47, 407
Tiān, 天, heaven 3, 28, 49, 73, 106, 135–7, 158, 190–1, 251–2, 263, 272, 352–5, 369, 407
Tiānmìng, 天命, Mandate of Heaven 49
Tiāntāi, 天台, Jp. Tendai 51, 306–8, 389, 394, 396–7, 404, 407
Tillich, Paul 417 n.5
Timaeus 20
  see also Plato
Tipler, Frank J. 259
tiqqûn, repair 225, 298, 391, 407
tīrthaṅkara 46, 189, 392, 394, 408
Torah 41–2, 108, 195–7, 225, 388, 392, 400, 408
tradition 3–4, 13–16, 415 n.1
trikāya, Three Bodies theory, Ch. *sānshēn*, 三身 332, 408
Trinity 43, 254, 324, 380, 408
Tǔdìgōng, 土地公, God of the Soil and the Ground 49

Übermensch, overman 229
see also Nietzsche
Udayana 276–7, 408
Umāsvāti 244, 408, 418 n.5
Unmoved Mover 20, 66, 256, 280–4, 341, 377, 408
see also Aristotle, cosmological proofs
Upaniṣads 24, 45–6, 90, 98–101, 119–20, 130–2, 153, 155–6, 185–7, 212, 243, 275, 279, 327, 379, 408–9
upāya, Ch. *fāngbiàn*, 方便, useful means 159, 220, 408–9
see also Vimalakīrti Nirdeśa

vāda 24, 89–90, 408, 420 n.22
Vaiśeṣika 24, 47, 156, 185, 246–7, 275–7, 311, 409
Vaiśeṣika Sūtras 246–7, 392
Vaiṣṇavite 47–8, 241, 309–10, 379, 409
varṇa, caste 187, 212–13, 275, 330, 379, 383, 409
vedanā, feeling 99
Vedānta 24–5, 47, 90, 98–9, 132, 152–4, 156, 185–6, 310, 350–1, 368, 409, 416 n.5, 423 n.15
Advaita Vedānta 24, 132–3, 152–3, 156, 186, 200–1, 211–12, 214, 247, 310–11, 351; *see also* Śaṅkara
Dvaita Vedānta 25, 154, 156, 186, 247, 275; *see also* Madhva
Viśiṣṭādvaita Vedānta 24, 153–4, 156, 186, 247, 275, 278, 351–2; *see also* Rāmānuja
Vedas 24–5, 45–7, 90, 155–6, 185–7, 275–8, 330, 377, 389, 395, 397, 408–9, 411, 416 n.4
Vedic religion (aka Brahmanism) 24, 45–7, 185, 213, 250, 263, 379, 406, 409
Vimalakīrti Nirdeśa (aka *Vimalakīrti Sūtra*) 212–14, 220, 333–4, 409
Vimalakīrti 333
Viṣṇu 47–8, 154, 186–7, 309, 330, 337, 379, 409
Voltaire 363–4

wakȟáŋ, sacred or powerful 137–8, 237, 239, 262, 273, 409
Wakȟáŋ Tȟáŋka, great mysterious sacred 52, 138, 160–1, 180–1, 183, 239–40, 272–3, 335, 355–6, 369, 397, 404, 409–10, 417 n.1, 425 n.17, 436 n.7, 436–7 n.8
Wakiŋyaŋ, Thunder Beings 389, 409, 436–7 n.8
wanáǧi yúhapi, keeping of the ghost/spirit 181, 410
Wáng Yángmíng, 王陽明 252
Weddle, David 329
wéi shì, 為是, that's it which deems 74, 411
White Buffalo Calf Woman 52, 75, 138, 180–2, 263, 335, 380, 410, 436–7 n.8
wičháša wakȟáŋ and *wíŋyaŋ wakȟáŋ*, holy man and woman 33, 75, 101, 181, 335, 410, 416 n.9, 442–3 n.19
will (cetanā) 99–100
Wiredu, Kwasi 76–7
wiwáŋyaŋg wačhipi, Sun Dance 183, 410
worship, 39, 41–2, 47–8, 51, 53, 157, 184–5, 188, 222, 360, 378, 389, 392, 403, 405, 409, 411
Wovoka 302, 335, 356, 387, 410
wúwéi, 無爲, non-action 107, 136, 191, 410
wǔxíng, 五行, five material phases 50, 249, 251, 269–70, 305, 410

xīn, 心, heart-mind 134–5, 189–91, 216–17, 251–2, 270, 386, 403–4, 410
xìng, 性, human nature 133–7, 190–2, 217–19, 354, 384, 403–4, 410–11
Xúnzǐ, 荀子 135–7, 158, 354–5, 384, 410–11, 429 n.19

yajña, fire rituals 45, 395, 411
Yánluó Wáng, judge of the underworld, 閻羅王 49
yáng, 陽, active energy 49–50, 157, 248–9, 262–3, 269–72, 305, 317, 331, 389, 406, 411, 432 n.3, 436 n.5
YHWH 41, 109–10, 124, 163, 197, 221, 225, 229, 252, 254–5, 279, 297, 323–4, 348, 360–1, 363, 375, 382, 384, 392, 395–6, 403–4, 411
yì, 義, moral rightness 73–4, 107, 134–5, 137, 190, 217–19, 251, 389, 411
Yìjīng, 易經, divination manual 248, 269, 411
yīn, 陰, passive energy 49–50, 157, 248–9, 269–72, 305, 317, 331, 406, 411, 432 n.3, 436 n.5
yīn shì, 因是 74, 411
Yoga Sūtra 327, 329
Yoga/*yoga* 24, 26, 47, 185–9, 213, 327–30, 384, 392, 399–400, 403, 411, 416 n.10
  see also Patañjali
Yorùbá 14, 30–3, 39, 53–5, 61, 65, 69, 76–8, 88, 102–4, 119–20, 128–9, 133, 161–3, 173, 183–5, 210–11, 240–2, 274–5, 296, 303–5, 317, 336–8, 358–9, 368–9, 375, 377–8, 384–5, 387–8, 390, 394, 398–9, 403, 411, 415 n.1, 416 n.10, 417 n.2, 431 n.9, 440 n.10, 443 n.28
yuga 309–10, 409, 412
yuwípi 335–6, 412, 442–3 n.19

Zàoshén, 灶神, Stove God 49–50
zazen, sitting meditation, Jp. 座禅; Ch. *zuò chán*, 坐禪 334, 383, 412
Zen 412
  see also Buddhism: Chán/Zen Buddhism
Zhāng Zài 270
zhì, 智, moral wisdom 134–5, 190, 217–18, 251, 336, 393, 402, 411–12
Zhōu Dūnyí, 周敦頤 270–1, 412
Zhū Xī, 朱熹 190–1, 217–18, 250–2, 270–2, 386–7, 412, 432 n.23, 434 n.17, 436 n.3, 5
Zhuāngzǐ, 莊子 28–9, 74, 84–5, 158–9, 191, 216–17, 219, 249, 354, 381, 410–12, 419–20 n.12
zìrán, 自然, natural spontaneity 107, 412
Zōhar 254–5, 412
zōngjiào, 宗教, religion 26–7, 413
Zoroastrianism 14